Chiara Valentini (Ed.)
Public Relations

Handbooks of Communication Science

Edited by
Peter J. Schulz and Paul Cobley

Volume 27

Public Relations

—

Edited by
Chiara Valentini

DE GRUYTER
MOUTON

Università della Svizzera italiana

Faculty of Communication Sciences

The publication of this series has been partly funded by the Università della Svizzera italiana – University of Lugano.

ISBN 978-3-11-055229-4
e-ISBN (PDF) 978-3-11-055425-0
e-ISBN (EPUB) 978-3-11-055260-7
ISSN 2199-6288

Library of Congress Control Number: 2020948094

Bibliographic information published by the Deutsche Nationalbibliothek
The Deutsche Nationalbibliothek lists this publication in the Deutsche Nationalbibliografie; detailed bibliographic data are available on the Internet at http://dnb.dnb.de.

© 2021 Walter de Gruyter GmbH, Berlin/Boston

Cover image: Oliver Rossi/Photographer's Choice RF/Gettyimages
Typesetting: Dörlemann Satz, Lemförde
Printing and Binding: LSC Communications, United States

www.degruyter.com

Preface to *Handbooks of Communication Science* series

This volume is part of the series *Handbooks of Communication Science*, published from 2012 onwards by de Gruyter Mouton. When our generation of scholars was in their undergraduate years, and one happened to be studying communication, a series like this one was hard to imagine. There was, in fact, such a dearth of basic and reference literature that trying to make one's way in communication studies as our generation did would be unimaginable to today's undergraduates in the field. In truth, there was simply nothing much to turn to when you needed to cast a first glance at the key objects in the field of communication. The situation in the United States was slightly different; nevertheless, it is only within the last generation that the basic literature has really proliferated there.

What one did when looking for an overview or just a quick reference was to turn to social science books in general, or to the handbooks or textbooks from the neighbouring disciplines such as psychology, sociology, political science, linguistics, and probably other fields. That situation has changed dramatically. There are more textbooks available on some subjects than even the most industrious undergraduate can read. The representative key multi-volume *International Encyclopedia of Communication* has now been available for some years. Overviews of subfields of communication exist in abundance. There is no longer a dearth for the curious undergraduate, who might nevertheless overlook the abundance of printed material and Google whatever he or she wants to know, to find a suitable Wikipedia entry within seconds.

'Overview literature' in an academic discipline serves to draw a balance. There has been a demand and a necessity to draw that balance in the field of communication and it is an indicator of the maturing of the discipline. Our project of a multi-volume series of *Handbooks of Communication Science* is a part of this coming-of-age movement of the field. It is certainly one of the largest endeavours of its kind within communication sciences, with almost two dozen volumes already planned. But it is also unique in its combination of several things.

The series is a major publishing venture which aims to offer a portrait of the current state of the art in the study of communication. But it seeks to do more than just assemble our knowledge of communication structures and processes; it seeks to *integrate* this knowledge. It does so by offering comprehensive articles in all the volumes instead of small entries in the style of an encyclopedia. An extensive index in each *Handbook* in the series, serves the encyclopedic task of find relevant specific pieces of information. There are already several handbooks in sub-disciplines of communication sciences such as political communication, methodology, organizational communication – but none so far has tried to comprehensively cover the discipline as a whole.

https://doi.org/10.1515/9783110554250-201

For all that it is maturing, communication as a discipline is still young and one of its benefits is that it derives its theories and methods from a great variety of work in other, and often older, disciplines. One consequence of this is that there is a variety of approaches and traditions in the field. For the *Handbooks* in this series, this has created two necessities: commitment to a pluralism of approaches, and a commitment to honour the scholarly traditions of current work and its intellectual roots in the knowledge in earlier times.

There is really no single object of communication sciences. However, if one were to posit one possible object it might be the human communicative act – often conceived as "someone communicates something to someone else." This is the departure point for much study of communication and, in consonance with such study, it is also the departure point for this series of *Handbooks*. As such, the series does not attempt to adopt the untenable position of understanding communication sciences as the study of everything that can be conceived as communicating. Rather, while acknowledging that the study of communication must be multifaceted or fragmented, it also recognizes two very general approaches to communication which can be distinguished as: a) the semiotic or linguistic approach associated particularly with the humanities and developed especially where the Romance languages have been dominant and b) a quantitative approach associated with the hard and the social sciences and developed, especially, within an Anglo-German tradition. Although the relationship between these two approaches and between theory and research has not always been straightforward, the series does not privilege one above the other. In being committed to a plurality of approaches it assumes that different camps have something to tell each other. In this way, the *Handbooks* aspire to be relevant for all approaches to communication. The specific designation "communication science" for the *Handbooks* should be taken to indicate this commitment to plurality; like "the study of communication", it merely designates the disciplined, methodologically informed, institutionalized study of (human) communication.

On an operational level, the series aims at meeting the needs of undergraduates, postgraduates, academics and researchers across the area of communication studies. Integrating knowledge of communication structures and processes, it is dedicated to cultural and epistemological diversity, covering work originating from around the globe and applying very different scholarly approaches. To this end, the series is divided into 6 sections: "Theories and Models of Communication", "Messages, Codes and Channels", "Mode of Address, Communicative Situations and Contexts", "Methodologies", "Application areas" and "Futures". As readers will see, the first four sections are fixed; yet it is in the nature of our field that the "Application areas" will expand. It is inevitable that the futures for the field promise to be intriguing with their proximity to the key concerns of human existence on this planet (and even beyond), with the continuing prospect in communication sciences that that future is increasingly susceptible of prediction.

Note: administration on this series has been funded by the Universita della Svizzera italiana – University of Lugano. Thanks go to the president of the university, Professor Piero Martinoli, as well as to the administration director, Albino Zgraggen.

Peter J. Schulz, Universita della Svizzera italiana, Lugano
Paul Cobley, Middlesex University, London

Acknowledgments

The journey to this handbook started in spring 2017, when I was still working at Aarhus University in Denmark. It has taken almost three years to complete the handbook, due in part to the numerous events that have occurred in my life. I have become a mother of three children, moved from Denmark to Sweden and then to Finland, and changed jobs. Being an academic, a mother, and the partner of a businessman who is always traveling was not easy. It required a lot of planning, management and, above all else, emotional support. However, it was doable. I hope that other female academics will be encouraged by my example and pursue projects alongside familial obligations. A lot can be achieved with perseverance, determination, and a goal-oriented mindset.

A handbook of this magnitude would not have been possible without the support of the large community of inspiring, engaging and accessible public relations scholars, with whom I had the great pleasure of discussing and sharing my thoughts on this volume. Over the years, I have been blessed by a number of mentors and friends who have shaped me in various ways and have been instrumental in opening doors to international collaborations, journals, handbooks and initiatives. In particular, I would like to thank the following for their friendship, help and support: Jennifer Bartlett, Günter Bentele, Toni Muzi Falconi, Finn Frandsen, Vincent Hazleton, Robert L. Heath, Øyvind Ihlen, Winni Johansen, Michael Kent, Dean Kruckeberg, Jaakko Lehtonen, Gianpietro Mazzoleni, Juan Carlos Molleda, Stefania Romenti, Betteke van Ruler, Krishnamurthy Sriramesh, Cynthia Stohl, Maureen Taylor, Ralph Tench, Katerina Tsetsura, Giampietro Vecchiato, Marita Vos, and Ansgar Zerfass.

There is no doubt that this editorial project would have not been as successful without the involvement of dedicated and compassionate contributors. Their intellectual impact is what makes this handbook special, and I am very grateful for their work, flexibility, patience, and accommodation. Each and every contributor to this handbook has earned a special place in my heart. I would also like to remember Ronel Rensburg, a delightful public relations scholar and friend from South Africa, who was invited to contribute to the project but sadly passed away too early.

Further, I would like to thank Timothy W. Coombs and Lee Edwards for their valuable comments on my early drafts of the introductory and concluding chapters. They inspired me with their creativity and excellence, and I am grateful for their friendliness and accessibility. I am also grateful to my current institution, Jyväskylä School of Business and Economics. Specifically, I would like to thank Dean Hanna-Leena Pesonen and Vice Dean of Research Vilma Luoma-aho for providing me with the freedom and time to pursue this editorial project. Vilma Luoma-aho has also been a caring friend and trusted colleague over the years. She continually inspires me and is a role model for what she has accomplished as a mother of two.

In addition, I am very grateful to Paul Cobley and Peter J. Schulz, the main editors of the Handbooks of Communication Science series, for inviting me to contribute to this editorial project with a volume on public relations to this important effort and,

https://doi.org/10.1515/9783110554250-202

more importantly, for giving me the liberty to decide on and organize the contents of this volume. Next, I would like to thank Barbara Karlson and Michaela Göbels, the in-house editors for the Handbooks of Communication Science series, for their time, energy, responsiveness, and cordiality and for helping to make this volume possible, despite several delays. Also, I appreciate Dave Rimmer for diligently copy-editing all the chapters and paying attention to detail. His work strengthened this handbook.

Last but not least, I would like to thank my husband, Marko, and my children for their unconditional love and for being very patient with me as I took time to complete this and many other projects. Also, thanks to my parents, Livio and Ornella, who supported me in achieving my dreams and becoming an international scholar. This handbook is dedicated to all of them.

Chiara Valentini

Contents

Part III – Theories of Public Relations

Part IV – Recent Theorizing in Public Relations

Afterwords

Chiara Valentini

Introduction

Chiara Valentini

1 Public relations and social influence: Understanding the roots of a contested profession

Abstract: This chapter introduces the reader to the field of public relations by offering an overview of its core function and purpose. It is argued that public relations is a profession and discipline in the field of communication science that is situated at the crossroads of other social influence disciplines. Then, the chapter presents and discusses three major points of contention in the discipline: the function of public relations, the name, and its object. Next, the chapter proposes partly solving these contentions by moving away from the dichotomic view of public relations as either a managerial function or a socio-cultural practice, and instead embrace a more fluid understanding of what public relations does based on the idea of *organizing*. The last part of the chapter introduces the structure of the handbook and its four distinctive parts.

Keywords: public relations function; object; social influence; persuasion; organizing

1 Introduction

Humans, like animals, have always tried to exercise some form of social influence and change the preferences or behaviors of an individual or group. Being able to exercise social influence is an important skill for survival, as humans and animals can facilitate important group dynamics to save themselves from extinction or starvation. In humans, social influence often takes the shape of persuasion, which is an "active attempt by an individual, group, or social entity (e. g., government, political party, business) to change a person's beliefs, attitudes, or behaviors by conveying information, feelings, or reasoning" (Cacioppo et al. 2018: 129). Communication plays a key role in helping humans to achieve social influence via persuasion. In the Classical period, persuasion was considered a "rhetorical art"; old Greek rhetors had to master persuasion to exercise social influence (Heath and Bryant 2000). The body of literature on persuasion is vast and encompasses several disciplines, including communication, psychology and social psychology, neuroscience, marketing, advertising, and public relations.

The dominant understanding of public relations is linked to the concept of persuasion as a form of social influence (Miller 1989). It is generally conceptualized as *a specialized communication function in charge of building, supporting and maintaining positive images as well as respectful and constructive relations with publics and stake-*

https://doi.org/10.1515/9783110554250-001

holders through communication and non-communication activities. To achieve these goals, social influence may be exercised in different forms and at different levels. Given the scale and reach of public relations work, there is no doubt that public relations, like other communication disciplines, is highly dependent upon persuasion as a way to produce changes in people's opinions, behaviors, and attitudes. Sometimes, the changes occur in the target audience; other times, changes occur in the persuaders (Heath and Bryant 2000) who can persuade themselves when it is necessary to change in order to reach a common ground with the target audience.

Although there is nothing inherently wrong with the use of persuasion, the public relations profession has received more criticism than other communication professions for using it. There is a general misconception that public relations is an amoral practice that perpetuates the interests of those in power with no or limited consideration of the implications of its actions for minorities, other voices, and society at large (Lamme and Russell 2010; Coombs and Holladay 2014). Some of the derogative names assigned to public relations include spin, propaganda, demagogy, and pseudo-event (L'Etang and Pieczka 1996). Historically, public relations saw its development during wartime propaganda and post war to push commercial interests in the first half of the 20th century. Today it is often associated with "wicked" individuals and/or organizations that recurrently make headlines in newspapers and media outlets. While it is true that still too many public relations cases involve malpractice or unethical practices, this does not mean that ethical and good public relations does not exist (Coombs and Holladay 2014). Indeed, research on public relations, activism and social engagement shows that public relations can serve more noble purposes and drive positive changes in society (Sommerfeldt 2013; De Moya and Bravo 2016; Taylor and Kent 2016; Toledano 2016). For example, it can increase the inclusiveness and engagement of different social actors and construct new forms of relations and living.

The social influence that characterizes public relations (of which persuasion is one form) should not be seen as creepy. As Heath and Bryant (2000: 174) noted, "persuasion should [...] allow people the power of self-determination" and social influence is necessary to cope with the challenges that humans have had to face since the dawn of civilization. Rather than seeing social influence in public relations as ethically wrong, what we need is a better understanding of the role that public relations plays as an institutional force that shapes our society and culture (Edwards 2018).

One of the aims of this handbook is to show that public relations is neither a manipulative profession nor a candid, unbiased one. According to Fitzpatrick and Gauthier (2003: 195), "criticism results from either a misunderstanding of or lack of appreciation for the function of public relations". Through reading this handbook, the reader will gain an understanding of the roots of this profession; what it does, how and for what purposes; and become aware of its fundamental questions and issues. It is hoped that this will help readers understand the delicate and often difficult task of balancing the interests that ethical public relations professionals need to consider on a daily basis, and the impact that public relations can have on how diverse social actors think and act on realities that are constructed or co-constructed around them.

In the following, an overview of some of the major points of contention regarding public relations is offered in order to introduce the reader to the field. Many of those points are further articulated, discussed, and advanced in other chapters of this handbook. In addition, the reader is introduced to the various terminologies, approaches, and views that scholars contributing to this handbook have used to present and elaborate on diverse topics.

2 Points of contention in public relations

There are many points of contention among public relations scholars and professionals. In the following, I review three major points that are further discussed in the contributions of this handbook.

2.1 Function of public relations

One of the major points of contention in public relations is the function of the profession. What public relations is and does, and whether it should be considered a profession or a practice, are hotly debated. For some, public relations lacks a clear, defined function in organizations, which can compromise the credibility of the profession (Thurlow 2009) and can make theory-building efforts more difficult to be successful or meaningful (Ferguson 2018).

Historically, public relations is situated in organizational structures with other communication and non-communication functions. Thus, many marketing scholars and professionals consider public relations to be one element of the communication mix that exists alongside advertising, sales promotions, events and experiences, publicity, and direct and personal sales (Moss et al. 1997; Kotler and Keller 2009). For advertisers, public relations is a form of unpaid, spontaneous publicity (Arens 2006; Bivins 2009). For journalists, it is a low-level reporting practice (Merkel et al. 2007; Macnamara 2014; Yoo and Samsup 2014). The problem here is not just semantic, but fundamentally an issue of recognition by other professions. The identity of public relations has been, and still is, contested because public relations professionals frequently work to support other organizational functions and often adopt practices from other professions in order to be more effective. One example of this is media relations activities; through the years, these activities have become increasingly strategic, adapting content production to the media logics that journalists tend to follow in order to increase the credibility of content and increase its reach (Ihlen and Pallas 2014). Arguably, this capacity to adapt and borrow knowledge to perform tasks should be seen as a positive thing, but it can create confusion regarding competence and expertise among different communication-based professions and raise professional encroachment problems. That is why some scholars have suggested departing from its original name to explain its core identity; to them, public relations should be understood as a profession about relations and relating with public(s) in the public sphere (Verčič et al. 2001; Bentele and Nothhaft 2010).

Another point of contention is related to the boundaries of public relations activities, which, most of the time, are based on their professional function. Traditionally, public relations professionals were in charge of activities that involved crafting, producing, and delivering messages through different channels and in different formats. However, an increasing number of public relations activities today, particularly those at the senior level, involve the creation and maintenance of relationships and constructive flows of communication and interactions among groups of individuals, such as consumers, customers, clients, suppliers, employees, political actors, activists, or communities.

This variation in public relations activities has led some scholars to define their function based on the effects they produce. Those who see public relations as having a symbolic function primarily believe that its main role is to construct and manage positive images and reputations, whereas those who see it as a behavioral function identify its main role as producing positive behavioral effects by, for example, building and maintaining good relationships with publics and stakeholders (Grunig J. 1993). The latter function has been perceived as superior because it is considered to involve less persuading and instead focus on reaching a common understanding that can help establish mutually beneficial relationships. Yet, it can be argued that social influence exists even in the behavioralist view in the form of, for instance, personal influence, which has been shown to be highly relevant for building and maintaining good relationships (Valentini 2010). Other scholars, particularly those who view public relations through a rhetorical lens, see this distinction as artificial and forced. For them, symbolic actions can produce noticeable behavioral effects, and behaviors often perform a symbolic function.

Although the debate on the nature of public relations is not yet settled, another debate has emerged based on the functionalistic view of public relations, according to which public relations is a function in organizations. In such debates, scholars wonder whether public relations should be defined as a specific managerial activity, thus limiting public relations to organizations, or as a social and cultural practice in its own right (Edwards 2018). The latter view detaches public relations from the mainstream understanding of an organizational function, instead positioning it as a sort of social agent with performative and agentic effects in multiple domains and contexts.

As some scholars have noted (Grunig J. 1993; Ihlen and Verhoeven 2009), the symbolic and behavioralist views are not mutually exclusive; when practiced ethically, they can coexist and serve each other's purposes. For example, constructing a positive image of an organization, individual, or entity (symbolic function) may help public relations' efforts to reach out and build relationships with publics and stakeholders (behavioral function). Conversely, good relationships can support the public image of an organization.

Thus, public relations is more than just another organizational function, if we narrowly define organizations as "a stable association of persons engaged in concerned activities directed to the attainment of specific objectives" (Valentini 2018: 2). For some time, organizational theorists have proposed abandoning this concept of an organization – a stable structure – in favor of the concept of *organizing*, a more fluid idea that includes developing collective structures and practices in which communication can play an important constitutive role (Weick 1979; 1995; Robichaud and Cooren 2013). From a post-structuralist approach, I argue that seeing public relations as an *organizing function* instead of an organizational function represents what public relations has done and can do for publics, stakeholders, and societies, as a powerful force that impacts opinions, behaviors, societal norms, cultures, and ways of thinking. Understanding public relations as an organizing function emphasizes agency rather than the loci of functions, and it can better illustrate the back-and-forth movement and translation between the actions of public relations and their interpretation by professionals as well as publics (Weick 1979). The notion of organizing could bring some closure to the debate on whether public relations is an organizational function, as it allows for a more fluid definition of what public relations is and does for/to organizations, publics, societies, and cultures.

2.2 Name of public relations

The questions and debates outlined above raise the issue of the name of public relations, which has become imperative to address. Several educational programs in universities across the world have changed their names to "strategic communication", "corporate communication" or "communication management". Should public relations evolve with the latest development of tasks, activities, and professional needs? Should it change its name to reflect its newer identity?

Perhaps because of the bad legacy of the term "public relations", or perhaps because the profession has developed new venues of interest and become more integrated, professionals across the world use a variety of different names and titles to describe public relations. The debate regarding this is more animated among academics than professionals, as the latter do not seem to see a problem in switching names. According to the European Communication Monitor, most professionals prefer to use the term "corporate communication" in their professional titles, followed by "strategic communication" and "public relations" (Zerfass et al. 2011).

Scholars who position themselves within the strategic communication field do not want to be confused with public relations scholars. Although they recognize the common roots of these fields, in their view, strategic communication is a different field. Specifically, strategic communication is defined as "the practice of deliberate and purposive communication that a communication agent enacts in the public sphere on behalf of a communicative entity to reach set goals" (Holtzhausen and Zerfass 2013: 284). It can encompass activities related to management, marketing, public relations, technical communication, political communication, and information/social marketing campaigns (Hallahan et al. 2007). Unlike public relations, it is perceived to offer an integrative perspective on all goal-oriented communications of an organization (Frandsen and Johansen 2018). Today, it is the preferred term to describe public relations activities for non-corporate entities; for instance, it is commonly used to define communication functions in public sector organizations and government entities (Nielsen and Salomonsen 2012; Valentini 2013; Fredriksson and Pallas 2016).

In the business world, "corporate communication" has emerged as the preferred term, although there are some country-specific preferences for professional names due to different historical reasons and influence from professional bodies. Similar to strategic communication, it is claimed that corporate communication is much more than public relations. It is used as an umbrella term to describe a variety of communication forms and formats, including public relations, public affairs, and employee, customer, and stockholder communications (Cornelissen 2017). Corporate communication is also like strategic communication in that it is goal-oriented, focusing on managing and coordinating different forms of communication to provide a consistent image of an organization to all its stakeholders (van Riel 1995).

This terminological issue may seem ridiculous at times, but it is important to epistemologically reflect on the meanings of names and their impact on how the profession of public relations is understood by practitioners, the general public and by other communication and non-communication professions. The different nuances of the terms used to describe communication professionals' identity can lead the research community to investigate different issues, ask different research questions, and thus theorize differently on this discipline. Yet, I argue that this problem could be partially solved if we understand that public relations, strategic communication, corporate communication, and communication management are *organizing* functions, rather than organizational functions, and focus on understanding, exploring, and analyzing their different practices and their impact on organizations, publics, stakeholders, and societies. From this perspective, contention regarding terminology becomes less important because the unifying element across these very similar communication professions is their capability to organize something for or on behalf of someone.

While this handbook primarily focuses on public relations, an attentive reader will notice that the reflections and discussions parallel questions and issues raised in the strategic and corporate communication disciplines. As this matter is quite important for the evolution of public relations, some contributors have purposely decided to use either of these terms instead of "public relations" to emphasize the view and perspective adopted in their discussion.

2.3 The object of public relations

The third point of contention concerns the object of public relations. Does public relations deal with publics, stakeholders, or both? Early conceptual developments in public relations are grounded on the work of Dewey (1927), in which the public is predominantly regarded from a situational perspective as a group of individuals with whom public relations interacts (Rawlins and Bowen 2005). Yet, other perspectives, such as mass media, agenda building, and homo narrans, have also been identified in public relations research (Vasquez and Taylor 2001). Most public relations literature considers publics to be groups of individuals who face a similar problem, recognize it, and organize themselves to address it, regardless of whether they have a direct interest in any organization involved with the issue (Dewey 1927).

During the last forty years, the management school of thinking has taken several stances on public relations vocabulary. During the 1980s, public relations started to become more interested in relationship management, which may have led to more interest in drawing upon management terminology. The term "stakeholder" emerged as an alternative way to describe groups of individuals who directly impacted or are impacting the operations of an organization and whose interests are closely tied to the organization's business (Freeman 1984). However, J. Grunig and Repper (1992) warn that "stakeholder" and "public" are not interchangeable: "Stakeholders are people who are linked to an organization because they and the organization have consequences on each other" (127), whereas publics "arise on their own and choose the organization for attention" (128). Essentially, publics are groups of individuals that form in response to a particular problem, not necessarily because they possess a stake or interest in the organization, and they are defined through their communications. In contrast, stakeholders are defined by the management of an organization, and they may not be consciously aware that they are part of a stakeholder group.

Yet, a clear distinction between the two terms is not always so evident. In addition to the terminological dispute (Mackey 2006), the distinction between stakeholders and publics has dissolved for the most part, and so has the distinction between primary and secondary stakeholders (Ihlen 2008). Kruckeberg and Vujnovic (2010) go even further and claim that the concept of publics is dead in contemporary society. Without taking such a radical view, and considering that prioritization and management are key interests for any organization, I argue that societal expectations regarding organizations' responsibilities have extended so far that it is almost impossible not to look at a broad spectrum of specialized and non-specialized interests. The relations and interactions among organizations, publics, and stakeholders are so complex and nonlinear that it no longer makes sense to distinguish between publics and stakeholders. In part, this broadening is the result of the increasing complexity of today's environment (Hurth 2017). It is evident that public relations must be able to navigate and adapt to this environment in order to build, support and maintain relations and interactions with a variety of different stakeholders and publics, whose interests often collide and may be irreconcilable. To overcome this challenge, public relations is asked to perform a number of very different organizing activities at the societal, cultural, political, economic, and interpersonal levels.

In this handbook, both terms (i.e. stakeholders and publics) have been used, sometimes interchangeably and sometimes with specific reference to the original differentiation. In fact, it is evident from the contributions that there is contention regarding the concepts among authors. This partially reflects the authors' preferences and partially their academic roots and philosophical stances. While the terms may vary and carry different meanings, there is one thing that remains stable: the object of public relations. Public relations aims at exercising some form of social influence on other social actors and agents via communication to achieve symbolic and/or behavioral effects. Terminological discussions are important, but we must not forget that all public relations deals with many different social actors, exercises some influence and performs an organizing role while interacting, constructing, and deconstructing the environment in which activities take place.

3 The structure of this handbook

The purpose of this handbook is to present and offer a deeper understanding of the public relations profession and the body of knowledge that public relations scholars have developed over the years. The reader is offered a compilation of key classical *public relations theories* and *recent theorizing in public relations* as well as key models and concepts. The section on public relations thoeries contains those theories that are considered classical public relations contributions, whereas the section on recent theorizing in public relations deals with recent theorizing efforts undertaken by scholars to expand the body of knowledge. The theories, concepts and models presented in this volume are explained, and critically discussed to offer an understanding of the theoretical and practical contributions of public relations as an applied communication science. It is important to note that the handbook does not include all theoretical perspectives in the field. For instance, political and not-for-profit-related topics in the public relations discipline have been purposively left out since other volumes on these specific topics exist within the De Gruyter Mouton collection. Furthermore, deliberate choices had to be made about what to include and exclude in the part on emergent theoretical developments, as it was not possible to cover all new thinking in the field from the last ten years within one volume.

The chapters are organized into four thematic parts: Part I – History, identity and practice; Part II – Core functions of public relations; Part III –Theories of public relations; and Part IV – Recent theorizing in public relations. This handbook is structured to take the reader on a journey to explore, first the profession (part I and II), and later the discipline of public relations (part III and IV). Part I delves into what the profession is and how it has developed and the major debates on how the profession should move and how it is affecting society. Part II focus on professional activities and functions that are typically undertaken by public relations. The last two parts are dedicated to the theoretical contributions of public relations as distinct communication discipline.

3.1 Part I – Public Relations: History, Identity, and Practice

Part I presents and discusses questions related to the origins, evolution, and identity of public relations as a profession and field of study from a global perspective. In Chapter 2, Rodriguez-Salcedo and Watson take the reader on an historical "excursion" regarding the origins and roots of public relations around the world. Although limited by the chapter length, the authors show that the roots of this profession are much deeper and more culturally varied that we may realize, and so are the meanings that people around the world ascribe to this profession.

Following this, Chapter 3 reviews and discusses the specific contributions and roles women had and have in the development and professionalization of public relations. As Tooth and Aldoory emphasize, women are the largest group of professionals in many societies, and hence they play a great role in determining what public relations can accomplish within organizational settings and the larger societies in which organizational public relations operates.

Speaking of professional influence, in Chapter 4, Fawkes questions the premise of considering public relations as a distinct profession. She explores the tensions between different forces that shape professional identity and the resulting identity conflicts, particularly those regarding ethical responsibility. She concludes with suggestions for shaping this profession's identity through the development of global capabilities.

Continuing the discussion of the identity of public relations, in Chapter 5, van Ruler addresses the important question of what value public relations may offer to organizations and society by discussing how public relations can enhance a professional reflective culture in which societal expectations are part of the organizational public relations practice.

Taking this as a point of departure, in Chapter 6, Bartlett and Hurst address the fundamental nature of legitimacy in public relations. After explaining and offering a reading of key legitimacy literature, they discuss the idea that vying for legitimacy and reputation has become a central part of the practice of public relations related to explaining organizations and maintaining support.

The last chapter in Part I, Chapter 7, is a piercing discussion of one of the main criticisms of public relations through the years, which concerns its presumed power to influence others. Weaver introduces the reader to the paradoxes of power and control that constitute its identity as well the main critique of this profession and suggests some reflections on how to address power in public relations.

3.2 Part II – Core Functions of Public Relations

Part II addresses some of the core functions of the public relations profession today. While there are differences across organizational settings and activities, the contributors focus on the activities that are expected of one who is competent in public relations.

This part starts with a chapter on one classical public relations activity, media relations. In Chapter 8, Tsetsura provides a critical overview of media relations approaches, from agenda-setting and framing to journalist–public relations relationships. This is done to understand the complexity of relationship-building with traditional media and non-traditional stakeholders who have their own mediated channels.

Next, in Chapter 9, Etter, Winkler, and Pleil elaborate on how social media have developed over the last 15 years from a niche area to disruptive and dominating phenomena in the context of public relations. The authors offer four approaches to understand the development of social media research and practice and then discuss the contributions to public relations.

In line with the symbolic view of public relations, in Chapter 10, Murtarelli, Romenti, and Carroll introduce the reader to two parallel sets of understandings pertaining to image and reputation management. The chapter highlights the role of public relations in managing image and reputation, illustrates its contributions to construct and maintain positive images and a good reputation on behalf of an organization, individual or entity, and identifies opportunities and risks that professionals could face in the current competitive environment.

Speaking about risks to image and reputation, in Chapter 11 Diers-Lawson and Pang examine the field of strategic issue and crisis management as an important public relations activity involving management of risk to minimize or mitigate dangers in order to preserve an organization's image. The authors conclude by offering some insights into the strategic management of crises, issues, and risks.

The next two chapters take a social turn and discuss the function of public relations in the context of stakeholder and societal engagement and social advocacy. In Chapter 12, Holladay and Tachkova describe how stakeholder theory provides a foundation for understanding organization–stakeholder engagement processes. In doing so, they help position public relations as an engagement activity that creates value through corporate social responsibility and sustainable development. In Chapter 13, Williams and Sommerfeldt advance our notion of public relations as a practice that involves social influence by focusing on social advocacy as a specific public relations activity that can strengthen connections between an organization, its constituent publics, and society. Through the lens of *communitas*, which is an orientation to serve the community and the public sphere, these authors discuss how public relations can serve the public good and be a positive force in society.

The last chapter addresses the important question of how to measure and evaluate the impact of public relations activities. In Chapter 14, Macnamara reviews the current state of practice and the latest evaluation frameworks and models that are used internationally. In addition, he outlines the key concepts and principles for the three stages of formative, process and summative evaluation. Macnamara concludes by offering suggestions for best practices and new directions for the future of measurement and evaluation.

3.3 Part III – Theories of Public Relations

Part III presents main theories and theoretical perspectives related to public relations. The theories and models discussed here are considered part of classical public relations theory, although some more recent versions of well-known theories are included with a theoretical review that can lead to reflections for future theorizing and a critical evaluation of the applicability of the theory to practice. An attentive reader may find similarities between the concepts and ideas presented in this part and those of other disciplines. Much public relations theory is an interdisciplinary melting pot as scholars have used concepts and ideas from other disciplines to bring new lines of thinking to the field of public relations. Paraphrasing J. Grunig (personal communication 22 February 2017), usually, concepts from other disciplines must be adapted to fit to public relations problems. Thus, even though the theories presented in this part were constructed based on concepts from many other disciplines, they can be considered classical public relations theories.

In Chapter 15, J. Grunig and Kim introduce the reader to the evolution of thought surrounding the *Four models of public relations* and their relevance and applicability to today's professional world. The four models, which describe four different ways of communicating and conducting public relations, are considered early classical public relations theoretical contributions.

In Chapter 16, Hung-Baesecke, Chen, and Ni present another classical public relations theory, *Excellence theory*. The scholars offer an overview of its origins, developments and contributions to the body of knowledge in public relations. They conclude by advancing some ideas for future research topics derived from this theory.

Chapter 17 introduces one of the least studied models of public relations, the *Personal influence model*. Sriramesh and Fisher warn that personal influence, as a form of social influence exercised by public relations professionals on other individuals, is practiced widely across cultures and not just in collective societies. The authors conclude by offering their thoughts on the importance of personal influence in the public relations field as well as avenues for further research.

Chapter 18 draws the reader's attention to rhetoric and its important function in persuasive communications (and thus in public relations). Through a compelling review and discussion, Heath, Waymer and Ihlen introduce the *Rhetorical theory of public relations* and discuss its normative and instrumental functions in public relations. According to the scholars, the rhetorical theory offers a theoretical ground to help public relations construct discourses for the strategic purpose of managing relatedness. While this theory focuses on textual enactment, the next chapter deals with stance enactment in communication processes.

Chapter 19 presents another classical public relations theory, *Contingency theory*. Pang, Yan, and Cameron argue that this theory fulfils the requirements for being considered a grand theory of public relations since it explains the job of public relations, which is essentially to mitigate conflict by adapting communications. Contingency theory clarifies that this adaptation process is possible by enacting a variety of stances depending on the circumstances.

The idea of adaptability is also central in Chapter 20, which focuses on global public relations theories and theoretical approaches. Chaidaroon and Hou review and discuss four major approaches to studying and theorizing about global public relations. All these approaches share a general assumption that public relations practices involve meaning-making, discourse production and relationship-building, and that such activities must be adapted to different situational and contextual elements, of which culture plays a key role. The scholars remind readers that global public relations is both a product of globalization and an agent that produces economic, political and socio-cultural flows of globalization.

In Chapter 21, Ledingham, one of the major contributors to *Relationship management theory*, presents the roots of his thinking on relationship management, from the initial premises to its increasing relevance in contemporary practice and definition of the public relations profession.

The concept of relations is central in Chapter 22, where Vujnovic, Kruckeberg, and Starck explain the roots of *Community-building theory* and its subsequent development into an *Organic theory of public relations*. Both theories postulate a normative, societal role of public relations. The scholars argue that public relations practitioners have an important responsibility to maintain and change societal relations. They are community-builders who, through communication, should strive to maintain and restore a sense of community.

This sense of community can be enhanced by dialogic communications. As Lane notes in Chapter 23, much research on public relations that deals with community, relationships, and similar topics focuses on dialogue. This could be associated with the desire of professionals and scholars to better understand the type of communication that can help to build and maintain positive relationships with publics and stakeholders. Lane offers an incisive review of the evolution of another classical theory, the *Dialogic theory of public relations*, linking it to the wider philosophical discussion of dialogue as a concept, and offering suggestions for future theorizing.

The last chapter in Part III deals with the identification and classification of publics in public relations. In Chapter 24, Kim, Tam, and Chon present another established public relations theory, the *Situational theory of publics*, as well as its origins and its evolution into the *Situational theory of problem-solving*. As these scholars noted, for public relations, it is paramount to understand how publics behave when specific issues arise and what type of communication may be needed. This understanding helps practitioners to identify the best strategies for responding to demands. The main assumptions of these theories is that we must see communication as a process that individuals undertake to manage problematic life situations.

3.4 Part IV – Recent Theorizing in Public Relations

The last section of this handbook addresses emerging theories for public relations that are not part of the classical tradition but were developed in other disciplines and have resonated with some public relations scholars, as well as efforts to further theorize about public relations. These scholars have tried to translate and adapt classical knowledge from disciplines such as sociology, management, organizational and cultural studies, and philosophy, and reposition it to tackle complex problems.

In Chapter 25, Hazleton and Tydings review a classical sociological theory (i. e. social capital theory) and link it with the behavioralist view of public relations, which emphasizes the impact of building social capital in relationships. These authors propose three theoretical constructs to advance social capital theory and facilitate its use as a practical theory for the community of public relations professionals.

Chapter 26 takes a different route, deconstructing the identity of public relations based on the Scandinavian idea of institutionalism. Through a provoking discussion, Fredriksson, Ivarsson, and Pallas challenge the idea of a public relations function or role. For them, public relations is a management idea, and as such, its essential purpose is to achieve better management. This understanding, the scholars argue, would allow for multiple interpretations of what public relations is and does in different organizations over time without imposing one single view. It would also calm the terminological debates between "public relations", "strategic communication", "corporate communication" and others, since such distinctions are irrelevant if public relations has the flexibility to be translated and adapted across contexts and situations.

Chapter 27 also focuses on current professional challenges caused by the instability, volatility, and uncertainty of the environments in which public relations operates. The reader is introduced to *Actor–Network Theory*, which Somerville argues can offer important insights into the practice of public relations. From an Actor–Network Theory perspective, all human, technological, textual, or natural entities are important "social" actors, and they can all acquire power by placing themselves at the center of a network. Hence, understanding diverse social actors' behaviors and the dynamics of social influence can help a public relations professional to influence other actors' positions in a way that benefits the organization or entity on whose behalf the professional is acting.

Moving towards management, in Chapter 28, Olkkonen and Luoma-aho introduce the idea of managing stakeholder expectations. According to them, expectations provide organizations with information and cues about stakeholders' and publics' values, interests, experiences and knowledge, which are important for strategic public relations planning. After introducing the field of expectations and its relevance, the scholars advance propositions for a *Relationship expectation theory* in public relations.

Chapter 29 provides an understanding of what culture is and how it impacts public relations activities. Curtin offers an overview of the nexus of public relations and cultural theories and presents acute reflections on how culture is translated across different approaches and epistemological lines of thinking. She concludes by elaborating on the contribution of culture to our understanding of different practices of public relations.

The last chapter of Part IV deals with ethics and ethical theories. In Chapter 30, Bowen and Bhalla discuss ethical issues and challenges facing public relations from an organizational perspective in an increasingly global environment. These authors introduce the overarching concepts of normative (ideal) and positive (descriptive) ethics, followed by the two most prominent forms of normative ethics: utilitarianism and deontology. The chapter concludes by offering suggestions for how to include more ethical thinking in contemporary public relations decision-making.

The last two chapters of this handbook offer the reader some critical thoughts about public relations and some conclusions. In Chapter 31, Bourne and Edwards call for more reflexivity and scrutiny of how public relations operates, emphasizing the effect of public relations on society. The scholars also invite giving more attention to diverse voices and to diversity in public relations. Chapter 32, written by Valentini, offers a meta-theoretical analysis of the so-called classical public relations theories presented in this handbook, and shows some continuities and discontinuities in the academic discourse about what public relations is and does and what knowledge we have.

4 Concluding thoughts

This handbook is part of a series of existing and forthcoming handbooks by de Gruyter Mouton that provides in-depth and broad perspectives on different communication topics. The handbook is one of the first of its kind as it tries to reach scholars, students, practitioners, and readers who are not familiar with public relations activities and theories. Yet, its contents go beyond an introduction to public relations; the scholars represented here have purposively worked to build coherent and critical texts that speak to multiple voices and views. Public relations is a multi-faceted profession, and thus it must be understood from a wide perspective based on solid theoretical foundations in other communication and non-communication disciplines.

The handbook brings together scholars from different parts of the world and from very different theoretical and disciplinary traditions. It includes old and new schools of thinking, as well as established and emergent scholars. The diversity of these perspectives is considered a strength of this handbook, as it encapsulates several variations and understandings of public relations. Scholars and practitioners alike can utilize this handbook as an account of what public relations is, does, and contributes to. In reviewing the public relations discipline, this collective work fills some important gaps in the knowledge and stimulates further thought and action. I hope you enjoy reading this handbook and feel inspired to push boundaries while exploring existing or new lines of thinking. The profession and discipline of public relations will benefit from future theorizing *in* and *for* public relations, and I hope you will consider contributing to the advancement of our professional and disciplinary understanding of this topic.

References

Arens, William F. 2006. *Contemporary advertising*. New York: McGraw-Hill

Bentele, Günter & Howard Nothhaft. 2010. Strategic communication and the public sphere from an European perspective. *International Journal of Strategic Communication* 4(2). 93–116

Bivins, Thomas. 2009. *Mixed media: moral distinctions in advertising, public relations, and journalism*. New York: Routledge,

Cacioppo, John T., Stephanie Cacioppo & Richard E. Petty. 2018. The neuroscience of persuasion: A review with an emphasis on issues and opportunities. *Journal of Social Neuroscience* 13(2). 129–172.

Coombs, Timothy W. & Sherry J. Holladay. 2014. *It's Not Just PR: Public Relations in Society*, 2nd edn. Chichester, UK: Wiley Blackwell.

Cornelissen, Joep. 2017. *Corporate communication: A guide to theory and practice*, 5th edn. London: sage

De Moya, Maria & Vanessa Bravo. 2016. The role of public relations in ethnic advocacy and activism: A proposed research agenda. *Public Relations Inquiry* 5(3). 233–251.

Dewey, John. 1927. *The Public and Its Problems*. Chicago: Swallow Press.

Edwards, Lee. 2018. *Understanding public relations. Theory, culture and society*. London: Sage.

Ferguson, Mary Ann. 2018. Building theory in public relations: Interorganizational relationships as a public relations paradigm. *Journal of Public Relations Research* 30(4). 164–178.

Fitzpatrick, Kathy & Candace Gauthier. 2003. Toward a professional responsibility theory of public relations ethics. *Journal of Mass Media Ethics* 16(2/3). 193–212.

Frandsen, Finn & Winni Johansen. 2018. Strategic communication. In Craig R. Scott & Laurie Lewis (eds), *International Encyclopedia of Organizational Communication*. Malden, MA: Wiley Blackwell.

Fredriksson, Magnus & Josef Pallas. 2016. Diverging principles for strategic communication in government agencies. *International Journal of Strategic Communication* 10(3). 153–164.

Freeman, Edward R. 1984. *Strategic Management: A Stakeholder Approach*. Cambridge: Cambridge University Press.

Grunig, James E. 1993. Image and Substance: From symbolic to behavioral relationships. *Public Relations Review* 19(2). 121–139.

Grunig, James E. & Fred C. Repper. 1992. Strategic management, publics, and issues. In James E. Grunig (ed.), *Excellence in Public Relations and Communication Management*, 117–157. Hillsdale, NJ: Lawrence Erlbaum Associates.

Hallahan, Kirk, Derina R. Holtzhausen, Betteke van Ruler, Dejan Verčič & Krishnamurthy Sriramesh. 2007. Defining strategic communication. *International Journal of Strategic Communication* 1(1). 3–35.

Heath, Robert L. & Jennings Bryant. 2000. *Human Communication Theory and Research*, 2nd edn. Mahwah, NJ: Lawrence Erlbaum Associates.

Holtzhausen, Derina R. & Ansgar Zerfass. 2013. Strategic communication: Pillars and perspectives on an alternative paradigm. In Krishnamurthy Sriramesh, Ansgar Zerfass & Jeon-Nam Kim (eds.), *Current trends and emergent topics in public relations and communication management*, 283–302. New York: Routledge.

Hurth, Victoria. 2017. Organizations as open systems that need purpose and integrated thinking. *Board Leadership: Innovative Approaches to Governance* 150. 1–8.

Ihlen, Øyvind. 2008. Mapping the environment for corporate social responsibility: stakeholders, publics and the public sphere. *Corporate Communications: an International Journal* 13(2). 135–146.

Ihlen, Øyvind & Josef Pallas. 2014. Mediatization of corporations. In Knut Lundby (ed.), *Mediatization of Communication*, Handbooks of communication science 21, 423–442. Berlin: De Gruyter Mouton.

Ihlen, Øyvind & Piet Verhoeven. 2009. Conclusions on the domain, context, concepts, issues, and empirical venues of public relations. In Øyvind Ihlen, Magnus Fredriksson & Betteke van Ruler (eds.), *Public relations and social theory: Key figures and concepts*, 322–340. New York: Routledge.

Kotler, Philip & Kevin L. Keller. 2009. *Marketing Management*, 13th edn. Upper Saddle River, NJ: Pearson Prentice Hall.

Kruckeberg, Dean & Marina Vujnovic. 2010. The death of the concept of *publics* (plural) in 21st century public relations. *International Journal of Strategic Communication* 4(2). 117–125.

Lamme, Margot O. & Karen M. Russell. 2010. Removing the spin. Toward a new theory of public relations history. *Journalism and Communication Monographs* 11(4). 281–362.

L'Etang, Jacquie & Magda Pieczka. 1996. *Critical perspectives in public relations*. London: Cengage Learning Emea.

Mackey, Steve. 2006. Misuse of the term 'stakeholder' in public relations. *PRism* 4(1). http://praxis. massey.ac.nz/prism_on-line_journ.html (accessed 28 January 2020).

Macnamara, Jim. 2014. Journalism–PR relations revisited: The good news, the bad news, and insights into tomorrow's news. *Public Relations Review* 40(5). 739–750.

Merkel, Bernd, Stephan Russ-Mohl & Giananni Zavaritt. 2007. *A Complicated, Antagonistic, Symbiotic Affair: Journalism, Public Relations and Their Struggle for Public Attention*. Lugano, Switzerland: Università della Svizzera Italiana.

Miller, Gerald R. 1989. Persuasion and public relations: Two p's in a pod. In Carl H. Botan & Vincent Hazleton (eds.), *Public Relations theory*, 45–66. Hillsdale NJ: Lawrence Erlbaum Associates.

Moss, Danny, Gary Warnaby & Louise Thame. 1997. Public relations or simply product publicity? In Danny Moss, Toby MacManus & Dejan Verčič (eds.), *Public relations research: an international perspective*, 135–158. London: International Thompson Business Press.

Nielsen, Jeppe Agger & Heidi Houlberg Salomonsen. 2012. Why all this communication? Explaining strategic communication in Danish local governments from an institutional perspective. *Scandinavian Journal of Public Administration* 16(1). 69–89.

Rawlins, Brad L. & Shannon A. Bowen. 2005. Publics. In Robert L. Heath (ed.), *Encyclopedia of Public Relations*. London: Sage.

Robichaud, Daniel & François Cooren. 2013. *Organization and Organizing: Materiality, Agency, and Discourse*. New York: Routledge.

Sommerfeldt, Erich J. 2013. The civility of social capital: Public relations in the public sphere, civil society, and democracy. *Public Relations Review* 39. 280–289.

Taylor, Maureen & Michael Kent. 2016. Nation building in the former Yugoslavia. A 20-year retrospective to understand how public relations rebuilds relationships in divided societies. In Ian Somerville, Owen Hargie, Maureen Taylor & Margalit Toledano (eds.), *International Public Relations. Perspectives from deeply divided societies,* 9–26. London: Routledge.

Thurlow, Amy. 2009. "I just say I'm in advertising": A public relations identity crisis? *Canadian Journal of Communication* 34. 245–263.

Toledano, Margalit. 2016. Advocating for reconciliation: Public relations, activism, advocacy and dialogue. *Public Relations Inquiry* 5(3). 277–294.

Valentini, Chiara. 2010. Personalised networks of influence in public relations: Strategic resources for achieving successful professional outcomes. *Journal of Communication Management* 14(2). 153–166.

Valentini, Chiara. 2013. Public relations in the public sector. The role of strategic communication in the Italian public administration. *Sinergie: Italian Journal of Management* 92. 93–113.

Valentini, Chiara. 2018. Communicatively constituted stakeholders: Advancing a communication perspective in stakeholder relations. In Adam Lindgreen, Francois Maon, Joelle Vanhamme, Beatriz Palacios Florencio, Christine Strong & Carolyn Vallaster (eds.), *Engaging with Stakeholders: A Relational Perspective on Responsible Business,* 65–79. New York: Routledge

Vasquez, Gabriel M. & Maureen Taylor. 2001. Research perspectives on "the Public". In Robert L. Heath (ed.), *Handbook of Public Relations,* 139–154. London: Sage.

Verčič, Dejan, Betteke van Ruler, Gerhard Bütschi & Bertil Flodin. 2001. On the definition of public relations: a European view. *Public Relations Review* 27(4). 373–387.

van Riel, Cees B. M. 1995. *Principles of Corporate Communication.* Harlow, UK: Prentice Hall.

Weick, Karl E. 1979. *The Social Psychology of Organizing,* 2nd edn. New York: McGraw-Hill.

Weick, Karl E. 1995. *Sensemaking in Organizations.* London: Sage

Zerfass, Ansgar, Piet Verhoeven, Ralph Tench, Angeles Moreno & Dejan Verčič. 2011. *European Communication Monitor 2011: Empirical insights into strategic communication in Europe.* Brussels: EACD, EUPRERA.

Yoo, Jae-Woong & Samsup Jo. 2014. How do journalists express their perceptions of public relations on Twitter? *Social Behavior & Personality: An International Journal* 42 (7). 1175–1182.

Part I – **Public Relations: History, Identity and Practice**

Natalia Rodríguez-Salcedo and Tom Watson

2 Public relations origins and evolution: A global perspective

Abstract: Public relations has ancient roots in promotional activities but is largely a communication phenomenon of the 20th century. Governments played a fundamental role in establishing communication activities in many regions and continents. These led to the formation of profession-like practices of public relations. From this base, trade associations were formed and education programmes introduced in many countries. Later, the agency sector developed and became internationalised. Although the main international influences on public relations have been from Germany, the United Kingdom and the United States, distinctive national forms of public relations based on cultural, political and social influences have been evolving in the second half of the 20th century and into the 21st. In general, public relations practice has thrived in its application and employment in countries with open economies and democratic institutions where free speech is less controlled.

Keywords: antecedents; corporate communication; culture; democratization; education; government; international; professionalization; proto-public relations; religion

1 Introduction

This chapter traces the formation of public relations as a practice from its earliest indications in the ancient world through four millennia to the end of the 20th century. The many antecedents of public relations were mainly methods of promotion and disseminating information. It was not until the late 19th century that the term "public relations" was first used in the United States, although public relations-like practices (also called proto-public relations) had long been evident.

But what is public relations? This chapter doesn't propose a single definition as it will show that there has been a wide range of cultural, managerial, political and religious influences upon the formation of theories and practices. There are, however, some characteristics that shape the wide variety of forms of public relations:

- It is a planned communication and/or relationship-building activity with strategic or deliberate intent (Lamme and Russell 2016). Some definitions emphasise the management of communications (Grunig J. and Hunt 1984; Broom and Sha 2013), the management of relationships (Coombs and Holladay 2006) and the creation and maintenance of reputation (Chartered Institute of Public Relations 2012).
- It seeks to create awareness and understanding among specific groups, often referred to as "publics" or "stakeholders", and engage their interest.

https://doi.org/10.1515/9783110554250-002

- It has the function of enabling participation in the public sphere, giving voice to organisations and institutions.
- The interest of the public should result in a mutually beneficial relationship or response, possibly as dialogue (Gutiérrez-García, Recalde, and Pinera-Camacho 2015). Thus, it is different from publicity which only seeks to disseminate messages.
- Therefore, in the nature of its operation, public relations is a two-way activity enacted through the media, which has been the gatekeeper of communication. With the rise of social media, public relations activity has increasingly become a form of direct communication, bypassing media scrutiny.
- Although the US public relations pioneer Edward L. Bernays proposed that "public relations attempts to engineer public support" (Bernays 1955: 4–5), the term "to engineer" is rejected by many as implying manipulation rather than truth-telling. Ethical communication is the bedrock of public relations.

This chapter will consider the antecedents of public relations (proto-public relations), as well as the formation and expansion of public relations in six major continental blocks – Asia, Australia and New Zealand, Middle East and Africa, Latin America, Europe and North America. It then reviews the development of public relations into a professional-style practice during the 20th century with particular reference to North America and the internationalisation of practices. The chapter concludes with a three-part reflection on the antecedents, the springboards (impetuses for expansion) and the restraints that affected public relations across the world.

2 How public relations began

When did public relations (or similar practices) begin? Suggestions include Sumerian wall-markings from 2000 BC (in modern Iraq) to the persuasive rhetoricians of Ancient Greece (400 BC) or proto-handbooks of election propaganda for candidates and the personality cults of Roman emperors. Al-Badr (2004) has claimed that a 4,000-year-old cuneiform tablet found in Iraq was similar to a "bulletin telling farmers how to grow better crops" and thus a form of promotional information. Cicero's brother advised him on how to win over public opinion if he wanted to become consul of the Roman Consulate in his epistolary *Commentariolum Petitionis* (Comments on Elections), a precedent of election campaigns handbooks (64 BC). Julius Caesar, when consul in 59 BC, published a daily news tablet or sheet called *Acta Diurna* (Daily Gazette) that offered information to the Roman populus and showed him as an active leader. In the Christian era, Brown (2015) has proposed that St Paul the Apostle was a 1st century example of a public relations practitioner because of his influence on others, the campaign he undertook to reach out and build relationships with faith communities and his writing and publication of "letters" (books) of the Bible. Other examples are the formation and promotion of saintly cults (Watson 2008), and the promotion of crusades by popes.

These examples are not public relations, because they were not "seen as strategically planned activity in medieval times and (...) did not use the framing of language and accumulated best practice that are applied now" (Watson 2008: 20). "They were PR-like but were not PR", hence it was "proto-public relations" (Watson 2008). This term is based on "proto", meaning "original" or "primitive" (OED 2005: 601), similar to the term "prototype". In the discussion of regional and continental evolution of public relations that follows, a thematic analysis is used and not all countries are referred to.

2.1 Asia

Around the world there were other antecedents of public relations. In China, activities can be traced for thousands of years occurring mainly at state level "with the intention of the ruler or the emperor to establish a credible reputation among his people, or to maintain a harmonious relationship with different sectors of society" (Hung-Baesecke and Chen 2014: 24). These occurred in three forms: collections of folklore and culture such as folk songs, lobbying between rival states in order to avoid war and prevent attacks, and diplomacy to open trade links such as the Silk Road across Asia. Chinese, Taiwanese and Vietnamese researchers point to Confucianism as an ancient and enduring influence on proto-public relations and modern practices. Keeping promises and valuing reputation, an emphasis on interpersonal relationships and "relational harmony", being firm on principles and ethics yet flexible on strategy and the importance of propriety led to the formation of proto-public relations based on *guanxi* (personal connections), which has both positive and negative aspects. It is also found in Vietnam as *quan hệ*, which also means "personal network" (Van 2014: 148). Confucianism emphasises "the importance of public opinion" (Wu and Lai 2014: 115) and has given a strong cultural base to modern public relations in East Asia. Proto-public relations in Thailand evolved through royal institutions from the 13th century onwards and was expressed in Buddhist religious beliefs and supported the nation's unity (Tantivejakul and Manmin 2011). King Rama IV, Chulalongkorn, in the late 19th century "used royal gazettes, printed materials, royal photographs and the release of information to the press" to provide clear evidence "of PR type activity to support national governance and imperialism avoidance" (Tantivejakul 2014: 130).

Although western forms of public relations are practised in Japan, it developed a culturally different form called *kouhou* which originally mean to "widely notify" (Yamamura, Ikari, and Kenmochi 2014: 64). The term first appeared in a leading newspaper and denoted an advertisement or announcement. In the Meiji restoration starting in 1867, older social and political structures were broken down during modernization although a more democratic society did not evolve. The "public did not exist, only the emperor's subjects did" (Yamamura, Ikari, and Kenmochi 2014: 64). However, the government formed news agencies to supply information to the rapidly expanding number of newspapers and "press agencies were the first organizations to systematically engage in the publicity business" (Yamamura, Ikari, and Kenmochi 2014: 64).

India, a British colony from the 18th century to 1947, has a proto-public relations history that goes back to the reign of King Ashoka (272–232 BC) whose edicts and inscriptions on rocks and pillars "were imperial communications to the subjects of his vast empire" (Vil'Anilam 2014: 35). During subsequent eras, rulers communicated with society through formal meetings at the emperor's court (Darbar), where representations were made and decisions given. In the first phase of India's communication history, until 1858, which Reddi (1999) calls a "propaganda" era, there was communication from the British-owned East India Company, and the first, short-lived newspaper was started in Calcutta in 1780. It was followed by the "publicity and information" era until independence. This period included the formation of the governmental Central Publicity Board during World War I, India's first organisational communication operation (Bardhan and Patwardhan 2004) and the development of public relations activities undertaken by Indian Railways.

2.2 Australia and New Zealand

Australia and New Zealand, both British colonies until the start of the 20th century, also saw government communication as the preparatory stage for public relations. In Australia, "Government attempts to inform, convince and persuade the widely spread population relied on and exploited PR strategies more than any single entity private enterprise could hope to achieve" (Sheehan 2014: 11). Promotional activities undertaken by the colonies that made up 19th century Australia attracted immigrants to new settlements and miners to the mid-century gold rush, as well as lobbying the colonial master in London about independence and trade issues. In New Zealand, the colony's promoters sought immigrants and investors, and positioned a future separated from Australia as an independent dominion of the British Empire. Galloway (2014: 14) comments that 19th century New Zealand "began to develop some skill in the press agentry then beginning to emerge in the United States" and that strategic publicity took place as early as the London Great Exhibition of 1851 and the Vienna International Exposition of 1873.

2.3 Middle East and Africa

In the Arab world, before technology accelerated the speed of communication, traditional gathering points such as the mosque and the *majlis* or *diwaniyya*, a public gathering place for men, were both formal and informal channels for the dissemination and discussion of news (Badran 2014). Antecedents have been tracked back 1,400 years to the era of the prophet Mohammed when the new religion began to be disseminated among the tribes of the Arabian Peninsula (Abdelhay-Altamimi 2014). Poetry was important in this culture and the poet "was considered to be the press secretary of the tribe, attacking the tribe's enemies, praising its accomplishments and strengthening the fighter's morale" (Fakhri, Alsheekley, and Zalzala 1980: 34). It is a tradition that is "alive and well" in the modern Arabian Gulf region (Badran 2014: 8). The practice of public relations, prior to the arrival of Western agencies and corporate communication departments, was limited to a protocol role of organising events and taking care of visitors (Abdelhay-Altamimi 2014; Badran 2014).

In colonial Africa of the 19th and early 20th century, proto-public relations was in the form of governmental information, often supporting the formation of newspapers in British colonies in Eastern and Southern Africa (Kiambi 2014; Natifu 2014) and Nigeria in West Africa (Ibraheem 2014). Kiambi has found evidence of a Colonial Office information methodology that may have been applied in African, Asian and Caribbean colonies in the early to mid-20th century.

2.4 Latin America

In Latin America, public relations dates from the mid-20th century onwards, and shows the influence of corporate communication from US-owned companies, although a distinctive Latin American model of public relations was to evolve in the second half of the century. Only in Argentina, a Spanish colony until 1810, is there clear evidence of publicity-type activities during the 19th century in support of the nascent nation and its ambition to attract investment from Europe. These included newspapers promoting political groups and the national interest, and a diplomatic lobbying campaign (Carbone and Montaner 2014).

Before World War II, the Ford and General Motors car companies played an important role in Argentina and some other continental markets through their introduction of US-style communication and promotional methods. Public relations commenced in Brazil during 1914 when a Canadian-owned tramway company in Sao Paolo set up a public relations department, but progress was very slow until the 1950s. In Central America, corporate public relations activity supported the Panama Canal in 1914. In Colombia, Mexico and Peru, public relations was gradually introduced as a professional communication practice from the 1950s onwards, aided by US influences.

In the 1950s, Latin American nations and communicators saw the opportunities offered by governmental and corporate communication and formed one of the first regional public relations associations (FIARP), which launched the Inter-American Public Relations Conference. This regular event did much to share knowledge and aid the formation and sustaining of professional association and higher education courses in public relations. Brazil, in a unique step, licenced public relations practitioners in a 1968 law.

By the late 20th century, Latin America had developed a regional form of public relations, which was reported by Molleda (2000) as the "Latin American School of Public Relations". Moving away from corporatist, pragmatic approaches, it offered public relations as a social role where the practitioner is a "change agent or conscience of the organization" (Molleda 2001: 513) rather than a promoter for the employer or client organisation.

Public relations' expansion in the continent was aided by reduced statism and economic planning, and the move from military dictatorships to more open economies and plural polities. From the 1980s, public relations practice, professionalisation and education began to thrive. There appeared to be a correlation in the profession's development between increased democracy and more open economies across the continent.

2.5 Europe

The European antecedents are subject to considerable debate. Some scholars (Boshnakova 2014; Lawniczak 2005, 2014) consider that public relations in Eastern Europe and Russia arose only after the fall of the Berlin Wall in 1989 and the collapse of the Soviet bloc, a result of new democratic politics. Others, however, have identified proto-public relations activity in preceding decades and centuries, including among former Soviet bloc nations such as Czechoslovakia, East Germany, Hungary, Romania and Yugoslavia (Hejlová 2014; Bentele 2015; Szondi 2014; Rogojinaru 2014; Verčič 2014).

In Western Europe, Germany's public relations history was the best developed, with evidence of organised strategic communication in the 18th century. Early proto-public relations activity can be traced to writers employed "as publicists and as state employees in the 1790s" and Karl Varnhagen von Ense, a "full time 'press officer' [was] hired by the Prussian Chancellor von Hardenberg during the Vienna Congress (1814–1815)", which sought to solve boundary issues arising from the French Revolution and the Napoleonic Wars (Bentele 2015: 48–49). In 1841, a central bureau of newspapers was started in Prussia, with a succeeding *Literarisches Kabinett* or *Büro* (Literary Cabinet or Bureau) continuing until 1920. "Official" newspapers were established and government-friendly newspapers given financial support. "Economic and technical progress also shaped PR's development" (Bentele 2015: 50). Coal mining and steel manufacturing were the basis of heavy industry; electronics and chemicals were innovative sectors. Krupp (steel), Siemens and AEG (electronics) and BASF, Bayer, Hoechst and Agfa (chemicals) were seeking national and international markets and set up the beginnings of systematic, planned corporate and marketing public relations. In 1867, a full-time "Literat" (man of letters) was appointed as the manager of

Krupp's corporate communications, followed in 1870 by a corporate press department which monitored coverage of the company in newspapers and prepared articles and brochures to promote Krupp and its products (Wolbring 2000). Other German companies also developed press relations operations. In much the rest of Western Europe, there is little evidence of proto-public relations or planned publicity and press relations that can be compared with the German experience.

Although the United Kingdom had well-organised practices for informational communications in colonies, this was not evident in the four home nations until after World War I. There were notable exceptions such as the Marconi Company, which issued news releases in 1910 about trans-Atlantic telegraph services. In the Netherlands, there was a long tradition of *voorlichting* (a literal translation of "Enlightenment") in which people were given information so they could participate in societal discussions. *Voorlichters* travelled around spreading news about health, farming, education and politics (Ruler and Cotton 2015). In Norway, socially radical policies were promoted by *potetprest* (potato priests of the Lutheran church) in public information campaigns in the mid–late 18th century aimed at alleviating poverty through the planting of potatoes. The priests used lectures, handbooks and their enthusiasm in these planned activities.

2.6 North America

The antecedents of public relations differed in North America. In the United States, they were evident in the 19th century in a wide range of activities. The term "public relations" was used in a variety of meanings and circumstances (Myers 2017). In Canada, public relations evolved from governmental practices (Thurlow 2017; Lee, Likely, and Valin 2017). Although it has been almost traditional to ascribe the formation of public relations as a consequence of press agentry and publicity for circuses in the second half of the 19th century, recent scholarship (Lamme and Russell 2010; Lamme 2015; Lamme et al. 2017) has shown that it was practised in fields as diverse as railways, religious organisations and travelling entertainment. The hucksterish image of early publicity was shaped by press agents who earned their living by selling stories about clients to newspapers, while publicists sought media coverage for their clients through the creation of events and promotional actions. By the turn of the 20th century, the first agencies were being established, but their methods had been shaped by earlier practitioners.

Canada's experience was very different. It was a British colony until 1867 and its communication practices "focused on public policy and government administration" (Thurlow 2017: 41). Programmes up to the 1930s were aimed at nation-building and included campaigns from agriculture and immigration departments. Emms (1995: 27) comments that Canada lacked the "flamboyant publicists, controversial big business promoters and high-profile PR counsellors" that could be found in their southern neighbour.

3 Expansion

In general, public relations was a 20th century phenomenon. During the first half of the century, its expansion was primarily in the United States with some disrupted progress in Germany. The United Kingdom's engagement with public relations commenced after World War I, but expanded more rapidly from 1945 onwards, as did that in much of Western Europe and other regions of the world outside of Eastern Europe. In Asia, Thailand established governmental communications in the 1930s but other nations in that continent and in Africa developed public relations structures after independence, which mainly came in the 1960s. The People's Republic of China was closed by its Communist government from 1949 until 1979, after which public relations practice was gradually introduced as the economy reopened. The advance of public relations in Latin America was varied as many countries were under forms of military government, often until the mid-1980s.

3.1 United States

The predominant models of public relations practices were developed in the United States from the final decades of the 19th century onwards. Although most countries have national approaches to public relations, there are "International PR" models of practice in general and specialist areas used by transnational corporations and international organisations that have derived from US practice.

The mostly widely imitated US innovation was the agency for communication activities. Cutlip (1994) names the Publicity Bureau of Boston, started by three former newspaper reporters as a "general press agent business" in 1900, as the first of this type. It lasted for only 12 years but represented universities and American Telephone & Telegraph (AT&T). It was followed in 1902 by a New York agency set up by another newspaperman, William Wolf Smith, whose agency was a "publicity business" aimed at assisting corporations counter press attacks and regulatory legislation. The third agency, Parker & Lee, which followed in 1904, is especially notable as one founder was the newspaperman Ivy L. Lee who became the first high-profile public relations adviser and a major influence on US practice until his early death in 1934. Lee's partner was George Parker, who had served as President Grover Cleveland's press agent in his three presidential campaigns. Apart from Parker, all founders of the pioneer agencies came from newspapers. This set the style of practice as media relations for publicity purposes. Ivy Lee became an adviser to the Pennsylvania Railroad and the magnate John D. Rockefeller. Lee set out the argument for companies to put their cases to the public: "If you go to the people and get the people to agree with you, you can be sure that ultimately legislatures, commissions and everybody else must give way in your favor" (Cutlip 1991). Although Lee is portrayed as a public relations pioneer, he favoured the term "publicity", as evidenced in his 1925 book, *Publicity: Some of the*

Things It Is and Is Not. He did not promote a clear, organized vision of public relations, but believed in the benefits of keeping the press informed about organisations and letting the editors decide what information was to be published (Morse 1906; Hiebert 1966: 48).

The agency business grew gradually. It was not until after World War I, in 1919, that the earliest active promoter of "public relations" as a term and a communications practice set up in business. This was Edward L. Bernays who, with his soon-to-be wife Doris Fleischman, started their agency in New York. Bernays' importance is more related to his capacity for personal publicity and his prolific writing in books such as *Crystallizing Public Opinion* (1923), *Propaganda* (1928) and *The Engineering of Consent* (1955), and less for his leadership in public relations in the 1920s and 1930s, when he was seen by peers as a relentless self-promoter. On starting his business, Bernays titled it Edward L. Bernays, Counsel on Public Relations, thus presenting the concept of "public relations counsel" as a higher professional skill and calling than those of "publicist" or "press agent". As a close relative of his double uncle Sigmund Freud, he engaged with developments in psychology and sociology, as well as with academic developments such as the study of public opinion. What was an art for Lee, was promoted as a science by Bernays. His importance, which rose amongst US practitioners from the 1950s until his death at 103 in 1995, was in promoting public relations as being more than the negotiation of coverage in the media, but still a persuasive communication activity on behalf of clients.

Public relations and publicity work grew through the 1920s until slowed by the Great Depression. It was a contested area. Tedlow (1979) found that media owners loathed press agents and publicists and called them "space grabbers" because they obtained coverage in newspapers for clients without the need to buy advertisements. They were also recruiting journalists to do their work, a practice that still continues.

3.2 Other countries – after World War I

In Europe, public relations and publicity activity expanded in Germany and the United Kingdom after World War I. In Germany, it was well developed in industry, national government and, especially, local and regional government. This came to a halt in 1933 when the Nazis came to power (Bentele 2015). The most important developments in the United Kingdom were the formation of the "first public relations agency", Editorial Services Ltd, by Basil Clarke in 1924 (Evans 2013). Clarke used the term "industrial propaganda", especially in relation to communication with employees. Propaganda, prior to its blackening in the Nazi era, was widely used in government and industry as a synonym for informational communication and awareness-creating publicity. Stephen Tallents, another British pioneer in the establishment of public relations, led the work of the Empire Marketing Board to develop trade and business among nations, dominions and colonies of the British Empire. He later went on to advise the

BBC and government departments and was the founding president of the Institute of Public Relations in 1948 (Anthony 2012). In France, a group of US professionals tried to set up a public relations company in 1924. They attempted to organize conferences about the discipline but did not draw big audiences. Apart from this failed North American attempt, several French companies, such as Renault and Péchiney, developed initiatives to manage relationships with their publics before World War II (Rodríguez-Salcedo 2012: 349).

Other countries that introduced public relations included Australia, whose first self-styled public relations adviser was George Fitzpatrick in 1929 (Gleeson 2012). Many of its state governments had information and publicity departments by 1930. In Thailand, the government set up a Publicity Division in 1933, modelled on German practices, to provide information to the public. It has since evolved into the Government Public Relations Department (GPRD) and now plays a major role in managing government communication and relations with media industries (Tantivejakul 2014).

3.3 World War II

During World War II, all combatants had established propaganda and information operations. In the United Kingdom, the Ministry of Information was the mainstay of internal propaganda and public information campaigns. It continued as the Central Office of Information for decades until its closure in 2011. L'Etang (2004: 59) notes that "by the end of the Second World War, the British State had invested heavily in a variety of propaganda activities to support political, economic, and diplomatic objectives."

In the United States, the armed forces had public relations staff who were trained to accompany units into war zones, as well as to keep domestic audiences informed. Many veterans who had spent the war in military public relations units drove the expansion of public relations in the US and internationally in the following decades. The main propaganda organisations in the United States were the Office of War Information (OWI), which focused on disseminating information worldwide, and the War Advertising Council, which produced public service announcements. Both provided platforms for public relations and publicity employment, although as Lee (2015) found, employment in government departments dropped rapidly as the war ended.

In Germany, a previously diverse media sector was forced to follow National Socialist doctrines after 1933 with information centralized under the Reich Ministry of Public Information and Propaganda headed by Propaganda Minister Goebbels. "Needless to say, the entire system of public communication gained a propagandist character" (Bentele 2015: 52). By the beginning of the war in the Pacific in 1941, Japan had an established information division in its Cabinet office and the "propaganda machine was in place" (Yamamura, Ikari, and Kenmochi 2014: 65).

3.4 1945 onwards

After the end of World War II in 1945, the expansion of public relations gathered pace, especially in North America and Western Europe. Eastern Europe, which was under Soviet control, and China, which would come under Communist Party rule in 1949, were extensive, highly populated exceptions. Asia, Africa and Latin America would follow later.

In Western Europe, American influence was at its height in the nations that had been affected by the wartime conflict. US funding of the European Recovery Program (the "Marshall Plan") encouraged the democratisation of politics, open economies and the reconstruction of infrastructure. In some countries, communicators travelled to the United States and were briefed on public relations and promotional activity. Belgium, which had pre-war experience of propaganda and promotional activity from industries in its colonies, sent economic missions to the United States "which led to the propagation of PR in different parts of Belgium" (Ruler and Cotton 2015: 92). These visits noted that successful companies nurtured their relationships with publics through communication that had human dimensions. Germany, France, Greece, the Netherlands and Italy also benefited from Marshall Plan linkages. German public relations historian Günter Bentele refers to the period from 1945 to 1958 as "New beginning and upswing" (Bentele 2015: 47).

In Greece, the exposure to American advertising agencies and public relations practices in the tourism market in the early 1950s was the springboard for the formation of early agencies (Theofilou 2015). In Italy, the United States Information Service (USIS) was very active in recruiting Italian staff, producing films and documents, offering exchange visits to its homeland, and assisting the Christian Democracy party (DC) to combat the influence of the Communist Party (Muzi Falconi, and Venturozzo 2015). Portugal and Spain, which were non-combatants in World War II and ruled by military dictatorships since the 1930s, were not part of the Marshall Plan funding and programmes. Development of their national public relations sectors would be delayed until the mid-1970s when both dictatorships broke down (Rodríguez-Salcedo and Watson 2017). Spain started its public relations sector during the final 15 years of the Franco regime but it was not until democracy returned in the mid-1970s that it gained momentum (Rodríguez-Salcedo 2015; Rodríguez-Salcedo and Xifra 2015). Portugal shrugged off the Salazar regime at the same time, but took a decade longer than its Iberian neighbour to develop a national public relations sector (Santos 2016).

3.4.1 Emergence of professional associations

Other aspects in the post-war expansion of public relations were the formation of professional associations and the introduction of university-level education. Although the Public Relations Society of America (PRSA) was formed in 1947, it had antecedent organisations that dated to 1936 (National Association of Accredited Publicity Directors). In the United Kingdom, the Institute of Public Relations (IPR) was launched in 1948 with the assistance of a trade union, the National Association of Local Government Officers. Other national bodies were formed around the same time: Australia (1949), Belgium (1953), Denmark (1950), Finland (1947), France (1949), Germany (1958), Greece (1960), Netherlands (1946), New Zealand (1954), Norway (1949), Spain (1961) and Sweden (1950). France had two associations in the early 1950s and they merged in 1955 (Rodríguez-Salcedo 2012: 351). It was the same with Italy, with three associations in the late 1950s which merged into a single organisation in 1970.

In 1955, after several years of talks, the International Public Relations Association (IPRA) was launched in London and, for around 15 years, became the crossroads for international discourse. Although IPRA was composed of individual senior practitioners, it played a leadership role in defining aspects of public relations practice such as codes of conduct and ethics, early planning of public relations education and training and seeking recognition for public relations as a profession. IPRA was important from 1955 to 1970 in promoting public relations through its congresses and publications and by bringing practitioners together. From some of these connections, networks of agencies were built, some being acquired by the US agencies as they extended their offices and resources around the world. Also in Europe, the Confédération Européenne des Relations Publique (CERP) was formed through the initiative of Lucien Matrat of France in 1959. Matrat was its first president and also a prominent member of IPRA. CERP's Research and Education wing later became the European Public Relations Education and Research Association (EUPRERA) in 2000. IPRA continues as an organisation, although its role of international coordination and leadership has been taken over by the Global Alliance for Public Relations and Communication Management.

3.4.2 Education

The education and training of practitioners was seen as a vital element in building the skills base of public relations and defining it as a professional activity. Although the first public relations course was offered at the University of Illinois in 1920, it was not until the late 1940s that the new professional associations actively started to discuss education. In the United States, Boston University established the first degree programme in 1947, although around ten courses were offered at other universities. The first Canadian university PR course was taught at McGill University in 1948, but the first university degree was not offered until 1977 by Mount Saint Vincent University (Wright 2011). For at least two decades, the United States was the leading provider of university-level studies, mainly in second- and third-tier establishments.

The professional associations had education and training as a priority. Sir Stephen Tallents said in his 1949 IPRA presidential address that members' "first function (...) was to educate themselves" (L'Etang 2004: 188). IPR drew up its first draft syllabus in

1954, although many senior members were dubious about the value of education. Sam Black, later an honorary professor of public relations and an internationally recognised educator, dismissed education as a requirement for practice: "It is not necessary to have had any specialised training to have a good public relations outlook. So much depends on common-sense and good taste" (L'Etang 2004: 190). He was to change his stance because he was one of the most widely travelled public relations educators and trainers, the author of several books and leader of some of IPRA's policy-making on university-level education.

IPRA took the lead in shaping international approaches to education. Its Gold Paper No. 2, *Public Relations Education Worldwide*, published in 1976, was primarily researched and written by the German public relations leader, Albert Oeckl. Unlike later Gold Papers, it proposed that public relations topics should be part of a general humanities degree. It was followed by three other Gold Papers in the succeeding 20 years (1982, 1990, 1997), all of them used by universities and national associations to prepare degree programmes and accreditation processes. Examples include Denmark, Russia, Ukraine and Zimbabwe. The Gold Papers increasingly focused education and training on skills for public relations practice, rather than a rounded syllabus. This is a tension that has long existed between practitioner organisation and universities around the world.

The adoption of public relations degree studies did not follow a continental or regional pattern. Early introductions, after the United States, were Japan (1951), Belgium (1957), Taiwan (1963), Thailand (1965), Turkey (1965), Spain (1968), Egypt (early 1970s), Mexico (1976), Australia (mid-1970s) and Saudi Arabia (1976). Much of Europe, both Eastern and Western, launched courses in the 1980s and 1990s. In many countries, public relations courses had been taught within other degree programmes or at diploma level for one or two decades. The introduction in Eastern Europe came from 1991 onwards, following the collapse of the Soviet bloc. The United Kingdom, which had started discussing education and training in 1948, waited 40 years before the first degrees commenced; first, a master's programme at Stirling University in 1988, followed in 1989 by bachelor's programmes at three universities.

3.4.3 International public relations

Western Europe became the target for American corporations as economies revived in the 1950s and 1960s. This impetus gave a platform for the establishment of international arms of major public relations agencies and for multinational corporations' corporate communication departments. The first agencies to expand from the United States were Hill & Knowlton, Burson-Marsteller and Barnet & Reef. Hill & Knowlton was established before World War II in Cleveland and then New York. Burson-Marsteller was set up in 1953 and Barnet & Reef, which no longer exists, started in 1959. The agencies began by linking with partners or associates in the new markets and later acquiring either the partner agency or another business. This enabled them to support American clients as they expanded into new territories and grow the agencies' businesses (Rodríguez-Salcedo and Gómez-Baceiredo 2017). This development and the corporate communication expansion also led to the use of common public relations and publicity approaches that could be planned and monitored from a central position. The outcome was that American models of public relations became known as "International PR", with ubiquitous practices attempted in many countries of greatly varying culture, politics and societies. They have been very successful, as shown by their decades of operation, but not in all countries. In Thailand, for example, international agencies have come and gone. Often, they tried to impose an international model of PR to satisfy clients, but failed to gain desired results because they did not appreciate Thailand's Buddhist values and relationship culture (Tantivejakul 2014).

4 Worldwide growth

During the 1970s, momentum built for the worldwide expansion of public relations practices. Already, the early international agency networks were in place, corporate public relations departments were growing as governments and multinational corporations sought to expand their influence, and the technology for faster communications, such as telephone, satellite communication and television, was evolving. News media were also expanding. In many Western countries, newspapers could be printed and distributed from several cities; television news was less reliant on film and able to access satellite-distributed material. All these developments sped up the news gathering and dissemination processes (Gorman and McLean 2009) and increased pressure on organisations to respond quickly. It was also the decade in the United States and Germany in which theoretical research began to flourish. James Grunig, a noted academic theorist, led the way in the United States by positioning public relations as a management function. His definition of public relations as "the management of communication between an organisation and its publics" (Grunig J. and Hunt 1984: 4) is the most commonly cited. Other academics began to undertake research, and the first academic journal, *Public Relations Review*, was established by Professor Ray Hiebert in 1975. For much of the next 20 years, American research and theorisation would dominate public relations, until the academic base became much more international.

Through the 1960s and 1970s, public relations was mainly focused on media relations. This was a reflection of the journalistic background of many entrants and the expectation of employers in companies and governments that media coverage was beneficial. Media relations remains a major part of PR practice today. This type of public relations would change as graduates who had studied public relations and related communication topics increasingly entered agencies and organisations from 1990s onwards.

5 1990s

After the fall of the Berlin Wall in 1989 and the collapse of the former Eastern Bloc, public relations began to flourish in these countries. For some, this development was wholly new as it arose from the introduction of democratic governments, while others interpreted the rapid growth of public relations as the continuation of practices from the former socialist countries. They argued that many former governmental communications and propaganda people left their old jobs and became PR entrepreneurs using many of the same techniques and contacts.

In the 1990s, Europe led the PR world in two areas. The first was the formation of the International Communications Consultants Association (ICCO) which brought the world's PR trade bodies together, and the second was the interpretation of the quality assurance (QA) movement into the public relations field. In addition to ICCO, the professional bodies developed the Global Alliance for Public Relations and Communication Management, which launched in 2002. In this decade, there was rapid expansion of public relations in consultancies, government and corporations. An important springboard was the privatisation of governmental entities in many countries, fuelling further internationalisation of agencies and corporate communication operations as companies moved rapidly into new markets through acquisition. Another sector to emerge strongly was public relations for non-profit organisations, such as charities and social organisations.

A second springboard was the introduction of specialist public relations for technology companies ("tech PR") from the mid-1990s onwards. This brought new types of expertise and communication methods such as email and the early Internet, which were used by practitioners and organisations as communication and promotional tools. The Web 1.0 period was the beginning of the biggest transformation of public relations practices and strategies since the end of World War II. Until then, technology change was relatively slow, with facsimile (fax) machines only recently replacing telex and post. With Web 1.0, the pace of change accelerated.

In Latin America, the ending of several military governments and controlled economies led to greater democracy in politics and open markets, which in turn fostered communication such as public relations, political communication and advertising. Watson (2015: 14) notes that, after restraints were eased, "PR grew in all forms, as did education and training." In the Middle East and Africa, a relatively liberal period allowed the expansion of public relations, especially as the media environment became much more open and international. In Israel, the period since 1995 has been a "golden age" for public relations (Magen 2014: 53).

Although the bursting of the dotcom bubble around 2001 slowed the growth of public relations, it was only temporary as employment continued to expand. For example, in 2004, it was estimated that 45,000 people worked in PR in the UK. By 2011, it had risen to about 60,000. Similar growth has been experienced in many countries. For example, the annual *European Communication Monitor* survey is sent to more than 30,000 mid-to-senior level corporate communicators in 43 countries.

6 Summary

In a study of the public relations histories of more than 70 countries, Watson (2015) analysed them using three aspects: the antecedents of modern public relations, the factors that aided the expansion of these practices (springboards), and the restraints that slowed growth.

- *Antecedents:* There were three common forms: early corporate communications (e. g. Krupp in Germany, railways in the United States); governmental information and propaganda methods, especially in British colonies and former colonies; and cultural influences linked to dominant religions (Buddhism, Confucianism and Islam) in North Africa, the Middle East and Asia.

- *Springboards:* Watson (2015: 12) identified a sequence of influences that frequently assisted the expansion of public relations: *Governmental PR → Corporate communication → Formation of a Professional Association → Education at universities and colleges → Establishment of Agencies.* There were exceptions, especially in the focus on nation-building and politicised communication in post-colonial societies in Asia and Africa, but this sequence was seen in many more countries. In post-World War II Western Europe and in Eastern Europe after 1989, there was strong influence from American models of practice, but these have been modified into national forms of public relations.

- *Restraints:* Since the middle of the 20th century, public relations has not expanded at a uniform rate, even in adjacent countries, for economic and political reasons. Among the historic reasons were closed or statist economies, one-party and military governments that stifled free expression and the media and thus the emergence of public relations. Propaganda was dominant in some countries (notably Eastern Europe) until democratic politics was allowed. And elsewhere public relations was practised as a protocol activity to support rulers and not to foster dialogue (Middle East).

Overall, public relations has expanded as a practice mostly in democratic environments in which there is an open economy. There are exceptions but these are mainly, as in the case of Spain in the 1960s, when the controlling regime was beginning to ease controls on the media and politics to improve economic conditions. By the second decade of the 21st century, public relations had become a major communication practice around the world. The very small beginnings, such as Krupp in Germany and the first US PR agency business in 1900, have led to widespread employment, extensive use of practices and increasing research and education. It has come a long way from circuses, regional steam railways and telephone companies publicising their activities to a very limited range of print media, particularly in an era of social media.

7 Future directions for public relations history

The history of public relations has established a sound base over the past decade. Research and scholarship now need to develop in four directions (Watson 2016), away from a comfortable defence of current theory and historical practices.

The first direction is that more effort is needed for outreach and connection with other areas of media and communication history. Some media historians regard public relations as being inherently unethical and manipulative of public opinion. Public relations historians need to be more involved in this debate and respond to the challenges and orthodoxies of media historians. Leaving public relations at the margins of communication and media history is to overlook the richness of the field and the insights into social and political history that it offers.

The second task is that the historiography (the way in which history is interpreted) of public relations needs to engage with major theoretical debates, such as postmodernism, postcolonialism, discourse, new annalistic and other approaches. Postcolonial approaches to the history of public relations in nations and regions that have been decolonized after World War II have already shown new, rich and alternative interpretations in Southeast Asia and Africa. For students and researchers, there are many other opportunities for new interpretations to be applied.

A third direction is for public relations historians to challenge the legends of public relations that exist in so many older texts that have relied overly on tales of "great men" who supposedly shaped the field but were mostly self-publicists undertaking activities established in the generation before them. Not only were "great women" (and women in general) overlooked but the vast extent of proto-public relations has been ignored. It is time for public relations historians to become "dangerous" (Watson 2014) and not only reject the legends but also suggest new research methodologies.

Fourth, more historical research is needed on the people who have populated public relations work, moving away from easy reference points such as "great men" and self-publicisers. These "big names" didn't do all the work, make judgements, agonize over ethics, establish professional bodies, and undertake teaching and research. These productive activities were undertaken by the great mass of people who have worked in public relations, publicity and communication by organizations over the last century and before. Oral history research, the development of archives and the adoption of new historiographic approaches offer real opportunities for new under-standing of workplace roles and the expansion of public relations around the world.

Overall, the future of the history of public relations will be shaped in two ways: by historians who move away from the current inward focus and on to more challenging approaches; and by greater inclusion of history in the public relations curriculum, especially at undergraduate level.

References

Abdelhay-Altamimi, Nawaf. 2014. Kingdom of Saudi Arabia. In Tom Watson (ed.), *Middle Eastern and African Perspectives on the Development of Public Relations: Other Voices*, 83–96. Basingstoke: Palgrave Macmillan.

Al-Badr, Hamoud Abdulaziz. 2004. *The Basics of Public Relations and Its Practices*. Riyadh: Dar Aloloom.

Anthony, Scott. 2012. *Public Relations and the Making of Modern Britain*. Manchester: Manchester University Press.

Badran, Badran A. 2014. The Arab States of the Gulf. In Tom Watson (ed.), *Middle Eastern and African Perspectives on the Development of Public Relations: Other Voices*, 5–21. Basingstoke: Palgrave Macmillan.

Bardhan, Nilanjana & Padmini Patwardhan. 2004. Multinational corporations and public relations in a historically resistant host culture. *Journal of Communication Management* 8(3). 246–263.

Bentele, Günter. 2015. Germany. In Tom Watson (ed.), *Western European Perspectives in the Development of Public Relations: Other Voices*, 44–59. Basingstoke: Palgrave Macmillan.

Bernays, Edward L. 1923. *Crystallizing Public Opinion*. New York: Boni & Liveright.

Bernays, Edward L. 1928. *Propaganda*. New York: Horace Liveright.

Bernays, Edward L. (ed.). 1955. *The Engineering of Consent*. Norman, OK: University of Oklahoma Press.

Boshnakova, Dessislava. 2014. Bulgaria. In Tom Watson (ed.), *Eastern European Perspectives on the Development of Public Relations: Other Voices*, 5–13. Basingstoke: Palgrave Macmillan.

Broom, Glen M. & Bey-Ling Sha. 2013. *Cutlip and Center's Effective Public Relations*, 11th edn. Englewood Cliffs, NJ: Prentice Hall.

Brown, Robert E. 2015. *The Public Relations of Everything – The Ancient, Modern and Postmodern Dramatic History of an Idea*. Abingdon: Routledge.

Carbone, Carolina & Manuel Montaner. 2014. Argentina. In Tom Watson (ed.), *Latin American Perspectives on the Development of Public Relations: Other Voices*, 5–16. Basingstoke: Palgrave Macmillan.

Chartered Institute of Public Relations. 2012. What is Public Relations, https://www.cipr.co.uk/content/careers-advice/what-pr (accessed 12 October 2017).

Coombs, W. Timothy & Sherry J. Holladay. 2006. Unpacking the halo effect: reputation and crisis management. *Journal of Communication Management* 10(2). 123–137.

Cutlip, Scott M. 1991. Public Relations Was Lobbying From the Start. Letter to *New York Times*, January 18, 1991. http://www.nytimes.com/1991/01/18/opinion/l-public-relations-was-lobbying-from-the-start-560791.html (accessed 15 October 2017).

Cutlip, Scott M. 1994. *The Unseen Power: Public Relations, a History*. Hillsdale, NJ: Lawrence Erlbaum.

Emms, Merle. 1995. *The origins of public relations as an occupation in Canada*. Montreal: Concordia University MA Thesis.

Evans, Richard. 2013. *From the Front Line: The Extraordinary Life of Sir Basil Clarke*. Stroud: Spellmount.

Fakhri, S., A. Alsheekley & F. Zalzala. 1980. *Public Relations*. Baghdad: Ministry of Higher Education and Research.

Galloway, Chris. 2014. New Zealand. In Tom Watson (ed.), *Asian Perspectives on the Development of Public Relations: Other Voices*, 14–19. Basingstoke: Palgrave Macmillan.

Gleeson, Damian John. 2012. George William Sydney Fitzpatrick (1884–1948): An Australian public relations "pioneer". *Asia Pacific Public Relations Journal* 13(2). 2–12.

Gorman, Lyn & David McLean. 2009. *Media and Society into the 21st Century: A Historical Introduction*, 2nd edn. Chichester: Wiley-Blackwell.

Grunig, James & Todd Hunt. 1984. *Managing Public Relations*. New York: Holt, Rinehart & Winston.

Gutiérrez-García, Elena, Mónica Recalde & Alejandra Pinera-Camacho. 2015. Reinventing the wheel? A comparative overview of the concept of dialogue. *Public Relations Review* 41(5). 744–753.

Hejlová, Denisa. 2014. The Czech Republic. In Tom Watson (ed.), *Eastern European Perspectives in the Development of Public Relations: Other Voices*, 25–40. Basingstoke: Palgrave Macmillan.

Hiebert, Ray Eldon. 1966. *Courtier to the Crowd: The Story of Ivy Lee and the Development of Public Relations*. Ames, IA: Iowa State University Press.

Hung-Baesecke, Chun-Ju Flora & Yi-Ru Regina Chen. 2014. China. In Tom Watson (ed.), *Asian Perspectives on the Development of Public Relations: Other Voices*, 20–33. Basingstoke: Palgrave Macmillan.

Ibraheem, Ismail Adegboyega. 2014. Nigeria. In Tom Watson (ed.), *Middle Eastern and African Perspectives on the Development of Public Relations: Other Voices*, 97–108. Basingstoke: Palgrave Macmillan.

Kiambi, Dane. 2014. Kenya. In Tom Watson (ed.), *Middle Eastern and African Perspectives on the Development of Public Relations: Other Voices*, 67–82. Basingstoke: Palgrave Macmillan.

Lamme, Margot Opdycke. 2015. *Public Relations and Religion in American History: Evangelism, Temperance, and Business*. New York: Routledge.

Lamme, Margot Opdycke & Karen Miller Russell. 2010. Removing the spin: Towards a new theory of public relations history. *Journalism Communication Monographs* 11(4). 280–362.

Lamme Margot Opdycke & Karen Miller Russell. 2016. Theorizing public relations history: The roles of strategic intent and human agency. *Public Relations Review* 42(5). 741–747.

Lamme, Margot Opdycke, Karen Miller Russell, Denise Hill & Shelley Spector. 2017. United States – Development and expansion of public relations. In Tom Watson (ed.), *North American Perspectives on the Development of Public Relations: Other Voices*, 21–35. Basingstoke: Palgrave Macmillan.

Lawniczak, Ryszard. 2005. *Introducing Market Economy Institutions and Instruments: The Role of Public Relations in Transition Economies*. Poznan: Piar.pl.

Lawniczak, Ryszard. 2014. Poland. In Tom Watson (ed.), *Eastern European Perspectives on the Development of Public Relations: Other Voices*, 54–66. Basingstoke: Palgrave Macmillan.

Lee, Mordecai. 2015. Government is different: A history of public relations in American public administration. In Burton St. John III, Margot Opdycke Lamme & Jacquie L'Etang (eds.), *Pathways to Public Relations: Histories of Practice and Profession*, 108–127. Abingdon: Routledge.

Lee, Mordecai, Fraser Likely & Jean Valin. 2017. Government Public Relations in Canada and the United States. In Tom Watson (ed.), *North American Perspectives on the Development of Public Relations: Other Voices*, 65–80. Basingstoke: Palgrave Macmillan.

L'Etang, Jacquie. 2004. *Public Relations in Britain – A History of Professional Practice in the 20th Century*. Mahwah, NJ: Lawrence Erlbaum.

Magen, Clila. 2014. Israel. In Tom Watson (ed.), *Middle Eastern and African Perspectives on the Development of Public Relations: Other Voices*, 51–66. Basingstoke: Palgrave Macmillan.

Molleda, Juan Carlos. 2001. International paradigms: The Latin American school of public relations. *Journalism Studies* 2(4). 513–530.

Morse, Sherman. 1906. An awakening in Wall Street. *American Magazine* 52(5). 457–463.

Muzi Falconi, Toni & Fabio Venturozzo. 2015. Italy. In Tom Watson (ed.), *Western European Perspectives in the Development of Public Relations: Other Voices*, 75–88. Basingstoke: Palgrave Macmillan.

Myers, Cayce. 2017. United States Antecedents and Proto-PR. In Tom Watson (ed.), *North American Perspectives on the Development of Public Relations: Other Voices*, 5–19. Basingstoke: Palgrave Macmillan.

Natifu, Barbra. 2014. Uganda. In Tom Watson (ed.), *Middle Eastern and African Perspectives on the Development of Public Relations: Other Voices*, 138–152. Basingstoke: Palgrave Macmillan.

OED. 2005. *Oxford English Dictionary*. Oxford: Oxford University Press.

Rodríguez-Salcedo, Natalia. 2012. Mapping public relations in Europe: Writing national histories against the US paradigm. *Communication & Society* 25(2). 331–374.

Rodríguez-Salcedo, Natalia. 2015. Contributions to the history of public relations in the midst of a dictatorship: First steps in the professionalization of public relations in Spain (1960–1975). *Journal of Public Relations Research* 27(3). 212–228.

Rodríguez-Salcedo, Natalia & Beatriz Gómez-Baceiredo. 2017. A herstory of public relations: Teresa Dorn, from Scott Cutlip to Burson-Marsteller Europe (1974–1995). *Journal of Public Relations Research* 29(1). 16–37.

Rodríguez-Salcedo, Natalia & Tom Watson. 2017. The development of public relations in dictatorships – Southern and Eastern European perspectives from 1945 to 1990. *Public Relations Review* 43(2). 375–381.

Rodríguez-Salcedo, Natalia & Jordi Xifra. 2015. Spain. In Tom Watson (ed.), *Western European Perspectives in the Development of Public Relations: Other Voices*, 123–138. Basingstoke: Palgrave Macmillan.

Rogojinaru, Adela. 2014. Romania. In Tom Watson (ed.), *Eastern European Perspectives in the Development of Public Relations: Other Voices*, 67–81. Basingstoke: Palgrave Macmillan.

Reddi, C. V. Narasimha. 1999. Notes on PR practice in India: Emerging new human environment – A challenge. *Asia Pacific Public Relations Journal* 1. 147–160.

Ruler, Betteke van & Anne Marie Cotton. 2015. Netherlands and Belgium. In Tom Watson (ed.), *Western European Perspectives in the Development of Public Relations: Other Voices*, 89–106. Basingstoke: Palgrave Macmillan.

Santos, Joao Moreira. 2016. Roots of public relations in Portugal: Changing an old paradigm. *Public Relations Review* 42(5). 792–800.

Sheehan, Mark. 2014. Australia. In Tom Watson (ed.), *Asian Perspectives on the Development of Public Relations: Other Voices*, 4–13. Basingstoke: Palgrave Macmillan.

Szondi, Gyorgy. 2014. Hungary. In Tom Watson (ed.), *Eastern European Perspectives in the Development of Public Relations: Other Voices*, 41–53. Basingstoke: Palgrave Macmillan.

Tantivejakul, Napawan. 2014. Thailand. In Tom Watson (ed.), *Asian Perspectives on the Development of Public Relations: Other Voices*, 128–143. Basingstoke: Palgrave Macmillan.

Tantivejakul, Napawan & Prichaya Manmin. 2011. The practice of public relations in building national unity: A historical view of the kingdom of Thailand. The Proceedings of the International History of Public Relations Conference 2011. Bournemouth University, 6–7 July. http://microsites.bournemouth.ac.uk/historyofpr/files/2010/11/IHPRC-2011-Proceedings.pdf (accessed 12 September 2017).

Tantivejakul, Napawan & Prichaya Manmin. 2011. The practice of public relations in building national unity: A historical view of the kingdom of Thailand. The Proceedings of the International History of Public Relations Conference 2011. Bournemouth University, 6–7 July. http://microsites. bournemouth.ac.uk/historyofpr/files/2010/11/IHPRC-2011-Proceedings.pdf (accessed 12 September 2017).

Tedlow, Richard S. 1979. *Keeping the Corporate Image: Public Relations and Business 1900–1950.* Greenwich, CT: JAI Press.

Theofilou, Anastasios. 2015. Greece. In Tom Watson (ed.), *Western European Perspectives in the Development of Public Relations: Other Voices*, 60–74. Basingstoke: Palgrave Macmillan.

Thurlow, Amy. 2017. Canada – Development and Expansion of Public Relations. In Tom Watson (ed.), *North American Perspectives on the Development of Public Relations: Other Voices*, 37–49. Basingstoke: Palgrave Macmillan.

Van, Loan T.H. 2014. Vietnam. In Tom Watson (ed.), *Asian Perspectives on the Development of Public Relations: Other Voices*, 144–157. Basingstoke: Palgrave Macmillan.

Verčič, Dejan. 2014. Slovenia. In Tom Watson (ed.), *Eastern European Perspectives in the Development of Public Relations: Other Voices*, 99–109. Basingstoke: Palgrave Macmillan.

Vil'Anilam, John V. 2014. India. In Tom Watson (ed.), *Asian Perspectives on the Development of Public Relations: Other Voices*, 34–47. Basingstoke: Palgrave Macmillan.

Watson, Tom. 2008. Creating the cult of a saint: Communication strategies in 10th century England. *Public Relations Review* 34(1). 19–24.

Watson, Tom. 2014. Let's get dangerous – a review of current scholarship in public relations. *Public Relations Review* 40(5). 874–877.

Watson, Tom. 2015. What in the world is public relations? In Tom Watson (ed.), *Perspectives on Public Relations Historiography and Historical Theorization*, 4–19. Basingstoke: Palgrave Macmillan.

Watson, Tom. 2016. Special section: Public relations history 2016 editor's preface. *Public Relations Review* 42(5). 739–740

Wolbring, Barbara. 2000. *Krupp und die Öffentlichkeit im 19. Jahrhundert: Selbstdarstellung, öffentliche Wahrnehmung und gesellschaftliche Kommunikation.* Munich: C.H. Beck.

Wright, Donald. 2011. History and development of public relations education in North America: A critical analysis. *Journal of Communication Management* 15(3). 236–255.

Wu, Yi-Chen & Ying-Ju Lai. 2014. Taiwan. In Tom Watson (ed.), *Asian Perspectives on the Development of Public Relations: Other Voices*, 114–127. Basingstoke: Palgrave Macmillan.

Yamamura, Koichi, Seiya Ikari & Takashi Kenmochi. 2014. Japan. In Tom Watson (ed.), *Asian Perspectives on the Development of Public Relations: Other Voices*, 63–77. Basingstoke: Palgrave Macmillan.

Elizabeth L. Toth and Linda Aldoory

3 Women in public relations: A feminist perspective

Abstract: Studies of women in public relations form a substantial body of knowledge today. Between 2005 and 2015, 70 gender-based academic and trade articles were published in public relations and strategic communication journals/trade journals. We consider gender to be an indelible influence on the shape of the public relations field and on public relations scholarship. We also believe that public relations as a communication function of organizations has a responsibility, and the women who make up the vast majority of public relations practitioners likewise, to be the ethical organizational voice that informs and contributes to the public interest. By addressing women's issues in public relations in this chapter, we hope to advance what public relations can accomplish within organizational settings and the greater societies in which organizational public relations operates. This chapter describes the historical beginnings of the research agenda on women and public relations and how this research developed. First, we define key terms, such as gender and feminism. Then, we address the critiques and challenges to feminist theory, including how feminist theory compares and contrasts with other public relations theoretical perspectives. Finally, we summarize how feminist theories of public relations might further evolve.

Keywords: women; gender; female; feminist; feminism

1 Introduction

Studies of women in public relations form a substantial body of knowledge today. Between 2005 and 2015, 70 gender-based academic and trade articles were published in public relations and strategic communication journals/trade journals (Place and Vardeman-Winter 2015: 3). According to Place and Vardeman-Winter (2015: 3), "the state of gender research in public relations is alive and healthy." We consider gender to be an indelible influence on the shape of the public relations field and on public relations scholarship. We also believe that public relations as a communication function of organizations has a responsibility, and the women who make up the vast majority of public relations practitioners likewise, to be the ethical organizational voice that informs and contributes to the public interest.

As feminist scholars, we adhere to Rakow's (2013: xiii–xiv) definition of public relations as "communicative activity used by organizations to intervene socially in and between competing discourses in order to facilitate a favourable position within a globalized context." By addressing women's issues in public relations in this chapter,

https://doi.org/10.1515/9783110554250-003

we hope to advance what public relations can accomplish within organizational settings and the greater societies in which organizational public relations operates.

This chapter describes the historical beginnings of the research agenda on women and public relations and how this research developed. First, we define key terms, such as gender and feminism. Then, we address the critiques and challenges to feminist theory, including how feminist theory compares and contrasts with other public relations theoretical perspectives. Finally, we summarize how feminist theories of public relations might further evolve.

2 Defining terms: Gender, feminism, feminist theory

L. Grunig, Toth and Hon (2001) noted that the terms "women," "woman," "female," "sex", "gender" and "feminine" are sometimes used interchangeably. This may be a practical consideration, perhaps to avoid boring the reader, but it also risks lumping all women into one category and possibly ignoring the diversity among them (Grunig, L., Toth and Hon 2001: 19). These authors concluded, "Woman may need to live with the tension between their individual identities and an affiliation with like others, an 'alliance of convenience,'" but it was understood that women are not homogeneous in their perceptions, actions, and lived experiences.

2.1 Gender

Definitions of gender in feminist research acknowledge the biological but also the individual and social meanings, reinforced through communication and intersecting with race, ethnicity, sexual orientation, and class, that create understandings of what it is to be female or male. Rakow (1989: 289) was among the first to call attention to the concept of gender as one that is in constant motion, a "way to organize and make sense of the worlds in which we live" rather than some universal meaning of what it means to be a woman or a man. L. Grunig, Toth and Hon (2001: 51) defined gender as a scheme based on biological differences for a way of dichotomizing people "such as asking respondents to check "male" or 'female' in the demographic portion of a survey." They argued that gender was also based on ascribed identities assigned to individuals by someone else or avowed identities or those that individuals declare about themselves. Their definition of gender links to Rakow's (1989: 289) position that gender is a construction with individual and societal involvement. Rakow wrote: "gender is not something we are but something we do and believe, it is performative" (1989: 289). Gender is not constructed in human relations alone but intersects with ethnicity, sexuality, class, and a range of other discourses, often in contradictory ways (Van Zoonen 1994: 3). Pompper and Jung (2013: 498) make the additional point that most gender research is about women though men have gender, too. We acknowledge the importance of gender studies with men and women, though besides Pompper's work, gender studies addressing men and masculinity have not been published in public relations scholarship.

2.2 Feminism

Definitions of feminism found in public relations scholarship emphasize the value of women's perspectives and the critique of a lack of gender critique. With a 1988 *Public Relations Review* special issue on women and public relations, L. Grunig introduced a definition of a feminism as "coming from a woman's point of view and having a transformative component: the empowerment of women" (1988: 48).

Other definitions of feminism have reinforced political and social dimensions, the role of communication, and the conditions of women's lives. Liao (2006: 106) stated, "Feminism grows out of social and political movements aiming to bring justice into society so the marginalized can choose their positions instead of being pushed into positions where they are." Aldoory (2009: 115) considered the process of revealing underlying symbols and meanings in media, in public relations, and in public relations products such as campaigns. Golombisky (2015: 391) quoted Kolmar and Bartkowski (2010: 2) in describing feminism as "attempts to describe, explain, and analyze the conditions of women's lives."

For L. Grunig, Toth and Hon (2000: 55), feminism shared four elements: the centrality of gender as an analytical category, the belief in equity and concomitant concern for oppression, an openness to all voices, and a call to action. Citing the differences in feminist thought, Fitch, James, and Motion (2016: 279) agreed in their reflections on feminism, public relations, and research that feminism is concerned with two objectives: "The first is descriptive: to reveal obvious and subtle gender inequities. The second is change-oriented: to reduce or eradicate those inequities." While scholars have argued for some major tenets bounding the feminist research, there are many different subdisciplines of feminism, such as "lesbian feminist; postmodern, poststructuralist, first-wave, third-world, or eco-feminist; Marxist or socialist or liberal or radical feminist; career, cross-cultural, global or mainstream feminist; nonaligned, proto-, psychoanalytic- and pro- or male feminist and so on" (Grunig, L., Toth and Hon 2001: 55).

2.3 Historical perspectives on gender in PR

Following World War 2, women of the late 1940s and '50s felt optimistic about a professional future in public relations, and historians suggest this might have led to a subsequent 1970s influx of women into the profession (Gower 2001; L'Etang 2015).

Unlike entry into most occupations by women, public relations was one of only a few occupations to show a "disproportionate" increase in female workers (Reskin and Roos 1990). While the U.S. led the world in opening public relations up to female employees, the United Kingdom, many European countries, and Russia were not far behind (Tsetsura 2014; Yeomans and Gondim-Mariutti 2016).

In the 1980s, the noticeable percentage increase of women into the public relations field led to public expressions of concern, which increased scholarly interest among researchers in the field (Toth 1988). Headlines in trade publications of the 1980s heralded women as becoming an issue for the field. Examples include: *A concern: Will women inherit the profession* (Bates 1983); *The women are coming, the women are coming* (Joseph 1985); and *Public relations numbers are up but the status is down* (Lesly 1988). These authors expressed the fears of practitioners that women would devalue the field of public relations and drive down salaries and the status of the profession. Similar debates were happening in European countries as well. In his 1985 survey on the impact of increasing numbers of women in public relations, Joseph (1985: 22) summarized mostly dire predictions along the lines of the following:

> More women will open PR agencies; there will be fewer PR jobs for men; competition for top PR jobs will increase between men and women; corporations will continue to expect less from women; more women will get promotions to top PR posts to fill EEO quotas; there will be a higher ethical performance; and many of the best PR women will leave to raise families and they will not return to full-time work in the field.

Very few voices accompanied the one claim in the Joseph survey of improved ethical performance due to women. Among those who sought to counter the narrative of women as "an issue" was Rakow (1989: 287), a U.S.feminist scholar who argued that the increasing numbers of women in public relations could be a "positive and desirable transformation." White women entering public relations would hold the values assigned to them by society, those of preferring cooperative and collaborative styles of interacting and organizing (Rakow 1989: 294–295); these are styles that could lead to advocating the social responsibilities of organizations.

In response to the concern about women entering public relations, the International Association of Business Communicators (IABC) and the Public Relations Society of America (PRSA) underwrote a series of studies on gender, salary, and status. The highly publicized studies included *The Velvet Ghetto* (Cline et al. 1986); *Beyond the Velvet Ghetto* (Toth and Cline 1989); a special issue of *Public Relations Review* (Grunig L. 1988); and *Under the Glass Ceiling* (Wright et al. 1991). Authors found significant evidence of gender disparities in professional practice.

In the 1990s, the PRSA underwrote several surveys of their members. These examined a set of variables, including salary, job satisfaction, roles and promotion to management, sexual harassment, and managerial traits (Serini et al. 1997; Serini et al. 1998a, 1998b; Toth et al. 1998). The results made their way into academic circles, and PRSA created a Task Force on Women in Public Relations in 1989, which continued until 2017 as the Committee on Work, Life, and Gender Issues. This early period of research culminated in a first book on U.S. women and public relations and how gender influenced practice (Grunig, L., Toth and Hon 2001).

3 Taking a feminist approach

Feminist approaches help to advance theories of why women are almost universally devalued by societies. Two such approaches are (1) a categorization of women's movements as waves; and (2) feminist thought as liberal or radical. Both of these feminist approaches have been applied to examinations of women in public relations.

3.1 Feminist waves

Waves represent generational periods of time when movements around women's issues were particularly strong across the world. In summary, the first wave of feminism between 1840 and 1920 focused on the equality of citizenry. The second wave was between 1960 and 1988 and focused on equal rights, workplace equality, and reproductive freedom. The third wave, between 1988 and 2010, included activism that rejected the idea of a singular value or goal for feminism. The fourth wave dates from 2008 forward and seeks to find a common ground between different groups linked around feminism (Looft 2017: 894). Yeomans and Gondim-Mariutti (2016) recount similar waves or lenses that provide a classification scheme for analyzing women's roles in public relations in the United Kingdom.

Using the waves approach, Gower (2001: 18), in her history of women in public relations, examined issues of *Public Relations Journal* between 1940 and 1972, and sought to explain the change in women's optimism about public relations careers. She found subsequent "murmurs of discontent" by the second half of the 1960s. Early women pioneers saw the field as a new profession with few barriers to entry, while the second generation had to deal with the feminine myth that women belong in the home (Gower 2001: 17). Pioneering women benefited from the first wave of feminism. A new sense of awareness by women in public relations followed the women's second wave or liberation movement, especially after 1965: "the reality was brought home to them that women faced discrimination in public relations just as in other professions" (Gower 2001: 20).

An exploratory study by Byers and Crocker (2012) of Canadian women junior academics did not find a correlation between feminist generations and the waves of feminism. They concluded that the waves framework did not capture the multiplicity of academic women's identities. The waves approach provided a theoretical starting point, but Byers and Crocker cautioned against generational generalizations.

3.2 Liberal, socialist and radical feminisms

The second approach, introduced by Steeves (1987) into public relations research, divided feminist studies into liberal feminism, socialist feminism, and radical feminism. Liberal feminism has had its most influence on feminism in America, according to Steeves (1987: 100). It represents an approach to feminist research that "focuses efforts on creating and changing laws to promote women's opportunities for professional and intellectual growth." Liberal feminists struggle for individual equality. Steeves critiqued liberal feminism as speaking "only to white, heterosexual, middle and upper-class women and incapable of addressing most women's concerns" (Steeves 1987: 95). Her example was of historical studies praising notable achievements of women.

Radical feminism often assumes innate differences between male and female and works to dismantle patriarchy, rather than making adjustments to the current sociological systems through legal changes. Radical feminists analyze the structures of power that oppress women, and believe those structures were originally based on a biological premise that males were superior to females. Typically, a goal of radical feminism is to create female-only spaces where the true value of women can be illuminated. As with the other types of feminism, radical feminism can be found all over the world.

Socialist feminism offers the "greatest potential for a comprehensive framework to address women's devaluation in communication," according to Steeves (1987: 97). Socialist feminism focuses on women's oppression as caused by oppressions by race, class, sexual orientation and cultural background (Steeves 1987: 105). Steeves described socialist feminists as seeking "theoretical and political balance in addressing multiple factors contributing to women's secondary status" (Steeves 1987: 97). For socialist feminists, the goal is collective over individual gains (Steeves 1987: 108). Some feminist solutions according to this approach include raising awareness about sexism in society, passing federal legislation that supports working parents and outlawing sexual harassment, and mandating equal representation for women in government (Hon 1995: 66–69). Socialist feminism has been more common in European countries (Gaido and Frencia 2018). However, authors and believers can now be found in all parts of the world. Simorangkir (2011: 34) addresses how feminism as a Western concept was attacked within a nationalist context in Indonesia, historically, and ultimately affected perceptions and status of women and men in public relations. According to the author, "most Indonesian feminists do not consider themselves feminists in the same sense as feminists in the West," and that today there are competing paradigms that overshadow any one feminist approach to research and practice in public relations.

4 Public relations' approach to feminist theory

Early feminist public relations scholars tended toward labeling their research either radical or liberal, as they attempted to explain the reasons for gender discrimination data in the field and to address solutions, but this dichotomization did not often work (Yeomans and Gondim-Mariutti 2016). In one earlier article that searched for explanations for gender discrepancies, Aldoory and Toth (2002) argued that the theory of human capital has been used to explain the differences found in the early PRSA and IABC studies. Human capital theory argues that differences in the amount of a person's human capital could predict many of the commonly observed gender differences in both productivity and earnings (Paglin and Rufolo 1990: 140). However, Aldoory and Toth (2002) held the years of experience, age, education, and education levels constant in a survey of 864 PRSA members so that salary gender comparisons would be equivalent. The authors reported that "when years of experience, job interruption, age, and educational level were accounted for, gender still made a significant impact on salary difference between men and women" (Aldoory and Toth 2002: 122). Thus, the human capital approach to considering certain factors as sources of change was not supported.

Research from different countries in the 2000s continued to show differences in pay and status, but often avoided labeling of gender work as feminist approach in presenting their data. The European Communication Monitor has consistently indicated pay discrepancies between men and women in public relations, and explanations run the gamut of perspectives (Zerfass et al. 2014, 2015). Frohlich and Peters (2007) examined the German agency sector and explored both gender stereotypes and organizational context to explain negative consequences on women in public relations. In a study of Russian public relations practitioners, Erzikova and Berger (2016) found that women who were top leaders in organizations still assumed traditional gender roles. They did not, however, identify these women as liberal feminists. In the U.S., Dozier, Sha and Shen (2013) reported an $8,305 a year difference in salary attributed to gender discrimination alone. In a survey of Chilean public relations practitioners, Mellado and Barria (2012) attributed gender as a factor that predicted professional roles, but did not bring in a feminist perspective in explaining the roles of women. Other researchers, such as Chen (2011), used human capital variables to predict career success for Taiwan agency public relations practitioners. While not necessarily a robust and comprehensive view of the gender differences found, the human capital factors continue to be part of the scholarly discourse in public relations.

There are scholars who have used more radical approaches to feminism and its framework for uncovering structures in public relations that oppress women even while they are the majority in numbers. Pompper (2007, 2011, 2012) has taken a radical feminist perspective throughout a number of studies that broadened the voices of women and how economic, professional, and supervisory systems need to be changed for purposes of equity. Vardeman-Winter's research has acknowledged and critiqued the study of White women in place of diverse women, while still benchmarking salary and status inequities (Vardeman-Winter 2011; Vardeman-Winter and Place 2017).

Feminist theories promised to look differently at women's lived experiences to seek out better explanations of gender bias, because statistics cannot do more than report the averages of large groups of people. *Toward a Feminist Theory of Public Relations* was a key article espousing feminist theory to explain the role of women in public relations. Based on long interviews and focus groups, Hon (1995) generated a number of factors to explain discrimination against women in public relations. Also, she identified a number of liberal/radical feminist strategies that can affect equity for women. Her findings led to building a feminist theory of public relations by explaining discrimination and positing a social agenda for combating women's subjugation.

There are several areas of public relations research that are relevant to the study of women, but two in particular seem closely aligned with a feminist approach to understanding gender discrimination. First, rhetorical public relations scholars search for ethical communication practices that can advance both organizations and their publics' interests. Heath (2009: 24) stated that the "the rationale for rhetorical theory is that it helps us understand the process of decision-making, collective efforts, and the give and take of conversation, debate, advocacy, accommodation, negotiation, and orative decision-making." The focus of rhetorical analysis can be the social collective that is continually shaping meanings, and feminist theory could add to rhetorical analysis by searching for a deeper commitment to the values, facts, identifications, and policy actions that affect women. Johnson and Quinlan (2015) published a feminist rhetorical analysis of a public debate in the 1914–1916 period on women's access to pro-Twilight Sleep, a procedure to help offset pain of delivery. Authors analyzed women activists and their communication tactics through use of a pamphlet, a collection of organizational documents, letters to the editor and books published (Johnson and Quinlan 2015). Johnson and Quinlan concluded that this movement changed the course of birthing from midwifery to the standard practice of hospital delivery. In keeping with other rhetorical case studies of activist group public relations, the technical sphere won over the public sphere and women lost ground in advocating for themselves regarding childbirth.

Second, public relations is intertwined with the critical perspective. Critical theory has as its goal contesting the ideological assumptions that undergird theory building (Martin 2003). It seeks to expose how powerful organizations dominate less powerful publics and to open up different research questions about organizations and their relationships to the public interest, thus liberating the intellectual domain (Dozier and Lauzen 2000). Critical theorists, like rhetorical theorists, focus on the symbolic processes of organizations but their efforts are not to contribute to a fully functioning society but to disrupt beliefs about society. Several feminist public relations scholars have addressed critical theory and gender in their work. Aldoory (2009) used critical theory to focus on gender and power in her analysis of public relations texts. Fitch, James and Motion (2016: 280) developed a feminist research agenda for public relations, arguing that "a critical research perspective considers how power is manifest in society, in organizational structures, in institutional processes and in occupational identities."

5 Critique of the current feminist perspective

What the statistics have told us about pay and advancement gender inequities have not changed much since the early 1980 PRSA audits. In a 2017 survey of 5,590 responses from employees of 51 agencies in North America done by Ketchum Global Research Analytics, men made $6,072 more a year than women when tenure, job type, education, field of study, location and ethnicity are held constant (Shah 2017). Men hold the bulk of the industry's leadership roles at the highest levels (Makovsky 2013; Risi 2016). However, while trade blogs and publications have flagged these inequities, their critique turns to individualist women solutions: more women for the boardroom; increased work flexibility; eliminate the stereotypes of women facing criticism for speaking up; and women need to promote themselves (Risi 2016). These suggestions continue to reinforce the assumption that women can change the inequities if they just try different strategies, that women can reason their way out of the inequity and devaluation issues. Public relations trade publications continue to feature individual women practitioners who have advanced to leadership positions. For example, the *Cision PR Newswire* blog (Rabin, June 1, 2017) ran a headline, "Successful Women in PR: Leaning in and Climbing Up," celebrating six women who have made it to the top of their organizations. This argument by individual example is used to offset the claims from many public relations salary surveys that women are more likely to be found in technical rather than managerial roles (Place and Vardeman-Winter 2015).

Feminist public relations scholars have critiqued themselves to advance theoretically the research on gender and public relations. Aldoory (2005: 672) called for a reconceived feminist paradigm for public relations because of the field's emphasis on "residual androcentrism, Modern, Western, and often elitist thought that implicitly undergirded gender studies in public relations." Aldoory urged a definition of gender as constructed socialization that included men and women because men are gendered as well as women. Constructed socialization also opens discourse about lesbian, gay, bisexual and transsexual experiences. Aldoory sought to extend conceptualizations of power beyond property to power as a discursive construction. Analysis of diversity/ inclusiveness needs to include perspectives of people of color rather than just White practitioners. "Diversity should be conceived and studied as situated knowledge, which influences the research participant, his/her performance and communication, the researcher, and his/her data collection and interpretations" (Aldoory 2005: 676).

Another critique argued for a shift from the lives of women in public relations (i.e. advancing improvements in the position of women public relations practitioners) to concerns about public relations in the lives of women (Rakow and Nastasia 2009: 262). Rakow and Nastasia identified the work of public relations gender scholarship as mostly written from a liberal feminist perspective that accepts the spheres of patriarchy and capitalism and seeks to work within these institutions. They called on gender scholars to turn to studies of "women who are the object of public relations discourses, those women who are outside the 'circle of men' whose knowledge is validated and replicated by public relations programs and campaigns" (Rakow and Nastasia 2009: 271). The authors wish to expose the lives of women who are subjugated by the "'relations of ruling' that characterize patriarchal, racist, and colonial societies." Daymon and Demetrious' (2014) edited book, *Gender and Public Relations,* is also a critical examination of public relations' social obligations.

6 How feminist public relations might evolve and look to the future

Scholars who have studied gender and public relations over the last three decades have provided a lens for the practice to reveal inequities based on gender identity and social constructions that surround males and females. Gender and power are reinforced through communication and organizational and individual behavior. Researchers today have sought to examine, critique and deconstruct norms, theories and human experience in order to define the public relations workplace as much more complex, fragmented and culturally nuanced.

6.1 Three renewed commitments

In addition to the critiques of feminist public relations research, Golombisky (2015), in a comprehensive summary of feminist public relations theory, called for three renewed commitments: (1) to reclaim Rakow's communication model of gender as performative; (2) to define diverse women through intersectionality and interstitialy; and (3) to build equity goals beyond the organization.

Her call to renew the feminist commitment to the conceptualization of gender as performative reminds us of the importance of the narratives of public relations women in their own right. Past narratives of how women public relations practitioners came to terms with the glass ceiling and how they make meaning of power (Wrigley 2002). Place (2012: 446) gave voice to how women public relations practitioners made meaning of power in their work, allowing for more nuanced constructions of influence, relationships, knowledge, access, negative force, and empowerment.

We have learned through narratives how gender is constructed in other cultures. Tsetsura (2011) revealed through one-on-one and focus-group interviews how Russian female public relations professionals thought of their work as a "real job," which is recognized and valued by the men in Russia. L' Etang (2014) provided evidence of constructed gendered perspectives of public relations practice, drawing on 27 oral histories from practitioners. Her findings of how British women gained access to public relations work in the 1940s, '50s and '60s were similar to those of Gower (2001). L'Etang (2014: 301) added to our understanding of gender and early practice by also learning how women resisted the public relations gender stereotypes and intrinsic qualities associated with them, such as domesticity, hospitality, empathy, and intuitions. Her participants gave voice to experiencing the male gaze and heteronormativity. Looking now at the social constructions revealed in these articles provides different facets of how gender is performed in different time periods, contexts, and cultures.

Golombisky (2015) called for a commitment to study feminist theory through intersectionality. She quoted Dill and Kohlman (2012: 403), arguing for an "emphasis on the interlocking effects of race, class, gender, and sexuality, highlight the ways in which categories of identity and structures of inequality are mutually constituted and defy separation into discrete categories of analysis."

Golombisky summarized the importance of standpoint theory to understand practitioners. For examples, Pompper has provided important research opening up the standpoints of Latinas (2007) and women of color (2011, 2012). See the work of Vardeman-Winter and Place (2017) summarizing the White workforce of public relations and the need to vigorously engage in intersectional research to reveal diverse practitioners' experiences. Golombisky also urged us as knowledge producers to explain our own standards, as for example done by Vardeman-Winter (2011) who reexamined her research findings from the standpoint of a White researcher.

Calling on her expertise as a women's studies scholar, Golombisky (2015: 408) challenged U.S. public relations feminist scholars to look into a world that "has become communicatively global, corporately neocolonial, and culturally diasporic." As our students and colleagues span the global, we have opportunities to build collaborations for women who are working to better societies through communication practices.

6.2 Propositions for the future

In addition to these renewed commitments to feminist theory, there are other suggestions for moving feminist public research forward.

1. Benchmarking studies are needed that measure inequities to help dispel the myth that equity now exists. Some in the field argue that there are no longer gender problems in the profession. By continually examining what jobs and roles women and men want and have, what job satisfaction looks like, and what salary levels are, researchers can clarify the gender disparities that still exist and compare them over time.

2. There are factors that have been virtually ignored in gender research that need to take priority in the future. For example, studies should explore the presence of micro-aggressions in the field, how these can be identified, and how they impact practitioners. Other areas of concern include client perceptions of male/female public relations practitioners and relationships, networking dynamics by gender, and the role of sexual harassment in the workplace.

3. Case studies should be used to reveal structures, policies, and barriers to gender equity and gender plurality. Multiple case studies would benefit the field by comparing different types of public relations practice, different organizations, and different genders enacting professional roles. Global, comparative case studies of gender would offer perspective on cultural, political, and national factors.

4. An innovative turn would be the use of participatory action methodology that engages public relations workers in the studies and centralizes their voice in the design, implementation, and analysis of the research. By separating researcher from practitioner, the findings from research often go unnoticed in the profession. Instead, researchers can create avenues of engagement for public relations practitioners where they are partners in the design of studies as well as the action that comes out of results.

5. More research should uncover and critique the use of gendered language in the workplace. In public relations, we are the experts who train others in how to best communicate, and yet we may not be looking inward to training ourselves in use of gender-oppressive language and micro-aggressions. Use of language such as "queen bee" diminishes women's equity in power as it suggests that the power the woman has is wrong, and men in the same role do not receive a similarly gendered moniker.

6. More research should help build our understanding of discourse analysis. Feminist and critical scholars have been employing this methodology, which asks the researcher to look more deeply at texts beyond their most immediate meanings. This form of analysis requires the rigorous process of reading and re-reading of texts as narratives that will reveal how gender meanings are built and reinforced.

7 Conclusion

Public relations research first examined gender because of the influx of women in the occupation, which threatened its status and salaries. Since then, feminist researchers have rightly identified the responsibilities of organizations and practitioners to go beyond a view of the occupation and its organizational functions to how and in what ways their enactment of gendered roles contributes to social justice in a global society. Feminist public relations scholars have contributed several lines of theory to this project. The challenges to research and practice outlined in this essay are meant to encourage researchers to seek further answers about how gender influences and is influenced by public relations practice.

References

Aldoory, Linda. 2005. A (Re)conceived feminist paradigm for public relations: A case for substantial improvement. *Journal of Communication* 5. 668–684.

Aldoory, Linda 2009. Feminist criticism in public relations: How gender can impact public relations texts and contexts. In Robert L. Heath, Elizabeth L. Toth, and Damion Waymer (eds.), *Rhetorical and Critical Approaches to Public Relations II*, 110–123. New York: Routledge.

Aldoory, Linda & Elizabeth L. Toth. 2002. Gender discrepancies in a gendered profession: A developing theory for public relations. *Journal of Public Relations* 14. 103–126.

Bates, Don. 1983. A concern: Will women inherit the profession? *Public relations Journal.* 6–7.

Byers, Michele & Diane Crocker. 2012. Feminist cohorts and waves: Attitudes of junior female academics. *Women's Studies International Forum* 35. 1–11.

Cline, Carolyn G., Elizabeth Toth, Judy Van Slyke Turk, Lynne Masel Walters, Nancy Johnson & Hank Smith. 1986. *The Velvet Ghetto: The Impact of the Increasing Percentage of Women in Public Relations and Business Communication.* San Francisco: IABC Foundation.

Chen, Yi-Ning Katherine. 2011. Social capital, human capital, and career success in public relations in Taiwan. *Chinese Journal of Communication* 4. 430–49.

Daymon, Christine & Kristin Demetrious. 2014. *Gender and Public Relations: Critical Perspectives on Voice, Image and Identity.* London: Routledge.

Dill, Bonnie Thornton & Marla H. Kohlman. 2012. Intersectionality: A transformative paradigm in feminist theory and social justice. In Sharlene J. Hesser-Biber (ed.), *Handbook of Feminist Research: Theory and Praxis*, 2nd edn. 154–174. Los Angeles: Sage.

Dozier, David M. & Martha M. Lauzen. 2000. Liberating the intellectual domain from the practice: Public relations, activism, and the role of the scholar. *Journal of Public Relations Research* 23. 3–22.

Dozier, David M., Bey-Ling Sha & Hongmei Shen. 2013. Why women earn less than men: The cost of gender discrimination in U.S. public relations. *Public Relations Journal* 7. 1–15.

Erzikova, Elina & Bruce K. Berger. 2016. Gender effect in Russian public relations: A perfect storm of obstacles for women. *Women's Studies International Forum* 56. 28–36.

Fitch, Kate, Melanie James & Judy Motion. 2016. Talking back: Reflecting on feminism, public relations and research. *Public Relations Review* 42. 279–287.

Frohlich, Romy & Sonja B. Peters. 2007. PR Bunnies caught in the agency ghetto? Gender stereotypes, organizational factors, and women's careers in PR agencies. *Journal of Public Relations Research* 19(3). 229–254.

Gaido, Daniel & Cintia Frencia. 2018. "A clean break": Clara Zetkin, the socialist women's movement, and feminism. *International Critical Thought* 8. 277–303.

Golombisky, Kim. 2015. Renewing the commitments of feminist public relations theory from velvet ghetto to social justice. *Journal of Public Relations Research* 27. 389–415.

Gower, Karla K. 2001. Rediscovering women in public relations: Women in the Public Relations Journal, 1945–1972. *Journalism History* 27. 14–21.

Grunig, Larissa A. 1988. A research agenda for women in public relations. *Public Relations Review* 14(3). 48–57.

Grunig, Larissa A. 2006. Feminist phase analysis in public relations: Where have we been? Where do we need to be? *Journal of Public Relations Research* 1. 115–140.

Grunig, Larissa A., Elizabeth L. Toth & Linda C. Hon. 2000. Feminist values in public relations. *Journal of Public Relations Research* 12. 49–68.

Grunig, Larissa A., Elizabeth L. Toth, & Linda C. Hon. 2001. *Women in Public Relations: How Gender Influences Practice*. New York: Guilford Press.

Heath, Robert L. 2009. The rhetorical tradition: Wrangle in the market place. In Robert L. Heath, Elizabeth L. Toth, and Damion Waymer (eds.), *Rhetorical and Critical Approaches to Public Relations II*, 17–47. New York: Routledge.

Hon, Linda C. 1995. Toward a feminist theory of public relations. *Journal of Public Relations Research* 7. 27–88.

Johnson, Bethany & Margaret M. Quinlan. 2015. Technical versus public spheres: A feminist analysis of women's rhetoric in the twilight sleep debates of 1914–1916. *Health Communication* 3. 1076–1088.

Joseph, Ted. 1985. The women are coming, the women are coming. *Public Relations Quarterly*. 21–22.

Kolmar, Wendy K. & Frances Bartkowski. 2010. *Feminist Theory: A Reader*. 3rd edn. Boston: McGraw Hill.

L'Etang, Jacquie. 2015. "It's always been a sexless trade"; "It's clean work"; "There's very little velvet curtain": Gender and public relations in post-Second World War Britain. *Journal of Communication Management* 19(4). 354–370.

Liao, Hsiang-Ann. 2006. Toward an epistemology of participatory communication: A feminist perspective. *Howard Journal of Communication* 17. 101–118.

Lesly, Philip. 1988. Public relations numbers are up but the status is down. *Public Relations Review* 14. 3–7.

Looft, Ruxandra. 2017. #girlgaze: photography, fourth wave feminism and social media advocacy. *Journal of Media and Cultural Studies* 31. 892–902.

Martin, Joanne. 2003. Feminist theory and critical theory: Unexplored synergies. In Mats Alvesson and Hugh Willmott (eds.), *Studying Management Critically*, 66–91. London: Sage.

Makovsky, Ken. 2013. Women in leadership in PR. https://www.forbes.com/sites/kenmakovsky/2013/02/25/davos-blog-1-women-in-leadership-in-pr/#13dd90233238 (accessed 27 November 2019).

Mellado, Claudia & Sergio Barria. 2012. Development of professional roles in the practice of public relations in Chile. *Public Relations Review* 38. 446–453.

Paglin, Morton & Anthony M. Rufolo. 1990. Heterogeneous human capital, occupational choice, and male-female earnings differences. *Journal of Labor Economics* 8. 123–144.

Place, Katie. 2012. Power-control or empowerment? How women public relations practitioners make meaning of power. *Journal of Public Relations Research* 34. 435–450.

Place, Katie & Jennifer Vardeman-Winter. 2015. *Status Report: Public Relations Research 2005–2015*. Miami: Lillian Lodge Kopenhaver Center for the Advancement of Women in Public Relations.

Pompper, Donalyn. 2007. The gender-ethnicity construct in public relations organizations: Using feminist standpoint theory to discover Latinas' realities. *The Howard Journal of Communication* 18. 291–311.

Pompper, Donalyn. 2011. Fifty years later: Mid-career women of color against the glass ceiling in communications organizations. *Journal of Organizational Change Management* 24. 464–486.

Pompper, Donalyn. 2012. On social capital and diversity in a feminized industry: Further developing a theory of internal public relations. *Journal of Public Relations Research* 17. 69–86.

Pompper, Donalyn & Taejin Jung. 2013. Outnumbered yet still on top, but for how long? Theorizing about men working in the feminized field of public relations. *Public Relations Review* 39. 497–506.

Rabin, Julia. 2017. Successful women in PR: Leaning in climbing up. https://www.prnewswire.com/
    blog/successful-women-in-pr-leaning-in-%20climbing-up-20753.html. *Cision PR Newswire*
    (accessed on 17 November 2019).
Rakow, Lana. 1989. From the feminization of public relations to the price of feminism. In Elizabeth
    L. Toth and Carolyn G. Cline (eds.), *Beyond the Velvet Ghetto*, 287–298. San Francisco: IABC
    Foundation.
Rakow, Lana. 2013. Forward. In Christine Daymon and Kristin Demetrious (eds.), *Gender and Public
    Relations: Critical Perspectives on Voice, Image, and Identity*. New York: Routledge.
Rakow, Lana & Diana I. Nastasia. 2009. On feminist theory of public relations: An example from
    Dorothy E. Smith. In Oyvind Ihlen, Betteke van Ruler & Magnus Fredriksson (eds.), *Public
    relations and social theory: Key figures*, 252–277. Hoboken, NJ: Taylor and Francis.
Reskin, Barbara F. & Patricia A. Roos. 1990. *Job queues, gender queues: Explaining women's inroads
    into male occupations*. Philadelphia: Temple University Press.
Risi, Jennifer. 2016. Public relations agencies are dominated by women. So why are all their leaders
    men? https://qz.com/631499/public-relations-agencies-are-dominated-by-women-so-why-
    are-all-their-leaders-men (accessed on 27 November 2019).
Serini, Shirley A., Elizabeth L. Toth, Donald K. Wright & Arthur G. Emig. 1997. Watch for falling glass:
    Women, men, and job satisfaction in public relations. *Journal of Public Relations Research* 9(2).
    99–118.
Serini, Shirley A., Elizabeth L. Toth, Donald K. Wright & Arthur G. Emig. 1998a. Power, gender, and
    public relations: Sexual harassment as a threat to the practice. *Journal of Public Relations
    Research* 10(3). 193–218.
Serini, Shirley A., Elizabeth L. Toth, Donald K. Wright & Arthur G. Emig. 1998b. An examination of
    managerial traits by men and women in public relations. Paper presented at the International
    Communication Association conference, Jerusalem, 23 July.
Shah, Aarti. 2017. Why do PR firms pay women, people of color less? *The Holmes Report*, https://
    www.holmesreport.com/long-reads/article/why-do-pr-firms-pay-women-people-of-color-less
    (accessed 27 November 2019).
Simorangkir, Deborah. 2011. The impact of the feminization of the public relations industry in
    Indonesia on communication practice. *International Journal of Strategic Communication* 5. 26–48.
Steeves, Leslie H. 1987. Feminist theories and media studies. *Critical Studies in Mass
    Communication* 4. 95–135.
Toth, Elizabeth L. 1988. Making peace with gender issues in public relations. *Public Relations Review*
    14(3). 36–47.
Toth, Elizabeth L. & Carolyn G. Cline. 1989. *Beyond the Velvet Ghetto*. San Francisco: IABC Research
    Foundation.
Toth, Elizabeth L., Shirley A. Serini, Donald K. Wright & Arthur G. Emig. 1998. Trends in public
    relations roles: 1990–1995. *Public Relations Review* 24(2). 148–163.
Tsetsura, Kathryn. 2011. Is public relations a real job? How female practitioners construct the
    profession. *Journal of Public Relations Research* 23. 1–23.
Tsetsura, Kathryn. 2014. Constructing public relations as a women's profession in Russa. *Revista
    Internacional de Relaciones Publicas* 8(4). 85–110.
Vardeman-Winter, Jennifer. 2011. Confronting whiteness in public relations campaigns and research
    with women. *Journal of Public Relations Research* 23. 412–441.
Vardeman-Winter, Jennifer & Katie R. Place. 2017. Still a lily-white field of women: The state of
    diversity in public relations practice and research. *Public Relations Review* 43. 326–336.
Wright, Donald K., Larissa A. Grunig, Jeffrey K. Springston & Elizabeth L. Toth. 1991. *Under the
    glass ceiling: An analysis of gender issues in American public relations*. PRSA Foundation
    Monographs Series 1(2). New York: PRSA Foundation.

Wrigley, Brenda J. 2002. Glass ceiling? What glass ceiling? A qualitative study of how women view the glass ceiling in public relations and communications management. *Journal of Public Relations Research* 14. 27–55.

Yeomans, Liz & Fabiana Gondim-Mariutti. 2016. Different lenses: Women's feminist and postfeminist perspectives in public relations. *Revista Internacional de Relaciones Publicas* VI(12). 85–106.

Zerfass, Ansgar, Dejan Verčič, Piet Verhoeven, Angeles Moreno & Ralph Tench. 2014. *European communication monitor 2014. Excellence in strategic communication – key issues, leadership, gender and mobile media. Results of a survey in 42 countries.* Brussels: EACD/EUPRERA, Helios Media.

Zerfass, Ansgar, Dejan Verčič, Piet Verhoeven, Angeles Moreno & Ralph Tench. 2015. *European communication monitor 2015. Creating communication value through listening, messaging and measurement. Results of a survey in 41 countries.* Brussels: EACD/EUPRERA, Helios Media. van Zoonen, Lisbet. 1994. *Feminist media studies.* Thousand Oaks, CA: Sage.

Johanna Fawkes

4 Public relations and the problems of professional identity

Abstract: Public relations' identity is shaped by various forces: the demands and constraints of being a professional, which apply to other professions as well; the identity(ies) preferred by public relations as a sector; those conferred on PR by others; and the particular roles adopted by or enforced on individual practitioners. The choices of ethical image reflect the confusion which permeates the profession. This chapter explores the tensions between these forces and the resulting identity conflicts, particularly regarding ethical responsibility. It closes with suggestions emerging from recent research taking a capability approach to public relations as a global profession.

Keywords: professional identity; professionalism; professional ethics; capability approach

1 Introduction

This chapter explores the collective identity of public relations (PR) as a profession and the multiple identities of individual public relations practitioners. The establishment of a collective professional identity is an essential stage in securing professional status, as this chapter discusses. This is no easy task due to competing factors, such as rival occupational groups who desire the same status, and to divisions among practitioners and academics. None of these factors is unique to public relations; study of ancient professions like the clergy and medicine reveal long disputes for supremacy in the church and on the ward. Among newer groups there is often less cohesion as the occupational group is still evolving. The section on professionalism helps set the scene for PR in particular by reminding us how widespread these issues are.

Broader examination of professional struggles also frames the discussion about how the public relations profession is presented – by academics, by professional bodies and by critics. This reveals how different sections within the practice seek to embrace or distance themselves from the term public relations itself. The situation is further complicated in PR by the proliferation of metaphors used to describe the individual practitioner: ethical guardian, corporate conscience, cab for hire, advocate in the marketplace of free speech are some of the examples considered in this chapter.

Problems with jurisdiction, definition, terminology and core concepts are outlined – including identity structures beyond professional role, such as gender and ethnicity. Recent research into building a global capability framework for public relations may help create a more meaningful identity, a way of telling others what it is public

https://doi.org/10.1515/9783110554250-004

relations can do. This emphasises the potential of PR, the contribution it can make, in the right context. It also reinforces the position that identity cannot be reduced to a simple sentence in complex and hybrid fields like PR.

The chapter is organised around a sequence of problems or issues that concern public relations' professional identity:

1. What is a profession?
2. Is public relations a profession?
3. Identity issues for PR as a whole
4. Identity issues for individual practitioners
5. Ethics, identity and the professional project
6. Reframing the profession through a capability approach.

The aim of the chapter is not to define the identity of public relations as a profession, but to consider the tensions between different views of the field. Identity is rarely imposed successfully; it emerges through reflection and observation. This chapter considers professional identity to be socially constructed rather than assembled from a collection of tasks.

2 What is a profession?

The term professional is used very loosely in public relations literature, yet is the foundation of many claims to reputation, autonomy and social value. It is used as if its meaning is self-evident, though associations may vary from "doing a decent job" or "getting paid" through "objectivity" to aspects of appearance, such as suits and briefcases or even masculinity and whiteness.

The description offered by a major US report into public relations education illustrates this:

> If you work in public relations, or teach it, you probably have used the word "profession" from time to time. Indeed, when we define public relations in its broadest sense – as an essential management function that helps an organization and its publics build relationships that enable them to understand and support one another – a case can certainly be made that public relations is a profession (PRSA 2006: 11).

Gregory describes public relations professionalism as "taking education and training as seriously as other professions (...) and [joining] the appropriate professional body" (Gregory 2009: 275). However, the case for the professional status of public relations proves to be somewhat elusive on closer inspection.

Professions are usually seen as originating in clergy, medical work and law (15th century), with changes in the Industrial Revolution (19th century) and the introduction of nationalised bureaucracies for managing society (20th century). Recent decades have seen the emergence of knowledge workers (21st century), the broad grouping in which public relations resides. Similar developments can be found across European countries, with differences beyond the region. It is interesting to note that the older professions, particularly medicine and law, continue to earn respect and have not lost professional status, despite being joined by so many new occupations. Freidson (1994) distinguishes between the older professions that have legally protected licences to practice and those less prestigious occupations that are protected by professional bodies. The discussion in this chapter focuses on the latter group, to which public relations belongs.

The study of professions can be broadly grouped into what are sometimes called *trait* or *functionalist* approaches and those considered to be based in understanding of *power* or *revisionist* approaches. The first grouping has its roots in the work of founding sociologist Emile Durkheim (1858–1917), who stresses the positive rewards of social duty, including the creation of "solidariness" within groups and societies. He theorises the role of groups and institutions as buffers between excessive state domination and individual alienation, including the family, religious institutions and "occupational groups" or professions. This somewhat idealistic approach was adopted – and adapted – as part of the wider, functionalist approach spearheaded by US scholar Talcott Parsons (1951). Parsons endowed professions with a moral purpose that was not always evident empirically (Sciulli 2005), while the detailed discussion focused on definitions and descriptions of professional work (its *traits*), rather than scrutiny of moral claims. This view dominates the field and underpins the role of professional bodies and codes of ethics in most western professional or occupational groups.

From the mid-1960s, this concept of professionalism was critiqued and challenged by the power approach (or *revisionists*, to use Sciulli's 2005 term) drawing on the seminal work of Max Weber (1864–1920) following the English translation of his *Theory of Social and Economic Organisation* in 1964. While both are concerned with the division of labour in society, Weber is more critical than Durkheim about the role of professions and their acquisition and maintenance of power over others. As Sciulli (2005: 917) puts it,

> revisionists also consider the rise of expert occupations with monopolies in the services market to be, if anything, a malevolent force in civil society, not a salutary addition. They reject outright as apologetic and ideological Parsons' conjecture that professions contribute in any way, let alone intrinsically, to social integration as opposed to social control.

One of the leading scholars of professionalism, Magali Larson (1977) draws on Weberian analysis to critique what she terms the "professional project", the means whereby a group of workers evolve through occupational status to form a profession, a movement that involves creating professional monopolies, guarding them in jurisdictional contests and mythologising their achievements. She deploys Weber's model of the ideal-typical profession, by which desired characteristics and domains are outlined, not as a descriptor of reality but as a benchmark or reference point, suggesting professions have proceeded as if the idealised version was descriptive rather than prescriptive. Larson emphasises professionalism as a dynamic process of securing and maintaining social status, "the process by which producers of special services sought to constitute *and control* a market for their expertise. (...) Professionalization appears also as a collective assertion of special social status and as a collective process of upward social mobility" (1977: xvi; emphasis in original). Revisionists, such as those cited above, consider the trait approach moribund and inflexible; yet professional bodies and practitioners still tend to conceive of professions according to their core tasks.

Despite these disputes, it is worth closing this brief overview of professionalism literature with Cooper's (2004: 61–63) definitions of a profession as comprising:
- esoteric knowledge – theoretical or technical – not available to the general population;
- commitment to social values, such as health or justice;
- national organisation to set standards, control membership, liaise with wider society;
- extra-strong moral commitment to support professional values.

3 Is public relations a profession?

Those scholars who have seriously asked whether public relations warrants professional status (Bivins 1993; Breit and Demetrious 2010; Pieczka and L'Etang 2001; Sriramesh and Hornaman 2006; van Ruler 2005) have tended to conclude in the negative as it meets some but not all of the criteria of a profession outlined above, given the open entry to this work and the difficulty of imposing ethical and other standards on the membership. L'Etang (2008: 26) goes further, suggesting that "only when practitioners have a good facility to understand and carry out a variety of research can the occupation move forwards to professional status". And of course, unlike medicine or law, anyone can practise PR; as Macnamara (2012) points out, only 3,000 practitioners belonged to the Australian professional body in 2009 out of an estimated 21,000 potential members, a point made earlier by van Ruler (2005) regarding European representation. However, undaunted by the difficulty of controlling practitioners, the field has strenuously sought professional status, because

> that would give credibility and reputation to the industry, increase the accountability and credibility of practitioners, enhance the quality of work produced by practitioners, and give practitioners greater opportunities to contribute to organizational decision making (Sriramesh and Hornaman 2006: 156).

In other words, professional status is good for business. The last point is particularly poignant as it speaks to the longing to be taken seriously in the boardroom and looks to professionalism as offering a path to that table. This is also consistent with Larson's understanding of the professional project, the means by which an occupational group improves its social standing.

This debate is contextualised by van Ruler (2005: 161) who summarises the literature of professions to produce four models of professions applicable to public relations:

1. *knowledge model*, in which professionalisation develops from expertise, with a commitment to both the client and society;
2. *status model*, whereby an organised elite secure power and autonomy;
3. *competition model*, which focuses on the client's demands and evaluation in competition with other professionals; and
4. *personality model*, which is suggested as the development of experts who build a reputation with clients by virtue of expertise and personal charisma.

Van Ruler finds that the knowledge model is strongly represented in US literature, with the competition model endorsed by others, though she points out that the first is over-reliant on the 'body of knowledge', while the second leads to confused identity – she argues that public relations needs a professional 'brand'.

Sriramesh and Hornaman's (2006: 157) survey of literature suggests that for public relations to be accepted as a profession (which the majority of their sources say has not yet happened), it must satisfy the following criteria:

1. Maintaining a code of ethics and professional values and norms
2. Commitment to serve in the public interest and be socially responsible
3. Having a body of esoteric, scholarly knowledge
4. Having specialised and standardised education, including graduate study
5. Having technical and research skills
6. Providing a unique service to an organisation and the community
7. Membership in professional organisations
8. Having autonomy in organisations to make communication-related decisions.

This summary is close to the definitions explored above, though it's not clear which of these hurdles PR fails to leap. Pieczka and L'Etang (2001) are critical scholars of public relations who challenge assertions made about public relations' professionalism. They believe open access to practice and unenforceable ethics provide obstacles to professional status, noting a tendency to describe what public relations professionals *do* (the trait approach), rather than reflect on their wider role which, they say, is due to "professionalisation efforts that necessarily rely on an idealistic understanding of the profession (Pieczka and L'Etang 2001: 229). As they say, most approaches to professionalism in public relations rely on a very optimistic view of the profession in society, based on Durkheim and Talcott Parsons' benign understanding of professionalism, concepts abandoned by the sociology of professionalism in the 1970s. Their view, that public relations is not a profession, is shared by McKie and Munshi (2007: 102) who note that the concepts of public relations as a profession that are prevalent in core texts tend to reinforce idealised versions of the field.

Of course, public relations is not alone in finding the concept elusive and this chapter will continue to use the term, because as Cheney (2010: 7) points out, "occupation (...) is not as suggestive of lifestyle, social pressures and one's place in society". I particularly like Brown and Duguid's (2001) phrase "community of practice" because it includes academics and other commentators, not just practitioners, and this chapter uses the term profession in this encompassing spirit.

4 Identity issues for public relations as a whole

Public relations could be considered to have a blurred identity in that it has difficulty defining the field, as explored further below. Students and practitioners will be familiar with being told public relations is "like journalism/marketing/sales etc". While problems with border control are not unique to public relations, they are very strong in this area. The power or revisionist school of professional study suggests that professions emerge from "jurisdictional struggles" (Abbott 1988):

> A jurisdictional claim made before the public is generally a claim for the legitimate control of a particular kind of work. This control means first and foremost a right to perform the work as professionals see fit. Along with the right to perform the work as it wishes, a profession normally also claims rights to exclude other workers as deemed necessary, to dominate public definitions of the tasks concerned, and indeed to impose professional definitions of the tasks on competing professions. Public jurisdiction, in short, is a claim of both social and cultural authority (Abbott 1988: 60).

Professions are then defined as emerging entities in which "dimensions of difference" (Abbott 1995: 870) – such as the introduction of examinations for apothecaries – form a boundary between surgeons and apothecaries, but within the larger entity of physicians. Abbott shows how social work emerged and defined itself against other occupational groups from the 1920s onwards, offering a useful parallel with public relations, as both groups have had to struggle for legitimacy. This struggle is intensified by ever greater pressures from economic, social, technological and other global factors, contributing to what some scholars see as the end of professions (Adams 2010; Broadbent, Dietrich, and Roberts 1997; Leicht and Fennell 2001).

Returning to public relations, Abbott's perspective enriches understanding of the field's relationship with neighbouring occupations like journalism, marketing or legal and human resources functions. This approach is used by Pieczka and L'Etang

(2001: 227) to suggest journalism and marketing operate as "jurisdictional compet-itors" for the field, and this issue is explored further by Hutton (1999, 2001, 2010) who considers that public relations' failure to identify its core concept threatens its very survival, given the superior self-theorising of marketing as a discipline. He cites the loss of jobs from public relations to other elements of an organisation, such as the legal, human resources and/or marketing departments. He notes that tra-ditionally there have been tensions between public relations and marketing, and there is certainly an overlap between aspects of social marketing, for example, and the core functions of public relations. McKie and Munshi (2007:102–103) note the "clear potential for misunderstanding and conflict in such divided core definitions", echoing Hutton's concerns about core concepts, but add that, despite this confu-sion, "professionalism comes close to the status of a mantra whose repetition is enough to ensure success for public relations in the third millennium". This is con-sistent with the critical stance of challenging assertions, and stresses the dangers of using the concept of professionalism without due attention to the requirements of that claim.

More recently, McKie and Willis (2012) explore Hutton's (2010) warnings from a complexity perspective, agreeing that advertising and marketing hegemonies have marginalised public relations. There is resonance here with the neo-institutional approaches to professionalism outlined by Bartlett, Tywoniak, and Hatcher (2007), among others. Briefly, this approach applies insights from biology and botany to suggest organisations and institutions come to resemble similar bodies over time, until one element finds points of divergence and starts a new direction (which if suc-cessful, will encourage other entities to adopt its choices). To extend the relationship with the natural sciences, L'Etang's (2011) calls for anthropological examination of the field. While most text books don't yet reflect these developments, scholars are leaving the old trait approach way behind in seeking to understand public relations as an occupational group (see, for example, chapter 8 in Edwards 2018).

A further confusion arises from conflicting conceptualisations of public relations as a promotional practice and as strategic counsel. As an educator and researcher, I have come across many university courses that share the name public relations but that offer completely different curricula – with one group, usually based in media and journalism departments, providing wide experience in media production and design but wholly lacking in business, management or organisational theory or practice; and another based in business schools, which covers accounting, for example, but not media practice (Tench and Fawkes 2005). Recent experience con-firms this division is not obsolete. So, is the problem one of core definition or simple labelling?

4.1. Problems with terminology

One legacy of the trait approach is in the continual problems with defining the field. Do we produce strategic advice or pseudo-events to use Daniel Boorstin's (2012 [1961]) phrase? The obvious answer is "both", but there is intense pressure to emphasise the former over the latter. For most of the past half-century, the main push has been to locate public relations firmly in the management discipline, ensuring that education in the field includes management theory and practice. Despite this effort, 84 per cent of senior practitioners throughout Europe cited the lack of understanding of communication practice within top management as their main barrier to professionalisation (Zerfass et al. 2013).

A further terminological problem is that "public relations" is rejected in many countries, with preference given to organisational, corporate or strategic communication or communication management (Christensen and Cornelissen 2011; Cornelissen 2017; Heath and Gregory 2015; Hallahan and Verčič 2007). Research among practitioners revealed that the term "strategic communication" is preferred (Macnamara et al. 2018; Zerfass et al. 2013).This ongoing debate over the naming of the field points to an ambiguity that is encapsulated by Edwards (2011), who discusses the various attempts to define the field and characterises the different approaches that exist. The varying foci of the authors she cites range from the management of communication, relationships, reputation, organisational identity and stakeholder engagement.

Many practitioners identify themselves by their specialisms, such as investor relations, or claim that political communication is quite distinct from the promotional aspects of those who are involved with products and/or media relations. It is a peculiar state when the component parts of a field are pulling away from other elements that contribute to that practice (Jeffrey and Brunton 2012; Thurlow 2009). For example, Thurlow's research with Canadian practitioners found many public relations people preferred to say they worked in advertising, because the latter field is better understood and subject to less ethical criticism. Thus, the problems of public relations' identity as a whole derive from within the field as well as from its external critics. In recent years, there has been an upsurge of interest in aspects which were neglected in the management approach, including public relations as a promotional practice (for example Edwards 2018; Cronin 2018). This work builds on cultural and sociological approaches, viewing public relations as social force generating social content suitable for meta-analysis. While conceptually robust and placing communication strongly in its social context, it may be a while before texts, curricula and professional bodies revise the professional goal of achieving recognition as a management role. Having looked at the overall identity of the profession, the next question concerns the identity of individual practitioners and how that is generated.

5 Identity issues for public relations practitioners

There is a wide range of writing on the formation and maintenance of professional identity from the fields of social psychology and organisational theory. For example, Dent and Whitehead's (2002) discussion of performativity, drawing on Goffman (1959) and Lyotard (1984), emphasises the hollowness at the heart of performing a professional identity. They go on to explore how professional self and identity (including gender and professionalism) are constructed and maintained across different work sites and in a variety of professional cultures. They find that professionalism has become managerialised, embedded in the employing organisation, just as management has become professionalised, so that the boundaries of what constitutes a profession are now blurred beyond recognition. A review of literature on teachers' professional identity concludes:

> What these various meanings have in common is the idea that identity is not a fixed attribute of a person, but a relational phenomenon. Identity development occurs in an intersubjective field and can be best characterised as an ongoing process, a process of interpreting oneself as a certain kind of person and being recognised as such in a given context (Beijaard, Meijer, and Verloop 2004: 108).

It is interesting that their review found divergent interpretations of identity, including self-image, professional roles in the workplace and images of teachers held by society, and suggests similar variations could be found in other professions' discussions of identity. Many of the approaches concerned the development of the self as a teacher, generally meaning the development of reflective skills and adjustments in self-understanding. These insights are clearly relevant to other professionals, including public relations and communication managers.

The formation of professional identity in public relations is less explored than in teaching, though there are notable exceptions. Daymon and Surma (2012) for example draw on the work of Wenger (1998), who rejects the dichotomy between individual and society, suggesting identity is socially constructed through the engagement with the practices, routines and stories of each social milieu. They are particularly interested in the multiple, fluid identities that women navigate in negotiating personal and professional spaces.

Their description resonates with Bourdieu's concept of "habitus", which Edwards (2010) uses to understand how professional identity is built, particularly among black and ethnic minority entrants to the profession.

> The professional habitus plays a significant role in defining what it is to be "a professional" and, like the other processes that define professional jurisdiction, its character is linked to the political, social and economic circumstances from which the profession has emerged (Edwards 2010: 206)

Edwards cites Bourdieu's (2000) observation that new entrants to a profession "fall into line with the role (...) try to put the group on one's side by declaring one's recognition of the rule of the group and therefore of the group itself" (Bourdieu 2000). This is particularly salient in observing how race and gender become institutionalised in professional identities, welcoming some and excluding others (Edwards 2018: 155). Most writers on professional identity ground their work in social identity theory (e. g. Haslam 2004) or the social constructionist view of identity (e. g. Broadbent, Dietrich and Roberts 1997). Here narratives of self are shaped by professional identity, which extends far beyond remuneration, as "the 'I' cannot talk with the authority of a professional, cannot give an account of itself as a professional, unless the discursive association is prior held and legitimised in the eyes of others" (Broadbent, Dietrich and Roberts 1997: 4). This discursive professional identity distinguishes between objective examination of discourses and language from the outside and the "subjective perspective of a particular participant in a community of practitioners who attaches particular meaning, significance, values and intentions to their ideas or utterances" (Kemmis 2009: 29).

This is only recently echoed in public relations scholarship, which has tended to assess roles using management rather than sociological theory. Tsetsura's (2010) exploration of social construction and its relevance to public relations challenges this assumption, as do the contributions of above-cited writers like Edwards, Daymon and Surma.

5.1 Competing identities

The above section outlined some of the ways in which a professional identity is constructed. This section looks at particular identities available to practitioners. While the social constructionist position can argue that these are fluid and the practitioner moves between them, there are some conceptual roadblocks between identities, particularly concerning ethics.

I have argued elsewhere (e. g., Fawkes 2007, 2010, 2012 and 2015) that these different identities embody different approaches to ethics and hence lead to different degrees of professionalism. The following table summarises those arguments, suggesting how PR identities are constructed within the academic community. The section below unpacks the ideas contained in the table. (For more detail about public relations' ethics, see Chapter 30.)

Table 1: A taxonomy of identities in public relations

Term	Theoretical school of origin	Description	Research	Images
Boundary spanner	Excellence/ systems theory	Represents the public to the organisation and vice versa	J. Grunig et al. 1992; White and Dozier 1992	Diplomat
Relationship manager	Relationship management	Responsible for building and maintaining internal and external relationships	Ledingham and Bruning 2001; Hon and J. Grunig 1999	Carer Trust manager
Advocate (1)	Rhetoric/ persuasion	Argues the case for the client/employer in democratic context	Heath 2001; Porter 2010	Orator
Advocate (2)	Marketplace theory Free speech	Argues the case for the client/employer in marketplace	Fitzpatrick and Bronstein 2006	Lawyer
Propagandist	Critical	Distorts the truth to protect client	Miller and Dinan 2008; Ewen 1996	Con merchant/ snake oil sales

The commitment to practice to a strong ethical standard is an essential element of claiming professional status (Cooper 2004). This entails balancing duties to client and duties to society, something which many professionals find challenging, particularly where those clients may undertake lawful but harmful business, as in fossil fuels, tobacco or arms. Challenges also arise when practitioners are asked to emphasise some aspects of a situation over others, for example stressing the food work a charity does to offset claims of abuse. In everyday practice, ethics is always present (see Fawkes 2018 for a fuller exploration of the harm in public relations).

The boundary spanner role, founded in the excellence school, makes the highest claims for ethical purity. Bowen (2007: 275) declares that excellence ethics conform closely to Kant's imperatives, finding that "ethics is a single excellent factor and the common underpinning of all factors that predict excellent public relations". Most writing from the excellence perspective on ethics draws on the systems theory (McElreath 1996) which underpins this approach. For example, Bowen (2008: 273) asserts that systems theory "provides a normative theoretical framework to explain why public relations is the best suited function to advise senior management on matters of ethics". This is the discourse which generates the "ethical guardian" image, which persists as an idea, despite L'Etang's (2003) challenge that public relations practitioners do not have the training to take on such a role. The relationship manager draws on similar approaches to ethics, with a strong reliance on codes to maintain professional standards.

Rhetorical approaches to public relations ethics often deploy aspects of virtue ethics (Baker and Martinson 2002; Edgett 2002; Harrison and Galloway 2005; Pater and van Gils 2003). Ideas of advocacy are found here, as rhetoric is less hostile to persuasion and seeks to balance multiple demands rather than perform idealized acts. Heath (2007) explores the tension between the symmetry proposed as the basis of ethics in the excellence approach and the ethical aspects of advocacy, noting J. Grunig's (2001) acceptance that not all ethical dialogue can be symmetrical, or there would be no room for debate. Rather, argues Heath, ethical advocacy requires equal access to the structures and platforms of debate. Porter (2010: 128) goes further, suggesting that "rhetoric provides a framework for ethical public relations", demonstrating, like the Bowen quote above, that ethical approaches to public relations are framed by competing theoretical lenses.

However, the strongest articulation of advocacy ethics is based in marketplace theory rather than virtue ethics (Fitzpatrick and Bronstein 2006). This model recognizes that public relations often plays a more asymmetrical or persuasive role than is encompassed by the boundary spanner, is strongly located in US jurisprudence and, while uncritical of free market morality, does acknowledge the need for awareness of factors such as access, process, truth and disclosure (Fitzpatrick 2006).

So far in this chapter, the nature of professional identity has been considered as a complex, fluid issue, essential to the creation of a distinct profession but the cause of tensions among and within practitioners who are faced by a number of potential identities to navigate. This is particularly true of the ethical identities available and the implications of seeing oneself as either a diplomat or a cab-for-hire. While some of the literature (Bowen 2008) urges public relations people to act as ethical guardians or corporate consciences, other research (Bowen et al. 2006) suggests a resistance to this role. I have suggested elsewhere that this proves a serious split identity for practitioners who either wear the saintly robes of the ethical conscience or apparently abandon them for the dirty business of making a living (see Fawkes 2012 for details). The final section of this chapter offers a new way forward for understanding the complex and changing nature of the profession that will allow individuals and professional groups to assess their own identities within a broader framework.

6 Reframing the profession

Earlier parts of this chapter identified the difficulties public relations faces in defining itself as a profession. This section summarises a two-year project undertaken by the University of Huddersfield for the Global Alliance (GA) to construct a framework that would help professional bodies worldwide to more accurately describe the scope of the field (Gregory and Fawkes 2019). In response, a nine-country academic research partnership was created, representing institutions in seven regions (Asia, Scandinavia, Europe, Africa, Australasia, North America, South America) who agreed to work with their national and regional professional associations and employers on a country-based research project. The results from each country were synthesised to form a matrix comprising the core capabilities of public relations as a profession (i. e. applied across the field, not expected of each individual). The brief from the GA was that the research should offer practical value to GA affiliated professional bodies and their members worldwide; reflect cultural and regional variations in public relations as a global profession; be forward-looking in its approach; and meet academic standards for rigour.

Unlike previous work on public relations competencies, (Gregory 2008; Manley and Valin 2017; Tench et al. 2013) which focus on the skills required of individual PR practitioners at different career stages, this research expanded concepts of capability in professions. For example. Lester (2014, 2016) has developed a holistic model that incorporates the needs of individual practitioners in a profession and the requirements of the profession as a whole, particularly in their societal role. The research design was also influenced by the capability approach (CA) developed by the Nobel prize-winning economist Amartya Sen (1999) with significant contributions from the philosopher Martha Nussbaum (2000, 2002). It has gained currency as an applied approach to development and global sustainability in recent years (Robeyns 2006), but has also been applied to educational development, health issues and the development of professions – for example, midwifery in sub-Saharan Africa. The core concepts of the capability approach are summarised by Walker and Unterhalter (2007: 2–7) as the centrality of a person's (or group's) well-being to human flourishing, distinctions between the capacity to flourish and the functioning or demonstration of valued achievements, and the freedom to choose what is valued. It is an approach that stresses potential and identifies obstacles to achieving potential (internal and external) rather than describing existing skill sets.

This offered valuable insights for researching not only what practitioners considered to be the core capabilities of the public relations profession as a whole, but also what might prevent individuals – and the profession – from realising their potential. Using a mix of expert panels, surveys and focus groups in each participating country, the research team identified a set of eleven capability statements, which describe an aspect of public relations seen as core to the discipline, together with sets of sub-capabilities, which provide more detail and depth to the eleven statements. While individual country-based research showed some (often minor) differences in emphasis, there was strong agreement that the final set of statements reflected the views of practitioners and academics consulted across the continents (see Table 2).

It is important to note that the framework is not a definitive statement and that it encompasses everything the profession is capable of, whether in an organisation or more generally. No individual will be expected to perform across all these indicators. It allows for specialisms within teams and within the occupational group as a whole. The table encourages individuals and managers to identify personal or team strengths and highlights other capabilities that may or may not be relevant to the particular workplace. This flexibility and practical application should help address issues of identity at the level of individual practitioner, group or department, and for the profession as a whole.

Table 2: Global capability framework for public relations and communication management. Source: Fawkes et al. 2018: 5–6

Type of capability	Capabilities	Sub-capabilities
	To align communication strategies with organisational purpose and values	– You set clear communication objectives that are aligned to organisational objectives and then see them through – You act as an architect of communication plans, enacting the purpose, values and policies of the organisation – You understand how communication can – and cannot – help an organisation realise its objectives
	To identify and address communication problems proactively	– You create short- and long-term narratives to facilitate communication with multiple organisational stakeholders – You identify opportunities to design organisational communication, and outline core content – You develop integrated communication operations
Communication capabilities	To conduct formative and evaluative research to underpin communication strategies and tactics	– You use research to listen to and understand situations before, during and after communication and relationship-building activities – You manage research design, data collection and analysis to improve communication outcomes – You establish evaluation systems to demonstrate the impact of communication
	To communicate effectively across a full range of platforms and technologies	– You have command of communication specialties, such as investor relations, and understand the optimum channels for specific stakeholders – You communicate effectively across paid, earned, shared and owned (PESO) channels – You have or can source strong written and visual skills to create and tell stories that engage and connect with diverse publics. – You synthesise complex concepts and convert them to simple, clear and relevant content

Tab. 2: (continued)

Type of capability	Capabilities	Sub-capabilities
Organizational capabilities	To facilitate relationships and build trust with internal and external stakeholders and communities	– You identify, analyse and listen to stakeholders and their communication needs – You develop stakeholder engagement strategies and partnerships that are mutually beneficial – You communicate sensitively with stakeholders and communities across a range of cultural and other values and beliefs
	To build and enhance organisational reputation	– You identify, analyse and strategically advise on key issues and risks for the organisation. – You help the organisation to define and enact its purpose and values – You help shape organisational culture and its processes – You understand and manage key intangible assets (e. g. brand, culture, sustainability)
	To provide contextual intelligence	– You see the bigger picture – socially, culturally, politically, technologically and economically – You identify strategic opportunities and threats, issues and trends – You operate in a connected world, demonstrating broad understanding of local and global diversity in culture, values and beliefs
Professional capabilities	To provide valued counsel and be a trusted advisor	– You combine a long-term perspective with the agility to manage crises – You offer strategic counsel to executive management, particularly regarding the interests of multiple stakeholders – You influence organisational decision-making and development – You negotiate with empathy and respect for all parties
	To offer organisational leadership	– You are part of or have access to the executive management team and help build internal alliances within the organisation – You demonstrate communication leadership by encouraging management based on dialogue – You demonstrate business and financial acumen through sound knowledge of the organisation's business and core processes

Tab. 2: (continued)

Type of capability	Capabilities	Sub-capabilities
	To work within an ethical framework on behalf of the organisation, in line with professional and societal expectations	– You consider business objectives in the light of society's expectations – You clarify the consequences of a proposed action on others, ensuring potential outcomes are understood by decision-makers – You understand and apply ethical frameworks – You recognise and observe the societal obligations of professionals
	To develop self and others, including continuing professional learning	– You take responsibility for your own continuous professional development, through a range of activities including training and education – You participate in industry events, represent the industry in public, and educate others on the role and value of public relations to employers and clients – You are able to offer professional guidance that involves, motivates and contributes to personal and team development

7 Conclusion

This chapter has considered in general the range of challenges facing any emerging profession seeking to establish its identity, and in particular the difficulties for public relations in agreeing its name, its functions and its role in organisations and in society more widely. These present serious disadvantages for any group seeking to secure its social status in a fast changing and fluid communications environment. The fragmentation of the field into older specialisms, such as internal communication or investor relations, as well as rapidly evolving fields like artifical intelligence and public relations, mean the core identity of the field is very unclear, as Hutton (1999) suggested over twenty years ago. Given that the number of people working in the practice and the membership of professional bodies has continued to grow in that period, some may say it is of no concern. However, there is a clear link between being a professional and being socially responsible, at the individual and collective levels; to lose professional identity runs the risk of losing ethical direction.

References

Abbott, Andrew. 1988. *The System of Professions: An Essay on the Division of Expert Labor*. Chicago: University of Chicago Press.

Abbott, Andrew. 1995. Things of boundaries. *Social Research* 62(4). 857–882.

Adams, Tracey L. 2010. Profession: A useful concept for sociological analysis? *Canadian Review of Sociology/Revue canadienne de sociologie* 47(1). 49–70.

Baker, Stacey & David L. Martinson. 2002. Out of the red-light district: Five principles for ethically proactive public relations. *Public Relations Quarterly* 47(3). 15–19.

Bartlett, Jennifer, Stephane Tywoniak & Caroline Hatcher. 2007. Public relations professional practice and the institutionalisation of CSR. *Journal of Communication Management* 11(4). 281–299.

Beijaard, Douwe, Paulien C. Meijer & Nico Verloop. 2004. Reconsidering research on teachers' professional identity. *Teaching and Teacher Education* 20(2). 107–128.

Bivins, Thomas H. 1993. Public relations, professionalism and the public interest. *Journal of Business Ethics* 12. 117–126.

Boorstin, Daniel J. 2012 [1961]. *The Image: A guide to Pseudo-Events in America*. New York: Vintage Books.

Bourdieu, Pierre. 2000. *Pascalian Meditations*. Oxford: Polity.

Bowen, Shannon A. 2007. The extent of ethics. In E. L. Toth (ed.), *The Future of Excellence in Public Relations and Communication Management*. 275–297. Mahweh, NJ: Lawrence Erlbaum.

Bowen, Shannon A. 2008. A state of neglect: Public relations as 'corporate conscience' or ethics counsel. *Journal of Public Relations Research* 20(3). 271–296. doi:10.1080/10627260801962749

Bowen, Shannon A., Robert L. Heath, Jaseub Lee, Graham Painter, Frank J. Agraz, David McKie & Margalit Toledano. 2006. *The Business of Truth: A Guide to Ethical Communication*. San Francisco: International Association of Business Communicators.

Breit, Rhonda & Kristin Demetrious. 2010. Professionalisation and public relations: An ethical mismatch. *Ethical Space* 7(4). 20–29.

Broadbent, Jane, Michael Dietrich & Jennifer Roberts. 1997. *The End of the Professions? The Restructuring of Professional Work*. London: Routledge.

Brown, John. S. & Paul Duguid. 2001. Knowledge and organization: a social-practice perspective. *Organization Science* 12(2). 198–213.

Cheney, George. 2010. *Just a Job? Communication, Ethics, and Professional Life*. Oxford & New York: Oxford University Press.

Cooper, David E. 2004. *Ethics for Professionals in a Multicultural World*. Upper Saddle River, NJ: Prentice Hall.

Cornelissen, Joep. 2017. *Corporate communication: A Guide to Theory and Practice*. Los Angeles: SAGE.

Cronin, Anne M. 2018. *Public Relations Capitalism: Promotional Culture, Publics and Commercial Democracy*. New York: Palgrave MacMillan.

Daymon, Christine & Anne Surma. 2012. The mutable identities of women in public relations. *Public Relations Inquiry* 1(2). 177–196.

Dent, Mike & Stephen Whitehead. 2002. Configuring the new professional. In Mike Dent & Stephen Whitehead (eds.), *Managing Professional Identities: Knowledge, Performativity and the 'New' Professional*, 1–18. London: Routledge

Edgett, Ruth. 2002. Toward an ethical framework for advocacy. *Journal of Public Relations Research* 14(1). 1–26.

Edwards, Lee. 2010. 'Race' in public relations. In Robert L. Heath (ed.), *The SAGE Handbook of Public Relations*, 205–222. Thousand Oaks, CA: SAGE Publications.

Edwards, Lee. 2011. Public relations and society: a Bourdieuvian perspective. In L. Edwards & C. E. M. Hodges (eds.), *Public Relations, Society & Culture: Theoretical and Empirical Explorations*. London: Routledge.

Edwards, Lee. 2018. *Understanding Public Relations: Theory, Culture and Society*. Thousand Oaks, CA: SAGE Publications.

Ewen, Stuart. 1996. *PR!: A Social History of Spin*. New York: Basic Books.

Fawkes, Johanna. 2007. Public relations models and persuasion ethics: A new approach. *Journal of Communication Management* 11(4). 313–331.

Fawkes, Johanna. 2010. The shadow of excellence: a Jungian approach to public relations ethics. *Review of Communication* 10(3). 211–227.

Fawkes, Johanna. 2012. Saints and sinners: Competing identities in public relations ethics. *Public Relations Review* 38(5). 865–872. doi:DOI 10.1016/j.pubrev.2012.07.004

Fawkes, Johanna. 2015. *Public Relations Ethics and Professionalism: The Shadow of Excellence*. London: Routledge.

Fawkes, Johanna. 2018. Harm in public relations. In P. Lee Plaisance (ed.), *Communication and Media Ethics*, 273–294. Boston & Berlin: De Gruyter.

Fawkes, Johanna, Anne Gregory, Jesper Falkheimer, Elena Gutierrez-Garcia, Ronel Rensburg, Gabriel Sadi, Alex Sevigny, Marianne Sison, A. Thurlow, Katerina Tsetsura, Katharina Wolf. 2018. *Building a Global Capability Framework for the public relations and communication management profession*. hud.ac/ect (accessed June 2018)

Fitzpatrick, Kathy. 2006. Baselines for ethical advocacy in the 'marketplace of ideas'. In Kathy Fitzpatrick & Carolyn Bronstein (eds.), *Ethical Public Relations: Responsible Advocacy*, 1–17. Thousands Oaks, CA: SAGE Publications.

Fitzpatrick, Kathy & Carolyn Bronstein. 2006. *Ethics in Public Relations: Responsible Advocacy*. Thousand Oaks, CA & London: SAGE Publications.

Freidson, Eliot. 1994. *Professionalism Reborn: Theory, Prophecy, and Policy*. Cambridge: Polity.

Goffman, Erving. 1959. *The Presentation of Self in Everyday Life*. New York: Doubleday Anchor.

Gregory, Anne. 2008. Competencies of senior communication practitioners in the UK: An initial study. *Public Relations Review* 34(3). 215.

Gregory, Anne. 2009. Ethics and professionalism in public relations. In R. Tench & L. Yeomans (eds.), *Exploring Public Relations*, 2nd edn, 273–289. Harlow, Essex: Pearson Education.

Gregory, Anne and Johanna Fawkes. 2019. A global capability framework: Reframing public relations for a changing world. *Public Relations Review* 45(3). 101781

Grunig, James E. 2001. Two-way symmetrical public relations: Past, present and future. In R.L.Heath (ed.), *The Handbook of Public Relations*, 11–30. Thousands Oaks, CA: SAGE Publications.

Grunig, James E., David M. Dozier, William P. Ehling, Larissa A. Grunig, Fred C. Repper & John White. 1992. *Excellence in Public Relations and Communication Management*. Hillsdale, NJ: Lawrence Erlbaum.

Hallahan, Kirk & Dejan Verčič. 2007. Defining strategic communication. *International Journal of Strategic Communication* 1(1). 3–35.

Harrison, Karey & Chris Galloway. 2005. Public relations ethics: A simpler (but not simplistic) approach to the complexities. *Prism* 3.

Haslam, S. Alexander. 2004. *Psychology in Organizations: The Social Identity Approach*, 2nd edn. London: SAGE Publications.

Heath, Robert L. 2001. A rhetorical enactment rationale for public relations: The good organisation communicating well. In R. L. Heath & G. Vasquez (eds.), *Handbook of Public Relations*, 31–50. Thousand Oaks, CA: SAGE Publications.

Heath, Robert L. 2007. Management through advocacy: reflection rather than domination. In James E. Grunig, Elizabeth L. Toth, & Larissa A. Grunig (eds.), *The Future of Excellence in Public Relations and Communications Management*. Mahwah, NJ: Lawrence Erlbaum Associates.

Heath, Robert L. & Anne Gregory. 2015. *Strategic Communication*. Los Angeles: SAGE Publications.

Hon, Linda C. & James E. Grunig. 1999. *Guidelines for measuring relationships in public relations*. https://www.instituteforpr.org/wp-content/uploads/Guidelines_Measuring_Relationships.pdf (accessed January 2018).

Hutton, James G. 1999. The definition, dimensions and domain of public relations. *Public Relations Review* 25(2). 199–214.

Hutton, James G. 2001. Defining the relationship between public relations and marketing. In Robert L. Heath (ed.), *The Handbook of Public Relations*, 205–214. Thousand Oaks, CA: SAGE Publications.

Hutton, James. G. 2010. Defining the relationship between public relations and marketing: Public relations' most important challenge. In Robert L. Heath (ed.), *The SAGE Handbook of Public Relations*, 509–522. Los Angeles: SAGE Publications.

Jeffrey, Lynn & Margaret Brunton. 2012. Professional identity: How communication management practitioners identify with their industry. *Public Relations Review* 38(1). 156–158. doi:DOI 10.1016/j.pubrev.2011.09.005

Kemmis, Stephen. 2009. Understanding professional practice: A synoptic framework. In Bill Green (ed.), *Understanding and Researching Professional Practice*, 19–38. Rotterdam: Sense Publishers.

Robeyns, Ingrid. 2006. The capability approach in practice. *Journal of Political Philosophy* 14(3). 351–376.

L'Etang, Jacquie. 2003. The myth of the 'ethical guardian': An examination of its origins, potency and illusions. *Journal of Communication Management* 8(1). 53–67.

L'Etang, Jacquie. 2008. *Public Relations: Concepts, Practice and Critique*. Los Angeles: SAGE Publications.

L'Etang, Jacquie. 2011. Imagining public relations anthrolopogy. In Lee Edwards & Caroline E. M. Hodges (eds.), *Public Relations, Society & Culture: Theoretical and Empirical Explorations*, 15–32. London: Routledge.

Larson, Magali S. 1977. *The Rise of Professionalism: A Sociological Analysis*. Berkeley & London: University of California Press.

Ledingham, John A. & Stephen D. Bruning. 2001. *Public Relations as Relationship Management: A Relational Approach to the Study and Practice of Public Relations*. 2nd edn. Mahwah, NJ & London: Lawrence Erlbaum Associates.

Leicht, Kevin T., & Mary L. Fennell. 2001. *Professional work: a sociological approach*. Malden, MA: Blackwell Publishers.

Lester, Stan. 2014. Professional standards, competence and capability. *Higher Education, Skills and Work-Based Learning* 4(1). 31–43.

Lester, Stan. 2016. Communicating Professional Competence. http://devmts.org.uk/parn2017.pdf (accessed June 2017).

Lyotard, Jean-François. 1984. *The Postmodern Condition: A Report on Knowledge*. Manchester: Manchester University Press.

Macnamara, Jim R. 2012. *Public Relations: Theories, Practices, Critiques*. Frenchs Forest, NSW: Pearson Australia.

Macnamara, Jim, Ansgar Zerfass, Ana Adi & May O. Lwin. 2018. Capabilities of PR professionals for key activities lag: Asia-Pacific study shows theory and practice gaps. *Public Relations Review* 44(5). 704–716.

Manley, Dustin & Jean Valin. 2017. A global body of knowledge. *Public Relations Review* 43. 56–70.

McElreath, Mark P. 1996. *Managing Systematic and Ethical Public Relations*. 2nd edn. Madison, WI: Brown and Benchmark.

McKie, David & Debashish Munshi. 2007. *Reconfiguring Public Relations: Ecology, Equity and Enterprise*. London: Routledge.

McKie, David & Paul Willis. 2012. Renegotiating the terms of engagement: Public relations, marketing, and contemporary challenges. *Public Relations Review* 38(5). 846–852. doi:http://dx.doi.org/10.1016/j.pubrev.2012.03.008

Miller, David, & William Dinan. 2008. *A Century of Spin: How Public Relations Became the Cutting Edge of Corporate Power*. London: Pluto Press.

Nussbaum, Martha C. 2000. *Women and Human Development: The Capabilities Approach*. Cambridge & New York: Cambridge University Press.

Parsons, Talcott. 1951. *The Social System*. London: Routledge and Kegan Paul.

Pater, Alberic, & Anita van Gils. 2003. Stimulating ethical decision-making in a business context: Effects of ethical and professional codes. *European Journal of Management* 21(6). 762–772.

Pieczka, Magda & Jacquie L'Etang. 2001. Public relations and the question of professionalism. In Robert L. Heath (ed.), *The Handbook of Public Relations*, 223–235. Thousand Oaks, CA: SAGE Publications.

Porter, Lance. 2010. Communicating for the good of the state: A post-symmetrical polemic on persuasion in ethical public relations. *Public Relations Review* 36. 127–133.

PRSA. 2006. *The Professional Bond: public relations education in the 21st century*. https://apps.prsa.org/SearchResults/view/6I-2006/0/The_Professional_Bond_Public_Relations_Education_i#.XinBuGhKiCo (accessed February 2018).

Sciulli, David. 2005. Continental sociology of professions today: Conceptual contributions. *Current Sociology* 53(6). 915–942.

Sen, Amartya. 1999. *Development as Freedom*. New York: Knopf.

Sriramesh, Krishnamurthy & Lisa Hornaman. 2006. Public relations as a profession: An analysis of curricular content in the United States. *Journal of Creative Communications* 1(2). 155–172.

Tench, Ralph & Johanna Fawkes. 2005. Mind the gap, exploring different attitudes to public relations education from employers, academics and alumni. Paper presented at the Alan Rawel/CIPR conference, Lincoln, UK. March.

Tench, Ralph, Ansgar A. Zerfass, Piet Verhoeven, Dejan Verčič, Angeles Moreno & Ayla Okay. 2013. *Competencies and Role Requirements of Communication Professionals in Europe. Insights from quantitative and qualitative studies*. Retrieved from Leeds, UK.

Thurlow, Amy B. 2009. "I just say I'm in advertising": A public relations identity crisis? *Canadian Journal of Communication* 34(2). 245–263.

Thøger Christensen, Lars, & Joep Cornelissen. 2011. Bridging corporate and organizational communication: Review, development and a look to the future. *Management Communication Quarterly* 25(3). 383–414.

Tsetsura, Katerina. 2010. Social construction and public relations. In Robert L. Heath (ed.), *SAGE Handbook of Public Relations*, 163–175. Thousand Oaks, CA: SAGE Publications.

van Ruler, Betteke. 2005. Professionals are from Venus, scholars are from Mars. *Public Relations Review* 31. 159–173.

Walker, Melanie & Elaine Unterhalter. 2007. *Amartya Sen's capability approach and social justice in education*. New York: Palgrave Macmillan.

Weber, Max. 1964. *The theory of social and economic organization*. New York: The Free Press.

Wenger, Etienne. 1998. *Communities of Practice: Learning, Meaning and Identity*. Cambridge: Cambridge University Press.

White, John & David M. Dozier. 1992. Public relations and management decision making. In James E. Grunig (ed.), *Excellence in Public Relations and Communication Management*, 91–108. Hillsdale, NJ: Lawrence Erlbaum Associates.

Zerfass, Ansgar A., Dejan Verčič, Ralph Tench, Piet Verhoeven & Angeles Moreno. 2013. *European communication monitor: Annual survey on future trends in communication management and public relations*. http://www.communicationmonitor.eu/ (accessed January 2018).

Betteke van Ruler

5 Public relations as a reflective practice

Abstract: In our digital and mediated age, organizations live in a public arena of very dynamic, ongoing constructions of meanings, expressed by often self-employed stakeholders. In order to cope with this arena, organizations need to be able to continuously adapt to change. Public relations can be seen as the field that organizes the coping mechanisms for adaptation to change by means of its reflective practice. The reflective approach offers a public view instead of a public's view. To understand the impact of a reflective perspective, we need to see communication from a diachronic or evolutionary perspective instead of the classic persuasion or mutual understanding models. Through this lens on communication, interaction is focused on the social actions of all actors in their relationship with the communication process itself and not so much in their relationship with the other actor(s). In a reflective model of public relations, the basic concepts are reflection, enactment, and sensemaking. These concepts help to reveal how public relations produces society and how societal legitimation is an organizational constraint in which listening is a vital aspect. A reflective approach to public relations will alter public relations research, practice and education to a large extent.

Keywords: public relations; reflective public relations; diachronic communication model; enactment; sensemaking; public relations practice; public relations research; public relations education

1 Introduction

In our digital and mediated age, organizations live in a public arena of very dynamic, ongoing constructions of meanings, expressed by often self-employed stakeholders. In order to cope with this arena, organizations need to be able to continuously adapt to change (Bennett and Lemoine 2014). Public relations can be seen as the field that organizes the coping mechanisms for adaptation to change by means of its reflective practice.

1.1 A reflective perspective

A reflective[1] perspective offers a public or societal view of public relations. It focuses on the idea that organizations need to relate to society as a whole instead of to certain publics or stakeholders (see also Van Ruler 2016, 2018; Van Ruler and Verčič 2003,

---

1 Like Holmström (2004), I use "reflectivity" instead of "reflexivity," for two reasons. First, this is because of the psychological behavioral connotations of the word "reflexivity" (which suggests a rather

https://doi.org/10.1515/9783110554250-005

2005). Such a societal perspective was also the basis for Olasky's (1989) alternative exposition of U.S. public relations history, especially in his differentiation between "public" and "private" relations, but it has never become mainstream in public relations theory. Contemporary theories of public relations mainly focus on management/organization as one actor in the public relations process and the publics/target groups/stakeholders as the other actors. Moreover, they look for either pure organizational gain or a balance between organizational and stakeholder benefits. Most of these theories have been developed from a (social-) psychological, a systems, or a rhetorical perspective on public relations, and most focus on relationships between organizations and their management on the one hand, and certain individuals or groups of individuals on the other. It is doubtful whether these perspectives are sufficient to help organizations to earn long-term societal legitimacy in these VUCA times (Volatile, Uncertain, Complex and Ambiguous, see Bennett and Lemoine 2014).

A reflective approach is derived from the social sciences rather than behavioral or managerial sciences, and takes, consequently, a public view instead of defining a view of the publics. From a reflective point of view, public relations is not just a phenomenon to be described and defined, a practice of certain professionals, or a way of viewing relationships between parties. It is primarily a strategic process of seeing an organization from a societal or public point of view. The primary concerns of public relations when taking a reflective approach are an organization's inclusiveness and preservation of the "social license to operate" (RSA 1995; Boutilier 2017).

Contemporary organizations face two challenges that are of fundamental importance for their survival: being good and being visible. An organization has to be good in the sense that it supplies good, high-quality products or services at an appropriate price. However, being good also means that organizations are able to demonstrate that they operate in a way that will sustain their social legitimacy. While the brand is important in terms of the product, so is the company behind the brand. This implies that an organization must relate to society at large in order to learn what is acceptable and what is not, and is able to show how it acts accordingly (or explain why not). This is all about communication in the context of the organization and its policies and behaviors, and is normally seen as the domain of public relations, in which communication is a basic process.

Public relations literature normally embraces the notion of communication as part of its operation, but mainly as a tool to be used in an appropriate way and rarely as a key concept that needs to be defined, acknowledged, and discussed, let alone as a dynamic process of meaning creation. Paraphrasing Toth (1992: 12), we could say that the most obvious contribution to be made by communication scholars to research in

---

routine action, or "reflex"), while here I refer to "reflection" as a conscious cognitive process. Second, another reason concerns the etymology of the word "reflexivity." "Reflexum" is the perfectum of the Latin verb "reflecto." Reflexive refers, therefore, more to a state, while I prefer to see it as an ongoing process.

the field of public relations is the much richer delineation of what is meant by communication and how communication can build societal legitimation and trust, but can also undermine and break them.

1.2 The role of communication in mainstream public relations approaches

One widespread approach to public relations relies on the concept of corporate communication (Argenti 1994; Dolphin 1999; Cornelissen 2014; Van Riel 1995, 2000), also referred to as the reputation approach. This concept is – although often implicitly – built on the public relations approach of founding father Edward Bernays (1923, 1955), who claimed that public relations is basically a means of engineering the consent of the masses. Although rarely discussed and usually seen as a rather simple tool (Van Ruler 2018), communication is seen as a one-way instrument to alter or maintain a positive reputation by creating consent for the policy and deeds of an organization. This is what J. Grunig called two-way *asymmetrical* public relations (see chapter 15 in this book).

J. Grunig (1989, 1992) developed a two-way *symmetrical* model of public relations to contrast it with the public relations concept advocated by Bernays and his successors. This two-way symmetrical model is, without doubt, the most widespread approach to public relations in the academic community across the world. In a subsequent overview of his work, J. Grunig (2001) proposed replacing "symmetrical" with "dialogical," due to criticism of the former term. Dialogue is needed to reach a mutual understanding of how an organization should behave in a symmetrical way, as he explains in the 2001 article. Looking at public relations journals, we indeed see that many researchers now talk about dialogical public relations, and often with the same meaning as J. Grunig when he spoke about symmetrical public relations. For example, Kent and Taylor (2002) stated that the concept of dialogue enhances public relations research because it delivers an ethical orientation for positive organizations in terms of public relationships, while Golob and Podnar (2011) claimed that dialogue enhances public relations because it helps organizations activate a process of mutual understanding.

A brief overview of mainstream public relations approaches allows us to conclude that alongside the concept of corporate communication/asymmetrical public relations, the symmetrical model also remains dominant, although now often called dialogical public relations. It remains to be seen whether these asymmetrical and symmetrical approaches are helpful to organizations in the public arena of very dynamic, ongoing constructions of meanings that we now live in.

1.3 The missing element

In 1996, Castells labeled the 21st century "the information age" (Castells 1996; see also Castells 2010). Time or space no longer limits information, and it is hard to know who possesses certain information and who does not. In addition, while internet use is increasing dramatically, it is almost impossible to know what information people have and who is submitting what information to whom. Nor can organizations even try to know what others are doing with that information; how they construct their meanings and to whom they convey them.

Thanks to the internet, the public sphere – in the definition of "what is potentially known to and can be debated by all" (Hollander 1988) – is exploding vigorously and people are able to openly express their feelings about organizations and their behaviors. It is doubtful whether we can still label them as "publics" in the sense of people who are willing to listen and open up, since they much more frequently act as senders and, consequently, as participants in meaning construction in relation to the issue at hand. Moreover, they barely act as negotiators with the organization, but more as expressors of their feelings to anyone who is willing to listen. It certainly no longer makes sense to see the organization as the sender and stakeholders as the receivers. Stakeholders are senders as well. Moreover, stakeholders change over time, are rarely found to be groups in a sociological sense, tend to respond more to others than to the organization itself, and are predominantly bound by issues-related values or just meanings that are circulating.

The context of modern public relations is, consequently, much more complex than a notion of symmetrical or dialogical communication with relevant publics implies. Public relations works for publics and with publics, but also in public, in the open, as the German communication scholar, Oeckl (1976), used to say, and its "working" or effects can be found in the meaning of the consequences in society. It is in this public sphere that public opinions and public feelings develop. By communicating, people in organizations construct and reconstruct public meaning – they themselves the actors who communicate in public. However, each individual is only one actor, often completely outvoted by many other voices. Thus, organizational senders are far from sole senders of the self. The public sphere is created by whoever is contributing to these meaning constructions. This is why we may call the public sphere the "communication battlefield" of organizations.

Organizational actors have at best a supporting role on this battlefield, and often only act as extras. This is complicated by changes to this battlefield itself over time, as well as to the issues concerned, and those occupying the field. However, what complicates matters even more is the fact that meanings develop very quickly and cannot be attached to certain stakeholders. Classic asymmetrical and symmetrical public relations approaches cannot explain what we should do with these new aspects.

In this chapter, I will first discuss communication as a basic concept in public relations and argue that a diachronic or evolutionary view of communication could be more profitable than the classic persuasion or mutual understanding models with respect to preserving a social license to operate. Second, I will discuss the concepts of reflection, enactment, and sensemaking as basic concepts in such a diachronic view of communication and will show how public relations produces society and how societal legitimation presents an organizational constraint, in which listening is a basic aspect. Third, I will discuss what a reflective approach to public relations means for public relations theory, practice, and education.

2 Communication as a basic public relations concept

There are many ways to define communication (Craig and Muller 2007; Littlejohn 1983, 1987; Littlejohn and Foss 2011). In essence, communication is about meaning creation. Meaning can be explained as the "whole way in which we understand, explain, feel about and react towards a given phenomenon" (Rosengren 2000: 59). The crucial question, then, is whose meaning is created and what this means for interpreting the world, and which lens on communication fits today's public relations challenges.

2.1 The concept of meaning

The concept of meaning has two dimensions: a denotative and a connotative one. The denotative meaning of a phenomenon is the one found in a dictionary. It is the literal or overt meaning that is shared by most people. The connotative meaning refers to subjective associations. For example, a dog is denotatively a four-legged domestic animal, and most people would agree on this. However, for some, the word "dog" contains connotations of fear, while for others it contains connotations of tenderness. Many communication scientists emphasize that the connotative meaning is the steering factor of communicative behavior. In asymmetrical public relations models, this is indeed emphasized, but only at the receiving end of the communication; for example, the target groups who should be willing to alter their feelings about the subject. In mutual understanding approaches, the emphasis is not so much on connotation as on the building of a new, denotative meaning. Thus, in public relations, meaning is used in different ways. However, in both mainstream approaches to public relations, meaning is usually seen as static. In symbolic interactionism, meaning has a different sense, as Sandstrom (2008: 4927) explains, as it is seen as arising in the ongoing processes of interaction between people. From this perspective, meaning is not seen as static but as a very dynamic, evolutionary process in its connotative as well as in its denotative dimensions. Thus, we can find two mainstream views on communication, namely as a one-way persuasive process in which the receiver should alter their connotative meaning, and as a two-way process in which actors should create a new, denotative meaning. However, there is yet another approach to communication, in which meaning is created in an ongoing, diachronic process. I will discuss all three approaches in the following sections.

2.2 Communication as a one-way persuasive process

Early mass communication theories used to focus on communication as a one-way process in which a sender influences a receiver. During the 1960s, Bauer (1964) concluded that there are two different views regarding the idea of these influences. The first of these, which he describes as the social model, "is (…) one of the exploitation of man by man. It is a model of one-way influence: the communication does something to the audience, while to the communicator is generally attributed considerable latitude and power to do what he pleases to the audience" (1964: 139). Bauer called his second model "the scientific model of communication as a transactional process in which parties each expect to give and take from the exchange approximately equitable values" (1964: 319). Although this scientific model allows for influence, it is not a linear causal model.

Bauer stated that, while research shows that the scientific model is by far the more adequate of the two, it is the social model that is dominant. Bauer's social model of one-way influence is equivalent to J. Grunig's two-way asymmetrical model. However, Bauer uses "one-way" because of the presumed linear causality. Indeed, it is questionable whether the concept of "two-way" is adequate to describe the social model, as the receiver is seen as the object, who is only able to receive or, in the case of some feedback systems, to answer the sender's questions. The receiver is not seen as a full participant in the process, and the same is true of J. Grunig's two-way asymmetrical model. That is why I prefer to describe asymmetrical communication as "controlled one-way" communication (Van Ruler 2004a). Thayer (1968: 129–130) used to call this a "synchronic" view of communication because the sender attempts to synchronize the psychological state (e. g., the connotative meaning) of the receiver with their own.

One-way communication approaches imply that meanings in the nervous system of one person can be deposited in the nervous system of another, Barnlund (2009) explains. However, good communication is not that simple, he claims (2009: 13): "Limiting communication to the sending of messages impoverishes the process and renders at least one participant impotent. (…) Such emotional distancing creates, to use the phrase of Martin Buber's, an I-It rather than an I-Thou relation. One is not likely to approach or expose himself to an unresponsive façade."

Although a one-way approach might still be viable in some areas of communication research, most recent approaches to the concept of communication view it as a fundamental two-way process that is interactive by nature and participatory at all levels (Servaes 1999). This involves the paradigmatic change of a sender/receiver-orientation into an actor-orientation (e. g., a process in which all actors can be active and take initiative) (see e. g., Bentele, Steinmann, and Zerfass 1996; Putnam and Pacanowsky 1983; Thayer 1987). That is why the emphasis in communication theory is currently on communication as a process in which meanings are created and exchanged (Craig and Muller 2007; Littlejohn and Foss 2011; Rosengren 2000). This is, however, done in different ways, as a process of creating shared meaning in direct interaction processes or as an ongoing process in which meanings as such interact. The key difference between these two approaches is the concept of interaction. This will be discussed in the following sections.

2.3 Communication as a process of creating shared meaning

For some communication scientists, communication is a process that creates a shared meaning, that is, a new denotative or overt meaning, which we normally call consensus (see e. g., Schramm 1965). This is equivalent to the symmetrical approach to public relations. A glance at public relations journals and the annual international public relations conferences allows us to conclude that such a two-way approach is favored in public relations over one-way approaches. The basic concept of communication in these two-way public relations models is communication as a process of mutual understanding between persons. The key aspect of this model is the relationship between A and B, which involves a communication process about X (something out there) and the meaning A and B give to this X. Newcomb (1953) postulated this as a "strain to symmetry," resulting in a widening of the area of agreement by engaging in communication. That is to say, where there is balance, each participant will resist change, and where there is imbalance, attempts will be made to restore equilibrium.

The premise in all balance models is that people will always search for consistency (Stappers, Reijnders, and Moeller 1990). In public relations, this is often described as consensus building between dependent parties about the meaning of the issue at hand. The parties with which organizations need to build consensus are called their publics or stakeholders. Consequently, in symmetrical approaches, public relations above all concerns negotiation with important stakeholders on how the organization should behave, or as Pieczka (2016: 79) concluded, "J. Grunig's own use of a game theory term to describe this process as creating a 'win-win zone,' makes it clear that dialogue here is synonymous with bargaining," and on seeking a state of equilibrium. We may conclude that in symmetrical public relations, communication is – although rarely debated as such – usually seen taking a balance model approach (for an overview, see Van Ruler 2004a).

A key concept in the symmetrical or dialogical model of public relations is "interaction." From a psychological perspective, interaction is usually seen from the angle of person-to-person interaction or group interaction, as in Bales' interaction process analysis or Fisher's interaction analysis (for an overview, see Littlejohn 1983: 227–240), in which people respond to each other. This idea can also be found in relational communication theory as constructed by Bateson (1979). He concluded that every interpersonal exchange bears a message that contains the substance or content of the communication as well as a statement about the relationship. Watzlawick, Beavin, and Jackson (1967) called this latter part of the message "metacommunication." They claimed that relationships emerge from the interaction between people. People set up all kinds of interaction rules and these govern their communicative behaviors. By obeying the rules, the participants sanction the defined relationship. In these models, interaction is focused on how people engage in conversations with each other and literally converge. To emphasize the difference from other dialogical approaches, I prefer to call this a "direct reciprocal dialogue" model.

2.4 Communication as a diachronic, evolutionary process

In large parts of the communication science field, the emphasis today lies much more on the fact that communication creates intersubjectively new meanings as such (see e. g., Putnam and Pacanowsky 1983). The key word in this approach is also dia-logue, but in the classical meaning of the Greek *dia-logos*, which literally means "a free flow among people of words and their interpretations" (Matson and Montagu 1967). This is not necessarily a conversation between two or more people in the literal sense. Dialogue and interaction, therefore, have a different meaning to that of rela-tional approaches, as discussed above. Here, interaction is not necessarily a process between two or more people. That is why "two-way" fails to describe this approach to communication.

Interaction comes from Latin and means not only direct reciprocal dialogue but also "to act upon each other and have influences on each other" (Neumann 2008). It may refer to feedback processes and to direct interaction between people, but also to a more abstract concept of interaction which concerns how people relate to other mean-ings in developing their own meanings. In the symmetrical or dialogical public rela-tions model, interaction is narrowed to concrete interactions between people who are literally engaged in conversation with each other. Viewing communication through an evolutionary lens, interaction is seen as the dynamic interplay between actors in their role as senders and receivers, by which the consequences of the communicative transactions as such are influenced (Stappers, Reijnders and Moeller 1990). In this view of communication, interaction is focused on the social action of all actors in their relationship with the communication process itself and not so much in their relation-ship with the other person(s). This should be seen as a virtual, reflective process at the level of the interpretations made by senders and receivers, which influences the meaning they give to a message and, consequently, the effects of the message. Seen through this lens, actors are not necessarily related or in proximity to each other.

This more reflective concept of interaction fits the diachronic view of commu-nication held by Thayer (1968, 1987), stipulating that communication is an ongoing process of learning, in which meanings develop through developing cognitions and feelings. While this is interactive by nature, it does not necessarily lead to one shared meaning; in a diachronic view of communication, meaning construction is not static but a dynamic and ongoing process. It is interactive because people consider the meanings of other people, but not because people literally interact. While Thayer favored this diachronic view of communication, Dance (1970) proposed a helical model to reflect the fact that communication is an essentially dynamic and exponential process that changes participants, contexts, and the future probabilities of communication, thereby focusing on the evolutionary process of meaning construction itself. For this reason, I prefer to call this approach to communication a diachronic or evolutionary approach.

Such a diachronic or evolutionary view of how communication works fits both the modern network idea of organizations as players in an arena (or even on a battlefield) of meaning constructions, as we can learn from Latour's constructivist actor-network theory (for an explanation of actor-network theory in public relations, see Verhoeven 2009), and the concept of "organizations as arenas of social worlds that give a lens to understand agency and collective learning in organizations" (Huysman and Elkjaer 2006). Looking at communication from such a perspective urges us to take a different stance toward public relations as well.

2.5 Communication in public relations

What makes public relations special is that its focus is on meaning creation by the actors involved in solving problems in an organization's daily relationship to society. It is a myth to believe that this is done only via two-way communication, as Australian public communication scholar Macnamara (2016a: 339) convincingly shows. Although some countries are famous for neo-corporatism and their consensus building approach to societal problems (Van Ruler 2004b), it is indeed unrealistic to claim that, even in these countries, management acts only through direct, concrete interaction, and that everyday organizational communication is restricted to dialogue or negotiation. In practice, it is difficult to choose between directive and purely interactive management, as Hersey and Blanchard (1993) have already showed. That is why it is unrealistic to have only the choice of one-way or two-way communication as the basic concept in public relations; everyone attempts to inform and persuade others, and everyone engages in dialogues and negotiations now and then. Thus, the persuasive and mutual understanding approaches are not in conflict, they are strategies that can be used in certain situations and may, consequently, not function as a basic approach to communication when talking about public relations. Moreover, in environments characterized by uncertainty, uniqueness, and value conflict, "an art of problem framing, an art of implementation, and an art of improvisation" (Schoen 1987: 13) are needed. A diachronic, evolutionary view of communication fits such an environment and can be seen as a solid conceptual basis for a reflective approach to public relations.

3 Reflective public relations

Organizations (and their public relations professionals) must address the dynamics of the digitized and mediated world, in which meanings are constructed by various people in a very dynamic way. Authoritative management is outdated, but going too far in the other direction is also not feasible. A reflective approach helps organizations adapt to change and at the same time express and debate the non-negotiable values.

This is why I am convinced that we should replace the classic one-way and two-way models of public relations with reflective public relations, in which the organization reflects on and debates what is going on in the outside world as well as in the organization itself. This also requires having conversations about what this means for enacting the organization and in relating to society at large, instead of creating relationships with certain publics or stakeholder groups (see Van Ruler and Verčič 2003, 2005; also Holmström 2004, 2008).

This is all the more necessary because, as Ihlen and Verhoeven (2012) stated: "Some of the most profound social changes are related to the downfall of social authorities. Decisions have to be legitimized on a continuous basis. From this, we argue, stems the idea that trust, legitimacy, understanding, and reflection are crucial concepts for public relations." Today, a permanent reflection on legitimacy is indeed conditional for the survival of an organization (Holmström 2008; Ihlen and Verhoeven 2012; Van Ruler and Verčič 2003, 2005).

3.1 The concept of reflection

In both communication science and organization science, symbolic interactionism has inspired some scholars to take a constructionist view of reality. Analyzing Dewey, who claimed that society does not exist through communication but in communication (Dewey 1916: 5), Carey (1975) developed a constructionist approach to mass communication, in opposition to the more common transmission view, and he called his approach a ritual view. If one examines a newspaper in terms of a transmission view of communication, one sees the medium as an instrument for disseminating news. A ritual view of communication will focus on how the world is portrayed and confirmed in the news. Writing about and reading the news should thus be seen as a ritual act. News is not so much information but drama, telling stories, he claims.

German communication scholars were the first to introduce a constructionist approach to public relations theory (Bentele and Ruhl 1993; Bentele 1997; Faulstieg

1992). The basic premise of this view is that human beings reflect the other to themselves and social reality in a dynamic process. Hence, constructing social reality is a
shared process of ongoing meaning construction (Bentele and Ruhl 1993: 12). In this
view, reflective interpretation and conceptualization of meanings are at the forefront
in a constant process of deconstruction and reconstruction (Van Nistelrooij 2000:
275). Krippendorf (1994) – a constructionist communication scientist – mentions the
"recursiveness" of communication: it is an ongoing social process of deconstruction
and reconstruction of interpretations. Hence, Faulstieg (1992) and other constructionist public relations scholars state that public relations involves not so much interaction between human beings, but is rather a form of societal action as such. In this
process, sensemaking (cf. Weick 1995) is what makes public relations really reflective.

From a reflective point of view, public relations is not just a phenomenon to be
described and defined, or a way of viewing relationships between parties. It is primarily a strategic process of viewing an organization from the "outside" or by taking
a "public" view, while deconstructing and reconstructing the organization, in terms
of its societal actions, in a constant process. Or, as Falkheimer and Heide (2016: 167)
claim, being reflexive (as they call it) in public relations means leaving behind traditional, functionalistic thinking and uncovering what has usually been taken for
granted. This concerns enactment and sensemaking.

3.2 Enactment and sensemaking

Public relations scholar Heath (1994) describes public relations as an enactment
process. The meaning public relations managers give to their company, the market,
environment, customers, themselves, and their jobs, affects their job performance.
"They enact their jobs as actors enact the scripts in plays" (Heath 1994: vii), and this
is why role playing is in fact communication, he says. The focal points of organizational communication analysis, Heath argues (1994: 2), are the acts people perform
that are meaningful to themselves and others, along with their thoughts about organizing and working. At the heart of this analysis is an interest in knowing how people
in and around companies create and enact meaning, which is in fact a sensemaking
approach to the study of organizational performance.

Looking at public relations from this point of view, it is impossible to see communication simply as transmission (see Dervin and Foreman-Wernet 2004) and continue
to focus on the traditional logic supporting the idea that the receiver deficits in the
communication process (Dervin 2004: 19). Sensemaking involves placing stimuli in
some kind of framework, and can be seen as a thinking process that uses retrospective accounts to explain and redress surprises, constructing meaning, interacting in
pursuit of mutual understanding and patterning: "In order to convert a problematic
situation to a problem, a practitioner must do a certain kind of work. He must make
sense of an uncertain situation that initially makes no sense" (Weick 1995: 6–7).

This problem setting is a process in which, interactively, we name the things to which we will attend, and frame the context in which we will attend to them (Schoen 1983: 40). Sensemaking is grounded as much in deduction from well-articulated theories as it is in induction from specific cases of struggle to reduce ambiguity. Sensemaking is, however, driven by plausibility rather than accuracy. The concept of organizational sensemaking is based in action theory, seen as the propositions people have to guide their behaviors (Weick 1995: 21). This also refers to the basic symbolic interactionist Thomas theorem, which states that it is not facts but the interpretation of facts that steers people's actions. People – and thus managers also – tend to frame situations so as to make a problem solvable. Sensemaking comes to life in communication through the way in which people frame the meanings in their heads (Entman 1993; Goffman 1974). Thus, framing is basically an interactive cultural process (D'Angelo 2002) that reveals the social reality (De Vreese 2003) and may work as myth (Van Ruler 1997). Problematizing the concepts of enactment and sensemaking helps to uncover what has been taken for granted. In reflective public relations, this is key in the daily work of its practitioners.

3.3 Public relations produces society

A reflective approach focuses on how we understand reality and how we can produce knowledge about this reality and give meaning to it. Reality is not seen as "something out there." Such a view on reality as something human beings construct themselves was popularized by one of the most frequently cited works in the social sciences, *The Social Construction of Reality* by Berger and Luckmann (1966).

According to Berger and Luckmann (1966), reality is a quality pertaining to phenomena we recognize as having a being independent of our own volition; we cannot wish them away. Knowledge is the certainty that phenomena are real and that they possess specific characteristics. The sociology of knowledge is therefore concerned with the analysis of the social construction of reality, and social structure can be seen as an essential element of the reality of everyday life. "At one pole of the continuum are those others with whom I frequently interact in face-to-face situations – my inner circle, as it were," they explain. "At the other pole are highly anonymous abstractions, which by their very nature can never be available in face-to-face interaction. Social structure is the sum total of these typifications and of the recurrent patterns of interaction established by means of them" (Berger and Luckmann 1966: 48).

What is seen as appropriate is not a fact but also not random. "Culture defines which act is appropriate and which is not" (Heath 1994: 5). Culture leads people to share a vocabulary that carves reality into meaningful units. However, enactments themselves also develop culture, which is why the process in which organizational work is being done itself produces culture and, consequently, society, as Faulstieg (1992) stated, and is in itself an ongoing process.

Macnamara (2016a: 340) concludes that public relations is rather organization-centric, exerting persuasive control by focusing on one-way dissemination of
organizational messages, making attempts at persuasion on behalf of and in the
interest of power elites. "Such an approach is likely to promote further alienation and
dislocation between corporations, business, industry, governments, as well as other
types of organizations and their publics. (...) In short, PR and strategic communication
management are more anti-social than they are social," he claims, and I agree. In the
end, classic persuasive approaches to public relations and strategic communication
seem to produce a notion of society in which people are seen as objects and in which
mistrust is normal. Considering that organizations need social legitimation in order
to survive, as sociologist Zijderveld (2000) explains, the consequences of this kind of
public relations are far-reaching for society as such.

3.4 Societal legitimation as an organizational constraint

The most important concept in societal legitimation is the concept of listening. In this
respect, Macnamara (2016a: 343) quotes Heath and Coombs (2006: 346), who noted:
"Today's public relations practitioners give voice to organizations, and this process
requires the ability to listen." Manamara makes the criticism that public relations
practitioners go on to narrowly configure listening by saying "listening gives a foundation for knowing what to say and thinking strategically of the best ways to frame
and present appealing messages." (Macnamara, 2016a: 343). In other words, if public
relations practitioners listen, they only listen to reply, not to understand, let alone
to bring what they hear into decision-making in the organization. Good listening is
the "missing essential in public communication," Macnamara (2016b: 3) laments.
According to Macnamara (2016a: 340), PR practitioners are overwhelmingly engaged
in establishing an "architecture of speaking" in organizations, as well as pursuing the
one-way "work of speaking," with little infrastructure for, or commitment to, listening
in a more integrative way.

Organizational workers use all kinds of strategies, including the manipulation of
frames (persuasion) in order to get things done, even if there are conflicting interests.
The constraint in this manipulation is public legitimacy, which, because of increased
public counteraction, has become increasingly necessary for business to address if
it is to survive. This new, broadened business paradigm requires a greater degree of
reflective self-control by management, and this leads to what Schoen (1983) called
the dilemma of rigor or relevance, which all professionals experience sooner or later.

Rigor develops technical rationality yet depends on internally consistent but normative theories to achieve clearly fixed ends. In contrast, relevance develops reflective
rationality, focusing on the right solution in the right context, with doubt, therefore,
located more in the situation than in the mind. The task of the professional/manager
is to make sense of the situation and construct the appropriate meaning for it, and

the way to do this is by enacting his or her meanings and reconsidering them; that is, reflection-in-action and reflection on the communication-in-action (cf. Schoen 1983). This is the art of sensemaking and should be seen as the core business of public relations as a reflective practice.

3.5 Public relations as a concept of viewing an organization

From a reflective point of view, public relations deconstructs and reconstructs reality in an ongoing and interactive way. That is why we should not see public relations as merely a phenomenon to be described and defined, or a way of viewing relationships between parties. It is primarily a strategic process of viewing an organization from the "outside," or taking a "public" view, while deconstructing and reconstructing reality in a constant process by reflectively making sense of interactions.

More precisely, it is also a way of viewing an organization as merely an empirical realization of an institution. Consequently, what the organization represents (the institution) is much more important than the organization itself (Zijderveld 2000). In referring to organizational activity, management theory usually focuses on the concept of "organization," while sociologists view an organization more as an "institution." Zijderveld (2000: 35) claims these two concepts are not alternative explanations but different dimensions: All organizations are also institutions. He states that it does make a difference whether a university, a corporation, or a union is seen as an organization or an institution. The concept of "organization" focuses on functional rationality, the division of staff and line functions, on formal structures of command, on hierarchies of power and on decision-making processes. The concept of "institution," however, reveals a different kind of reality, which can be thought of in terms of value or substantial rationality. Seeing a corporation or an administration as an "institution" means there is less concern for the careful matching of ends and means, and more for a definition of the ends to be realized (Zijderveld 2000: 95).

Thus, the concept of "organization" is economic and administrative, while the concept of "institution" is social. The organizational dimension gives an organization economic legitimacy and trustworthiness. From the perspective of "organization," the focus is on societal values, but only from the perspective of a functional rationality instrumental to economic and administrative reasoning. From the perspective of "institution," societal values are the bottom line. This is why it is only the institutional dimension that gives an organization societal legitimation and trustworthiness.

Institutions are traditional and collective patterns of behavior, ways of acting, thinking, and feeling. "Social behavior is essential for the survival of human beings, while institutions – as traditional patterns of behavior – ensure, by taking for granted the order and security needed for actions to be successful" (Zijderveld 2000: 16). A corporation is the realization of the institution of the "economy," an administration is the realization of the institution of the "state." Moreover, institutions are not institutes, which come and go. Institutions are more long-lasting; they are ways of acting, thinking, and feeling realized in historically and culturally rooted institutes.

While the organizational dimension is important for short-term survival, the institutional dimension is more important for long-term survival. Institutions are creations of human beings, established to survive as social entities. As a consequence, they only exist as long as they are seen to be meaningful by their society. What a society considers as meaningful (i. e. socially legitimate) is a social construction itself, based in the dynamic structure of the empirical realizations of its institutions. This is where reflective public relations comes in. It is not so much the organization but the institution that is represented and enacted.

4 Discussion

Viewing organizations from a public and institutional point of view has quite a few consequences for public relations. It urges us to view public relations not only as a form of messaging to or dialogue with stakeholders, but as a means to cope with and co-produce social reality. This has significant consequences for public relations research, practice and education.

4.1 Consequences for public relations research

Seeing interaction from a reflective, constructionist point of view, social interaction is an ongoing process. This means that researching public relations as a discrete process no longer makes sense. Even campaigning should be seen as an ongoing process, and evaluation should, consequently, also be seen in a different way (see Van Ruler 2019). However, it goes much further than this. Reflective public relations should not aim at its own general theory of public relations. It should, above all, be interested in a theory of organization in the context of societal legitimacy, which opens a broader space of questioning at different levels of analysis.

Reflectivity stands in contrast to linear causality: it is an ongoing, interactive process and not a discrete, linear one. Along these lines, reflectivity must be seen as the core concept of social interaction because it provides a better explanation for what happens than does causality. While human beings find themselves reflected in their relations to the other and the social group as a whole, their knowing is reflective knowing. From this perspective, reflective public relations is a matter of social interaction, seen as the dynamic interplay between social actors in their roles as senders and receivers, by which the consequences of the communicative transactions as such are influenced. Research should thus focus on the social actions of all actors in their personal relationship with the communication process itself, and not so much on their relationship with other person(s). Research should be much more focused on processes of meaning creation and sensemaking, and should consider this as an ongoing and very dynamic process. Seen through this lens, actors are not necessarily related or in proximity to each other. This literally means that we need much more time-series research and research into the dynamic of public as well as organizational frames on issues. Moreover, it certainly means that the meanings the organization gives to its reality should not be seen as "natural" or as merely negotiable, but considered in relation to developing meanings of its reality in society.

If we believe that public relations practitioners should be aware of the fact that reality is not "something out there," then, of course, researchers should not claim this either. Falkheimer and Heide (2016: 165) lament that most public relations research is "boxed-in" research. While reflective public relations is oriented to how organizations relate to society, their approach presents a plea for a reflexive research paradigm, as described by Alvesson and Sköldberg (2009) in their seminal work *Reflexive Methodology*. "The reflexive turn within academic theorizing is a result of an increasing interest among scholars to be aware of, and discuss, the active role they have in constructing the reality that is to be researched. This turn stands in contrast to the still dominant belief that researchers have an objectivist status", as Falkheimer and Heide conclude (2016: 163). This leads to boxed-in research:

> This kind of research often is rather uncreative and uninteresting and only tries to bridge a small knowledge gap that has been identified, leading to results with little relevance for either scholars or practitioners. (…) First there is the perspective box, which means that the scholar always uses the same theoretical framework, e. g. image repair theory or agenda-setting theory. Second there is a domain box, meaning that a scholar specializes in one small field, e. g. nation branding or social media use, and mainly replicates earlier studies. Third, there is a methodology box, where the scholar consistently applies the same method approach and technique in empirical research. (2016: 165)

As Macnamara (2016b: 308) adds on this point: "Despite a heavy focus on quantitative research in late modernity, numbers and proved hypotheses rarely if ever tell the full story about people and their concerns. As well, there is always more that all researchers can do to listen, including being conscious of our own unavoidable subjectivity and applying reflexivity."

4.2 Consequences for public relations practice

In a large Delphi study, my Slovenian colleague Dejan Verčič and I came to the conclusion that in Europe public relations plays four main roles (Van Ruler and Verčič 2002). The managerial and operational roles are similar to the dominant paradigm of the one-way and two-way models. In this Delphi research project on the identity of public relations, participants also claimed other roles. First, they mentioned a reflective role, involving analyzing standards and values in society and discussing these with organization management in order to adjust the standards and values of the organization to ensure social legitimacy. Second, they saw an educational role, which involves helping members of the organization to become sensitive to social demands and expectations, as well as being communicatively competent to respond appropriately to those social demands. This led to the four Cs of good public relations practice (Van Ruler 2012: i) Counselling of the (management of the) organization to maintain social legitimacy, ii) Coaching of the members of the organization to act accordingly, iii) Conceptualization of communication programs, and iv) Creation of appropriate tools and actions.

In a reflective approach, publics are no longer seen as mere audiences, but as senders as well (although not necessarily oriented at the organization). This is why listening is a key element in reflective public relations. Scharmer (2009) identified four listening strategies. First, *downloading* means listening by selecting what is already known and what confirms one's opinion. Second, while downloading is the most common listening strategy, an *empathic listening* strategy – listening without judgment by trying to grasp the perspective of the other and critically considering one's own – is conditional for a constructive understanding. Empathic listening thus also means listening for the place the other person is speaking from. This is a typical strategy employed by therapists. Third, another common listening strategy is *object-focused listening*, that is, listening by focusing on new information to confirm one's own story. Finally, Scharmer believes in *generative listening*, which means carefully balancing different types of listening so that a new understanding will emerge.

Reflective public relations means that organizations reinvent themselves, as Tench et al. (2016: 44) call this process. Successful organizations are notorious for their bias toward action. They must reflect on their actions in words and deeds (which "communicate" as well) and learn from this. "Through communication people and organizations expose themselves to the world, through communication they interact with the world and through communication they reflect their own identity, values and interests. Organizational learning is a process of continuous, iterative communication with the environment" (Tench et al. 2016: 45). Public relations (or communication management, as it is sometimes called) is the function in, or for, the organization that knows how to do this.

Consequently, reflective public relations is also a new approach to practical measurement methodology. At the 2014 AMEC Conference, Macnamara (2014) called for a shift from looking back to looking forward. Nevertheless, in public relations planning models there is no role for measurement other than as evaluation at the end; in other words, looking back. The consequence of this view for measurement is that accommodating change is not seen as a role for public relations practice. Rather, change is most likely seen as a negative attack on continuity. In contrast, reflective public relations is always focused on looking forward, and prefers formative evaluation. This is why reflective public relations is agile and sees strategy development as well as daily action as part of an ongoing reflective practice (Van Ruler 2015, 2019). There is yet another consequence to be considered from a reflective public relations point of view, and that is the position of public relations departments in the organizational structure. Contrary to most public relations approaches, Macnamara (2016a: 343) prefers a role outside the dominant coalition, in the manner of legal counsel and auditors. This echoes the plea of Lauzen and Dozier (1992, 1994), who claimed that public relations should not be obedient to management but more distant, having a more reflective role.

4.3 Consequences for public relations education

Reflective public relations education does not take the organization but instead society as its point of departure. In the reflective approach, public relations serves the same kind of function as journalism and advertising, insofar as they all contribute to a flow of information and its meanings and to the development of meanings in and of society per se. They all contribute to the development of the public sphere, in terms of size ("How many people are involved in public life?"), in level ("What is the level at which we discuss public matters?") and in quality ("What are the frames used in the debates?"), and this echoes Carey's (1975) cultural approach to communication. Theory building in public relations is closely related to journalism in many European countries, not because the practitioners must deal with journalists, but because of these overlapping functions in society.

A reflective approach to public relations also means that it involves shifting public relations out of management theory, placing it in the entirely different environment of social theory, as Macnamara (2016a: 341) and for example Ihlen and Van Ruler (2009) also claim. This is exactly why Ihlen and Van Ruler (2009) introduced a project in which a variety of public relations scholars presented social theories as alternative perspectives on public relations by studying the latter as a social phenomenon. Social theory can help to make sense of public relations at the societal, organizational and individual levels. Contrary to most public relations approaches, a socially oriented view is not directed toward management problems, but rather toward the relationship that public relations has with the society in which it is produced and with the social systems it co-produces, Ihlen and Van Ruler claim (2009: 3). Sociological theories are not only applicable at the societal level but also at the organizational and individual levels, by viewing organizations and their practitioners from a societal, public perspective.

Using social theory does not mean that public relations cannot be taught in management schools. As Ihlen and Verhoeven (2012) stated, organizational approaches to public relations should be supplemented with societal approaches that expose what public relations is in society today, rather than only focusing on the organizational level. However, this needs an educational environment with a broad and modern view of the role of organization and management.

Moreover, Ihlen and Verhoeven (2012) also advise not only focusing on the effectiveness of public relations, but also on its broader consequences in society. Regarding education, this has to do with the plea to open up more perspectives on public relations than the one-sided or two-sided functionalist perspectives that are still very dominant. Most education favors concepts such as trust and legitimacy, but some see them as important concepts because they are a means to realizing organizational goals, while others see them as ends in themselves. This distinction is quite significant, Ihlen and Verhoeven (2012) warn. We may see the concept of power and the distribution of it at the heart of these discussions, but we rarely enter into these kinds of discussions with our students.

4.4 Final remarks

Languages, as the most important systems of vocal signs, build up semantic fields or zones of meaning that are linguistically circumscribed (cf. Heath 1994, 2001). While it is possible to say that human beings have a certain nature, it is more significant to say that human beings construct their own nature, or simply, that we produce ourselves. This self-production is always, by necessity, a social enterprise, as Berger and Luckmann (1966) argue. Human beings produce a human environment together, with the totality of its socio-cultural and psychological formations. This not only occurs at a private level but also at an organizational level. It may be that a given social order precedes any individual organism's development, but social order is still a human product, or, more precisely, an ongoing human production.

By playing roles, the individual participates in a social world; by internalizing these roles, the same world becomes subjectively real to the individual. Roles represent institutional order, although some of these, however, symbolically represent that order in its totality more than others. Such roles are of great strategic importance in society, since they represent not only this or that institution, but also the integration of all institutions into a meaningful world, and these are the roles that have a special relationship to the legitimating apparatus of society. Historically, these roles have most commonly been allocated to political and religious institutions, but this is no longer the case, as it is said that NGOs and corporations now have more power than politics and religion. This is where reflective public relations find its core.

According to Berger and Luckmann (1966: 110), legitimation (the term comes from Weber), as a process, is best described as a "second-order" objectifying of meaning. Its function is to make objectively available and subjectively plausible the "first-order" objectifying that has been institutionalized. It embodies the institutional order by ascribing cognitive validity to its objectivized meanings and, in turn, justifies them. However, in the modern world there is always a rivalry between definitions of reality, and social structure can predict the outcome. This is why we need to reflect on public relations first of all from a public point of view.

Reflective public relations is not just another strategy for public relations practitioners but a completely alternative approach to organization and management. People in organizations use all kinds of strategies, including the manipulation of frames (persuasion) in order to get things done, even if there are conflicting interests. As I have argued here, the constraint in this manipulation is public legitimacy, which, because of increased public counteraction, has become increasingly necessary for business to survive. This new, broadened business paradigm requires a larger degree of reflective self-control by management, and agile ways of working in which change is part of daily life. Reflective public relations should therefore have its constraint in the management approach of the organization.

References

Alvesson, Mats & Kaj Sköldberg. 2009. *Reflexive methodology: New vistas for qualitative research*, 2nd edn. London: Sage.

Argenti, Paul A. 1994. *Corporate communication*. Burr Ridge, IL: Irwin.

Barnlund, Dean C. 2009 [1968]. Communication: The context of change. In C. David Mortensen (ed.), *Communication Theory*, 6–26. New Brunswick, NJ: Transaction Publishers.

Bateson, Gregory. 1979. *Mind and nature: A necessary unity.* New York: E.P. Dutton.

Bauer, Raymond A. 1964. The obstinate audience: The influence process from the point of view of social communication. *The American Psychologist* 19. 319–328.

Bennett, Nathan & G. James Lemoine. 2014. "What VUCA really means for you" *Harvard Business Review* January–February 2014. https://hbr.org/2014/01/what-vuca-really-means-for-you (accessed 21 December 2018).

Bentele, Gunter. 1997. Public relations and reality: A contribution to a theory of public relations. In Danny Moss, Toby MacManus and Dejan Verčič (eds.), *Public relations research: An international perspective*, 89–109. London: International Thompson Business Press.

Bentele, Gunter & Manfred Ruhl (eds.). 1993. *Theorien öffentlicher Kommunikation* [Theories of public communication]. Munich: Ölschläger.

Bentele, Gunter, Horst Steinmann & Ansgar Zerfass (eds.). 1996. *Dialogorientere Unternehmens-kommunikation. Grundlagen, Praxiserfahrungen, Perspektiven*. [Dialogue-oriented Corporate Communication, Basics, Praxis, Perspectives]. Berlin: Vistas.

Berger, Peter L. & Thomas Luckmann. 1966. *The social construction of reality. A treatise in the sociology of knowledge.* New York: Penguin Books.

Bernays, Edward. 1923. *Crystallizing public opinion*. New York: Boni and Liveright

Bernays, Edward. 1955. *The Engineering of Consent*. Norman: University of Oklahoma Press.

Boutilier, Robert. 2017. *A Measure Of The Social License To Operate For Infrastructure And Extractive Projects*. http://dx.doi.org/10.2139/ssrn.3204005 (accessed 3 February 2018).

Carey, James W. 1975. A Cultural Approach to Communication, *Journal of Communication* 2(1). 1–22.

Castells, Manuel. 1996. *The Rise of the Network Society: The Information Age: Economy, Society and Culture Volume I*. Oxford: Blackwell Publishers.

Castells, Manuel. 2010. *The Rise of the Network Society: The Information Age: Economy, Society and Culture Volume I*, 2nd edn. Malden, MA: Wiley-Blackwell.

Cornelissen, Joep. 2014. *Corporate communication: a guide to theory and practice*. Thousand Oaks, CA: Sage.

Craig. Robert T. & Heidi L. Muller (eds.). 2007. *Theorizing communication, readings across traditions.* Thousand Oaks, CA: Sage.

Dance, Frank E. X. 1970. A helical model of communication. In Kenneth K. Sereno and C. David Mortensen (eds.), *Foundations of communication theory*, 130–107. New York: Harper and Row.

D'Angelo, Paul. 2002. News framing as a multiparadigmatic research program: A response to Entman, *Journal of Communication* 52(4). 870–888.

De Vreese, Claes. 2003. *Framing Europe. Television news and European integration.* Amsterdam, NL: Aksant Academic Publishers.

Dewey, John. 1916. *Democracy and education: An introduction to the philosophy of education.* New York: Macmillan. https://www.gutenberg.org/files/852/852-h/852-h.htm (accessed 1 February 2018)

Dervin, Brenda. 2004. Communication gaps and inequities: Moving toward a reconceptualization. In Brenda Dervin and Lois Foreman-Wernet (eds.), *Sense-making methodology reader. Selected writings of Brenda Dervin*, 17–46. Cresskill, NJ: Hampton Press.

Dervin, Brenda & Lois Foreman-Wernet (eds.). 2004. *Sense-making methodology reader. Selected writings of Brenda Dervin.* Cresskill, NJ: Hampton Press.

Dolphin, Richard R. 1999. *The fundamentals of corporate communications.* Oxford: Butterworth Heinemann.

Entman, Robert. 1993. Framing: Toward clarification of a fractured paradigm, *Journal of Communication* 43(4). 51–58.

Falkheimer, Jesper & Mats Heide. 2016. A reflexive perspective on public relations: on leaving traditional thinking and uncovering the taken-for-granted. In Jacquie L'Etang, David McKie, Nancy Snow and Jordi Xifra (eds.), *The Routledge handbook of critical public relations*, 162–172. London: Routledge.

Faulstieg, Werner. 1992. *Oeffentlichkeitsarbeit. Grundwissen: kritische Einführung in Problemfelder* [Public relations. Basics: critical introduction into problems]. Bardowick: Wissenschaftlicher Verlag.

Goffman, Ervin. 1974. *Frame analysis. An essay on the organization of experience.* Boston: Northeastern University Press

Golob, Ursa & Klement Podnar. 2011. Corporate social responsibility communication and dialogue. In Øyvind Ihlen, Jennifer L. Bartlett and Steve May (eds.), *The handbook of communication and corporate social responsibility*, 231–251. Oxford: Wiley-Blackwell.

Grunig, James E. 1989. Symmetrical presuppositions as a framework for public relations theory. In Carl H. Botan and Vincent Hazleton Jr. (eds.), *Public relations theory*, 17–44. Hillsdale, NJ: Lawrence Erlbaum.

Grunig, James E. 1992. Communication, public relations, and effective organizations: An overview of the book. In James E. Grunig (ed.), *Excellence in public relations and communication management*, 1–28. Hillsdale, NJ: Lawrence Erlbaum.

Grunig, James E. 2001. Two-way symmetrical public relations: Past, present, and future. In Robert L. Heath (ed.), *Handbook of public relations*, 11–30. Thousand Oaks, CA: Sage.

Heath, Robert L. 1994. *Management of corporate communication. From interpersonal contacts to external affairs.* Hillsdale, NJ: Lawrence Erlbaum.

Heath, Robert L. 2001. Shifting foundations. Public relations as relationship building. In Robert L. Heath (ed.), *Handbook of public relations*, 1–9. Thousand Oaks, CA: Sage.

Heath, Robert L. & Timothy Coombs. 2006. *Today's public relations: An introduction.* Thousand Oaks, CA: Sage.

Hersey, Paul & Ken H. Blanchard. 1993. *Management of organizational behavior.* Englewood Cliffs, CA: Prentice Hall.

Hollander, Ed. 1988. *Lokale communicatie en locale openbaarheid. Openbaarheid als communicatiewetenschappelijk concept* [Local communication and local public sphere. Public Sphere as communication scientific concept]. Nijmegen: Katholieke Universiteit Nijmegen dissertation.

Holmström, Susanne. 2004. The reflective paradigm of public relations. In Betteke van Ruler and Dejan Verčič (eds.), *Public relations and communication management in Europe, A nation-by-nation introduction to public relations theory and practice*, 121–134. Berlin: Mouton de Gruyter.

Holmström, Susanne. 2008. Reflection: Legitimising late modernity. In Ansgar Zerfass, Betteke van Ruler & Krishnamurthy Sriramesh (eds.), *Public relations research, European and international perspectives and innovations*, 235–250. Wiesbaden: Verlag für Sozialwissenschaften.

Huysman, Marleen & Bente Elkjaer. 2006. *Organizations as arenas of social worlds; towards an alternative perspective on organizational learning?* Paper presented at the OLKC 2006 Conference at the University of Warwick, Coventry, 20–22 March.

Ihlen, Øyvind, & Betteke van Ruler. 2009. Introduction: Applying social theory to public relations. In Øyvind Ihlen, Betteke van Ruler & Magnus Fredriksson (eds*.), Public relations and social theory, key figures and concepts*, 1–20. New York: Routledge.

Ihlen, Øyvind & Piet Verhoeven. 2012. A public relations identity for the 2010s. *Public Relations Inquiry* 1(2). 159–176.

Kent, Michael & Maureen Taylor. 2002. Toward a dialogic theory of public relations, *Public Relations Review* 28. 21–37.

Krippendorf, Klaus. 1994. A Recursive theory of communication. In David Crowley and David Mitchell (eds.), *Communication theory today*, 78–104. Cambridge: Polity Press.

Lauzen, Martha M. & David M. Dozier. 1992. The Missing Link: The public relations manager role as mediator of organizational environments and power consequences for the function. *Journal of Public Relations Research* 4. 205–220.

Lauzen, Martha M. & David M. Dozier. 1994. Issues management mediation of linkages between environmental complexity and management of the public relations function. *Journal of Public Relations Research* 6. 163–184.

Littlejohn, Stephen W. 1983. *Theories of human communication*, 2nd edn. Belmont, CA: Wadsworth.

Littlejohn, Stephen W. 1987. *Theories of human communication*, 3rd edn. Belmont, CA: Wadsworth.

Littlejohn, Stephen W. & Karen A. Foss. 2011. *Theories of human communication*, 10th edn. Long Grove Ill: Waveland Press.

Macnamara, Jim. 2014. *Breaking the PR measurement and evaluation deadlock: A new approach and model*. Paper presented at the AMEC International Summit on Measurement "Upping the Game," Amsterdam, 11–12 June. http://amecinternationalsummit.org/wp-content/uploads/2014/06/Breaking-the-PR-Measurement-Deadlock-A-New-Approach-and-Model-Jim-Macnamara.pdf (accessed 20 December 2018).

Macnamara, Jim. 2016a. Socially integrating PR and operationalizing an alternative approach. In Jacquie L'Etang, David McKie, Nancy Snow and Jordi Xifra (eds.), *The Routledge handbook of critical public relations*, 335–348. London: Routledge.

Macnamara, Jim. 2016b. *Organizational listening, The missing essential in public communication*. New York: Peter Lang.

Matson, Floyd W. & Ashley Montagu (eds.). 1967. *The human dialogue, perspectives on communication*. New York: The Free Press.

Neumann, W. Russell. 2008. Interaction. In Wolfgang Donsbach (ed.), *The international encyclopedia of communication*, 2305–2309. Malden, MA: Blackwell Publishing.

Newcomb, Theodore M. 1953. An approach to the study of communicative acts. *Psychology Review* 60. 393–404.

Oeckl, Albert. 1976. *PR-Praxis. Der Schlüssel zur Öffentlichkeitarbeit* [Public relations practice. The key to public relations]. Düsseldorf: Econ.

Olasky, Marvin N. 1989. The aborted debate within public relations: An approach through Kuhn's paradigm. In James E. Grunig and Larissa A. Grunig (eds.), *Public relations research annual* 1, 87–96. Hillsdale, NJ: Lawrence Erlbaum.

Pieczka, Magda 2016. Dialogue and critical public relations. In Jacquie L'Etang, David McKie, Nancy Snow and Jordi Xifra (eds.), *The Routledge handbook of critical public relations*, 76–87. New York: Routledge.

Putnam, Linda L. & Michael E. Pacanowsky (eds.). 1983. *Communication and organizations. An interpretive approach.* Beverly Hills, CA: Sage.

Rosengren, Karl E. 2000. *Communication: an introduction.* London: Sage.

RSA 1995. *Tomorrow's company.* London: The Royal Society for the Encouragement of Arts, Manufactures and Commerce.

Sandstrom, Kent. 2008. Symbolic Interaction. In Wolfgang Donsbach (ed.), *The international encyclopedia of communication*, 4927–4933. Malden, MA: Blackwell Publishing.

Schoen, Donald A. 1983. *The reflective practitioner: How professionals think in action.* New York: Basic Books.

Schoen, Donald A. 1987. *Educating the reflective practitioner: Toward a new design for teaching and learning in the professions.* San Francisco: Jossey-Bass Publishers.

Schramm, Wilbur. 1965. How communication works. In W. Schramm (ed.), *The process and effects of mass communication*, 3–26. Urbana: University of Illinois Press.

Scharmer, C. Otto. 2009. *Theory U: Leading from the future as it emerges.* San Francisco: Berrett-Koehler.

Servaes, Jan. 1999. *Communication for development. One world, multiple cultures.* Creskill, NJ: Hampton Press.

Stappers, James G., Toon A. D. Reijnders & Willen A. J. Möller. 1990. *De werking van massamedia. Een overzicht van inzichten* [How media work; an overview of insights]. Amsterdam, NL: Arbeiderspers.

Tench, Ralph, Dejan Verčič, Ansgar Zerfass, Angeles Moreno & Piet Verhoeven. 2016. *Communication excellence. How to develop, manage and lead exceptional communications.* Cham: Palgrave McMillan.

Thayer, Lee 1968. *Communication and communication systems.* Homewood, IL: Richard D. Irwin.

Thayer, Lee. 1987. *On communication, essays in understanding.* Norwood, NJ: Ablex.

Toth, Elizabeth L. 1992. The case for pluralistic studies of public relations: rhetorical, critical and system perspectives. In Elizabeth L. Toth and Robert L. Heath (eds.), *Rhetorical and critical approaches to public relations*, 3–16. Hillsdale, NJ: Lawrence Erlbaum.

Van Nistelrooij, Antonie. 2000. *Collectief organiseren. Een sociaal-constructionistisch onderzoek naar het werken met grote groepen* [Collective organizing. A social-constructionistic research project into large scale group work]. Utrecht, NL: Lemma.

Van Riel, Cees B. M. 1995. *Principles of corporate communication.* London: Prentice Hall.

Van Riel, Cees B. M. 2000. Corporate communication orchestrated by a sustainable corporate story. In Majken Schultz, Mary Jo Hatch and Mogens Holten Larsen (eds.), *The expressive organization. Linking identity, reputation, and the corporate brand*, 157–181. Oxford: Oxford University Press.

Van Ruler, Betteke. 1997. Communication: magical mystery or scientific concept? Professional views of public relations practitioners in the Netherlands. In Dany Moss, Toby MacManus and Dejan Verčič (eds.), *Public relations research: An international perspective*, 247–263. London: International Thomson Business Press.

Van Ruler, Betteke. 2004a. The Communication Grid, introduction of a model of basic communica-
tion strategies in public relations practice, *Public Relations Review* 30(2). 123–143.
Van Ruler, Betteke 2004b. Public relations in Europe, the Dutch case. In Betteke van Ruler and Dejan
Verčič (eds.), *Public relations and communication management in Europe. A nation-by-nation
introduction to public relations theory and practice*, 261–276. Berlin & New York: Mouton De
Gruyter.
Van Ruler, Betteke. 2012. *Met het oog op communicatie, reflecties op het communicatievak* [With
an eye on communication. Reflections on the job of communication professionals]. Den Haag:
Boom/Lemma.
Van Ruler, Betteke. 2015. Agile public relations planning: The reflective communication scrum.
Public Relations Review 41. 187–194.
Van Ruler, Betteke. 2016. Public relations: Too little emphasis on communication. *Communication
management review* 1(1). 6–27.
Van Ruler, Betteke. 2018. Communication theory: An underrated pillar on which strategic
communication rests. *International Journal of Strategic Communication* 12(4). 367–381.
Van Ruler, Betteke. 2019. Agile communication evaluation and measurement. *Journal of
Communication Management* 23(3). 265–280.
Van Ruler, Betteke & Dejan Verčič. 2002. *The Bled manifesto on public relations*. Ljubljana: Pristop.
Van Ruler, Betteke & Dejan Verčič. 2003. *Reflective communication management, a public
view on public relations*. Paper presented at 53rd Annual Conference of the International
Communication Association "Communication in Borderlands," San Diego, 23–27 May.
Van Ruler, Betteke & Dejan Verčič. 2005. Reflective communication management, future ways for
public relations research. In Pamela J. Kalbfleisch (ed.), *Communication yearbook* 29. 239–274.
Mahwah, NJ: Erlbaum.
Verhoeven, Piet. 2009. On Latour: actor-network-theory (ANT) and public relations. In Oyvind Ihlen,
Betteke van Ruler and Magnus Fredriksson (eds.), *Public relations and social theory, key figures
and concepts*, 166–186. New York: Routledge.
Watzlawick, Paul, Janet Beavin & Don Jackson. 1967. *Pragmatics of human communication: A study
of interactional patterns, pathologies, and paradoxes*. New York: Norton.
Weick, Karl E. 1995. *Sense making in organizations*. Thousand Oaks, CA: Sage.
Zijderveld, Anton C. 2000. *The Institutional imperative. The interface of institutions and networks*.
Amsterdam: Amsterdam University Press.

Jennifer Bartlett and Bree Hurst

6 Public relations and legitimacy

Abstract: This chapter highlights the links between legitimacy and public relations, providing insights into how and why public relations is practiced. Specifically, this chapter defines legitimacy, and charts the evolution of public relations practices as they are related to legitimacy. It also discusses the legitimacy of the practice of public relations in society and its implications, as well as the legitimacy of the profession of public relations more broadly. The chapter acknowledges the idea that vying for legitimacy and reputation has become a central part of the practice of public relations in explaining organisations and maintaining support. It also underscores that when the profession of public relations is questioned as to its legitimacy, theoretically we may well argue that its existence, influence and power is a central part of contemporary society – whether used by the establishment or the people.

Keywords: legitimacy; pragmatic legitimacy; moral legitimacy; cognitive legitimacy; profession.

1 Introduction

When van Ruler and Verčič (2005) suggested legitimacy is at the heart of public relations, it provided a lens through which to consider the effects of public relations work and public relations as a societal function. Whichever way the literature deals with legitimacy, its focus is on how and why public relations is practiced. However, concurrently there are broader questions about the legitimacy of public relations work and the profession itself. Questions in this arena ponder the professionalisation of the field, as well as the power and influence public relations can have on organisations and on society more generally. This chapter explores the concept of legitimacy through defining its meaning, attributes and application, before examining the various implications this has for how we view public relations practice.

Various public relations texts (Cutlip, Center, and Broom 2006; L'Etang 2014) refer to the history of public relations reaching back to ancient times as leaders and spokespeople sought to narrate and interpret the story of society or to persuade and advocate for specific interests. Often this storytelling and advocacy has been the privilege of the rich and the powerful with the means to further their own interests. However we can also reach back into history to see how the people have likewise harnessed these tools to create change and further causes of democracy and equality. The American and French revolutions, anti-war demonstrations, the Arab Spring (National Geographic 2019) and the #MeToo (Me Too 2018) movement suggest that the people's interest can harness power and create influence to further social good.

https://doi.org/10.1515/9783110554250-006

Yet popular media portray public relations as corporate or government spin, "propaganda" and the privilege of the rich and powerful. These two variations of the purpose and influence of public relations raise questions about the very legitimacy of public relations and the work it does. In this chapter we explore the notion of legitimacy and consider what this means for the work of public relations. First we will define legitimacy, then explore the work of public relations. Finally the chapter will address questions about the legitimacy of public relations as a societal function before raising final questions.

2 Defining legitimacy

While the term legitimacy is widely used in common parlance, interest in the notion of legitimacy as a field of organisational study emerged in the 1970s alongside open systems theory. This shift in understanding and definitions of organisations and of the managers of those organisations redefined thinking about organisations as rational efficient entities to complex organisational arrangements with cultural, symbolic and technical imperatives (Scott 1987). Theoretically this shift in thinking took place in organisational theory and the re-emergence of neo-institutional theory (DiMaggio and Powell 1983; Meyer and Rowan 1977), population ecology (Hannan and Freeman 1977) and resource dependency (Pfeffer and Salancik 1978) perspectives. Public relations texts such as *Effective Public Relations* (Cutlip, Center, and Broom 2006) likewise picked up this perspective on organisations in their explanations and description of the field.

Early definitions of legitimacy focused on congruence between societal expectations and organisational practices (Meyer and Scott 1977; Parsons 1967; Pfeffer and Salancik 1978). Taking this perspective shifted conceptualisations of organisations from agency perspectives in which a strategic manager operated on behalf of owners to achieve specific outcomes, to a broader notion of the organisation operating within wider societal arrangements and where organisational boundaries were more fluid and open. It also meant that organisational practices and outcomes were not defined by the organisation or the manager, but that a range of other insiders and outsiders had influence – either explicitly or implicitly – on managerial decisions. One might argue that this subsequent entanglement of efficiency and legitimacy as organisational drivers has been a catalyst for the growth of public relations around this period and some definitions of public relations practitioners as boundary spanners (Cutlip, Center, and Broom 2006), ferrying intelligence and interpretation between the inside and outside of the organisations.

Suchman (1995) was instrumental in exploring and articulating the notion of legitimacy, which has had wide influence in organisational and communication literatures. Based in neo-institutional and strategic approaches in the organisational theory tradition, this paper was seminal in marrying the external influences of societal meanings and expectations with strategic managerial attempts to respond and manage in line with those expectations to achieve organisational and operational outcomes. It would be remiss not to include his much-cited definition of legitimacy: "Legitimacy is a generalized perception or assumption that the actions of an entity are desirable, proper, or appropriate within some socially constructed system of norms, values, beliefs, and definitions. Inherent is the notion of an organisational or societal entity or practice." (Suchman 1995: 574)

Perceptions are integral to this definition, which makes the idea of legitimacy somewhat intangible and fluid, leaving conceptualisations of what is legitimate up for negotiation and constant reconstruction. Meyer and Rowan (1977) provide important insight when they suggest legitimacy is the absence of critique and alignment with taken-for-granted assumptions of how things will operate. They have a mechanism of ceremony, inspection and evaluation that reflects on the centrality of myths and symbols as the foundation of principles of legitimacy (Waeraas 2009). This may mean that practices are being carried on as taken-for-granted or business-as-usual arrangements and that they have not come up for questioning. Legitimacy therefore refers to a credible shared account or rationale of the organisation and its practices (Jepperson 1991; Suchman 1995). However, if the organisation or practices are potentially contentious, it becomes important for the rationale to show value. Suchman (1995) reminds us of these types of important distinctions despite the overall definition as generalised assumption of appropriateness.

Another related organisational perspective that incorporates external influence on the organisation – resource dependency theory (Pfeffer and Salancik 1978) – also refers to legitimacy. However in this perspective, legitimacy is conceptualised as a resource to be acquired for use by the organisation to garner reputation or other resources. This view is morally problematic, as Suchman reminds us that organisations can not just extract legitimacy from the environment like a "feat of cultural strip mining" (Suchman 1995: 576). However this objectification of legitimacy perhaps underpins the notion of social licence to operate, which is commonly referred to in practice, especially in relation to corporate social responsibility.

Inherent to the main body of work around legitimacy is social construction of reality (Berger and Luckmann 1967) and taken-for-grantedness (Zucker 1977). Berger and Luckmann's (1967) contribution to our understanding of our realities is that our shared assumptions about reality are jointly constructed by multiple social actors. This aligns with constructionist insights on public relations' role in shaping meanings of organisational and societal action (Heide 2009). Zucker (1977) brings psychological insights about our cognitive assumptions about our world. Importantly, and central to a constructionist perspective, we rely on these taken-for-granted assumptions of the world because they provide the social lubricant for navigating our world (Berger and Luckmann 1967). We do not assess every single encounter or situation – we rely on our assumptions of the world because they display the requisite symbols of being appropriate and legitimate. The institutional perspective imbues the external environment and cultural significance of the organisation and its activities.

3 Suchman and forms of legitimacy

In his seminal and widely referenced article, Suchman (1995) presents important insights in articulating three forms of legitimacy. These are useful to examine as they begin to allow us to consider the theoretical bases of legitimacy as a platform from which to consider empirical studies and public relations practices. The three forms of legitimacy are pragmatic, moral and cognitive legitimacy.

3.1 Pragmatic legitimacy

Pragmatic legitimacy is essentially an exchange-based form of legitimacy. Drawing inspiration from ideas of exchange and value to the individual from Pfeffer and Salancik (1978) and Dowling and Pfeffer (1975), this form of legitimacy is focused on an immediate audience in relation to the organisation. This audience is interested in the benefit to them from the relationship with the organisation. Therefore their assessment of the organisation's appropriateness is linked to the value which comes to them from their organisational exchange.

Suchman (1995) suggests there are some related variations to this exchange-based pragmatic legitimacy that provide an extension to this resource dependency-inspired body of work. One he calls dispositional legitimacy, where the immediate audience has a sense that even if there is not an immediate exchange relationship in play at the time, there is still a sense that the organisation has their interests at heart. This remains aligned with central principles of legitimacy related to perceptions of appropriateness that are inherent in this view. Another variation is related to legitimacy from audiences having the sense that they have some influence on the organisation. This might lead us to contemporary parallels inspired by systems theory and engagement and dialogue where stakeholders are able to be involved and consulted on decisions and matters related to the organisation.

3.2 Moral legitimacy

Moral legitimacy takes a social interest perspective around perceptions that the organisation is engaged in practices which are the "right thing to do". Inspired by work by Aldrich and Fiol (1994), moral legitimacy rests on normative evaluations of organisations and their practices. Berger and Luckmann (1967)'s social construction of reality principles are integral to this view, as these evaluations are related to the audience or stakeholder's socially constructed view of the world. This does suggest that normative standards are potentially open to being influenced by self-interests. This has important implications for a common critique of the influence and ethics of public relations practices (e. g. Grunig J. and Hunt 1984) and questions about their influence on society.

However, Suchman suggests there are some forms of moral legitimacy that are more immune to potential manipulation by self-interests but which still are related to societal expectations of the right things to do. These are aligned to consequential, structural, procedural and, in some forms, reputational demands. For example, we take it for granted that corporations pursue profit; that hospitals have nursing care, surgery etc. and not construction; or that there are procedures to go through to enrol in education institutions. The final reputational element is that there are individuals or leaders who have additional kudos or legitimacy because they display attributes of greater social good.

While these forms of moral legitimacy are more immune to individual self-interest due to their broader societal nature, a raft of subsequent research has focused on processes of institutionalisation and of shifting and maintaining institutional arrangements (Lounsbury and Crumley 2007; Suddaby and Greenwood 2005). As examples in subsequent paragraphs will illustrate, public relations can be involved in this type of work in terms of reframing and reconceptualising accepted practices and norms.

3.3 Cognitive legitimacy

Suchman's (1995) final category is cognitive legitimacy. Key themes in this category are the inevitability or necessity of social arrangements, organisations, actions and the like. This form of legitimacy is distinct from evaluation and whether we think something is right or wrong but just inevitable (Jepperson 1991). Zucker (1978) describes this form of legitimacy as existing distinctively from actors or situations per se, existing as cognitive arrangements where we cannot conceive of the situation continuing in their absence. For DiMaggio and Powell (1983), cognitive legitimacy relates to the comprehensibility of a situation. In other words, it is about the rationalisation of the world, and the creation of plausible stories that embody the notion of taken-for-grantedness.

In related frameworks of legitimacy, public relations can be informed by three pillars of legitimacy, based on the foundations of how and why social and organisational arrangements are legitimate – regulative, normative and cognitive (DiMaggio and Powell 1983; Scott 1991). These variations of Aldrich and Fiol's (1994) socio-political categories cover a range of legitimacy dimensions that we can relate to specific social actors. Regulative dimensions refer to legal and regulatory arrangements which shape and legitimate organisational actions. It is important to note that these include both hard and soft regulation, such as industry codes of practices common in neoliberal economies. Normative legitimacy relates to practices that are shaped by the actions of actors which create taken-for-granted practices. These include the role of education and professional standards that dictate the types of practices used in various organisational and social roles. This dynamic is central for our subsequent discussion on the professionalisation of public relations. As well as shaping "best practice", this category also includes the carrying and transfer of practices between organisations and individuals by "carriers", such as consultants who transfer new knowledge. Cognitive legitimacy has some references to Zucker (1977) and fundamental meanings of the reality of the world.

In summary, these definitions highlight a number of key dynamics that are germane to our interest in the concept of legitimacy for public relations. The first is based in the foundations of the social construction of reality and the fact that norms, rules and meanings are constructed by various social actors. This view is facilitated by conceptualisations of organisations having cultural drivers around symbols, myths and rationalisations, rather than a rational view of the organisation. The second is that the notion of legitimacy is based in the development of plausible congruent scripts explaining social and organisational arrangements. Suchman (1995) suggests the role of the actors are relevant in the genesis of legitimacy – from an exchange relationship between audience/stakeholder and the organisation; a social meaning the audience holds in relation to broader social values; and the inevitability and taken-for-grantedness of practices. These elements lay the foundations for considering the role of legitimacy for public relations and its work in framing and meaning-making, managing relationships and persuasion. The normative pillars of legitimacy may also provide explanatory power for discussions of the legitimacy of public relations as a profession and its role in society. It is no coincidence that the public relations profession has blossomed alongside the evolution of organisational theory and discussions of legitimacy in organisational theory.

4 Public relations as the work of legitimacy

Legitimacy is frequently revisited as a concept in public relations literature, being used as a rationale and as a technique of the profession. For example, the emergence of corporate social responsibility in both theory and practice across many disciplines has also highlighted legitimacy as a concern of public relations. As in most scholarly fields, academics in public relations intermittently re-engage with concepts and theories, and legitimacy is certainly one such case. Here the focus of the literature is examined to understand public relations' use, inspiration and interpretation of legitimacy. In doing so, we note that public relations' treatment of legitimacy takes place alongside advances in a range of other disciplines. The work presented begins in the 1990s, even though legitimacy is frequently referred to in earlier public relations texts (Grunig J. and Hunt 1984).

4.1 The 1990s

As discussed in the prior section, the multilevel turn in organisational theory elevated the importance of legitimacy to understanding organising and organisations. The role of communication and public relations like practices to manage legitimacy during crises and in issues began being investigated in the organisational and management literature. One seminal paper at that time was the use of impression management and institutional theory to examine how advocacy groups used illegitimate actions to garner legitimacy for their cause (Elsbach and Sutton 1992). This was followed up by another seminal paper related to the process of legitimation of the cattle industry during a crisis (Elsbach 1994). This focus on crisis, impression management and image repair was prevalent in the public relations literature with legitimacy being referred to both overtly and implicitly (Benoit 1995; Benoit and Brinson 1994; Hearit 1995).

Other scholars were promoting the notion of legititmacy related to the principles of public relations practice and its role in society, albeit with different takes on the theme. Robert Heath (1997) argued that a rhetorical perspective supports the legitimacy of public relations as a valued means for voice in society more broadly. Meanwhile, consistent with this turn in the literature, communication and legitimacy was being theorised in the communication journals as a driver and rationale for communication strategy (Jensen 1997; Metzler 1995). In this view, a communication strategy should aim at driving an organization or entity towards more legitimacy. These perspectives are also aligned with the spirit of the Habermasian lens (Habermas 1975) on public relations and the relationships between communication, institutions and legitimacy. In particular, links have been made between Habermas' concept of the public sphere (see Ihlen and van Ruler 2009), as well as the importance of legitimacy in ensuring the validity of communication (see Burkart 2007).

4.2 The 2000s

The 2000s kicked off with claims that legitimacy was an important concern for public relations even without crisis (Boyd 2000). The term legitimacy became more prominent in titles of public relations scholarship in that time, perhaps reflecting the recognition of legitimacy as a concept of importance for explaining the rationale for public relations. For example, legitimacy featured as central topics in handbooks defining the key interests of the field (Cornelissen 2004; Metzler 2001). Bridges (2004) suggested legitimacy was one of the central explanations of the gaps between organisational practice and societal expectations, and as such is one of the central explanations of the type of problem to which public relations practice attends. Some scholars went so far as to suggest legitimacy was the key driver for public relations, and as such provided its central rationale (van Ruler and Verčič 2005).

By the mid to late 2000s, organisation theory scholars noted that institutional theory – with legitimacy as its central rationale – was the most used organisation theory in leading management journals such as Academy of Management, replacing culture as the dominant perspective. This blurring of public relations, communication and organisational theory perspectives burgeoned in this period. Notable and germane to public relations is the paper (Suddaby and Greenwood 2005) on rhetorical strategies for legitimation showing how professions used rhetoric to legitimate new boundaries around professions. Perhaps reflective of this, legitimacy and legitimation from a Weberian perspective (Waeraas 2009), were presented as a foundational theory for public relations in the volume on social theory and public relations. Waeraas (2009: 301) suggests legitimacy makes three key contributions to our understanding of public relations: for understanding the purpose and practice of public relations; as a rationale for public relations justifying an organisation's right to existence; and as a driver for public relations practice in building attractive and symbolic meaning of the organisation.

One possible reason for the resurgence of interest in legitimacy is related to the corporate social responsibility movement. As corporate social responsibility became a concern for corporations and governments around the world, public relations practitioners and academics found a perfect ground for their work of managing perceptions and aligning organisational meanings and practices with societal expectations. This was also seen in management literatures (Palazzo and Scherer 2006) as organisations sought to redefine themselves as having financial, social and environmental responsibilities. Public relations scholars likewise presented empirical evidence of how public relations practices were harnessed to reposition the meaning of organisational responsibility and how practices were rationalised (Bartlett 2007; Bortree 2009; Rahaman, Lawrence, and Roper 2004).

4.3 The 2010s

Legitimacy, especially using institutional theory as a basis, has continued to build and grow as an arena of public relations scholarship from scholars in the USA, Europe and Australasia (Frandsen and Johansen 2013; Fredriksson and Pallas 2015; Fredriksson, Pallas, and Wehmeier 2013; Le and Bartlett 2014; O'Connor and Shumate 2010; O'Connor, Parcha, and Tulibaski 2017). There is a large body of work related to how legitimacy is managed, which led from the foundational perspectives of the past few decades.

Another emergent strand of the literature considers the relationships between the concepts of legitimacy and reputation. Both of these concepts are based on relationships among various societal actors (Galaskiewicz 1985), and with the images or perception they form as a result of these relationships. However, while parallels between these concepts are apparent, another seminal paper defines important differences between the seemingly related terms of reputation and legitimacy (Deephouse and Carter 2005; Deephouse and Suchman 2008). These differerences are explicity explored conceptually through a communication and public relations lens (Bartlett, Pallas, and Frostenson 2013), and highlights the implications for communicators. With both concepts being prevalent in practice, the relationship between legitimacy and reputation remains an area for further studies, thus contributing to our insights on legitimacy in public relations.

5 Legitimacy of the public relations profession

If the previous section has examined the way the public relations practices are related to legitimacy, we also raise the question of the legitimacy of public relations. This is addressed in two ways. The first is related to the legitimacy of the practice of public relations in society and its implications. The second is the legitimacy of the profession of public relations.

5.1 Legitimacy and the influence of public relations

At the heart of these questions is querying the power, influence and indeed legitimacy of some societal actors having the resources and ability to shape meanings of organisational actions. In addition, these questions extend to the legitimacy of managing the reputations and image restoration of organisational actors, especially around their image restoration, rhetorical and operational actions, with all the consequences this has. For example, what are the implications of entire industries being considered inappropriate, such as coal mining or red meat farming? And conversely, what are the implications for shareholders and firm-owners of organisations making significant contributions to social and environmental initiatives? These types of controversial and contested meanings are central to the questions of the influence that some can have on society. Indeed, the legitimacy of the activities within some of the cited studies referred to in the prior section are subject to inquiry here.

Discussions of the legitimacy of the work of public relations tend to be covered in the critical public relations literature rather than the normative, which tends to deal with the idea that notions of symmetry (Grunig J. 2001) or rhetorical principles (Heath 1997) will deal with these issues of power. Critical arguments explicitly address the role of power and influence wielded by public relations. Through popular media and everyday parlance, public relations is portrayed as having significant influence on society and is regarded with concern and lack of respect. Relational perspectives are offered as a means to deal with these concerns (Edwards 2006) to rethink the power of public relations.

One common framing of public relations is as propaganda and spin. The connotations of propaganda relate to misinformation, persuasion and deceit. Spin or spin doctoring are more recent terms for framing situations to the benefit of the one in the position of power. Public relations scholars interrogate this and consider the implications and role of ethics in public relations practice and in the professional accreditation and education around those in the field (Fawkes 2007). In a practical sense, of course, this is about one party seeking to frame situations and actions in their favour. Framing is a classic concept in communication and alongside rhetoric and persuasion. If we reflect on the Suchman principles of legitimacy presented earlier, we are reminded that reality is socially constructed and therefore is shaped by the social actors around the situation. Likewise Waaeras (2009) reminds us of the Weberian basis of legitimacy (which underpins institutional theory with its central principle of legititmacy), the principle of myths reminds us that beliefs are constructed, and subsequently that they have a plausible rationale (Ashforth and Gibbs 1990). This means nothing is value-neutral, nor free of power and influence. However, as the public relations literature (Fawkes 2007; L'Etang 1997; Waeraas 2009) and professional guidelines reflect, this power should be laden with ethical concerns and duty of care.

5.2 Legitimacy of public relations as a profession

Another key strand of literature related to the legitimacy of public relations is about its status as a profession. Whether public relations has status as a profession, and whether its practitioners are professional and ethical in engaging in the work of persuasion, framing etc., as discussed in chapters 4 and 30 of this handbook, are some of the key questions raised.

Certainly public relations, under various names, has been practiced across several millenia and back to ancient Greece. Much of the literature then flags modern public relations emerging from the Industrial Revolution and growth in various media technologies that allowed the public to be engaged with public and organisational issues. We can see a further period of incredible growth in the Western world since the 1950s and the influx of upward mobility, consumerism and education. In the 21st century, access to information across the globe has further accelerated with Web and mobile technologies (Bartlett, J. and Bartlett, G. 2012). It is now estimated that spending on public relations is worth billions of dollars each year (Moloney 2006).

Public relations is not unique in its interest in its status as a profession. Professionalisation of so-called new or organisational professions (Hwang and Powell 2009) is of interest across diverse occupations such as nursing, accounting, journalism and others. The professionalisation of public relations has been of interest at least from the 1990s, especially but not exclusively via work from United Kingdom scholars (L'Etang 2013).

Professionalisation literature falls into three key streams of research (Thomas, R. and Thomas, H. 2014):

- Essential characteristics of professions,
- Sociological strategies enacted by professional associations, and
- Role of corporate entities in professionalisation.

Public relations literature has been strong in the essential characteristics of the profession approach to professions. This strand of work is interested in whether occupations can be considered professions. Criteria marking professions in this literature include: a unique body of technical knowledge; existence of a professional association as a central mechanism for monitoring and managing knowledge and the professionals; ethical standards guiding members' practice in the societal interest; and recognition of status and income. This constitutes institutionalisation of an arena of work (Suddaby and Viale 2011).

L'Etang and Pieczka (2006) offered important coverage of this body of work and the professionalisation project. Emerging from the sociological perspectives of Abbott (1988) and the emergence of new professions, their work has focused on this approach. We have seen the growth of public relations degree programmes, especially since the 1970s, laying claim to a discrete body of knowledge for those training to engage in this profession. These are the types of claims of a profession to legitimate itself as a profession.

One might argue that public relations is legitimate by the sheer size of the number of people and organisations practicing public relations backed by the number of degree qualifications and professional associations related to the field. With our original definitions of legitimacy, a level of taken-for-grantedness and lack of questioning, in this case as to its role in society, we might surmise that, overall, public relations as a profession is legitimate because it is taken for granted. However we do get recurrent questioning about the practices of public relations from time to time around certain situations. We also face the "it's just PR", "it's spin" etc. taunts, as referred to earlier. However, in the main, the prevalence of public relations is a taken-for-granted practice.

Professional associations play an integral role in organising and defining professionals and their work and behaviour, seeking to achieve occupational closure (Noordegraaf 2011; Thomas, R. and Thomas, H. 2014). As such, professional associations play an important role in creating demarcation lines around the occupation and practices of public relations and, in theory, creating barriers to entry to the profession. The public relations professional associations which emerged after World War II – for example the PRSA in the USA; PRIA in Australia; and Institute of Public Relations (IPR, now CIPR) in the United Kingdom for example, provided an important platform for the establishment of public relations as a profession (Watson 2015). Public relations professional associations are now found throughout the world, further reflecting the growth and indeed legitimacy of the public relations profession. One of the important professionalisation practices of these associations is done via defining and rewarding "best practice", usually through industry awards. These awards define attributes of best practice for the profession, requiring award entrants to demonstrate how their work aligns with these standards. This process of professionalising through normative legitimacy (Suchman 1995) is illustrative of the institutionalisation process taking place.

6 Discussion, conclusions and implications

One might argue that the growth in interest in legitimacy and indeed the expansion of the public relations industry, particularly in the western world, are functions of neoliberalism and a shift away from regulation and clearer definitions of legalities and appropriateness. If we draw on both Weber's principles of rational versus charismatic pillars, or institutional theory's perspectives on mimetic pillars of replication of practices considered appropriate, we can see explanations for why there is a greater need for organisations to continually build and maintain support for their practices and even their existence.

Therefore, vying for legitimacy and reputation become central to explaining organisations and maintaining support. Simultaneously, having this legitimating account heard and given credibility within a dense informational environment with multiple stakeholders and advocates championing their cause provides an additional challenge for organisations. More recently we have seen a renewed focus in public relations on storytelling and narrative as tools to legitimate and to make sense within the cacophony of voices and comments around organisations and ideas. It also provides a means to cut through the information overload perpetuated through social media and hyper-marketing efforts.

Legitimacy potentially will remain an important concept for conceptualising public relations as a conservative mood moves into social and political agendas around the world. For example, we may recast both ceremonial displays of compliance with accepted norms, as well as creating an absence of dissent (Meyer and Rowan 1977), within the work of public relations. This reminds us of the power of public relations, wielded both by organisations and by the people via public opinion and advocacy, to shape society and contest status quo. No doubt, this leads to the ongoing questioning of the legitimacy of public relations itself and its role in society.

Ironically, these shifts in the structures of society coincide with a broader recasting of the roles of professions as institutional structures, and our theorising of them. Traditional professions in arenas such as medicine, law and religion are arguably losing their historical power with the emergence of so-called organisational professions. As professions such as public relations, human resources, procurement etc. pursue their ambitions of accreditation and resource acquisition, the notion of professional status is being eroded. When public relations is questioned as to its legitimacy, theoretically we may well argue that its existence, influence and power is a central part of contemporary society – whether used by the establishment or the people.

References

Abbott, Andrew. 1988. *The system of professions: An essay on the division of expert labour.* Chicago: University of Chicago Press.

Aldrich, Howard. E. & C. Marlene Fiol. 1994. Fools rush in? The institutional context of industry creation. *Academy of Management Review* 19(4). 645–670.

Ashforth, Blake. E. & Barry W. Gibbs. 1990. The double-edged sword of organizational legitimation. *Organization Science* 1. 177–194.

Bartlett, Jennifer Lea. 2007. *The Web of Institutionalised Legitimacy: Building a model of legitimacy as a raison d'etre for public relations practice.* Brisbane: Queensland University of Technology PhD thesis.

Bartlett, Jennifer Lea & George Bartlett. 2012. Kaleidoscopes and Contradictions. In Sandra Duhe (ed.), *New Media and Public Relations*, 2nd edn., 13–20. New York: Peter Lang.

Bartlett, Jennifer Lea, Josef Pallas & Magnus Frostenson. 2013. Reputation and Legitimacy: accreditation and rankings to assess organizations. In Craig E. Carroll (ed.), *The Handbook of Communication and Corporate Reputation*, 530–544. West Sussex, UK: John Wiley & Sons Inc.

Benoit, William L. 1995. *Accounts, excuses, and apologies: A theory of image restoration strategies.* Albany: State University of New York Press.

Benoit, William L. & Susan L. Brinson. 1994. AT&T: "Apologies are not enough". *Communication Quarterly* 42(1). 75–88.

Berger, Peter L. & Thomas Luckmann. 1967. *The social construction of reality: A treatise in the sociology of knowledge.* New York: Anchor Books.

Bortree, Denise Sevick. 2009. The impact of green initiatives on environmental legitimacy and admiration of the the organization. *Public Relations Review* 35(2). 133–135.

Boyd, Josh. 2000. Actional legitimation: No crisis necessary. *Journal of Public Relations Research* 12(4). 341–353.

Bridges, Janet A. 2004. Corporate issues campaigns: Six theoretical approaches. *Communication Theory* 14(1). 51–77.

Burkart, Roland. 2007. On Jurgen Habermas and public relations. *Public Relations Review* 33. 249–254.

Cornelissen, Joep. 2004. *Corporate Communications: Theory and Practice.* London: Sage.

Cutlip, Scott M., Allen H. Center & Glen M. Broom. 2006. *Effective public relations*, 9th edn. New Jersey: Prentice Hall.

Deephouse, David L. & Suzanne M. Carter. 2005. An Examination of Differences Between Organizational Legitimacy and Organizational Reputation. *Journal of Management Studies* 42(2). 329–360.

Deephouse, David L. & Mark Suchman. 2008. Legitimacy in organizational institutionalism. In Royston Greenwood, Christine Oliver, Kerstin Sahlin & Roy Suddaby (eds.), *The Sage Handbook of Organizational Institutionalism*, 49–77. London: Sage.

DiMaggio, Paul J. & Walter W. Powell. 1983. The iron cage revisited: Institutional isomorphism and collective rationality in organizational fields. *American Sociological Review* 48. 47–160.

Dowling, John & Jeffrey Pfeffer. 1975. Organizational legitimacy: Social values and organizational behavior. *Pacific Sociological Review* 18. 122–136.

Edwards, Lee. 2006. Rethinking power in public relations. *Public Relations Review* 32(3). 229–231.

Elsbach, Kimberly D. 1994. Managing organisational legitimacy in the California cattle industry. *Administrative Science Quarterly* 39(1). 57–88.

Elsbach, Kimberly D. & Robert I. Sutton. 1992. Acquiring organisational legitimacy through illegitimate actions: A marriage of institutional and impression management theories. *Academy of Management Journal* 35(4). 699–738.

Fawkes, Johanna. 2007. Public relations models and persuasion ethics: a new approach. *Journal of Communication Management* 11(4). 313–331.

Frandsen, Finn & Winni Johansen. 2013. Public relations and the new institutionalism: In search of a theoretical framework. *Public Relations Inquiry* 2(2). 205–221.

Fredriksson, Magnus & Josef Pallas. 2015. Strategic communication as institutional work. In Derina Holtzhausen & Ansgar Zerfass (eds.), *The Routledge handbook of strategic communication*, 143–156. New York & London: Routledge.

Fredriksson, Magnus, Josef Pallas & Stefan Wehmeier. 2013. Public relations and neo-institutional theory. *Public Relations Inquiry* 2(2). 183–203.

Galaskiewicz, Joseph. 1985. Interorganizational relations. *Annual Review of Sociology* 11. 281–304.

Grunig, James E. 2001. Two-way symmetrical public relations. In Robert L. Heath (ed.), *Handbook of Public Relations*, 11–30. Thousand Oaks, CA: Sage.

Grunig, James E. & Todd Hunt. 1984. *Managing public relations*. New York: Holt, Rinehart and Winston.

Habermas, Jürgen. 1975. *Legitimation crisis*. USA: Beacon Press.

Hannan, Michael T. & John Freeman. 1977. The population ecology of organizations. *American Journal of Sociology* 82. 929–964.

Hearit, Keith Michael. 1995. "Mistakes were made": Organizations, apologia, and crises of social legitimacy. *Communication Studies* 46(1–2). 1–17.

Heath, Robert L. 1997. Legitimate 'perspectives' in public relations practice: A rhetorical solution. *Australian Journal of Communication* 24(2). 55–63.

Heide, Mats. 2009. On Berger: A social constructionist perspective on public relations and crisis communication. In Oyvind Ihlen, Betteke van Ruler & Magnus Fredriksson (eds.), *Public Relations and Social Theory: Key Figures and Concepts*, 43–61. New York: Routledge.

Hwang, Hokyu & Walter W Powell. 2009. The rationalization of charity: The influences of professionalism in the nonprofit sector. *Administrative Science Quarterly* 54(2). 268–298.

Ihlen, Oyvind & Betteke van Ruler. 2009. Introduction: Applying social theory to public relations. In Oyvind Ihlen, Betteke van Ruler & Magnus Fredriksson (eds.), *Public Relations and Social Theory: Key Figures and Concepts*, 1–20. New York: Routledge

Jensen, Inger. 1997. Legitimacy and strategy of different companies: A perspective of external and internal public relations. In Danny Moss, Toby MacManus & Dejan Verčič (eds.), *Public Relations Research: An International Perspective*, 225–246. London: International Thomson Business Press.

Jepperson, Ronald L. 1991. Institutions, institutional effects and institutionalism. In Walter R. Powell & Paul J. DiMaggio (eds.), *The new institutionalism in organizational analysis*, 143–163. Chicago: University of Chicago Press.

L'Etang, Jacquie. 1997. Public relations and the rhetorical dilemma: Legitimate perspectives, persuasion, or pandering? *Australian Journal of Communication* 24(2). 33–53.

L'Etang, Jacquie. 2013. Public relations: A discipline in transformation. *Sociology Compass* 7(10). 799–817.

L'Etang, Jacquie. 2014. Public relations and historical sociology: Historiography as reflexive critique. *Public Relations Review* 40(4). 654–660.

L'Etang, Jacquie & Magda Pieczka. 2006. Public Relations: Critical debates and contemporary practice. Mahwah, NJ: Lawrence Erlbaum Associates.

Le, Jenny & Jennifer Lea Bartlett. 2014. Managing impressions during institutional change – The role of organisational accounts in legitimation. *Public Relations Inquiry* 3(3). 341–360.

Lounsbury, Michael & Ellen T. Crumley. 2007. New practice creation: An institutional perspective on innovation. *Organization Studies* 28(7). 993–1012.

Me Too. 2018. *Me Too – About*. https://metoomvmt.org/about/ (accessed on 25 November 2019).

Metzler, Maribeth S. 1995. *A communicative theory of organizational legitimacy*. New York: Rensselaer Polytechnic Institute PhD thesis.

Metzler, Maribeth S. 2001. The centrality of organisational legitimacy to public relations practice. In Ronald L. Heath (ed.), *The Handbook of Public Relations*, 321–334. Thousand Oaks, CA: Sage Publications.

Meyer, John W. & Brian Rowan. 1977. Institutionalized organizations: Formal structure as myth and ceremony. *American Journal of Sociology* 83(2). 340–363.

Meyer, John W. & W. Richard Scott. 1977. Centralization and the legitimacy problems of local government. In John W. Meyer & W. Richard Scott (eds.), *Organizational Environments: Ritual and Rationality*, 199–215. Beverley Hills, California: Sage Publications.

Moloney, Kevin. 2006. *Rethinking Public Relations: PR Propaganda and Democracy*, 2nd edn. London: Routledge.

National Geographic. 2019. What was the Arab Spring and how did it spread? https://www.nationalgeographic.com/culture/topics/reference/arab-spring-cause/ (accessed on 14 October 2019.

Noordegraaf, Mirko. 2011. Remaking professionals? How associations and professional education connect professionalism and organizations. *Current Sociology* 59. 465–488.

O'Connor, Amy & Michelle Shumate. 2010. An economic industry and institutional level of analysis of corporate social responsibility communication. *Management Communication Quarterly* 24(4). 529–551.

O'Connor, Amy, Joshua M. Parcha & Katherine L.G. Tulibaski. 2017. The institutionalization of corporate social responsibility communication: An intra-industry comparison of MNCs' and SMEs' CSR reports. *Management Communication Quarterly* 31(4). 503–532.

Palazzo, Guido & Andreas Georg Scherer. 2006. Corporate legitimacy as deliberation: A communicative framework. *Journal of Business Ethics* 66(1). 71–88.

Parsons, Talcott. 1967. A paradigm for the social analysis of social systems and change. In N. J. Demerath III & Richard A. Peterson (eds.), *System, change and conflict*, 189–212. New York: The Free Press.

Pfeffer, Jeffrey & Gerald R. Salancik. 1978. *The external control of organizations*. New York: Harper & Row.

Rahaman, Abu Shiraz, Stewart Lawrence & Juliet Roper. 2004. Social and environmental reporting at the VRA: institutionalised legitimacy or legitimation crisis? *Critical Perspectives on Accounting* 15(1). 35–56.

Ruler, Betteke van & Dejan Verčič. 2005. Reflective communication management, future ways for public relations research. *Communication Yearbook* 29. 239–273. Scott, W. Richard. 1987. *Organizations: Rational, natural and open systems*, 2nd edn. Englewood Cliffs, NJ: Prentice Hall.

Scott, W. Richard. 1991. Unpacking institutional arguments. In Walter W. Powell & Paul J. DiMaggio (eds.), *The New Institutionalism in Organizational Analysis*, 164–182. Chicago: The University of Chicago Press.

Suchman, Mark C. 1995. Managing legitimacy: Strategic and institutional approaches. *Academy of Management Review* 20(3). 571–610.

Suddaby, Roy & Royston Greenwood. 2005. Rhetorical strategies of legitimacy. *Administrative Science Quarterly* 50. 35–67.

Suddaby, Roy & Thierry Viale. 2011. Professionals and field-level change: Institutional work and the professional project. *Current Sociology* 59(4). 423–442.

Thomas, Rhodri & Huw Thomas. 2014. 'Hollow from the start'? Professional associations and the professionalisation of tourism. *The Service Industries Journal* 34(1). 38–55.

Waeraas, Arild. 2009. On Weber: Legitimacy and legitimation in public relations. In Oyvind Ihlen, Betteke van Ruler & Magnus Fredriksson (eds.), *Public Relations and Social Theory: Key Figures and Concepts*, 301–322. New York: Routledge.

Watson, Tom. 2015. *Perspectives on public relations historiography and historical theorization: Other voices*. London: Palgrave Macmillan UK.

Zucker, Lynne. G. 1977. The role of institutionalization in cultural persistence. *American Sociological Review* 42. 726–743.

Zucker, Lynne. G. 1978. Institutional theories of organizations. *Annual Review of Sociology* 13. 443–644.

C. Kay Weaver
7 Public relations, power and control

Abstract: This chapter examines how power and control have been theorised in connection to the role that public relations plays in social culture. Exactly whether and how public relations and its practitioners wield power in society and are able to assert control over citizens are contested matters. Whether we conclude that public relations is a powerful tool, or not, and to what ends it is used, is dependent on our theoretical perspective. The chapter considers how Excellence theory and its liberal-pluralist underpinnings, and Marxist, postcolonial, and poststructuralist theories variously conceptualise power and control in, and through, public relations. In identifying the motivating factors behind particular theoretical constructions of power and control in public relations, the chapter demonstrates how theorising is itself a political act seeking to influence how we make sense of phenomena. Only when we understand the politics of theory and how theories variously represent public relations, are we able to reflect on the ethics of public relations practice. This chapter aims to assist public relations practitioners and scholars to grasp the nuanced debates about the role that public relations plays in society, and the contribution that it makes to shaping social culture, peoples and our futures.

Keywords: public relations; power; control; culture; society; Excellence theory; liberal pluralism; Marxist theory; postcolonial theory; poststructuralist theory

1 Introduction

How power and control is understood in discussions of the impacts that public relations has on society and culture and how people think and behave is dependent on the particular theoretical lens that we apply in that discussion. There are many different and contested perspectives on the issue of whether public relations is able to assert power over and control what we do and how we think. These perspectives are informed by the many different ways in which the concepts of power and control are themselves theorised in terms of who has power in society, and how they are granted that power.

When considering the power and control that public relations might wield in society, it has to be acknowledged that the communication practices that it employs – media relations, lobbying, community and public engagement, promotion, for example – are used to support a vast array of organisational, political, profit and non-profit and activist causes, many of which can even be in opposition to each other. As a case in point, public relations strategies are used in support of the interests of the powerful gun lobby and National Rifle Association in the US; they are also used by

https://doi.org/10.1515/9783110554250-007

those who want to restrict gun ownership. We should not, then, make broad sweeping claims about the power and control that public relations has in society as it can be used in many and varied ways by different groups and to different ends. What we can do is develop an understanding of the politics of different theories to make sense of how and why they make certain claims as to whether public relations practice can assert power and control over people, and how those theories position public relations as a communicative practice in relation to democracy. This is important because, ultimately, where there have been concerns expressed about how public relations can be used to powerful ends, and to control people, this is related to whether it is subverting democratic values of accountability, transparency, civil society, participation and inclusion in decision-making (Edwards 2016).

This chapter explores how the relationship between public relations, power and control have been theorised in Excellence, Marxist, postcolonial, and poststructural theories of public relations. In examining how these perspectives talk about public relations, power and control, a key consideration has to be given to how public relations as a practice is itself theoretically constructed. Before examining these theoretical approaches, we should first asses what is meant by the terms power and control.

2 Defining power and control in the public relations context

Power is generally understood as the ability to have an effect on, or over, something or someone. *Having power* involves the capacity to determine your own actions, but can also mean having the ability to make others do something that they may not have otherwise done (Wrong 2017). The latter aspect of power involves domination and enforcement, and the effect that it produces is a consequence of the fear of not complying – maybe the person will be punished or otherwise negatively suffer if they fail to do what is expected or demanded of them. This connects power to control (Wrong 2017). When a person has power, they have the power to control themselves, another person, peoples, outcomes and/or events, though they may not necessarily choose to assert that power and control. Power and control exist in degrees and can be contested and challenged. The exception to this is a situation of absolute power, in which, through their position as, for example, an absolute monarch or dictator, a person is able to assume absolute authority to do as they chose without being accountable to others. In such an example, power is usually associated with corruption, abuse and win-lose relationships (McMillan 2016)

Power should not always be perceived in negative terms of *power over* and associated with repression, force and abuse. Power can also be seen positively in terms of *power with*, which involves achieving and promoting power through support, collaboration, collective strength and unity (Berger 2005). This sort of power involves people, groups and/or organisations, for example, coming together to enhance each other's power. In this context, power is not associated with control over, but sharing control and agency. The notion of *power to* is similar to *power with,* in that it involves people and groups being empowered through, for example, education and leadership development. Once a person, group or organisation does have a sense of their own *power to,* they can be described as having *power within*; that is, they have a sense of self-worth, agency and ability to control and determine their own life, its direction and achievements.

In the context of public relations, care must be taken in terms of how its power is described. As a type of communication practice, public relations is generally not used to instil fear in people to the extent that they comply with messages communicated through organisational channels, the media, promotional materials, or the like. If this were the case we would likely label the communication "propaganda", which is "associated with control and is regarded as a deliberate attempt to alter or maintain a balance of power that is advantageous to the propagandist" (Jowett and O'Donnell 2006: 3). It should be acknowledged that the distinctions between public relations and propaganda are not necessarily obvious (Weaver, Motion, and Roper 2006), and that there are those (Stauber and Rampton 1995; Miller and Dinan 2008) who argue that public relations is simply another name for propaganda.

The power that public relations communication has is most usually not considered in terms of actual power, but rather in terms of symbolic power. The concept of symbolic power originated with Pierre Bourdieu (1991) and positions language as a medium of power through which social structures are represented and accepted as normal. Language, which includes all forms of spoken, written and visual representation, presents particular narratives of reality and encourages audiences to perceive phenomena in particular ways. Few would question that public relations is involved in the strategic representation and promotion of ideas, arguments, positions, symbols, labels and meanings, all of which are designed to inform how we understand and make sense of the people, organisations or groups represented in that communication. The extent to which people are controlled by these representations is, as is discussed further below, dependent on how we theorise the position of the audience, or public, in the communication process. The next section considers the Excellence theory of public relations, which at its very core was concerned with issues of power and control.

3 Excellence theory, power and control in liberal-pluralist capitalism

The Excellence theory of public relations is an important starting-point for the examination of how power and control are theorised in public relations scholarship (see chapter 16). This is because its architects sought to identify ethical idealistic ways of undertaking public relations activity that involved processes "of compromise and negotiation and not a war of power" (Grunig J. and White 1992: 39). The Excellence theorising of public relations aimed to change the dominant pejorative view of public relations as a communicative practice used to help organisations to get people to believe and/or do what those organisation wanted them to do, and thereby assert control over them.

J. Grunig and Hunt (1984) identified four models of public relations practice: press agentry, public information, two-way asymmetric, and two-way symmetric (see chapter 15). Press agentry is a publicity and promotion model which uses manipulative persuasion – *power over* – in efforts to shape and thereby control the thoughts and actions of audiences. Messages which use hype to get us to buy products or believe in certain ideas are generally of this type. The accuracy of the content of the message is not of concern to the sender. This compares with the public information model where the message does contain accurate objective information, but the sender has not conducted any research on their audience to understand their existing attitudes or behaviours, and is not seeking feedback or to build a relationship with that audience. Public information messages aim to make audiences perceive phenomena and act on objective information – such as taking evasive action to protect oneself in the eventuality of an earthquake – but still involve the communication having *power over* that audience. In contrast, J. Grunig and Hunt (1984) identified two-way *a*symmetrical communication as based on research into the intended audiences' beliefs, attitudes and behaviours. Two-way asymmetrical communication is still designed to empower and be of benefit to the sender in that it seeks to produce, or control, audience behaviour in ways that the sender has deemed appropriate. The two-way symmetrical model of public relations is the only one which seeks to equally *empower* the sender and receiver of the communication in that the sender, through dialogue, is seeking information on what the audience wants in a given situation. An example of two-way symmetrical public relations would be an organisation engaging in a dialogue with its publics about whether it should invest in fossil fuel or alternative green technologies.

Because press agentry, public information and two-way asymmetrical communication all, in one way or another, involve attempts to persuade audiences to adopt certain attitudes and behaviours, J. Grunig and Hunt (1984) deemed them to be unethical. The communicative approaches judged to be unethical involve the message sender attempting to have persuasive communicative *power and control over* the receiver-audience. The only form of public relations upheld in Excellence theory as ethical is the two-way symmetrical model. This model depicts a relationship of equals between the organisation and the public – with each having an equal right and ability to put forward ideas in their dialogic encounter, and having equal authority about the decision outcome that is reached in that encounter. Two-way symmetrical public relations is, therefore, depicted as offering a relationship of *power with* between an organisation and its publics, and even a *power to* model given the organisation actively promotes a dialogic relationship with its audience. In effect, J. Grunig and White (1992), following Kruckeberg and Starck (1988), argued for an approach to public relations practice which involved "an active attempt to restore a sense of community" (Grunig J. and White 1992: 42). This Excellence perspective also advocates for a relationship of control mutuality, where "Control mutuality means that both the organization and the stakeholder have the same amount of control over the relationship" (Coombs and Holladay 2007: 27).

Excellence theorists have always acknowledged that they are advocating for an idealistic approach to public relations practice – where power and control is mutually shared by an organisation and its publics in a win-win scenario. Yet, we must consider the type of political democracy that these ideas are grounded in to understand how the relationship between the organisation and the public can be one of equals, and to assess if this ideal *power with* model is possible to achieve.

The notion that an organisation and its publics are able to engage in a dialogic relationship of a kind where each have an equal ability to present their respective ideas, views and positions on an issue, and come to the best decision about how to move forward, is an idealism of free market capitalist liberal-pluralism. This posits power as dispersed in a democracy, as ideally unconstrained by government regulation and interference, and different groups as capable of gaining social representation and influence. Within the capitalist liberal-plural democracy, the position that appeals to the greatest number of people will prevail. Excellence theorists were, however, aware that in capitalist democracies elite privileged groups will attempt to maintain their hold on financial and social power and actively work to prevent others from successfully challenging that power. Consequently, J. Grunig (1989) described "issue-group liberalism" as a better reflection of how the American political landscape operates, with public-issue groups across the political left and right variously attempting to pressurize organizations, corporations and governments to support their interests and causes. According to J. Grunig, such groups play a crucial role "in limiting organisational autonomy" (1989: 22), and forcing organisations to engage in public relations work. Indeed, the voices of diverse special interest groups are welcomed into democratic public debate, where it is argued that, in the marketplace of ideas, the public will evaluate competing messages and claims and come to decide which position best fits with the public interest.

Excellence theorists have, however, been extensively critiqued for failing to consider the relationships of power and control that play out in the public sphere in capitalist liberal-plural democracies. They are particularly criticised for failing to acknowledge the power that organisations have in this context – as financial institutions, as motivated to make profits for shareholders, as employers, as purveyors of information, and as having many more resources available to them than unorganised members of the public (Leitch and Neilson 2001). Coombs and Holladay have argued that "Excellence theory may offer a naive conceptualization of power in the organization-stakeholder relationship because it does not recognize that organisations have the upper hand when it comes to deciding whether, and under what conditions, to engage in dialogue" (Coombs and Holladay 2007: 54). Largely as a consequence of their engagement with critical social theories, other scholars have consequently sought to advance more sophisticated theorising of power and control in the public relations discipline. Those most opposed to the Excellence argument that public relations can be used to positively create relations of *power with*, and control mutuality, are Marxist communication theorists.

4 Marxist theories of public relations, power and control

Marxist theorists of public relations attribute it with a very significant, though largely hidden, amount of power and control in society. For these theorists, public relations plays a central role in supporting capitalism, and capitalists, to dominate how societies are run, and determine their cultural imperatives, political biases and structures of power. Marxist scholars Miller and Dinan argue that public relations has always been implicated in capitalism's exploitation of the working-class and that its history is one "intimately linked with the power of capital" (2003: 193). They, like Ewen (1996), point to the strong ties between the evolution of public relations and the power that corporate capitalism has secured not only over the Western world, but over much of the globe.

   Public relations emerged as a communication resource in support of Western capitalism in the late 19th century, when the American progressive press were posing challenging questions about the social effects of the great inequalities that existed between the wealth and political power of the bourgeoisie and the poor disenfranchised working class under industrialisation (Ewen 1996). At this time the working class were being forced into abject poverty as a result of the poor wages and working conditions afforded to them by manufacturers and factory owners who sought to minimise production costs to maximise profits. This gave rise to worker protests and strikes not only in the US but in many parts of Europe. Initially, the bourgeoisie were blamed by governments and the press for causing unrest among their employees. But by the 20th century, "Amid a burgeoning of militant working politics, at home and abroad, fears of revolt from below began to overshadow the problem of corporate greed" (Ewen 1996: 60). Consequently, the press became a vehicle that those representing the interests of corporations used to manage public opinion about labour activism, and American public relations was born.

   From a Marxist perspective, those with the most money have the greatest ability to employ public relations staff and/or consultancies to promote their messages throughout society. They do this through, for example, the press, orchestrated public relations campaigns, and lobbying of local, regional and national governments. The ability to control social outcomes that this power grants the capital-owning class was amply demonstrated after the First World War when worker militancy and unionism was again on the rise in the US and UK, with coal miners, dock and rail workers protesting about poor wages and working conditions. In both countries, the response from capitalist industrialists was to lobby governments to prevent the introduction of laws to protect workers. They also ran public relations campaigns which portrayed strikers as a "bewildered herd" (Miller and Dinan 2008: 31) threatening social order, safety and democracy. They depicted the power of the working class, were it to be unleashed, as irrational, violent, animalistic and needing to be controlled. In the UK, public relations tactics were also used to educate the public about the importance of the industrial capitalist class to the wealth and well-being of the nation, and to gain public sympathy for the needs and interests of big business (Miller and Dinan 2008).

A century later, many argue that public relations continues to uphold the power and control of capitalist interests in society, and that 21st century communication contexts are further enabling the ease with which this can be achieved. As news companies struggle to identify profitable business models in digital environments and the social and political value placed on journalism weakens, public relations communication is increasingly used to fill news space (Sissions 2012; Weaver 2016). For Marxist theorists this points to an ongoing and urgent need to expose the powerful role that public relations can play in social culture in extending and defending the reach of global capitalism and "private circuits of power" (Miller and Dinan 2003: 194). These scholars also point out how public relations is a wealth-generating industry in its own right, and how it is usurping other forms of democratic communication in the context of privately owned capitalist social media economies.

Miller and Dinan (2000) have demonstrated how this kind of Marxist-informed research can be undertaken through the political economy analysis of the growth of public relations firms in the UK during the latter quarter of the 20th century. They show how the public relations industry grew at an exponential rate in the UK in the 1980s – a time when "the government privatization programme provided a key financial boost for the PR industry and more importantly helped the industry to develop new markets in financial PR in Britain and in privatization work abroad" (Miller and Dinan 2000: 14). The role played in the privatization and deregulation programmes by public relations involved persuading an initially reluctant public to believe that nationalized industries were a burden on taxpayers, and that they should take advantage of opportunities to become shareholders in the newly privatised organisations. Even the British Labour Party, traditionally regarded as representing workers' rights and the interests of trade unions, in the 1990s developed close associations with business and invested heavily in public relations. Its rebranding of the party as "New Labour" and use of media management to produce two landslide election victories in 1997 and 2001, have been described as "the most effective public relations campaigns of all time" (Day 2002).

Miller and Dinan's approach to investigating the power and influence of public relations, by researching surges in company mergers, concentrations and conglomerations, also illustrates the powerful reach of private consultancies extending into other services. Large global public relations firms now provide advice on accounting, auditing, reputation management, investor relations, and even competitive intelligence and surveillance (Miller and Dinan 2003). Thus, the public relations industry that protects the interests of what is now a transnational capitalist class and the colonising power of global capital and its flows is intractably bound up in those interests itself. Because postcolonial theories of public relations are aligned with some of the perspectives on the power that public relations wields in societies advocated for by Marxist scholars, these are considered in the next section.

5 Postcolonial approaches to public relations and the power of transnational capital

Postcolonial theory, as Dutta and Pal (2011: 197) explain, "primarily engages with the dominant power of the West that imperializes developing nations by advancing the modernist logic of progress and development to justify global capitalism". Like Marxist perspectives, postcolonial theory is concerned with how the power of capital and capitalism is used to dominate and control non-Western and developing countries – those predominantly in the Global South. However, postcolonial theory extends this critique by "attend[ing] to the interplays of culture and power in processes of communication within the realm of geopolitics, unequal power relationships, and colonial relationships of exploitation and oppression" (Dutta 2016: 248). Like Marxists, postcolonial theorists are unlikely to use the term public relations unproblematically, often labelling it "spin" (Munshi and Kurian 2005), or propaganda – terms that better describe their view on how it assists the transnational capitalist class to gain power and control in developing countries.

Whereas Excellence theorists advocate an ideal ethical model of public relations as supporting dialogue between organisations and publics, and ethical public relations as creating *power with*, postcolonial theorists describe this "language of participatory development and grass-roots driven empowerment" (Dutta 2016: 25) as exploitative and culturally *disempowering*. Dutta notes how "Public relations has emerged on the political economy of transnational capitalism as a key actor in the management of public opinion, public policies, and resources at a global level" (2012: 202). This has involved transnational public relations companies, many of which are owned by larger corporate conglomerates with a range of different types of financial interests, be it in media companies, transport, mining or agricultural, for example, using public relations techniques to silence subaltern voices and privilege White Western narratives in the Global South.

Munshi and Edwards (2011) cite an example of this in a communication campaign supported by major multinational corporations designed to combat AIDS in Africa. They state that this campaign "projects a magical transformation of sick people in

Africa into healthy ones because of the medicines provided by the choreographed philanthropy of Western corporations and consumers. This narrative not only privileges the White Western worldview, but also erases race" (Munshi and Edwards 2011: 353). The campaign failed to acknowledge how the spread of AIDS in Africa is linked to poverty and inequality and the imperatives of capitalism which continue to make it impossible for African nations to rise out of national debt. This privileging of Western individualistic narratives in humanitarian campaigns is extremely common (Dogra 2012, Thompson and Weaver 2014). In these terms, postcolonial theorists argue that "the dominant function of public relations (...) [is to] perpetuate dominant knowledge claims that serve the status quo" (Dutta 2014: 257).

Postcolonial theorists do, however, see opportunities for challenging the power and control that transnational corporations have managed to assert over the Global South. Writers such as Smith (1999), Dutta (2016), and Dutta and Pal (2011) argue that notions of knowledge, ethics, informed consent, community participation and dialogue can be reframed and reinterpreted in ways that support subaltern and indigenous communities to co-create and advance decolonizing processes. To do this requires the disruption of taken-for-granted assumptions, structures of knowledge, power and control, and high levels of reflexivity on the part of those involved – whether it be scholars writing and theorising about public relations, public relations practitioners, or community participants and activists. Dutta (2016: 258) positions this cultural-centred approach as working "towards learning the language of public relations as an inverted strategy for resisting the co-optation of subaltern cultures, and formulating creative strategies from the grassroots to disrupt the structures of state, market, and civil society, while simultaneously putting forth alternative rationalities of cultural, social, political, and economic organizing". Here Dutta evokes ideas of contested knowledges and the ability to challenge and disrupt dominant structures of power and control, and to use public relations techniques to do this. In making this argument, Dutta is underlining how who has power and control in society is determined by who is in control of the prevailing social and cultural narratives in that society. These theoretical ideas have their roots in poststructural theories of power, some of which have been applied to study the role that public relations plays in social culture. These are examined in the next section.

6 Poststructural theories of public relations, power and control

At the heart of all poststructural theorising is a concern with understanding issues of power and control in society. This is equally the case where there is a focus on understanding how power is symbolically represented in and through communication practices. Poststructural theories have been used to identify how public relations is involved in the production of knowledge in society, and expose the systems of power and control that support the production and extension of particular knowledges and versions of truth. Public relations, as a communicative practice, is implicated in the production, promotion and extension of knowledge because it is used to advocate for the interests, and, therefore, the power and control, of those who pay for it. Public relations is, as Edwards (2006: 231) states, "a form of symbolic production generating symbolic power". The works of poststructural theorists such as Bourdieu, Foucault and Fairclough have been especially influential in informing theorising of the symbolic power structures that public relations is part of.

Bourdieu (1991) theorises power in relational terms where unconscious norms, values and rules determine the symbolic meaning of attributes – a simple example is the meaning of male and female – in particular contexts, or habitus. Bourdieu, as Edwards (2006: 230) has outlined, "characterizes certain professionals – journalists, politicians, public relations practitioners – for whom language is at the heart of their work, as symbolic producers, transforming or disguising interests into disinterested meanings and legitimizing arbitrary power relations". In these terms, public relations practitioners unconsciously reinforce the dominant power structures of society. From Bourdieu's (1991) perspective, they exercise symbolic violence on audiences by failing to reveal the real interests of the organizations that they represent – which are predominantly invested in legitimizing the activities of the organisation and maximising profits for their owners and shareholders.

Critical discourse theory provides a useful complement to Bourdieu's theory of power as it considers how public relations texts are implicated in constructing symbolic and material relationships of power and control. Discourses are, in their simplest form, a set of statements. Yet as Foucault (1996: 35) outlined, a discourse comprises "the existence of a rule of formation for all its objects, for all its operations, for all its concepts, and for all its theoretical options". Discourses symbolically structure how we make sense of and understand the truth of the world around us. That is, they support particular *regimes of truth*, and different discursive positions will compete to establish their regime of truth as *the truth*.

Drawing on Foucault and Fairclough's theories of discourse and power, Motion and Leitch (1996) identify public relations as a discursive practice that is strategically used to shape and determine public support for organisational activities. They argue that public relations practitioners "strategically deploy texts in discursive struggles over sociocultural practices. The aim of such discursive struggles is to maintain or to transform these sociocultural practices and the values and attitudes which support them and which they embody" (1996: 298). Motion and Leitch describe public relations practitioners as "discourse technologists" (1996: 298), whose aim it is to strategically advantage those with the power to employ them. Yet critical discourse analysis also provides a route through which to consider public relations as a "legitimate tactic in the struggle for and negotiation of *power*" (Motion and Weaver 2005: 50; emphasis in original). It provides scholars with a tool to "investigate how public relations practice uses particular discursive strategies to advance the hegemonic power of particular groups and to examine how these groups attempt to gain public consent to pursue their organizational mission" (Motion and Weaver 2005: 50).

As Edwards (2006) has pointed out, there are many voices and interests in society competing to have their discursive perspective on issues dominate how those issues are understood. Challenging Marxists perspectives, she stresses that public relations competes with "marketers, journalists, analysts and critics, to maintain its position in the field of communication. The power that public relations actually exerts [is] much more complex than suggested by arguments presenting it as a simple mouthpiece for corporate interests." (Edwards 2006: 230). This also suggests a need to consider how public relations can be used for social good, and how groups other than corporations use it in efforts to manage and control the discursive framing of issues.

7 Public relations, power, control, resistance and the social good

One of the advantages of poststructural theorising is that, in considering issues of power in communication, it has also encouraged researchers to think about whether and how public relations can be used to bring power and legitimacy to groups and organisations that are traditionally *disempowered*. In this context, scholars have turned to examine how activist and humanitarian organisations have utilised public relations methods to promote their interests and causes.

A leading proponent of research into activism in the public relations discipline, Demetrious (2006), has called for greater attention to be paid to the use of public communication by grassroots organisations. She predicted that these groups "will become adept in the traditional areas of public relations such as relationship management and the use of specialised communication tactics" (2006: 99). Similarly calling for activism to be embraced in public relations scholarship, rhetorical theorists Heath and Waymer (2009) positioned activism as playing an important function in social debate and decision-making. They declared "the role of the activist organization in the issue dialogue (...) is a vital part of issues management" (Heath and Waymer 2009: 195–196). Smith and Ferguson presented a similar argument, asserting that "activists are co-creators of the relationships between organizations and their public, contributing to the development and resolution of issues and, ultimately, to social good" (2010: 396). When considering claims made by scholars such and Heath and Wayner, and Smith and Ferguson, it must be appreciated that their perspectives are underpinned by a belief in the functionality of a dialogic model of public relations. This perspective often fails to fully recognise the challenges activist groups face in engaging in public debate and dialogue, challenges often caused by lack of access to financial and human resources to support that engagement.

Another challenge posed for interest groups in fully embracing public relations as a communications tool is that, as Demetrious (2006: 107) has written, "'public relations' has specific connotations for activists as a self-serving capitalist activity deeply rooted in exploitative corporate history and tradition. 'PR' for activists is therefore a loaded term". Furthermore, where public relations has also been used in attempts "to support the channelling of resources and the acquisition of power and influence as to mitigate suffering" (Lugo-Ocando and Hernandex-Toro 2016: 226), fundraising and awareness campaigns often leverage on discourses of pity in order to stimulate public donation. Such narrative framing ultimately undermines the self-determination and control of those people about which the campaign speaks – those in need of resources and empowerment.

However, there have been examples of public relations campaigns successfully challenging corporate and elite groups and interests. Henderson (2005), Motion, Leitch, and Weaver (2015) and Weaver (2010; 2014) identified activist use of public relations techniques to draw public attention to and protest against the commercial release of genetically engineered organisms into the environment in New Zealand. In this work, activists demonstrated considerable skill in their use of discursive communication techniques to popularise public dissent and support for non-mainstream perspectives on the risks of genetically engineered foods. Toledano (2016), looking at the very different issue of the Israeli-Palestinian conflict, has demonstrated how a highly experienced public relations practitioner who had worked in the Israeli commercial sector, and following the tragic death of her son at the hands of a Palestinian sniper, used her skills to promote reconciliation and peace between Israelis and Palestinians. In another example, Munshi and Kurian (2016: 405) suggest that public relations can be used to promote social justice and sustainable citizenship, where "sustainable citizenship encompasses building active relationships among a variety of publics to empower those without power".

8 Concluding remarks

How we theorise power and control in connection to public relations is determined by our own understandings, beliefs and biases about how societies operate, how culture is created, maintained, shared, communicated and changed. None of the theoretical positions – Excellence, Marxist, postcolonial or poststructural – considered in this chapter argue that public relations should have great power and control in society. All agree that its potential for power and control needs to be constrained, or, at the very least, that there should be transparency about whether, and by who, public relations is being used to advocate for certain organisations, groups, causes and discursive positions. There also is implicit agreement that if it is to be recognised as an ethical profession, public relations work needs to be less hidden from view, more honest about what it is and not disguised as journalism and community relations, for example, and that organisations should be open about their spending on public relations activities. There is less agreement about the nature of the societies that we live in and how public relations is involved in (re)producing structures of power and control in those societies. Those advocating a liberal-pluralist view that public relations can contribute to healthy democracy, public dialogue and decision-making, and Marxists who argue that public relations always advantages the capitalist class, along with postcolonialists who consider it as contributing to the disempowerment of the Global South, will always disagree about the power that public relations wields. Poststructuralists, in turn, are generally cynical about claims that public relations can contribute to dialogic decision-making simply because of the power imbalances and inequities across groups in society. Yet poststructuralists are more positive about the potential that public relations has to promote social causes and social good. What is clear from considering these various positions is that when we are talking about power and control in connection to public relations, we need to think carefully about what type of society we are articulating when we claim that public relations has the power to influence and control people, societies and culture, or not.

References

Berger, Bruce K. 2005. Power over, power with, and power to relations: Critical reflections on public relations, the dominant coalition and activism. *Journal of Public Relations Research* 17(1). 5–28.

Bourdieu, Pierre. 1991. *Language and symbolic power*. Cambridge: Polity Press.

Coombs, W. Timothy & Sherry J. Holladay. 2007. *It's not just PR: Public relations in society*. Malden, Oxford & Carlton: Blackwell Publishing.

Day, Julia. 2002. New Labour wins PR accolade. *The Guardian*. https://www.theguardian.com/media/2002/mar/28/marketingandpr.politics (accessed 28 January, 2018)

Demetrious, Kristin. 2006. Active voices. In Jacquie L'Etang & Magda Pieczka (eds.), *Public relations: Critical debates and contemporary practice*, 93–107. London: Lawrence Erlbaum.

Dogra, Nandita. 2012. *Representations of global poverty: Aid, development and international NGOS*. London. IB Tauris.

Dutta, Mohan Jyoti. 2012. Critical interrogations of global public relations. In Krisnamurthy Sriramesh & Dejan Verčič (eds.), *Culture and public relations: Links and implications*, 202–217. London & New York: Routledge.

Dutta, Mohan Jyoti. 2014. A postcolonial critique of public relations. In Jacquie L'Etang, David McKie, Nancy Snow & Jordi Xifra (eds.), *The Routledge handbook of public relations*, 248–260. London & New York: Routledge.

Dutta, Mohan Jyoti. 2016. A postcolonial critique of public relations. In Jacquie L'Etang, David McKie, Nancy Snow & Jordi Xifra (eds.), *The Routledge handbook of critical public relations*, 248–260. London & New York: Routledge.

Dutta, Mohan Jyoti & Mahuya Pal. 2011. Public relations and marginalization in a global context. In Nilanjana Bardhan & C. Kay Weaver (eds.), *Public relations in global contexts: Multi-paradigmatic perspectives*, 195–225. New York & London: Routledge.

Edwards, Lee. 2006. Rethinking power in public relations. *Public Relations Review* 32(3). 229–231.

Edwards, Lee. 2016. The role of public relations in deliberative systems. *Journal of Communication* 66(1). 60–81.

Ewen, Stuart. 1996. *PR! A social history of spin*. New York: Basic Books.

Foucault, Michel. 1996. *Foucault Live (Interviews 1966–1984)*. New York: Semiotext(e)

Grunig, James E. 1989. Sierra club study shows who become activists. *Public Relations Review* 15(3). 3–24.

Grunig, James E & Todd Hunt. 1984. *Managing public relations*. New York: Holt, Rinehart & Winston.

Grunig, James E & Jon White. 1992. The effect of worldviews on public relations. In James E. Grunig (ed.), *Excellence in public relations and communication management*, 31–64. Hillsdale: Lawrence Erlbaum.

Heath, Robert L & Damion Waymer. 2009. Activist public relations and the paradox of the positive: A case study of Frederick Douglass' "Fourth of July Address". In Robert Heath, Elizabeth L. Toth & Damion Waymer (eds.), *Rhetorical and critical approaches to public relations*, 195–215. New York: Routledge.

Henderson, Alison. 2005. Activism in 'paradise': Identity management in a public relations campaign against genetic engineering. *Journal of Public Relations Research* 17(2). 117–137.

Jowett, Garth S. & Victoria O'Donnell. 2006. *Propaganda and persuasion*. 4th edn. Thousand Oaks, London & New Delhi: Sage.

Kruckeberg, Dean & Kenneth Starck. 1988. *Public relations and community: A reconstructed theory*. New York: Praeger.

Leitch, Shirley & David Neilson. 2001. Bringing publics into public relations: New theoretical frameworks for practice. In Robert L. Heath (ed.), *Handbook of public relations*, 127–128. Thousand Oaks, London & New Delhi: Sage.

Lugo-Ocando, Jairo & Manuel Hernandex-Toro. 2016. Public relations and humanitarian communication. In Jacquie L'Etang, David McKie, Nancy Snow & Jordi Xifra (eds.), *The Routledge handbook of critical public relations*, 226–234. London & New York: Routledge.

McMillan, M. E. 2016. *From the First World War to Arab Spring. What's really going on in the Middle East?* London: Palgrave Macmillan.

Miller, David & William Dinan. 2000. The Rise of the PR industry in Britain, 1979–98. *European Journal of Communication* 15(1). 5–35.

Miller, David & William Dinan. 2003. Global public relations and global capitalism. In David Demers (ed.), *Terrorism, globalization and mass communication: Papers presented at the 2002 Centre for Global Media Studies Conference*, 193–214. Spokane: Marquette Books.

Miller, David & William Dinan. 2008. *A century of spin: How public relations became the cutting edge of corporate power*. London: Pluto Press.

Motion, Judy & Shirley Leitch. 1996. A discursive perspective from New Zealand: Another worldview. *Public Relations Review* 22(3). 297–309.

Motion, Judy, Shirley Leitch & C. Kay Weaver. 2015. Popularizing dissent: A civil society perspective. *Public Understanding of Science* 24(4). 496–510.

Motion, Judy & C. Kay Weaver 2005. A discourse model for critical public relations research: The Life Sciences Network and the battle for truth. *Journal of Public Relations Research* 17(1). 49–67.

Munshi, Debashish & Priya Kurian. 2005. Imperializing spin cycles: A postcolonial look at public relations, greenwashing, and the separation of publics. *Public Relations Review* 31(4). 513–520.

Munshi, Debashish & Priya Kurian. 2016. Public relations and sustainable citizenship: Towards a goal of representing the unrepresented. In Jacquie L'Etang, David McKie, Nancy Snow & Jordi Xifra (eds.), *The Routledge handbook of public relations*, 405–414. London & New York: Routledge.

Munshi, Debashish & Lee Edwards. 2011. Understanding 'race' in/and public relations: where do we start and where should we go? *Journal of Public Relations Research* 23(4). 349–367.

Sissons, Helen. 2012. Journalism and public relations: A tale of two discourses. *Discourse and Communication* 6(1). 273–294.

Smith, Linda Tuhiwai. 1999. *Decolonizing methodologies: Research and indigenous peoples*. London & New York: Zed Press.

Smith, Michal F. & Denise P. Ferguson. 2010. Activism 2.0. In Robert L. Heath (ed.), *The SAGE handbook of public relations*, 395–408. London: Sage.

Stauber, John Clyde & Sheldon Rampton. 1995. *Toxic sludge is good for you: Lies, damn lies and the public relations industry*. Monroe, ME: Common Courage Press.

Thompson, Briar & C. Kay Weaver. 2014. The challenges of visually representing poverty for NGO communication managers in New Zealand. *Public Relations Inquiry* 3(3). 377–393.

Toledano, Margalit. 2016. Advocating for reconciliation: Public relations, activism, advocacy and dialogue. *Public Relations Inquiry* 5(3). 277–294.

Weaver, C. Kay. 2010. Carnivalesque activism as a public relations genre: A case study of the New Zealand group Mothers Against Genetic Engineering. *Public Relations Review* 36(1). 35–41.

Weaver, C. Kay. 2014. Mothers, bodies, and breasts: Organising strategies and tactics in women's activism. In Christine Daymon & Kristin Demetrious (eds.), *Gender and public relations: Critical perspectives on voice, image and identity*, 108–131. London & New York: Routledge.

Weaver, C. Kay. 2016. Who's afraid of the big bad wolf? Critical Public Relations as a cure for Media Studies' fear of the dark. In Jacquie L'Etang, David McKie, Nancy Snow & Jordi Xifra (eds.), *The Routledge handbook of public relations*, 261–273. London & New York: Routledge.

Weaver, C. Kay, Judy Motion & Juliet Roper. 2006. From propaganda to discourse (and back again): Truth, power, the public interest and public relations. In Jacquie L'Etang & Magda Pieczka (eds.), *Public relations: Critical debates and contemporary practice*, 7–21. London: Lawrence Erlbaum.

Wrong, Dennis. 2017. *Power: Its forms, bases and uses*. London: Taylor & Francis.

Part II – **Core Functions of Public Relations**

Katerina Tsetsura

8 Public relations as media relations

Abstract: This chapter provides an overview of approaches to understanding media relations, from focusing on agenda-setting and framing to journalist-public relations practitioner relations, to understand the complexity of relationship-building with traditional media and non-traditional stakeholders who have their own mediated channels. This chapter reviews the first years of media relations development and describes theories, frameworks, and concepts that help to better understand and explain various aspects of media relations. The chapter also examines current theoretical approaches to contemporary media relations research and practice. It concludes with recommendations for future studies and proposes several directions, including the need to address auto-communication effects of media relations, among others.

Keywords: journalism; transparency; trust; truth; agenda-setting; media catching; framing; strategic mediatization; dialogue; auto-communication

1 Introduction

Media relations has been part of public relations since its beginnings. The earliest forms of public relations were connected to media relation practices (Supa 2014). But what is media relations? According to Supa and Zoch (2009: 2), "Media relations is the systematic, planned, purposeful and mutually beneficial relationship between a public relations practitioner and a mass media journalist." Media relations is unquestionably an important component of public relations. Mass media are a basic means through which corporations can communicate with their audiences and are thereby a useful tool for public relations practitioners. In addition, after clients, the media are the second-most important audience for public relations of large international companies (Alfonso and De Valbuena Miguel 2006). Therefore, it is important that public relations practitioners have a good relationship with the people who work for and in the media industry.[1]

This chapter provides an overview of the contemporary theories, approaches, and frameworks of media relations and describes their roles in public relations, including framing theory, agenda-setting theory, media catching, theory of mediatization and strategic mediatization, dialogic communication, the media model mediation, a relational paradigm, and media transparency. The chapter begins with an excur-

---

1 Acknowledgment: The author would like to thank Johanna Trafalis for her help in preparing this chapter.

https://doi.org/10.1515/9783110554250-008

sion into the history of media relations; it then examines media relations theories and approaches and concludes with an invitation to re-examine the ways in which scholars think about media relations in the 21st Century.

2 Early years of media relations

Practices of media relations have been evident in the USA since the 18th century, and even earlier in other countries (Supa 2014). Indeed, some of the first practices of media relations were similar to today's practices, including media conferences and interviews (Van Ruler and Verčič 2004). During its early years, media relations was associated with the word publicity and public relations in general (Pimlott 1951). Examples of typical media relations tactics included writing and disseminating news releases, media pitches, media alerts, backgrounders, etc.; organizing news conferences (or press conferences, as they were previously called in the era of the print-only media), media tours; and establishing and maintaining relations with journalists and offering them newsworthy story ideas and information (Supa 2014). For a long time, media relations was considered a main function of public relations (Grunig J. 1990). With the passing of time, other areas of public relations evolved, and media relations was no longer perceived as a sole function of public relations. Media relations is now defined as a strategic sub-field of public relations, with its goal of communicating between the organization and the media. However, media relations once again has become a vital piece of public relations after the rise in the popularity of independent and alternative online news media (Supa and Zoch 2009). With the rise of the number of online influencers and citizen journalists, nowadays organizations strive to establish and maintain relations with people who share views publicly (predominantly online) with followers to reach desired audiences with organizations' messages, including potential and current consumers (Freberg et al. 2011). This renewed interest in media relations, establishing and maintaining the interest of those who can share information with your target audiences, is multipled by a century-long pursuit of influencing agenda-settings of traditional media. As such, media relations, relations with the media representatives, in a traditional or contemporary sense, those who have access to mediated channels of communication, is still a big part of what public relations practitioners do. The next section focuses on the phenomenon of media catching, which helps media practitioners to better understand how journalists decide to search for information and what they do with the information they receive.

3 Media relations and media catching

Media catching has been characterized as a turnaround of the original media relations communication arrangements (Waters, Tindall, and Morton 2010). Contrary to media pitching, in which media relations practitioners provide news ideas to journalists, media catching allows journalists to ask for data and information that they need for their news stories (Erzikova, Waters, and Bocharsky 2018). Media relations practitioners are not necessarily connected to these stories (Tallapragada et al. 2012).

The media catching concept has long been known in public relations practice. Journalists have depended on trustworthy representatives of organizations to assist them with the production of news stories. Media catching succeeds by creating a two-sided channel of communication and not necessarily a one-sided channel (Tallapragada et al. 2012). Media catching has lately gained popularity among journalists and media relations practitioners. Many media catching groups have been created in recent years. The HARO group, for example, is a media-catching group on a social networking site that was created by Peter Shankman in November 2007. The HARO group responds not only to journalists and to media relations practitioners, but also to any person who wants to join the group and become a source of information. Another example of media catching is the media request service *Pressfeed.ru* (Erzikova, Waters, and Bocharsky 2018).

Researchers have argued that media catching has changed the nature of media relations (Erzikova, Waters, and Bocharsky 2018). Media catching helps journalists get answers and information that would otherwise be difficult to obtain. Because of media catching, various interrelationships between journalists and media relations practitioners have been developed. Depending on which organizations answer the inquiries, journalists might choose which ones to consult (Tallapragada et al. 2012). Therefore, media catching has made media relations more competitive. At the same time, the opportunity to reach certain media has increased with media catching.

Generally, media catching can be helpful to media relations practitioners and journalists because of a two-sided communication flow between the two groups. However, the communication objective of media relations practitioners has not changed. This means that the practitioners must be ethical, objective, and honest. In addition, sometimes journalists may receive a one-sided or incomplete story through media catching if they do not seek additional sources to cover the issue. Media catching can also be quite slow (Waters, Tindall, and Morton 2010).

4 The practice of media relations

Darnowski et al. (2013) estimated that 80 % of public relations practitioners use media relations every week. Media relations practitioners work with the media and attempt to foster healthy relationships with journalists to increase positive brand coverage without the need of advertisements (Johnston 2008). Media relations practitioners are "pre-reporters" for journalists, providing information that journalists need to accomplish their work (Supa and Zoch 2009: 9). The dominant roles of media relations practitioners are to create and maintain strong relationships with the media, to expand media coverage, and to assure that the coverage of an organization is timely, error-free, and favorable (Edwards 2012). The next section focuses on explaining how public relations sees its interactions with news media and journalists.

5 Media relations and the relational paradigm

The relational paradigm argues that people are shaped by the relationships they have with one another. People are not separate entities, but are part of a world that is interrelated. According to the relational paradigm, to know is to use. The relational paradigm changes the perception of a fixed world that is composed of people, things, and their properties to a world that is formed by relationships and networking (Wachtel 2002). The relational paradigm supports the contention that organizations' relationships with different target audiences should be directed strategically following the mutual benefit principle. Since the relational paradigm has gained recent dominance, public relations is seen as a process of relationship management. Relationship management emphasizes the process of forming and maintaining positive and long-term relationships between organizations and their publics. It is essential for public relations practitioners to administer relationships with the media in congruence with relationship maintenance strategies, such as directness, positivism, splitting of duties, networking, and commitment (Taskiran 2016).

Media relations often relies on the relational approach because media professionals consider that a strategy of openness gives the best and most effective results to their communication with public relations practitioners. The relational paradigm has established the importance of media relations to public relations and considers media as an entity that needs to reach out to other audiences, such as consumers, publics, public institutions, service providers, shareholders, and investors (Taskiran 2016).

The relational paradigm has underlined the importance of public relations by establishing the concept that its practitioners need to establish and develop relationships and communication between organizations and their publics. The relational paradigm has helped public relations to gain importance as a separate field of study and has brought its focus on the importance of establishing and maintaining relationships between the media and public relations practitioners (Taskiran 2016).

6 Theoretical frameworks explaining media relations

Theories and frameworks that can explain media relations can be placed into three categories. The first category includes theories that relate to guiding the public's way of thinking, specifically framing theory and agenda-setting theory. The second category includes the theory of mediatization, strategic mediatization, and dialogic communication theory. These theories fall into the same category because they help media practitioners to strengthen their voices and positions. Finally, the third category includes a relational paradigm and the mediating media model, because both share the same goal of providing a solid theoretical framework to guide media practitioners. The next sections discuss each of these three categories in more detail.

6.1 Media relations and framing theory

Framing theory began with sociologist Erving Goffman in 1974. He postulated that people use arrangements of data to coordinate and to comprehend information (Goffman 1974). Gamson and Modigliani (1989) defined a frame as a concept or event that establishes and gives context to the events linked to an issue. Framing helps in the collection of specific parts of a story that need to be mediated. Through framing, certain ideas are forwarded to the public (Entman 1993). Media relations practitioners commonly use framing to achieve their goals and objectives. Framing is one of the most common analytical methods utilized in media relations. Framing is an important tool by which key messages are communicated to the public in such a way that unwanted storylines are avoided (Edwards 2012).

Framing is important in media relations because news and ideas today are mediated continuously and rapidly. Framing allows media relations practitioners to handle a continuous massive flow of information, allowing them to mediate and engage in conversation by constructing their own meanings for each story they communicate. With the help of framing, media relations practitioners categorize this flow of information and make sure that the information is in accordance with the frame (Edwards 2012). Framing is literally a "filter of information," because it allows the desired information to be communicated and blocks the unwanted information (Holladay and Coombs 2013: 103).

Because of its ability to explain how people perceive information, framing theory has affected media relations and its practice. With the assistance of framing theory, strategic communication managers can promote their desired objectives by appropriately designing their messages. The influence on media frames has accompanied media and public relations throughout history. For example, in 1908, media practitioners of *The New York Times* used framing theory to promote the New York to Paris auto race (Holladay and Coombs 2013). Framing theory has been used continuously in media relations, and effective use of framing has had a tremendous impact on how information is perceived and reported. Framing has become a critical tool for media relations practitioners to maximize their effectiveness and to have a strong say in the information that is being communicated. Since media relations practitioners frame by filtering properties, framing can turn negative information into positive information and vice versa (Edwards 2012). Gatekeepers use framing to communicate ideas about information and events, and media relations has largely taken its shape from this theory.

Framing theory is one of the most widespread theories used in media relations and media studies in general. This theory, though, has a history that must be taken into consideration. First, framing theory is an anthropocentric theory. When using this theory, media practitioners are often tempted to filter the information in a way that fits their own subjective cognition, and many times they overlook the broad picture of what they want to communicate. Then, a lot of objective crucial information is ignored (Ytterstad 2015). Another drawback is that framing theory is "a strategic approach to truth" (Ytterstad 2015: 7), with its main assumption that human beings are overtly strategic in all communication. A framing paradigm, some have argued, views the audience as "cognitive misers who resist processing" information (Entman 2009: 333). A single issue framing, for example, is believed to be appropriate (if not highly desired) in many instances, and, therefore, the totality of reality can easily be lost. Finally, framing theory can include an under-appreciation of the significance of undeveloped meaning (Ytterstad 2015). Framing theory with its organizing power is a tool that can easily guide media relations practitioners to communicate certain aspects of the perceived reality as primary, leaving behind the important meaning of what is intended to be communicated (Reese 2007).

6.2 Media relations and agenda-setting theory

Agenda-setting theory is also commonly used in media relations. The media influence is discussed, but has little impact on the conclusion of these discussions in light of media relations (McCombs and Shaw 1972). This theory says news media have the capability to affect how important the topics of the public agenda are perceived to be (McCombs and Reynolds 2002). Media relations practitioners commonly use agenda-setting theory to achieve organizational content planning and to reach the target audience on time. According to the agenda-setting theory, all information that comes from public relations practitioners will contribute to the media agenda and will also contribute to the public's agenda.

Agenda-setting theory can bring organizational content and a wide range of target audiences together through the power of control (Taskiran 2016). Agenda-setting theory is widely used because it helps media practitioners to better understand how audiences receive and process information. With the help of agenda-setting theory, media relations practitioners can construct and influence the social personality of the organization (Ginesta, Ordeix, and Rom 2017). The implementation of this theory can help media relations practitioners gain recognition and reputation for the organizations they are working for, through a way of better understanding the media coverage process and in finding ways to dessiminate strategic messages of the organization. The theory has helped broaden the development of media relations.

Critics of the agenda-setting theory argue that the effects of the theory are temporary because the public's attention is like a cycle that moves from strong interest to gradual decline (Soroka 1999). Another aspect that has been highlighted by critics of agenda-setting theory is that only certain topics and agendas are communicated to the public, thus restricting the sphere of information. In that sense, a traditional function of journalists as gatekeepers is perceived to be a drawback in the eyes of media relations practitioners whose opportunities to present many topics to the audiences are minimized. Moreover, because the agenda is being set by the media, both in everyday life and in politics, people and politicians prioritize some actions over others to fit the agenda set by the media (Schroeder 2018). Can the same be said about organizations? Of course, paying attention to organizations' media coverage is essential, and actions of organizations can sometimes be influenced by media coverage. However, in today's world, many organizations also choose to pay attention to agendas set, not only by the traditional media, but also by other target publics, including influencials, activists, and employees.

6.3 Media relations and theory of mediatization

Another theory that has impact on media relations is the theory of mediatization. Mediatization refers to a long-term process of increasing influence of the media and the news media logic, defined as "the institutional, technological, and sociological characteristics of the news media, including their format characteristics, production and dissemination routines, norms, and needs, standards of newsworthiness, and to the formal and informal rules that govern news media" (Strömbäck 2011: 373). At its core, this theory highlights how news media affect other political elites, institutions, and organizations and explains the constitutive rules of communication (Altheide 2004). It also shows how mass media become a central point of present-day activities of society (Hjarvard 2008). Unlike the media effect approach, which looks at "the use of media for communicating meaning," mediatization theory focuses on long-lasting structural transformations where the media play a determining institutional role in social and cultural praxis (Hjarvard 2013: 2).

Mediatization has helped mass media move into the center of the activities of contemporary societies. Through mediatization, society has become increasingly dependent on media and their logic. One typical example is the connection between sports and media, which has resulted in the creation of mega sporting events. These events attract a huge number of spectators throughout the world through a mediatization process (Kettner-Høeberg and Lopez 2015). Because mediatization explains influence of the media on politics and the government, this theory has helped to update media relations practices at a governmental level. Specifically, media logic helps to understand that political decisions can be influenced by the global media coverage.

Mediatization theory takes into account that media continuously affect the audience to a great extent. The drawback of this theory is that it does not explain all of the different aspects of social life that are mediatized. Mediatization does not differentiate cultural and political spheres and, as a result, it operates in the same way in both spheres. Therefore, this theory loses its potential to understand the differences of the process among various stakeholders (Schroeder 2018). Moreover, even though mediatization has many advocates, the theory has not been uniformly understood. Mediatization theory is gaining popularity in a today's world driven by mediated politics (such as announcements of major political decisions by the world's leaders on Twitter followed by extensive traditional media coverage of such announcements). Several media researchers argue that media reasoning provokes the loss of independence and the loss of free thoughts and actions. Especially in the world of politics, the political arena has become theatrical, to a large extent, as politicians satisfy the demands of the media (Ampuja, Koivisto, and Väliverronen 2014).

6.4 Media relations and strategic mediatization

This new concept was suggested by Zerfass, Verčič, and Wiesenberg (2016). Strategic mediatization changes what used to be the fundamental boundaries among advertising and media relations, mass media, and other noncore media organizations, which are making content to be sources or multipliers. Strategic mediatization considers mediatization to be a concept that evaluates the relationship between advancements in media and communications and differences in culture and society (Couldry and Hepp 2013). The phenomenon of mediatization invites us to rethink "the interrelations between changes in media and communications on the one hand, and changes in culture and society on the other" (Couldry and Hepp 2013: 199). Strategic mediatization is a new practice that has replaced traditional mass media practices with new communicative channels, such as social media. These channels have both technical and social characteristics, depending on the society (Zerfass, Verčič, and Wiesenberg 2016). For example, when advertising a product, companies look for ways to relate their product or service with the issues central to society's contemporary discourse to attract the public's attention.

Strategic mediatization has changed the way in which organizations, public relations, and advertising professionals, and the public communicate. Strategic mediatization provides new opportunities for media relations by intermingling on one hand with society and culture and on the other hand with organizations, public relations, advertising, and marketing. This way, strategic mediatization opens up the way for new collaboration practices in media relations (Zerfass, Verčič, and Wiesenberg 2016).

Because strategic mediatization searches for interrelations between changes in media on the one hand and changes in culture and society on the other, the approach has several drawbacks. Specifically, applying strategic mediatization in the context of marketing public relations can be a challenge because it would require continuous adaptation of the messages to different societal and cultural contexts. Applying the same cultural elements in organizational messages across societies simply might not work. Additionally, the challenge of having to renegotiate the organization's own corporate values if those messages go into conflict with the values established and/or advocated by a society can be enomorous. Consequently, applying this approach broadly is tedious and maybe an unattainable process. For strategic mediatization to give positive results, it should take cultural sensitivity into account.

6.5 Media relations and dialogic communication theory

The dialogic communication theory argues that preserving dialogue is an important aspect of a prosperous relationship between organizations and their publics. Dialogic communication can help organizations by raising their trustworthiness and public reinforcement, making their image better and minimizing governmental interference through transparency (Ledingham and Bruning 2000). Public relations can ease dialogic communication by making channels and procedures for dialogic communication (Kent and Taylor 2002). According to this theory, organizations should be willing to communicate with publics in truthful and ethical ways to generate successful communication channels between them and the publics (Kent, Taylor, and White 2003). Moreover, the dialogic communication theory seeks to attain practical value through all communication channels: person-to-person, as well as various online channels of communication (e. g., the web, videos, photographs, downloadable documents, blogs, social media) (Pettigrew and Reber 2011). Dialogic communication is a widely argued for as a tool for communication between mass media practitioners and their audiences because it opens up many different avenues to their relationships (Pettigrew and Reber 2011).

Dialogic communication has positively influenced media relations. Recent research has found that strong dialogic orientation is positively associated with better organization media relationships (Lee and Hemant-Desai 2014). However, the practice of media relations to provide information to journalists may be an obstacle to the development of dialogic relationships between organizations and the news media. This is a structural limitation of the dialogic theory (Lee and Hemant-Desai 2014).

Another criticism is that media practitioners do not practice dialogic communication theory to enact its full potential (Noddings 1984). Many times, practitioners do not succeed in practicing the aspects of this kind of communication. According to Noddings (1984), the purpose of dialogue is to understand the reality of one another and to be able to share each other's feelings. If this is not the case, the conversation is not a dialogue (Noddings 1984). When engaging in dialogue, we exchange and negotiate our ways of thinking. Critics of the dialogic communication theory claim that, most of the time, practitioners do not know the meaning of dialogue and organizations are not committed to a true dialogue with the publics (Lane and Bartlett 2016). (For more information on dialogue and dialogic communication theory, see Chapter 23 in this book.) For many scholars, dialogue is considered an ideal form of communication. Critics of the dialogic communication theory claim that dialogue is not practical in organizations because it takes time and effort and, at times, might become perilous (Kent and Theunissen 2016).

6.6 Media relations and the mediating the media model

Pang's (2010) mediating the media model provides practitioners with a complete framework to improving media relations. The model identifies two influencers in media relations: internal (journalist mindset, journalist routines, and newsroom routines) and external (extra-media forces and media ideologies). Internal influences are found to be more prevalent than are external ones. The model invites journalists to consider how media relations practitioners work to understand the profession (Pang 2010). It explains the ways in which journalists work with information sources and gather, analyze, and present information. The model can also help media relations practitioners better understand what to do to reach and influence the media.

The mediating the media model is relatively new to media relations. It needs more research to be accurately evaluated and more time to be used more broadly. Recent studies examine the ways in which organizations can use the mediating the media model to attain effective relations with social media influencers (Pang, Chiong, and Begam Binte 2014). Media relations practitioners can achieve effective media relations once they understand and correctly apply internal and external influences (Pang, Chiong, and Begam Binte 2014).

The mediating the media model is a useful tool for media relations practitioners that opens up new horizons and potential for the development of media relations. A drawback for the mediating the media model is that, because it is relatively new, media relations practitioners have not yet completely applied this model in practice.

7 Media transparency as a contemporary issue for media relations

Media transparency is a building block for professional media development, based on trust between the media and the audience (Tsetsura and Kruckeberg 2017). Honesty, independence of opinion, fair judgment, and traditional news values are the main factors that define journalistic principles and media credibility. If one or several of these principles are violated, the audience has a right to know what has influenced journalistic decisions (Craig 2008). The absence of any direct and indirect influence is central to the concept of media transparency. Lack of disclosure of influences and constraints that have been placed on journalists, editors, and the media in which articles or programs appear is often referred to as non-transparency or media opacity. Publishing news in exchange for a payment or a favor compromises a traditional function of mass media in society and undermines media's roles as gatekeepers (Craig 2007; Tsetsura and Kruckeberg 2017). Non-transparent practices can be found worldwide. Understanding how public relations practitioners who work for organizations can influence the news is at the heart of media non-transparency studies (Tsetsura and Kruckeberg 2017).

Media opacity is defined as a favorable condition for any form of payment for news coverage or any other influence on editorial and journalists' decisions that is not clearly stated in the finished journalistic product. Media opacity takes place in many countries (Tsetsura and Kruckeberg 2017). Some critics have advocated that such media practices are part of some cultures in regions throughout the world, but a growing number of studies has shown that culture is not a sole determining factor in the decision-making processes of journalists and public relations practitioners in cases of media opacity. Almost 85 percent of the professionals who are members of international organizations, including the the International Public Relations Association, International Press Institute, and International Federation of Journalists, condemn these practices as unprofessional and unethical (Tsetsura and Kruckeberg 2017). Explaining these practices solely as a result of cultural differences might be a simplistic and somewhat naïve way of understanding and analyzing the problem. Rather than justifying these practices as solely cultural distinctions, and the political, economic, historical, societal, and environment factors (Tsetsura and Valentini 2016), as well as the level of professional development and practice and the development of ethical conduct, should be accounted for when one attempts to determine whether media relations practices in a certain country might be perceived as corrupt or unethical. Understanding global media relations practices and their influence on global society is at the heart of media transparency and media opacity studies.

Media opacity is defined as a conscious lack of media transparency (Tsetsura and Kruckeberg 2017). In transparency, no hidden influences exist in the process of gathering/disseminating news and other information that is presented by the media.

If any influences exist, they have been clearly identified in the end product in the media. *Hidden influences* include incentives that may be extended by public relations practitioners or that are solicited by news media or their representatives. These may be monetary and non-monetary payments, free products or services, or, by contrast, threats to influence the financial well-being or editorial content of the media (Tsetsura and Kruckeberg 2017).

Media opacity in the news gathering/dissemination process is a significant threat to societies. Influences that are hidden through news media opacity may change our perception of what we consume as *news*, and, in the words of Tsetsura and Kruckeberg (2017: 90), can create "incomplete truth that can only be regarded as an insidious attempt to inappropriately and unethically manipulate and control people that must be viewed as a threat to citizens and marketplace consumers as well as to society at large." When media relations practitioners pay bribes for their media releases to be disseminated in the news media or when other hidden influences amend the perceptions of information that people consume as news, "a betrayal of trust occurs because journalists and their news media are promoting the illusion among consumers that the news that journalists have gathered and that the news media have disseminated is accurate, complete, and unbiased" (Tsetsura and Kruckeberg 2017: 90).

Thus, transparency in production and dissemination of news in the media is essential and universal. Transparency should be the norm for all societies, and both media relations practitioners and journalists should strive for the transparent exchange and presentation of information. If media transparency, as Tsetsura and Kruckeberg (2017) argue, has an increased intrinsic and, thereby, economic value, then truth through news media transparency can be positioned and effectively presented through the reiteration of publicly declared codes of ethics by both professions. Efforts from both sides, media and public relations practitioners, may also help address issues that are arising as the news media lose their trust among people throughout the world and compete with a growing number of mediated conversations and exchanges on social media among groups that have no connection to the traditional societal institutions of the media. Examination of media non-transparency allows us to understand how hidden influences on the media by various information sources may affect information exchange patterns and processes and, more importantly, what implications these non-transparent practices may have on the levels of trust toward the media as a societal institution – and toward media and public relations practitioners.

8 Challenges for media relations

Media relations still faces many challenges. First, no established theory has been specifically developed to explain media relations in the context of public relations, with the possible exception of a normative theory of media transparency (Tsetsura and

Kruckeberg 2017). Future researchers should strive to create a theoretical framework for media relations and its practice (Supa and Zoch 2009). The continued advancement of new communication technologies provides a challenge to media relations researchers to create original and useful ways to investigate media relations and its functions. Therefore, future research must examine the influence of technology on the relationship of journalists and media relations practitioners (Supa and Zoch 2009) and on understanding the impact that trust and transparency have on media relations and relationships (Tsetsura and Kruckeberg 2017). Most importantly, future research must differentiate media relations as a sub-field of its own and, at the same time, must maintain the connection between media relations and public relations (Supa and Zoch 2009).

Future scholars of media relations should reevaluate their approach to this sub-field of public relations. First, it is important for the next generation of scholars to problematize a concept of media and to reconceptualize what counts as media today. Do we refer only to the traditional societal institutions as the media? Or do we accept and cogitate on the meaning of the media as any form of hybrid (mass, highly targeted group, or individualized) mediated information exchange in the virtual public sphere, between and among individuals who may or may not exist, who may or may not know one another, who may live next door to each other or may be on the opposite sides of the planet (and yet may communicate with each other in real time), and who may or may not have any undisclosed reasons to communicate certain messages?

Do we consider bloggers and other influentials to be media representatives? Do we regard as media social media platform companies, such as Twitter, Instagram, Facebook, or even search engines such as Google, as some would argue?

If a traditional relationship-building continuum were between a journalist and a public relations practitioner, do we now draw new continua, such as practitioner-blogger, practitioner-platform, or even practitioner-bot/algorithm?

Do media relations practitioners then attempt to communicate and to establish and maintain relationships with these individual producers of information, agents, and voices of certain groups of publics? If so, how do media relations practitioners select, from a vast sea of mediated information suppliers, those who have established levels of trust with their readers and/or viewers?

Most importantly, do we examine media relations – or media relationships? As an increasing number of research studies in media relations addresses strategic functions of communication and provides opportunities to utilize statistical power to predict responses of publics and mediated relations, we tend to lose sight of the simple humanistic function of media relations – a straightforward idea that relationship-building happens at the level of individuals first, not amorphous groups and companies. As such, is media relations about understanding organization-public relationships – or rather about understanding the needs and wants of one individual who communicates on behalf of an organization and another individual who seeks information to share with others? The underlying issue of trust at the individual level further contributes to development of trust at the institutional and societal levels (Tsetsura and Luoma-aho 2010). Hence, perhaps scholars need to go back to understanding the basics of human interaction between two professionals: a public relations specialist and a media representative (a journalist, an influencer, or an information disseminator, depending on which definition of the media one adopts). Importantly, a media representative should also be a professional, in a broad sense of this word (a person who understands and subscribes to the commonly agreed principles of conduct and ethical behavior as a disseminator of information), to be considered media relations.

Finally, the future of media relations is in understanding the power and the limits of media in delivering information to stakeholders. If a company is a media company that has its own media channels, then what scholars need to focus on is how we understand our own channels of communication and whether we pay enough attention to our own employees who are now members of the growing new media (e. g., online informational networks, social or otherwise, and forums).

One way to think about the connection between internal stakeholders and media relations is to consider auto-communication. Auto-communication can help public relations professionals better understand the outcomes of their ongoing interactions with the media and the consequences of communicating via mediated channels. Auto-communication is concerned with communication about organizational identity within a broad context because it explains how externally directed messages may influence internal publics (Christensen 1997). Christensen (1997) argued that external media play a large role in the process of auto-communication. As such, external media grant authority and status to messages and may influence how internal stakeholders evaluate communication from their own organizations (Cheney et al. 2014). Morsing (2006) gleaned that employees, for instance, are more dedicated readers of organizations' CSR messages than are any external stakeholders. Such communication may influence the desire of managers to identify closely with the organization (Morsing 2006). Auto-communication can also have dysfunctional aspects, as organizations may become self-centered, even narcissistic, in their communication (Ganesh 2003). "While external audiences rarely care about the specifics of an organization's identity, members (and managers in particular) are often so deeply involved in the organization's expressions of identity that they lose touch with the issues of stakeholder relevance and interest," Cheney et al. (2014: 703) concluded.

The concept of auto-communication can enrich one's understanding of how strategic communication through the media, which is intended for external publics, is consumed and perceived by internal stakeholders. The auto-communication effect should be accounted for in public relations practice, particularly when campaigns are focused on external stakeholders, but do not clearly reflect on a possibility of the internal communication processes as a result of external messaging. One way to think about the future of media relations is to consider mediated communication with internal audiences that happen organically, that is, as a result of external communication strategies and efforts. That means public relations scholars and practitioners need to take a closer look at the ways in which they create and disseminate mediated messages and need to account for possible consequences of auto-communication as a result of such messaging.

Media relations is becoming increasingly complex and comprehensive. As it moves forward, the media relations legacy will continue to thrive (that is, typical ways in which practitioners interact with journalists and traditional media representatives will still need our attention). However, increasingly, media relations scholars and practitioners will need to focus on the complexity of relationship-building with non-traditional stakeholders who have their own mediated channels: bloggers, various types of influentials, and their own employees. And, despite the fact that media are changing and journalism is experiencing drastic transformation, what certainly is clear is that media relations will continue to be one of the most important areas of public relations.

References

Alfonso, Gonzàlez-Herrero & Ruiz De Valbuena Miguel. 2006. Trends in online media relations: Web-based corporate press rooms in leading international companies. *Public Relations Review* 32(3). 267–275.

Altheide, David L. 2004. Media logic and political communication. *Political Communication* 21. 293–296.

Ampuja, Marko, Juha Koivisto & Esa Väliverronen. 2014. Strong and weak forms of mediatization theory. *NORDICOM Review* 35. 111–123.

Cheney, George, Lars T. Christensen & Stephanie L. Dailey. 2014. Communicating identity and identification in and around organizations. In Linda L. Putnam & Dennis K. Mumby (eds.), *The SAGE Handbook of organizational communication*, 3ʳᵈ ed., 695–716. Thousand Oaks, CA: Sage.

Christensen, Lars T. 1997. Marketing as auto-communication. *Consumption Markets & Culture* 1(3). 197–227.

Couldry, Nick & Andreas Hepp. 2013. Conceptualizing mediatization: Contexts, traditions, arguments. *Communication Theory* 23(3). 191–202.

Craig, David A. 2007. The case: Wal-Mart public relations in the blogosphere. *Journal of Mass Media Ethics* 22. 215–128.

Craig, David A. 2008. Journalists, government, and the place of journalism across cultures. *Journal of Mass Media Ethics* 23. 158–161.

Darnowski, Christina, Marcia DiStaso, Hilary Fussell Sisco & Tina McCorkindale. 2013. March. What influences professionals to identify as public relations specialists? Paper presented at the International Public Relations Research Conference, Miami, FL. 6–10 March.

Edwards, Maryn. 2012. Is any press good press? Framing media content and the reunion(s) of Take That: 2005–2010. *Popular Music History* 7(2). 143–157.

Entman, Robert. 1993. Framing: Toward a clarification of a fractured paradigm. *Journal of Communication* 43. 51–58.

Entman, Robert. 2009. Framing media power. In Paul D'Angelo & Jim A. Kuypers (eds.), *Doing news framing analysis: Empirical and theoretical perspectives*, 331–356. New York: Taylor & Francis.

Erzikova, Elina, Richard Waters, & Konstantin Bocharsky. 2018. Media catching: A conceptual framework for understanding strategic mediatization in public relations? *International Journal of Strategic Communication* 12(2). 145–159.

Freberg, Karen, Kristin Graham, Karen McGaughey & Laura Freberg. 2011. Who are the social media influencers? A study of public perceptions of personality. *Public Relations Review* 37(1). 90–92.

Gamson, William & Andre Modigliani. 1989. Media discourse and public opinion: A constructionist approach. *American Journal of Sociology* 95. 1–37.

Ganesh, Shiv. (2003). Organizational narcissism: Technology, legitimacy and identity in an Indian NGO. *Management Communication Quarterly* 16(4). 558–594.

Ginesta, Xavier, Enric Ordeix & Josep Rom. 2017. Managing content in cross-cultural public relations campaigns: A case study of the Paris terrorist attacks. *American Behavioral Scientist* 61(6). 624–632.

Goffman, Erving. 1974. *Frame analyses: An essay on the organization of experience.* Cambridge, MA: Harvard University Press.

Grunig, James E. 1990. Theory and practice of interactive media relations. *Public Opinion Quarterly* 35(3). 18–23.

Hjarvard, Stig. 2008. The mediatization of society: A theory of the media as agents of social and cultural change. *Nordicom Review* 29(2). 105–134.

Hjarvard, Stig. 2013. *The mediatization of culture and society.* New York: Routledge.

Holladay, Sherry & W. Timothy Coombs. 2013. The great automobile race of 1908 as a public relations phenomenon: Lessons from the past. *Public Relations Review* 39(2). 101–110.

Johnston, Jane. 2008. Media relations: Issues and strategies (1st edn.). Sydney: Allen & Unwin Academic.

Kent, Michael L. & Maureen Taylor. 2002. Toward a dialogic theory of public relations. *Public Relations Review* 28(1). 21–37.

Kent, Michael L. & Petra Theunissen. 2016. Elegy for mediated dialogue: Shiva the Destroyer and reclaiming our First Principles. *International Journal of Communication* 10. 4040–4054.

Kent, Michael L., Maureen Taylor & William J. White. 2003. The relationship between Web site design and organizational responsiveness to stakeholders. *Public Relations Review* 29(1). 63–77.

Kettner-Høeberg, Helle & Bernat López. 2015. The Vuelta goes glocal: Changes in the Vuelta a España's communication strategy and media relations under the new Amaury Sport Organization's management. *Catalan Journal of Communication & Cultural Studies* 7(2). 181–196.

Lane, Anne & Jennifer Bartlett. 2016. Why dialogic principles do not make it in practice – and what we can do about it. *International Journal of Communication* 10. 4074–4094.

Ledingham, John A. & Stephen D. Bruning. 2000. A longitudinal study of organization-public relationships dimensions: Defining the role of communication in the practice of relationship management. In John A. Ledingham & Stephen D. Bruning (eds.), *Public relations as relationship management: A relational approach to public relations,* 55–69. Mahwah, NJ: Lawrence Erlbaum.

Lee, Seow Ting & Mallika Hemant Desai. 2014. Dialogic communication and media relations in non-governmental organizations. *Journal of Communication Management* 18(1). 80–100.

McCombs, Maxwell E. & Donald L. Shaw. 1972. The agenda-setting function of mass media. *The Public Opinion Quarterly* 36(2). 176–187.

McCombs, Maxwell & Amy Reynolds. 2002. News influence on our pictures of the world. In Jennings Bryant & Dolf Zillmann (eds.), *Media effects: Advances in theory and research,* 2nd edn., 1–18. Mahwah, NJ: Lawrence Erlbaum.

Morsing, Mette. 2006. Corporate social responsibility as strategic auto-communication: On the role of external stakeholders for member identification. *Business Ethics: A European Review* 15(2). 171–182.

Noddings, Nel. 1984. *Caring: A feminine approach to ethics and moral education*. Berkeley, CA: University of California Press.

Pang, Augustine. 2010. Mediating the media: A journalist-centric media relations model. *Corporate Communications: An International Journal* 15(2). 192–204.

Pang, Augustine, Vivien H. E. Chiong, & Nasrath B. B. A. Hassan. 2014. Media relations in an evolving media landscape. *Journal of Communication Management* 18(3). 271–294.

Pettigrew, Justin E. & Bryan H. Reber. 2011. Journalists' opinions and attitudes about dialogic components of corporate websites. *Public Relations Review* 37(4). 422–424.

Pimlott, John A. R. 1951. *Public relations and American democracy*. Princeton, NJ: Princeton University Press.

Reese, Stephen D. 2007. The framing project: A bridging model for media research revisited. *Journal of Communication* 57(1). 148–154.

Schroeder, Ralph. 2018. Towards a theory of digital media. *Information, Communication & Society* 21(3). 323–339.

Soroka, Stuart. 1999. Policy agenda-setting theory revisited: A critique of Howlett on Downs, Baumgartner and Jones, and Kingdon. *Canadian Journal of Political Science* 32(4). 763–772.

Strömbäck, Jesper. 2011. Mediatization of politics: Toward a conceptual framework for comparative research. In Erik P. Bucy & Lance R. Holbert (eds.), *Sourcebook for political communication research: Methods, measures, and analytical techniques*, 367–381. New York: Routledge.

Supa, Dustin W. & Lynn M. Zoch. 2009. Maximizing media relations through a better understanding of the public relations-journalism relationship: A quantitative analysis of changes over the past 23 years. *Public Relations Journal* 3(4). 1–28.

Supa, Dustin W. 2014. The academic inquiry of media relations as both a tactical and strategic function of public relations. *Research Journal of the Institute for Public Relations* 1(1). https://instituteforpr.org/academic-inquiry-media-relations-tactical-strategic-function-public-relations/ (accessed 16 March 2020).

Tallapragada, Meghnaa, Ilin C. Misaras, Kimberly Burke & Richard D. Waters. 2012. Identifying the best practices of media catching: A national survey of media relations practitioners. *Public Relations Review* 38(5). 926–931.

Taskiran, Hatun B. 2016. The media relations field in public relations: Evaluations of relationship maintenance strategies by Turkish media professionals. *İstanbul Üniversitesi İletişim Fakültesi Dergisi* 50(1). 35–56.

Tsetsura, Katerina & Dean Kruckeberg. 2017. *Transparency, public relations and the mass media: Combating the hidden influences in news coverage worldwide*. New York: Taylor and Francis/Routledge.

Tsetsura, Katerina & Vilma Luoma-aho. 2010. Innovative thinking or distortion of journalistic values? How the lack of trust creates non-transparency in the Russian media. *Ethical Space: The International Journal of Communication Ethics* 7(4). 30–38.

Tsetsura, Katerina & Chiara Valentini. 2016. The "holy" triad in media ethics: A conceptual model for understanding global media ethics. *Public Relations Review* 42(4). 573–581.

Van Ruler, Betteke & Dejan Verčič. 2004. *Public relations and communication management in Europe: A nation-by-nation introduction to public relations theory and practice*. Berlin: Walter de Gruyter.

Wachtel, Paul L. 2002. Probing the boundaries of the relational paradigm. *Psychoanalytic Dialogues* 12(2). 207–225.

Waters, Richard, Natalie Tindall & Timothy Morton. 2010. Media catching and the journalist-public relations practitioner relationship: How social media are changing the practice of media relations. *Journal of Public Relations Research* 22(3). 241–264.

Ytterstad, Andreas. 2015. Framing global warming: Is that really the question? A realist, Gramscian critique of the framing paradigm in media and communication research. *Environmental Communication* 9(1). 1–19.

Zerfass, Ansgar, Dejan Verčič & Markus Wiesenberg. 2016. The dawn of a new golden age for media relations? How PR professionals interact with the mass media and use new collaborative practices. *Public Relations Review* 42. 499–508.

Michael Etter, Peter Winkler, and Thomas Pleil

9 Public relations and social media

Abstract: With an international perspective, this chapter elaborates how social media have developed over the last fifteen years from a niche topic to an industry-disruptive and dominating phenomenon in public relations. The chapter will analyse how public relations theory and practice have embraced this development from four approaches: dialogue-centric approaches, crisis-centric approaches, user-centric approaches, and data-centric approaches. The chapter closes with a conclusion and recommendations for future research.

Keywords: social media; public relations; dialogue; crisis; big data

1 Introduction

More than for any other technological innovation over the last fifteen years, public relations scholars and practitioners alike have debated the disruptive potential of social media for strategic communication and related developments in content marketing. The term social media refers to a range of new information and communication technologies (ICT), such as online social networks (e. g. Facebook), micro-blogs (e. g. Twitter), video platforms (e. g. YouTube), or wikis (e. g. Wikipedia), that enable their users to create and share content, interact with each other, and organize at little to no cost (Kaplan and Haenlein 2010). Over the last years, social media have supported existing and created new public relations functions and job profiles in organizations. While initially often used for more peripheral functions and minor roles with the aim to engage consumers online (e. g. "social media managers" or "community managers"), social media are increasingly integrated in strategic organizational considerations. For example, they are used by high-level executives, such as CEOs, for fast and direct information dissemination towards various stakeholders, or they are increasingly used for crisis management (Coombs and Holladay 2012). While public relations understands social media on a general level as enabler of public interaction and engagement, digital marketing, more narrowly, borrows user-centric content strategies from public relations for commercial purposes. The impact of social media on these disciplines has often been referred to as a paradigm shift and is discussed as both opportunity and threat for organizations.

Opportunities for organizations are identified from afforded interactions, dialogue, and beneficial content co-creation. This more optimistic and beneficial view is often reflected in studies and best cases, such as the Primark case, which showed how consumers defended reputation attacks on the clothing brand in social media (Jones, Temperley, and Lima 2009). Challenges, on the other hand, derive from the speed and

https://doi.org/10.1515/9783110554250-009

loss of control over interaction and content creation. In prominent and vividly discussed examples the threat for organizations and their reputations is made evident. An often-cited case is the seminal social media crisis of Nestlé in the year 2010, when social media was used by civil society actors to shame the company's use of palm oil in Nestlé's products (e. g. Etter and Vestergaard 2015; Coombs and Holladay 2012).

2 Four approaches

Overall, scholars have agreed that social media are a phenomenon that needs to be taken seriously and that opens interesting avenues for research. The way to approach and evaluate the phenomenon itself is debated. While some scholars have argued to use established public relations models and theories, others have advocated to rethink existing theories and develop new ones, which finds most vivid expression in four approaches that we will review more in detail below.[1] Concretely we focus on "dialogue-centric approaches" and "crisis and issue-centric approaches", which both are enacted by the main principle of participation in social media. Furthermore, we focus on "user-centric approaches" and "data-centric approaches", which are driven by the principle of optimization by organizations.

2.1 Dialogue-centric approaches

Dialogue-centric approaches and related, often normative-oriented theories originated three decades ago and still dominate the international academic public relations debate. These approaches root in the ideal of dialogue, which proposes that organizations communicate with their publics oriented towards mutual understanding and outcomes that serve both the organization's and the public's interests (Kent and Taylor 2002; Grunig J. and Hunt 1984).

In the Anglo-American rooted debate, scholars have applied the normative focus of dialogue and relationship-building and conceptually applied it to social media (e. g. Seltzer and Mitrook 2007; Taylor and Kent 2014). Based on this normative focus, scholars have conducted numerous empirical studies that investigate how these potentials, promises, and normative ideals are met (e. g. Bortee and Seltzer 2009; Bruning, Dials, and Shirka 2008; DiStaso and McCorkindale 2013; Kelleher 2009; Kent, Taylor, and White 2003; Men and Tsai 2012, 2013, 2014; Saffer, Sommerfeldt, and Taylor 2013; Sundstrom and Levenshus 2017; Yang and Taylor 2010; Khang, Ki, and Ye 2012).

---

[1] Parts of this chapter further elaborate on ideas developed in a chapter on online public relations by two of the authors published in a German handbook (Winkler and Pleil 2018).

The vast amount of empirical research has revealed that organizations often do not live up to initial promises and expectations of dialogue and relationship-building. As possible reasons for the lack of dialogue, scholars have mentioned the novelty of the technology, risk aversion, and the lack of resources and management support for their implementation (e. g., Etter 2013; Briones, Liu, and Jin 2011; Castelló, Etter, and Nielsen 2016).

In the Anglo-American scholarship, these findings have led to a more cautious approach towards the promises of social media in public relations research over the last years (Lane 2014; Macnamara 2010; Sommerfeldt and Kent 2015; Yang and Taylor 2015). On the one hand, we can observe a reaffirmation of normative claims, such as the call for more dialogue and symmetry in social media, whereby scholars have highlighted discrepancies between instrumental goals (such as reputation maintenance, and related economic outcomes, such as sales, etc.) and the social orientation through dialogue (Taylor and Kent 2014). On the other hand, scholars have proposed an analytic move away from classic dyadic relationships between organization and publics, towards a networked understanding of multiple organization-public relationships online (Himelboim, Moon, and Suto 2014; Kent, Sommerfeldt, and Saffer 2016; Sommerfeldt 2013; Sommerfeldt and Kent 2015; Valentini 2018). This shift is also reflected in recent work that calls for new approaches that more strongly consider the diversity, but also polarization and tensions, of the digitized society (Valentini, Kruckeberg, and Starck 2012).

In the European public relations debate, scholars have similarly developed dialogue-oriented models, such as the situtative phase model (Pleil 2007) that is rooted in the four-phase model by J. Grunig and Hunt (1984). These models are less normative with regard to dialogue, but rather situative. Furthermore, these models consider how a power shift from organizations to their publics has created new challenges for organizations. Accordingly, scholars propose how organizations can manage these new challenges, for example by finding the right balance between openness and flexibility (Macnamara and Zerfaß 2012; Linke and Zerfaß 2013; Pleil 2015).

Empirical studies by European scholars have also investigated the application of dialogue and interaction in various contexts, such as for CSR communication or the engagement with fans, in social media (Etter 2013; Ingenhoff and Kölling 2010; Linke and Zerfaß 2012; Moreno et al. 2015; Röttger, Stahl, and Zerfaß 2014; Rußmann 2015; Rühl and Ingenhoff 2015; Thummes and Malik 2015; Wiencierz, Moll, and Röttger 2015; Zerfaß and Droller 2015; Zerfaß et al. 2014). And similarly to Anglo-American studies, these works find that interactive potentials are often not applied by practitioners, which has dampened initial hopes for the dialogue-oriented application of social media in public relations practice (Elving and Postma 2017).

In the European debate, the reflection of these findings has led to a more fundamental critical turn than in the Anglo-American scholarship. First, the general fit between established dialogue and relationship-oriented public relations approaches for a social media environment is fundamentally questioned. Scholars argue that not only organizations, but also users themselves, seem not very interested in deliberative dialogue but rather use the tools for self-presentation (Valentini 2016) and self-optimization purposes (Sandhu 2015). Second, European scholars suggest overcoming interpersonal dialogic and relationship theories that are central to established public relations approaches, and instead turn towards language-focused (Valentini, Romenti, and Kruckeberg 2016; Romenti, Murtarelli, and Valentini 2014) and technology-sensitive approaches (Winkler and Wehmeier 2015). Third, the European debate explores broader changes in the networked public sphere, whereby scholars identify increased pressure for transparency (Raupp 2011), the volatility of attention dynamics (Bentele and Nothhaft 2010), orientation towards affect and scandalization (Imhof 2015), and new asymmetries through algorithms (Winkler 2014, 2015) as main challenges for dialogue-orientation and deliberation in social media.

In sum, for both Anglo-American and European dialogue-centric approaches we can observe an interesting shift. The initially appealing idea of applying traditional, mostly normative public relations models to social media is tempered by empirical studies that show that these ideals are hardly met. In reaction, new models and understandings, such as language-focused or technology-sensitive models, have emerged, which take actual use, conditions, and limitations of social media more strongly into account.

2.2 Crisis and issue-centric approaches

The empowerment of users through social media technologies and perceptions of increased risks and challenges for organizations have resulted in a strong interest from crisis and issues-centric approaches in public relations. These approaches mainly follow two broader, interrelated streams of investigation. The first one explores descriptively the qualitative changes that social media bring to crisis situations and the new ways for detecting and possibly managing issues. The second one, more prescriptively, examines how these changes can be tackled by organizations through new forms of crisis communication and issue-monitoring. Scholars have thereby reexamined established concepts and theories on mainly crisis communication, and developed new ones.

With the rise of social media, public relations scholars have debated early how organizations can make use of these new technologies in crisis situations. Like dialogue-centric approaches, crisis and issue-centric approaches developed high expectations for social media, which were hailed to support practitioners in better managing or preventing crises (e. g. Gonzalez-Herrero and Smith 2008). Besides the affordances of speed, interactivity, and direct access to publics, scholars have emphasized the possibility to monitor online publics and identify emerging issues in social media to detect signals of early crises, predict the levels of reputation threats, and develop crisis response strategies accordingly (e. g. Coombs and Holladay 2012).

However, empirical studies have shown mixed results about the use of social media for crisis communication and issue management. While some scholars find that social media are helpful to monitor online publics (Coombs and Holladay 2012), reduce negative impact on reputation, create mutual understanding (Roshan, Warren, and Carr 2016), and engage in dialogue during a crisis (Romenti, Murtarelli, and Valentini 2014), others have shown that practitioners hardly embrace social media's assumed potential. For example, as with the dialogue-centric approaches, empirical studies reveal that organizations do not make great use of interactive features to interact with publics in crisis situations (e. g. Ki and Nekmat 2014) and make only limited use of the social monitoring features to detect possible reputation threats (Graham and Avery 2017).

With the empowerment of publics through social media, scholars have also laid more focus on the active role of users. Studies investigated not only how users increasingly use social media to receive information about a crisis (e. g. Veil, Buehner, and Palenchar 2011), but also how they actively participate in crises situations or even initiate a crisis, which creates new challenges for organizations (Veil, Buehner, and Palenchar 2011; Albu and Etter 2016). The concern that any user may potentially initiate a crisis, by posting corroborating messages in social media, has particularly resonated with practitioners. The perception of threat has been fuelled by several cases, which have shown how little incidents gained large-scale attention through viral diffusion and eventually led to wide negative reactions (Pfeffer, Zorbach, and Carley 2014; Albu and Etter 2016). Studies have shown, indeed, that content by social media users can influence crisis perceptions (Etter, Fleck, and Mueller 2017) or the intention to speak out on social media (Zheng, Liu, and Davison 2018).

With the new attention to different actors who participate in the co-creation of a crisis, European scholars have developed a strong interest in framing theory and analysis in order to investigate how the different actors frame a crisis and influence each other (e. g. Schultz, Utz, and Göritz 2011; Etter and Vestergaard 2015; Van de Meer et al. 2014; Valentini and Romenti 2011). In sum, this work has shown that news media still play a major role in influencing the public framing of a crisis. Others have highlighted that not only actors, but even the medium itself has an influence on how crises develop and are percieved (Schultz, Utz, and Göritz 2011).

Conceptually, mainly Anglo-American scholars have initially applied established models, such as the situational crisis communication theory (SCCT) (DiStaso, Vafeiadis, and Amaral 2015). However, over time scholars have argued that new models are needed to accommodate for changing crisis dynamics in social media. For example, Jin and Liu (2010) introduced the social media mediated crisis communication model, which grasps the complexity and interconnectedness of the networked public sphere (Austin, Liu, and Jin 2012; see also Etter, Ravasi, and Colleoni 2019). Conceptual development is also advanced by Schultz, Utz, and Göritz (2011), who introduce the notion of secondary crisis communication, which captures the practice of users to further disseminate crisis information. Furthermore, Coombs and Holladay (2012) introduce the notion of "sub-arenas", which describes the online realm, where stakeholders react to and visibly interpret corporate crises. Romenti, Murtarelli, and Valentini (2014) conceptualize new forms of dialogues between organisations and publics in social media during and after crises.

Over the years, the perception of increased risk has given way to a more realistic picture of the actual reputation threats in social media. While cases of consumer firestorms still emerge from time to time and gain large media attention, scholars and practitioners have realized that these incidents happen way less often than expected and might have less impact than feared. Indeed, the question has arisen as to what extent users in social media have an actual impact on reputations, sales, and other performance outcomes. Coombs and Holladay (2012) emphasize that negative comments and activism in social media alone do not necessarily constitute a crisis. Accordingly, they introduce the term "paracrisis", which resembles a crisis, but does not need a crisis team and can be handled at an early stage.

In sum, crisis and issue-centric approaches have early identified potential opportunities and threats for crisis situations and issue management in social media. To better understand the new crisis dynamics, and the role of the active users and publics in crisis situations, scholars have developed models and expanded existing ones. Over the years, the more nuanced understanding of the actual crisis dynamics and power dynamics has provided a more realistic perception of actual reputation threats in social media.

2.3 User-centric approaches

User-centric approaches to social media and digital marketing have highlighted new habits and expectations of online users. These approaches are based on the understanding of the practical field of content strategy, which takes the user's perspective as a starting-point for communication planning (Halvorson and Rach 2012). User-centric approaches emphasize that the aim of content marketing is not to persuade publics or brand organizations, but to offer and create useful content for users (Solis and Breakenridge 2009; Phillips and Young 2009).

The debate in user-centric approaches often evolves around the optimization of (content) design and technological aspects. Social media are thereby mainly seen as means to an end – especially for content creation and distribution – in the context of customer journeys. The focus is thereby typically on owned media, i. e. content created by users themselves for organizational purposes (Eck and Eichmeier 2014). While broadly established in practice, to date there is only little academic research on user-centric approaches in public relations (Verčič, D., Verčič, A., and Sriramesh 2015).

One of the most prominent ideas from the user-centric approach is "social listening", which is based on on online monitoring techniques (Aßmann and Pleil 2014).

These techniques are used to systematically collect and analyze comments in social media to use them for flexible planning and measurement of communication strategies (Halvorson and Rach 2012). While the large amount of data in social media is often approached with a quantitative approach, Macnamara (2014) argues that interpretative-qualitative methods should receive more attention to better understand perceptions, behaviour, and interactions of users. An approach that follows this call is "persona modelling" (Spies 2015), which creates typologies of users for communication planning. Similarly, "empathy mapping" (Ferreira et al. 2015; Endrissat, Islam, and Noppeney 2016) seeks to identify user attitudes for further strategic planning.

The insights from these methods often feed into agile planning models, such as Scrum, which are not only popular with practitioners, but also find attention in public relations research (van Ruler 2015). These agile planning models, which were originally developed in the context of IT, are applicable for any kind of communication planning – offline and online – and are particularly valuable in fast-changing communication environments (van Ruler 2015), such as in the context of social media. These models emphasize flexible adaption in contrast to the linear planning process, whereby the illusion of control is replaced with iterative and flexible consideration of user feedback (van Ruler 2015; Gulbrandsen and Just 2016). This flexibilization, however, requires the reorganization of processes within organizations (Hergert, 2018), such as decentralizing communication functions with less emphasis on consistency and control (Christensen, Firat, and Torp 2008; Castelló, Etter, and Nielsen 2016) and a stronger importance of interdisciplinary collaboration, emergent strategies, and informal relationships within organizations (Smith 2013; Winkler and Etter 2018).

Another user-centric approach, which has gained increasing attention in recent years, is digital storytelling (Bailie and Urbina 2013). As a popular form of content strategy, digital storytelling finds wide application in employee and consumer communication, business-to-business, or employer branding. Storytelling puts the user's needs and emotions at the centre and seeks to develop a consistent plot through different channels (Fordon 2018). However, scholars have also critically argued that this form of content strategy largely rests on "emotional persuasion" (Sammer 2017) and neglects the full interactive potential of social media (Wehmeier and Winkler 2015).

In contrast, co-creation strategies give users a more prominent role. Co-creation strategies are based on the idea that many users create better content than a few selected experts (Wolf 2016). Furthermore, scholars have argued that the participation through social media technologies increases the identification with content (Siakas, D. and Siakas, K. 2016). Accordingly, co-creation strategies have found application in various fields, such as brand communication, innovation communication, or employer branding. This broad application blurs disciplinary borders and is reflected in changing professional practices and roles. For example, social media enable every employee to become a spokesperson for an organization (Zerfaß and Pleil 2015), and, hence, enable a flexible integration of employees for content strategies. Critically, scholars have mentioned that employee integration for social media strategies needs a cautious approach, because social media often blur the boundaries of public and professional spheres, and might lead to the corporate colonization of the private spheres of employees (Banghart, Etter, and Stohl 2018). In sum, user-centric approaches have been hailed for their focus on the needs of individual users. However, these approaches lack critical reflection on underlying economic drivers and public implications of individualistic user centrism.

2.4 Data-centric approaches

Data-centric approaches have only recently emerged in public relations research and practice. These approaches evolve around strategic or ethical questions of the use of different sorts of user data retrieved from social media and other online platforms. These approaches depart from the assumption that systematic data analysis will lead to better decision-making, but could also lead to a more targeted distribution of content. Early developments of these approaches can be found in the debate around measurements of inputs, outcomes, and outputs, while a more recent focus has shifted to social media platforms that generate large volumes of data, also called big data. This recent focus on big data practices and digital methods for public relations has not only been researched from a strategic and practice-oriented perspective, but increasingly by more critical scholars who highlight questions of power and control. These critical reflections have been paralleled with greater scrutiny by regulators, such as the recent GDPR (General Data Protection Regulation) by the European Union, and a series of data breaches and scandals, such as that around Cambridge Analytica.

The use of big data is discussed in different ways in public relations and digital marketing. While some scholars see a potential to regain control over public communication processes, others problematize new dependencies and responsibilities of public relations. The regaining of control over public communication is attractive for practitioners, particularly after a perceived loss of control in social media. Big data and analytics hold the promise to regain control through prediction models, micro-targeting, and immediate measurement of impact.

The debate on big data and control mainly problematizes trace data, which users create using social media, often without being aware how the data is used by organizations. The data is mainly sourced from social media networks (Parks 2014), aggregated through automated data mining tools, and subsequently analysed with new digital methods, such as opinion mining and sentiment analysis (Etter et al. 2018), which increasingly draw on machine-learning techniques and computational linguistics. These new techniques and methods are often used to address traditional questions of public relations, related to information diffusion and opinion formation. For example, they allow the analysis of users' attitudes and interests, which are used to create fine grained user typologies for micro-targeting. Furthermore, public relations scholars have argued that the analysis of big data sets supports practitioners not only for decision-making (Wiencierz and Röttger 2016), but also for the justification of decisions in an organizational context and for the better prediction of the consequences of their decisions (Wiesenberg, Zerfaß, and Moreno 2017).

Overall, the debate on big data in public relations is only in its nascence. A meta-analysis of journal articles by Wiencierz und Röttger (2017) reveals that big data finds less attention and legitimation in public relations scholarship, as opposed to more marketing and advertising-oriented journals. Accordingly, Kent and Saffer (2014) call for a stronger orientation towards conceptual embeddedness of these technologies and highlight the so far underused strategic potential of big data for public relations. Weiner and Kochhar (2016) make similar arguments in a white paper and call for an integration of big data in public relations that promises higher performance outcomes. In contrast to overall affirmative approaches to an instrumental use of big data in public relations, Holtzhausen and Zerfass (2015) and Wiesenberg, Zerfaß, and Moreno (2017) suggest a more balanced approach, with an evaluation of risks and benefits of big data use depending on the situational context. The study by Wiesenberg, Zerfaß, and Moreno (2017) on European communication directors shows that practitioners often have only a basic understanding of big data, acknowledge its practical relevance, but lack technical knowledge and skills to embrace the technology.

A critical approach to data-oriented public relations highlights the responsibilities of public relations practitioners with regard to new data practices, including the use of artificial intelligence (e. g. Galloway and Swiatek 2018). The concerns revolve around the delegation of decision-making to non-human entities, such as algorithms, the lack of transparency of access and use of data, and the power concentration by a few central players. Collister (2015) addresses, as one of the first scholars, the problem of increased delegation of decision by highlighting how algorithms make the selection of messages and interactions in social media, the public presentation and visibility of organizations through search engines, and the understanding and relevance of stakeholders through micro-targeting in public relations. He concludes that the PR scholarship fails to keep pace with the technological development and calls for new frameworks and concepts to understand new practices. Galloway and Swiatek (2018) caution PR scholars and practitioners alike to look beyond the immediate effects of automation, but also consider wider societal implications of artificial intelligence. Finally, Wiencierz (2018) analyses public relations codes of ethics and explores how big data practices that serve the public interest can be communicated in these codes. The author suggests that adherence to established codes in public relations also increases public trust in big data practices that serve the public interest.

Besides these reflections, scholars have highlighted that the current power and data concentration by a few companies requires the creation of a new advocacy role of public relations. Holtzhausen (2016), for example, calls for a role of public relations as an organizational activist (Holtzhausen 2012) that explicitly opposes data-based discrimination of certain societal groups and demands algorithmic accountability for the responsible use of user data. The question remains whether such a role for public relations is realistic and desirable.

In sum, we can observe two counter-trends in the current data-oriented public relations debate. On the one hand, there is a trend that understands big data and analytics as a chance to regain control over public relations in social media. Accordingly, this stream calls for a fast adoption of new skills and competences. On the other hand, a more critical trend focuses on new dependencies and new responsibilities for the discipline.

3 Conclusions

This chapter has reviewed four of the most prominent approaches in public relations that deal with social media as opportunity and challenge. Based on this review, we propose for the most established and dominant dialogue-centric approach, to overcome established, overtly normative conceptions of dialogue and relationships, and further develop more analytically grounded concepts that apply the discourse dynamics and affordances of social media instead.

For crisis and issue-centric approaches, we propose further conceptualization and empirical research in order to understand the new dynamics during crises in social media and their interdependencies with established crisis communication logics. Particularly interesting will be to further investigate the conditions under which negative reactions in social media have substantive consequences for organizations.

For user-centric approaches, we see a chance in increased interdisciplinary exchange with neighbouring content-driven areas of strategic communication to develop a better understanding of new communication roles and practices without losing focus on their broader organizational and public implications.

Finally, for data-centric approaches we emphasize an understanding of public relations as a public-interest-oriented discipline that can address new challenges that arise with new dependences and the challenges of organizational big data practices. In sum, social media, after one and a half decades, still proves to have highly transformative yet often unexpected impact on the professional and academic understanding of public relations and its key concepts.

References

Albu, Oana & Michal Etter. 2016. Hypertextuality and social media: A study of the constitutive and paradoxical implications of organizational Twitter use. *Management Communication Quarterly* 30(1). 5–31.

Aßmann, Stefanie & Thomas Pleil. 2014. Social Media Monitoring: Grundlagen und Zielsetzungen. In Ansgar Zerfaß & Manfred Piwinger (eds.), *Handbuch Unternehmenskommunikation: Strategie – Management – Wertschöpfung*, 585–604. Wiesbaden: Springer.

Austin, Lee, Fisher Liu & Yan Jin. 2012. How audiences seek out crisis information: Exploring the social-mediated crisis communication model. *Journal of Applied Communication Research* 40(2). 188–207.

Avery, Elizabeth J., Melissa Graham & Sejin Park. 2016. Planning makes (closer to) perfect: exploring United States' local government officials' evaluations of crisis management. *Journal of Contingencies and Crisis Management* 24(2). 73–81.

Bailie, Rahel & Noz Urbina. 2013. *Content Strategy: Connecting the dots between business, brand, and benefits*. Laguna Hills: XML Press.

Banghart, Scott, Michael Etter & Cynthia Stohl. 2019. Organizational boundary regulation through social media policies. *Management Communication Quarterly* 32(3). 337–373. DOI: 0893318918766405 (accessed 20 January 2020).

Bentele, Guenther & Howard Nothhaft. 2010. Strategic communication and the public sphere. *International Journal of Strategic Communication* 4. 93–116.

Bortee, Denise & Trent Seltzer. 2009. Dialogic strategies and outcomes: An analysis of environmental advocacy groups' Facebook profiles. *Public Relations Review* 35. 317–319.

Briones, Rowena, Betch Kuch Liu & Yan Jin. 2011. Keeping up with the digital age: How the American Red Cross uses social media to build relationships. *Public Relations Review* 37(1). 37–43.

Bruning, Stephen, Melissa Dials & Amanda Shirka. 2008. Using dialogue to build organization-public relationships, engage publics, and positively affect organizational outcomes. *Public Relations Review* 34. 25–31.

Castelló, Itziar, Michael Etter & Finn Årup Nielsen. 2016. Strategies of legitimacy through social media: The networked strategy. *Journal of Management Studies* 53(3). 402–432.

Christensen, Lars, Andrea Firat, & Simon Torp. 2008. The organisation of integrated communications: Toward flexible integration. *European Journal of Marketing* 42(3/4). 423–452.

Collister, Simon. 2015. Algorithmic public relations: materiality, technology and power in a post-hegemonic world. In Jacquie L'Etang, David McKie, Nancy Snow, & Jordi Xifra (eds.), *The Routledge handbook of critical public relations*, 360–371. New York: Routledge.

Coombs, Timothy & Sherry Holladay. 2012. The paracrisis: The challenges created by publicly managing crisis prevention. *Public Relations Review* 38(3). 408–415.

DiStaso, Marcia & Tina McCorkindale. 2013. A benchmark analysis of the strategic use of social media for fortune's most admired US companies on Facebook, Twitter and YouTube. *Public Relations Journal* 7(1). 1–33.

DiStaso, Marcia, Michail Vafeiadis, & Carla Amaral. 2015. Managing a health crisis on Facebook: How the response strategies of apology, sympathy, and information influence public relations. *Public Relations Review* 41(2). 222–231.

Eck, Karing & Dirk Eichmeier. 2014. *Die Content-Revolution im Unternehmen: Neue Perspektiven durch Content-Marketing und -Strategie*. Freiburg: Haufe.

Elving, Wim & Rosa Postma. 2017. Social Media: The dialogue myth? How organizations use social media for stakeholder dialogue. In Betteke van Ruler, Iekje Smit, Øyvind Ihlen, & Stefania Rometi (eds.), *How strategic communication shapes value and innovation in society*, 123–142. Bingley: Emerald.

Endrissat, Nada, Gazi Islam, & Claus Noppeney. 2016. Visual organizing: Balancing coordination and creative freedom via mood boards. *Journal of Business Research* 69(7). 2353–2362.

Etter, Michael. 2013. Reasons for low levels of interactivity: (Non-) interactive CSR communication in Twitter. *Public Relations Review* 39(5). 606–608.

Etter, Michael, Davide Ravasi, & Elanor Colleoni. 2019. Social media and the formation of organizational reputation. *Academy of Management Review* 44(1). 28–52.

Etter, Michael, Matthes Fleck & Roy Mueller. 2017. The influence of social media comments on crisis perception. Paper presented at the EUPRERA conference in London, 13–14 October.

Etter, Michael & Anne Vestergaard. 2015. Facebook and the public framing of a corporate crisis. *Corporate Communications: An International Journal* 20(2). 163–177.

Etter, Michael, Elanor Colleoni, Laura Illia, Katia Meggiorin & Antonio D'Eugenio. 2018. Measuring organizational legitimacy in social media: Assessing citizens' judgments with sentiment analysis. *Business & Society* 57(1). 60–97.

Ferreira, Bruna, Silva Williamson, Oliveira Edson & Tayana Conte. 2015. *Designing personas with empathy map.* Proceedings of the 27th International Conference on Software Engineering and Knowledge Engineering, 501–505. doi:10.18293/SEKE2015-152 (accessed 20 January 2020).

Fordon, Anja. 2018. *Die Storytelling-Methode: Schritt für Schritt zu einer überzeugenden, authentischen und nachhaltigen Marketing-Kommunikation.* Wiesbaden: Springer.

Galloway, Chris & Lukasz Swiatek. 2018. Public relations and artificial intelligence: It's not (just) about robots. *Public Relations Review* 44(5). 734–740.

Gonzalez-Herrero, Alfonso & Suzanne Smith. 2010. Crisis communications management 2.0: Organizational principles to manage crisis in an online world. *Organization Development Journal* 28(1). 97–105.

Grunig, James & Hunt, Timothy. 1984. *Managing public relations.* Fort Worth: Holt, Rinehart and Winston.

Gulbrandsen, Ibb & Sine Just. 2016. *Strategizing communication.* Kopenhagen: Samfundslitteratur.

Halvorson, Kristina & Melissa Rach. 2012. *Content strategy for the web.* 2nd edn. Berkeley: New Riders.

Herget, Josef. 2018. Agile Methoden zur Gestaltung der Unternehmenskultur: Dynamiken der Veränderungsfähigkeit für einen Kulturwandel nutzen. In Josef Herget & Herbert Strobl (eds.), *Unternehmenskultur in der Praxis: Grundlagen – Methoden – Best Practices*, 243–256. Wiesbaden: Springer.

Himelboim, Itai, Bitt Moon & Ryan Suto. 2014. A social networks approach to public relations on Twitter. *Public Relations Review* 26. 13–22.

Holtzhausen, Derina R. 2016. Datafication: Threat or opportunity for communication in the public sphere? *Journal of Communication Management* 20(1). 21–36.

Holtzhausen, Derina R. 2012. *Public relations as activism. Postmodern approaches to theory and practice.* New York: Routledge.

Holtzhausen, Derina R. & Ansgar Zerfass. 2015. Strategic communication: Opportunities and challenges of the research area. In Derina R. Holtzhausen & Ansgar Zerfass (eds.), *The Routledge handbook of strategic communication*, 3–17. New York: Routledge.

Imhof, Kurt. 2015. Die Online-Geschichtsphilosophie der PR-Forschung. In Olaf Hoffjann & Thomas Pleil (eds.), *Strategische Onlinekommunikation. Theoretische Konzepte und empirische Befunde*, 13–30. Wiesbaden: Springer VS.

Ingenhoff, Diana & Martina Kölling. 2010. Web sites as a dialogic tool for charitable fundraising NPOs: A comparative study. *International Journal of Strategic Communication* 4(3). 171–188.

Jin, Yan & Liu Fisher. 2010. The blog-mediated crisis communication model: Recommendations for responding to influential external blogs. *Journal of Public Relations Research* 22(4). 429–455.

Jones, Brian, John Temperley & Anderson Lima. 2009. Corporate reputation in the era of Web 2.0: the case of Primark. *Journal of Marketing Management* 25(9–10). 927–939.

Kaplan, Andreas & Michael Haenlein. 2010. Users of the world, unite! The challenges and opportunities of Social Media. *Business Horizons* 53(1). 59–68.

Kelleher, Tom. 2009. Conversational voice, communicated commitment, and public relations outcomes in interactive online communication. *Journal of Communication* 59(1). 172–188.

Kent, Michael & Adam Saffer. 2014. A delphi study of the future of new technology research in public relations. *Public Relations Review* 40(3). 568–576.

Kent, Michael, Erich Sommerfeldt & Alanedam Saffer. 2016. Social networks, power, and public relations: Tertius Iungens as a cocreational approach to studying relationship networks. *Public Relations Review* 42(1). 91–100.

Kent, Micheal & Maureen Taylor. 2002. Toward a dialogic theory of public relations. *Public Relations Review* 28(1). 21–37.

Kent, Michael, Maureen Taylor & William White. 2003. The relationship between web site design and organizational responsiveness to stakeholders. *Public Relations Review* 29(1). 63–77.

Khang, Hyoungkoo, Eyun-Jung Ki & Lan Ye. 2012. Social media research in advertising, communication, marketing, and public relations, 1997–2010. *Journalism & Mass Communication Quarterly* 89(2). 279–298.

Ki, Eyon-Jung & Elmie Nekmat. 2014. Situational crisis communication and interactivity: Usage and effectiveness of Facebook for crisis management by Fortune 500 companies. *Computers in Human Behavior* 35. 140–147.

Lane, Anne. 2014. Toward understanding the (lack of?) significance of dialogue to the practice of public relations. *Journal of Asia Pacific Public Relations* 15(1). 123–142.

Linke, Anne & Ansgar Zerfaß. 2012. Future trends of social media use in strategic communication: Results of a delphi study. *Public Communication Review* 2(2). 17–29.

Linke, Anne & Ansgar Zerfaß. 2013. Social media governance: regulatory frameworks for successful online communications. *Journal of Communication Management* 17(3). 270–286.

Macnamara, Jim. 2010. Public relations and the social: How practitioners are using, or abusing, social media. *Asia Pacific Public Relations Journal* 11(1). 21–39.

Macnamara, Jim. 2014. *Breaking the PR measurement and evaluation deadlock: A new approach and model.* Paper presented at the AMEC International Summit on Measurement "Upping the Game", Amsterdam, 11–12 June.

Macnamara, Jim & Ansgar Zerfaß. 2012. Social media communication in organizations: The challenges of balancing openness, strategy, and management. *International Journal of Strategic Communication* 6(4). 287–308.

Men, Rita & Wan-Hsiu Tsai. 2012. How companies cultivate relationships with publics on social network sites: Evidence from China and the United States. *Public Relations Review* 38. 723–730.

Men, Rita & Wan-Hsiu Tsai. 2013. Beyond liking or following: Understanding public engagement on social networking sites in China. *Public Relations Review* 39. 13–22.

Men, Rita & Wan-Hsiu Tsai. 2014. Perceptual, attitudinal, and behavioral outcomes of organization-public engagement on corporate social networking sites. *Journal of Public Relations Research* 26. 417–435.

Moreno, Angeles, Christina Navarro, Ralph Tench & Ansgar Zerfaß. 2015. Does social media usage matter? An analysis of online practices and digital media perceptions of communication practitioners in Europe. Public Relations Review 41(2). 242–253.

Parks, Malcolm. 2014. Big data in communication research: Its contents and discontents. *Journal of Communication* 64(2). 355–360.

Pfeffer, Juergen, Thomas Zorbach & Kathleen Carley. 2014. Understanding online firestorms: Negative word-of-mouth dynamics in social media networks. *Journal of Marketing Communications* 20(1–2). 117–128.

Phillips, David & Phillip Young. 2009. *Online public relations: A practical guide to developing an online strategy in the world of social media*. 2nd edn. London: Kogan Page.

Pleil, Thomas. 2007. Online-PR zwischen digitalem Monolog und vernetzter Kommunikation. In Thomas Pleil (ed.), *Online-PR im Web 2.0*, 10–32. Konstanz: UVK.

Pleil, Thomas. 2015. Online-PR. Vom kommunikativen Dienstleister zum Katalysator für ein neues Kommunikationsmanagement. In Günther Bentele, Romy Fröhlich & Peter Szyszka (eds.), *Handbuch der Public Relations*, 3rd edn., 1017–1038. Wiesbaden: Springer VS.

Raupp, Juliane. 2011. Organizational communication in a networked public sphere. *Studies in Communication/Media* 1. 73–93.

Romenti, Stefania, Grazia Murtarelli & Chiara Valentini. 2014. Organisations' conversations in social media: applying dialogue strategies in times of crises. *Corporate Communications: An International Journal* 19(1). 10–33.

Roshan, Mina, Matthew Warren & Rodney Carr. 2016. Understanding the use of social media by organisations for crisis communication. *Computers in Human Behavior* 63. 350–361.

Röttger, Ulrike, Juergen Stahl & Ansgar Zerfaß. 2014. *Leadership in communication management: Enduring and emerging challenges in Germany, Austria and Switzerland. In Bruce K. Berger & Juan Meng (eds.), Public relations leaders as sensemakers. A global study of leadership in public relations and communication management*, 186–200. New York: Routledge.

Rühl, Christopher & Diana Ingenhoff. 2015. Communication management on social networking sites: Stakeholder motives and usage types of corporate Facebook, Twitter and YouTube pages. *Journal of Communication Management* 19(3). 288–302.

Rußmann, Uta. 2015. Die Ö Top 500 im Web: Der Einsatz von Social Media in österreichischen Großunternehmen. Eine Bestandsaufnahme. *Medien Journal. Zeitschrift für Medien- und Kommunikationsforschung* 39(1). 19–34.

Saffer, Adam, Erich Sommerfeldt & Maureen Taylor. 2013. The effects of organizational Twitter interactivity on organization-public relations. *Public Relations Review* 39. 213–215.

Sammer, Petra. 2017. Von Hollywood lernen? Erfolgskonzepte des Corporate Storytelling. In Annika Schach (ed.), *Storytelling: Geschichten in Text, Bild und Film*, 13–32. Wiesbaden: Springer Fachmedien Wiesbaden.

Sandhu, Swaran. 2015. Dialog als Mythos: normative Konzeptionen der Online-PR im Spannungsfeld zwischen Technikdeterminismus und strategischem Handlungsfeld. In Olaf Hoffjann & Thomas Pleil (eds.), *Strategische Onlinekommunikation. Theoretische Konzepte und empirische Befunde*, 57–74. Wiesbaden: Springer VS.

Sundstrom, Beth & Abbey B. Levenshus. 2017. The art of engagement: Dialogic strategies on Twitter. *Journal of Communication Management* 21(1). 17–33.

Schultz, Friederike, Sonja Utz & Anja Göritz, A. 2011. Is the medium the message? Perceptions of and reactions to crisis communication via Twitter, blogs and traditional media. *Public Relations Review* 37(1). 20–27.

Seltzer, Trent & Michael Mitrook. 2007. The dialogic potential of weblogs in relationship building. *Public Relations Review* 33(2). 227–229.

Siakas, Dimitrios & Kerstin Siakas. 2016. User orientation through open innovation and customer integration. In Christian Kreiner, Rory O'Connor, Alexander Poth & Richard Messnarz (eds.), *Systems, software and services process improvement*, 325–341. Cham: Springer.

Smith, Brian. 2013. The internal forces on communication integration: Co-created meaning, interaction, and postmodernism in strategic integrated communication. *International Journal of Strategic Communication* 7(1). 65–79.

Solis, Brian & Deirdre Breakenridge. 2009. *Putting the public back in public relations: How social media is reinventing the aging business of PR*. New Jersey: Pearson.

Sommerfeldt, Erich. 2013. Networks of social capital: Extending a public relations model of civil society in Peru. *Public Relations Review* 39(1). 1–12.

Sommerfeldt, Erich & Michael Kent. 2015. Civil society, networks, and relationship management: Beyond the organization-public dyad. *International Journal of Strategic Communication* 9. 235–252.

Spies, Michael. 2015. *Branded interactions: creating the digital experience*. London: Thames & Hudson.

Taylor, Maureen & Michael Kent. 2014. Dialogic engagement: Clarifying foundational concepts. *Journal of Public Relations Research* 26(5). 384–398.

Thummes, Kerstin & Maja Malik. 2015. Beteiligung und Dialog durch Facebook? Theoretische Überlegungen und empirische Befunde zur Nutzung von Facebook-Fanseiten als Dialogplattform in der Marken-PR. In Olaf Hoffjann & Thomas Pleil (eds.), *Strategische Onlinekommunikation. Theoretische Konzepte und empirische Befunde*, 105–130. Wiesbaden: Springer VS.

Valentini, Chiara. 2016. Is using social media "good" for the public relations profession? A critical reflection. *Public Relations Review* 41(2). 170–177.

Valentini, Chiara. 2018. Social Media. In Robert L. Heath and Winni Johansen (eds.), *International Encylopedia of Strategic Communication*. Wiley: Blackwell.

Valentini, Chiara, Dean Kruckeberg, & Kenneth Starck. 2012. Public relations and community: A persistent covenant. *Public Relations Review* 38(5). 873–879.

Valentini Chiara & Stefania Romenti. 2011. Blogging about crises: The role of online conversations in framing Alitalia's performance during its crisis. *Journal of Communication Management* 15(4). 298–313.

Valentini, Chiara, Stefania Romenti & Dean Kruckeberg. 2016. Language and discourse in social media relational dynamics. A communicative constitution perspective. *International Journal of Communication* 10. 4055–4073.

van der Meer, Toni & Piet Verhoeven. 2013. Public framing organizational crisis situations: Social media versus news media. *Public Relations Review* 39(3). 229–231.

van Ruler, Betteke. 2015. Agile public relations planning: The reflective communication scrum. *Public Relations Review* 41(2). 187–194.

Veil, Shari, Tara Buehner & Michael Palenchar. 2011. A work-in-process literature review: Incorporating social media in risk and crisis communication. *Journal of contingencies and crisis management* 19(2). 110–122.

Verčič, Dejan, Ana Verčič & Krishnaumurthy Sriramesh. 2015. Looking for digital in public relations. *Public Relations Review* 41(2). 142–152.

Watkins, Brandi & Regina Lewis. 2014. Winning with apps: A case study of the current branding strategies employed on professional sport teams' mobile apps. *International Journal of Sport Communication* 7(3). 399–416.

Wehmeier, Stefan & Peter Winkler. 2015. Personalisierung und Storytelling in der Online-Kommunikation. In Ansag Zerfaß & Thomas Pleil (eds.), *Handbuch Online-PR. Strategische Kommunikation in Internet und Social Web*, 2nd edn., 455–466. Konstanz: UVK.

Weiner, Michael & Susan Kochhar. 2016. *Irreversible: The public relations big data revolution*. IPR white paper. Gainesville: Institute for Public Relations.

Wiencierz, Christian. 2018. *Vertrauen in gemeinwohlorientierte Big-Data-Anwendungen. Ethische Leitlinien für eine datenbasierte Organisationskommunikation*. In Kerstin Liesem & Lars Rademacher (eds.), *Die Macht der Strategischen Kommunikation. Medienethische Perspektiven der Digitalisierung*, 109–126. Baden-Baden: Nomos.

Wiencierz, Christian & Ulrike Röttger. 2016. Trust in organizations: The significance and measurement of trust in corporate actors. In Bernd Blöbaum (ed.), *Trust and Communication in a Digitized World*, 91–111. Wiesbaden: Springer VS.

Wiencierz, Christian, Ricardo Moll & Ulrike Röttger. 2015. Stakeholderdialog auf Facebook – Entschuldigung und Verantwortungsübernahme als vertrauensfördernde Reaktion auf Online-Beschwerden in sozialen Netzwerken. In Olaf Hoffjann & Thomas Pleil (eds.), *Strategische Onlinekommunikation. Theoretische Konzepte und empirische Befunde*, 131–154. Wiesbaden: Springer VS.

Wiesenberg, Markus, Ansgar Zerfaß & Angeles Moreno. 2017. Big data and automation in strategic communication. *International Journal of Strategic Communication* 11(2). 95–114.

Winkler, Peter. 2014. *Eine PR der nächsten Gesellschaft. Ambivalenzen einer Disziplin im Wandel.* Wiesbaden: Springer Gabler.

Winkler, Peter. 2015. Wider die reine Netzwerkrhetorik – Plädoyer für eine netzwerksoziologisch informierte Online-PR. In Olaf Hoffjann & Thomas Pleil (eds.), *Strategische Onlinekommunikation. Theoretische Konzepte und empirische Befunde*, 31–56. Wiesbaden: Springer VS.

Winkler, Peter & Michael Etter. 2018. Strategic communication and emergence. A dual narrative framework. *International Journal of Strategic Communication* 12(2). 382–398. DOI: 10.1080/1553118X.2018.1452241 (accessed 20 January 2020).

Winkler, Peter & Thomas Pleil. 2018. Online Public Relations. In Wolfgang Schweiger & Klaus Beck (eds.), *Handbuch Online-Kommunikation*, 2nd edn., 451–478. Wiesbaden: Springer VS. DOI: 10.1007/978-3-658-18017-1_18-1 (accessed 20 January 2020).

Winkler, Peter & Stefan Wehmeier. 2015. New modes of participation in online-PR: Understanding texto-material networks. In Enric Ordeix, Valérie Carayol & Ralph Tench (eds.), *Public relations, values and cultural identity*, 307–324. Brussels: Peter Lang.

Wolf, Bernie. 2016. Inspiration by swarms. In Patrick Siarry, Lhassane Idoumghar & Julien Lepagnot (eds.), *Swarm intelligence based optimization*, 20–38. Cham: Springer.

Yang, Aimei & Maureen Taylor, M. 2015. Looking over, looking out, and moving forward: Positioning public relations in theorizing organizational network ecologies. *Communication Theory* 25(1). 91–115.

Yang, Kenneth & Yowei Kang. 2015. Exploring big data and privacy in strategic communication campaigns: A crosscultural study of mobile social media users' daily experiences. *International Journal of Strategic Communication* 9(2). 87–101.

Yang, Aimei & Taylor, Maureen. 2010. Relationship-building by Chinese ENGOs' websites: Education, not activation. *Public Relations Review* 36(4). 342–351.

Zerfaß, Ansgar & Miriam Droller. 2015. Kein Dialog im Social Web? Eine vergleichende Untersuchung zur Dialogorientierung von deutschen und US-amerikanischen Nonprofit-Organisationen im partizipativen Internet. In Olaf Hoffjann & Thomas Pleil (eds.), *Strategische Onlinekommunikation. Theoretische Konzepte und empirische Befunde*, 75–104. Wiesbaden: Springer VS.

Zerfaß, Ansgar & Thomas Pleil. 2015. Strategische Kommunikation in Internet und Social Web, in A. Zerfaß & T. Pleil (eds.), *Handbuch Online-PR. Strategische Kommunikation in Internet und Social Web*, 2nd edn., 39–86. Konstanz: UVK.

Zerfaß, Ansgar, Ralph Tench, Angeles Moreno, Piet Verhoeven, Dejan Verčič & Juergen Klewes. 2014. *Mind the gap: How the public and public relations professionals value leadership and social media. Results of the ComGap study in 10 European countries.* London: Ketchum/EUPRERA.

Zheng, Bowen, Hefe Liu, & Robert Davison. 2018. Exploring the relationship between corporate reputation and the public's crisis communication on social media. *Public Relations Review* 44(1). 56–64.

Grazia Murtarelli, Stefania Romenti, and Craig E. Carroll

10 Public relations as image and reputation management

Abstract: A general call for overcoming the distinction between the concepts of image and reputation seems to be emerging in the public relations field. The recurring counter-position of the two concepts is part of the larger debate over the symbolic communication-based function versus the behavioral function of public relations. The aim of this chapter is to conciliate the two perspectives by reviewing the literature about image and reputation management. The chapter highlights the role of public relations in managing image and reputation and illustrates its contribution, but also identifies opportunities and risks that professionals could face in the current competitive environment. The chapter has four main parts. The first section examines the concept of image. The second addresses the concept of reputation. The third section guides readers beyond the distinction between the two concepts and discusses the implications for and the contribution of public relations professionals in managing and evaluating image and reputation. The final section explores possible future trends in public relations and communication research.

Keywords: corporate image; corporate reputation; image management; reputation management; online reputation; image measurement; reputation mechanisms; corporate perceptions; intangibles; identity

1 Introduction

Among key public relations functions, image and reputation management are central to public relations' daily activities because they represent the starting-point for stimulating and affecting stakeholders' opinions and behaviors, as well as for supporting mutual understanding between organizations and their stakeholders. Yet the term *corporate image* has developed a negative connotation within the competitive environment. Various public relations and marketing scholars have emphasized the ephemeral and manipulative nature of corporate image management and related it to the construction of public impressions that appeal to an external audience (Bernstein 1984; Caillouet and Allen 1996; Williams and Moffitt 1997). Public relations and communication professionals have been oriented toward image-building or image-enhancing processes in order to construct, improve, or manipulate an organization's public appearance (L'Etang 2009). If images are manipulated, bolstered, and boosted by public relations professionals, then the function might deal "with shadows and illusions rather than reality" (Grunig J. 1993: 124–125), taking on aspects of propaganda and spin-doctoring (L'Etang 2009).

https://doi.org/10.1515/9783110554250-010

Such a negative view has been reinforced by the recurring counter-position of the concepts of image and reputation. The distinction between the two concepts can be viewed as part of the larger debate over the symbolic communication-based function (public relations as image building) versus the behavioral function (public relations as relationship management). According to J. Grunig (1993), "symbolic and behavioral relationships are intertwined like strands of a rope" (1993: 123), and

> when symbolic (communication-based) relationships are divorced from behavioral relationships (grounded in actions and events), public relations practitioners reduce public relations to the simplistic notion of image building [which] offer[s] little of value to the organizations they advise because they suggest that problems in relationships with publics can be solved by using the proper message – disseminated through publicity, or media relations – to change an image of an organization. (Grunig J. 1993: 136)

Consequently, a call to overcome the distinction between the concepts of image and reputation has emerged in both academic and professional circles. This chapter aims to transcend this debate by conciliating the two perspectives and to provide useful insights for public relations professionals, who are increasingly required to simultaneously play the roles of image-maker/visual communication manager, reputation manager, and relationship builder. Hence, this chapter reviews the literature on image and reputation management to outline the role of public relations in managing corporate image and reputation; it is structured as follows. The first section examines the opportunities and risks of image management for public relations scholars and practitioners. The second explores the role of public relations professionals as reputation managers. The third discusses the implications for and the contribution of public relations functions to managing image and reputation. The final section discusses potential future trends in research.

2 Opportunities and risks of image management by public relations

Image can be explored as one of the dimensions of reputation, public esteem – the degree to which a firm is liked, trusted, admired, and regarded (Carroll 2009). Image can be described as external publics' perceptions about organizational behaviors, activities, and achievements. From this perspective, image can play a vital role in projecting corporations and their objectives, visions, missions, and strategies into stakeholders' minds. Organizational scholars have emphasized the informational content of a corporate image and its function as an organizational signal (Riordan, Gatewood, and Bill 1997; Hatch and Schultz 1997), focusing on the communicative impact of organizational *skin, bones,* and *soul* (Fairholm 2009) and the internal issues related to the concept of image, which can be described as "the way 'organizational elites' would like outsiders to see the organization. This orientation highlights top management's concern with projecting an image of the organization that is based (ideally) on identity" (Gioia, Schultz, and Corley 2000: 65–66).

The organizational view allows us to highlight the positive influence that image can have on organizational processes and members at different levels. If we consider image as strongly linked to organizational culture and identity, effective image management can benefit an organization in the following ways: First, *by focusing on external constituencies, image can serve as an organizational signaling element with strong informative power,* helping an organization position itself within the competitive markets by conveying "information about otherwise unobservable characteristics of the organization, which are important to the market choices of potential stakeholders" (Riordan, Gatewood, and Bill 1997: 402). Image projects the essence of the organization to its various constituencies in order to achieve organizational objectives (Olins 1995). Images can shape organizational understanding and sense-making (Dutton, Dukerich, and Harquail 1994) by affecting stakeholders' decisions with a consequent impact on quality, satisfaction and loyalty (Andreassen and Lindestad 1998; Nguyen and Leblanc 2001; Lai, Griffin, and Babin 2009).

Second, *by focusing on internal constituencies, corporate image can help employees better understand which activities are proper and coherent with the organizational portrait members have developed* (Gioia, Schultz, and Corley 2000). Images can support employees in understanding themselves and their role within an organization, as well as in aligning their decisions and behaviours to serve the same purpose (Hatch and Schultz 1997). Images can also make organizations more or less attractive to current or future employees. As Turban and Greening (1997) noted, by signaling favorable information about organizations, images can help attract more and better qualified employees.

As effective image management could positively impact organizations, public relations and communication professionals are required to develop an intimate understanding of what image is. In doing so, however, they risk being considered part of a pseudo-managerial profession who manage "pseudo-events, pseudo-action and pseudo-structures, i. e. phenomena which have the purpose of producing effects on people's impressions and definition of reality" (Atvesson 1990: 373).

The following table summarizes the definitions and categories of corporate/organizational image from different perspectives.

Table 1: Definitions of corporate/organizational image (Source: adapted from Carroll 2008)

Labels	Definition	Authors
Construed external image	Mental associations that organization members believe others outside the organization hold about the organization	Dutton, Dukerich, and Harquail 1994; Gioia, Schultz, and Corley 2000
Defining image	Central images in an organization, such as root metaphors and archetypes, that give definition to the organization	Carroll 1995; Merrin 2005
Desired future image	Mental associations about the organization that organization leaders want important audiences to hold	Gioia, Schultz, and Corley 2000
Perceived Image	The perceptions held by insiders or outsiders	Barich and Kotler 1991; Balmer and Greyser 2006
Projected Image	The nonverbal image emitted by an organization	Gioia, Schultz, and Corley 2000
Refracted Image	The image passed on by third parties such as the news media, advertising agencies, government regulators, analysts, and pundits through some form of medium	Rindova and Fombrun 1999

Considering the different labels and definitions, we can observe that some of the definitions of images (*refracted, desired future image, and projected*) are communicatively built, meaning that they follow certain communication combinations and schemata settled by organizations. In such cases, corporate image could be defined by taking into account its functional components, i. e. measurable and tangible elements such as the reliability of products and their quality or price (Kennedy 1977; Martineau 1958; Stern, Zinkhan, and Jaju 2001).

The last three definitions of image (*perceived, desired,* and *construed*) are more cognitive, based mostly on mental associations and perceptive schemata or on emotional components such as stakeholders' perceptions, beliefs, or interpretations (Stern, Zinkhan, and Jaju 2001). From this perspective, image is the sum of interactions from experiences, impressions, opinions, and feelings of stakeholders vis-à-vis the organization (Worcester 2009).

Thus, corporate image is a multidimensional concept: "rarely will a single factor completely reflect the 'personality' of an organization. Also, it is unlikely that all the groups with which an organization interacts will have the same image at a particular point in time" (Dowling 1986: 112). The multidimensional nature of the concept compels public relations and communication professionals to explore (a) what are the different dimensions of corporate image, (b) what determinants contribute to the formation and management of corporate image, and (c) which techniques can be used to evaluate the dimensions of corporate image (Spector 1961).

Corporate image dimensions. Corporate image has been described as the total sum of perceptions of corporate personalities and features that stakeholders develop by experiencing the organization (Spector 1961). However, stakeholders may perceive the same features of an organization even if they have different experiences of it, and conversely, different groups of stakeholders may have the same experiences with the organization but may develop different perceptions of its corporate image (Spector 1961). Thus, it is necessary "to isolate the salient image dimensions for each group of interest to the organization" (Dowling 1986: 112). The following table synthesizes some examples of corporate image's dimensions.

Table 2: Corporate image dimensions (Source: personal elaboration 2019)

Dimensions	Features	Authors
Attitude and behavior	Positive feelings; sentiment or affect; behaviors; status	Tran et al. 2015; Carroll 2008
Dynamism	Pioneering approach; flexibility; activisms and goal orientation; modern; investments in R&D; new product development	Spector 1961; Dowling 1986
Cooperation	Being friendly and well liked; cares about local community; degree of familiarity	Specto, 1961; Dowling 1986; Tran et al. 2015
Reliability	Being persuasive; business wise and well-organized	Spector 1961; Dowling 1986
Ethics	Being ethical; reputable and respectful; equal opportunity employer; socially and environmentally responsible; protecting jobs of local workers	Spector 1961; Dowling 1986; Tran et al. 2015
Successfulness	Control of finance and high self-confidence; competent management; sound financial condition; regular dividend payments; sound financial investments	Spector 1961; Dowling 1986

Attitude and behavior are linked to the positive feelings and behaviors corporate images could refer to as well as to the status and sentiment images stimulate in stakeholders (Carroll 2008). *Dynamism* relates to a firm's pioneering or innovative approach. *Cooperation* refers to a firm's capacity to be familiar with and close to local communities. *Reliability* is linked to being perceived as well-organized and wise in the ways of business, while *ethics* refers to being perceived as ethical and respectful toward internal and external environments. Finally, *successfulness* is related to a firm's ability to manage finance, employees, and investments. If companies seek to derive any value from research on their image, communication professionals should know which are the "meaningful characteristics that reflect the dimensions the respondents use when they evaluate the corporations' image" (Spector 1961: 47).

Image determinants and formation process. Corporate images are based on stakeholders' experiences and perceptions of organizations or on organizational media communication (Kennedy 1977; Dowling 1986). More precisely, "sources of a company's image are extensive, and they are both person determined (people observing the company will selectively perceive different aspects of the company's communications) and object determined (people are simply forming their image of the company based on their reality of that company)" (Kennedy 1977: 110). To create or modify a corporate image, the first step is to focus on the *object-determined criteria*, meaning the information shared by organizations with their publics. Thus, organizations need to clearly define their *objective company criteria* (Kennedy 1977: 124) or *formal company policies* (Dowling 1986: 111), which are attributes or facts within an organization that could be identified by anyone looking for information about it. These terms refer to that information which is not open to personal interpretations by publics, such as that related to products, prices, corporate policies, and physical conditions (Dowling 1986). The second step consists of taking into account the *person-determined criteria*, meaning *company personnel's perception* (Kennedy 1977) or *employees' image* (Dowling 1986), and the *external group perception* (Kennedy 1977) or *external groups' image of the company* (Dowling 1986). *Person-determined criteria* refer to the different perceptions and interpretations of stakeholder sub-groups (internal or external). Different interpretations of the corporate image could reflect the communication that employees receive from the internal environment or their needs, norms, and values (Dowling 1986). Additionally, external groups of stakeholders contribute to modifying corporate image by evaluating corporate products and behaviors. Product usage and media communication, for instance, could positively or negatively influence stakeholders' experiences (Kennedy 1977).

In the image formation process, communication, corporate personality, and corporate identity are strongly linked (Abratt 1989; Tran et al. 2015). Organizations first define their personality and identity. Personality should be defined "before the company is formed by deciding on what it is to do, what it shall believe in, [and] how it shall operate all factors which constitute a corporate personality" (Abratt 1989: 67). Corporate identity can be defined as "an assembly of visual cues – physical and behavioral by which an audience can recognize the company and distinguish it from others and which can be used to represent or symbolize the company" (Abratt 1989: 68). Then the organization must translate personality and identity into "understandable tangible and intangible corporate image variables" (Tran et al. 2015: 102).

Corporate image evaluation. Since corporate image can be seen as an intangible asset, communication professionals need to implement effective evaluative techniques for measuring it. Van Riel, Stoeker, and Maarhuis (1998) articulated six different measurement techniques related to corporate image, as summarized in the following tables.

Table 3: Measurement techniques for corporate image (Sources: Carroll 2008; Mohan 1993; Treadwell and Harrison 1994; van Riel, Stroeker, and Maathuis 1998)

Measurement Techniques	Output	Usefulness
Attitude scales	Ranking of attributes capturing stakeholders' comparison between the organization and its competitors	Useful for collecting data that are representative of specific stakeholders' groups and comparable over time.
Content analysis	Media portrayals in terms of topics and favorability	Useful for determining audiences' likely degree of trust, admiration, and respect for an organization
Q-Sort	Deep insights into respondents' feelings about the company	Useful to investigate coherence between organizations' announcements and stakeholders' opinion
Photosort	Photographs symbolizing organizational values and the degree of stakeholders' appreciation	Useful as a projective technique with briefing aims
Laddering	Stakeholders' unstructured thoughts and mental links with the company	Useful for the study of the corporate image
Kelly Repertory Grid	List of attributes of corporate images	Useful for eliciting attributes of corporate image
Natural grouping	List of words associated w corporate image	Useful to measure the overall associations induced about the organization
Surveys	Perceptions of attractiveness or agreement with the image, or construal of other people's views	Allows for description and correlations of antecedents and outcomes

Measurement techniques for corporate image could differ depending on the type of collected data or the type of statistical procedure. Dowling (1988), for instance, distinguishes between attribute-based scaling procedures and non-attribute-based scaling procedures.

Attribute-based scaling procedures are useful to measure corporate image using a detailed set of attributes that respondents rate. The most common measurement techniques include snake plots, factor analysis, and joint space multidimensional scaling

(MDS). Non-attribute-based scaling procedures can be used to describe organizations by creating a list of attributes.

The most common measurement techniques include unstructured interviews, focus groups, object scoring methods, ordered scaling, the Kelly Repertory Grid, and simple space multidimensional scaling (MDS) (Dowling 1988; van Riel, Stroeker, and Maathuis 1998).

3 Public relations professionals as reputation managers

After exploring the concept of image, investigating reputation and the role of public relations as a reputation management function can help professionals to face current and future trends within the field. Image and reputation are interrelated concepts. As mentioned above, image can be considered a component of reputation, but reputation is also considered a type of image (Dutton, Dukerich, and Harquail 1994; Carroll 2009).

Organizational reputation refers to what is generally said about an organization that "defines" it – what it is about, what it stands for, what it does, with whom it associates, and/or how it deviates from (or exceeds) social expectations – or what it is material to know (Carroll 2016). The concept of reputation has been explored by a wide range of academic disciplines which have examined different dimensions from their own perspectives. While this multi-perspective approach has stimulated an increasing interest in the concept of reputation among researchers and professionals, it has also emphasized its definitional problem. Reputation can be explored according to seven different disciplinary areas (Carroll 2013; Fombrun and van Riel 1997): accountancy, economics, marketing, organizational behavior, sociology, strategy, and communication.

Accountants view reputation as an intangible asset with financial worth that can play a relevant role in creating competitive advantage for the organization (Rindova and Fombrun 1999; Romenti 2016). *Economists* consider reputation an informative signal of organizational attractiveness, or of the quality of products and features, addressed to all stakeholders (Kreps and Wilson 1982; Fombrun and van Riel 1997; Romenti 2016). *Marketers* consider reputation synonymous with corporate image, as it is based on the pictures stakeholders create in their minds from the information at their disposal (Lippmann 1922; Balmer 1995; Romenti 2016). *Organizational scholars* view reputation as strictly linked to the concepts of organizational culture and identity. According to them, reputation is based on the sense-making experience of employees, which, in the case of a strong culture and identity, could affect how internal stakeholders perceive and interpret the organizational reality and how they present themselves and the organization to external stakeholders (Dutton and Dukerich 1991; Fombrun and van Riel 1997; Romenti 2016). *Sociologists* view reputation as an indicator of legitimacy, since it is based on the satisfaction of the social expectations expressed by multiple stakeholders and on the interactional norms characterizing the institutional field in which the organization-stakeholder relationships occur (Fombrun and van Riel 1997; Romenti 2016). *Strategists* have underlined the dual nature of corporate reputation: it can be viewed as an intangible asset but also as a barrier to imitation by competitors, since reputation is based on a firm's specific and unique internal features (Fombrun and van Riel 1997; Romenti 2016). Finally, *communication scholars* define reputation as what is generally said about an organization (Carroll 2013, 2015). It is nurtured by direct experiences with the company, the word of mouth, and direct communication implemented by the organization (Fombrun 1996; Romenti 2016).

Continued work on defining reputation has unfolded in two directions, one still focused on perceptions – lending itself to quasi-analytic, multivariate modeling – and the other focused on reputation as claims (Whetten and Mackey 2002), with a focus on content and what people say.

In the first direction, organizational reputation can be thought of as a multidimensional concept comprising five dimensions: public prominence, public esteem, properties/attributes, plexes and positioning (Carroll 2010, 2015; Lange, Lee, and Dai 2011). Organizational prominence concerns an organization's top-of-mind awareness, publicity, and familiarity among the public. Before a firm can be said to have a reputation, people must be familiar with it. This raises the question of whether all firms even have reputations; some do not. Public esteem is the degree to which an organization is liked, trusted, admired, regarded, or respected by the public. The third dimension, properties/attributes, concerns what the organization has a reputation for. Although some organizations are known for being known (often termed "celebrity"), this third dimension concerns organizational traits or performance levels. Reputation attributes can be thought of in various ways, the most common of which deal with organizational performance or competencies, such as executive leadership, workplace performance, corporate social responsibility/citizenship, products and services, and financial performance. This list of attributes has been expanded in recent years to include governance, ethics, innovation, efficiency, dependability, quality, and reliability. Corporate social responsibility has also been broken down into several areas such as workforce diversity, environmental performance, and philanthropy. Concerning the fourth dimension, plexes, Carroll (2015) argues that plexes are the network connections an organization has to the larger reputational ecosystem. Plexes are similar to corporate associations. Plexes can also be an organization's connections to public issues and current events; its supply chain or its place in the industry; its stance on social, economic, and political issues; and how well the organization treats (and is treated by) others. The concept of plexes focuses on an organization's linkages. Finally, the fifth dimension, positioning, refers to how all of these other elements connect together as a whole in a particular sequence, as well as how that sequence is timed.

In the second direction, focusing on reputation as claims, the AC4ID Framework (Carroll, Greyser and Schreiber 2011) identifies several types of organizational reputation that are often juxtaposed with one another. The *actual reputation* captures the perception-based dimension of the first direction, as observed by individual stakeholders. The *communicated reputation* refers to the reputation promoted or communicated by the organization itself, either through controllable media (advertising, marketing, public relations, or sponsorships) or uncontrollable media (word of mouth, news reports, commentary, or social media). The *conceived reputation* refers to the co-constructed view of reputation as constituents "make sense" of an organization's reputation publicly. *Construed reputation* refers to what top management believes other people think (or another stakeholder thinks) is the organization's reputation. The *covenanted reputation* refers to the reputation created by the brand's promises or stakeholders' expectations. The *ideal reputation* refers to what market research reveals as the organization's optimal positioning of itself, given the economic, industry, or political realities the organization faces within its market; the ideal reputation is based on data. The *desired reputation* refers to the aspirations of organizational leaders, regardless of what the data or others tell them is feasible. Both views of reputation today place a greater focus on assessments, estimation, judgement, and opinions as social facts more than mere perceptions, and point to the multiple nature of reputation, which is evaluative, perceptual, and communicative.

The evaluative nature of reputation and the increasing interest in its measurement. First of all, reputation has an evaluative nature, as it is considered one of the "most important strategic resources" of an organization (Flanagan and O'Shaughnessy 2005: 445). Like other intangible assets, it plays a competitive role, as it helps organizations distinguish themselves from competitors, affects stakeholders' perception of quality, reduces information asymmetry, improves market prominence, and contributes to value creation (Boyd, Bergh, and Ketchen 2010). It represents the deep evaluation (respect, esteem, estimation) of an organization's image, and more specifically, it amounts an evaluation of the organization's strategic type by specific groups of stakeholders such as customers or alliance partners (Rindova et al. 2005). Its value is determined through the interactions and interrelationships among multiple attributes, both internal and external to the firm (Barney 1991; Roberts and Dowling 2002). Due to its evaluative nature, it is possible to identify several antecedents to the dimensions of reputation previously discussed.

The quality of products, and consequently the perceived quality dimensions, can be affected by organizational inputs used in the production processes and by the quality of the organization's productive assets (or knowledge assets). Prominence can also be affected by certifications from institutional intermediaries, such as media rankings, and by affiliation with high-status actors (Rindova et al. 2005). As an intangible asset, reputation can vary in terms of prominence (level of accumulation) and in terms of quality (level of stock).

The evaluative nature of reputation has stimulated academic and professional research into its measurement, and specifically into defining reliable paths for measuring its value. As Helm and Klode (2011: 87) noted, corporate reputation can be considered as a "driver of corporate performance"; but, in order to be managed, corporate reputation must first be measured (Gardberg and Fombrun 2002).

The perceptual nature of reputation. Second, reputation has a perceptual nature. Similar to corporate image, corporate reputation refers to the perceptions of an organization, but differently from image, it is "built up over a period of time and it focuses on what it does and how it behaves" (Balmer 1998: 971). As Wartick (2002: 374) described the process, "some individual, group, or larger human collective gathers and processes information about past actions of a business and draws conclusions (i. e. overall appeal) about a business's future prospects". Reputation can be considered an aggregation of individual impressions, characterized by three main features: the role of perception and impression, the importance of time, and the relevance of interactions.

The crucial role of perceptions means that "reputation can develop somewhat independent of reality, and is thus socially constructed" (Walker 2010: 369). In this regard, Highhouse, Brooks, and Gregarus (2009) have developed an illustrative model of the individual impression development process applied to corporate reputation with the aim of explaining how the individual's impression of an organization is formed and how it constitutes corporate reputation when it is aggregated with other individual impressions. As the following table shows, the model is based on three main phases: cues signaling corporate attributes; images in the minds of constituents; and finally, impressions of corporations.

Table 4: An illustrative model of the individual impression development process (Source: Highhouse, Brooks, and Gregarus 2009)

1. Cues signaling corporate attributes	2. Images in the minds of constituents	3. Constituents impressions of corporation
– Organizational investments – External factors	– Market Image – Employer image – Financial Image – CSR image	– Respectability – Impressiveness

According to the model, it is possible to identify specific cues signaling corporate attributes. These could be manipulated directly by organizations through actions such as organizational investments in social capital, human capital, product development, and diversification, but also through advertising, public relations, and CSR policy. Cues could also be beyond organizational control and be related to external factors, such as word of mouth and media exposure. Cues could affect the different images of a company in the minds of its different constituents, such as its market, employer, financial, and CSR images. By taking into consideration the aggregate perceptions of all stakeholders, the perceptual perspective on reputation emphasizes two relevant features: reputation is a social and a collective concept. Viewing reputation as an aggregate perception invites communication professionals to consider two main elements: reputation is often issue-specific, and it can vary according to stakeholder group (Walker 2010). In managing perceptual reputation, then, it is crucial to ask which issue reputation is related to and according to whom (Lewellyn 2002).

The communicative nature of reputation. Finally, reputation has a communicative nature. The concept of reputation is linked to stakeholders' expectations of organizations and to the ability of organizations to cultivate, nurture, and maintain effective relationships within the competitive scenario. In this regard, three operative terms can be linked to reputation: expectations, diversity, and competition. Carroll, Greyser, and Schreiber (2011: 460) argued that "reputation is what stakeholders say about the expectation of an organization's value vis-à-vis an organization's peers and competitors". Carroll, Greyser, and Schreiber (2011) took into consideration the expectations of value expressed by stakeholders; the non-monolithic character of reputation, which is stakeholder-group specific; and finally, the competitive nature of the concept, which helps an organization to build value and to take value from its competitors.

The relational nature of the term has stimulated research into the role of emotions in attributing legitimacy to an organization and developing trust and loyalty towards it (Kim and Lennon 2013; de Albornoz, Plaza, and Gervás 2012). If organizations ignore or disregard stakeholders' expectations, their behavior could affect emotional aspects of the organization-stakeholder relationship, negatively impacting corporate reputation (MacMillan et al. 2005). According to Alsop (2004), the emotional bond between organizations and their stakeholders is crucial to the most enduring reputations. Emotions can affect organization-stakeholder relationships and behaviors, as "a consumer's emotional attachment (...) induces a state of emotion-laden readiness that influences his or her allocation of emotional, cognitive, and behavioral resources toward a particular target" (Park and MacInnis 2006: 17). Being able to recognize and manage stakeholders' emotions could represent a challenge for reputation managers, as it affects how communication professionals could and should interpret their publics' behavior and how they can help organizations to develop empathic communication initiatives.

4 Beyond distinctions: implications for and contribution of the public relations function

If we can move beyond the recurring distinction between image and reputation, image and reputation management can change and shape our thinking of public relations as profession. Transcending the traditional distinction between image and reputation means that communication professionals can turn their focus to three main issues: understanding whether image and reputation can be managed and how; exploring whether image and reputation can be engaged directly or indirectly; and finally, recognizing that a professional needs to be in charge of managing corporate image and reputation within a company.

As to the first issue, some scholars have expressed the possibility of managing both image and reputation as strategic assets of an organization; from this perspective, image and reputation are viewed as both liability and capital, and thus are owned by organizations. This view contrasts with that of organizational communication scholars who view image and reputation as co-constructed by different constituents, such as an organization, its members, external audiences, and other stakeholder groups.

Regarding the second issue, reputation should be engaged directly or indirectly. The direct approach is based on organizational-public relationships that are reputation-based and reputation-mediated; the indirect approach implies that organizations are not involved in managing reputation but rather in developing relationships that could indirectly affect the corporate reputation.

Concerning the third issue – the recognition of a person in charge for managing, developing, and protecting organization's reputation – this responsibility is shared among different roles: the chief executive officer (CEO), the board of directors, the chief communication officer (CCO), and every member of the organization. In any case, communication and public relations professionals need to be aware of the impact of organizational image and reputation on their aims and performance. Effectively enhancing organizational reputation requires professionals able to strategically manage image and reputation as intangible assets of an organization (Dowling 1993; Rindova, Williamson, and Petkova 2010). They also need to carefully manage organizational reputational intelligence concerning the internal or external environment (Carroll, Greyser, and Schreiber 2011), taking into account cognitive, affective, and behavioural information about the various stakeholders and publics who play relevant roles in image and reputation-building strategies. Finally, communication professionals need to nurture interdependencies and cultivate complex relationships, as both image and reputation are socially constructed concepts based on relational and interactional dynamics (Boyd, Bergh, and Ketchen 2010). Given this scenario, the public relations function could contribute to the management of organizational image and reputation at different levels.

First, in managing the image formation process, the PR function helps organizations in transforming personality and identity into coherent corporate image components. It also provides support in converting corporate image from awareness to familiarity, then to favorability, and finally, to trust and advocacy (Tran et al. 2015). Its role is to assure consistency and congruency between the corporate image and reality (Abratt 1989).

Second, public relations can act as a bridging function, helping the organization to understand how individuals place the organization in specific categories, such as marketing or product categories, specific industries or organizational forms, or even organizational positions on critical issues.

Finally, the reflective function of public relations can help professionals support an organization in evaluating the management of its reputational risk (Brivot, Gendron, and Guénin 2017; Graafland 2017). The concept of reputational risk is becoming not only "a strategic management category but also a logic of organizing" or "an important cognitive frame and reflexive orientation" (Power et al. 2009: 309). The reflective function of public relations is crucial, as it assists in selecting information from publics that could help organizational members balance their behaviors and initiatives.

5 Future research

Communication scholars exploring the concepts of image and reputation will have multiple future streams of research they can follow (Carroll 2017). These include (a) the link between image, reputation, and organizational communication routines; (b) the management of the dark side of reputation; (c) the ethical issues related to reputation management; (d) the moderating role of organizational culture and its impact on corporate image and reputation; and (e) the effects of online dynamics on the concept of reputation.

The link between image, reputation, and organizational communication routines. Communication scholars have underestimated the impact of image and reputational issues on ordinary communication activities, and vice versa. Reputation, for instance, has been investigated in relation to exceptional communicative scenarios such as crisis management. A possible stream of research could focus on analyzing how to exploit the communicative resources at the disposal of professionals for routine communication behavior, with the aim of implementing image and reputation-building processes.

Managing the dark side of reputation. Recently, some companies have implemented aggressive reputation-management tactics, such as creating fraudulent reviews by exploiting less-resourced individuals or manipulating online information processes to hide the truth. These companies, called "brand bullies," are expert in demolition rather than in enhancement of reputation. Research in this area could focus on specific concepts such as executive hubris, fake news management, and political influence.

Ethical issues related to the reputation management process. Increasingly, corporate reputation has been related to ethical and moral issues: to build a good reputation, a pattern of ethical behavior is crucial. Some examples come from the internal context and more specifically from employee-management strategies and tactics. Reputation has been explored as an intangible asset useful in attracting a talented workforce, but little attention has been paid to the workforce compensation, leaving the impression that a good corporate reputation justifies poor pay systems (Carroll 2013). Relevant to this, communication scholars could focus more on the linkages among reputation, accountability, and ethics.

The moderating role of organizational culture and its impact on corporate image and reputation. The perceptual nature of reputation has encouraged analyses of the moderating role of the culture in the image and reputation management process (Flatt and Kowalczyk 2008; Bartikowski et al. 2011). Most of the research has focused on the role of organizational culture, identifying culture as a factor that can significantly influence the development and management of reputation (Flatt and Kowalczyk 2008). Since organizational culture impacts organizational strategy definition and implementation, it could also influence image and reputation-building strategies (Weigelt and Camerer 1988). Few studies have examined the role of individual culture in the image and reputation development process. Cultural values, habits, and issues could affect how individuals perceive corporate reputation and develop their impressions over time. Communication scholars could deepen our knowledge in this area by conducting empirical research comparing how these processes work in different cultures.

Effects of online dynamics on reputation. Current measurement models have focused on offline reputation, underestimating the effect of online dynamics and the concept of digital reputation. Romenti et al. (2015: 261) have defined digital reputation "as the quantity and quality of coverage of different organizational issues in the digital environment, as threats of online discussions among relevant nodes of networks, or as a reflection of real (offline) reputation." Models and methods for measuring online reputation have been predominantly developed at the professional level (for instance, the RepTrak® Pulse score by the Reputation Institute) and few scholars have focused their attention on the topic (Romenti et al. 2015). Therefore, communication scholars could focus on developing models, measurement techniques, and methods that integrate offline and online reputation.

To sum up, we invite communication scholars to move beyond traditional research avenues in order to take into account new theoretical and practical phenomena such as the link between reputation and communication satisfaction, internal stakeholders' empowerment, stakeholders' well-being, and routine communication processes such as listening and feedback management.

References

Abratt, Russell. 1989. A new approach to the corporate image management process. *Journal of Marketing Management* 5(1). 63–76
Alsop, Ronald J. 2004. Corporate Reputation: anything but superficial – the deep but fragile nature of corporate reputation. *Journal of Business Strategy* 25(6). 21–29.

Andreassen, Tor Wallin & Bodil Lindestad. 1998. The effect of corporate image in the formation of customer loyalty. *Journal of Service Research* 1(1). 82–92.

Atvesson, Mats. 1990. Organization: from substance to image? *Organization Studies* 11(3). 373–394.

Balmer, John M. T. 1995. Corporate branding and connoisseurship. *Journal of General management* 21(1). 24–46.

Balmer, John M. T. 1998. Corporate identity and the advent of corporate marketing. *Journal of Marketing Management* 14(8). 963–996.

Balmer, John M. T. & Stephen A. Greyser. 2006. Corporate marketing: Integrating corporate identity, corporate branding, corporate communications, corporate image and corporate reputation. *European Journal of Marketing* 40(7/8). 730–741.

Barich, Howard & Philip Kotler. 1991. A framework for marketing image management. *MIT Sloan Management Review* 32(2). 94.

Barney, Jay. 1991. Firm resources and sustained competitive advantage. *Journal of Management* 17(1). 99–120.

Bartikowski, Boris, Gianfranco Walsh & Sharon E. Beatty. 2011. Culture and age as moderators in the corporate reputation and loyalty relationship. *Journal of Business Research* 64(9). 966–972.

Bernstein, David. 1984. *Company image and reality: A critique of corporate communications*. New York: Taylor & Francis.

Boyd, Brian K., Donald D. Bergh & David J. Ketchen Jr. 2010. Reconsidering the reputation-performance relationship: A resource-based view, *Journal of Management* 36(3). 588–609.

Brivot, Marion, Yves Gendron & Henry Guénin. 2017. Reinventing organizational control: Meaning contest surrounding reputational risk controllability in the social media arena. *Accounting, Auditing & Accountability Journal* 30(4). 795–820.

Caillouet, Rachel Harris & Myria Watkins Allen. 1996. Impression management strategies employees use when discussing their organization's public image. *Journal of Public Relations Research* 8(4). 211–227.

Carroll, Craig E. 1995. Rearticulating organizational identity: Exploring corporate images and employee identification. *Management Learning* 26(4). 467–486.

Carroll, Craig E. 2008. Organizational Image. In Wolfgang Donsbach (ed.), *International Encyclopedia of Communication*, 3464–3469. Oxford: Wiley-Blackwell.

Carroll, Craig E. 2009. The Relationship between Media Favorability and Firms' Public Esteem. *Public Relations Journal* 3(4). 1–32.

Carroll, Craig E. (ed). 2010. *Corporate Reputation and the news media: Agenda-setting within business news coverage in developed, emerging, and frontier markets*. New York: Routledge

Carroll, Craig E. 2013. The future of communication research in corporate reputation studies. In Craig E. Carroll (ed.), *The Handbook of Communication and Corporate Reputation*, 590–596. Oxford: Blackwell.

Carroll, Craig E. 2015. Matching dimensions of reputation and media salience for feedback, alignment, and organizational self-awareness. *Vikalpa: Journal for Decision Makers* 40(4). 480–485.

Carroll, Craig E. (ed.). 2016. *The SAGE encyclopedia of corporate reputation*. Thousand Oaks, CA: Sage Publications.

Carroll, Craig E. 2017. Reputation. In C. R. Scott & L. K. Lewis (eds.), *The International Encyclopedia of Organizational Communication*. New York: John Wiley & Sons.

Carroll, Craig E., Stephen A. Greyser & Elliot Schreiber. 2011. Building and maintaining reputation through communications. In C. Caywood (ed.), *The International Handbook of Strategic Public Relations & Integrated Communications*, 457–476. New York: McGraw-Hill.

de Albornoz, Jorge C., Laura Plaza & Pablo Gervás. 2012. SentiSense: An easily scalable concept-based affective lexicon for sentiment analysis. *LREC* 12. 3562–3567.

Dowling, Grahame R. 1986. Managing your corporate images. *Industrial Marketing Management* 15(2). 109–115.

Dowling, Grahame R. 1988. Measuring corporate images: A review of alternative approaches. *Journal of Business Research* 17(1). 27–34.

Dowling, Grahame R. 1993. Developing your company image into a corporate asset. *Long Range Planning* 26(2). 101–109.

Dutton, Jane E. & Janet M. Dukerich. 1991. Keeping an eye on the mirror: Image and identity in organizational adaptation. *Academy of Management Journal* 34(3). 517–554.

Dutton, Jane E., Janet M. Dukerich & Celia V. Harquail. 1994. Organizational images and member identification. *Administrative Science Quarterly*. 239–263.

Fairholm, Matthew R. 2009. Leadership and Organizational Strategy. *Innovation Journal* 14(1). 1–16.

Flanagan, David J. & Kenneth C. O'Shaughnessy. 2005. The effect of layoffs on firm reputation. *Journal of Management* 31(3). 445–463.

Flatt, Sylvia J. & Stanley J. Kowalczyk. 2008. Creating competitive advantage through intangible assets: The direct and indirect effects of corporate culture and reputation. *Journal of Competitiveness Studies* 16(1/2). 13–30.

Fombrun, Charles J. 1996. *Reputation*. Boston: John Wiley & Sons.

Fombrun, Charles J. & Cies B. van Riel. 1997. The reputational landscape. *Corporate Reputation Review* 1(2). 5–13.

Gardberg, Naomi A. & Charles J. Fombrun. 2002. The global reputation quotient project: First steps towards a cross-nationally valid measure of corporate reputation. *Corporate Reputation Review* 4(4). 303–307.

Gioia, Dennis A., Majken Schultz & Kevin G. Corley. 2000. Organizational identity, image, and adaptive instability. *Academy of Management Review* 25(1). 63–81.

Graafland, Johan. 2017. Religiosity, attitude, and the demand for socially responsible products. *Journal of Business Ethics* 144(1). 121–138.

Grunig, James E. 1993. Image and substance: From symbolic to behavioral relationships. *Public Relations Review* 19(2). 121–139.

Hatch, Mary Jo & Majken Schultz. 1997. Relations between organizational culture, identity and image. *European Journal of Marketing* 31(5/6). 356–365.

Helm, Sabrina & Christian Klode. 2011. Challenges in measuring corporate reputation. In Sabrina Helm, Kerstin Liehr-Gobbers & Christopher Storck (eds.), *Reputation Management*, 87–110. Berlin: Springer.

Highhouse, Scott, Margaret E. Brooks & Gary Gregarus. 2009. An organizational impression management perspective on the formation of corporate reputations. *Journal of Management* 35(6). 1481–1493.

Kennedy, Sherril H. 1977. Nurturing corporate images. *European Journal of Marketing* 11(3). 119–164.

Kim, Jiyoung & Sharron J. Lennon. 2013. Effects of reputation and website quality on online consumers' emotion, perceived risk and purchase intention: Based on the stimulus-organism-response model. *Journal of Research in Interactive Marketing* 7(1). 33–56

Kreps, David M. & Robert Wilson. 1982. Reputation and imperfect information. *Journal of Economic Theory* 27(2). 253–279.

Lange, Donald, Peggy M. Lee & Ye Dai. 2011. Organizational reputation: A review. *Journal of Management* 37(1). 153–184

L'Etang, Jacquie. 2009. Public relations and diplomacy in a globalized world: An issue of public communication. *American Behavioral Scientist* 53(4). 607–626.

Lai, Fujun, Mitch Griffin & Barry J. Babin. 2009. How quality, value, image, and satisfaction create loyalty at a Chinese telecom. *Journal of Business Research* 62(10). 980–986.

Lewellyn, Patsy G. 2002. Corporate reputation: Focusing the zeitgeist. *Business & Society* 41(4). 446–455.

Lippmann, Walter. 1922. *Public Opinion*. New York: Hartcourt Brace.

MacMillan, Keith, Kevin Money, Steve Downing & Carola Hillenbrand. 2005. Reputation in relationships: Measuring experiences, emotions and behaviors. *Corporate Reputation Review* 8(3). 214–232.

Martineau, Pierre. 1958. Sharper focus for the corporate image. *Harvard Business Review* 36(6). 49–58.

Merrin, William. 2005. *Baudrillard and the media: A critical introduction*. Cambridge: Polity.

Mohan, Mary Leslie. 1993. *Organizational communication and cultural vision: Approaches for analysis*. Albany, NY: SUNY Press.

Nguyen, Nha. & Gaston Leblanc. 2001. Corporate image and corporate reputation in customers' retention decisions in services. *Journal of Retailing and Consumer Services* 8(4). 227–236.

Olins, Wally. 1995. *The new guide to identity*. London: Gower.

Park, C. Whan & Deborah J. MacInnis. 2006. What's in and what's out: Questions on the boundaries of the attitude construct. *Journal of Consumer Research* 33(1). 16–18.

Power, Michael, Tobias Scheytt, Kim Soin & Kerstin Sahlin. 2009. Reputational risk as a logic of organizing in late modernity. *Organization studies* 30(2–3). 301–324.

Rindova, Violina P. & Charles J. Fombrun. 1999. Constructing competitive advantage: The role of firm-constituent interactions. *Strategic Management Journal* 20(8). 691–710.

Rindova, Violina P., Ian O. Williamson & Antoaneta P. Petkova. 2010. Reputation as an intangible asset: Reflections on theory and methods in two empirical studies of business school reputations. *Journal of Management* 36(3). 610–619.

Rindova, Violina P., Ian O. Williamson, Antoaneta P. Petkova & Joe Marie Sever. 2005. Being good or being known: An empirical examination of the dimensions, antecedents, and consequences of organizational reputation. *Academy of Management Journal* 48(6). 1033–1049.

Riordan, Christine M., Robert D. Gatewood & Jodi Barnes Bill. 1997. Corporate image: Employee reactions and implications for managing corporate social performance. *Journal of Business Ethics* 16(4). 401–412.

Roberts, Peter W. & Grahame R. Dowling. 2002. Corporate reputation and sustained superior financial performance. *Strategic Management Journal* 23(12). 1077–1093.

Romenti, Stefania. 2016. *Misurare il capitale comunicativo.: Modelli e indicatori di performance della comunicazione per le imprese*. Milano: Franco Angeli.

Romenti, Stefania, Chiara Valentini, Grazia Murtarelli & Eleonora Cipolletta. 2015. A reputation measurement model for online stakeholders: concepts, evidence and implications. In Enric Ordeix, Valérie Carayol & Ralph Tench (eds.), *Public Relations, Values and Identity*. Brussels: Peter Lang. 253–274.

Spector, Aaron J. 1961. Basic dimensions of the corporate image. *The Journal of Marketing* 25(6). 47–51.

Stern, Barbara, George M. Zinkhan & Anupam Jaju. 2001. Marketing images: Construct definition, measurement issues, and theory development. *Marketing Theory* 1(2). 201–224.

Tran, Mai An, Bang Nguyen, T.C. Melewar & Jim Bodoh. 2015. Exploring the corporate image formation process. *Qualitative Market Research: An International Journal* 18(1). 86–114.

Treadwell, Donald F. & Teresa M. Harrison. 1994. Conceptualizing and assessing organizational image: Model images, commitment, and communication. *Communications Monographs* 61(1). 63–85.

Turban, Daniel B. & Daniel W. Greening. 1997. Corporate social performance and organizational attractiveness to prospective employees. *Academy of Management Journal* 40(3). 658–672.

van Riel, Cees B., Natasha Els Stroeker & Onno Johannes Maria Maathuis. 1998. Measuring corporate images. *Corporate Reputation Review* 1(4). 313–326.

Walker, Kent. 2010. A systematic review of the corporate reputation literature: Definition, measurement, and theory. *Corporate Reputation Review* 12(4). 357–387.

Wartick, Steven L. 2002. Measuring Corporate Reputation: Definition and Data. *Business & Society* 4(4).

Weigelt, Keith & Colin Camerer. 1988. Reputation and corporate strategy: A review of recent theory and applications. *Strategic Management Journal* 9(5). 443–454.

Whetten, David A. & Alison Mackey. A social actor conception of organizational identity and its implications for the study of organizational reputation. *Business & Society* 41(4). 393–414.

Williams, Sheryl L. & Mary Anne Moffitt. 1997. Corporate image as an impression formation process: Prioritizing personal, organizational, and environmental audience factors. *Journal of Public Relations Research* 9(4). 237–258.

Worcester, Robert. 2009. Reflections on corporate reputations. *Management Decision* 47(4). 573–589.

Audra Diers-Lawson and Augustine Pang

11 Strategic crisis management: State of the field, challenges and opportunities

Abstract: This chapter examines the field of strategic crisis management and argues that over the last 50–60 years the field has developed from one focused on post-crisis image recovery to one that highlights the importance of risk management to minimize or mitigate risks for organizations in order to preserve an organization's image. The chapter first explores the development and changes in the field, then highlights the internationalization occurring in research, as well as the continuing need for diverse, non-Western voices in the field to emerge, and finally explores the crisis management life cycle as a way to engage stakeholders and mitigate risks to an organization's reputation with its stakeholders. We conclude the chapter by discussing what professionals can do to manage issues, risks and crises.

Keywords: Crisis management; risks; issues; life cycle; reputation; image; scanning; monitoring; stakeholder relationship

1 Introduction

Organizations are, literally, experiencing and battling issues of some form or another every day. Due to the vulnerability of the organization to both internal and external uncertainties, no organization is immune from crises. The reality is the inevitability of challenges. If preserving a good image is the paramount task of public relations (Pang 2012), then the role of public relations remains ever relevant and increasing in importance as it manages the interrelated concepts of issues, risks and crises. This chapter offers an overview of the development of crisis management, the state of crisis management, how crisis management can be examined through a life cycle and how public relations professionals can respond, as well as identifying the challenges for public relations professionals to consider in managing issues, risks, and crises.

2 Crisis management: How far have we travelled?

From the first study of crises and crisis communication in the mid-20th century to the turn of the century, crises were generally thought of as a "low probability, high-impact event that threatens the viability of the organization and is characterized by ambiguity of cause, effect, and means of resolution, as well as by a belief that decisions must be

https://doi.org/10.1515/9783110554250-011

made quickly" (Pearson and Clair 1998: 60). This definition of crisis was supported by the small body of research that had emerged throughout the previous 40 years.

However while both practitioners and academics recognized that crises are challenging because they are often ill-structured and complex (Mitroff, Alpaslan, and Green 2004), they had also witnessed a growing and diverse number of crises, such as the 1989 Exxon Valdez oil spill in Alaska (Taylor 2014), the tainted blood scandal from the American Red Cross in the early 1990s (Hilts 1990), Enron's accounting scandal of 2001 (Seeger and Ulmer 2003), and the terrorist attacks of 2001 (Argenti 2002). As a result of the risks posed by modern crises in an information-rich world, the research interest in crisis management and crisis communication began to grow substantially.

These new experiences with crisis demonstrated that crises can affect all types of organizations. The causes of the crises can range from circumstances entirely out of an organization's control to careless mistakes of individuals within an organization to systematic breakdowns or inefficiencies (Argenti 2002; King 2002; Pearson and Clair 1998; Reilly 1987). With the growth of interest in crises, crisis management, and crisis communication, how we define a crisis has also evolved. Instead of thinking of crises as low-probability and high-impact events with ambiguous causes and outcomes, we should be thinking of crises differently:

A crisis is typically defined as an untimely but predictable event that has actual or potential consequences for stakeholders' interests as well as the reputation of the organization (...) That means a crisis can harm stakeholders and damage the organization's relationship with them (...) Respond well and survive the crisis; respond poorly and suffer the death of the organization's reputation or perhaps itself (Heath and Millar 2004: 2).

Heath and Millar's (2004) definition of crisis provides us with a few important characteristics of crises that seem to be consistent across different types of crisis, in different parts of the world, and with different levels of blame and severity. First, crises are inherently public in nature (Moore 2004); therefore, to understand crisis management, we ought to understand the nature of crisis communication. In fact, what should be clear in Heath and Millar's definition of crisis is strategic planning around crisis risk ought to be an inherent part of doing business in the 21st century. Second, while crises happen to or because of an organization, organizations do not exist in isolation. Crises affect people – people within the organization, its community, country, and the region(s) in which it operates. This means that crisis management and crisis communication should always be focused on the people and groups with an interest in the organization and its activities – that is, its stakeholders (Freeman 1999; Jin, Pang, and Cameron 2012). Third, a core stake at risk in a crisis is the relationship between an organization and its stakeholder(s). If the relationships fail, then outcomes of that failure can range from reputational damage to the failure of the organization and/or its mission. Likewise, if the relationship is strengthened, then an organization can prosper despite the crisis – or perhaps even because of the crisis.

This definition of a crisis also suggests there are two parts to crisis response. The first is the material crisis response – that is, solving the problem that triggered the crisis. The material crisis response can include mitigating the effects of the crisis, recovery of control of the situation, fact-finding, and/or damage control. If we think of crisis management as the material part of crisis response, then it is clear that it is intertwined with risk management and crisis communication. Jindal, Laveena, and Aggarwal (2015) define crisis management as a process allowing organizations to deal with major problems that pose a threat to the organization and/or its stakeholders. For organizations, crisis management is a learned behavior that focuses on mitigation and control of the internal and external dynamics of the crisis itself; yet it is not like being a mechanic that finds a problem in the car and fixes it – it is still about managing people and their decisions.

The second part is crisis communication. Crisis communication involves three equally important elements:
- Stakeholder Relationship Management: Managing, building, or rebuilding stakeholder relationships,
- Narrating the Crisis: Media engagement, direct stakeholder engagement across different platforms of communication – from face-to-face to social media,
- Communication Strategy Development and Implementation: A campaign-based approach using measurable objectives, good intelligence, and continual evaluation of the effectiveness of the approach.

2.1 A brief history of the growth of crisis management research

In addition to the growth and emergence of crisis studies as a field of practice in public relations and business studies more broadly, in the last several years there has also been an interest in reflecting on the field. There have been three such analyses of crisis research in recent years. One tracked public relations scholarship trends (Kim et al. 2014), one examined crisis communication's interdisciplinary approach (Ha and Boynton 2014), and one analyzed all available research connected to crisis research across academic journals (Diers-Lawson 2017a, 2017b). Diers-Lawson (2017a, 2017b) provides three key changes in the research, theory development, and changes in the field over time.

Initially, the field was increasingly data-driven. The first wave of crisis research focused on questions of what crises are, how they fit within the communication and management domains, as well as "best practices." These are important pieces, but they are typically not empirical; instead they are meant for reflection and conceptual growth or development. The second wave of crisis research focused on the organization and its crisis response, emphasizing applied research and case studies that provided the groundwork for much of the theoretical developments of the late 1990s. As the field has been able to better define itself and understand the nature of crisis response from the organization's perspective, the third wave has emerged – research focused on the stakeholder. Here, the core questions focus on stakeholder reactions to crises, crisis response, and how that can affect the organization. Yet, some researchers argue that the third wave is unlikely to have a significant impact on practice because "historically, many practitioners have not made routine use of academic research on crisis communication that is and has long been available" (Lehmberg and Hicks 2018: 358).

Second, conceptual interests in crises have changed. In recent years, we have seen less of a focus on crisis management, internal crisis management, and crisis planning evidenced in the research. In part, this is probably attributable to the emergence of the third wave of crisis research and a move away from non-data-driven "best practices" pieces. However, the field's lack of focus on internal crisis management is potentially problematic. During a talk in 2014 at the University of Manchester, Brian Gilvary – BP's chief financial officer throughout the 2010 Gulf of Mexico crisis – indicated that the hardest part of managing the financial side of the crisis was supporting the emotional experience for his employees as they watched the events unfold and were experiencing the crisis themselves. Yet, we see little new research emerging focusing on the employee experience of a crisis.

Third, crisis research is increasingly global. When we talk about crisis research, the voices we have heard in the past were disproportionately American, with about 60 percent of all empirical journal articles in crisis communication published since 1953 researching from an American point of view (Diers-Lawson, 2017a, 2017b). Though there has been a meaningful growth in research from Europe and Asia, the overwhelming majority of research has been dominated by Western voices, representing 83 percent of all crisis communication journal articles. Further, there is little research in crisis communication from the southern hemisphere. And this is the embarrassing reality – we know very little about crises, crisis management, and crisis communication across much of the world – especially the developing world.

Though this is a weakness in the field at present, the positive side is that this has been significantly changing with a decrease in U.S.-centric research, an increasing focus on Europe, an increasing focus on China, and overall a more global approach to crisis research. It is also important to note that this is not a grand conspiracy; rather, a reflection of the access to organizations, news, and information about crises by the academics who research crises. As our field grows and changes, research is also becoming more diverse. Additionally, as we become increasingly global, we will be able to get more views from practitioners and researchers representing voices from across the world. Moreover, the field of conflict studies tends to be less considered. It has only been in the last few years that questions about emergent global conflicts have begun to emerge within traditional studies of crises and crisis management. The two fields of study – conflict studies and crisis – were pursued by different scholars and typically people in different departments of study with little overlap. That too seems to be changing as the interconnectedness of issues, organizations, and stakeholders is increasingly recognized.

2.2 Crisis management in the 21st century

Certainly, crisis research will continue to develop and change with time. Inasmuch as it is useful to have a broad overview of crisis research, it is also useful to understand the influence that different fields have on research and practice connected to the field. This influences the present as much as do questions of culture, changing technologies, and stakeholders. Not surprisingly, much of the focus for crisis research is connected to management and business, communication and language, and the social sciences and humanities. However, research in crisis communication is applied across most fields of practice.

3 Crisis management and the intersection of risk, issues, and crisis

Since we discussed what crises are and began to differentiate between crisis management and crisis communication, we should deepen our understanding of crises in applied contexts. A crisis can represent any situation from a customer-service crisis played out on social media to major disease outbreaks or armed conflicts around the world. There are three characteristics that all crises share:
– They are inherently public,
– Organizations trying to manage crises do not exist in isolation; rather, there are complex relationships that influences the choices organizations make,
– A core stake at risk in a crisis is the relationship between an organization and its stakeholder(s).

If we assume that there are many different types of crises, but they all share these three characteristics, then we can focus on understanding the process connecting risk management through crisis response. By focusing on the process, it should become clear that communication and management are both necessary and complementary, but have different responsibilities throughout the process. This means that responding to crises is both a public relations and a management function. We also made the point that one of the key shifts in our understanding of crises in the last couple of decades was that crises should not be considered surprises. In fact, Heath and Millar (2004) argue that crises should not be viewed as unpredictable, just untimely. This means that modern crisis management and communication is as much about risk management as it is about responding to crises once they emerge.

3.1 Risks and risk detection

Risk is often a difficult concept for social or behavioral scientists to unpack because much of what we must manage is peoples' perception of risk rather than the probability that a crisis will happen (Freundberg 1988). For example, an engineer can calculate the probability that a bridge will fail, or an infectious disease expert can calculate the spread of disease based on population density and a number of other factors; however in many cases, risk management is not about the material risk but about the reduction of the perception of risk via the communication of information about the risk.

One of the challenges in this process is that technical information must be translated and that public decisions about risk are not always rational (Freundberg 1988). In exploring reactions to the impact of disease, epidemics, and bioterrorism, Covello et al. (2001) identified 15 factors that influenced peoples' perception of risk. Though the 15 factors are all very different, what is consistent is that the unknown, uncontrollable, or nebulous make people less willing to accept the credibility of threats; however, at the same time, once people judge risks to be "real" those factors that made us resistant to accepting them as credible also mean that they are perceived as greater threats. Put simply, people often bury their heads in the sand, pretend that the risk is not real until it is unavoidable, and then may overestimate the negative effects it could have.

Risk detection is a natural starting-point in the process; before an organization can plan to minimize the risks that it or its stakeholders could experience, those risks must be known (Comfort 2007; Dilenschneider and Hyde 1985; Hayes and Patton 2001; Heath 1998a; Kash and Darling 1998; Ritchie 2004; Stacks 2004). From there, the risk has to be evaluated in the second step in as objective and effective way as possible so that a straightforward judgment of the likelihood and severity of the risk can be made (Comfort 2007; Dilenschneider and Hyde 1985; Freundberg 1988; Massey and Larsen 2006).

The third step is the communication of risk (Comfort 2007). However, as Freundberg (1998) pointed out, this is challenging because technical information does not always translate directly. Furthermore, peoples' perceptions of risks are affected by a number of factors (Covello et al. 2001). Nevertheless, communicating risk is vital to ensure that relevant stakeholders, like members of the organization, regulators, the media, and those directly affected, can appropriately understand the situation and are prepared to deal with it (Johansson and Härenstam 2013; Ley et al. 2014). Thus, the communication of risk focuses on exchanging knowledge essential to managing the risk.

Finally, sharing information then allows for the organization and mobilization of a collective response to reduce risk and respond to danger (Comfort 2007; Dilenschneider and Hyde 1985; Heath 1998b). The mobilization of collective response includes communication-related tasks such as issue management, managing stakeholder relationships, developing communication plans and protocols, and staff development

(Hayes and Patton 2001; Heath 1998a; Heath and Millar 2004; Johansson and Hären-stam 2013; Kash and Darling 1998; Perry, Taylor, and Doerfel 2003; Reilly 2008). It also includes management-related tasks like developing teams and decision-making systems to facilitate the process (Hayes and Patton 2001; Horton 1988; Jindal, Laveena, and Aggrawal 2015; Nunamaker, Weber, and Chen 1989).

A starting-point in understanding what crisis communication does in the real world is to think of it as an integral part of helping organizations manage risk. This means that the role for crisis communication is not just about management or public relations – it has evolved from being "corporate public relations" to a part of life-saving interventions across industries.

3.2 Issues and the issue-management process

Clearly, what happens during the risk-detection process is that issues relevant to an organization and/or its stakeholders emerge. Therefore, the final step in the risk-detection process is to connect it with other processes that allow organizations to mobilize and manage risk. Issues management is one of those processes that organizations can effectively use in order to minimize or mitigate risk, crisis, and conflict. In this context, issues should be thought of as a controversial gap between an organization's behavior and their stakeholders' expectation. The resolution of these differences can lead to important consequences for organizations (Heath 2002; Heath 2004; Heath and Gay 1997). While the resolution of an issue might lead to positive outcomes for an organization, the issue is always a risk.

It is also important to note that there are a lot of risks organizations face that do not emerge as issues organizations must manage, so in order for an issue to emerge, there are two necessary conditions before we can classify a risk an issue:
- There is an expectancy violation,
- There is the potential for controversy as a result of the expectancy violation.

Thus, when we ask "what is an issue?" in the context of issues management, we begin with the assumption that the organization has violated an expectation. From there, we should think about two additional components associated with issues. First, we should expect that stakeholders and organizations might differ in their perspectives and interests connected to an issue. Though we discuss the complexities of environments, stakeholders, and the implications of different points of view throughout this text, suffice to say that while organizations and stakeholders might be concerned about the same issue, their perspectives are rarely the same. As such, organizations need to be able to understand the different perspectives on issues and the likely risk to the organization of these contestable points of difference if they are to help manage the issue (Breakwell 2000; Freberg and Palenchar 2013; Ginzel, Kramer, and Sutton 1993; Scott and Lane 2000; Slovic 1987).

Second, we should think of managing issues as distinctive from more common processes like SWOT analysis, because in this context there is always inherent risk associated with emergent issues. A SWOT analysis is a general discussion of an organization's strengths, weaknesses, opportunities, and threats and is a vital part of ensuring that an organization is prepared for crises (Coombs 2014). It is distinctive from issues management because issues management focuses on the weaknesses that could develop into crises or conflicts.

When we adopt a stakeholder-centered view of organizations and crisis management, we also need to think about issues management as a process that is more than just managing an organization's risks, but also as a process that manages the relationships between organizations and their stakeholders. Heath's (2002) perspective on issues management is stakeholder-centered in that he argues that it is stewardship for building, maintaining, and repairing relationships with stakeholders and stake seekers. He argues that successful issues management:

- Enhances an organization's ability to plan and manage its activities,
- Enhances an organization's ability to behave in ethical and socially responsible ways, as a part of routine business,
- Enhances an organization's ability to monitor its environment,
- Enhances the organization's ability to develop strategic dialogue to manage relationships more effectively.

However, for issues management to be successful, organizations cannot be reactionary – they must view this as an anticipatory process. In his analysis of issues management, Meng (1992) identified a five-stage issues life cycle encompassing the potential, emerging, current, crisis, and dormant stages of an issue (see Figure 1). In simple terms, as the issue moves through the first four stages, the issue attracts more attention and becomes less manageable from the organization's point of view (Heath and Palenchar 2009; Meng 1992).

To borrow from a health care analogy – early detection is the best approach to managing issues, which is in both the organization's and the stakeholders' interests. If an organization is able to identify issues before they are triggered by an event, whistleblower, the media, consumers, or any one of the organization's internal or external stakeholders then the organization has more opportunities to meaningfully address the issue. However, as the issue matures, the number of engaged stakeholders, publics, and other influencers expands and positions on the issue become more entrenched, meaning that the choices available to the organization necessarily shrink (Elsbach, Sutton, and Principe 1998; Heath and Palenchar 2009; Kernisky 1997; Meng 1992; Pang, Cropp, and Cameron 2006; Seeger et al. 2001).

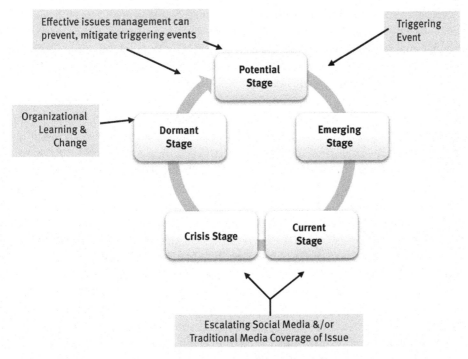

Figure 1: Adaptation of Meng's (1992) issues management process (see Diers-Lawson 2020)

4 Managing crisis through a life cycle: Current frameworks

Now that we have explained crisis, risks, and issues, the next question we seek to answer is where they fit in the study of crisis management. Pang (2013a) argued that strategic crisis management is a dynamic, ongoing process through a life cycle. For instance, Coombs (2019) argued for a three-staged approach – pre, during, and post crisis. Others such as Fearn-Banks (2017) and James, Crane, and Wooten (2013) argued for a five-staged approach – detection, prevention/preparation, containment, recovery, and learning. George (2012) argued for a three-phase approach, similar to Coombs' (2010) approach. At each step of the life cycle, key tasks are recommended for organizations to engage in. This paper adopts Wilcox, Cameron, and Reber's (2015) proactive-strategic-reactive-recovery framework as its theoretical lens and posits the key tasks.

The proactive phase is the time before crisis occurs. Gonzalez-Herrero and Pratt (1996) described it as the birth stage; Fink (1986) called it the prodromal stage; Meyers (1986) called it the pre-crisis stage; and Turner (1976) calls it the normal point. Coombs (2019), Ulmer, Sellnow, and Seeger (2007), and George (2012) called it the pre-crisis stage. Fearn-Banks (2017) called it the detection stage, while James, Crane and Wooten (2013) described it as the signal detection stage. During this phase, scholars recommended that organizations begin the tasks of scanning the environment for possible issues, tracking emerging issues, and crisis planning. Sturges (1994) described it as a time the organization is actively internalizing all this information.

The strategic phase is the time when issues and risks have been identified and some may be showing signs of emergence. Gonzalez-Herrero and Pratt (1996) called it the growth stage; Fink (1986) called it the acute phase; Meyers (1986) called it the crisis stage; and Turner (1976) called it the incubation phase. Coombs (2019), Ulmer, Sellnow, and Seeger (2007) and George (2012) called it the pre-crisis stage. Fearn-Banks (2017) and James, Crane, and Wooten (2013) called it the prevention/preparation stage. Sturges (1994) described it as the time when the organization is instructing and sharing with its stakeholders what needed to be done.

The reactive phase is the time when the crisis explodes. Gonzalez-Herrero and Pratt (1996) called it the maturity phase; Fink (1986) called it the chronic phase; Turner (1976) called it the precipitating/rescue and salvage phase; Meyers (1986) called it the crisis phase. Coombs (2019), Ulmer, Sellnow, and Seeger (2007) and George (2012) called it the crisis stage. Fearn-Banks (2017) called it the containment stage while James, Crane, and Wooten (2013) described it as the containment/damage control stage. Scholars recommended this as the time when organizations engage in crisis communication, which predominantly means managing the media. Sturges (1994) described it as a time when organizations need to instruct and share with stakeholders their action plans.

The recovery phase is the time when the crisis has subsided. Gonzalez-Herrero and Pratt (1996) called this the decline phase; Fink (1986) called it the resolution phase; Turner (1976) called it the cultural readjustment phase; Meyers (1986) called it the post-crisis phase. Coombs (2010), Ulmer, Sellnow, and Seeger (2007) and George (2012) called it the post-crisis stage. Fearn-Banks (2017) called it the recovery and learning stages while James, Crane, and Wooten (2013) described it as the business recovery stage. Wilcox, Cameron, and Reber (2015) described it as a time when the organization needed to restore battered and bruised reputation. Sturges (1994) argued that this is the time when organizations adjust to the new landscape and internalize what it had learned from the experience.

Based on the literature, what has been consistent thus far have been, first, regardless of the number of stages or phases scholars have conceptualized, that four distinct stages have emerged:
- Stage 1: Detection/Prevention;
- Stage 2: Planning/Preparation;
- Stage 3: Crisis response/containment;
- Stage 4: Crisis recovery/resolution/learning.

The life cycle operates in a loop. After one cycle is completed, scholars recommend that they loop back into what Pauchant and Mitroff (1992) described as organizational learning or interactive crisis management.

Second, the tasks recommended have been geared towards identifying and managing the external threat(s). Frandsen and Johansen (2011: 348) argued that crisis researchers have primarily focused on the "external dimension of crisis communication, and in particular on the crisis response strategies applied by organizations in crisis, in their communication with external stakeholders (such as customers, media, politicians, and NGOs), to protect or restore an image or reputation that has been threatened or damaged by the crisis." Third, the tasks to be undertaken appeared mechanical, operational and functional, with the assumption that carrying them out would stand the organization in good stead. There appears to be lack of strategic thinking on how the different tasks collectively impact the organization; a holistic view of where the tasks fit into the bigger purpose of organization; a goal or vision that the organization should aspire to. Strategic thinking, in this case, should involve a process in which the organization uses the crisis occasion as a platform to showcase, reaffirm, reexamine, and reenact its mission, values, and operations (Lerbinger 2006).

Thus, while these prescriptive suggestions may provide organizations with sufficient guidance before, during and after crises, we argue there are gaps and challenges that current frameworks have not addressed. The chapter concludes by suggesting a revised framework for strategic crisis management.

5 Crisis management in the profession. How should public relations respond?

The role of PR assume heightened importance as the communication landscape becomes dynamic and ever-changing. Yet, the tasks of PR to preempt and prevent crises remain grounded in fundamentals of PR functions. These involve:

Scanning. The first step in effective issues management is the application of both informal and formal research in order to develop actionable intelligence about the organization, its stakeholders, and its operational environment. Put more simply, the scanning phase in issues management is ongoing and devoted to collecting and organizing information relevant to the organization. Scanning does not focus on analyzing the information, merely on developing a systematic approach for identifying information to analyze. Bridges and Nelson (2000) argue that scanning is important because it ensures the organization is prepared for emergent threats. The central objective for scanning is to understand the organization's environment, its stakeholders, and the intersection between them (Aldoory, Kim, and Tindall 2010; Coombs 2004; Shepard, Betz, and O'Connell 1997; Sutcliffe 2001). Bridges and Nelson (2000) identify four ways to segment an organization's environment in the scanning process. First, the social segment refers to monitoring an organization's reputation by collecting information about what different stakeholders might be saying about it. Second, the economic segment refers to collecting economic forecasts and breaking economic news reflecting the economic trends that might signal risk for the organization. Third, the political or regulatory segment focuses on collecting information about trends or shifts in governmental processes that will affect the organization's operations. Finally, the competitive segment refers to collecting information about an organization's competitors to provide intelligence about the industry as an early warning of risks. Scanning is often overlooked, but an effective and simple scanning plan can ensure that the best information is getting used so that the organization can monitor issues. To borrow from the adage, garbage in is garbage out.

Monitoring. Once the information is collected in the scanning process, then the work of monitoring the information begins. When the scanning system reveals an issue that could be emerging or have the potential to emerge, a decision to actively monitor the issue must be made. There are nearly an infinite number of issues that organizations could monitor; however, no organization has infinite resources; therefore, monitoring is a strategic decision to devote resources to an issue. For that reason, Heath and Gay (1997) suggest that monitoring should only occur after a potential issue meets three criteria:

- The issue is growing in legitimacy as signaled by coverage by journalists and/or other opinion leaders in legacy or social media,
- The issue offers a quantifiable threat relative to the organization's markets or operations,
- The issue is championed by an individual, group, or institution with actual or potential influence.

The monitoring process is a way to connect issues with relevant stakeholders so that the organization can make informed strategic decisions about the best ways to proceed with risk mitigation. Likewise, organizations need to be able to track issues easily with information available at a glance that can be developed into strategic recommendation reports. In issues management, this is often accomplished with a risk register. A risk register is a log or basic database used to identify risks, their severity, and action steps that can be taken. It needs to provide a snapshot glance to determine what is going on in an organization's environment – it is an organizational tool to provide actionable information at a glance for the organization. Risk registers are meant to be adaptable and living documents regularly updated.

Decision-making. The monitoring phase of the process and creation or updates to the risk register will create an evaluation of particular issues and threats; however, based on categorization and good judgment, we have to begin to allocate proper resources to managing issues. An organization's values and its culture will influence the decision process.

Prioritization is the first component of good decision-making in issues management. It determines which issues demand organizational response and, therefore, the allocation of resources. Although there are many ways to analyze issues using open access and proprietary models, there are four common-sense assessments of issues that should guide prioritization:
1. What are the consequences and who will have to face the consequences of the issues?
2. How likely is the issue to affect the organization?
3. How much impact will the issue have? No two issues are equal and should not be treated as such.
4. When is the impact, if it happens, likely to occur? In a context of limited resources, sometimes organizations have to balance timescale, severity, and probability.

Prioritization is not a decision that is made once – issues can be moved up or down on an agenda for action or simply back for continued monitoring depending on the prioritization and urgency of the issue. Prioritization is also often determined by the stakeholders involved (Henriques and Sadorsky 1999). Second, organizations must assess their strategic options. Like any other management discipline, robust issues-management strategy emerges from sound data, diverse viewpoints, and ingenuity. Credible information and identifying realistic and measurable objectives provides the foundation for effective anticipatory and responsive strategy development. Building on previous research in anticipatory risk management (see Ashley and Morrison 1997), the decision-making process in issues management has four components:
1. Organizations must identify and choose among different risk mitigation options.
2. Organizations must identify the opportunity costs associated with risk mitigation.
3. Organizations must identify the residual risk that remains, even after risk-mitigation efforts.
4. Once risk-mitigation decisions are taken, who or what department is responsible for executing different elements of the risk mitigation plan?

Finally, during the decision-making process, the organization takes action; however, this can be easier said than done as the greatest barriers to effective issues management typically includes the lack of clear objectives and an unwillingness or inability to act (Jaques 2009).

Evaluation. After actions are taken, there is an evaluation stage. The issues-management process begins and ends with data or intelligence. This process should also be a learning process, where we better understand what went well that we should replicate in the future, and what needs to be addressed now or should be addressed differently in the future (see Figure 2).

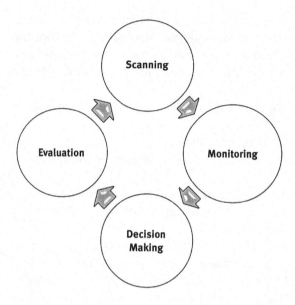

Figure 2: Issues management process overview (see Diers-Lawson 2020)

6 Conclusion: Current approaches – and gaps in crisis thinking

Another task for public relations professionals to consider is how to manage risks, issues, and crisis through the life cyle. This chapter concludes by elucidating the current approaches, and highlight the gaps.

As discussed, four stages had been identified.

Stage 1: Detection/Prevention. The tasks recommended appeared straightforward: Scan the environment for possible issues, track emerging issues, and engage in crisis planning.

The gap: Understanding the internal dimensions of one's organization. Based on Pang's (2013a) framework, the internal dimension of crisis management has, by and large, been unexplored (Frandsen and Johansen 2011). One internal dimension is the role management plays or does not play in crisis planning. Arguably, underlying the reasons why organizations do not prepare could be the lack of management impetus, where the organization is more concerned about operational priorities and profit considerations.

If management is the vital support or stumbling block to crisis planning, the gap should address the relationship crisis planners have with their top management. Another dimension is the organization's relationship with its employees. Frandsen and Johansen (2011: 353) argued that organizations must begin to examine the relationship they have with these internal stakeholders, as they have a "stronger and more complex psychological dimension than most of the other stakeholders. Employees are 'closer' to the organization." They proposed two ways in which employees can be harnessed in crisis planning: (1) the employees as receivers (where the management actively shares information with them at different stages of the crisis); and (2) the employees as senders (where the management works with them to gather information about how the crisis is developing on the ground or on the web).

Stage 2: Planning/Preparation. The tasks recommended appeared straightforward: risk communication and activating the crisis plan.

The gap: Seeking to understand the emotional upheavals of stakeholders. Based on Pang's (2013a) framework, evidence increasingly shows that, in times of crises, stakeholders are not shy from demonstrating their emotions. Indeed, understanding stakeholders' emotions should dominate organization radar (Coombs 2010). While there have been pockets of studies examining emotions (for instance, see Choi and Lin 2009; McDonald, Sparks, and Glendon 2010; Ni and Wang 2011), thus far arguably the only framework to comprehensively understand stakeholder emotion is the Integrated Crisis Mapping model (ICM) proposed by Jin, Pang, and Cameron (2012). The authors argued that understanding the emotional upheavals stakeholders face in a crisis can equip organizations to design the appropriate strategies to address stakeholder needs.

Stage 3: Crisis response/containment. The tasks recommended appeared straightforward: Managing the media.

The challenge: Managing developments in social media. Based on Pang's (2013a) framework, the advent of the Internet has increasingly empowered stakeholders, giving them a platform to instantaneously connect and share ideas. Siah, Bansal, and Pang (2010) argued that the new media is a double-edged sword. On one hand, they provide new platforms and means for organizations to communicate with stakeholders; on the other hand, the same platforms and means can be used to escalate crisis for the organization. While top management still use successful and positive media coverage as a key indicator to assess effectiveness (Pang and Yeo 2009), the challenge for organizations is to monitor social media and heightens the need for crisis managers to understand what works across multiple media platforms. Four phenomena relating to social media are observed. First, paracrises. A paracrisis is a "publicly visible crisis threat that charges an organisation with irresponsible or unethical behaviour" (Coombs and Holladay 2012: 409). It is not a full-blown crisis, but a threat, also known as a warning sign or prodrome, which can escalate into crisis. Second, how crises are increasingly triggered online and escalated within the social media environment, and gain credibility offline when reported in mainstream media. The pervasiveness of social media has changed the way mainstream media operates and prioritizes news content. Increasingly, it is becoming more difficult for mainstream media to ignore content originating from social media (Pang, Nasrath, and Chong 2014). A third phenomenon observed is social media hype. As netizens increasingly take to social media to question organizations, it leads to a frenzy of hype. Pang (2013b) described social media hype as a netizen-generated hype that causes a huge interest in the social media spheres, triggered by a key event and sustained by the self-reinforcing quality in its ability for users to engage in discussion. This is characterized by (1) a key trigger event which captures the attention of the public; (2) a sharp increase in interest levels, rising within 24 hours after a particular event; (3) interest waves, where there are the ebbs and falls in user interest surrounding the key trigger event; (4) sustaining and spreading of interest across different mediums, including traditional media, as well as various social media platforms.

A fourth phenomenon is how stakeholders utilize social media to parody the official online accounts of organizations. Wan et al. (2015) described this as parody social media. Parody social media accounts can emerge in three ways: (1) the actual crisis or paracrisis functioning as a trigger event, prompting those who create crisis information for others to consume to act; (2) smouldering issues from a crisis/paracrisis that is mishandled by the organization, resulting in frustrated stakeholders creating the account; (3) the organization chose to ignore issues, resulting in an information vacuum (Pang 2013c), which the parody social media account emerged to fill.

Stage 4: Crisis recovery/resolution/learning. The task recommended is restoring battered and bruised reputation.

The challenge: Image management. Based on Pang's (2013a) framework, organizations need to be more cognizant of image-management efforts. The difference between image and reputation is that the latter is what others think of the organization's track record (Wilcox, Cameron, and Reber 2015). This track record is based on economic performance, social responsiveness, and ability to deliver on goods and services. Gray and Balmer (1998: 697) argued that this "evolved over time as a result of consistent performance" while image is the "mental picture" that stakeholders have of an organization. Reputation takes time to build up, but image can be constructed by organizations. After a crisis is over, organizations can be proactive in engaging in different image work to reconstitute itself to its stakeholders, a challenge that appeared to be overlooked. Pang's (2012) image-management model offers one perspective. Image management is a dialogic process in which organizations and stakeholders communicate with one another (Massey 2004). Even though this is collaborative, the organization should take the lead in constructing its image. Gray and Balmer (1998) argued that the corporate communication should be at the forefront of such efforts.

> One way organizations can build positive images through the media (offline and online) is through framing (Sturges 1994). Hallahan (1999) suggested that practitioners can operate as "frame strategists, who strive to determine how situations, attributes, choices, actions, issues and responsibility should be posed to achieve favorable objectives." Framing is analogous to telling one's story (Heath 2004) and to constructing meanings with one's audience (Heath 2004).

Thus, the more positive a story the organization tells of itself, the more it fills the information vacuum (Pang 2013c), or what people get to know, of the organization. Effective framing can be executed if organizations have strong media relations (Pang 2010). Beyond the mainstream media, organizations can tap on websites, blogs and micro-blogging services like Twitter and Facebook. Websites were the first electronic frontier in engaging in dialogic communication (Pang, Mak and Shin 2018).

The tasks for public relations professionals remain increasingly critical. The work is cut out for professionals to be ahead of the curve by being strategic in thinking and ever-ready to employ tactics to manage evolving risks, issues, and crises.

References

Aldoory, Linda, Jeong-Nam Kim & Natalie Tindall. 2010. The influence of perceived shared risk in crisis communication: Elaborating the situational theory of publics. *Public Relations Review* 36(2). 134–140.

Ashley, William C. & James. L. Morrison. 1997. Anticipatory management: Tools for better decision making. *Futurist* 31(5). 47–51.

Argenti, Paul A. 2002. Crisis communication: Lessons from 9/11. *Harvard Business Review* 80(12). 103–109.

Breakwell, Gail. M. 2000. Risk communication: Factors affecting impact. *British Medical Bulletin* 56(1). 110–120.

Bridges, Janet A. & Richard A. Nelson. 2000. Issues management: A relational approach. In John A. Ledingham & Stephen D. Bruning (eds.), *Public relations as relationship management: A relational approach to the study practice of public relations*, 95–115. Mahwah, NJ: Lawrence Erlbaum.

Choi, Yoonhyeung & Ying-Hsuan Lin. 2009. Consumer responses to Mattel product recalls posted on online bulletin boards: Exploring two types of emotion. *Journal of Public Relations Research* 21(2). 198–207.

Comfort, Louise K. 2007. Crisis management in hindsight: Cognition, communication, coordination, and control. *Public Administration Review* 67(1). 189–197.

Covello, Vincent T., Richard G. Peters, Joseph G. Wojtecki & Richard C. Hyde. 2001. Risk communication, the West Nile virus epidemic, and bioterrorism: responding to the commnication challenges posed by the intentional or unintentional release of a pathogen in an urban setting. *Journal of Urban Health* 78(2). 382–391.

Coombs, W. Timothy. 2004. Impact of past crises on current crisis communication: Insights from Situational Crisis Communication Theory. *The Journal of Business Communication* 41(3). 265–290.

Coombs, W. Timothy. 2010. Parameters for crisis communication. In W. Timothy Coombs & Sherry J. Holladay (eds.), *Handbook of Crisis Communication*, 17–53. Malden, MA: Wiley-Blackwell.

Coombs, W. Timothy. 2014. *Ongoing Crisis Communication: Planning, Managing, and Responding: Planning, Managing, and Responding*. Thousand Oaks, CA: Sage.

Coombs, W. Timothy. 2019. *Ongoing Crisis Communication*, 5th edn. Thousand Oaks, CA: Sage.

Coombs, W. Timothy & Holladay, Sherry J. 2012. The paracrisis: The challenges created by publicly managing crisis prevention. *Public Relations Review* 38. 408–415. doi:http://dx.doi.org/10.1016/j.pubrev.2012.04.004 (accessed 29 January 2020).

Diers-Lawson, Audra. 2017a. Crisis Communication. Oxford Research Encyclopedia of Communication. https://oxfordre.com/communication/view/10.1093/acrefore/9780190228613.001.0001/
acrefore-9780190228613-e-397 (accessed 29 January 2020).

Diers-Lawson, Audra. 2017b. A state of emergency in crisis communication an intercultural crisis
communication research agenda. *Journal of Intercultural Communication Research* 46(1). 1–54.

Diers-Lawson, Audra. 2020. *Crisis communication: Managing stakeholder relationships*. London:
Routledge.

Dilenschneider, Robert L. & Richard. C. Hyde. 1985. Crisis communications: Planning for the
unplanned. *Business Horizons* 28(1). 35–38.

Elsbach, Kimberly D., Robert I. Sutton & Kristine E. Principe. 1998. Averting expected challenges
through anticipatory impression management: A study of hospital billing. *Organization Science*
9(1). 68–86.

Fearn-Banks, Kathleen. 2017. *Crisis Communications*. 5th edn. New York: Routledge.

Fink, Stephen. 1986. *Crisis management: Planning for the inevitable*. New York: AMACOM.

Frandsen, Finn & Winni Johansen. 2011. The study of internal crisis communication: Towards an
integrative framework. *Corporate Communications: An International Journal* 16(4). 347–361

Freberg, Karen & Michael J. Palenchar. 2013. Convergence of digital negotiation and risk challenges:
Strategic implications of social media for risk and crisis communications. In H.S.N. Al-Deen
& J.A. Hendricks (eds.), *Social Media and Strategic Communications*, 83–100. Palgrave
Macmillan: London.

Freeman, R. Edward. 1999. Divergent stakeholder theory. *Academy of Management Review* 24(2).
233–239.

Freundberg, William R. 1988. Perceived risk, real risk: Social science and the art of probabilistic risk
assessment. *Science* 242. 44–49.

George, Amiso M. 2012. The phases of crisis communication. In Amiso M. George & Cornelius B.
Pratt (eds.), *Case studies in crisis communication*, 31–50. New York: Routledge Taylor and
Francis.

Ginzel, Linda. E., Roderick. M. Kramer & Robert. I. Sutton. 1993. Organizational impression
management as a reciprocal influence process: The neglected role of the organizational
audience. *Research in Organizational Behavior* 15. 227–266.

Gray, Edmund R. & John M. T. Balmer. 1998. Managing corporate image and corporate reputation.
Long Range Planning 31(5). 695–702

Gonzalez-Herrero, Alfonso & Cornelius B. Pratt. 1996. An integrated symmetrical model for
crisis-communications management. *Journal of Public Relations Research* 8(2). 79–105.

Ha, Jin Hong & Lois Boynton. 2014. Has crisis communication been studied using an interdisciplinary
approach? A 20-year content analysis of communication journals. *International Journal of
Strategic Communication* 8(1). 29–44.

Hallahan, Kirk. 1999. Seven models of framing: Implications for public relations. *Journal of Public
Relations Research* 11(3). 205–242.

Hayes, Deborah & Mark Patton. 2001. Proactive crisis-management strategies and the archaeo-
logical heritage. *International Journal of Heritage Studies* 7(1). 37–58.

Heath, Robert L. 2002. Issues management: Its past, present, and future. *Journal of PublicAffairs*
2(2). 209–214

Heath, Robert L. 2004. Crisis preparation: Planning for the inevitable. In Dan P. Millar & Robert L.
Heath (eds.), *Responding to Crisis: A Rhetorical Approach to Crisis Communication*, 33–35.
Mahwah, NJ: Lawrence Erlbaum Associates.

Heath, Robert L. & Christine. D. Gay. 1997. Risk communication: Involvement, uncertainty and
control's effect on information scanning and monitoring by expert stakeholders. *Management
Communication Quarterly* 10(3). 342–359.

Heath, Robert L. & Michael J. Palenchar. 2009. *Strategic Issues Management*. 2nd edn. Thousand Oaks, CA: Sage.

Heath, Robert. 1998a. Dealing with the complete crisis – the crisis management shell structure. *Safety Science* 30(1). 139–150.

Heath, Robert. 1998b. Looking for answers: suggestions for improving how we evaluate crisis management. *Safety Science* 30(1). 151–163.

Heath, Robert L., & Dan P. Millar. 2004. A rhetorical approach to crisis communication: Management, communication processes, and strategic responses. In Dan P. Millar & Robert L. Heath (eds.), *Responding to Crisis: A Rhetorical Approach to Crisis Communication*, 1–18. Mahwah, NJ: Lawrence Erlbaum Associates.

Henriques, Irene, & Perry Sadorsky. 1999. The relationship between environmental commitment and managerial perceptions of stakeholder importance. *Academy of Management Journal* 42(1). 87–99.

Hilts, Phillip J. 1990. Red Cross faulted on tainted-blood reports. *New York Times*, 11 July. https://www.nytimes.com/1990/07/11/us/red-cross-faulted-on-tainted-blood-reports.html (accessed 8 March 1999).

Horton, Thomas R. 1988. *Crisis management. Management Review* 77(9). 5–8.

James, Erika. H, Bret Crane & Lynn. P. Wooten. 2013. Managing the crisis lifecyle in the information age. In Andrew J. DuBrin (ed.), *Handbook of Research on Crisis Leadership in Organizations*, 177–192. Northampton, MA: Edward Elgar Publishing.

Jaques, Tony. 2009. Issue and crisis management: Quicksand in the definitional landscape. *Public Relations Review* 35(3). 280–286.

Jindal, Shivali, Laveena Laveena & Apoorv Aggarwal. 2015. A comparative study of crisis management – Toyota v/s General Motors. *Scholedge International Journal of Management & Development* 2(6). 1–12.

Jin, Yan, Augustine Pang, & Glen T. Cameron. 2012. Toward a Publics-Driven, Emotion-Based Conceptualization in Crisis Communication: Unearthing Dominant Emotions in Multi-Staged Testing of the Integrated Crisis Mapping (ICM) Model. *Journal of Public Relations Research* 24. 266–298.

Johansson, Anders, & Malin Härenstam. 2013. Knowledge communication: a key to successful crisis management. *Biosecurity and Bioterrorism: Biodefense Strategy, Practice, and Science* 11(S1). 260–263. doi:10.1089/bsp.2013.0052 (accessed 29 January 2020).

Kash, Toby. J., & John. R. Darling. 1998. Crisis management: prevention, diagnosis and intervention. *Leadership & Organization Development Journal* 19(4). 179–186.

Kernisky, Debra. A. 1997. Proactive crisis management and ethical discourse: Dow Chemical's issues management bulletins 1979–1990. *Journal of Business Ethics* 16(8). 843–853.

Kim, Soo-Yeon, Myung-Il Choi, Bryan H. Reber & Daewoo Kim. 2014. Tracking public relations scholarship trends: Using semantic network analysis on PR Journals from 1975 to 2011. *Public Relations Review* 40(1). 116–118.

King, Granville I. 2002. Crisis management and team effectiveness: A closer examination. *Journal of Business Ethics* 41(3). 235–249.

Lehmberg, Derek & Jeff Hicks. 2018. A 'glocalization' approach to the internationalizing of crisis communication. *Business Horizons* 61(3). 357–366.

Lerbinger, Otto. 2006. *Corporate public affairs: interacting with interest groups, media, and government*. Mahwah, NJ: Lawrence Erlbaum.

Ley, Benedikt, Thomas Ludwig, Volkmar Pipek, Dave Randall, Christian Reuter & Torben Wieden-hoefer. 2014. Information and expertise sharing in inter-organizational crisis management. *Computer Supported Cooperative Work (CSCW)* 23(4–6). 347–387.

Massey, E. Joseph 2004. Managing organizational images: Crisis response and legitimacy restoration. In Dan P. Millar & Robert. L. Heath (eds.), *Responding to a crisis: A rhetorical approach to crisis communication*, 233–246. Mahwah, NJ: Lawrence Erlbaum.

Massey, Joseph E. & John P. Larsen. 2006. Crisis management in real time: How to successfully plan for and respond to a crisis. *Journal of Promotion Management* 12(3–4). 63–97.

McDonald, Lynette M., Beverley Sparks & A. Ian Glendon. 2010. Stakeholder reactions to company crisis communication and causes. *Public Relations Review* 36. 263–271.

Meng, Max. 1992. Early identification aids issues management. *Public Relations Journal* 48(3). 22.

Meyers, C. Gerald. 1986. *When it hits the fan: Managing the nine crises of business*. New York: Mentor.

Mitroff, Ian, M. Can Alpaslan & Sandy E. Green. 2004. Crises as ill-structured messes. *International Studies Review* 6(1). 165–182.

Moore, Simon. 2004. Disaster's future: The prospects for corporate crisis management and communication. *Business Horizons* 47(1). 29–36.

Ni, Lan & Qi Wang. 2011. Anxiety and uncertainty management in an intercultural setting: The impact on organization-public relationships. *Journal of Public Relations Research* 23(3). 269–301.

Nunamaker, Jay F., Sue E. Weber & Minder Chen. 1989. Organizational crisis management systems: Planning for intelligent action. *Journal of Management Information Systems* 5(4). 7–31.

Pang, Augustine. 2010. Mediating the Media: A journalist-centric model in managing the media by corporate communication practitioners. *Corporate Communications: An International Journal* 15(2). 192–204.

Pang, Augustine. 2012. Towards a crisis pre-emptive image management model. *Corporate Communications: An International Journal* 17(3). 358–378.

Pang, Augustine. 2013a. Strategic crisis management: Gaps and challenges across the life cycle. Paper presented at 27th Annual Australia and New Zealand Association of Management Conference at Hobart, Tasmania, 4 December.

Pang, Augustine. 2013b. Social media hype in times of crises: Nature, characteristics and impact on organizations. *Asia Pacific Media Educator* 23(2). 309–336.

Pang, Augustine. 2013c. Dealing with external stakeholders during the crisis: Managing the information vacuum. In Andrew J. Dubrin (ed.), *Handbook of Research on Crisis Leadership in Organizations*, 209–229. Northampton, MA: Edward Elgar Publishing.

Pang, Augustine, Fritz Cropp & Glen T. Cameron. 2006. Corporate crisis planning: Tensions, issues, and contradictions. *Journal of Communication Management* 10(4). 371–389.

Pang, Augustine, Begam Nasrath & Aaron Chong. 2014. Negotiating crisis in the social media environment: Evolution of crises online, gaining credibility offline. *Corporate Communications: An International Journal* 19(1). 96–118.

Pang, Augustine, Angela Mak & Wonsun Shin. 2018. Integrated CSR communication: Toward a model encompassing media agenda building with stakeholder dialogic engagement. In Adam Lindgreen, Joelle Vanhamme, Francois Maon & Rebecca Mardon (eds.), *Communicating Social Responsibility in the Digital Era*, 158–175. London: Routledge.

Pang, Augustine & Su Lin Yeo, 2009. Winning respect: Transformation to professionalization of public relations in Singapore. *Media Asia* 36(2). 96–103.

Pauchant, C. Thierry, & I. Ian Mitroff. 1992. *Transforming the crisis-prone organization*. San Francisco: Jossey-Bass.

Perry, Danielle C., Maureen Taylor & Marya L. Doerfel. 2003. Internet-based communication in crisis management. *Management Communication Quarterly* 17(2). 206–232.

Pearson, Christine M., & Judith A. Clair. 1998. Reframing crisis management. *Academy of Management Review* 23(1). 58–76.

Reilly, Anne. H. 1987. Are organisations ready for a crisis? *Columbia Journal of World Business* 22(1). 79–87.

Reilly, Anne H. 2008. The role of human resource development competences in facilitating effective crisis communication. *Advances in Developing Human Resources* 10(3). 331–351.

Ritchie, Brent W. 2004. Chaos, crises and disasters: a strategic approach to crisis management in the tourism industry. *Tourism management* 25(6). 669–683.

Scott, Susanne. G. & Vicki. R. Lane. 2000. A stakeholder approach to organizational identity. *Academy of Management Review* 25(1). 43–65.

Seeger, Matthew W., Beth Heyart, Elizabeth A. Barton & Sonya Bultnyck. 2001. Crisis planning and crisis communication in the public schools: Assessing post Columbine responses. *Communication Research Reports* 18(4). 375–383.

Seeger, Matthew W. & Robert R. Ulmer. 2003. Explaining Enron: Communication and responsible leadership. *Management Communication Quarterly* 17(1). 58–84.

Shepard, Jon M., Michael Betz & Lenahan O'Connell. 1997. The proactive corporation: Its nature and causes. *Journal of Business Ethics* 16(10). 1001–1011.

Siah, Joanna A. M., Namrata Bansal & Augustine Pang. 2010. New media and crises: New media – a new medium in escalating crises? *Corporate Communications: An International Journal* 15(2). 143–155.

Slovic, Paul. 1987. Perception of risk. *Science* 236. 280–285.

Stacks, Don W. 2004. Crisis management: Toward a multidimension model of public relations. In Dan P. Millar & Robert L. Heath (eds.), *Responding to Crisis: A Rhetorical Approach to Crisis Communication*, 37–49. Mahwah, NJ: Lawrence Erlbaum.

Sturges, David L. 1994. Communication through crisis: A strategy for organizational survival. *Management Communication Quarterly* 7(3). 297–316.

Sutcliffe, Kathleen M. 2001. Organizational environments and organizational information processing. In Fredric M. Jablin & Linda L. Putnam (eds.), *The New Handbook of Organizational Communication: Advances in Theory, Research, and Method*, 197–230. Thousand Oaks, CA: Sage.

Taylor, Alan. 2014. Remembering the Exxon Valdez Oil Spill. *The Atlantic*. https://www.theatlantic.com/photo/2014/03/remembering-the-exxon-valdez-oil-spill/100703/ (accessed 16 October 2019).

Turner, Barry. 1976. The organizational and interorganizational development of disasters. *Administrative Science Quarterly* 21. 378–397.

Ulmer, Robert R., Timothy L. Sellnow & Matthew W. Seeger. 2007. *Effective Crisis Communication*. Thousand Oaks, CA: Sage.

Wan, Sarah, Regina Koh, Andrew Ong & Augustine Pang. 2015. Parody social media accounts: Influence and impact on organizations during crisis. *Public Relations Review* 41. 381–385.

Wilcox, Dennis, Glen T. Cameron & Bryan H. Reber. 2015. *Public relations: Strategies and tactics*, 11th edn. 248–276. Boston: Pearson Allyn & Bacon.

Sherry J. Holladay and Elina R. Tachkova

12 Public relations for stakeholder and societal engagement

Abstract: Public relations uses relationship building and stakeholder engagement to pursue organizational objectives. This chapter describes how stakeholder theory provides a foundation for understanding organization-stakeholder engagement processes. Engagement connects management with external and internal stakeholders to understand and make decisions based on shared interests and value creation. Organizations also are expected to engage with society as a whole to create value through corporate social responsibility and sustainable development. Ethical engagement with stakeholders and society should benefit the social evaluation of the organization.

Keywords: Corporate social responsibility; engagement; reputation; stakeholder; stakeholder engagement; strategic management; sustainability

1 Introduction

The concept and practice of stakeholder and societal engagement through public relations have grown in importance as social media and other digital platforms provide the technological affordances for more direct communication between organizations and stakeholders. Technology has enabled e-commerce as well as other forms of two-way communication between consumers and businesses. Organizations can more easily share current information with stakeholders or "invade" social media sites with unsolicited offers for products and services. The economic interests of organizations have encroached upon digital spaces in ways that parallel the increasing influence of business in society as a whole. Corporations have become the dominant institutions in modern society, eclipsing the roles of governments and NGOs/non-profit organizations.

The digital environment empowers people to voice concerns and to organize virtually to discuss business-related issues ranging from the abstract (e. g., What should be the role of business in society? How can capitalism create a sustainable world?) to the specific (e. g., How can we persuade organization X to end its unfair labor practices? How does organization Y survive despite its poor customer service record?). Organizations are understandably concerned about how they are discussed and evaluated online and offline and how those conversations may affect them. Thus it is important for organizations to monitor conversations and media coverage about their operations and citizenship behaviors to understand peoples perceptions. The Center for Corporate Citizenship defines *corporate citizenship* as "how a company exercises its rights, obligations, privileges and overall corporate social responsibility within our local and

https://doi.org/10.1515/9783110554250-012

global environments" (Boston College Center for Corporate Citizenship 2019). The concept of corporate citizenship offers a broad view of the relationship of business to society. The concepts of corporate reputation and corporate social responsibility reputation are more narrowly focused.

Corporate reputation is based on people's evaluations of what they know about the organization and is a valuable intangible asset. Reputation differs from *corporate identity* – how the organization thinks of itself, including its basic characteristics – and *corporate image* – the mental image the organization seeks to project to tell people who it is (Walker 2010). Reputation Institute is a global consulting firm focused on assessing perceptions of organizations and offering guidance on how firms can build their credibility. Reputation Institute uses seven dimensions to assess an organization's overall reputation: citizenship, governance, workplace, financial performance, leadership, products and services, and innovation (Reputation Institute 2019: 2). *Corporate social responsibility* (CSR), the responsibility of businesses for their impacts on society (European Commission 2011: 6), is the primary driver of overall corporate reputation. Reputation Institute assesses an organization's CSR reputation via three dimensions: (1) *citizenship* (has a positive societal influence and is environmental responsible), (2) *governance* (is open and transparent and behaves ethically), and (3) *workplace* (is concerned about employee well-being and offers equal opportunities). Their research demonstrates that organizations prioritizing CSR over profits have a stronger overall corporate reputation than organizations that focus only on financial performance. Consumers care about an organization's values and reward socially responsible companies (Reputation Institute 2015).

Stakeholder expectations for interaction with organizations over a range of issues are a feature of contemporary society. However, stakeholder engagement is not merely interaction. Though stakeholder engagement has been defined in many ways (see Greenwood 2007 for a review), our use of the term follows Freeman's (1984) stakeholder theory. According to Freeman, engagement is a communication process based on *shared interests* and *value creation*. Public relations performs a boundary-spanning role by connecting management with external and internal stakeholders through engagement to understand and make decisions based on mutual interests.

Despite frequent references to "engagement" within the study of communication, the concept of engagement is inconsistently conceptualized (Johnston 2014; Johnston and Taylor 2018). Johnston (2018) broadly defines engagement as "a dynamic multi-dimensional relational concept featuring psychological and behavioral attributes of connection, interaction, participation, and involvement, designed to achieve or elicit an outcome at individual, community, organization, or civic levels" (Johnston 2018: 19). Her definition and engagement taxonomy notes engagement can be both a state (cognitive, affective, and behavioral engagement) and process (interaction, participation, etc.) occurring at micro, meso, and macro levels. As used in public relations, engagement generally refers to communication processes and outcomes consistent with democratic ideals of participation and transparency (Pieczka 2018).

This chapter focuses on how public relations processes facilitate organizations' engagement with stakeholders and society as a whole. It does so by explaining key concepts including public relations, stakeholders, and stakeholder engagement. The second section in this chapter elaborates on the nature of stakeholder engagement by describing how formalized reporting frameworks guide engagement over sustainability, and then discussing how stakeholder engagement informs the practice of corporate social responsibility and sustainability. The chapter concludes by identifying weaknesses in current research and recommending areas where future research could benefit our understanding and practice of stakeholder engagement.

1.1 Public relations, stakeholders, and stakeholder engagement

Public relations has been defined as "the management function that establishes and maintains mutually beneficial relationships between an organization and the publics on whom its success or failure depends" (Cutlip, Center, and Broom 1994: 2). As a management function, public relations contributes to the strategic direction of the organization by understanding and communicating with interdependent stakeholders (publics) who can influence the organization's operations. Public relations processes are used to understand, meet, and influence expectations to align their needs with those of the organization so that each receives something of value.

Though the definition of PR focuses on mutually beneficial relationships, "mutual" is unlikely to translate into "equal" in all respects. For example, an organization provides employment opportunities and philanthropic activities for a community and the community provides a workforce and tax breaks. Contributions are "comparable" but dissimilar.

In addition, an organization's interest in stakeholders as strategic resources may be qualitatively different than a stakeholder's interest in the organization. Mutually beneficial relationships represent an ideal, but in reality the benefits derived from these relationships are probably neither similar nor equal. Nor are these relationships mutually influential in terms of power. Because of their material and symbolic resources, organizations may exercise power more easily and often at the expense of others (Cheney and Christensen 2001; Dawkins 2014). The boundary-spanning function of public relations is likely to reveal tensions between the interests of the organization and interests of stakeholders and thus expose ethical dilemmas for parties in the relationship (Dawkins 2014; Holtzhausen 2012).

The abuse of relationships through the unbridled pursuit of organizational interests at the expense of stakeholder and societal interests is unethical, unsustainable, and destined to fail. Critiques of public relations' research and practice often claim it promotes organizational goals at the expense of stakeholder and societal interests. However, as demonstrated by organizational scandals involving deception, misconduct, and abuse of stakeholder trust in the relationship, stakeholders can publicly challenge organizations to keep them in check. Stakeholders grant a social license to operate based on their perceptions of legitimacy and their social approval of an organization (e. g., Bundy and Pfarrer 2015; Heath 2006; Sethi 1977). Stakeholders can withdraw support when the organization ignores interdependence and fails to create value for stakeholders.

Stakeholder engagement processes are one way to address concerns about shared interests and the influence of organizations in contemporary society. To better understand stakeholder engagement as a public relations function, the concept of *stakeholder* must be elaborated. McKie and Willis (2012: 850) note that public relations is essentially a "field whose strategic raison d'être is shaped by stakeholders." In the public relations literature, the most influential definition of stakeholder is offered by Freeman, a strategic management scholar who developed stakeholder theory and the idea of "managing for stakeholders." Freeman defined a stakeholder as "any group or individual who can affect or is affected by the achievement of the firm's objectives" (1984: 25). This definition is consistent with public relations' view of the importance of mutually beneficial relationships and dialogue. Stakeholders have a legitimate stake in the organization's core purpose, its decisions, and actions. Freeman (1984) divided stakeholders into two groups: those who are foundational to a firm's objectives and activities (primary stakeholders such as customers, suppliers, employees, communities, and financiers) and those secondary stakeholders that can affect an organization's objectives (the government, media, competitors, consumer advocates, and interest groups including NGOs, economic, and professional associations). Not every individual is a stakeholder; simply being aware of an organization does not make a person a stakeholder.

According to Freeman (1984), mutually beneficial relationships with stakeholders influence (or in the future might have the potential to influence) the objectives, strategic direction, and performance of an organization. The various relationships are based on different interests or areas of concern. A single stakeholder group cannot create value for itself or others; it is through interaction and decision making that value is created. Managers must understand the stakeholders for whom they create value as well as the methods of value creation, thus forcing them to see connections between the world of business and the world of ethics. This means engagement is a moral and strategic imperative. Value creation requires purposeful, transparent communication to identify, understand, and address stakeholder interests as well as organizational interests. Action-oriented stakeholder engagement directs resources toward cultivating and maintaining relationships to align interests and create value. Dawkins' (2014) discussion of "good faith" stakeholder engagement similarly advocates for transparency, dialogue, and power neutralization. However, Freeman tends to be more optimistic about collaboration and generally avoids discussion of power imbalances, focusing instead on the power of mutual interests in creating ethical engagement.

1.2 Engagement within public relations research

Public relations often uses the term *stakeholder engagement* to differentiate it from forms of engagement commonly used in other disciplines such as Marketing and Education where engagement may be described as anything from the amount of time consumers spend on a website to psychological states produced through active learning (e. g., Johnston 2018). However, despite growing interest in stakeholder engagement within the public relations discipline, the term is fraught with inconsistent conceptualizations and operationalizations. For example, Taylor and Kent (2014: 386–388) examined how "engagement" was treated in extant public relations research and found most engagement-related research reflected only the organization's perspective (was organization-centric), focused on one-way communication rather than interaction or relationships, and was described as non-routine communication occurring within a particular context. Their conclusions echoed common criticisms of organization-centric approaches to engagement with stakeholders.

Taylor and Kent (2014) identified five contexts in which engagement has been studied in public relations research: social media engagement, employee engagement, corporate social responsibility engagement, civic engagement and social capital, and dialogic engagement. Of particular interest to this chapter is the use of stakeholder engagement and its value to the CSR context. They found research has conceptualized CSR engagement as "organizations being transparent and open to public questions and scrutiny" and "enacting corporate initiatives deemed beneficial to local stakeholders (...) where engagement is equated with doing good deeds and interacting with the community" (Taylor and Kent 2014: 386). They note research within the last two contexts, civic engagement and dialogic engagement, are more likely to view public relations as a philosophy or activity rather than a tool used by organizations to accomplish their objectives. Civic engagement context concerns how public relations is used to build social capital, help communities solve problems, and promote democratic ideals (Sommerfeldt 2013; Taylor 2010), and dialogic engagement describes how dialogic principles provide a foundation for dialogue and ethical communication between organizations and stakeholders (Kent and Taylor 2002).

1.3 Viewing engagement as decision-making

An alternative conceptualization of stakeholder engagement was proposed by Coombs and Holladay (2018a) who envision engagement as *participation in decision-making*. In general, viewing engagement as participation in decision-making is consistent with Freeman's (1984) stakeholder theory, because both view decision-making as central to engagement. Coombs and Holladay's communication-focused definition integrates the decision-making emphasis of stakeholder theory with concerns over power in the stakeholder-organization relationship. Drawing upon the public participation and decision-making literatures, they define *stakeholder engagement* as "the dynamic interplay of stakeholder and organizational actions designed to define the communicative nature and parameters of joint decision-making efforts" (280). This definition recognizes that engagement is most useful when it develops decisions that create shared value within a context where both parties may communicate to seek and exercise power to influence the situation in which decisions are made. Hence, engagement should not be viewed as one process controlled by the organization, but rather as a range and series of processes that negotiate the various ways organizations and stakeholders enact engagement.

Coombs and Holladay (2018a) claim engagement varies along two dimensions: (1) the communicative nature of the interaction, and (2) the control of engagement parameters. The former refers to the view of communication (its directionality, as in one-way and two-way communication), and the latter refers to who initiates the engagement to establish the topic of discussion. The two dimensions were used to create a matrix of four categories describing the nature of engagement: (1) *organizational statement* designed to limit interaction, characterized by one-way communication from the organization, (2) *stakeholder contestation* (i. e., a challenge to organizational practices), using one-way communication from the stakeholder designed to prompt engagement, (3) *consultative*, two-way communication where engagement parameters are controlled by the organization, and (4) *dialogic*, two-way communication where the organization and stakeholders share control of the engagement parameters. The resulting matrix demonstrates engagement and refers to a range of processes related to empowerment (control) and communication for decision-making. It also envisions how engagement may be initiated by stakeholders (stakeholder contestation) to motivate organizations to consider their concerns. As used in the literature, the term "stakeholder engagement" positions the organization as the party that determines if and how engagement will occur. However, the concept *of stakeholder contestation* acknowledges stakeholders also act to propose engagement.

Stakeholder contestation can be used to challenge an organization's operations when they seem irresponsible or immoral (Lerbinger 1997). These accusations may result from the organization's failure to recognize shared interests and interdependence. If stakeholders or others who are not viewed as stakeholders expect an organization to engage with them over an issue they believe concerns them, but the organization fails to recognize a need for engagement, stakeholders may press the organization through stakeholder contestation. Stakeholders use contestation to increase their *salience* to the organization (Mitchell, Agle, and Wood 1997) by claiming to share interests and acting in ways to demonstrate interdependence. For example, if stakeholders perceive a problem with organizational operations (e. g., a product doesn't perform as expected or poses risks, or an organization's latest advertisement is insensitive to an ethnic group), they may engage in one-way communication – contestation – to stimulate engagement. Through online actions such as virtual protests – including taking over the organization's Twitter account or creating derisive memes – or offline boycotts, protesting stakeholders seek to attract attention from sympathetic stakeholders who join and/or prompt the organization to acknowledge shared interest and respond through consultative or dialogic communication engagement (Cisnek 2016; Coombs and Holladay 2015a, 2015b, 2018a, 2018b). However, the organization may also choose to ignore the bid and respond through one-way communication (organizational statement). Both organizations and stakeholders can use public relations processes to initiate, enact, and respond to engagement.

Overall, the definition of engagement and its associated matrix reflects a *contingency approach,* arguing that there are different types of engagement that can be used fruitfully in different situations with varying degrees of dissensus and consensus. For example, the nature of the engagement process shifts when stakeholder contestation leads to consultative or dialogic processes. The model also envisions how one-way communication by an organization (organizational statement) may be perceived as sufficient and satisfactory for some types of engagement. For instance, an organization typically uses one-way communication when posting financial and non-financial reports to its website. This information-sharing illustrates one way to "close the loop" and report the results of engagement (Hurst and Ihlen 2018; Pedersen 2006). The information may be relevant to a several stakeholder groups due to the content and nature of its connections with the organization. However, the content may not prompt a need for consultation or dialogue. In some cases, stakeholder groups may have engaged with the organization to contribute to the report contents, as would be the case with GRI or AA1000 Stakeholder Engagement Standard reporting. No further consultation or dialogue is needed at this point due to their previous involvement and knowledge. However, a stakeholder group other than the one(s) directly involved in the report may seek engagement over the report if it questions the validity of its contents.

If a decision is required in complex situations of high uncertainty, stakeholder engagement in the form of dialogue (two-way communication where control of the engagement parameters is shared) may be required to ensure decision making will reflect the interests of the parties involved, will use the expert knowledge each brings to the relationship, and will address the moral dimensions of the decision and the decision making process.

Finally, it should be noted that defining engagement in this way acknowledges that engagement processes may be ongoing and open-ended rather than a single, well-defined episode resulting in a decision (Yang 2018). The interdependent relationships are often long-lived, and many decisions may be needed to maintain the viability of the organization and create value. Thus, conceptualizing *stakeholder engagement* as "the dynamic interplay of stakeholder and organizational actions designed to define the communicative nature and parameters of joint decision-making efforts" (Coombs and Holladay 2018: 80) offers a view of engagement that includes both organization- and stakeholder-initiated engagement, and is consistent with conceptualizations of public relations and stakeholder theory.

2 Stakeholder engagement and corporate social responsibility

2.1 Formal reporting of stakeholder engagement processes

The issues or topics over which organizations and stakeholders engage vary, as does the extent to which the engagement processes are formalized and guided by recognized stakeholder engagement reporting frameworks such as AccountAbility's AA1000 Stakeholder Engagement Standard (AA1000SES) and the Global Reporting Initiative Standards. These standards describe "what a good-quality stakeholder engagement process looks like" (AccountAbility 2015: 7). The documents are open-source, non-proprietary, and complement the GRI's Standards for Sustainability Reporting. They justify the importance of engagement and engagement reporting, offer comprehensive guidance on engagement, and can be applied at micro, meso, and macro levels. The information and standards could benefit all parties participating in engagement, not simply the organization proposing engagement. Growing interest in this type of reporting means public relations practitioners should understand how to apply the frameworks.

According to AA1000SES, "Stakeholder engagement should be aligned with organizational objectives to improve performance of the organization through learning from stakeholders, resulting in outcomes such as product and service improvements, and better management of risk and reputation" (AccountAbility 2015: 15). The document provides guidance for establishing the purpose of the engagement, including scope, mandate, and stakeholders; planning the engagement by profiling and mapping stakeholders; determining engagement levels and methods, and drafting a plan; preparing for engagement by mobilizing resources, building capacity, and identifying and preparing for engagement risks; implementing the plan by inviting and briefing stakeholders, engaging with stakeholders, documenting the engagement and its outputs; developing an action plan and communication of the engagement outputs and action plan; and finally, monitoring and evaluating the engagement, learning and improving, following up on the action plan, and reporting on the engagement. The report itself is a form of stakeholder engagement.

Overall, systematic reporting of stakeholder engagement processes should provide transparent accounts of shared interests, decision-making processes, and actionable outcomes of engagement. Research examining report contents found that organizations may use reporting to enhance their legitimacy, but often fall short in describing their motivations for engaging and how the information and plans influenced future behavior (Crawford and Clark 2011; Devin and Lane 2014; Hurst and Ihlen 2018). If stakeholders believe their needs are not met, they could challenge the organization to provide more complete disclosure. More research is needed at this meta-level of engagement to identify the extent to which reporting facilitates information-sharing and fulfills the goals of the engagement process, especially the process of "closing the loop" (Devin and Lane 2014). Stakeholders who participated in the process may be best-suited for assessing the value of these reports, especially descriptions of the ways in which the products or outcomes of engagement were used to "close the loop."

2.2 Stakeholder engagement and corporate social responsibility

Thus far we have described stakeholder engagement as an important public relations function that contributes to ethical decision-making and shared value. Using the previously described reporting frameworks may improve the quality of engagement by guiding participants through a planned process designed to accomplish specific goals. An area of public relations over which engagement is likely to occur is corporate social responsibility (CSR) (for reviews see Bartlett 2011; Hurst and Ihlen 2018). As described in an earlier section, *corporate social responsibility* includes the expectation that business will do more than make a profit and make positive contributions to society (Carroll and Shabana 2010). CSR-related engagement may be prompted by numerous factors, most notably discussions over "what counts" as CSR and what organizations "should do" to be socially responsible, what Hurst and Ihlen (2018) call "mapping of responsibilities." Understanding stakeholder expectations, developing new initiatives, and communicating about CSR are among the more complex tasks facing public relations. Describing the role of public relations in CSR, Bartlett notes that "historically, theoretically and practically there is a strong link between public relations and CSR" (2011: 73). Globalization, access to information, and concerns over environmental and social sustainability have intensified interest in CSR.

There is no single, accepted definition of CSR. The European Commission (EC) describes CSR as "the responsibility of enterprises for their impact on society" (European Commission 2011: 6). The EC directs organizations to:

> have in place a process to integrate social, environmental, ethical, human rights and consumer concerns into their business operations and core strategy in close collaboration with their stakeholders, with the aim of: maximising the creation of shared value for their owners/shareholders and for their other stakeholders and society at large; and identifying, preventing and mitigating their possible adverse impacts.

The definition also includes *sustainability* as a facet of CSR. *Sustainable development* is defined as "development that meets the needs of the present without compromising the ability of future generations to meet their own needs" (United Nations 1987). These definitions clearly identify *society* as a stakeholder of all organizations. Thus, making for shared interests and value creation requires organizations to engage with society as a whole in addition to its other stakeholders. Because public relations cannot engage literally with an entire society, others must serve as proxy.

Stakeholder engagement is important to CSR because definitions of "responsible behavior" are socially constructed, not fixed; moreover, expectations for responsible behavior vary across time and with prevailing norms and laws in different cultural contexts. To act in accordance with macro, meso, and micro-level values and expectations, organizations must engage in dialogue to listen and cocreate the meaning of responsible behavior (Coombs and Holladay 2018; Morsing and Schultz 2006). Ignoring differences between actual and expected "responsible behavior" may provoke stakeholder-initiated critiques with negative consequences for the organization's legitimacy, social license to operate, and reputation (Lange and Washburn 2012; Lerbinger 1997; Sethi 1977).

In some cases, organizations are aware of societal expectations due to widely known criticisms of an industry. An example will illustrate how an industry issue will also be viewed as a societal issue that may be addressed (but not resolved) by an individual organization to improve its social responsibility practices and reputation. H&M Group, a fast fashion company, is aware of criticism directed at the industry as a whole and at them specifically (e. g., human rights, environmental damage, supply chain transparency, etc.). Concerns over the negative impacts of fast fashion have led some consumers to consider alternatives ranging from purchasing "ethical fashion" through renting clothing to simply buying less clothing. Thus, fast fashion companies like H&M Group are motivated to reform many of their operations to reduce the taint of fast fashion. H&M Group reports that it engages and makes decisions with numerous stakeholder groups to manage a range of concerns that pose threats to its reputation as a responsible organization. H&M Group describes its actions at its "Engaging Stakeholders" website: "We believe it is important to hold a continuous and open dialogue with our stakeholders. A multitude of diverse voices and insights help us innovate and prioritise actions within our sustainability work" (H&M Group 2019). H&M Group reports engagement with customers, communities, suppliers, peers, NGOs, INGOs, policymakers, and investors, and participates in several multi-stakeholder initiatives. As the company explains, "It is no secret (or surprise) that the challenges we face are too complex for any company to tackle alone, no matter their size. By acknowledging this complexity, we can approach these issues in a holistic way and, working together, create systematic change" (H&M Group 2019). More detailed information is available at its website. Through this type of one-way reporting (Morsing and Schultz 2006), H&M Group engages to reassure readers it understands their expectations and has the ability to create value for stakeholders as well as society. H&M Group acknowledges problems in the industry as threats (threats to value creation, CSR reputation, and overall corporate reputation). It describes the issues over which it engages with partners through information-sharing tools geared to those specific stakeholder relationships (e. g., stakeholder surveys, meetings, partnerships, direct dialogue, media analyses, etc., which are examples of both one-way and two-way communication). It also reports productive decision-making across relevant stakeholder networks to create shared value in the present and future.

In comparison to other organizations in its industry, H&M Group's website seems to offer more specific information by listing stakeholders, engagement tools, and the organization's commitments to responsible behavior. This example was presented to demonstrate how the information on its website, including additional reports to support website content, is one-way communication controlled by the organization. However, the report (and the organization behind the report and the organization's actions) may be interpreted in different ways and generate different perceptions and evaluations across different stakeholder groups. The following draws upon the H&M Group example to demonstrate various ways stakeholders may make sense of the information and how it could affect its reputation.

Some stakeholders may be impressed by the mere existence and public sharing of the report. Others might read the information and conclude H&M is a good corporate citizen, or is at least moving in the right direction. These groups are satisfied with the one-way engagement. Different stakeholders may question the report's accuracy and depth and demand more detailed information about changes in business practices and tangible outcomes derived from the engagement processes (stakeholder contestation). Financial shareholders may wonder how this type of reporting might affect the bottom line. Was engagement good for business? Management may want to know if providing the information had a positive effect on the organization's reputation in the industry. Will *society* believe H&M Group to be a good corporate citizen?

The point is that stakeholders will have different interpretations of the "meaning" of the report and derive different conclusions about value creation, including those related to its social responsibility. And, as discussed in the context of engagement, assessments are likely based on perceptions of mutual interest. How does it benefit various stakeholder groups? How does it benefit society? When will we see changes based upon the engagement described in the report? Does the socially constructed nature of CSR make it possible to determine which organizations create value for society and thus are socially responsible? How do we evaluate – assign a monetary or subjective value to – CSR? How can we meaningfully "punish" organizations that fail to meet expectations for social responsibility? Even the application of "objective" reporting frameworks to these questions will not provide answers. Definitive answers to these values-based questions are elusive and drive the need for additional research.

3 Conclusions and directions for future research

This chapter used the lens of stakeholder theory (Freeman 1984) to describe how public relations facilitates engagement for decision-making that creates value. Because Freeman's definition of stakeholder centers on mutual interest and is frequently applied in public relations research, it offered a reasonable route for exploring engagement. However, Freeman's approach is not grounded in communication.

Though it draws on systems theory, a common touchstone in public relations research and practice, it shares a weakness with systems theory: It has little to say about principles of effective stakeholder communication and does not address how to respond to conflicting interests among stakeholder groups. Freeman's recommendation to create a "new" solution that integrates the conflicts may be easier said than done. However, using *dialogic* (two-way) communication to share information, cocreate meaning, and demonstrate commitment and authentic concern for the relationship may create transformative processes and outcomes. From an alternative perspective, value may arise from dissensus and contestation that changes relationships as well as decision-making (Cisnek 2016; Coombs and Holladay 2015a, 2018; Holtzhausen 2012). Challenges may move engagement to a tipping point that provides the conditions for dialogue.

Stakeholder theory reveals flaws in the assumption that business exists only to generate profit for shareholders. A single mutually beneficial relationship will not ensure longevity. Engagement connects relevant stakeholders to an organization and stakeholders to society to *improve decision-making* which *benefits* stakeholders at a macro level. Stakeholder concerns for sustainable value creation explain why they should engage with an organization as well as why they, along with the organization, should engage with society. Stakeholders derive value from the opportunity to live in unpolluted neighborhoods, to spend leisure time in unspoiled natural settings, and to be associated with an organization with a strong CSR reputation. When an organization's activities create value for society, the organization is more likely to be seen as socially responsible.

Public relations should engage to "listen" to the economic, social, and environmental interests of society. The environment cannot speak for itself, but interest groups can. The "voice" of the climate crisis has heightened concerns about issues such as cradle-to-cradle production, externalities, and social impact assessments. The social dimension of society may now include issues the organization formerly viewed as irrelevant to its operations. But through contestation or by identifying opportunities for value creation the organization may engage over an unanticipated social issue.

We propose future research in several general areas of engagement. First, stakeholder theory generally assumes relevant stakeholders are willing to engage because they have a stake in decisions. However, how should public relations approach "reluctant stakeholders"? A reluctant stakeholder group could ignore or deny mutual interests. A different stakeholder may anticipate a power imbalance will present a barrier to promised dialogue. Presumably the organization would try to convince the reluctant stakeholder of the need to engage. This situation might occur when a stakeholder believes "It's not my problem" (i. e., "I have no stake in this") or "They don't have to listen to me" (i. e., "My lack of power translates to lack of voice"). What tactics might be used to create value in a way that attracts reluctant stakeholders? Could a version of stakeholder contestation be effective in demonstrating the need for engagement? How does engagement concerning society compare to other forms of engagement?

The discussion of engagement as participation in decision-making (Coombs and Holladay 2018a) suggests it may need to be viewed as a process with shifts in control of the parameters. Would it be useful to identify if and how patterns (sequences) occur under different circumstances (e. g., power, the complexity of the decision, access to resources such as time available for decision-making)? What would constitute "breaking points" in a long history of engagement?

Researchers have noted that there is a lack of research on how the "products" of planned engagement are used once the engagement concludes (Crawford and Clark 2011; Devin and Lane 2014; Hurst and Ihlen 2018). Research is needed to better understand why this may happen. How do organizations and stakeholders "make sense" of the lack of follow-up? What are the challenges in reporting on post-engagement? Are there material barriers or simply disinterest in using the information? If stakeholders fail to see implementation of recommended actions, how does this affect their orientation to future engagement opportunities?

The concept of dialogue has begun to dominate discussions of engagement (e. g., Taylor 2018; Taylor and Kent 2014). Because it is discussed in detail in Chapter 23 and other chapters, dialogue is not a focus in this chapter. Though dialogue represents an ideal form of engagement, is it necessarily required for ethical and effective decision-making (i. e., reaching decisions providing mutual benefits)? The practice of public relations may be served when research examines whether dialogue is always desirable. Given that dialogic principles can be difficult to learn, challenging to enact, and time-consuming, should dialogue be our preferred option for engagement?

Lastly, how are the next generations of public relations practitioners preparing to engage CSR and other stakeholders? CSR is a complex topic that can be approached in different ways and is heavily influenced by culture. The use of formal and informal reporting standards discussed earlier is prevalent in some industries but not others. Nevertheless, graduates should understand the value of standards and learn from these reporting frameworks. How can we best prepare students to use social auditing methods? What CSR-related knowledge might graduates bring to their first jobs? Are they prepared for engagement at micro, meso, and macro levels? Students should understand methods of engagement and how they can be used in various contexts.

References

AccountAbility. 2015. AA1000 Stakeholder engagement standard (AA1000SES). www.accountability. org/standards/ (accessed 15 December 2019).
Bartlett, Jennifer L. 2011. Public relations and corporate social responsibility. In Øyvind Ihlen, Jennifer Bartlett & Steve May (eds.), *The Handbook of Communication and Corporate Social Responsibility*, 67–86. Malden, MA: John Wiley & Sons.

Boston College Center for Corporate Citizenship. 2019. Corporate citizenship. https://ccc.bc.edu/content/ccc/research/corporate-citizenship-news-and-topics/corporate-citizenship.html (accessed 15 December 2019).

Botan, Carl. 1997. Ethics in strategic communication campaigns: The case for a new approach to public relations. *Journal of Business Communication* 34 (2). 188–202.

Bundy, Jonathan & Michael D. Pfarrer. 2015. A burden of responsibility: The role of social approval at the onset of a crisis. *Academy of Management Review* 40(3). 345–369.

Carroll, Archie B. & Kareem M. Shabana 2010. The business case for corporate social responsibility: A review of concepts, research and practice. *International journal of management reviews* 12(1). 85–105.

Cheney, George & Lars Thøger Christensen. 2001. Public Relations as contested terrain: A critical response. In Robert L. Heath (ed.), *Handbook of public relations*, 167–182. Thousand Oaks, CA: Sage.

Ciszek, Erica. 2016. Digital activism: How social media and dissensus inform theory and practice. *Public Relations Review* 42(2). 314–321.

Coombs, William T. & Sherry J. Holladay. 2015a. How activists shape CSR: Insights from internet contagion and contingency theories. In Ana Adi, Georgina Grigore & David Crowther (eds.), *Corporate social responsibility in the digital age,* 93–104. Bingley, UK: Emerald Publishing.

Coombs, Timothy & Sherry J. Holladay. 2015b. CSR as crisis risk: Expanding how we conceptualize the relationship. *Corporate communications: An International Journal* 20(2). 144–162.

Coombs, William T. & Sherry J. Holladay. 2018. Activist Stakeholders Challenging Organizations: Enkindling Stakeholder-Initiated Engagement. In Kim A. Johnston & Maureen Taylor (eds.), *The Handbook of Communication Engagement*, 269–283. Hoboken, NJ: Wiley-Blackwell.

Crawford, Elise Perrault & Cynthia Clark Williams. 2011. Communicating corporate social responsibility through nonfinancial reports. In Øyvind Ihlen, Jennifer Bartlett & Steve May (eds.), *The Handbook of Communication and Corporate Social Responsibility,* 338–357. Malden, MA: John Wiley & Sons.

Cutlip, Scott M., Allen H. Center & Glen M. Broom. 1994. *Effective public relations* (7th edn.). Upper Saddle Ridge, NJ: Prentice-Hall, Inc.

Dawkins, Cedric. 2014. The principle of good faith: Toward substantive stakeholder engagement. *Journal of Business Ethics* 121p (2). 283–295.

Devin, Bree L. & Anne B. Lane. 2014. Communicating engagement in corporate social responsibility: A meta-level construal of engagement. *Journal of Public Relations Research* 26(5). 436–454.

European Commission. 2011. Communication from the commission to the European parliament, the council, the European economic and social committee and the committee of the regions: A renewed EU strategy 2011–14 for corporate social responsibility. https://ec.europa.eu/growth/industry/corporate-social-responsibility_en (accessed 12 December 2019).

European Commission. No date. Corporate social responsibility & responsible business conduct. https://ec.europa.eu/growth/industry/corporate-social-responsibility_en (accessed 12 December 2019).

Freeman, Robert E. 1984. *Stakeholder management: Framework and philosophy.* Cambridge: Cambridge University Press.

Greenwood, Michelle. 2007. Stakeholder engagement: Beyond the myth of corporate responsibility. *Journal of Business Ethics* 74(4). 315–327.

H&M Group. 2019. Engaging stakeholders. https://hmgroup.com/sustainability/vision-and-strategy/stakeholder-engagement.html (accessed 17 December 2019).

Heath, Robert L. 2006. Onward into more fog: Thoughts on public relations' research directions. *Journal of Public Relations Research* 18(2). 93–114.

Holtzhausen, Derina. R. 2012. *Public relations as activism: Postmodern approaches to theory & practice.* New York: Routledge.

Hurst, Bree & Øyvind Ihlen. 2018. Corporate social responsibility and engagement: Commitment, mapping of responsibilities, and closing the loop. In Kim Amanda Johnston & Maureen Taylor (eds.), *The handbook of communication engagement*, 133–147. Hoboken, NJ: Wiley-Blackwell Publishing.

Johnston, Kim A. & Maureen Taylor. 2018. Engagement as communication: Pathways, possibilities, and future directions. In Kim A. Johnston & Maureen Taylor (eds.), *The handbook of communication engagement*, 1–15. Hoboken, NJ: Wiley-Blackwell Publishing.

Johnston, Kim A. 2014. Public relations and engagement: Theoretical imperatives of a multidimensional concept. *Journal of Public Relations Research* 26(5). 381–383.

Johnston, Kim A. 2018. Toward a theory of social engagement. In Kim Amanda Johnston & Maureen Taylor (eds.), *The handbook of communication engagement*, 19–32. Hoboken, NJ: Wiley-Blackwell.

Kent, Michael L. & Maureen Taylor. 2002. Toward a dialogic theory of public relations. *Public Relations Review* 28(1). 31–37.

Lane, Anne & Michael L. Kent. 2018. Dialogic engagement. In Kim A. Johnston & Maureen Taylor (eds.), *The handbook of communication engagement*, 61–72. Hoboken, NJ: Wiley-Blackwell.

Lange, Daniel & Nathan T. Washburn. 2012. Understanding attributions of corporate social irresponsibility. *Academy of Management Review* 37(2). 300–326.

Lerbinger, Otto. 1997. *The crisis manager: Facing risk and responsibility.* Mahwah, NJ: Lawrence Erlbaum Associates

Mckie, David & Paul Willis. 2012. Renegotiating the terms of engagement: Public relations, marketing, and contemporary challenges. *Public Relations Review* 38(5). 846–852.

Mitchell, Ronald K., Brandley R. Agle & Donna J. Wood. 1997. Toward a theory of stakeholder identification and salience: Defining the principle of who and what really counts. *Academy of Management Review* 22(4). 853–886.

Morsing, Mette & Majken Schultz. 2006. Corporate social responsibility communication: Stakeholder information, response and involvement strategies. *Business Ethics: A European Review* 15(4). 323–338.

Pieczka, Magda. 2018. Critical perspectives of engagement. In Kim A. Johnston & Maureen Taylor (eds.), *The handbook of communication engagement*, 549–568. Hoboken, NJ: Wiley-Blackwell.

Pedersen, Esben Rahbek. 2006. Making corporate social responsibility (CSR) operable: How companies translate dialogue into practice. *Business and Society Review* 111(1). 137–163.

Reputation Institute. 2019. Corporate responsibility drives "good" business. https://www. reputationinstitute.com/csr-reptrak (accessed 12 December 2019).

Reputation Institute. 2015. Why corporate brands are more important today in consumer goods. file:///G:/0 %20Engagement%20chapter%20struture/CSR/Corporate-Reputation-Importance-in-Consumer-Goods.pdf (accessed 14 December 2019).

Sethi, S. Prakash. 1977. *Advocacy advertising and large corporations: Social conflict, big business image, the news media, and public policy.* Lexington, MA: Lexington books.

Sommerfeldt, Erich J. 2013. The civility of social capital: Public relations in the public sphere, civil society, and democracy. *Public Relations Review* 39(4). 280–289.

Taylor, Maureen & Michael L. Kent. 2014. Dialogic engagement: Clarifying foundational concepts. *Journal of Public Relations Research* 26(5). 384–398.

Taylor, Maureen. 2010. Public relations in the enactment of civil society. In Robert L. Heath (ed.), *The SAGE handbook of public relations*, 5–15. Thousand Oaks, CA: Sage Publications

Taylor, Maureen. 2018. Reconceptualizing public relations in an engaged society. In Kim A. Johnston & Maureen Taylor (eds.), *The handbook of communication engagement*, 103–114. Hoboken, NJ: Wiley-Blackwell Publishing.

United Nations. 1987. Report of the world commission on environment and development: Our common future. https://sustainabledevelopment.un.org/content/documents/5987our-common-future.pdf (accessed 9 December 2019).

Walker, Kent. 2010. A systematic review of the corporate reputation literature: Definition, measurement and theory. *Corporate Reputation Review* 12(4). 357–387.

Yang, Aimei. 2018. Conceptualizing strategic engagement: A stakeholder perspective. In Kim A. Johnston & Maureen Taylor (eds.), *The handbook of communication engagement*, 221–229. Hoboken, NJ: Wiley-Blackwell Publishing.

Gareth T. Williams and Erich J. Sommerfeldt

13 Social advocacy and public relations: Building communitas in the public sphere

Abstract: Public relations as a field has long struggled to assert its role within organizational hierarchies and in clarifying the nature of its interactions with publics. Paramount goals in this pursuit have been to solidify its role as a management function and to identify what unique value public relations offers an organization. Some theorists have suggested social advocacy as a way in which public relations can offer unique benefits to an organization by strengthening connections between the organization, its constituent publics, and society. Many examples of social advocacy exist within the literature, but are accompanied by questions of what constitutes ethical advocacy – and what constitutes ethical public relations in general. However, extant literature approaches the topic from many diverse and even opposing points of view and theoretical bases. In addition, unaligned terminologies obfuscate the overall narrative about social advocacy and public relations. This chapter compiles influential and relevant literature and examines the concepts of social advocacy through the lens of *communitas*, or an orientation to serve the community, and the public sphere.

Keywords: activism; advocacy; civil society; communitas; corporate social responsibility; issue advocacy; public relations; public sphere

1 Introduction

Advocacy has been a core function of public relations for the entire history of the field (Cancel et al. 1997). Public relations scholarship has framed effective and ethical advocacy as essential for public relations to achieve its aspirant identity as a distinct profession and part of organizational management (e. g. Dozier and Lauzen 2000; Edgett 2002; Grunig J. 2000). Publicly representing an individual, organization, or an idea is an accepted part of public relations practice. As such, the role of public relations as an advocate is clear, despite some lingering questions as to how most ethically to enact that advocacy (Edgett 2002). Significantly less clear, however, is the part of public relations in *social* advocacy.

The potential contributions of public relations to *society* rather than to *organizations* is a question of significant debate in recent scholarship. Retrospectives of public relations literature have shown that most scholarship has examined the role of public relations in increasing organizational effectiveness, most often within the context of for-profit organizations (e. g., Pasadeos, Berger, and Renfro 2010). A smaller stream of literature has attempted to theorize the role of public relations in making communities or societies more effective. For example, a number of works have focused on the

https://doi.org/10.1515/9783110554250-013

ability of public relations to serve a community-building function (Kruckeberg and Starck 1988; Hallahan 2004; Valentini, Kruckeberg, and Starck 2012). Public relations scholars have also discussed the possibilities for public relations to build civil society (Taylor 2010), facilitate the emergence of public spheres and democratic discussion (Raupp 2011; Sommerfeldt 2013), and ultimately contribute toward making communities and societies more fully functional (Heath 2006).

Building on the work of Heath (2006), Kruckeberg and Starck (1988), Taylor (2010), Sommerfeldt (2013) and others, we consider social advocacy as a means by which public relations can help an organization shape and more deeply participate in the society in which it operates. Social advocacy is an avenue by which public relations can build and maintain relationships with a spectrum of publics, identify and address organizational and societal power structures to benefit both the organization and society. By engaging in ideological collaboration with publics, organizations can cultivate relationships and shared meaning to ensure strong and resilient bonds and cultivate the capacity for the public to determine its own self-interest. Organizational social advocacy can help ensure and reinforce enfranchisement. The field's professional identity can be significantly improved and developed through critical consideration of the role social advocacy can play in public relations (Dozier and Lauzen 2000; Heath 2006). In such work to shape society, however, public relations practitioners must ensure ethical and mutually beneficial practices.

2 Social advocacy: In search of a definition

Many important concepts in the public relations literature have been accused of being manifestly "primitive terms" – undefined notions that appeal to intuition, an assumed common knowledge or generally understood meaning. For example, in their 1997 article, Broom, Casey, and Ritchey argued that "relationship," to that point in time, had been treated a primitive term in the public relations literature and lacked clear meaning and focus. Similarly, "dialogue" has been misunderstood and inappropriately operationalized by innumerable studies (Paquette, Sommerfeldt, and Kent 2015). Clear and consistent use of terms is essential to meaningful theoretical operationalization and the generation of heuristic research. Thus, we must first attempt to define what we mean by social advocacy before we can unpack its implications for public relations praxis.

Of the scattered scholarly texts that utilize the term "social advocacy" within and without public relations, none have made explicit attempts to define it. Independently, the terms social and advocacy have relatively clear meanings. "Social" applies to the attributes of society, which "consists of multiple collectivities, people living in groups with varying degrees of agreement, permeability, trust, power, and independence," and such collectivities "[share] views of reality and identification to coordinate their activities" (Heath 2006: 96). Edgett (2002: 1) defined advocacy as "publically representing an individual, organization, or idea with the object of persuading a target audience to look favorably upon – or accept the point of view of – the individual, organization, or idea". Social advocacy, upon first consideration, might simply be the act of participating in the activities of a collectivity to shape society as the public representation of an organization.

While working for the "public interest" may be a theme of social advocacy, Heath (2006) has argued that "the public interest" is too varied, complex, and conflicting a moniker for guiding public relations practice. Indeed, as will be discussed later, what is in the "public interest" is often not determined by the public, but by those with the resources and power to influence what issues enter into fora of public debate. As public relations is often construed as an organizational or corporate function – and one designed to serve organizational ends – a more precise and heuristically useful definition should perhaps be situated within an organizational context.

Other, perhaps related, concepts in the literature might easily be mistaken for social advocacy. Organizations may take stands on public issues – for example, Dodd and Supa (2015: 287) presented *corporate social advocacy* as the "taking of a public stance on a controversial social-political issue by corporations, most often in the form of a CEO statement." A working definition of social advocacy seemingly should also be differentiable from *corporate social responsibility* (CSR) efforts. Scholars have framed CSR as corporations fulfilling their economic, social, environmental, and philanthropic duties to society – working to meet the responsibilities and taking actions beyond their legal obligations and economic or business aims (Carroll 1991; Capriotti and Moreno 2007). Yet, CSR may be undertaken to legitimate the business itself rather than with genuine intent to serve the "public interest." Indeed, current CSR communication research focuses more on what to communicate to publics (Lee and Shin 2010), how to communicate (Wigley 2008), and where to communicate (Avery et al. 2010; Capriotti 2011) to reap the best rewards for the organization.

The only source – to our knowledge – that has attempted to explicitly define social advocacy in the context of public (and strategic) communication, is the Council on Accreditation (COA) – an international, independent, non-profit, human service accrediting organization. COA defines social advocacy as "[t]aking action to promote or prevent changes in policies or practices that impact entire groups of people," with a purpose to "[p]romote positive change and eliminate social, economic, and environmental injustice in social institutions, systems, legislation, and practices that affect individuals, families, groups, and communities" (COA 2017). The definition offered by the COA suggests social advocacy may serve different issues, social sectors or arenas, such as the environment and social and economic injustices.

The above definition is intuitive and pleasing, if still a bit reductive for our purposes. Is it enough that organizations work to influence supposedly "public" issues for such actions to constitute social advocacy? If so, social advocacy arguably becomes nearly indistinguishable in practice from better understood functions such as CSR or even issues management. And, as this literature tells us, such efforts are not necessarily concerned with the "public" interest, but rather the best interest of the organization. Advocacy, in and of itself, is an inherent quality of existence – social actors will seek to have their views prevail. But, the real challenge of truly *social* advocacy may be to balance organizational interests with those of others – reflecting a *communitas* rather than *corporatas* orientation to public dialogue and advocacy (Heath 2006).

3 Social advocacy and communitas

At its core, *communitas* is a concept wherein individuals and organizations recognize they are inextricably bound together, and that they must act for the good of the community. Communitas is central to Heath's (2006) vision of public relations working to build a fully functioning society. Fully functioning society theory (FST) offers a logical framework through which to examine public relations as a social advocacy function. Heath (2006) connects the responsibility of public relations to duties of responsible corporate citizenship, including an appreciation for responsible persuasion and its application in societal decision making. This role of organization as a "worthy citizen" underscores the utility of social advocacy for public relations in conjunction with fully functioning society theory (Heath, Waymer, and Palenchar 2013). Heath (2006: 105) explained:

> [T]he concept of communitas features the symbolic and instrumental reality of community as transcending the structures and functions of individuals and organizations. Identification is vital to this concept, as people see themselves and the organizations in the community as bound together. It is instrumental because it brings people together in harmony. As a consequence, organizations that foster communitas are seen as making an instrumental contribution to the full functioning of society.

When identified as part a community, individuals and organizations can work for its betterment. At the other end of a communicative and ethical spectrum, organizations with a *corporatas* orientation work to dominate and manipulate social interactions. Partisan exploitation and stratification of power and status are the norm in *corporatas* – building community becomes irrelevant (Heath 2006).

If an organization is to fulfil its role as an agent capable of shaping a fully functioning society, to be truly "social," as in part of a society, its social advocacy must attempt to influence environmental, social, or economic issues in ways that embody the spirit of communitas. Heath (2006: 106–107) distinguished communitas from corporatas through communication variables such as open, respectful, two-way communication based on listening and sharing information; building trust among publics by being reliable, non-exploitative, and dependable; cooperating to make sure that the needs of both the organization and stakeholders are met; fostering compatible views, mutual understanding, and shared interests with stakeholders; and display-ing a sense of commitment to the community by being involved and investing in it. In short, organizations that pursue relationships based on respect, trust, and dignity are focused on the good of its publics, stakeholders, and community. Social advocacy efforts that join people together on projects of social justice and social significance can, in turn, foster greater mutual respect and understanding. This benefits the long-term interests of the organization, the stability of the community, and the enfranchise-ment of community stakeholders.

Organizations have values and goals. As an organization attempts to achieve these goals, it should build relationships based on common values and meanings, and "acquire the resources it needs that, ultimately, will be in the best interests of all" (Tilson 2011: 46). Thus, we propose as the definition of social advocacy in public relations: *Publically representing collective interests to influence, promote, or prevent changes in policies or social practices that impact individuals, groups, organizations, and communities with a purpose to promote shared values.* The key to this definition is that the *telos* is not public perception of the organization or engagement with the organization, but the structures and mores of the society in which the organization and its interlocutors participate. This definition situates social advocacy squarely within the bounds of Heath's (2006) fully functioning society theory (FST) and its call for responsible advocacy in the spirit of communitas. Our definition suggests that, in order to practice social advocacy, an organization must have open and trusting rela-tionships with its community and that the views of the organization and community are aligned. If not aligned, the process of achieving shared understanding is at least done with respect for the others' interest.

Public relations scholars have, for some time, argued that the practice of dialogue and two-way communication can be used to help communities. Heath's (2006) per-spectives were built on the earlier work of scholars like Kruckeberg and Stark (1988), who argued that organizations should participate in their communities, and that organizational interests and community interests are often one and the same. Public relations can help organizations and publics "build a community where dialogue and mutual understanding can take place" (Valentini, Kruckeberg, and Starck 2012: 874). To use the customary systems terminology, in performing their boundary-spanning function, public relations should seek to solicit meaningful input from the environ-ment and generate outputs intent on building common zones of meaning (Heath 2006). See Chapter 22 in this book for a more detailed explanation of the perspective.

The key to social advocacy research – which may or may not coincide with CSR or corporate social advocacy – is consideration of the means by which an organiza-tion can contribute to or influence its community and society, and understanding the motives behind such communication. By participating in the strata of communications and activities that shape a society (i. e. public sphere), an organization participates in the creation and (re-)formation of a community. It collaborates with co-creators of the society for the "collective enactment of narratives [and] shared meaning made public through voices in unified competition" (Heath 2006: 97) to enhance societal operation and build the mechanisms by which it operates.

4 Social advocacy in the public sphere

The use of the terms "influence" and "promote" in our definition of social advocacy makes explicit the intention to persuade. Persuasion is the goal of social advocacy. However, the target of persuasion is not stakeholders' perception of the organization and its legitimacy – as is so often the case with traditional public relations efforts such as CSR – but their perception of issues. Such issues or factors may include social norms assumed by the public, regulations enacted by the government, policies proposed by the public or maintained by the government, and other environmental factors that affect or could affect the community or communities in which the organization exists. This is not to say organizations cannot advocate for positions on social issues that might benefit themselves. The challenge is to uphold the value of public discourse "while determining how to subsume partisan interests to societal interests" (Heath 2006: 108).

Indeed, discourse is also essential to our definition of social advocacy, as it is similarly essential to understandings of public relations. Discourse, as the means by which public relations "[agents] shape the environments in which organizations operate and how they generate and attract resources and affect, and are affected by other interested voices" (Heath 2011: 418) is essential to the social advocacy process. Public relations agents must represent a point of view within the public sphere of debate. Through discourse – enacted via public relations strategies – voices for social advocacy are able to compete in the "agentic discursive wrangles in the public arena" (Heath, Waymer, and Palenchar 2013: 274) – in other words, participate in dialogue in the public sphere.

A few scholars in public relations have argued that public relations can add value to society by enabling organizational participation in the public sphere, and by supporting the social structures and institutions that check state power (e. g., Sommerfeldt 2013; Taylor 2010; Taylor, 2011; Yang and Taylor 2013). The public sphere provides a mechanism though which public relations theory conceptualizes the relationship between the organization and the public (Leitch and Motion 2010). Indeed, considerable academic discussion on ethical public relations is founded on a pluralistic, Habermasian model of equal parties engaged in constructive discourse that, by each educating the other, seek to improve and optimize society (cf. Sommerfeldt 2013). Early research in the Excellence Theory tradition of public relations (cf. Grunig J. 1992) was founded on the presupposition that public relations could only achieve its fullest potential in pluralistic societies, wherein multiple voices compete with each other for power and influence. Extensive criticism of this view points out that normative pluralism ignores inherent power imbalances within society, making the notion of equal voice in public debate impossible (e. g. Fraser 1990; Roper 2005), a subject to which we return later.

Ethical organizational communication and social advocacy demands a perspective that extends beyond the priorities of the organization (Heath 2006) and reflects the needs of society. Reflexive public relations accommodates the notion as well (cf. van Ruler and Verčič 2005). Focusing on the good of society as well as the originating organization is an effective means to build relationships. By making issues of social concern public within the public sphere, public relations can work to ensure the representation of competing interests – including their own. In working to ensure the interests of the organization and that of its constituent community are aligned, or in the benevolent process of alignment, public relations facilitates enfranchisement in public issue debate.

Public relations is the public advocacy function by which agents representing social interests make their views known within the public sphere, for the public sphere rests on the principle of "publicity" (Sommerfeldt 2013). Issues must become public to become the subject of public debate. Social advocacy as we now know it, the pure and the tainted, the ethical and unethical, the earnest and the ulterior, the aspirational and the nihilistic, is sewn from the attainment of a critical publicity for issues within the public sphere. If a democratic state is dependent upon the celebration of diversity to "preserve freedom of thought and expression" (Hauser and Blair 1982: 145), social advocacy plays an essential role. Hegel and Mill described debate as a means by which society could sustain multiple competing notions of what constitutes truth (Self 2010). Indeed, if political concerns are only manifested in the public sphere when articulated, the rhetorical act of the social advocate plays an essential role giving social concerns standing as "theory, belief, or value" (Hauser and Blair 1982: 163). The public sphere therefore provides a compelling theoretical rationale in which to ground research on public relations and social advocacy – providing the forum in which actors engage in constructive, rational discourse to determine the best course for society in the spirit of communitas.

The greatest benefit of a thriving public sphere in a democratic society is that the public generates the conception of itself, of its own publicity – "individuals fighting to give direction to their lives" – rather than that concept being dictated by more powerful organizational actors or the government itself (Rogers 2012: 2). This fight, according to John Dewey (1927), is both the animating force behind the very concept of "publics," and a force that requires maintenance and sensitive attention, less it expire. It also allows publics to identify social and political priorities and advocate for those priorities or align themselves with others already advocating for them. The public sphere and civil society make both public relations and social advocacy possible and essential.

5 Power, ethics, and the public sphere

Power and motive are central issues for ethics in public relations. Ethical considerations become of particular import when discussing social advocacy. Unethical social advocacy practices may have roots in perceiving the public as "a means to an organization's end goal" (Vasquez and Taylor 2001: 139). Such efforts, like those associated with CSR practice, often conceal a profit motive in the shell of social advocacy. Alternately, social advocacy may manifest as a policy interest. These often ultimately benefit the organization's profit motive. One oft-cited example is the work of prominent think tanks to simultaneously counter tobacco regulations, attribution of acid rain to industrial sources, greenhouse gas emissions standards (specifically), and climate change regulation (in general) (Oreskes and Conway 2011). The common denominator in these efforts is not the issues themselves, but general opposition to government regulation through the ideal of unrestrained free market capitalism. While broad patterns can become apparent when viewing organizational activity at the portfolio level, publics are rarely incisive (or interested) enough to undertake such a granular examination of organizational communication strategies.

Examples of faux-social advocacy campaigns abound in contemporary practice. For example, public relations agents have created the false appearance of a grassroots movement in the form of front groups to undercut legitimate grassroots or earnest social advocacy efforts. Organizations may also present a false image of environmental conscientiousness to boost public perception. These tactics often co-opt genuine dialogue and public debate to "pre-empt, counter, engage with, accommodate, undermine, frame, etc., the arguments and claims of pressure groups," (Hansen 2010: 51). When greenwashing, public relations firms sometimes employ a "good cop/bad cop" approach to social advocacy, on the one hand seeking to project an issue-friendly (e. g., a "green" environmentalist image) to appeal to one ethic of the public, and on the other labelling advocates for that cause as terrorists and extremists, and not to be trusted by the public (Rowell 1996: 106–107). This manipulation can lure the public into trusting the corporate interest over that of the activist social advocate, and view the corporation as the true advocate with the public's interests at heart. "Industry cannot win purely with a public relations drive and therefore needs to initiate a pro-industry activist movement (...) the end result is people fighting for industry, but with all the hallmarks of fighting for themselves" (Rowell 1996: 13). By deceiving the public into thinking they are supporting their own interests while in fact helping bolster a commercial organization's interests, social advocacy is turned into a tool of manipulation and control (i. e. *corporatas*).

The public relations industry has gained a reputation for espousing these deceptive tactics, including some of the most prominent firms in the industry (Rowell 1996: 108). To use a famous example from the 1960s – the early years of environmental activism – when threatened by an anti-agricultural chemical wave of public opinion following the publication of Rachel Carson's *Silent Spring*, Monsanto Chemical Company published "The Desolate Year," an imitation/parody of Carson's prose that painted an apocalyptic picture of a world without agricultural chemicals (Monsanto Chemical Company 1962). Paradoxically, the image was that chemicals are necessary for the natural environment of Earth to thrive in an ideal, verdant state, and removal of the benevolent influence of manufactured chemicals produced an insect-intensive Armageddon.

The overt partisanship with which powerful corporations use public relations to further narrow self-interest raises an important consideration: is there a place for organizational communication in the public sphere? As an actor rather than a private citizen, the role for organizations in the Habermasian conceptualization of the sphere at first seems indistinct and inappropriate until interpreted through a theatrical lens, as by Hauser and Blair (1982: 158): "The significance of the sphere is not, however, that it provide visibility to the persons in it nor that it receive institutional recognition. It is important in that it provides an audience for public actors." As public actors, organizations ostensibly have good standing to participate in rational-critical debate on issues of public concern (cf. Sommerfeldt 2013). But Habermas bemoaned organizational influences in the public sphere, accusing corporate mass-media functions of advertising and public relations of co-opting the ability of the public to self-determine its own publicity – that is, what is thought to be of critical importance for public debate. He distinguished between *success-oriented strategic action* and *understand-oriented communicative action*, the former's goal to control and direct and the latter to achieve mutual understanding (cf. Self 2010). The concentration of power within organizations – for organizations exist to consolidate power resources (Heath and Palenchar 2008) – would initially (and often rightly) suggest organizations attempt to shape public discourse more for control and direction (corporatas) rather than mutual understanding (communitas): "Corporations are not in the business of giving everyone an equal voice and chance for discussion; they are focused on increasing profit margins. Discourse ethics' requirement of the actual participation by all affected also creates logistical difficulties for organizations" (Meisenbach, 2006: 57).

Indeed, the literature on dialogue in public relations (Kent and Taylor 2002) has made clear the difficulty of enacting full and open communication between an organization and its publics, due to the inherent risk involved in such communication and the unwillingness of organizations to surrender their inherently more powerful position. That said, realization of the Habermasian model of rational-critical, representative discourse in a practicable framework could provide a useful guide by which scholars and practitioners would "get closer to an ideal of ethical organizational communication" (Meisenbach 2006: 58).

While equal power or solidarity between an organization and a public may not be possible to attain, genuine aspirations to work in partnership with publics and establish common zones of meaning, as opposed to exploiting a common interest, is essential for genuine social advocacy. Thus, common public relations efforts like CSR and issues management may be taken to be genuine social advocacy if grounded in

communitas. A defensive facet of advocacy in public relations is an issues management function: anticipating and responding to issues identified by publics before they
threaten the organization (Grunig J. and Repper 1992). Social advocacy, if practiced
from a communitas orientation, allows organizations to proactively engage publics
and identify common priorities on issues of public policy, society, and other common
interests. Jaques (2006: 417) asserted that "issue management has the potential to
become a bridging process between activists and their natural targets, principally big
business and big government." The power of "issue advocacy" is particularly prominent in contemporary Internet-mediated engagement of interested publics (Hestres
2014). Through such advocacy, organizations can motivate publics to expand their
engagement to activist roles and to solicit expanded attention from media.

In an asymmetric society, advocacy and accommodation may provide superior
strategies for public relations than normative models of collaboration and consensus (Hallahan 2000). Activism can overcome power dynamics and improve the target
organization itself. Power dynamics in organizational dominant coalitions (cf. Grunig
J. 1992) impact or constrain efforts by public relations practitioners. Practitioners must
consider means to overcome these power dynamics and engage in activism to "serve
the voices of the many" (Berger 2005: 6). A shift to an activist public relations role,
as articulated in postmodern public relations literature, could both improve organizational relationships with stakeholders and internal power dynamics (Holtzhausen
2012).

The very act of vocalizing an opinion (or discourse, to set a higher bar) has power,
as "language of communication has its meaning wholly as it represents some other
order of reality (...) one does not act through language but conveys what stands behind
language (...) to engage in the rhetorical act is to exercise power" (Hauser and Blair
1982: 151–152). The concept of the rhetorical act as a defining act of the public is combined with situational theory of publics in the *homo narrans* model (Vasquez and
Taylor 2001). This communication-centred theory helps illumine internal functions
and communication within publics (Botan and Soto 1998). Such an approach may
become increasingly relevant as digital media render the public sphere in channels of
communication that are more visible and accessible for study.

Public relations practitioners can assume an advocacy role to influence publics by
engaging with activist groups and social movements. This also highlights a problem
in an organizational conceptualization of social advocacy. If undertaken as a means
by which to exploit the favour of a desired audience or to leverage social forces to an
organizational advantage, the public relations practitioner is trivializing the struggles
of the people upon whom the organization depends. Exploitation of social advocacy
for organizational gain is certainly an ethically problematic undertaking, one of many
the public relations practitioner encounters.

Earnest embrace of ethical practice can begin to counter the negative public perception of the field of public relations. Edgett (2002) asserts the need for an ethical
framework of advocacy within the field of public relations if the field is to achieve

status as a respected profession. Incorporation of advocacy as a necessary function of public relations is reinforced by Fawkes (2007). Fawkes (2007) builds on Edgett (2002) to argue that, rather than attempting to divorce itself from persuasion and an attendant perception of propaganda, public relations needs to explore ethical approaches that recognize persuasion as an intrinsic part of the field and not anathema to an ethical profession. Several authors affirm that even explicit persuasion can be conducted ethically (Fawkes 2007; Meisenbach 2006; Messina 2007).

Organizations wishing to persuade publics may also appropriate already accepted positions to frame a new discourse (Leitch and Motion 2010). Contemporary U.S. theories of public relations are criticized for not obligating ethical practice or commitment to a societal good above the good of the organization (Bowen 2010: 570–571). Excellence theory is singled out for particular criticism as advocating for power within the organizational management and not obligating use of that power in an ethical or mutually beneficial manner (Bowen 2010).

6 Digital media, advocacy, and the public sphere

Erosion or corruption of the ideal of the public sphere has long been lamented. Sprawling megalopolises, fast and isolating modes of transportation, mass broadcast media, and even proliferation of special interest groups are cited as culprits. The traditional role of journalists as information gatekeepers, collecting and vetting information for public digestion, has been upended. Public trust in media has eroded with segmentation of sources of information, and new media throve on ideology over impartiality, leaving it up to the consumer to be sceptical or swayed, as befits their viewpoint (Kruckeberg and Vujnovic 2010).

This fragmentation of and global access to media may have rendered the concept of defined publics – and any attempt to segment and target publics – as *potentially* impracticable (Kruckeberg and Vujnovic 2010). Normative models of public relations that previously dominated scholarship appear to be giving way to communication-based participatory models (Vasquez and Taylor 2001). The Hegelian construct of debate as driver of society and Habermasian public sphere has reached its latest realization in social network media (Self, 2010). This media-centred (r)evolution of public engagement and meaning making is not new. Habermas traces the evolution of the public sphere in parallel to the evolution of communication and media, and the subsequent expansions in public power from the 18th to the 20th century. As such, digital media may provide a platform to revive fora in which public spheres may arise (Hiebert 2005), though the capacity of such platforms to enact traditional notions of rational-critical debate has been questioned (Dahlgren 2005; Freelon 2010).

Digital media platforms are effective tools for organizing and connecting publics, to "shift power from the owners of the means of production to the masses" (Hon 2015:

313). Returning to the debate of ethics in social advocacy, Hiebert (2005: 8) necessarily hedges the bet with the dangers of this new paradigm: "Of course, much effort is being put into making those technologies even greater tools of propaganda, mind control, and hegemony than anything before." Social and interactive media "with murky sourcing" revitalize the conceptualization of publics as a process of evolution and iteration rather than neat segments that align and disperse in patterns by citing (Self 2010: 90). It is into this context that the public relations practitioner of today and tomorrow must wade to "join the conversation" (Self 2010: 90). Note the egalitarian tone of the charge.

7 Conclusion

Despite the potential for public relations to serve the public interest, and working to support the structures and institutions that make society a better place to live, an inherent weakness of public relations is "the profession's reputation for being partisan and self-serving" (Heath 2006: 94). Yet, this weakness provides an opportunity for professional growth. By working to serve the interests of society, rather than the interests of the communicator or organization, public relations professionals can simultaneously add value to society and become more expert and ethical communicators. Projects aimed at diffusing tensions, fostering understanding, partnerships, and public participation work to establish a sense of communitas, and may demonstrate the role that public relations can play in truly social advocacy. Disingenuous or manipulative efforts to shape society will exacerbate the inherent weakness of public relations identified by Heath (2006) and impede future relationship-building and engagement.

Internet searches for the term "social advocacy" and "public relations" result in innumerable sites cataloguing campaigns by social justice and activist groups – with a notable skew to social media campaigns. However, social advocacy public relations is not limited to social justice organizations, activist groups, or digital media platforms. Heath (2006) argued that a significant problem in the positioning of public relations theory and research is the common association of the practice with business, and especially large corporations. All organizations need and can engage in public relations. Accordingly, all organizations can work for the betterment of the communities and societies in which they operate. Social advocacy can be practiced by any organization – public or private sector – including non-profits and grassroots advocacy groups, for-profit entities, nongovernmental organizations (NGOs) and think tanks, and even governmental organizations.

Social advocacy offers many essential opportunities for public relations to realize disciplinary goals, including chances to shed its negative public aura, to cultivate resilient ties with stakeholders and publics, to turn organizational power structures to its advantage, to assert its rightful place among organizational management func-tions, and to actively improve societal and global processes through an ethical frame-work of practice. Social advocacy can also be leveraged by public relations practi-tioners to address power structures within an organization and to establish itself as a management function. These benefits directly address issues at the core of many debates regarding the identity and purpose of public relations, which are rooted in the twin needs for the field to claim a distinct identity in the social science constellation and to firmly establish itself as a distinct, ethical, and respected professional practice.

References

Avery, Elizabeth, Ruthann Lariscy, Ellie Amador, Tanya Ickowitz, Charles Primm & Abbey Taylor. 2010. Diffusion of social media among public relations practitioners in health departments across various community population sizes. *Journal of Public Relations Research* 22(3). 336–358.

Berger, Bruce. 2005. Power over, power with, and power to relations: Critical reflections on public relations, the dominant coalition, and activism. *Journal of Public Relations Research* 17(1). 5–28. https://doi.org/10.1207/s1532754xjprr1701_3 (accessed 26 November 2018).

Botan, Carl & Francisco Soto. 1998. A semiotic approach to the internal functioning of publics: Implications for strategic communication and public relations. *Public Relations Review* 24(1). 21–44.

Bowen, Shannon. 2010. The nature of good in public relations. In Robert Heath (ed.), *The SAGE handbook of public relations*, 569–583. Thousand Oaks, CA: SAGE Publications.

Broom, Glen, Shawna Casey & James Ritchey. 1997. Toward a concept and theory of organization-public relationships. *Journal of Public Relations Research* 9(2). 83–98. https://doi.org/10.1207/s1532754xjprr0902_01 (accessed 26 November 2018).

Cancel, Amanda, Glen Cameron, Lynne Sallot & Michael Mitrook. 1997. It depends: A contingency theory of accommodation in public relations. *Journal of Public Relations Research* 9(1). 31–63. https://doi.org/10.1207/s1532754xjprr0901_02 (accessed 26 November 2018).

Capriotti, Paul. 2011. Communicating corporate social responsibility through the internet and social media. In Øyvind Ihlen, Jennifer Bartlett & Steve May (eds.), *The Handbook of Communication and Corporate Social Responsibility*, 358–378. Oxford: Wiley-Blackwell. https://doi.org/10.1002/9781118083246.ch18 (accessed 26 November 2018).

Capriotti, Paul & Ángeles Moreno. 2007. Corporate citizenship and public relations: The importance and interactivity of social responsibility issues on corporate websites. *Public Relations Review* 33(1). 84–91. https://doi.org/10.1016/j.pubrev.2006.11.012 (accessed 26 November 2018).

Carroll, Archie. 1991. The pyramid of corporate social responsibility: Toward the moral management of organizational stakeholders. *Business Horizons* 34(4). 39–48. https://doi.org/10.1016/0007-6813(91)90005-G (accessed 26 November 2018).

COA. 2017. Social Advocacy – Council on Accreditation. http://coanet.org/standard/soc/purpose.pdf (accessed 17 December 2017).

Dahlgren, Peter. 2005. The Internet, public spheres, and political communication: Dispersion and deliberation. *Political Communication* 22(2). 147–162. https://doi.org/10.1080/10584600590933160 (accessed 26 November 2018).

Dewey, John. 1927. *The public and its problems*. New York: Holt

Dodd, Melissa & Dustin Supa. 2015. Testing the viability of corporate social advocacy as a predictor of purchase intention. *Communication Research Reports* 32(4). 287–293. https://doi.org/10.1080/08824096.2015.1089853 (accessed 26 November 2018).

Dozier, David & Martha Lauzen. 2000. Liberating the intellectual domain from the practice: Public relations, activism, and the role of the scholar. *Journal of Public Relations Research* 12(1). 3–22. https://doi.org/10.1207/S1532754XJPRR1201_2 (accessed 26 November 2018).

Edgett, Ruth. 2002. Toward an ethical framework for advocacy in public relations. *Journal of Public Relations Research* 14(1). 1–26. https://doi.org/10.1207/S1532754XJPRR1401_1 (accessed 26 November 2018).

Fawkes, Johanna. 2007. Public relations models and persuasion ethics: a new approach. *Journal of Communication Management* 11(4). 313–331. https://doi.org/10.1108/13632540710843922 (accessed 26 November 2018).

Fraser, Nancy. 1990. Rethinking the public sphere: A contribution to the critique of actually existing democracy. *Social Text* 25/26. 56–80. https://www.jstor.org/stable/466240 (accessed 26 November 2018).

Freelon, Deen. 2010. Analyzing online political discussion using three models of democratic communication. *New Media & Society* 12(7). 1172–1190, https://doi.org/10.1177/1461444809357927 (accessed 26 November 2018).

Grunig, James (ed.). 1992. *Excellence in public relations and communication management.* Hillsdale, N.J: Lawrence Erlbaum Associates.

Grunig, James. 2000. Collectivism, collaboration, and societal corporatism as core professional values in public relations. *Journal of Public Relations Research* 12(1). 23–48. https://doi.org/10.1207/S1532754XJPRR1201_3 (accessed 26 November 2018).

Grunig, James & Fred Repper. 1992. Strategic management, publics, and issues. In James Grunig (ed.), *Excellence in public relations and communication management*, 117–157. Hillsdale, N.J: Lawrence Erlbaum Associates.

Hallahan, Kirk. 2000. Inactive publics: the forgotten publics in public relations'. *Public Relations Review* 26(4). 499–515. https://doi.org/10.1016/S0363-8111(00)00061-8 (accessed 26 November 2018).

Hallahan, Kirk. 2004. "Community" as a foundation for public relations theory and practice. *Communication Yearbook* 28(1). 233–279. https://doi.org/10.1207/s15567419cy2801_7 (accessed 26 November 2018).

Hansen, Anders. 2010. *Environment, media and communication.* London & New York: Routledge.

Hauser, Gerald & Carole Blair. 1982. Rhetorical antecedents to the public. *Pre/Text* 3. 139–167.

Heath, Robert. 2006. Onward into more fog: Thoughts on public relations' research directions. *Journal of Public Relations Research* 18(2). 93–114. https://doi.org/10.1207/s1532754xjprr1802_2 (accessed 26 November 2018).

Heath, Robert. 2011. External organizational rhetoric: Bridging management and sociopolitical discourse. *Management Communication Quarterly* 25(3). 415–435. https://doi.org/10.1177/0893318911409532 (accessed 26 November 2018).

Heath, Robert & Michael Palenchar. 2008. Strategic issues management: Organizations and public policy challenges Thousand Oaks, CA: Sage Publications.

Heath, Robert, Damion Waymer & Michael Palenchar. 2013. Is the universe of democracy, rhetoric, and public relations whole cloth or three separate galaxies? *Public Relations Review* 39(4). 271–279. https://doi.org/10.1016/j.pubrev.2013.07.017 (accessed 26 November 2018).

Hestres, Luis. 2014. Preaching to the choir: Internet-mediated advocacy, issue public mobilization, and climate change. *New Media & Society* 16(2). 323–339. https://doi.org/10.1177/1461444813480361 (accessed 26 November 2018).

Hiebert, Ray. 2005. Commentary: new technologies, public relations, and democracy. *Public Relations Review* 31(1). 1–9. https://doi.org/10.1016/j.pubrev.2004.11.001 (accessed 26 November 2018).

Holtzhausen, Derina. 2012. *Public relations as activism: postmodern approaches to theory & practice*. New York: Routledge.

Hon, Linda. 2015. Digital social advocacy in the Justice for Trayvon Campaign. *Journal of Public Relations Research* 27(4). 299–321. https://doi.org/10.1080/1062726X.2015.1027771 (accessed 26 November 2018).

Jaques, Tony. 2006. Activist "rules" and the convergence with issue management. *Journal of Communication Management* 10(4). 407–420. https://doi.org/10.1108/13632540610714836 (accessed 26 November 2018).

Kent, Michael & Maureen Taylor. 2002. Toward a dialogic theory of public relations. *Public Relations Review* 28(1). 21–37.

Kruckeberg, Dean & Kenneth Starck. 1988. *Public relations and community: a reconstructed theory*. New York: Praeger.

Kruckeberg, Dean & Marina Vujnovic. 2010. The death of the concept of publics (plural) in 21st century public relations. *International Journal of Strategic Communication* 4(2). 117–125. https://doi.org/10.1080/15531181003701921 (accessed 26 November 2018).

Lee, Ki-Hoon & Dongyoung Shin. 2010. Consumers' responses to CSR activities: The linkage between increased awareness and purchase intention. *Public Relations Review* 36(2). 193–195. https://doi.org/10.1016/j.pubrev.2009.10.014 (accessed 26 November 2018).

Leitch, Shirley & Judy Motion. 2010. Publics and public relations: Effecting change. In Robert Heath (ed.), *The SAGE handbook of public relations*, 99–110. Thousand Oaks, CA: SAGE Publications.

Meisenbach, Rebecca. 2006. Habermas's discourse ethics and principle of universalization as a moral framework for organizational communication. *Management Communication Quarterly* 20(1). 39–62. https://doi.org/10.1177/0893318906288277 (accessed 26 November 2018).

Messina, Alex. 2007. Public relations, the public interest and persuasion: an ethical approach. *Journal of Communication Management* 11(1). 29–52. https://doi.org/10.1108/136325407 10725978 (accessed 26 November 2018).

Monsanto Chemical Company. 1962. The Desolate Year. *Monsanto Magazine* 42(4). 4–9.

Oreskes, Naomi & Erik Conway. 2011. *Merchants of doubt: how a handful of scientists obscured the truth on issues from tobacco smoke to global warming*. New York: Bloomsbury Press.

Paquette, Michael, Erich Sommerfeldt & Michael Kent. 2015. Do the ends justify the means? Dialogue, development communication, and deontological ethics. *Public Relations Review* 41(1). 30–39. https://doi.org/10.1016/j.pubrev.2014.10.008 (accessed 26 November 2018).

Pasadeos, Yorgo, Bruce Berger & R. Bruce Renfro. 2010. Public relations as a maturing discipline: An update on research networks. *Journal of Public Relations Research* 22(2). 136–158. https://doi.org/10.1080/10627261003601390 (accessed 26 November 2018).

Raupp, Juliana. 2011. Organizational communication in a networked public sphere. *Studies in Communication | Media* 0(1). 71–93. https://doi.org/10.5771/2192-4007-2011-1-71 (accessed 26 November 2018).

Rogers, Melvin. 2012. Introduction: Revisiting The Public and its Problems. In John Dewey, *The public and its problems: an essay in political inquiry*, 1–29. University Park, PA: Pennsylvania State University Press.

Rowell, Andrew. 1996. *Green backlash: global subversion of the environmental movement*. London & New York: Routledge.

Self, Charles. 2010. Hegel, Habermas, and community: The public in the new media era. *International Journal of Strategic Communication* 4(2). 78–92. https://doi.org/10.1080/1553 1181003704651 (accessed 26 November 2018).

Sommerfeldt, Erich. 2013. The civility of social capital: Public relations in the public sphere, civil society, and democracy. *Public Relations Review* 39(4). 280–289. https://doi.org/10.1016/j.pubrev.2012.12.004 (accessed 26 November 2018).

Taylor, Maureen. 2010. Public relations in the enactment of civil society. In Robert Heath (ed.), *The SAGE handbook of public relations*, 5–15. Thousand Oaks, CA: SAGE Publications.

Taylor, Maureen. 2011. Building social capital through rhetoric and public relations. *Management Communication Quarterly* 25(3). 436–454. https://doi.org/10.1177/0893318911410286 (accessed 26 November 2018).

Tilson, Donn. 2011. Public relations and religious diversity: A conceptual framework for fostering a spirit of *communitas*. *Global Media Journal* 4(1). 43–60.

Valentini, Chiara, Dean Kruckeberg & Kenneth Starck. 2012. Public relations and community: A persistent covenant. *Public Relations Review* 38(5). 873–879. https://doi.org/10.1016/j.pubrev.2012.06.001 (accessed 26 November 2018).

Van Ruler, Betteke & Dejan Verčič. 2005. Reflective communication management, future ways for public relations research. *Communication Yearbook* 29(1). 239–273. https://www.researchgate.net/publication/238318570_Chapter_8_Reflective_Communication_Management_Future_Ways_for_Public_Relations_Research (accessed 26 November 2018).

Vasquez, Gabriel & Maureen Taylor. 2001. Research perspectives on "the public". In Robert Heath & Gabriel Vasquez (eds.), *Handbook of public relations*, 139–154. Thousand Oaks, CA: Sage Publications.

Wigley, Shelley. 2008. Gauging consumers' responses to CSR activities: Does increased awareness make *cents*? *Public Relations Review* 34(3). 306–308. https://doi.org/10.1016/j.pubrev.2008.03.034 (accessed 26 November 2018).

Yang, Aimei & Maureen Taylor. 2013. The relationship between the professionalization of public relations, societal social capital and democracy: Evidence from a cross-national study. *Public Relations Review* 39(4). 257–270. https://doi.org/10.1016/j.pubrev.2013.08.002 (accessed 26 November 2018).

Jim Macnamara

14 Public relations measurement and evaluation

Abstract: The interrelated and integrated processes of measurement and evaluation have long been a challenge for public relations and communication management practitioners, with reviews showing "stasis", the use of invalid methods, and even a "deadlock" in the reporting of results of projects and campaigns. In particular, the field has struggled to present credible evidence of *outcomes* and *impact*, most often reporting *activities* and *outputs*. These terms derive from program logic models that are increasingly being applied, together with theory of change and other performance measurement theories and concepts to develop frameworks, models, and standards for measurement and evaluation of public relations and communication. This chapter reviews the current state of practice and the latest frameworks and models used internationally and outlines the key concepts and principles for the three stages of formative, process and summative evaluation. It concludes by identifying best practice and new directions for the future of measurement and evaluation, which researchers refer to as "the alpha and omega of strategy".

Keywords: measurement; evaluation; theory of change; program logic models; evaluation frameworks

1 Introduction

This chapter examines what is collectively one of the most discussed and often most troublesome aspects of public relations – measurement and evaluation. The terms "measurement" and "evaluation' are often used interchangeably, and not infrequently measurement is used as an umbrella term for the range of activities involved in these practices. However, there is an important difference and both processes need to be understood and integrated for effective reporting and accountability.

Measurement, as the term suggests, involves the taking of measures. In the case of public relations, measures can include the volume and favourability of media publicity, levels of awareness among target audiences, or the number of inquiries or registrations received following a campaign. Measures are often expressed as *metrics* (i. e. numbers).

Evaluation is an important further step focussed on assessing the value of results within certain context and parameters. In PR, value is usually related to the extent to which results align to an organization's objectives. Value can be financial, or it may be non-financial, such as achieving the support of key stakeholders or generating inquiries about a new service or product.

https://doi.org/10.1515/9783110554250-014

An important principle informing measurement and evaluation is that, to be credible, they must be undertaken in a rigorous way, usually based on research – not simply be anecdotal or based on subjective opinion. Valente defines the evaluation process as "the systematic application of research procedures to understand the conceptualization, design, implementation, and utility of interventions" (Valente 2001: 106), where "interventions" are the activities undertaken to influence awareness, attitudes or behaviour. In simple terms, the processes of measurement and evaluation are required to provide evidence that the objectives of public relations are achieved.

Today, all functions in organizations are expected to provide accountability and to report to senior management against objectives, key performance indicators (KPIs), on balanced scorecards, or other reporting methods, and an evidence-based approach is now a common requirement in management in both the public and private sectors (Wright et al. 2016). Also, measurement and evaluation afford learning about what is effective and what is not, thus informing strategy and facilitating learning and improvement.

This chapter summarizes program evaluation theory that has been developed and applied widely in a number of fields before giving a brief history of the development of PR measurement and evaluation (collectively referred to as "evaluation" hereafter for simplicity, and because measurement is an integrated part of the evaluation). It then reviews four contemporary models of PR and communication identifying their key features and important advances that they represent, as well as continuing gaps and limitations. Finally, based on recent research, this chapter presents conclusions and recommendations for future directions to further improve evaluation practice and demonstrate the value of effective public relations.

2 Theory of change and program theory

Well before it became a *cause célèbre* in PR, evaluation was a major focus of study and practice in international development, public administration, and education, and recently also has become a major focus in performance management in business. A body of *program theory* and *theory of change* has been developed through the work of researchers such as (in chronological order) Edward Suchman (1967); Carol Weiss (1972); Joseph Wholey (1970, 1979, 1983, 1987); Claude Bennett (1976); Huey Chen and Peter Rossi (1983); Leonard Bickman (1987); Mark Lipsey (1993); and others. Program evaluation is a central focus of program theory and theory of change, which explore how programs can be designed and implemented to achieve their objectives.

It is important for PR evaluators to understand the body of knowledge in relation to program evaluation generally, and this provides a context in which to review current models and approaches to evaluation of PR. Program evaluation has been advanced most notably in the disciplinary field of public administration, being developed first in relation to human service programs such as the delivery of social services and health promotion campaigns, but it has spread to a wide range of fields from agricultural programs and construction projects to the testing of military hardware. Rossi, Lipsey, and Freeman say that program evaluation based on program theory and theory of change is "useful in virtually all spheres of activity in which issues are raised about the effectiveness of organized social action" and note its relevance for advertising, marketing, and other communication activities (2004: 6).

2.1 Theory of change

Theory of change, which emerged from research in environmental and organizational psychology, provides a broad overview of how a program is intended to work, identifying the basic stages that lead from planning to demonstration of effectiveness in achieving its objectives, with particular emphasis on outcomes and impact. Theory of change also provides broad principles that apply to all types of programs that seek to influence or change human attitudes and/or behaviour. However, theory of change models usually provide little detail of activities to be undertaken or how these will be evaluated. Program theory and program logic models help inform practical application.

2.2 Program theory

Program theory involves the conceptualization of how a specific program is intended to work and includes identification of a "chain of activities" that are expected to produce the intended impacts stated in the program objectives. Rossi, Lipsey, and Freeman (2004) identify three key, interrelated components of a program theory: (1) the program impact theory; (2) the utilization plan; and (3) the program's organizational plan. Thus, while this approach starts with theory, it moves quickly towards practical implementation. The program impact theory, in simple terms, is the theoretical projection of what a program will achieve – that is, its desired effect and impact. This must be more than an aspirational statement. Program impact theory is a *causal* theory, designed to describe the cause and effect sequence that leads to the desired impact. Rossi, Lipsey, and Freeman note that the utilization plan is "usefully depicted as a flow chart" that tracks the various stages and elements in a program (2004: 142), while the organizational plan describes the management actions necessary, such as assigning the resources required and planning and implementing activities to achieve the desired effect.

2.3 Program logic models

The various stages and elements of a program theory are very commonly explicated in program logic models, a graphic illustration of the processes in a program from pre-program planning to its outcomes and impact. Use of the term "program logic model" and its basic construction is most commonly attributed to Joseph Wholey's (1979) text, *Evaluation: Promise and Performance* and is also informed by Claude Bennett's (1976) *The Seven Levels of Evidence*. Program logic models were used by the US Agency for International Development (USAID) in the 1970s, and have since been extensively applied in public administration across a wide range of sectors. Early program logic models developed for USAID and other organizations identified the causally connected stages of programs as "inputs", "outputs", achievement of the "project purpose", and achievement of the "program goal" (Practical Concepts Inc. 1971, 1979).

However, the Kellogg Foundation, which has been a leader in the field of program evaluation and program logic models for several decades, advocates a widely used model that identifies five stages in programs as "inputs", "activities", "outputs", "outcomes", and "impact" (see Figure 1). This serves as a planning model as well as an evaluation framework, facilitating identification and assessment of the adequacy of resources and other inputs as well as later stages. In communication and PR programs, inputs can include baseline data, formative research, and pre-testing, which indicate that this stage should not be overlooked, as it is in some PR evaluation models.

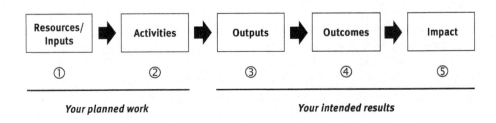

Figure 1: The basic structure of a classic program logic model (Kellogg Foundation 2004)

The University of Wisconsin Extension program (UWEX), another leader in the field, describes the components of basic program logic models in its guide as "inputs", "outputs", and "outcomes" (Taylor-Power and Henert 2008: 20). In addition, more advanced versions of the UWEX model segregate outputs into "activities" and "participation", making it quite similar to the Kellogg Foundation model, and split outcomes into short-, medium-, and long term – what are also called proximal and distal outcomes. When this is done, long-term (distal) outcomes are synonymous with impact (see Figure 2).

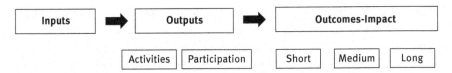

Figure 2: A more advanced program logic model (Taylor-Power and Henert 2008: 5)

As the UWEX *Developing a Logic Model: Teaching and Training Guide* notes, "many variations and types of logic models exist" (Taylor-Power and Henert 2008: 2). The Kellogg Foundation similarly says that "there is no one best logic model" (2004: 13). However, a broadly common approach to evaluation is evident that uses theory of change, program theory, and program logic models to plan, manage, and evaluate programs in stages most widely described as "inputs", "activities", "outputs", "outcomes", and "impact", sometimes with outcomes broken into short-, medium-, and long-term, in which long-term outcomes equate to impact. Armed with this knowledge, of which more details are available in general texts on evaluation (e. g. Funnell and Rogers 2011; Knowlton and Phillips 2013; Wholey, Hatry, and Newcomer 2010), we can then look at approaches, models and frameworks of evaluation for PR and communication.

3 The long and winding road to PR value

Evaluation of PR and closely related practices such as corporate communication and what some refer to today as strategic communication, has been undertaken in some form since the late 19th century when media monitoring came into common use (Lamme and Russell 2010). For instance, Tom Watson (2012) reported that the first press clipping agencies were established in the US and UK in the late 1800s. Discussion of research-based evaluation of PR dates back to Edward Bernays, identified in much (albeit US) PR literature as the "father of public relations" (Guth and Marsh 2007: 70). Watson points out that, whereas fellow US PR pioneer Ivy Lee regarded his practice as an art, Bernays saw PR as an applied social science that should be planned using opinion research and "precisely evaluated" (2012: 391). Arthur Page also advocated and used opinion research in the early 20th century, according to historical studies (Likely and Watson 2013: 144).

    Evaluation of PR has become a subject of intense focus since the late 1970s, according to historical reviews and texts on the topic (Likely and Watson 2013; Watson 2012; Watson and Noble 2014). In an analysis of PR evaluation over the past 40 years, Fraser Likely and Tom Watson say a conference organized and chaired by Jim Grunig at the University of Maryland in 1977 was a "prime catalyst" for scholarly attention to evaluation of PR, as well as a special issue of *Public Relations Review* on "Measuring the effectiveness of public relations" published in the same year (2013: 144). Other landmark publications in the reported "flowering of research" that occurred in the 1970s and the early 1980s included the work of Glen Broom and David Dozier (Broom and Dozier 1983; Dozier 1984, 1985), along with the advocacy of Jim Grunig (Grunig J. 1979, 1983) and that of some leading practitioners such as Walter Lindenmann of Ketchum (1979, 1980). However, a number of studies show that J. Grunig's *cri de coeur* about lack of evaluation in practice uttered in the early 1980s has continued to echo across the PR and corporate communication landscape. J. Grunig wrote in 1983:

> Lately, I have begun to feel more and more like the fundamentalist minister railing against sin; the difference being that I have railed *for* evaluation in public relations practice. Just as everyone is against sin, so most public relations people I talk to are for evaluation. People keep on sinning, however, and PR people continue not to do evaluation research. (Grunig J. 1983: 28)

A few years later in one of the first books on the subject, John Pavlik (1987) compared PR evaluation to the search for the Holy Grail, a view echoed by Jacqui L'Etang in the 21st century when she noted that "evaluation has become and remains something of a 'holy grail' for public relations" (2008: 26). This concern is supported by the following research findings and analysis.

3.1 "Stasis" and "deadlock"

Evaluation of PR has been described as being in a state of "stasis" (Gregory and Watson 2008; Macnamara and Zerfass 2017) and being caught in a "deadlock" (Macnamara 2015), even well into the 2010s. In particular, studies have shown a narrow focus on measuring "outputs" such as the volume of media publicity, audience reach, social media posts, and website and video views, with comparatively little focus on demonstrating "outcomes" or "impact" (Macnamara and Zerfass 2017; Zerfass et al. 2012; Zerfass et al. 2015). For example, the 2015 *European Communication Monitor*, a survey of more than 2,000 communication professionals across 41 European countries, reported that more than 80 per cent still rely on counting the volume of publicity as their main method of evaluation (Zerfass et al. 2015: 72).

3.2 "Reinventing the wheel"

Furthermore, historical analysis has shown that PR evaluation has gone down a path of "reinventing the wheel" by frequent introduction of new measures and methods rather than adopting evaluation models and methods based on *theory of change* and *program theory*, which are foundational theories of evaluation (Macnamara & Likely

2017). Despite extensive literature on evaluation in fields such as international development, public administration, and education, which use program logic models identifying key stages as *inputs*, *activities*, *outputs*, *outcomes*, and *impact* (Taylor-Power and Henert 2008; Kellogg Foundation 2004), would-be PR evaluators have created new terms such as "outgrowths", "outflows" and "outtakes", as well as metrics that have no social science basis.

3.3 AVEs and "vanity metrics"

Recent studies have shown that up to one-third of PR practitioners still use invalid metrics such as advertising value equivalents (AVEs) (USC and The Holmes Report 2016), along with "vanity metrics" (Bartholomew 2016: 97), such as high volumes of internet clicks, "followers", or "likes" as indications of communication effectiveness.

It is ironic that a large section of the PR industry seeks to compare itself to advertising when studies show that advertising has long been criticized for reliance on "reach" and "recall" metrics rather than evidence of outcomes or impact of communication on target audiences (Macnamara 2018). Despite recent advances to incorporate sophisticated methods such as customer journey mapping and data analytics as well as traditional social science research methods such as audience surveys and focus groups (Macnamara 2018), independent marketing consultant Jerry Thomas says that advertising has "the poorest quality-assurance systems and turns out the most inconsistent product of any industry in the world" (2008: 1). Also, the PESO model of media use (paid, earned, shared, and owned), which has traditionally been dominated by paid media advertising, is increasingly shifting with increased use of shared and owned media and a relative decline in paid advertising (Macnamara et al. 2016). The PR industry is thus short-sighted and misguided in seeking to compare its work to advertising.

Also, despite the growing importance of social media and opportunities for real-time analysis of audience response and advanced techniques such as *influencer mapping* using social network analysis (SNA), evaluation of online communication is often focussed on relatively meaningless metrics, as observed by PR evaluation specialist Don Bartholomew (2016: 97). As online content marketer Sujan Patel wrote in *Forbes* magazine:

> The number of social media followers your social profiles have attracted is one of the vainest of all the vanity metrics you can attract, yet it often consumes far too much of the company's attention. Repeat after me – just because someone follows you does not mean they're engaged with your brand. (Patel 2015: 9)

3.4 Classic PR evaluation models

There have been many models of evaluation of varying quality developed for PR over the past 40 years. These are not reviewed here as they have been widely discussed in journal articles and reviewed in texts such as *Evaluating Public Relations: A Best Practice Guide to Public Relations Planning, Research and Evaluation* (Watson and Noble 2014) and *Evaluating Public Communication: Exploring New Models, Standards, and Best Practice* (Macnamara 2018). The purpose here is to focus on contemporary models and future directions for how these can inform practice as well as ongoing research and theory-building. However, a brief reflection on some of the PR evaluation models that have been published and widely promoted over the past few decades is informative. These include the following:

- The *planning, implementation, impact (PII)* model developed by Scott Cutlip, Alan Center and Glen Broom (1985) in the sixth edition of the text *Effective Public Relations*. As the name suggests, this identified three stages of programs as planning, implementation, and impact, and visualized and described progress as a series of steps.
- The *PR effectiveness yardstick* developed by US research practitioner Walter Lindemann (1993). This also arranged programs into three stages, but described these as "outputs", "outgrowths" and "outcomes", with evaluation at each stage described as basic, intermediate, and advanced respectively (Lindemann 1993: 8).
- The *unified model of evaluation* first presented in a paper by Paul Noble and Tom Watson (1999) at a transnational communication congress in Europe in Berlin. This identified four stages as "input", "output", "impact", and "effect" (Noble and Watson 1999: 20). An important feature of this model is that it introduced feedback loops to PR evaluation models for the first time, although the creators of other models claim that feedback from each stage to inform progress and allow fine-tuning of strategy is implicit in the models.
- In the same year, Michael Fairchild and Nigel O'Connor (1999)[1] produced the first edition of the *IPR Toolkit for Measurement and Evaluation* which, while not including a model as such, advocated three stages called "outputs", "outtakes", and "outcomes" in what they called the PRE (planning, research, evaluation) process.
- In the early 2000s, PR researchers working in the Deutsche Public Relations Gesellschaft (DPRG) and Gesellschaft Public Relations Agenturen (GPRA) in Germany produced the first of a series of *communication controlling* models, which identify four stages of PR programs as "input", "output", "outcome", and

---

[1] The first IPR Toolkit is often cited as Fairchild (1999). Michael Fairchild confirms that Nigel O'Connor, then Head of Policy of the UK Institute of Public Relations (IPR), was the Project Manager for the work and that he and O'Connor worked together on the 'Toolkit' (M. Fairchild, personal communication, May 24, 2016), thus confirming the citation by Caroll and Stacks (2004) as Fairchild and O'Connor (1999) and the second edition as Fairchild and O'Connor (2001).

"outflow" (DPRG/GPRA 2000), thus introducing yet another term to PR evaluation terminology alongside "outgrowths" and "outtakes" and the more traditional stages of "inputs", "outputs", "outcomes" and "impact". Recent writing on this model emphasizes that communication controlling is more than a model for evaluation. For example, drawing on the writing of Ansgar Zerfass (2007, 2010), who has championed this model, Julia Huhn, Jan Sass, and Christopher Storck point out that "from a management accountancy perspective, the term "controlling" stands for the full management cycle comprising the planning, implementation, monitoring and evaluation of an organization's communication activities" (2011: 11). The creators and proponents of this model are aware of negative interpretations of the term "control" in the context of PR. However, they note that this model uses the term to denote processes in the same way that financial controlling refers to processes related to financial management and reporting (Huhn, Sass, and Storck 2011: 4).

3.5 The "march to standards"

Scholars and practitioners recognize evaluation as a major challenge, and since 2010 a number of initiatives have been launched in an attempt to develop standards and best practice in evaluation – what one industry paper refers to as the "march to standards" (Marklein and Paine 2012). Recent significant steps include adoption and promulgation of The Barcelona Principles in 2010 and in updated form in 2015[2] (AMEC, 2010, 2015) and establishment of the Coalition for Public Relations Research Standards and the Social Media Measurement Standards Conclave in 2011 (Conclave 2011/2013). These initiatives have involved a range of professional organizations, most notably the International Association for Measurement and Evaluation of Communication (AMEC), the Institute for Public Relations (IPR), and the Council of Public Relations Firms (CPRF), supported by the Global Alliance for Public Relations and Communications Management; the International Association of Business Communicators (IABC); the Public Relations Society of America (PRSA); the UK Chartered Institute of Public Relations (CIPR); the Society for New Communications Research (SNCR); the Federation Internationale des Bureaux d'Extraits de Presse (FIBEP); the Word of Mouth Marketing Association (WOMMA); and the Digital Analytics Association (DAA). As well, these organizations consulted with the Media Ratings Council (MRC); the Interactive Advertising Bureau (IAB); the American Association of Adver-

---

2 The principles were adopted at the second European Summit on Measurement hosted by the International Association for Measurement and Evaluation of Communication (AMEC) in Barcelona by more than 200 delegates from 33 countries.

tising Agencies (AAAA); the Association of National Advertisers (ANA); and the Web Analytics Association (WAA).

More recently, an international Task Force on Standardization of Communication Planning and Evaluation Models has been established under the auspices of the IPR Measurement Commission[3] and has attempted to identify or define standards for evaluation of PR (Macnamara and Likely 2017). Recent developments in terms of models for PR evaluation are outlined in the next section, which gives examples some of the latest models and frameworks in use, as well as Section 5, which examines recommendations for the future.

4 Major contemporary evaluation models for PR and communication

Five contemporary models of PR and communication evaluation are reviewed in the following. This range of models is analyzed because the field of PR and communication evaluation continues to be characterized by diversity, and each of the first four models reviewed is widely promoted by industry and professional bodies. Comparison shows the evolution of PR and communication evaluation, as well as continuing gaps and shortfalls. These deficiencies are addressed in the fifth model, which attempts to integrate the findings of 40 years of research and represent best practice.

4.1 European Commission model

A model widely used in Europe is that developed by the European Commission (EC) Directorate-General for Communication (DG COM), as it is applied to EC PR and communication campaigns across the 27 member states in continental Europe. The model is applied in conjunction with the EC's *Better Regulation Guidelines* (European Commission 2015a), its *Toolkit for the Evaluation of Communication Activities* (European Commission 2015b), and its *External Communication Network Code of Conduct on Measurement and Evaluation of Communication Activities* (European Commission 2015c). The European Commission's DG COMM administered an external communication budget of €378 million in 2015 (US$422 million) (European Commission 2015d). Thus, evaluation is important in terms of accountability and governance.

While the EC evaluation model broadly incorporates a program logic model approach, it deviates in two key respects. Figure 3 shows that the EC model suggests that communication begins with "activities" such as organizing events and distrib-

---

3 http://www.instituteforpr.org/ipr-measurement-commission

uting information. This overlooks the important "inputs" stage of planning during which formative evaluation is recommended to identify audience awareness, perceptions, attitudes, needs, interests, and channel preferences. Thus, this model is contrary to evaluation theory that identifies three stages of evaluation: *formative* (also referred to as *ex-ante*), *process*, and *summative* (also referred to as *ex-post*) (Bauman and Nutbeam 2014). Without formative evaluation, communication proceeds without audience insights and without baseline data for later comparison, which makes summative evaluation difficult if not impossible. Second, this model shows the second stage in the process of PR/communication as "relevance". The suggestion that the relevance of communication to audiences and/or to the organization should be determined after activities have been implemented is clearly flawed. Relevance is one of the key elements of SMART objectives and should be determined as part of setting communication objectives before activities are conducted and even before inputs are assembled. While the EC model omits "inputs" and ambiguously positions "relevance", it should be noted that the extensive guidelines on evaluation provided by the EC DG COMM do explain SMART objectives and advocate formative as well as process and summative evaluation.

Another interesting feature of the EC model is that, while communication objectives are derived (i. e. come down) from the organization, all results at output, outtake and outcome stages are conceptualized as flowing "upwards" to the organization, as shown by the arrows in Figure 3. This characteristic and its implications will be further discussed later in more detail.

4.2 UK Government Communication Service model

Another widely used contemporary evaluation approach is the UK Government Communication Service (GCS) Evaluation Framework (Government Communication Service 2015). This was developed in 2015 and has been implemented since early 2016 for evaluating UK government communication in which more than £300 million a year is invested and for which evaluation in mandatory. The framework includes a program logic model (see Figure 4) supported by an evaluation guide (a small booklet). To implement the framework, the GCS has established an Evaluation Council made up of senior GCS staff as well as external experts such as social researchers and academics, which reviews proposed communication campaigns before implementation. Also, the GCS has implemented an intensive professional development program that produces "evaluation champions" among GCS staff working across the civil service.

The GCS evaluation model follows evaluation program theory and program logic models more closely than does the EC model by including "inputs" as the first stage and noting that this should include formative evaluation, such as "pre-testing" (see Figure 4). The GCS evaluation model also emphasizes the use of qualitative as well as quantitative research.

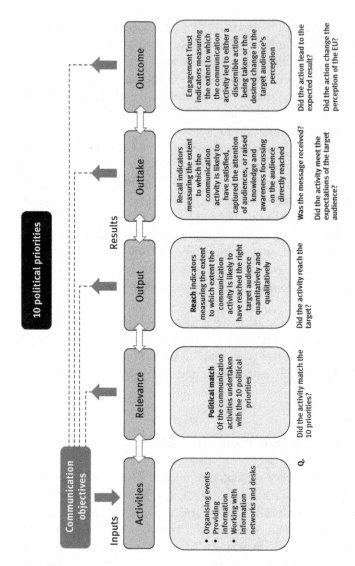

Figure 3: Evaluation model developed and used by the European Commission Directorate-General for Communication (European Commission 2015)

However, despite involving the external expertise of social researchers and academics, the GCS evaluation model maintains several features of earlier PR evaluation models that warrant review. One is the inclusion of "outtakes" as a stage before "outcomes". This is not a significant variation, as "outtakes" – a term created by Michael Fairchild (1997) in early UK Institute of Public Relations (IPR) models and later adopted by Walter Lindenmann (2003) in the US – equate to short-term outcomes as described by Taylor-Power and Henert (2008). However, of more significance is that, like the EC

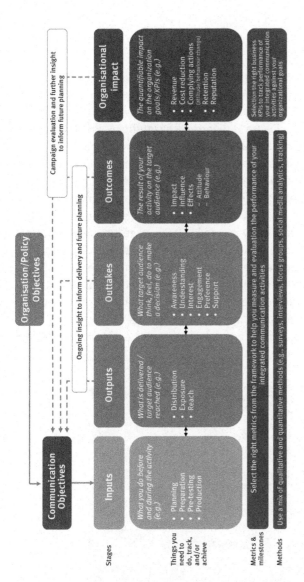

Figure 4: The UK Government Communication Service Evaluation Framework (Government Communication Service 2015)

model, communication objectives as conceived as being derived from the organization and all results of communication including the final stage of "impact" are seen as flowing to the organization. Neither this widely used model nor the EC model include stakeholders, publics, or society at any point in the process of public communication. This seems to be a serious omission in a model designed to guide the public communication of government in a democracy.

4.3 AMEC Integrated Evaluation Framework

In 2016, AMEC launched its Integrated Evaluation Framework (IEF) to replace the former AMEC Valid Metrics Framework. After a period of international consultation, this was upgraded to the AMEC Integrated Evaluation Framework 2.0 in May 2017 (AMEC 2017a). The AMEC IEF (see Figure 5) represents a significant breakthrough in several ways. The first noteworthy feature is that the IEF is an online application, not a static model that simply illustrates processes. Users can enter data such as their communication objectives and then progressively add data related to "inputs" (e. g. formative research findings such as baseline awareness or compliance rates, pre-test results, etc.), followed by data describing "activities", "outputs", "outcomes", and finally "impact". Data entry is aided at each stage by pop-up information tabs, which provide users with tips about what types of data are relevant to that stage. Multiple evaluation reports can be created, saved, and produced as PDF files and printed if required. The online application is also supported by a taxonomy of evaluation that provides definitions of each stage, examples of what occurs at each stage, and a list of relevant metrics and appropriate methods for generating those metrics. Thus, the AMEC IEF is a major advance in tools for evaluation of PR and communication.

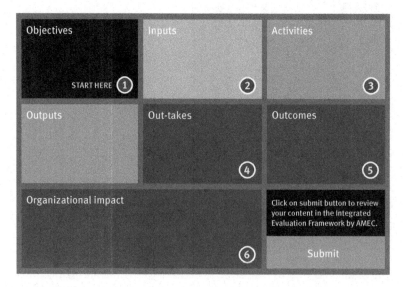

Figure 5: The AMEC Integrated Evaluation Framework 2.0 (AMEC 2017a)

The AMEC IEF differs from other evaluation models for PR and communication and most classic program logic models in that it reports in six stages including "outtakes" as well as "outcomes" (see Figure 3). As with the GCS model, "outtakes" can be regarded as synonymous with short-term outcomes in classic program logic models such as the UWEX model (Taylor-Power and Henert 2008) and "outcomes" interpreted as long-term outcomes.

However, one of the major failings in evaluation of PR has been what Glen Broom calls the "substitution problem" (2009: 358) – that is, the use of measures from one level as alleged measures at a higher level. An example is the reporting of the volume of publicity (an "output") as an alleged "outcome". Emeritus professor of PR James Grunig also has identified this problem, pointing out that many practitioners use "a metric gathered at one level of analysis to [allegedly] show an outcome at a higher level of analysis" (2008: 89). It is likely that separating "outtakes" and "outcomes" in a six-stage model will add to practitioners' confusion and exacerbate the "substitution problem".

Also, despite bringing evaluation into the digital online age and for all its functionality, the AMEC Integrated Evaluation Framework 2.0 does not include stakeholders, publics, or society at any step or stage. While the contemporary models reviewed here and some others such as the "communication controlling" model (Huhn, Sass, and Storck 2011; Zerfass 2010) aptly recognize the need for evaluation to align outcomes and impact to organizational goals and objectives, the omission of stakeholders, publics and society from consideration is contrary to program evaluation theory (e. g. Kellogg Foundation 2004; Taylor-Power and Henert 2008; Wholey, Hatry, and Newcomer 2010) and also contrary to disciplinary best practice such as Excellence theory. PR Excellence theory calls for evaluation to be conducted at (a) programme, (b) functional (e. g. department or unit), (c) organizational and (d) societal levels (Grunig, L., Grunig, J. and Dozier 2002: 91–92).

4.4 New South Wales Government Communication Evaluation Framework

The first evaluation model to explicitly recognize stakeholders, publics, and society as integral in the practices of PR and strategic communication and be designed to evaluate two-way communication was developed by the strategic communications branch of the New South Wales Department of Premier and Cabinet in Australia. This model was developed in consultation with academics in 2016–2017 for application across the state government, which spends around AUD$100 million a year on advertising and other forms of public communication. The DPC (2016) model shown in Figure 6 applies a classic five-stage program logic model customized to PR and communication. The information shown on the model at each stage is indicative rather than prescriptive. However, it highlights that evaluation should begin at the "inputs" stage with formative research to gain target audience insights and collect baseline data such as existing audience awareness levels, perceptions, and channel preferences. Underneath indicative activities at each stage, the model lists suggested evaluation methods

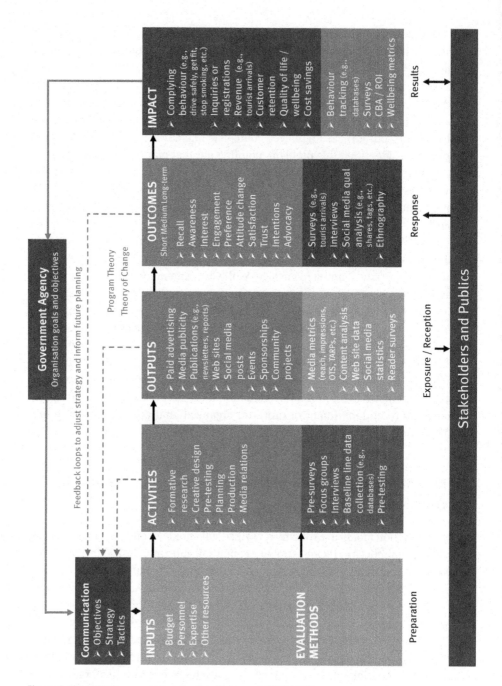

Figure 6: The NSW Government evaluation framework (DPC 2017)

such as literature review, pre-campaign surveys, focus groups or interviews, and database records analysis at the "inputs" stage, followed by pre-testing at the "activities" stage, and other appropriate methods throughout the program. The indicative information in the model clearly demarks the difference between activities, outputs, outcomes, and impact, and suggests evaluation methods that are appropriate for each.

Another subtle but important feature of the DPC model is that it shows that the "inputs" stage is informed by stakeholders, publics, and the interests of society, as well as the organization, as illustrated by the arrows (see Figure 6).

For example, stakeholder and public attitudes, perceptions, needs, and channel preferences as well as societal interests should inform planning and communication strategy. Furthermore, in addition to information and consideration flowing from external parties as well as the organization at the "inputs" stage, the model highlights that, while "outputs" flow outwards from the organization, evaluation of "outcomes" requires assessment of response from stakeholders, publics, and society to the organization. Finally, the arrows at the bottom of the model illustrate that impact is bi-directional. That is to say, impact on the organization as well as impact on stakeholders, publics, and society should be evaluated.

This model represents a further significant advance over traditional and even other contemporary models of evaluation for PR and communication because of its incorporation of true two-way communication, as well as concepts such as corporate social responsibility (CSR), towards publics and society. Other models are revealed as organization-centric. However, even this model can be shown to lack some key elements and considerations, and the DPC (2016) model was undergoing further development at the time of this research. Critical analysis reveals a number of shortcomings in this model and in evaluation theory for PR and communication generally.

1. Even though this model recognizes stakeholders, publics, and society and seeks input from them as well as the organization in planning public communication, the model shows that communication objectives are already determined prior to formative research. This means that communication objectives could be unrealistic or even in conflict with stakeholders and publics.

2. Like all program logic models, the stages are shown as separate "boxes" implying discrete stages when, in reality, the stages overlap. For example, journalist relations and production such as events and web content continue throughout a program or campaign.

3. Furthermore, the representation of stages as a row of boxes implies a linear "domino" progression along the "chain of activities", or what Charles Atkin and Vicki Freimuth describe as "preliminary or intermediate variables along the response chain" (2013: 58). In reality, progression is contingent on various milestones and evaluation must proceed iteratively, informed by feedback and process evaluation during each stage.

4. A major omission from this and all the models examined is that they do not recognize or suggest evaluation of context. Both internal and external context has a

major impact on whether or not communication is effective. For example, internal context includes availability of resources such as staff and budget, management decisions, product or service quality, and so on. External context includes economic, political, social, cultural, and competitive factors. For example, in addition to macro-societal, political, and economic shifts such as the UK voting to leave the European Union (*Brexit*), the election of Donald Trump as president of the USA, and economic recession in a number of European countries exacerbated by the arrival of unprecedented numbers of refugees, factors such as a competitor launching a new low-cost service, a new entrant to a market, or an unexpected crisis or scandal can radically affect a communication program.

5. Even though the DPC model recognizes the need to evaluate impact on stakeholders, publics and society as well as the organization, it and all other models focus on intended impact – i. e. what the organization wants to achieve. This and other models do not recognize, and therefore do not evaluate, unintended impact. By only evaluating outcomes and impact that the organization intends to create, evaluation may miss important reactions and responses and, accordingly, does not fully inform an organization. For example, an organization may succeed in selling its products or services or gaining approval for a development, but it might cause resentment among communities leading to longer-term opposition or reputation or brand damage.

4.5 An integrated approach

The gaps and shortfalls identified through critical analysis suggests directions for further development of evaluation models for PR and communication. Figure 7 represents an attempt to bring together learning from research in an expanded integrated evaluation model for PR and communication – that is, one that integrates the best features and some missing features from other models and also integrates an organization with its stakeholders, publics, and society rather than present a top-down, one-way flow of information and effects. This model is a further evolution of that developed collaboratively with the Public Relations Institute of Australia and published in its online guidelines (PRIA 2017).

The integrated model presented in Figure 7 seeks to address the shortcomings identified in existing models of evaluation, particularly by highlighting the two-way, interactive, and contingent nature of PR and communication, as follows.

– The integrated model shifts communication objectives from being a pre-determined antecedent to the communication program set unilaterally by the organization to being the result of both internal planning to achieve the organization's objectives and consideration of the views, needs, and interests of stakeholders, publics, and society. It proposes that setting communication objectives should be an iterative process and explicitly states that these should be SMART (specific,

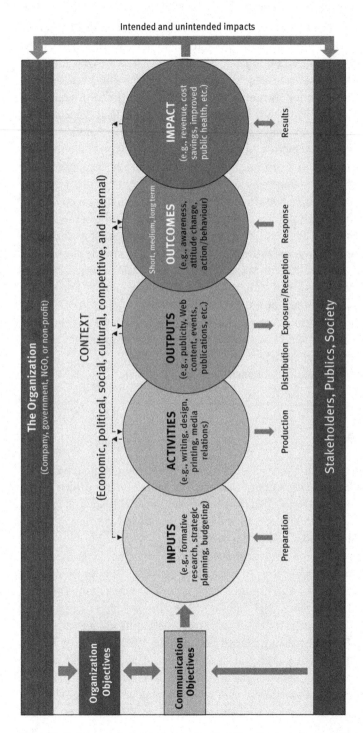

Figure 7: An integrated model of evaluation for PR and communication (Macnamara 2018)

measurable, achievable, relevant, and time-bound). None of the previous models emphasize that SMART objectives are a prerequisite for identifying what is to be evaluated and how outcomes and impact will be demonstrated. For example, if the objective is to "increase awareness", evaluation is not possible because there is no detail of pre-intervention awareness or what level is required. An objective to "increase awareness of Product X from 25 % to 70 % in the next 12 months" is measurable and therefore outcomes and impact are able to be reported.

– It recognizes that inputs, activities, outputs, outcomes, and impact are overlapping stages in a program and are contingent on feedback and response rather than a simple linear progression.

– It shows the ongoing iterative two-way nature of interaction between an organization and its stakeholders, publics and society generally, as represented in the arrows below each stage. Inputs flow into the organization, such as formative research as well as from the organization (e. g. budget and resources); outputs flow out from the organization to stakeholders, publics, and society; outcomes are evaluated by responses and reactions from stakeholders, publics, and society to the organization; and impact occurs in both directions.

– All stages of PR and communication are conducted within contexts and the internal and external context should be monitored and evaluated throughout, making adjustments to strategy if required.

– Unintended as well as intended impacts should be evaluated.

5 Conclusions

There has been considerable progress recently in the development of models, frameworks and guidelines for evaluation of PR. Contemporary models have drawn on the body of theory and knowledge developed in other disciplinary fields such as international development, public administration, and education, as well as being informed by human communication theory and media theory.

However, there are still gaps in PR evaluation theory and models, as identified in recent analyses (Likely and Watson 2013; Macnamara 2015, 2018; Macnamara et al. 2016) and as discussed here, and opportunities to further overcome the "stasis" and "deadlock" that has been reported. Practitioners should seek out and apply contemporary models as discussed, as these incorporate some significant advances over traditional models in PR textbooks published between the 1980s and early 2000s. It also should go without saying that practitioners should avoid invalid metrics such as advertising value equivalents (AVEs), which have been condemned by AMEC (2015, 2017b) and most professional communication organizations, and other methods involving what Tom Watson and Ansgar Zerfass (2012) refer to as "smoke and mirrors".

Beyond informing and guiding the processes of evaluation, contemporary evaluation models can also make a broader contribution to the theory and practice of PR and communication. Evaluation models identify key steps and requirements of planning, as well as the intent and underlying logic of PR and communication programs. Ray Pawson and Nick Tilley (1997, 2001), who developed what is called "realist evaluation", say that advanced evaluation identifies "what works in which circumstances and for whom?" rather than merely "does it work?" (as cited in Better Evaluation 2016: 2). In simple terms, evaluation models reveal *what* is intended to be done *to whom, how,* and *whose interests* are served. As such, evaluation models provide a strategic overview of PR and communication programs from beginning to end. In their summary of 10 years of findings from *The European Communication Monitor*, Ralph Tench and colleagues say it well in their description of evaluation as "the alpha and omega of strategy" (Tench et al. 2017: 91).

This reinforces the concept of formative as well as summative evaluation (before and after) and the importance of having SMART communication objectives. Major challenges for the future remain the linking of PR and communication to organizational objectives so that they are relevant. Both the *European Communication Monitor* (Zerfass et al. 2017) and the *Asia Pacific Communication Monitor* (Macnamara et al. 2018) have found that practitioners struggle with showing how PR and communication support organizational goals and objectives. At the same time as serving organizational objectives, both practitioners and academics need to develop an expanded approach to evaluation as highlighted in this chapter. To comply with Excellence, dialogic and other contemporary theories of PR that emphasize two-way communication and mutuality, evaluation needs to give greater consideration to stakeholders at all stages, from setting objectives to evaluating impact. Best practice evaluation involves looking well beyond measuring what the organization puts out.

References

AMEC (Association for Measurement and Evaluation of Communication). 2010. Barcelona Declaration of Measurement Principles. London. http://amecorg.com/2012/06/barcelona-declaration-of-measurement-principles (accessed 1 July 2017).

AMEC (Association for Measurement and Evaluation of Communication). 2015. Barcelona principles 2.0. London. http://amecorg.com/barcelona-principles-2-0 (accessed 1 July 2017).

AMEC (Association for Measurement and Evaluation of Communication). 2017a. AMEC integrated evaluation framework. London. https://amecorg.com/amecframework (accessed 1 July 2017).

AMEC (Association for Measurement and Evaluation of Communication). 2017b. The definitive guide: Why AVEs are invalid. London. https://amecorg.com/2017/06/the-definitive-guide-why-aves-are-invalid (accessed 2 July 2017).

Atkin, Charles & Vicki Freimuth. 2013. Guidelines for formative evaluation research in campaign design. In Ronald Rice & Charles Atkin (eds.), *Public communication campaigns*, 4th edn., 53–68. Thousand Oaks, CA: Sage.

Bartholomew, Don. 2016. *Metrics man: It doesn't count unless you can count* (Zifei Chen, ed.). New York: Business Expert Press.

Bauman, Adrian & Don Nutbeam. 2014. *Evaluation in a nutshell: A practical guide to the evaluation of health promotion programs*, 2nd edn. North Ryde, NSW: McGraw-Hill.

Bennett, Claude. 1976. *Analyzing impacts of extension programs, ESC-575*. US Department of Agriculture Extension Service. Department of Agriculture, Extension Service: Washington, DC.

Better Evaluation. 2016. Realist evaluation. Melbourne, Vic. http://betterevaluation.org/approach/realist_evaluation (accessed 1 July 2017).

Bickman, Leonard. 1987. The functions of program theory. In Bickman, Leonard (ed.), *New Directions for Program Evaluation* 33. 5–18. San Francisco: Jossey-Bass. https://doi.org/10.1002/ev.1443

Broom, Glen & David Dozier. 1983. An overview: Evaluation research in public relations. *Public Relations Quarterly* 28(3). 5–9.

Broom, Glen. 2009. *Cutlip & Center's effective public relations*, 10th edn. Upper Saddle River, NJ: Pearson.

Chen, Huey & Peter Rossi. 1983. Evaluating with sense: The theory-driven approach. *Evaluation Review* 7(3). 283–302. doi.org/10.1177/0193841X8300700301

Conclave on Social Media Measurement Standards. 2011/2013. The standards. http://smmstandards.wixsite.com/smmstandards/reach-and-impressions (accessed 1 July 2017).

Cutlip, Scott, Alan Center & Glen Broom. 1985. *Effective public relations*, 6th edn. Englewood Cliffs, NJ: Prentice-Hall.

Dozier, David. 1984. Program evaluation and the roles of practitioners. *Public Relations Review* 10(2). 13–21.

Dozier, David. 1985. Planning and evaluation in public relations practice. *Public Relations Review* 11(2). 17–25.

DPC (Department of Premier and Cabinet). 2016. New South Wales government evaluation framework for advertising and communication. Sydney, NSW.

DPRG/GPRA (Deutsche Public Relations Gesellschaft and Gesellschaft Public Relations Agenturen). 2000. *PR-evaluation: Messen, analysieren, bewerten – empfehlungen für die praxis*. Booklet des Evaluationsausschusses von DPRG und GPRA 2. Bonn, Germany.

European Commission. 2015a. Better regulation guidelines. Brussels. http://ec.europa.eu/smart-regulation/guidelines/toc_guide_en.htm (accessed 1 July 2017).

European Commission. 2015b. Toolkit for the evaluation of communication activities. Brussels. http://ec.europa.eu/dgs/communication/about/evaluation/documents/communication-evaluation-toolkit_en.pdf (accessed 1 July 2017).

European Commission. 2015c. External communication network code of conduct on measurement and evaluation of communication activities. Brussels. http://ec.europa.eu/dgs/communication/about/evaluation/documents/code-of-conduct-measurement-evaluation-communication-activities_en.pdf (accessed 2 July 2018).

European Commission. 2015d. Synergies and efficiencies review: Report from the Working Group on External and Internal Communication. Brussels.

Fairchild, Michael. 1997. *How to get real value from public relations*. London: ICO.

Fairchild, Michael & Nigel O'Connor. 1999. *The public relations research and evaluation toolkit: How to measure the effectiveness of PR*. London: Institute of Public Relations.

Funnell, Sue & Patricia Rogers. 2011. *Purposeful program theory: Effective use of theory of change and logic models*. San Francisco: Jossey-Bass.

Government Communication Service (GCS). 2015. Evaluation framework. London: Cabinet Office, HM Government. https://gcs.civilservice.gov.uk/guidance/evaluation/tools-and-resources (accessed 1 July 2017).

Gregory, Anne & Tom Watson. 2008. Defining the gap between research and practice in public relations programme evaluation: Towards a new research agenda. *Journal of Marketing Communications* 24(5). 337–350. doi.org/10.1080/13527260701869098

Grunig, James. 1979. The status of public relations research. *Public Relations Quarterly* 20(1). 5–8.

Grunig, James. 1983. Basic research provides knowledge that makes evaluation possible. *Public Relations Quarterly* 28(3). 28–32.

Grunig, James. 2008. Conceptualizing quantitative research in public relations. In Betteke van Ruler, Ana Tkalac Verčič & Dejan Verčič (eds.), *Public relations metrics, research and evaluation*, 88–119. New York: Routledge.

Grunig, Larissa, James Grunig & David Dozier. 2002. *Excellent organizations and effective organizations: A study of communication management in three countries*. Mahwah, NJ: Lawrence Erlbaum.

Guth, D. & Marsh, C. 2007. *Public relations: A values-driven approach*, 3rd edn. Boston: Pearson Education.

Huhn, Julia, Jan Sass & Christopher Storck. 2011. Communication controlling: How to maximize and demonstrate the value creation through communication. Berlin: German Public Relations Association (DPRG). http://www.communicationcontrolling.de/fileadmin/communication controlling/sonst_files/Position_paper_DPRG_ICV_2011_english.pdf (accessed 1 July 2017).

Kellogg Foundation. 2004. *Logic model development guide*. http://www.epa.gov/evaluate/pdf/ eval-guides/logic-model-development-guide.pdf (accessed 25 November 2019).

Knowlton, Lisa & Cynthia Phillips. 2013. *The logic model guidebook: Better strategies for great results*, 2nd edn. Thousand Oaks, CA: Sage Publications.

Lamme, Margot & Karen Russell. 2010. Removing the spin: Towards a new theory of public relations history. *Journalism & Mass Communication Monographs* 11(4). 281–362.

L'Etang, Jacqui. 2008. *Public relations: Concepts, practice and critique*. London: Sage Publications.

Likely, Fraser & Tom Watson. 2013. Measuring the edifice: Public relations measurement and evaluation practice over the course of 40 years. In Krishamurthy Sriramesh, Ansgar Zerfass & Jeong Nam Kim (eds.), *Public relations and communication management: Current trends and emerging topics*, 143–162. New York: Routledge.

Lindenmann, Walter. 1979. The missing link in public relations research. *Public Relations Review* 5(1). 26–36.

Lindenmann, Walter. 1980. Hunches no longer suffice. *Public Relations Journal* 36(6). 9–13.

Lindenman, Walter. 1993. An 'effectiveness yardstick' to measure public relations success. *Public Relations Quarterly* 38(1). 7–9.

Lindenmann, Walter. 2003. Guidelines for measuring the effectiveness of PR programs and activities. Gainesville, FL: Institute for Public Relations. http://www.instituteforpr.org/ wp-content/uploads/2002_MeasuringPrograms.pdf (accessed 25 November 2017).

Lipsey, Mark. 1993. Theory as method: Small theories of treatments. *New Directions for Program Evaluation* 57. 5–38. https://doi.org/10.1002/ev.1637

Macnamara, Jim. 2015. Overcoming the measurement and evaluation deadlock: A new approach and model. *Journal of Communication Management* 19(4). 371–387. doi: 10.1108/JCOM-04-2014-0020

Macnamara, Jim. 2018. *Evaluating public communication: Exploring new models, standards, and best practice*. Abingdon, UK: Routledge.

Macnamara, Jim & Fraser Likely. 2017. Revisiting the disciplinary home of evaluation: New perspectives to inform PR evaluation standards. *Research Journal of the Institute for Public Relations* 2(2). 1–21.

Macnamara, Jim, May Lwin, Ana Adi & Ansgar Zerfass. 2016. 'PESO' media strategy shifts to 'SOEP': Opportunities and ethical dilemmas. *Public Relations Review* 42(3). 377–385. doi: 10.1016/ j.pubrev.03.001

Macnamara Jim & Ansgar Zerfass. 2017. Evaluation stasis continues in PR and corporate communication: Asia Pacific insights into causes. *Communication Research and Practice*. doi.org/10.1080/22041451.2017.1275258

Macnamara, Jim, Ansgar Zerfass, Ana Adi & May O. Lwin. 2018, Capabilities of PR professionals for key activities lag: Asia-Pacific study shows theory and practice gaps. *Public Relations Review* 44(5). 704–716. https://doi.org/10.1016/j.pubrev.2018.10.010

Marklein, Tim & Katie Paine. 2012. The march to standards. Presentation to the 4th European Summit on Measurement, Dublin, Ireland, June. http://amecorg.com/downloads/dublin2012/The-March-to-Social-Standards-Tim-Marklein-and-Katie-Paine.pdf (accessed 1 July 2017).

Noble, Paul & Tom Watson. 1999. Applying a unified public relations evaluation model in a European context. Paper presented to the Transnational Communication in Europe:Practice and Research Congress, Berlin, Germany. http://eprints.bournemouth.ac.uk/20486 (accessed 28 January 2020).

Patel, Sajun. 2015. Why you should ignore vanity metrics and focus on engagement. *Forbes*, May 13. http://www.forbes.com/sites/sujanpatel/2015/05/13/why-you-should-ignore-vanity-metrics-focus-on-engagement-metrics-instead/#59ea320a574e (accessed 25 November 2019)

Pavlik, John. 1987. *Public relations: What research tells us.* Newbury Park, CA: Sage.

Pawson, Ray & Nick Tilley. 1997. *Realistic evaluation.* London: Sage.

Pawson, Ray & Nick Tilley. 2001. Realistic evaluation bloodlines. *American Journal of Evaluation* 22. 317–324.

Practical Concepts, Inc. 1971. *The logical framework.* Approach and training materials developed for U.S. Agency for International Development. Washington. D.C. [Unpublished manuscript].

Practical Concepts, Inc. 1979. *The logical framework. A manager's guide to a scientific approach to design & evaluation.* Washington, DC. http://pdf.usaid.gov/pdf_docs/nabn963.pdf (accessed 2 July 2018).

PRIA (Public Relations Institute of Australia). 2017. Measurement and evaluation framework. Sydney, NSW. https://www.pria.com.au/resources/measurement-evaluation (accessed 1 July 2017).

Rossi, Peter, Mark Lipsey & Howard Freeman. 2004. *Evaluation: A systematic approach*, 7th edn. Thousand Oaks, CA: Sage.

Suchman, Edward. (1967). *Evaluative research: Principles and practice in public service and social action programs.* New York: Russell Sage Foundation.

Taylor-Power, Ellen & Ellen Henert. 2008. *Developing a logic model: Teaching and training guide.* Madison, WI: University of Wisconsin-Extension Program. https://fyi.uwex.edu/program development/files/2016/03/lmguidecomplete.pdf (accessed 11 January 2018).

Tench, Ralph, Dejan Verčič, Ansgar Zerfass, Angeles Moreno & Piet Verhoeven. 2017. *Communication excellence: How to develop, manage and lead exceptional communications.* London: Palgrave Macmillan.

Thomas, Jerry. 2008. Advertising effectiveness. Decision Analyst. http://www.decisionanalyst.com/publ_art/adeffectiveness.dai (accessed 1 July 2017).

USC (University of Southern California, Annenberg Center for Public Relations) and The Holmes Report. 2016. *Global Communications Report 2016.* www.holmesreport.com/docs/default-source/default-document-library/2016-global-communications-report.pdf?sfvrsn=2 (accessed 1 July 2017).

Valente, Thomas. 2001. Evaluating communication campaigns. In Ronald Rice & Charles Atkin (eds.), *Public communication campaigns*, 3rd edn., 105–124. Thousand Oaks, CA: Sage.

Watson, Tom. 2012. The evolution of public relations measurement and evaluation. *Public Relations Review* 38(3). 390–398. doi: https://doi.org/10.1016/j.pubrev.2011.12.018

Watson, Tom & Paul Noble. 2014. *Evaluating public relations: A best practice guide to public relations planning, research and evaluation*, 3rd edn. London: Kogan Page.

Watson, Tom & Ansgar Zerfass. 2012. ROI and PR evaluation: Avoiding 'smoke and mirrors'. Paper presented to the International Public Relations Research Conference, Miami, FL, March. http://www.instituteforpr.org/iprwp/wp-content/uploads/Watson-Zerfass-ROI-IPRRC-Miami-20121.pdf (accessed 1 July 2017).

Weiss, Carol. 1972. *Evaluative research: Methods of assessing program effectiveness*. Englewood Cliffs, NJ: Prentice Hall.

Wholey, Joseph. 1970. *Federal evaluation policy*. Washington, DC: Urban Institute Press.

Wholey, Joseph. 1979. *Evaluation: Promise and performance*. Washington, DC: Urban Institute Press.

Wholey, Joseph. 1983. *Evaluation and effective public management*. Boston: Little Brown & Co.

Wholey, Joseph. 1987. Evaluability assessment: Developing program theory. *New Directions for Program Evaluation* 33. 77–92. doi.org/10.1002/ev.1447

Wholey, Joseph, Harry Hatry & Kathryn Newcomer (eds.). 2010. *Handbook of practical program evaluation*, 3rd edn. San Francisco: Jossey-Bass.

Wright, April, Raymond Zammuto, Peter Liesch, Stewart Middleton, Paul Hibbert, John Burke & Victoria Brazil. 2016. Evidence-based management in practice: Opening up the decision process, decision-maker and context. *British Journal of Management* 27(1). 161–178. doi.org/10.1111/1467-8551.12123

Zerfass, Ansgar. 2007. Unternehmenskommunikation und kommunikationsmanagement: Grund-lagen, wertschöpfung, Integration [Corporate communication and communication management: Basics, value creation, integration]. In Manfred Piwinger & Ansgar Zerfass (eds.), *Handbuch Unternehmenskommunikation* [*Handbook of corporate communication*], 21–71. Wiesbaden: Gabler.

Zerfass, Ansgar 2010. Assuring rationality and transparency in corporate communications. Theoretical foundations and empirical findings on communication controlling and communication performance management. In Melissa Dodd & Koichi Yamamura (eds.), *Ethical issues for public relations practice in a multicultural world, 13th International Public Relations Research Conference*, 947–966. Gainesville, FL: Institute for Public Relations. http://iprrc.org/paperinfo_proceedings (accessed 1 July 2017).

Zerfass, Ansgar, Dejan Verčič, Piet Verhoeven, Angeles Moreno & Ralph Tench. 2012. *European communication monitor 2012: Challenges and competencies for strategic communication*. Brussels: European Association of Communication Directors (EACD), European Public Relations Education and Research Association (EUPRERA), and Helios Media. http://www.communicationmonitor.eu/european-communication-monitor-all-reports (accessed 1 July 2017).

Zerfass, Ansgar, Dejan Verčič, Piet Verhoeven, Angeles Moreno & Ralph Tench. 2015. *European communication monitor 2015*. Brussels: European Association for Communication Directors (EACD) and European Public Relations Education and Research Association (EUPRERA) in association with Helios Media, Berlin. http://www.communicationmonitor.eu/european-communication-monitor-all-reports (accessed 1 July 2017).

Zerfass, Ansgar, Angeles Moreno, Ralph Tench, Dejan Verčič. 2017. *European Communication monitor: How strategic communication deals with the challenges of visualisation, social bots and hypermodernity – Results of a survey in 50 countries*. Brussels: European Association for Communication Directors (EACD) and European Public Relations Education and Research Association (EUPRERA) in association with Quadriga Media. http://www.communicationmonitor.eu/european-communication-monitor-all-reports (accessed 12 January 2018).

Part III – **Theories of Public Relations**

James E. Grunig and Jeong-Nam Kim

15 The four models of public relations and their research legacy

Abstract: Research on the models of public relations began in the 1970s when J. Grunig used his situational theory of individual communication behavior to conceptualize public relations as the communication behavior of organizations. Organizational theories originally were used to explain public relations behaviors. Dependent behaviors evolved from one-way vs. two-way communication, to synchronic and diachronic modes, to four models and then four dimensions of public relations. Independent explanatory variables began with organizational structures, environments, technologies, and power structures, and eventually included education, knowledge, professionalism, gender, ideology and culture, schemas, conflict and activism, and empowerment of the public relations function. Research on the models culminated in the Excellence study, which showed that knowledge to practice different models, CEO preferences for different models, the actual practice of the models, and symmetrical internal communication practices correlated with excellence in public relations and greater value to organizations, publics, and society. The two-way symmetrical model as a normative standard for public relations is discussed, as well as the practice of the models in different countries, cultures, and organizations. Criticisms of the models are grouped and discussed, and comparisons are made to similar theories of digital public relations, relationship cultivation strategies, dialogic public relations, and organizational listening.

Keywords: Models and dimensions of public relations; organizational variables; public relations knowledge and professionalism; the models in Excellence theory; the two-way symmetrical model as a normative preference for public relations; global public relations; criticisms of the models; dialogical public relations; digital public relations; relationship cultivation strategies; organizational listening

1 Introduction

In the 1960s, when James Grunig was an undergraduate student studying agricultural journalism at Iowa State University (1960–64) and a graduate student at the University of Wisconsin studying agricultural economics and mass communication (1964–68), public relations was understood and taught mostly as a form of journalism. Public relations practitioners were assumed to be journalists-in-residence who wrote about the organizations that employed them for the media or who helped journalists cover their organizations (i. e., media relations). He experienced this type of public relations as a writer for the Iowa Agricultural Information Service at Iowa State, for

https://doi.org/10.1515/9783110554250-015

the U. S. Department of Agriculture in Washington, DC, for a farm magazine published by the International Harvester Co. in Chicago, and as a newsletter editor at the Land Tenure Center (an international research center) at the University of Wisconsin. The available textbooks went beyond this journalistic paradigm to maintain that public relations also was a management function and that it used theories of persuasion to guide its practices. However, only a few universities taught public relations separately from journalism, and few practitioners had ever read the textbooks or studied public relations as a planned (strategic) communication activity.

J. Grunig was surprised, therefore, when he took a course in public relations at the University of Wisconsin from Scott Cutlip, who was a coauthor of the leading public relations textbook (Cutlip and Center 1964) and widely considered to be the leading academic scholar of the field. A large and boisterous man, Cutlip marched across the front of the classroom writing "one-way" on one side of the blackboard and another "one-way" on the other side. Then, he drew an arrow between the two "one-ways" and stated vociferously that public relations should be a two-way practice. It was on that day that J. Grunig's thinking about the four models of public relations began.

The simple distinction between public relations as a one-way form of communication (as applied journalism) and as a two-way form of communication (involving research and listening as well as the dissemination of information) identified two rudimentary models of public relations. In addition, J. Grunig's education at the University of Wisconsin also influenced him to believe that not all public relations involved persuasion (generally defined as one party changing the attitudes or behavior of another).

Two programs of research at Wisconsin focused on a coorientational approach to communication – the idea that when two or more parties communicate, they are not necessarily trying to change the attitudes (orientations) or behaviors of the other (agreement in coorientational terms). They also could communicate to be aware of what other people think (accuracy), to co-construct cognitions (understanding), or to co-construct solutions to overlapping problems (for an overview of coorientation, see Kim, H.-S. 2003). These programs of research were Chaffee and McLeod's extensive study of coorientation itself (e. g. Chaffee and McLeod 1968; McLeod and Chaffee 1973) and Carter's (1965) study of communication and affective relations, which extended into his many years of research on communication and behavior (see, e. g., Dervin and Chaffee 2003). J. Grunig and Stamm (1973) followed these programs and conducted research on the coorientation of collectivities (such as organizations and publics).

The first article describing four models of public relations did not appear until J. Grunig (1984) published an article on the topic that was featured in a new journal, *Public Relations Research & Education*, which eventually became today's *Journal of Public Relations Research*; and J. Grunig and Hunt (1984) used the models as a framework for several chapters in their textbook *Managing Public Relations*. The four models did have antecedents, however, in previous research on communication behavior (Grunig, J. 1966, 1968) – research that helps to understand the origins of the models.

2 Antecedents of the models

Although J. Grunig is best known for his research on public relations, his early research in the 1960s and early 1970s focused on the communication behavior of individuals and eventually of a collectivity he defined as a public. He developed a theory of the role of communication in economic decision making (Grunig, J. 1966) that departed from the focus of communication research at the time, the effects of messages sent by "senders" to "receivers," to his focus on how the communication behavior of receivers affected when and how they actively seek information or passively process (acquire) information that comes their way without much effort on their part. He used this new focus to develop a theory of communication and development that challenged source-oriented theories such as the diffusion of innovations (e. g. Rogers 1962) or the role of media in changing traditional societies (e. g. Lerner 1958). In his doctoral dissertation, J. Grunig (1968) developed a theory of communication and economic decision making, which he applied in two studies of the communication behaviors of large landowners and peasant farmers in Colombia – two groups that were targets for communication programs designed to "modernize" their attitudes and behaviors about farming practices (Grunig, J. 1969, 1971).

Both studies showed that communication behavior could be explained by perceptions of the situations in which farmers lived and worked, and that constraints and opportunities available in their environments had to be changed before communication would have much effect in promoting economic development. Unfortunately, communication professionals in agricultural development organizations in Colombia typically disseminated messages that they thought would persuade recipients to be more modern without first seeking information from farmers in order to understand the problems they faced and the information that would be relevant to them in solving those problems. J. Grunig concluded that development was limited more by the behavior of organizations who were supposed to help their clients than by the traditional attitudes and behaviors of those clients.

After this research in Colombia, J. Grunig began to teach public relations in 1969 at the University of Maryland, where he used his theory of information and decision making to develop a situational theory of publics that fostered an extensive program of research that has continued for 50 years (Grunig, J. 1997), and which now has evolved into J.-N. Kim and J. Grunig's (2011) situational theory of problem solving (see chapter 24 in this book). That same theory of information and decision making also became a template for the first study of the public relations behavior of organizations – the primary antecedent theory of the models of public relations.

J. Grunig (1976) turned his attention to the organizational subdisciplines of sociology, psychology, and communication to identify independent variables that might explain dependent organizational communication variables (primarily public relations behaviors). Public relations behaviors in the 1970s generally were unsophisticated and seldom based on theoretical knowledge. Public relations practitioners mostly were described as "flacks," or manipulators of the media. Even though most public relations practitioners engaged in one-way, manipulative communication behaviors, a few (primarily those who had studied public relations formally) practiced informative two-way communication, which Robinson (1966) called applied social scientists.

In his first research on the public relations behaviors of organizations, J. Grunig (1976) adopted Thayer's (1968: 129–130) synchronic and diachronic modes of communication. Thayer said that "one could think of the difference between these models as the difference between *monologue* and *dialogue*," but he added that his less-familiar terms described the difference between the modes more completely, primarily because they included the purpose of the communication as well as its direction. Thayer's synchronic mode was persuasive in nature: "the sort of encounter in which one of the participants, Y, has as his objective either a) bringing the psychological state-of-affairs of another person, Z, from its present apparent-state-of-affairs to the state-of-affairs desired or intended by Y, or b) behavior achieving some intended-state-of-affairs through the actions or behavior of Z. In both cases Z is the 'sink' for Y's message ..." Thayer's diachronic mode, in contrast, "does not hinge upon the resolution of one or the other's intended-state-of-affairs, but upon a joint or cooperative effort to achieve *whatever* result comes from the encounter."

The synchronic and diachronic modes of communication were the dependent variables in J. Grunig's (1976) first study of the public relations behavior of organizations. In a survey of 216 organizations in the Washington-Baltimore area, J. Grunig measured 16 common public relations procedures and placed them either into the synchronic category (e. g. writing press releases, staging events, or contacting governmental officials) or the diachronic category (e. g. conducting surveys or informal research before a project and counseling management on public opinion). He also measured several other organizational communication variables, such as vertical and horizontal communication, orientation toward the organization or the public, and persuasion vs. understanding.

In addition to measuring the synchronic and diachronic modes of public relations, J. Grunig (1976) identified characteristics of organizations that practiced them – following up on the normative observation from his Colombian research that organizations might need to be changed before they would communicate in a way that would be beneficial to their publics. The research was primarily positive or descriptive –an attempt to explain why different types of organizations practiced each of the two modes of communication. J. Grunig searched the organizational literature and identified different structures, technologies, and environments that might explain why organizations practiced public relations as they did.

J. Grunig (1976) used general systems thinking to look for similarities in the behaviors of organizations and individuals – behaviors described in his situational theory of communication behavior. At the time, the situational theory consisted of two variables: problem recognition and constraint recognition. Problem recognition occurred when individuals perceived that something was missing in a situation, a perception that motivated them to communicate and solve the problem. Constraint recognition occurred when forces outside the control of the individual (the structure of a situation) prevented them from behaving in ways that might solve a problem.

At this individual level, the combinations of the two variables produced four types of situational behaviors: problem facing (high problem recognition, low constraint recognition), routine habit (low problem recognition, low constraint recognition), constrained (high problem recognition, high constraint recognition), and fatalistic (low problem recognition, high constraint recognition). J. Grunig (1976) used these four types of behaviors to classify variables in the organizational literature into types of organizations that might practice different kinds of public relations behaviors.

The organizational literature at the time generally placed organizations into two or more categories based on structural, technological, and environmental variables. A typical example was Burns and Stalker's (1961) distinction between mechanical and organic organizations. Mechanical organizations, structurally, generally were centralized, formalized, stratified, and not complex. They also tended to have mechanized technologies and to have static environments. Organic organizations were less centralized, less formalized, less stratified, more complex, had intensive and mediating technologies, and had dynamic, changing environments (see also Hage and Aiken 1970). J. Grunig (1976) placed these organizational variables into categories that would increase organizational problem recognition or that would produce constraints for the organization. He then hypothesized that his study would produce four types of organizations that mirrored his four types of individuals and asked which mode of communication (synchronic or diachronic) each type would practice.

Factor analysis of all of the organizational variables, however, produced only two types of organizations: problem solving (high problem recognition, low constraints) and fatalistic (low problem recognition, high constraints). The characteristics of these two types of organizations closely resembled those of organic and mechanical organizations. J. Grunig (1976) expected to find that problem solving organizations would use public relations to communicate diachronically, and fatalistic organizations would use it to communicate synchronically. The study, however, showed that problem-solving organizations were more likely to communicate both diachronically and synchronically than were fatalistic organizations. Even for problem-solving organizations, however, diachronic communication (information seeking and research) was rare.

J. Grunig (1976) was able to explain why this occurred because he also had measured the professionalization of the public relations practitioners in his survey based on their training, values, and how they evaluated their work. He distinguished between *professionals* and *careerists* and included these variables in a factor analysis with the organizational and communication variables. This analysis produced three types of organizations: problem solving organizations with professionals, problem solving organizations with careerists, and fatalistic organizations with careerists. A clear picture emerged: Problem solving organizations with professional public relations practitioners rather than careerists practiced diachronic as well as synchronic public relations. Structurally, this special type of problem-solving organization was small, new, and less formalized – thus allowing more autonomy to a professional public relations person. When organizations employed careerist public relations practitioners, however, both types of organizations practiced only synchronic public relations, although the fatalistic organizations did not communicate much at all.

This study served as a template for nearly a decade of research, mostly in the 1980s, on the public relations behavior of organizations. The two-way typology of diachronic and synchronic public relations proved to be limiting, however, and gave way to the four models of public relations. Nevertheless, the research continued to examine the extent to which similar organizational and professional variables explained how public relations is practiced.

3 Introduction of the four models of public relations

J. Grunig first used the term "models" to refer to types of public relations in a journal article (Grunig, J. 1984) and a textbook (Grunig, J. and Hunt 1984) published in the same year. J. Grunig frequently has told an anecdote of how he first thought of the four models while he was teaching a lesson on public relations history in his undergraduate course in public relations theory. Not an historian himself, J. Grunig found that teaching this history as a chronology of famous public relations practitioners was uninteresting and difficult for students to remember. So, he wrote the names of four historical figures on the blackboard who he believed exemplified fundamentally different ways of practicing public relations and said their practices fit into four models. P. T. Barnum exemplified a press agentry/promotional model, Ivy Lee a public information model, Edward L. Bernays a two-way asymmetrical model, and Scott Cutlip and similar public relations educators a two-way symmetrical model. In J. Grunig and Hunt (1984), he described these four models as evolutionary stages in the history of public relations, but the idea of stages in history was criticized by public relations historians. As a result, in an unpublished second edition of *Managing Public Relations,* he modified the history chapter substantially and wrote that examples of all four models could be found throughout history and that he no longer believed public relations evolved from press agentry to public information to two-way asymmetrical to two-way symmetrical.

3.1 Asymmetrical and symmetrical nomenclature

J. Grunig introduced two important changes in nomenclature in his two 1984 publications. First, he renamed Thayer's (1968) synchronic and diachronic modes of communication as asymmetrical and symmetrical purposes of public relations. Thayer chose the term synchronic because its purpose was to "synchronize" the behavior of another party with one's own. However, the opposing term, "diachronic," did not really fit what he had in mind when two parties communicate in order to jointly solve a problem or reach a state of affairs that was beneficial to both. An examination of the etymology of the two terms revealed that synchronic refers to "at one time" whereas diachronic refers to "at more than one time." The difference in the time sequence did not seem to fit what Thayer, or J. Grunig, had in mind.

After brainstorming with graduate students in a communication theory class, J. Grunig chose the terms asymmetrical and symmetrical as replacements. By asymmetrical, he meant that an individual or organization communicates in order to change the cognitions, attitudes, or behavior of another entity but not one's own. Symmetrical meant that a person or organization communicates with the understanding that the interaction could change either or both parties. These new terms were not perfect, however, as they often have been misunderstood, or misinterpreted, by critics of the models as meaning that symmetry meant that there must be a perfect balance in the intentions of a communicating party or completely balanced outcomes. Critics of the symmetrical model, in particular, often cited the infrequent occurrence of balanced intentions and effects to claim that the model was utopian and impractical. In contrast, J. Grunig (2001: 28) used the term symmetrical to refer to a public relations process and not necessarily to outcomes that must be achieved for communication to be successful – "a give-and-take process that can waver between advocacy and collaboration." In addition, by using the terms advocacy and collaboration, he acknowledged that the purpose of communication could fall on different points along a continuum from completely asymmetrical to completely symmetrical. L. Grunig, J. Grunig, and Dozier (2002) compared this combination of advocacy and collaboration in the symmetrical model with what Murphy (1991) called a mixed-motive model, Spicer (1997) called collaborative advocacy, and Raiffa (1982) called collaborative antagonism.

Although asymmetrical and symmetrical were not perfect choices of words, we believe that no better terminology has emerged over the years. Recently, public relations scholars (e. g. Kent and Taylor 2002) have used the terms dialogue and monologue to mean essentially the same thing as symmetrical and asymmetrical – terms that Thayer (1968) also considered but rejected in favor of synchronic and diachronic. Although monologue and dialogue are acceptable substitutes for asymmetrical and symmetrical, they mostly seem to describe the direction of communication (communication as telling vs. communication as conversing) and do not fully capture the purpose of communication as persuasive versus joint problem solving.

Evans (2017: 1–2), an emeritus professor of agricultural communication at the University of Illinois, used the two terms "honest broker" and "joint problem solver" to describe the role of an agricultural communicator – terms that are an intriguing substitute as a name for the two-way symmetrical model. He described the "the timeless principle of entering the communication process as a respectful partner with intended audiences rather than looking at them as 'targets' or groups to be manipulated for one's own purposes. (...) that is why I like to consider 'joint problem solving' as a useful goal for communicating, with 'honest broker' communications as a means to that goal."

The honest broker/joint problem solver model seems to be an alternative name for the two-way symmetrical model. However, because of their long-term use we continue to use the terms asymmetrical and symmetrical even though the terms invite misinterpretation.

3.2 Models of public relations as the dependent variables

J. Grunig (1984) said that conceptualizing only two types of public relations behavior was overly simple and not theoretically pleasing, and he said the same about only two types of organizations in organizational theory. To improve this conceptualization, he chose the term "models" to describe four types of public relations behavior – inspired by the title of the book *Models of Man* by Simon (1957), a psychologist, economist, and management scholar who had influenced J. Grunig's research on economic decision making and organizational theory. Although Simon mostly used mathematical models as descriptors of several types of individual and social behaviors, the concept of models also was, and still is, widely used to describe other kinds of theoretical representations.

J. Grunig (1984) explained that "scientists use the term 'model' to describe a simplified representation of reality. All models are false, in part, because they cannot represent all of reality. However, the human mind must rely on models because it can only isolate and grasp key variables that can be abstracted from reality. The mind cannot grasp all of reality. Models, by themselves, are not theories. A theory is an abstract idea in the mind of a scientist. The scientist expresses this theory through different types of representations, such as words, diagrams, mathematical equations, and other types of *models*. Therefore, the models of public relations are abstract representations of what public relations is and how it is practiced in the mind of a theorist.

J. Grunig (1984) pointed out that concepts such as one-way and two-way, synchronic and diachronic, and monologue and dialogue were limited because they failed to recognize that the sets of paired concepts did not describe all of the elements of communicative behaviors. For example, persuasive communication (synchronic or asymmetrical) can be one-way or two-way (monologue or dialogue);

one-way communication can be informative (symmetrical) without being synchronic or asymmetrical. As a result, he proposed four models of public relations based on the interactions of two variables – the *direction* and the *purpose* of public relations. The press agentry/publicity model was one-way and asymmetrical, the public information model was one-way and symmetrical, the two-way asymmetrical model was two-way and asymmetrical, and the two-way symmetrical model was two-way and symmetrical.

J. Grunig (1984) developed quantitative indices of eight variables for each of the four models, which he used in a study of 52 organizations of different types in the Washington, DC area that were interviewed by graduate students in the Seminar in Public Relations Management at the University of Maryland. These indices since have been used in many other studies of the models.

The four models have been depicted in diagrams and figures in several ways over the years, including a widely cited table in J. Grunig and Hunt (1984: 22). Subsequent research, however, revealed inaccuracies in this table, especially in the types of organizations practicing each model and the frequency of their practice. J. Grunig and L. Grunig (1992) later depicted the models on two continuua, which illustrate them reasonably well.

One continuum has the press agentry model on one end and the public information model on the other. This continuum is called "craft public relations" because it represents mostly the use of technical skills and does not require professional, managerial knowledge. The second continuum moves from the two-way asymmetrical model on the left to the two-way symmetrical model on the right. It represents "professional" public relations because practitioners usually have some theoretical knowledge of communication, social science, and management in addition to technical communication skills. Public relations is most likely to be practiced on the symmetrical end of the professional continuum when the organization and its senior managers are open to outside ideas and to change. But when conditions are not so favorable, public relations still can be practiced professionally on the asymmetrical end of the continuum. At that end, public relations practitioners – while trying to persuade publics to their organization's point of view – at least do research to evaluate the effectiveness of their persuasive work. Although Figure 1 separates the two continua, many practitioners use elements of both in their work. For example, many practitioners use techniques of the public information and press agentry models in communication programs even though they model these programs on one or both of the two-way modes.

Craft Public Relations

] _____ [

Propaganda ^   ^   Journalism
      Press Agentry Model   Public Information Model

Professional Public Relations

] _____ [

Asymmetrical ^   ^   Symmetrical
Two-Way Asymmetrical Model   Two-Way Symmetrical Model

Figure 1: Four models of public relations placed on two continua

3.3 Independent, explanatory variables for the four models

At this point in their development, the four models were components of a primarily positive, or descriptive, theory that related them to organizational and environmental characteristics that might explain why different organizations practice one or more of the models. J. Grunig and Hunt (1984: 43) followed the lead of management scholars who, in the 1950s, adopted a contingency approach to determining the best management practices for an organization. They pointed out that different models might be appropriate for different types of organizations in different environments. Although they said that "it will become obvious that we prefer the two-way symmetric model and will stress that model throughout this book, we recognize that there are organizations facing problems for which the other models provide the best solutions."

To describe the independent variables that he thought might explain the practice of the four models, J. Grunig (1984) constructed a theory that consisted of the product/service environment, the political/regulatory environment, and the values of the "dominant coalition" – a term developed by management scholars to describe the most powerful people in an organization who are most influential in making decisions. He theorized that the product/service environment would explain public relations activities that support an organization's marketing communication activities and that the political/regulatory environment would explain its public affairs activities (government relations and support for political positions).

The *product/service environment* was derived from Hage and Hull's (1981) typology of organizations that fit into four environmental niches. Just as J. Grunig had moved from a two-way typology of public relations behavior to four models, Hage and Hull had moved from Burns and Stalker's (1961) mechanical and organic organizations to a four-way typology based on the interactions of two variables, scale of demand and knowledge complexity. Hage and Hull (1981) used these concepts to describe both the environment and technology of an organization. Organizations with large-scale demand for their products or services in the environment used large-scale technology to produce the products or services. Similarly, an organization with complex knowledge in its environment had more complex tasks to perform and employed more specialized personnel. Hage and Hull used the economist's term "scale" rather than the more common concept of "size" because large organizations can produce a small number of products or services on a large scale or a large number of products and services on a smaller scale.

Hage and Hull (1981) identified four types of organizations. The first, a *traditional* organization, had both small scale and limited complexity. J. Grunig (1984) predicted that it would practice the press agentry model. The second, a *mechanical* organization, had low complexity and large scale. J. Grunig predicted that it would practice the public information model. The third, an *organic* organization, had high complexity and small scale. J. Grunig predicted that it would practice the two-way symmetrical model. The fourth type, the *mixed mechanical/organic* organization had high complexity and large scale. J. Grunig predicted that it would practice a combination of the two-way symmetrical and asymmetrical models.

For policy-related, public affairs activities, J. Grunig (1984) identified two environmental variables, constraints and uncertainty, which constituted what he called the *political/regulatory environment*. The organizational literature suggested that organizations prefer autonomy and try to dominate their environments. However, constraints and uncertainty produced by labor unions, pressure groups, activist publics, and regulatory agencies force organizations to adapt to, rather than dominate, their environments. To describe this environment, J. Grunig introduced a second typology based on high, medium, and low levels of constraints and high and low levels of uncertainty. He hypothesized that high uncertainty would lead to two-way communication and that constraints would explain the symmetry and asymmetry of public relations (a curvilinear relationship in which symmetry would be highest at medium levels of constraint and asymmetry would be highest at low and high levels).

The *values of the dominant coalition*, J. Grunig (1984) hypothesized (following Hage 1980), might explain the models practiced when an organization appears to make decisions that are "out of equilibrium" with either of these two types of environment. Quite often, an organization did not practice the model of public relations that would move it toward equilibrium with its environment because the powerful people who run the organization did not understand or value the advanced models of public relations even though they would help the organization adjust better to its environment.

3.4 Results of the environmental contingency theory

Results of this initial study provided some support for the three-dimensional contingency theory. The 15 organizations practiced all of the models to some extent. However, in five organizations the press agentry model was dominant. They were small, traditional organizations with few political problems and whose dominant coalitions valued press agentry as a means of producing and controlling consumer demand. The public information model was dominant in only one organization, the information unit of an agricultural college, mostly because of the journalistic training of its practitioners and the values of its dominant coalition, even though a mix of the two-way models would have fit its environment better. Nine organizations practiced combinations of the two-way models. In four, the two-way asymmetrical model was dominant and in five the two-way symmetrical model was dominant. J. Grunig (1984) concluded that these organizations mostly were in equilibrium with their environments.

Schneider [aka L. Grunig] (1985: abstract, 2) expanded on this initial study by administering a lengthy questionnaire and conducting qualitative interviews in 48 organizations, 12 of which fit into each of Hage and Hull's (1981) four types of organizations. She summarized the results as follows:

> The publicity model of public relations predominates. However, two-way asymmetric communication also characterizes the traditional organization. Mechanical organizations emphasize public information, with concomitant journalistic activities such as writing and editing (especially in-house publications). Organic organizations practice two-way symmetric communication more than does any other Hage-Hull type. They also emphasize internal communication. Mixed [mechanical/organic] organizations practice both models of two-way public relations. Practitioners in this type enjoy the greatest autonomy, support, and value by top management.

4 Program of research on the models in the 1980s

These two studies of the models of public relations stimulated nearly a decade a research by graduate students and faculty members at the University of Maryland to test the validity of the models and the reliability of their measures and to study a large number of independent variables that might explain why organizations practice the different models. Reviews of this literature were published in J. Grunig and L. Grunig (1989, 1992). These reviews provided extensive evidence that supported the validity and reliability of the models—that is, that the concept of the models was a good theory and that the models existed in reality and could be measured. However, they also encountered many blind alleys in pursuing independent variables that only partially explained why organizations practiced the models.

4.1 Organizational variables and the models

Several studies published during this period correlated the four models of public relations with the same organizational structure and technology variables that J. Grunig (1976) had included in his four types of organizations derived from the situational theory of publics. For the structural variables, J. Grunig and L. Grunig (1989) concluded that one-way models tend to be used in centralized organizations and two-way models in decentralized ones. Complex organizations, which employed more special- ists with higher education, correlated negatively with the asymmetrical models (press agentry and two-way asymmetrical); but they did not correlate at all with the public information and two-way symmetrical models. Stratified organizations generally did not use the two-way symmetrical model, but there were no consistent correlations with the other models. There also were some scattered empirical links between types of technology and the models, but J. Grunig and L. Grunig (1989: 50) concluded that technology was "an inconsistent explanatory variable for public relations behavior" and dropped it from further research.

J. Grunig and L. Grunig (1989) concluded that organizations chose both a struc- ture and one or more model of public relations to adapt to their environments, so they collapsed the structural variables into the Hage and Hull (1981) typology dis- cussed in the previous section. Although the initial studies by J. Grunig (1984) and Schneider [aka L. Grunig] (1985) found some support for the variables of the product/ service environment and the political/regulatory environment, the two reviews con- cluded that correlations between the models and the various environmental niches were modest. J. Grunig and L. Grunig (1989) concluded that organizations did have a tendency to practice an appropriate model for their environments and technologies. However, they also concluded that the logical relationships between the models and organizational and environmental variables probably were more of a normative ideal for how organizations should practice public relations than a positive explanation of their actual public relations behaviors.

It is important to note that J. Grunig and L. Grunig (1989) did not conclude that the models, especially the two-way symmetrical model, were entirely normative (i. e. an ideal that seldom appears in practice) – a claim frequently made erroneously by critics of the models. Rather, they concluded that the *relationship* between the models and organizational variables and environments is normative – an ideal that *would* help organizations interact with their environments most effectively if it were actually practiced.

4.2 Other explanations for practicing the models

The conclusion that organizational and environmental variables did not fully explain why public relations departments practice different models stimulated the search for other variables that might explain their use – variables that were reviewed by J. Grunig and L. Grunig (1989, 1992). Some of these had been researched in studies cited thus far and others were new.

4.2.1 Empowerment of the public relations function

In the previous section, we explained that the *values of the dominant coalition* might override the natural adjustment of an organization to its environment, especially when the most powerful decision makers believe they can exert power to control their environment. In such cases, they often believe that a one-way model would help them exert that power. When that occurs, it is imperative that the chief communication officer have access to the dominant coalition or be a member of that powerful group. J. Grunig and L. Grunig (1989) cited research by Pollack (1986) that showed exactly that – positive correlations of *representation of public relations in the dominant coalition* and the *autonomy of the public relations function* with both the two-way symmetrical and two-way asymmetrical models and negative correlations with the press agentry and public information models.

4.2.2 Education and professionalism

Most of the studies reviewed by J. Grunig and L. Grunig (1989) measured whether the public relations practitioners who completed questionnaires had been educated in public relations. In most studies, research showed positive correlations between such education and practice of the more sophisticated two-way models. In general, however, the correlations were small because not all public relations educational programs emphasized the two-way models.

Education in public relations is one indicator of professionalism, and professionalism has been correlated with the four models several times – including its strong relationship with diachronic communication in J. Grunig (1976). J. Grunig and L. Grunig (1992) also cited three other studies that found correlations between professionalism and the two-way models – especially the two-way symmetrical model.

4.2.3 Knowledge and the potential of the PR department

Correlations of the two-way models with education and professionalism suggest that practitioners who implement the two-way models do so because they have the necessary knowledge. Wetherell (1989) developed indices to measure the knowledge needed to practice each of the models – indices that were distinct from the measures of their actual practice. "The indices provided the strongest correlations to date (...) [with] the four models of public relations. [Practitioners] with knowledge needed for the two-way models were most likely to practice them. Those practicing the two-way models also had the requisite knowledge for the one-way models. Those practicing the one-way models, however, did not have the knowledge needed for the two-way models" (J. Grunig and L. Grunig 1992: 300).

J. Grunig and L. Grunig (1992) combined education, professionalism, and knowledge into a category they called the *potential of the public relations* department – the greater the potential, the more likely it was that a practitioner would practice the two-way models, especially the symmetrical model. This potential also included the extent to which a practitioner enacted a managerial role as well as a technical role (e.g. Dozier 1992). A practitioner who enacted a managerial role was more likely to practice the symmetrical model and to have access to the dominant coalition. Potential of the department also included the extent to which men and women had equal opportunity in the department.

4.2.4 Gender

According to J. Grunig and L. Grunig (1992: 302), "several feminist scholars have pointed out the similarity between the presuppositions of the two-way symmetrical model – such as cooperation, negotiation, and compromise – and the characteristics of women." Wetherell (1989) studied this relationship, but she did not find a difference in the extent to which women and men practiced the four models. In contrast to what might be expected, she found that both women and men with feminine characteristics preferred and were more likely to practice the one-way models, probably because they embodied traditional female roles in public relations. However, both men and women in a managerial role were more likely to practice the two-way symmetrical model if they had feminine characteristics.

Wetherell's (1989) study also showed that fewer women than men, and possibly those with feminine characteristics, were able to enact a managerial role. This finding has been well known to feminist scholars of public relations (e.g. Hon, Grunig, L., and Dozier 1992) – suggesting that empowerment of women and people with feminine characteristics to enact a managerial as well as a technical role is an important factor in increasing the extent to which the two-way symmetrical model, in particular, is practiced.

4.2.5 Ideology and culture

In section 2.3, we reviewed studies by J. Grunig (1984) and Schneider [aka L. Grunig] (1985) that conceptualized *values of the dominant coalition* as one explanation of why organizations often do not choose the most appropriate model of public relations for their environment. Although the evidence from several studies was not definitive, J. Grunig and L. Grunig (1989) concluded that the one-way models and to a lesser extent the two-way asymmetrical model were related to conservative political values, rigid organizational codes, and internal values. In contrast, liberal political values, flexible system codes, and external values were related to the two-way symmetrical model.

Ideology is a central component of organizational cultures, so Sriramesh, J. Grunig, and Buffington (1992) reviewed this literature and related it to the models of public relations, among several organizational and public relations variables. They identified two overarching types of culture from this literature, *authoritarian* and *participative*. They predicted that an authoritarian culture would be related to an asymmetrical worldview of public relations in an organization and that a participative culture would be related to a symmetrical worldview, which was supported by Buffington's (1988) research showing that similar characteristics of culture were related to the models of public relations.

4.2.6 Schema for public relations

J. Grunig and L. Grunig (1992) used the concept of schema from the literature on cognitive psychology to explain how the way in which senior managers understand public relations helps to explain how it is practiced in an organization. A schema is a large, integrated block of knowledge that provides a subjective theory about how the world operates. Several studies showed that many senior managers cannot understand public relations as anything other than media relations, which means that public relations people are forced to practice either the press agentry or public information models to match that schema. Many managers also confuse public relations with marketing, which typically forces their public relations staff to practice the press agentry or two-way asymmetrical models.

4.2.7 Conflict and activism

Organizations with dynamic, changing environments typically experience conflict with active publics and activist groups. As a result, J. Grunig and L. Grunig (1989) predicted that such conflict would motivate organizations to practice the two-way symmetrical model. Studies by Lauzen (1986) and L. Grunig (1986) found that organizations were more likely to try all of the models of public relations when they experienced activism and conflict, but that few of them used the two-way symmetrical model even though, theoretically, it would be most effective. However, not enough organizations in their studies used the two-way symmetrical model for the researchers to conclude that it was most effective.

4.3 Which kinds of organizations practice the models?

The research we have described to this point has used organizational, environmental, professional, and individual practitioner variables to explain why organizations practice some or all of the models of public relations. Another possible explanation is that different types of organizations, such as corporations, government agencies, nonprofits, sports organizations, or theatre groups practice different models because of the nature of their work or for historical reasons. J. Grunig and Hunt (1984: 22) published a widely cited table in which they estimated how many organizations practiced each model and the kinds of organizations that practiced them – 50 % public information, 20 % two-way asymmetrical, 15 % press agentry, and 15 % two-way symmetrical. They said they believed that press agentry was practiced most in sports, theatre, and product promotion; public information in government organizations, nonprofits, and some businesses; two-way asymmetrical in competitive businesses and public relations firms; and two-way symmetrical in regulated businesses and public relations firms.

J. Grunig and L. Grunig (1992) reported that 13 studies were conducted from 1984 to 1992 showing that J. Grunig and Hunt's (1984) predictions sometimes were accurate but at other times completely inaccurate. In particular, mean values for the indices of the models showed that public information was least frequently practiced and press agentry most frequently practiced. Public information, however, was most popular in government agencies, especially in scientific organizations, where journalistic training and norms were emphasized. The two-way asymmetrical and symmetrical models were never the dominant model in any of the studies, although their mean scores generally fell at the midpoint of the scales, indicating that many organizations within each category did practice them. When practiced, the two-way symmetrical was most common in government agencies, the military, and regulated utilities, and two-way asymmetrical in corporations. Schneider's [aka L. Grunig] (1985) study of public relations as practiced in the four Hage-Hull (1981) categories, however, showed that a mixture of the two-way models most often were practiced in mixed mechanical-organic organizations, which tended to be large corporations.

Other studies showed that different programs within an overall public relations function practiced different models, such as during a crisis (two-way symmetrical), community relations (two-way symmetrical), and marketing communication (two-way asymmetrical and press agentry). J. Grunig (1992) also reviewed literature showing that a system of symmetrical communication is a key component of employee communication programs. J. Grunig and L. Grunig (1992) concluded that these results, taken as a whole, suggested that organizations used different models strategically – at different times and for different types of publics for which they believed a different model would be effective. In short, different categories of organizations practiced particular models for historical reasons, but any kind of organization could and did use all of the models.

Wetherell (1989) helped explained these divergent results by measuring the four models in three different ways: the models respondents said their organizations *actually practiced*, the models they said *they preferred*, and the amount of *knowledge available* in the organization to practice each model. Press agentry and public information actually were practiced most, but respondents said they would prefer the two-way symmetrical and asymmetrical models if they were allowed to practice them. At the same time, respondents reported greater knowledge about how to practice the one-way models than the two-way models – most likely reflecting their journalistic backgrounds.

4.4 Are the models practiced in different countries?

In addition to research that asked whether different models are practiced by different categories of organizations and in communication programs for different publics, researchers also have studied whether the models are unique to the United States and similar Western countries or whether they are or can be practiced in countries with different histories, cultures, and political and economic systems. J. Grunig et al. (1995) compared studies of the models in India, Greece, and Taiwan. They found that all of the models were practiced in these countries but that the press agentry and public information models were dominant. Although practitioners expressed a desire to practice the two-way, more professional, models, most did not have the knowledge to do so. In these three countries, J. Grunig et al. concluded, the two-way symmetrical model seemed to be more of an ideal, normative model than it is in the United States because the conditions in and around organizations necessary for that model existed even less often than in the United States. Nevertheless, they concluded that the benefits of the symmetrical model seemed to be generic to different cultures and that it would be effective if it were practiced more widely.

J. Grunig et al. (1995) also identified two additional patterns of public relations practice in these three countries – personal influence and cultural interpretation. However, they expressed the realization that these potentially new models also existed in the United States – e. g. personal influence in lobbying and cultural interpretation in programs for culturally diverse publics. J. Grunig et al. (1995) acknowledged that these two patterns of practice might constitute new models, but they added that, most likely, they represented variations in the practice of the original four models.

4.5 The two-way symmetrical model as normative practice

The research reviewed thus far in this chapter has largely viewed the models of public relations as positive theory – that is, of different ways in which organizations actually practice public relations and of different organizational, environmental, and individual variables that might explain why organizations practice different models. We pointed out earlier, however, that J. Grunig and Hunt (1984) expressed a preference for the two-way symmetrical model over the others. J. Grunig and L. Grunig (1992) ended their chapter on the models by reviewing literature that suggested that the two-way symmetrical model was both more ethical (see, e. g., Pearson 1989) and more effective than the other models. That conclusion also has been reflected in several publications that have attempted to demonstrate that the two-way symmetrical model should be the normative model for public relations practice.

J. Grunig and collaborators (Grunig, J. 1989, 1994, 2000; Grunig, J. and Jaatinen 1999; Grunig, J. and White 1992) reviewed theories and research results from communication, philosophy of science, cognitive psychology, anthropology, management, political science, and ethics to establish the parameters of a symmetrical *worldview*, which they believed explained why the two-way symmetrical model should be a normative standard for public relations practice. A worldview is a type of theory that is more abstract than and encompasses the middle-range theoretical principles and hypotheses that characterize most social and behavioral science theories. It is a broad conceptual framework, consisting of presuppositions, values, and ideology, that the human mind uses to understand and practice a phenomenon such as public relations.

J. Grunig (1989), for example, identified internal orientation, closed system thinking, efficiency, elitism, conservatism, tradition, and central authority as presuppositions of an asymmetrical worldview. In contrast, symmetrical presuppositions included interdependence, open system thinking, moving equilibrium, equity, autonomy, innovation, decentralization of management, responsibility, conflict resolution, and interest group liberalism. J. Grunig and Jaatinen (1999) theorized that governments with a societal corporatist worldview (in which government and interest groups collaborate) are more likely to engage in symmetrical communication, whereas governments with a pluralist worldview (in which interest groups compete for government resources) or a corporatist worldview (in which powerful groups dominate government and interest groups) are more likely to engage in asymmetrical public relations. J. Grunig (2000), similarly, argued that collectivism, collaboration, and societal corporatism should be core professional values in public relations.

J. Grunig and White (1992: 53) concluded that symmetrical public relations fulfills an idealistic social role because it is based on a worldview that "presupposes that public relations serves the public interest, develops mutual understanding between organizations and their publics, contributes to informed debate about issues in society, and facilitates a dialogue between organizations and their publics." This idealistic social role, however, is not just an "ideal" normative theory that is seldom, if ever practiced. It differs from other idealistic concepts of communication because the two-way symmetrical model does not require an ideal set of conditions by both organizations and publics for it to be practiced, as does, for example, Habermas's (1984) ideal communication situation.

If both an organization and its publics must intend to enter a communicative exchange with a symmetrical worldview, two-way symmetrical communication will seldom occur. However, either an organization or a public (or an interest group representing it) can initiate an exchange with a symmetrical intent and achieve an outcome that is beneficial to both even though the other party does not participate actively. Organizations, for example, can conduct research on publics and their problems and make decisions that benefit publics as well as the organization without the public being aware that it is participating in a dialogue.

A normative theory prescribes how public relations should be practiced, whereas a positive theory describes how it is practiced. As J. Grunig and L. Grunig (1992) pointed out, however, a normative theory that is not or cannot be practiced in reality is not a good normative theory. Evidence must be provided that when the normative theory actually is practiced its theoretical outcomes and benefits do occur. They explained that each of the four models could be viewed as a normative theory – of how public relations should be practiced (and there are normative advocates for each of the models). However, they argued that the philosophical, ethical, and practical values of the two-way symmetrical model provide strong evidence that the model should be the ethical standard for excellent, professional public relations –evidence that was accumulated in a major study of public relations from 1985 to 2002.

5 Models of public relations and the Excellence study

The Excellence study was a 15-year project funded by the International Association of Business Communicators (IABC) Research Foundation (Grunig, J. 1992; Dozier with Grunig, L. and Grunig, J. 1995; and Grunig, L., Grunig, J., and Dozier 2002). The Excellence study, described in chapter 16 of this handbook, produced a general theory of public relations and communication management that incorporated a number of middle-range theories, including the models of public relations. The study addressed two research questions: 1) what is the value of public relations to organizations and to society and 2) what characteristics of a public relations function are most likely to increase this value.

The second research question was addressed by measuring 14 characteristics of public relations and statistically correlating those characteristics, through factor analysis, with the measures of public relations value (Grunig, L., Grunig, J., and Dozier 2002: 9). The models of public relations comprised four of these variables: 1) the actual practice of the models for eight communication programs (for employees, media, investors, community, customers, government, members, and donors), 2) the knowledge in the public relations department to practice each of the models, 3) the CEO's worldview of the public relations function (as reported by the CEO and as predicted for the CEO by the head of PR), and 4) by the presence of a symmetrical system of internal communication as measured in the employee questionnaires. These different measures of the models reflected the collective evidence about the models from the research during the 1980s, as discussed in Sections 3.2 and 3.3 above. As a result, the quantitative and qualitative data reported in the Excellence study provided the most comprehensive information ever collected on the models of public relations.

Results of the study strongly confirmed that the 14 characteristics of excellent communication were correlated with the measures of the value of public relations. The models of public relations were not the most important predictors of excellence or lack of excellence. The strongest predictor was a strategic managerial role for public relations. However, the models were highly intertwined with the strategic management approach. L. Grunig, J. Grunig, and Dozier (2002: 25–26) concluded that the four models provided an accurate, positive description of public relations practice and worldview. Practitioners and CEOs did think about public relations in these ways, and the four models did describe the way communication programs were conducted for different types of publics. However, the differences among the two one-way and the two two-way models typically blurred in the minds of CEOs and in the actual practice of some, but not all, programs. CEOs, in particular, viewed an excellent public relations function as including the two-way asymmetrical model as often as the two-way symmetrical model. Similarly, the knowledge to practice both the two-way symmetrical and asymmetrical models in the public relations function correlated equally with overall excellence.

L. Grunig, J. Grunig, and Dozier (2002) said they found the answer to this joint preference of CEOs by isolating a two-way component of the two-way asymmetrical model. CEOs liked the two-way asymmetrical model because they preferred the systematic use of research in that model. Most did not distinguish research conducted for symmetrical purposes from research conducted for asymmetrical purposes. Most CEOs did not want asymmetrical communication programs, although some exceptions appeared in the qualitative cases. Organizations that defined public relations as a marketing function, in particular, tended to see public relations only in asymmetrical or in one-way terms.

To follow up on this finding, the researchers isolated three dimensions underlying the four models – one-way vs. two-way, symmetry vs. asymmetry, and mediated or interpersonal techniques. They also suggested further research on a fourth dimension, the ethics of communication. The overlapping concepts and practices of the models that had been found before – such as practicing the two-way symmetrical, two-way asymmetrical, and public-information models concurrently – seemed to have occurred because an organization had a symmetrical public relations worldview, favored extensive research, and practiced mediated as well as interpersonal communication.

L. Grunig, J. Grunig, and Dozier (2002: 25–26) concluded, therefore, that excellent public relations could be described better using these underlying dimensions than by the four models. They said that "excellent public relations is research-based (two-way), symmetrical (although organizations constantly struggle between symmetry and asymmetry when they make decisions), and either based on mediated or interpersonal communication (depending on the situation and public)." It also is more ethical, although the researchers did not measure ethics as a component of the models in the Excellence study.

Subsequent to the Excellence study, four studies conducted in Taiwan and Korea successfully used the four dimensions of public relations to describe and analyze public relations practice in those countries (Huang 1997, 2007; Rhee 2002; Sha 1999). A review can be found in J. Grunig (2001).

L. Grunig, J. Grunig, and Dozier (2002) also reported that quantitative and qualitative data revealed that organizations typically turn to a symmetrical approach when activist pressure or a crisis makes an asymmetrical approach too costly. Then, the CEO tends to upgrade the communication function and hire a knowledgeable top communicator – although sometimes the top communicator comes first and convinces the CEO of the need to enhance the communication function. By and large, organizations practiced symmetrical public relations when the CEO understood its value and demanded it and the senior communicator and his or her communication staff had the knowledge to supply it. Much of that knowledge comes from the ability to do research, to understand publics, and to collaborate and negotiate – skills that excellent communicators must have.

Dozier with J. Grunig and L. Grunig (1995) and L. Grunig, J. Grunig, and Dozier (2002) also introduced a new continuum of symmetrical and asymmetrical communication in a two-way setting, responding to Murphy's (1991) suggestion of the need for a mixed-motive model. This continuum placed the organization's position (as defined by the dominant coalition) on one end and the public's position on the other, with a win-win zone in the middle. They said that one-way persuasive communication intended only to enhance the organization's position or the public's position would both be asymmetrical. Two-way communication used to move the public, the dominant coalition, or both to the win-win zone in the middle could be described either as a symmetrical or mixed-motive model.

5.1 Symmetrical communication inside the organization

In a separate chapter based on the employee questionnaires, L. Grunig, J. Grunig, and Dozier (2002: 28) analyzed data on a symmetrical system of internal communication and correlated it with organizational variables identified in previous research – organizational structure, culture, and diversity. They concluded: "This chapter demonstrates conclusively that excellent public relations will thrive most in an organization with an organic structure, participative culture, and a symmetrical system of communication and in which opportunities exist for women and racio-ethnic minorities. Although these conditions alone cannot produce excellent public relations, they do provide a hospitable environment for excellent public relations."

They added: "Our data show that when the public relations function was given the power to implement symmetrical programs of communication, the result was a more participative culture and greater employee satisfaction with the organization. However, we also found that symmetrical communication is not likely in an organization with a mechanical structure and authoritarian culture. Organic structure and symmetrical communication interact to produce a participative culture, and participative culture contributes strongly to employee satisfaction with the organization."

5.2 Countries and types of organizations

L. Grunig, J. Grunig, and Dozier (2002) also addressed the questions of whether public relations excellence occurred in all of the three countries and whether different models were practiced in different countries. They found that overall excellence was essentially the same in the United States, Canada, and the United Kingdom. Minor differences in the models were found in the United Kingdom: Heads of public relations thought their CEOs would prefer the two-way models more than did their counterparts in other countries (although the CEOs did not express a greater preference for those models). And, knowledge to practice press agentry and public information was higher in the UK, possibly because fewer PR heads reported having education in public relations there. Comparisons of corporations, government agencies, associations, and not-for-profit organizations showed no significant differences on the excellence scale or on any of the measures of the public relations models. Therefore, the study supported the idea that all of the models are and can be practiced in any organization in each of these three countries.

During and after the Excellence study, J. Grunig and L. Grunig worked with international and U.S. colleagues with international experience to determine if the symmetrical model could serve as a normative principle on a global basis (Verčič, Grunig, L. and Grunig, J. 1996; Grunig, L., Grunig, J., and Verčič 1998; Wakefield 1997, 2000). They included the principle of symmetry in three forms (practice of the symmetrical model, knowledge to practice it, and a symmetrical system of internal communication) among eight generic principles of public relations taken from the Excellence theory that they theorized would have to be adapted to, and practiced differently, in different cultural, political, and economic situations. They called this a global theory of generic principles and specific applications and found support for it in several studies – including the conclusion that the symmetrical model could serve as a normative principle throughout the world.

6 Criticisms of the models of public relations

The models of public relations have been one of the most researched topics in public relations from the 1970s to the present. They have been the subject of numerous articles, theses, and dissertations in many countries; and they have been incorporated into textbooks and classroom syllabi around the world. Whenever a theory becomes this ubiquitous, it eventually will be subject to criticism from scholars and practitioners with differing theoretical perspectives, worldviews, ideologies, and applied practices. Reviews of these criticisms, with responses to them, have been published by L. Grunig, J. Grunig, and Dozier (2002) and J. Grunig (2001, 2006). The details of the criticisms and the responses to them by J. Grunig and colleagues are lengthy and detailed, but certain themes can be isolated.

6.1 Descriptive value of the four models

There have been some criticisms of the descriptive, positive, value of the four models. For example, Cancel et al. (1997: 32) said: "The practice of public relations is too complex, too fluid, and impinged by far too many variables for the academy to force it into the four boxes known as the four models of public relations." The same could be said, however, about any model used to represent an abstract idea in real-world, operational terms. And, as we have discussed above, J. Grunig and colleagues have refined their theory of public relations behavior from these simplified "four boxes" into four continuous dimensions of public relations behavior, which allow a large number of combinations to describe public relations behaviors.

6.2 The symmetrical model denigrates persuasion and excessively accommodates publics

The criticism that the symmetrical model excessively favors publics at the expense of organizations originally came from scholars of communication and rhetoric, whose theorizing and careers have been devoted to the concept of persuasion. Miller (1989), for example, described public relations and persuasion as "two Ps in a pod." These critics argued that it is unreasonable for organizations to abandon their self-interests. They also seem to believe that organizations can help publics by persuading them to change their behaviors – especially in such areas as health communication and marketing or in cases where unreasonable, and perhaps unethical, activist groups make demands on organizations.

J. Grunig and colleagues have responded to this criticism by pointing out that the symmetrical model does not rule out persuasion – that organizations and publics seek to persuade each other, and themselves, as they negotiate, bargain, and attempt to resolve conflicts. However, they do this within a symmetrical framework of openness toward the other party and listening to publics before assuming that they know what is in a public's interest. At the same time, J. Grunig has said many times that he believes that persuasion is a poorly defined concept – that it is not clear whether the change sought from a persuasive message is a change in attention, cognition, attitude, or behavior, or all of them. In addition, he has said that persuasion is one of the least frequent effects of communication and that he believes scholars pay far too much attention to it (see, e. g., J. Grunig's [2003] description of Richard Carter's parable of the chicken that couldn't lay a golden egg).

One of the most elaborate criticisms of the symmetrical model came from Cameron and his colleagues, who proposed an alternative contingency theory of public relations (e. g. Cameron 1997 and Cancel et al. 1997; see chapter 19 in this handbook). They equated symmetry with accommodation and argued that it often is unethical to accommodate a morally repugnant public – such as the Hitlers of the world. They developed a continuum that placed accommodation on one end and advocacy on the other. They also formulated a theory with 87 contingent variables that affect whether an organization chooses to accommodate a public or advocate for its own interests.

In response, J. Grunig and colleagues argued that symmetry cannot be equated with accommodation because total accommodation of a public's interest at the expense of an organization's would be an asymmetrical outcome in favor of that public. L. Grunig, J. Grunig, and Dozier (2002: 357) also developed their own continuum that depicts the organization's position on one end and the public's on the other. Accommodating either the organization's or the public's position at the expense of the other lies at an asymmetrical position at one or the other end of the continuum. Symmetry lies in the middle of their continuum – a win-win zone that seeks a solution that both sides can accept.

Sha (2004) clarified the interaction of self-interest and other-interest in the symmetrical model by adopting Noether's theory of conservation and change, which for public relations means that an organization can behave symmetrically and also conserve its essential beliefs, principles, and purposes. Her study of the Democratic Progressive Party in Taiwan showed that the party engaged in open dialogue with its external publics about whether Taiwan should remain independent of China, but it also conserved its interest in gaining power and establishing an independent Taiwan.

6.3 The symmetrical model is utopian and normative only

Critical theorists, such as L'Etang (1996), Pieczka (1996), and Moloney (1997), have argued that public relations is necessarily partisan and undemocratic and that the symmetrical model is an unrealistic, utopian, attempt to make an essentially evil practice look good. In essence, they argue that the symmetrical model is normative only and that it is not, and cannot, actually be practiced. J. Grunig and colleagues have responded to this criticism by citing the extensive literature, discussed in this chapter, from the Excellence study and other research that has documented that symmetrical communication actually is practiced and that it is effective when practiced. At the same time, they have found that other models also are practiced, usually more frequently than the symmetrical model. And they have taken the role of critical scholars themselves when they have criticized unethical and ineffective public relations practices.

Pieczka (1996) also argued that symmetrical theorists believe that the model is the only way that public relations should be practiced – what she called a closed-minded attempt to impose a single view on others. J. Grunig and colleagues responded that the symmetrical theory is only one possible normative theory, but that critical theorists typically do not offer an alternative normative theory of how they think public relations should be practiced and generally are content to critique existing practice without acknowledging that public relations can be a positive force in society.

In a similar way to critical theorists, postmodern scholars, such as Bardan (2003) and Holtzhausen, Petersen, and Tindall (2003), have criticized the global theory of generic principles and specific applications, especially the symmetrical principle. They have maintained that postmodern conditions require different forms of public relations in each setting and that the symmetrical model cannot be used in non-Western settings. J. Grunig (2006) responded by interpreting Holtzhausen, Petersen, and Tindall's data from South Africa as showing that symmetrical communication was applied differently there (a specific application of the generic principle), rather than showing that symmetrical communication did not exist, which was their interpretation. Bardan reported that she could not find any practice of symmetrical communication in India, but J. Grunig responded that failure to find positive evidence that the theory actually is practiced does not falsify a normative theory. Rather, a normative theory can be tested only by studying the work of practitioners who have actually applied the principles to see if it has the effects conceptualized in the theory.

6.4 The symmetrical model is organization-centered and helps only the powerful

Just as persuasion theorists seem to believe that the symmetrical model helps only publics, some critical theorists have argued that it helps only organizations. Karlberg (1996) first suggested that researchers should study how activist groups as well as organizations can use the symmetrical model, a suggestion that J. Grunig and L. Grunig (1997) and J. Grunig (2001) responded to by proposing a five-step process of symmetrical communication to be used by activist groups.

Other critical scholars, however, have argued that powerful organizations that claim to practice the symmetrical model actually practice only an illusion of symmetry, which we have called a pseudo-symmetrical model, to give the impression that they care about their publics. Leitch and Neilson (2001: 129), for example, said that the symmetrical model is "simply absurd" because of the difference in power between organizations and publics. Cheney and Christensen (2001: 129), likewise, said that because of "the full extent of corporate power in the world today ... relatively unorganized and resource-poor groups or individuals (cannot) enter into even two-way symmetrical discussions." J. Grunig (2000) responded to this criticism by pointing out that activist groups actually have a great deal of countervailing power today and are not always at the mercy of corporations and other powerful interests. He also added that professionalism can provide public relations executives with the power to gain access to the dominant coalition and to represent the interests of publics in organizational decisions – an activist role for public relations championed also by the postmodern scholars Holtzhausen and Voto (2002).

7 The legacy of the symmetrical model in current research

The Excellence study found that a symmetrical worldview of public relations in an organization, knowledge in the public relations function to practice a research-based two-way model (both symmetrical and asymmetrical), and a symmetrical system of communication inside an organization are important components of excellent public relations. However, two other prominent concepts emerged from the study: 1) public relations as a strategic management function and 2) organization-public relationships as the both the value and the goal of public relations. In research since the Excellence study, as a result, the models of public relations have been integrated into these other two research programs, both of which of are described in other chapters of this handbook.

7.1 The strategic management approach to public relations

Kim et al. (2013) and J. Grunig (2018), among others, have described the strategic management approach to public relations. In that approach, public relations professionals participate in strategic decisions of an organization by conducting research on problems experienced by publics, either that they want organizations to help solve or that are created by the behaviors of organizations. By doing so, public relations provides a voice for publics in organizational decisions and a voice for management to explain its decisions to publics. In this way, the two-way, symmetrical, and ethical dimensions of the models of public relations are incorporated in the strategic management approach.

7.2 Relationship cultivation strategies

Huang (1997) was among the first scholars of the models of public relations to study organization-public relationships. J. Grunig and Huang (2000) conceptualized these relationships as developing in three stages: antecedents, processes, and outcomes. The process stage consisted of several strategies for cultivating relationships, which J. Grunig and Huang classified as either symmetrical or asymmetrical. Hon and J. Grunig (1999) developed scales to measure relationship outcomes, and J. Grunig (2002) developed qualitative methods for assessing both relationship outcomes and symmetrical and asymmetrical strategies for cultivating relationships. Hung (2007) and Ki and Hon (2006) further conceptualized relationship cultivation strategies and developed measures for them. J. Grunig (2006), therefore, described relationship cultivation strategies as the heir to the models of public relations; and the legacy of the models of public relations has been integrated in this way into research on organization-public relationships.

7.3 Digital media and symmetrical communication

Public relations in the 21st century has been dominated by the use of digital media, and an important theoretical and empirical research question is whether the symmetrical model can be practiced with these new media. J. Grunig (2009) observed that, as with other new media, such as television in the past, public relations practitioners tend to use the new media in the same way as the old. Therefore, he said that many practitioners continue to use one-way models of public relations with digital media to dump information on the general population. He then laid out an explanation of how public relations can be more global, strategic, two-way and interactive, symmetrical or dialogical, and socially responsible if it uses a strategic management approach to the profession rather than the symbolic-interpretive approach still used by many practitioners.

8 Theories and research similar to the symmetrical model

In recent years, two programs of research have carried on the tradition of the two-way symmetrical model of public relations – dialogic communication and organizational listening.

8.1 Dialogic public relations

The first and most extensive of these traditions focuses on the concept of dialogue, as originally conceptualized by Kent and Taylor (1998, 2002). Kent and Taylor's theory especially has been applied to digital communication. Kent and Taylor distinguished their theory of dialogic communication from the two-way symmetrical model by claiming that the symmetrical theory is organization-centered, which, as should be clear from the theory and research reviewed in this chapter, is an erroneous interpretation. The symmetrical model, like dialogic theory, focuses on both organizations and publics. In addition, Kent and Taylor cited many of the same dialogic theorists as J. Grunig and colleagues – e. g. Pearson (1989) (compare Grunig, J. and White 1992: 58–60) and Bakhtin (1981) (compare Grunig, L., Grunig, J., and Dozier 2002: 317).

Sommerfeldt and Yang (2018: 61), in a review of dialogic literature, also tried to separate dialogue from the symmetrical model by saying that one of the most frequent failings of the dialogic communication literature is "the frequent conflation of dialogue with symmetrical communication," which they said "equates any back and forth of communication with dialogue." The separation of the public relations literature into the two camps of symmetrical communication and dialogic communication also emerged in a bibliometric analysis of the literature on dialogue and digital dialogical communication (Morehouse and Saffer 2018: 79), which they described as "starkly torn between differing philosophical, theoretical, and conceptual assumptions."

It should be obvious from this chapter that the symmetrical model entails much more than "back and forth communication." In our view, symmetrical communication is a broader theory than dialogic communication, in that it includes public relations activities such as environmental scanning, formative and evaluative research, giving voice to publics in strategic management, counseling of management, issues management, use of digital media, crisis management, cultivation of relationships, and negotiating with activists, as well as interactive encounters with publics. Symmetrical communication, like dialogic communication, also can be used by organizations representing publics as well as by corporations, government agencies, nonprofit organizations, and associations.

Dialogic communication also seems to require a set of ideal conditions, which, as we said above, is a limitation of Habermas's (1984) ideal communication situation. These conditions are mutuality, propinquity, empathy, risk, and commitment (Kent and Taylor 2002). As Kent (2018) explained: "In other words, formal dialogue, also called 'genuine dialogue,' can only take place if the parties involved treat each other with respect, minimize power dynamics and exploitation, are taught how to interact ethically and effectively, and are willing to trust each other enough to self-disclose or share personal or sensitive information." Because these conditions are so difficult to achieve, the literature shows that dialogic communication also is difficult to achieve (Morehouse and Saffer 2018; Nothhaft, Seiffert-Brockmann and Thummes 2018). In contrast, organizations, or publics, can practice symmetrical communication in an attempt to develop relationships with the other party even if the other party does not reciprocate. Through research on the problems and views of publics, for example, it is possible for one party to understand the other without "genuine dialogue" taking place.

Nevertheless, symmetrical theory and dialogical theory share common goals (the interests of publics as well as organizations and the building of relationships), and the public relations discipline has benefitted by the research of both sets of scholars.

8.2 Organizational listening

Both the symmetrical model and dialogic communication require organizational listening in one way or another, but as Macnamara (2016: 104–110) found in a literature review, very little research has been done on listening. For the most part, he added, listening has been embedded in the concept of dialogue but has not been studied by itself.

Muzi Falconi (2014) emphasized the importance of a public relations function conducting formative and evaluative research in order to develop a "hard infrastructure" to implement a listening culture in an organization. Macnamara (2016), similarly, explicated a number of ways in which an organization can listen, such as listening through research, in social media, and public consultation. He also described a number of models of listening in case studies he analyzed. Listening, therefore, is a critical component of symmetrical public relations and research on the concept should enhance the practice of that model.

9 Conclusion: The continuing value of the models of public relations

The four models of public relations have had an enormous influence on the discipline of public relations, both academic and professional, for nearly 50 years. The symmetrical approach to public relations, although not universally accepted, has provided a normative standard for effective, ethical, responsible, and professional public relations. It also has spawned the development of related concepts such as the dimensions of public relations behavior, the strategic management approach to public relations, organization-public relationships, dialogical communication, and organizational listening. The models of public relations and the symmetrical worldview of the profession continue to appear in textbooks, syllabi, journal articles, and professional publications around the world. Although the models themselves always were simplistic, the research and theorizing they have spawned have been profound.

References

Bardan, Nilanjana. 2003. Rupturing public relations metanarratives: The example of India. *Journal of Public Relations Research* 15. 199–223.

Bakhtin, Mikhail M. 1981. *The dialogic imagination: Four essays by M. M. Bakhtin.* M. Holquist (ed.), C. Emerson & M. Holquist (trans.). Austin, TX: University of Texas Press.

Buffington, Jody. 1988. *CEO values and corporate culture: Developing a descriptive theory of public relations.* College Park, MD: MA thesis.

Burns, Tom & George M. Stalker. 1961. *The management of innovation.* London: Tavistock Publications.

Cameron, Glen T. 1997. The contingency theory of conflict management in public relations. In *Proceedings of the conference on two-way communication*, 27–48. Oslo: Norwegian Central Government Information Service.

Cancel, Amanda. E., Glen T. Cameron, Lynne M. Sallot & Michael A. Mitrook. 1997. It depends: A contingency theory of accommodation in public relations. *Journal of Public Relations Research* 9. 31–63.

Carter, Richard F. 1965. Communication and affective relations. *Journalism Quarterly* 42. 203–212.

Chaffee, Steven H. & Jack M. McLeod. 1968. Sensitization in panel design: A coorientational experiment. *Journalism Quarterly* 45. 661–669.

Cheney, George & Lars T. Christensen 2001. Public relations as contested terrain: A critical response. In Robert L. Heath (ed.), *Handbook of public relations*, 167–182. Thousand Oaks, CA: Sage.

Cutlip, Scott M. & Allen H. Center 1964. *Effective public relations*, 3rd edn. Englewood Cliffs, NJ: Prentice-Hall.

Dervin, Brenda & Steven H. Chaffee, with Lois Foreman-Wernet (eds.). 2003. *Communication: A different kind of horse race: Essays honoring Richard F. Carter.* Cresskill, NJ: Hampton Press.

Dozier, David M. 1992. The organizational roles of communications and public relations practitioners. In James E. Grunig (ed.), *Excellence in public relations and communication management*, 327–356. Hillsdale, NJ: Lawrence Erlbaum Associates.

Dozier, David M. with Larissa A. Grunig & James E. Grunig. 1995. *Manager's guide to excellence in public relations and communication management.* Mahwah, NJ: Lawrence Erlbaum Associates.

Evans, Jim. 2017. *The agricultural communicator as joint problem solver and honest broker: A "twin pillars" approach to teaching and practice.* Ag Comm Faculty Discussion Draft. Urbana, IL, University of Illinois, December.

Grunig, James E. 1966. The role of information in economic decision making. *Journalism Monographs* 3.

Grunig, James E. 1968. *Information, entrepreneurship, and economic development: A study of the decision-making processes of Colombian latifundistas.* Madison, WI: University of Wisconsin dissertation.

Grunig, James E. 1969. Information and decision making in economic development. *Journalism Quarterly* 46. 565–575.

Grunig, James E. 1971. Communication and the economic decision making processes of Colombian peasants. *Economic Development and Cultural Change* 19. 580–597.

Grunig, James E. 1976. Organizations and publics relations: Testing a communication theory. *Journalism Monographs* 46.

Grunig, James E. 1984. Organizations, environments, and models of public relations. *Public Relations Research & Education* 1(1). 6–29.

Grunig, James. E. 1989. Symmetrical presuppositions as a framework for public relations theory. In Carl Botan & Vincent T. Hazelton (eds.), *Public relations theory*, 17–44. Hillsdale, NJ: Lawrence Erlbaum Associates.

Grunig, James. E. (ed.). 1992. *Excellence in public relations and communication management.* Hillsdale, NJ: Lawrence Erlbaum Associates

Grunig, James E. 1994. World view, ethics, and the two-way symmetrical model of public relations. In Wolfgang Armbrecht & Ulf Zabel (eds.), *Normative aspekte de public relations*, 69–90. Opladen, Germany: Westdeutscher Verlag.

Grunig, James E. 1997. A situational theory of publics: Conceptual history, recent challenges and new research. In Danny Moss, Toby MacManus & Dejan Verčič (eds.), *Public relations research: An international perspective*, 3–46. London: International Thomson Business Press.

Grunig, James E. 2000. Collectivism, collaboration, and societal corporatism as core professional values in public relations. *Journal of Public Relations Research*, 12, 23–48.

Grunig, James E. 2001. Two-way symmetrical public relations: Past, present, and future. In Robert L. Heath (ed.), *Handbook of public relations*, 11–30. Thousand Oaks, CA: Sage.

Grunig, James E. 2002. *Qualitative methods for assessing relationships between organizations and publics.* Gainesville, FL: The Institute for Public Relations, Commission on PR Measurement and Evaluation. https://instituteforpr.org/wp-content/uploads/2002_AssessingRelations.pdf (accessed 12 December 2018).

Grunig, James E. 2003. Constructing public relations theory and practice. In Brenda Dervin & Steven H. Chaffee with Lois Foreman-Wernet (eds.), *Communication: A different kind of horse race: Essays honoring Richard F. Carter*, 85–115. Cresskill, NJ: Hampton Press.

Grunig, James E. 2006. Furnishing the edifice: Ongoing research on public relations as a strategic management function. *Journal of Public Relations Research* 18. 151–176.

Grunig, James E. 2009. Paradigms of global public relations in an age of digitalisation. *PRism* 6(2). http://www.prismjournal.org/fileadmin/Praxis/Files/globalPR/GRUNIG.pdf (accessed 12 December 2018).

Grunig, James E. 2018. Strategic behavioral paradigm. In Robert L. Heath and Winni Johansen (eds.), *The international encyclopedia of strategic communication*. Wiley Online Library. https://doi.org/10.1002/9781119010722.iesc0171 (accessed 12 December 2018).

Grunig, James E. & Larissa A. Grunig. 1989. Toward a theory of the public relations behavior of organizations: Review of a program of research. *Public Relations Research Annual* 1. 27–66.

Grunig, James E. & Larissa A. Grunig. 1992. Models of public relations and communication. In James E. Grunig (ed.), *Excellence in public relations and communication management*, 285–326. Hillsdale, NJ: Lawrence Erlbaum Associates.

Grunig, James E. & Larissa A. Grunig. 1997. *Review of a program of research on activism: Incidence in four countries, activist publics, strategies of activist groups, and organizational responses to activism.* Paper presented to the Fourth Public Relations Research Symposium. Bled, Slovenia, July.

Grunig, James E., Larissa A. Grunig, Krishnamurthy Sriramesh, Yi-Hui Huang & Anastasia Lyra. 1995. Models of public relations in an international setting. *Journal of Public Relations Research* 7. 163–186.

Grunig, James E. & Yi-Hui Huang. 2000. From organizational effectiveness to relationship indicators: Antecedents of relationships, public relations strategies, and relationship outcomes. In John A. Ledingham and Steve D. Bruning (eds.), *Public relations as relationship management: A relational approach to the study and practice of public relations*, 23–53. Mahwah, NJ: Lawrence Erlbaum Associates Publishers.

Grunig, James E. & Todd Hunt. 1984. *Managing public relations.* New York: Holt, Rinehart & Winston.

Grunig, James E. & Miia Jaatinen. 1999. Strategic, symmetrical public relations in government: From pluralism to societal corporatism. *Journal of Communication Management* 3. 218–234.

Grunig, James E. & Jon White. 1992. The effect of worldviews on public relations theory and practice. In James E. Grunig (ed.), *Excellence in public relations and communication management*, 31–64. Hillsdale, NJ: Lawrence Erlbaum Associates.

Grunig, James E. & Keith R. Stamm. 1973. Communication and coorientation of collectivities. *American Behavioral Scientist* 16. 567–591.

Grunig, Larissa A. 1986. Activism and organizational response: Contemporary cases of collective behavior. Paper presented to the Association for Education in Journalism and Mass Communication. Washington, DC. August.

Grunig, Larissa A., James E. Grunig & David M. Dozier. 2002. *Excellent public relations and effective organizations: A study of communication management in three countries.* Mahwah, NJ: Lawrence Erlbaum Associates.

Grunig, Larissa A., James E. Grunig & Dejan Verčič. 1998. Are the IABC's excellence principles generic? Comparing Slovenia and the United States, the United Kingdom and Canada. *Journal of Communication Management* 2. 335–356.

Habermas, Jurgen (Thomas McCarthy, trans.). 1984. *The theory of communication action,* Vol. 1 Boston: Beacon.

Hage, Jerald. 1980. *Theories of organizations: Form, process, & transformation.* New York: Wiley Interscience.

Hage, Jerald & Michael Aiken. 1970. *Social change in complex organizations.* New York: Random House.

Hage, Jerald & Frank Hull. 1981. A typology of environmental niches based on knowledge technology and scale. Unpublished Working Paper 1, Center for the Study of Innovation, Entrepreneurship, and Organization Strategy, University of Maryland, College Park, MD.

Holtzhausen, Derina. R., Barbara K. Petersen & Natalie T. J. Tindall. 2003. Exploding the myth of the symmetrical/asymmetrical dichotomy: Public relations models in the new South Africa. *Journal of Public Relations Research* 15. 305–341.

Holtzhausen, Derina R. & Rosina Voto. 2002. Resistance from the margins: The postmodern public relations practitioner as organizational activist. *Journal of Public Relations Research* 14. 57–84.

Hon, Linda Childers & James E. Grunig. 1999. *Guidelines for measuring relationships in public relations.* Gainesville, FL: The Institute for Public Relations, Commission on PR Measurement and Evaluation. http://www.instituteforpr.org/wpcontent/uploads/ Guidelines_Measuring_ Relationships.pdf (accessed 12 December 2018).

Hon, Linda Childers, Larissa A. Grunig & David M. Dozier. 1992. Women in public relations: Problems and opportunities. In James E. Grunig (ed.), *Excellence in public relations and communication management*, 419–438. Hillsdale, NJ: Lawrence Erlbaum Associates.

Huang, Yi-Hui. 1997. *Public relations, organization-public relationships, and conflict management.* College Park, MD: University of Maryland dissertation.

Huang, Yi-Hui. 2007. A revisit of symmetrical communication from an international perspective: Status, effect, and future research directions. In Elizabeth L. Toth (ed.), *The future of excellence in public relations and communication management: Challenges for the next generation*, 235–262. Mahwah, NJ: Lawrence Erlbaum Associates.

Hung, Chun-ju Flora. 2007. Toward the theory of relationship management in public relations: How to cultivate quality relationships. In Elizabeth L. Toth (ed.), *The future of excellence in public relations and communication management: Challenges for the next generation*, 443–477. Mahwah, NJ: Lawrence Erlbaum Associates.

Karlberg, Michael. 1996. Remembering the public in public relations research: From theoretical to operational symmetry. *Journal of Public Relations Research* 8. 263–278.

Kent, Michael. 2018. Dialogue. In Robert L. Heath and Winni Johansen (eds.), *The International Encyclopedia of Strategic communication*. Wiley Online Library. https://doi.org/10.1002/9781119010722.iesc0061 (accessed 12 December 2018).

Kent, Michael L. & Maureen Taylor. 1998. Building dialogic relationships through the World Wide Web. *Public Relations Review* 28(1). 273–288.

Kent, Michael L. & Maureen Taylor. 2002. Toward a dialogic theory of public relations. *Public Relations Review* 28. 21–37.

Ki, Eyun-Jung & Linda Childers Hon. 2006. Relationship maintenance strategies on *Fortune 500* company web sites. *Journal of Communication Management* 10. 27–43.

Kim, Hak-Soo. 2003. A theoretical explication of collective life: Coorienting and communicating. In Brenda Dervin and Steven H. Chaffee with Lois Foreman-Wernet (eds.), *Communication: A Different kind of horserace*, 117–134. Cresskill, NJ: Hampton Press.

Kim, Jeong-Nam & James E. Grunig. 2011. Problem solving and communicative action: A situational theory of problem solving. *Journal of Communication* 61. 120–149.

Kim, Jeong-Nam, Chun-Ju Flora Hung-Baesecke, Sung-Un Yang & James E. Grunig. 2013. The strategic management approach to reputation, relationships, and publics: The research heritage of the excellence theory. In Craig E. Carroll (ed.), *The handbook of communication and corporate reputation*, 197–212. Chicester, UK: Wiley-Blackwell.

Lauzen, Martha. 1986. *Public relations and conflict within the franchise system*. College Park, MD: University of Maryland dissertation.

Leitch, Shirley & David Neilson. 2001. Bringing publics into public relations: New theoretical frameworks for practice. In Robert L. Heath (ed.), *Handbook of public relations*, 127–138. Thousand Oaks, CA: Sage.

Lerner, Daniel. 1958. *The passing of traditional society*. New York: Free Press.

L'Etang, Jacquie. 1996. Public relations and rhetoric. In Jacquie L'Etang & Magda Pieczka (eds.), *Critical perspectives in public relations*, 106–123. London: International Thomson Business Press.

Macnamara, Jim. 2016. *Organizational listening: The missing essential in public communication*. New York: Peter Lange.

McLeod, Jack M. & Steven H. Chaffee. 1973. Interpersonal approaches to communication research. *American Behavioral Scientist* 16. 469–500.

Miller. Gerald. R. 1989. Persuasion and public relations: Two "Ps" in a pod. In Carl H. Botan & Vincent T. Hazleton, Jr. (eds.), *Public relations theory*, 45–66. Hillsdale, NJ: Lawrence Erlbaum Associates.

Moloney, Kevin. 1997. Teaching organizational communication as public relations in UK universities. *Corporate Communication: An International Journal* 2. 138–142.

Morehouse, Jordan & Adam John Saffer. 2018. A bibliometric analysis of dialogue and digital dialogic research: Mapping the knowledge construction and invisible colleges in public relations research. *Journal of Public Relations Research* 30. 65–82.

Murphy, Priscilla. 1991. The limits of symmetry: A game theory approach to symmetric and asymmetric public relations. *Public Relations Research Annual* 3. 115–132.

Muzi Falconi, Toni. 2014. Global stakeholder relationships governance: An infrastructure. In Toni Muzi Falconi with James E. Grunig, Emilio Galli Zugaro & Joao Duarte (eds.), *Global stakeholder relationships governance: An infrastructure*, 1–55. New York: Palgrave Macmillan.

Nothhaft, Howard, Jens Seiffert-Brockmann & Kerstin Thummes. 2018. From homo dialogicus to homo sapiens: Reconciling public relations research with the mind sciences. Paper presented to the International Communication Association, Prague, 24 July.

Pearson, Ron. 1989. *A theory of public relations ethics*. Athens, OH: Ohio University dissertation.

Pieczka. Magda. 1996. Paradigms, systems theory and public relations. In Jacquie L'Etang & Magda Pieczka (eds.), *Critical perspectives in public relations*, 124–156. London: International Thomson Business Press.

Pollack, Ruth A. 1986. *An organizational analysis of four public relations models in the federal government*. College Park, MD: MA thesis.

Raiffa, Howard. 1982. *The art and science of negotiation*. Cambridge, MA: Harvard University Press.

Rhee, Yunna. 2002. Global public relations: A cross-cultural study of the excellence theory in South Korea. *Journal of Public Relations Research* 14. 159–184.

Robinson, Edward J. 1966. *Communication and public relations*. Columbus, Ohio: Charles E. Merrill Publishing Co.

Rogers, Everett M. 1962. *Diffusion of innovations*. New York: The Free Press of Glencoe.

Schneider (aka Grunig), Larissa A. 1985. *Organizational structure, environmental niches, and public relations: The Hage-Hull typology of organizations as predictor of communication behavior*. College Park, MD: University of Maryland dissertation.

Sha, Bey-Ling. 1999. *Cultural public relations: Identity, activism, globalization, and gender in the Democratic Progressive Party on Taiwan*. College Park, MD: University of Maryland dissertation.

Sha, Bey-Ling. 2004. Noether's theorem: The science of symmetry and the law of conservation. *Journal of Public Relations Research* 16. 391–416.

Simon, Herbert A. 1957. *Models of man*. New York: John Wiley.

Sommerfeldt, Erich J. & Aimee Yang. 2018. Notes on a dialogue: Twenty years of digital dialogic communication research in public relations. *Journal of Public Relations Research* 30. 59–64.

Spicer, Christopher. 1997. *Organizational public relations: A political perspective*. Mahwah, NJ: Lawrence Erlbaum Associates.

Sriramesh, Krishnamurthy, James E. Grunig & Jody Buffington. 1992. Corporate culture and public relations. In James E. Grunig (ed.), *Excellence in public relations and communication management*, 577–596. Hillsdale, NJ: Lawrence Erlbaum Associates.

Thayer, Lee. 1968. *Communication and communication systems*. Homewood, IL: Richard D. Irwin.

Verčič, Dejan, Larissa A. Grunig & James E. Grunig. 1996. Global and specific principles of public relations: Evidence from Slovenia. In Hugh M. Culbertson & Ni Chen (eds.), *International public relations: A comparative analysis*, 31–65. Mahwah NJ: Lawrence Erlbaum Associates.

Wakefield, Robert I. 1997. International *public relations: A theoretical approach to excellence based on a worldwide Delphi study*. College Park, MD: University of Maryland dissertation.

Wakefield, Robert I. 2000. World-class public relations: A model for effective public relations in the multinational. *Journal of Communication Management* 5(1). 59–71.

Wetherell, Barbara J. 1989. *The effect of gender, masculinity, and feminity on the practice of and preference for the models of public relations*. College Park, MD: University of Maryland MA thesis.

Chun-Ju Flora Hung-Baesecke, Yi-Ru Regina Chen and Lan Ni

16 The Excellence Theory – origins, contribution and critique

Abstract: This chapter focuses on the Excellence Theory, developed by James E. Grunig and his colleagues. We provide an overview of this theory, discuss how this theory was developed, studies derived from this theory, and the contributions of the Excellence Theory to the body of knowledge in public relations. In addition, we also address and respond to the critiques on this theory and the next stage of the Excellence Theory. We believe, by laying out future research topics derived from the Excellence Theory, more insights can be provided into how public relations and communication management contribute to organizational effectiveness, stakeholder engagement, quality relationship, and reputation management.

Keywords: Excellence study of public relations; strategic management; ethics; strategic behavioral paradigm; publics; models of public relations; evaluations

1 Introduction

In this chapter, we discuss the Excellence Theory by starting with an overview of the Excellence Study, led by James Grunig (University of Maryland, USA) with team members including Larissa Grunig (the University of Maryland, USA), David Dozier (San Diego State University, USA), Jon White (then the Granfield School of Management, United Kingdom), William Ehling (then Syracuse University, USA), and Fred Repper (then Vice President of Public Relations for Gulf States Utilities, USA). The focus of the Excellence Theory is to *manage the organization's behaviours* in order to build mutually beneficial relationships with and/or form a positive reputation among publics. Organization-public relationships and/or reputation further contribute to the organization's effectiveness and the publics' interest (Grunig, J. and Grunig, L. 2008; Kim et al. 2013). We focus on depicting the development of the Excellence Theory as an outcome of the Excellence Study, its content, the contributions and criticisms on this research, what has been developed since the last Excellence book, *Excellent Public Relations and Effective Organizations*, was published in 2002, and the next stage of the Excellence Study.

https://doi.org/10.1515/9783110554250-016

2 The development of the Excellence Study

In 1984, a team of researchers, later known as the "Excellence Team", responded to a request for proposal from the International Association of Business Communicators (IABC) Foundation for a research project to investigate, "how, why, and to what extent communication affects the achievement of organizational objectives" (Grunig L. et al. 2002). The IABC awarded the US$400,000 grant for this Excellence Study to the Excellence Team in 1985. This research project included three parts: a comprehensive literature review consisting of research from communication, mass communication, management, organizational psychology, psychology, etc. to explore how public relations can contribute to organizational effectiveness (Grunig, J. 1992); a book for public relations practitioners supplemented with the data from parts of the research findings (Dozier, Grunig, L., and Grunig, J. 1995); and a third book published in 2002 containing the comprehensive qualitative and quantitative research data for public relations scholars (Grunig, L., Grunig, J., and Dozier 2002).

The Excellence Team developed the following two major research questions (Grunig, L., Grunig, J., and Dozier 2002: 4–5):
–   How does public relations make an organization more effective, and how much is that contribution worth economically?
–   What characteristics of a public relations function are most likely to make an organization effective?

With a very comprehensive literature review from different disciplines to help identify the characteristics of an excellent public relations program and function, the Excellence Team then developed a set of questionnaires, including an investigation on the propositions, hypotheses, and research questions on the variables relevant to the Excellence Theory. The quantitative survey was conducted among 327 organizations in the United States, Canada, and the United Kingdom; while 25 qualitative studies were employed with the most and least excellent public relations departments identified from the survey (Grunig, L., Grunig, J., and Dozier 2002).

When this research project was completed, the Excellence Team concluded from the research findings that public relations contributes to organizational effectiveness by incorporating stakeholders' goals into an organization's, and that the value of public relations lies in how it helps an organization develop and maintain quality relationships with strategic constituencies (Grunig, L., Grunig, J., and Dozier 2002). Based on the research findings and suggestions from the international public relations community, ten generic principles of excellence public relations were developed and were incorporated into part of the global public relations theory (Verčič, Grunig, J., and Grunig, L. 1996):
1.   Public relations is involved in an organization's strategic management that involves setting specific organizational goals, objectives and tasks to achieve such goals

2. Public relations is empowered by the dominant coalition or by a direct reporting relationship to senior management
3. The public relations function is an integrated one that combines all the communication-related practices into one major umbrella function
4. Public relations is a management function separate from other functions
5. The public relations unit is headed by a manager rather than a technician
6. The two-way symmetrical model of public relations is used
7. A symmetrical system of internal communication is used
8. Knowledge potential for managerial role and symmetrical public relations
9. Diversity is embodied in all roles
10. An organizational context exists for excellence

Furthermore, Verčič, J. Grunig, and L. Grunig (1996) contended that the applications of these principles of excellent public relations to different countries should take into account six specific contextual factors: culture, political system, economic system, media system, level of development, and extent of activism. (For more information on the global theory of public relations, see chapter 20 in this book).

3 Overview of the Excellence Theory

It is noted that the Excellence Theory is more like a general theoretical framework with many middle-range theories. These middle-range theories include theories of publics, public relations and strategic management, models of public relations, evaluation of public relations, employee communication, public relations roles, gender, diversity, power, activism, ethics and social responsibility, and global public relations (Grunig, J. 2008). A common misunderstanding in the public relations field is equating the Excellence Theory with the models of public relations, when in fact the models are only one component in the Excellence Theory (see chapter 15 in this book).

The Excellence Study has generated in all 14 characteristics of excellent public relations that contribute to effective organizations – at the program, departmental, and organizational levels. These characteristics are (Grunig, L. et al. 2002: 9):
– At the program level
    – public relations is managed strategically
– At the departmental level
    – A single or integrated public relations department
    – Separate function from marketing
    – Direct reporting relationship to senior management
    – Two-way symmetrical model
    – Senior public relations person in the managerial role

- – Potential for excellent public relations, which should include knowledge of symmetrical communication, knowledge of managerial role, academic training in public relations, and professionalism
  - – Equal opportunity for men and women
- – At the organizational level:
  - – A two-way symmetrical worldview
  - – Public relations director has the power in or with the dominant coalition
  - – Participative rather than authoritarian organizational culture
  - – Symmetrical system of internal communication
  - – Organic rather than mechanical organizational structure
  - – Turbulent, complex environment with pressure from activist groups

Having introducing an overview of the Excellence Theory, we are now discussing the research developed from this theory since 2002.

4 Studies developed from the Excellence Theory by other PR scholars since 2002

How has the Excellence Theory influenced the public relations research agenda since 2002? In L. Grunig, J. Grunig, and Dozier (2002), the Excellence Team has outlined several important topics: globalization of public relations practices, relationship building in strategic management, public relations ethics, and public relations and change (including new technology, feminization, globalization, downsizing, mergers, and acquisition). In this section, we discuss how other public relations scholars adopted the Excellence Theory in their research by offering some examples.

4.1 Excellence principles in the international settings

Despite numerous discussions as to whether or not the generic principles of excellent public relations can be applied in global and local contexts (e. g. Taylor and Kent 1999), some of these principles could still be applied to a different cultural setting (Taylor and Kent 2006). For instance, Schwarz and Fritsch (2014) took part of the generic principles of Excellent public relations surveying 440 NGOs to identify how their respective public relations functions could be considered "excellent", and how international NGOs coordinate strategic communication between headquarters and their local units. The findings of this research indicated that these international NGOs did not separate the public relations function from other management functions, and there was no integrated public relations under one coordination mechanism. Lim, Goh, and Sriramesh (2005) used four generic principles of public relations in analyzing how public relations was practiced in Singapore. The survey and in-depth interview data showed that the professional status of public relations was lower than that of advertising or marketing. In addition, public relations was not practiced strategically and was not a strategic business tool in Singapore. Valentini and Sriramesh (2014) applied the generic principles relevant to an organization's strategic management in investigating how public relations is practiced in different types of organizations in Italy. The study found that no matter what type of organization, few public relations practitioners were included in an organization's dominant coalition. In addition, public relations was valued more by senior management in non-profit organizations than in corporations and government agencies.

4.2 Relationship building in strategic management

The Excellence Study has demonstrated that public relations' values show in the quality of relationships it helps organizations to build with their publics by participating in an organization's strategic planning (Grunig, L., Grunig, J., and Dozier 2002). Being a part of an organization's dominant coalition, public relations helps to incorporate the publics' concerns and voices in the decision-making process. With this, public relations enables symmetrical communication with the publics and enhances quality relationship building.

Plowman (2005) contended that public relations is a strategic management function when it helps organizations to formulate the organization's approach to achieve the organizational goals. Hence, strategic public relations starts "when communication practitioners can identify potential problems in relationships with the organization's stakeholders" (Plowman 2005: 133). In addition, the results of the Excellence Study also showed that involving public relations in an organization's strategic management can contribute to organizational competitive advantage, organizational goals, and organizational effectiveness (Grunig, L., Grunig, J., and Dozier 2002).

To further demonstrate how public relations can contribute to an organization's strategic management, Dess, Lumpkin, and Eisner's (2007) strategic management concept was used in Men and Hung (2012)'s study exploring the value of organization-public relationships (OPR) in each step of an organization's strategic management. Their findings confirmed the Excellence Study's finding on the benefit of quality relationships in enhancing organizational competitiveness, effectiveness, and goal attainment since they showed quality relationships established with various strategic stakeholders in each stage of strategic management.

4.3 Relationship management

The Excellence Study also contributed to expanding the research agenda on relationship management by showing the values of public relations in establishing quality relationships with publics. Following Ferguson's (1984) call for a research focus on public relationships, the topic on relationship management has been one of the major PR ones since Broom, Casey, and Ritchey (1997) and Ledingham et al. (1997) started the research agenda on OPR. Huang and Zhang (2013) conducted a content analysis on 40 articles published between 2000 and 2011 in the topics of "organization-public relationships," "OPR," "relationship management," and "relationship building" from major public relations publishing outlets – *Journal of Public Relations Research*, *Public Relations Review*, *Journal of Communication*, *Journalism and Mass Communication Quarterly*, *Journal of Communication Management*, and *International Journal of Strategic Communication*. Their findings show: First, in terms of the themes of OPR research, the initial focus was on scale development, and later shifted to scale application on various topics and various contexts, such as corporate, non-for-profit, government, international, and internet. Second, Huang and Zhang's (2013) study identified the unique trend of investigation that 15.8 % of the OPR research was conducted in an international setting, especially in East Asia (e. g. Hung 2005; Hung and Chen 2009; Jo 2006). The contributions of these international studies are the cultural elements influencing OPR development, such as face and favor (Huang 2001), network (Jo 2006), and types of OPR (Hung 2005) could be included to enrich the research agenda. Third, various research focused OPR as relational outcomes (e. g. Bortree 2010; Ki and Hon 2009). Besides Huang's own scales (Huang 2001), most of the research adopted Hon and J. Grunig's (1999) scales on relationship outcomes – trust, control mutuality, satisfaction, commitment, communal and exchange relationships.

4.4 Ethics in public relations

L. Grunig, J. Grunig, and Dozier (2002) contended that ethics should be included as one of the generic principles of public relations. In their earlier work, J. Grunig and L. Grunig (1996) posited that the teleological and deontological ethical perspectives should be incorporated in public relations ethics. Bowen (2004) continued the discussion of public relations ethics by further incorporating the core concepts Kantian deontology (rationality and transcendentialism, the law of autonomy, the categorical imperative, dignity and respect, duty, and intention) in the ethical decision making in an organization's issues management process (for details, see chapter 30 in this book). Research on public relations ethics using the Excellence Theory can also be found in the research on autonomy in communication (Bowen 2006), risk communication (Bowen 2009), ethics in symmetrical communication (Bowen and Gallicano 2013), and in relationship management (Bowen, Hung-Baesecke, and Chen 2016).

5 Contributions of Excellence Theory to the body of knowledge in public relations research

The Excellence Theory makes two major contributions to theorizing public relations as an academic discipline. We are elaborating these contributions as follows:

5.1 Theorizing public relations in the strategic behavioral paradigm

The Excellence Theory, as the first *grand* theory of public relations, provides a solid theoretical foundation that explicates the value of public relations to organizational effectiveness at various levels (i. e. program, functional, organizational, and societal) and the factors influencing the public relations values, such as organizational structure, environments, culture, power, and individual skills and knowledge (Grunig, J. and Grunig, L. 2008). As a grand theory, the Excellence Theory was developed by bringing together several middle-level theories and empirical data collected by J. Grunig and his team (Grunig, L., Grunig, J., and Dozier 2002).

The Excellence Theory also moves public relations from the symbolic-interpretive paradigm to the strategic behavioural paradigm. Before the Excellence Theory, public relations scholars and practitioners predominantly adopted the symbolic-interpretive paradigm that views the function of public relations as to influence how publics interpret the behaviours of organizations via persuasion in order to "secure the power of the decision-makers who chose those behaviours and allow them to behave as they like without interference from publics" (Grunig, J. 2018). The Excellence Theory, on the other hand, advocates the strategic behavioural paradigm of public relations that "focuses on the participation of public relations executives in strategic decision-making so that they can help manage the behaviour of organizations rather than only interpret it to publics" (Grunig, J. 2018). The Excellence Theory now represents the most dominant paradigm of public relations research (Botan and Taylor 2004; Botan and Hazleton 2009; Huang, Y., Wu, and Huang, Q. 2017; Pieczka 2006; Sallot et al. 2003; Ki and Ye 2017; Ye and Ki 2012). It has attracted numerous applications, extensions, criticisms, and refinements. Research that elaborates and refines the Excellence Theory in the areas of publics, public relations models, organization-public relationships, reputation, ethics, empowerment, culture diversity and professionalism, public relations strategy in specialized areas and global practices, and evaluation and measurements has significantly contributed to the body of knowledge of public relations (see Toth 2007). The Excellence Theory has stood the test of time. Even though Y. Huang, Wu, and Q. Huang (2017) found that more research on digital public relations published between 2008 and 2014 applied the dialogic theory than the Excellence Theory, it is still the most used in global public relations research published between 2001 and 2014 (Ki and Ye 2017).

5.2 Being a global theory

Another contribution made by the Excellence Theory lies in its middle-ground theory of "generic principles and specific applications" in examining global public relations. The generic principles and specific applications of the Excellence Theory provide the first theoretical framework to study and compare/evaluate global public relations by looking at the infrastructural, geopolitical, legal, cultural, and media variables of a society where public relations practices (Kent and Taylor 2007; Sriramesh and Verčič 2009). As Ki and Ye (2017) claimed, the middle-ground theory of generic principles and specific applications is most applied in global public relations research, followed by Image Restoration Theory (Benoit 1995) and Hofstede's cultural dimension theory (1980). As a result, scholars have advanced the middle-ground theory by continuously and exploring additional generic principles and and explicating the specific applications in various contexts (Kent and Taylor 2007; Van Gorp and Pauwels 2007; Watson and Sallot 2001; Yun 2006). After introducing the contributions of the Excellence Theory, the next section will turn to the discussion about the most-seen criticisms schoalrs have posed to the theory.

6 Criticisms

While it makes significant contributions to the theory and practice of public relations, the Excellence Theory has received several academic criticisms over the years. A review of the major challenges and the Excellence Study team's responses is outlined below.

6.1 Critique on the Excellence Theory as a whole

6.1.1 Is Excellence Theory too normative, rigid, organization-centric, western-biased, and/or dominant?

The Excellence Theory, as a whole, has been criticized for being only normative (L'Etang 1996; Pieczka 1996), too rigid (Edwards and Hodges 2011), organization-centric (Kent and Taylor 1998; Theunissen and Wan Noordin 2012), Western biased (Macnamara 2012), and over-dominant to the extent that it limits theoretical development in public relations (Coombs 2009).

Critics argue the Excellence Theory is normative rather than pragmatic largely because they believe that the two-way symmetrical model is rare in practice (Murphy 1991; Macnamara 2012) and not the best model in most situations (Heath 1992; Cameron 1997; Cancel, Cameron, Sallot, and Mitrook, 1997; Cancel, Mitrook, and

Cameron 1999). The responses of J. Grunig and colleagues will be discussed in a latter section of critique on public relations models.

Edwards and Hodges (2011) challenged the rigid nature of the Excellence Theory, arguing its heavy focus on organization theory oversimplifies human behaviour. Leitch and Neilson (2001) further built onto this critique by arguing that Excellence Theory conceptualizes publics into fixed categories (latent, aware, active and activist) to be identified based on their communicative and behavioral actions toward an organization in a situation. They instead suggested segmenting publics by their enacted identity that is dynamically formed through their communication with others in the situation. Undoubtedly, the Excellence Theory has incorporated ideas other than organizational theories, including psychology theory, economics theory, (situational theory), co-orientation theory (Broom and Dozier 1990; Verčič 2008), relational/relationship theory (adapting from the interpersonal theory; Grunig, L., Grunig., J., and Dozier 2002; Hon and Grunig, J. 1999; Ledingham and Brunig 2001), rhetorical theory (Heath 1992), and feminist theory (Grunig, L., Grunig., J., and Dozier 2002). It is correct that the Excellence Theory has a focus on the strategic management approach, but rather than a limitation. Leitch and Neilson (2001) claim it should be seen as the elaboration of the Excellence Theory. Similarly, other scholars have criticized the Excellence Theory for being organization-centric (Holtzhausen and Voto 2002; Kent and Taylor 1998; McKie 2008). The Excellence Theory does indeed take an organizational perspective by managing organizational communication and behaviours. However, the theory advocates management decisions that balance the interests of organizations and publics. Its strategic behavioural paradigm makes the Excellence Theory more public-centric than the symbolic-interpretive paradigm of public relations because it focuses on the consequences of organizational behaviors on publics instead of how the behaviors are interpreted by organizations and/ or publics.

With its dominance in the public relations research, some scholars argue that the Excellence Theory has subsumed or marginalized alternative views/approaches (e. g. a postmodern approach) in public relations theory building (Pieczka 1996; Elwood 1995; Holtzhausen and Voto 2002; McKie 2008) and limits the theory development in public relations. To respond to the first criticism, J. Grunig and L. Grunig (2008) argued that the strategic behavioural paradigm of the Excellence Theory incorporates the modernist, symbolic-interpretive, and postmodern perspectives of Hatch (1997) on organizations. The Excellence Theory argues that "public relations provide public voice in management decisions (a postmodern perspective), and it helps organizations achieve their objectives because they use communication to establish mutually beneficial relationships with publics and behave in responsible, sustainable ways that are more likely to result in good relationships and favourable reputations (a modernist, or more accurately, an instrumental perspective)" (Grunig, J. 2018). Therefore, the Excellence Theory is semi-postmodernism (Grunig, J. and Grunig, L. 2008) and reflects societal corporatism rather than corporatism (Grunig, J. 2000).

The Excellence Theory was developed by a team of public relations scholars in the United States and the United Kingdom. Critics have questioned its western focus, "specifically, American with ontological, axiological and epistemological assumptions grounded in US positivism, functionalism and behaviourism that limit its application as a global theory" (Macnamara 2012: 370–371). Developing from a Western perspective is a limitation to the Excellence Theory. It, however, has drawn research conducted in various geographic locations (Grunig, J. 2006; Sriramesh 2004) to either test its applicability or obtain its advancement. Rather than margalizing other approaches, public relations literature has suggested that scholars have elaborated on the Excellence Theory by using theories from various paradigms (Coombs 2009; Toth 2007). For example, Kent and Taylor (2007) used the rhetorical generic theory to extend the Excellence theory in evaluating international public relations. The media sociology related to the socio-cultural approach of public relations (Edwards and Hodges 2011) has good potential for advancing the understanding of the effects of media (i.e. the specific application) on international public relations. The network theory and complexity theory can be applied to enhance the symmetrical tenet of the Excellence Theory; that is, how to balance the interest of the organization and the (multiple) publics.

6.1.2 Critique on the public relations models

The four models of public relations as a key middle-range theory of the Excellence Theory have received many criticisms from scholars and practitioners. The detailed discussions on criticisms of this topic can also be found in chapter 15 on public relations models in this book. We are now only focusing on the criticism on the significant limitations of the four models to capture the public relations practice in digitalization (Waddington 2013).

Social media allow individuals to easily connect and communicate with each other (Boyd and Ellison 2007), thus enabling conversations about an organization among individuals through online-mediated social networks. Philips and Young (2009) and Sheldrake (2011) argued that such peer-to-peer conversations are significant in influencing the behaviours of stakeholders and publics toward the organization. This phenomenon leads to Philips and Young's (2009) call for "the new PR" and Waddington's (2013) assertion that the four models are outdated in digital communication because the models fail to capture the influence of stakeholders on each other with respect to an organization or its competitors.

J. Grunig (2009) responded to Philips and Young's call (2009) by saying that organizations do not (and cannot) communicate with individuals who are not their publics because of their limited resources and time. While the digital media (including social media) empower individuals by enabling them to seek and exchange information with one another anywhere in the world, organizations should join conversations among their publics in order to source public voices for management decision-making (Grunig, J. 2009). J. Grunig (2009) thus concluded that digitalization facilitates the application of the Excellence Theory.

The free flow of information in digitalization triggers "a social trend in which people increasingly use technologies to get the information they need from each other, rather than from traditional institutions like corporations" (Li and Bernoff 2011: 9). The trend further results in (1) communication about organizations being more audience-centric and (2) an increasing level of layperson influence in society (Booth and Matic 2011). The trends lead to the public relations practice of online community building (e. g. fan pages) and influencer communication in order to tap into peer-to-peer communication about the organization when individual stakeholder members want to discuss the organization (Li and Bernoff 2011; Zerfass et al. 2016). These practices target both stakeholders and publics and can be seen as elaboration of the four models. For example, online-community communication can be the application of two-way asymmetrical and symmetrical models while influencer communication relates to the two-way asymmetrical model and the personal influence model/individual influence model (Grunig, J. et al. 1995; Toth 2000).

In short, the Excellence Theory is resilient to its critics. Nevertheless the criticisms have generated revisions of the theory and pinpointed areas for moving the theory to the next stage, which will be discussed in the next section.

7 The next stage of Excellence Theory

Just like any other theories that have been tested, applied, and critiqued, the Excellence Theory can and should be further extended and developed in the future to bring more theoretical and practical advancement to the public relations field. Corresponding to the diverse range of theories incorporated in the Excellence Theory, we argue that there are two general research directions for the next stage of the Excellence Theory: the subject matter or topic of study and the context of study. Subject matter or topic of study refers to the content area of research (e. g. research on publics) whereas the context of study refers to the circumstances in which various content areas can be applied (e. g. research on publics in the context of internal communication or community relations). As of now, both directions have yielded rich research impact. For example, theories of publics have evolved from the situational theory of publics to the situational theory of problem solving (Kim and Grunig, J. 2011) (see chapter 24 in this book). At the same time, the Excellence Theory has been tested in many different contexts, especially different geographical locations. However, more is needed on both fronts and the following section highlights a few directions.

7.1 Next stage of theory development based on subject matters or topics

For the subject matter or topic of study, the following key areas can be fruitful avenues for further theoretical development: publics, public relations models/practices, strategic management, and evaluation of public relations.

7.1.1 Publics

The study of publics, one of the key words in public relations, is critical. In recent years, more attention has been paid to studying the segmentation of and understanding of publics. However, more needs to be done to clarify possible confusions, integrate different streams of research, and bring in different perspectives to the study of publics.

First of all, the concepts of "stakeholder" and "public" are usually used interchangeably. As Ni, Wang, and Sha (2018) pointed out, there are three main distinctions between the two concepts: how they are connected with an organization, how active they are, and what type of entities they are. A stakeholder is defined mainly from an organizational standpoint in terms of whether an individual has a stake in an organization or not, whereas a public may or may not have a direct relationship with an organization. Typically, a stakeholder is less active than a public, although members in latent publics can be less active as well. Finally, a stakeholder is an individual and a public is typically a group of individuals, although multiple stakeholders can form a stakeholder group. There needs to be more studies that clearly distinguish between stakeholders and publics when they examine relationship management or stakeholder engagement activities. Stakeholder relationship management, rather than public relationship management, is commonly studied. Typically, current relationship management research in public relations use samples from general consumers, employees, or community members who are members of stakeholder groups rather than publics (e. g. Gallicano 2013; Hong and Yang 2009). Using primary stakeholder groups as preferred samples in relationship management studies does not offer sufficient understanding of the role of different levels of activeness in publics. In addition, more studies are needed to explore the evolution process from stakeholders to publics as well as the interaction between publics and stakeholders, their respective influence on each other.

7.1.2 Public relations models/practices

One of the primary focuses in the Excellence Theory is how organizations practice public relations in an excellent way so as to achieve both organizational and publics' interests. Historically, such practices have been focused on the public relations models theory and more recently relationship management theory. We believe that the future research in this line of research needs to address the following issues: a) clarifying theoretical and operational confusion among key concepts such as public relations models versus practices, relationship management, and engagement; b) identifying the mechanism of engaging in symmetrical communication, one of the most important yet most controversial concepts; c) examining the reverse mechanisms such as non-engaging or disengaging (e. g. Lievonen and Luoma-aho 2015; Lievonen, Luoma-aho, and Bowden 2018); and d) moving relationship management beyond organization-focused consequences.

First, given the evolution of the public relations models theory, from four distinctive models to four dimensions that can be configured differently (i. e. direction of communication, symmetry, channels of communication, and ethics) (Grunig, L., Grunig, J. and Dozier 2012), we argue that it is time to further clarify these four dimensions and integrate with other theoretical concepts and processes, especially those from relationship management and engagement, both of which are becoming increasingly important research directions. The current buzzword in public relations research and practice is engagement. Not much research has disentangled the difference among public relations practices, engagement, and relationship management. In fact, these three concepts are sometimes used interchangeably. Other times, public relations models and relationship management are used to illustrate the process of engagement, or the strategies organizations use to engage their publics. Given the conceptual and operational overlap between models of public relations and relationship management strategies, we need an integrated framework of how organizations interact with publics.

Second, the critical challenge in, and therefore partly the criticism on, symmetry as a key aspect of public relations models lies in the facts that a) organizations and publics are with power differential and thus it is not in the organizations' best interest to engage in symmetrical communication with the publics, and b) reconciling differences to reach a mutually agreeing outcome is very difficult. The essence of symmetry is therefore the willingness and ability to engage in not only genuine dialogue, but also negotiations that lead to productive results.

Future research should be conducted to further examine how exactly conflict management is to be managed, especially those conflicts based on value clashes which are seen more and more often. In addition, it is also important to examine theoretical models of how practitioners can gain and enhance their abilities to actually engage in such conflict management and therefore promote genuine symmetry with publics. While symmetry may not always be desired, under the circumstances of conflict management where different parties want to and need to reconcile differences and reach some kind of mutually agreeable solution in order to move forward, symmetry is critical. To that end, researching practitioner competency in fostering symmetry among organizations and publics in difficult situations can be a fruitful line of research (e. g. Ni, Wang, and Sha 2018).

Finally, it is important to start examining the consequences of relationship management that go beyond organization-centric ones. Currently, most studies on relationship management have examined organization-centered outcomes focusing on either reducing negative impact (e. g. negative consequences resulting from conflicts and crises) or increasing positive impact through various perceptual, attitudinal, communicative, and behavioral outcomes desired by organizations in different sectors (Ni, Wang, and Sha 2018). However, more studies should examine public-oriented outcomes, or outcomes that matter to the publics or stakeholders themselves. These public-centered outcomes include community empowerment, either health empowerment or identity development (e. g. Ni, Wang, and Sha 2018). In addition, the scope of research can be expanded to include stakeholder-to-stakeholder relationship management, inter-organizational relationship management, or diplomatic relationship management.

7.1.3 Strategic management

The Excellence Theory identified and examined some generic principles that describe the characteristics of excellent public relations at different levels and provide the internal and environmental context of the organization that increases the likelihood that the public relations function will be practiced in an excellent way. It is therefore important to study public relations practices both at the functional and program levels as well as examining the internal and external context of the organization. For example, at the function level, more studies are need to explore how the public relations function should be configured internally and aligned externally with other organizational functions. At the program level, more research needs to examine how strategic management is conducted in the iterative stages of research, planning, implementation, and evaluation.

In the organizational level, Men and Hung-Baesecke's (2012) research mentioned in an earlier section has demonstrated the intangible values quality relationships can enhance organizational effectiveness, competitive advantage, and achieving organizational goals. Research that integrates public relations with organizational strategic management is also needed beyond earlier studies such as Steyn (2007) and Ni (2009).

7.1.4 Evaluation of public relations

Evaluation of public relations efforts at multiple levels is at the root of the Excellence Theory, because the Excellence Study was essentially conducted to address the two grand research questions: effectiveness question (how does public relations add value to organizations and society) and excellence question (how to conduct public relations in an excellent way). Evaluation of public relations efforts to demonstrate its effectiveness has always been challenging and an ongoing line of research (see chapter 14 in this book for an overview). From a measurement and evaluation perspective, Volk (2016) acknowledged the lack of a comprehensive explanation on how communication brings value to organizations. She advocated a more holistic approach that includes "an interdisciplinary, multidimensional, and multi-indexed approach" (Volk 2016: 973) to demonstrate values of communication – not only to revenue generating and building intangible values but also to build indirect values to preventing risks and problem solving. Kim and Ni (2013) proposed an integrated framework of evaluating public relations programs, taking into consideration both short-term and long-term effects, process and outcome objectives, as well as following both persuasion and problem solving approaches. More studies can be conducted along these lines to further evaluation research efforts.

7.2 Next stage of theory development based on contacts

On the other hand, for the context of study, we believe it is important to bring in two overall perspectives – global and intercultural perspectives – and two different contextual conditions – organizational context and functional context.

7.2.1 Global and intercultural perspectives

Although sometimes used interchangeably, global and intercultural public relations are not the same but complement each other. The global approach to public relations suggests that universal principles of best public relations practices do exist and should be applied in different parts of the world with modifications and changes based on local infrastructure such as political system, level of economic development, level of activism, and legal system; local culture, which includes both societal and organizational cultures; and media environment, which includes media control, media outreach, and media access (e. g. Sriramesh and Verčič 2009).

On the other hand, the *intercultural* approach focuses on the actual process of interaction and communication among people with different cultural identifies and backgrounds. Such cultural groups are defined more broadly, not just national culture, and can exist both within a country and across borders. More studies need to examine in-depth intercultural interactions and effectiveness in different contexts.

7.2.2 Contextual conditions

Contextual conditions include two main types: organizational context and functional context. For organizational context, Excellence Theory can be extended to different types of organizations (e. g. corporations, non-profits, government, activist and advocacy groups, or organizations) because they have different needs for understanding publics, managing relationships, and engaging in strategic management. At the same time, different functional contexts have been examined, but not in terms of how the Excellence Theory can be applied or whether and how the Excellence Theory needs to be used or adjusted. Therefore this line of research should be expanded as well. They include employee communication, corporate social responsibility, crisis communication, community relations, and others.

To summarize, these two major directions (subject matter or topic vs. context) can stand alone or be intersected to form new clusters of research (see Table 1).

Table 1: Summary of future directions

	Publics	Public Relations Practices	Strategic Management	Evaluation of Public Relations
Global perspective	Understanding publics with different geographical locations and national cultures	Applicability and boundary conditions for the use of different public relations models/ practices	Commonality and unique characteristics of excellent public relations at multiple levels across geographic locations.	Both universal and unique methods of evaluation are needed across geographic locations.
Intercultural perspective	Understanding publics with different identities, relational contexts, and cultural value orientations, often within the same country.	Applicability and boundary conditions for possessing the worldviews, skill sets, and overall intercultural competencies for using different public relations models/practices	Commonality and unique conceptualization and characteristics of excellent public relations at multiple levels in intercultural interactions.	Common and unique methods of evaluation across cultural groups.
Organizational contexts	Understanding publics with different organizational contexts (e. g. corporations, non-profits, government, etc.)	Applicability and boundary conditions for the use of different public relations models/ practices in different organizational contexts (e. g. corporations, non-profits, government, etc.)	Internal and external context of public relations' role in strategic management that leads to excellence in different organizational contexts (e. g. corporations, non-profits, government, etc.)	Evaluation of public relations programs in different organizational contexts (e. g. corporations, non-profits, government, etc.)

Tab. 1: (continued)

	Publics	Public Relations Practices	Strategic Management	Evaluation of Public Relations
Functional contexts	Understanding publics with different functional contexts (e. g. employee communication, crisis communication, community relations, etc.)	Applicability and boundary conditions for the use of different public relations models/ practices different functional contexts (e. g. employee communication, crisis communication, community relations, etc.)	How strategic management is conducted in different functional contexts (e. g. employee communication, crisis communication, community relations, etc.)	Evaluation of public relations programs in different functional contexts (e. g. employee communication, crisis communication, community relations, etc.)

This discussion on the future directions of the Excellence Theory is by no means exhaustive. It is our hope that this suggestion on some potential areas of research can help more researchers to actively think about and engage in other future avenues of research so we can further extend and develop the Excellence Theory.

8 Conclusions

In this chapter, we have discussed how the Excellence Study began, and the theory developed from this research project. The Excellence Theory has provided indicators on how an excellent public relations department should be established, particularly in terms of how public relations should be practiced, the required support from the organizational level, and the qualification and knowledge required for a public relations practitioner to contribute to organizational effectiveness. By providing explanations and responding to criticisms directed at the Excellence Theory, we also hope to highlight the essence of the theory, and clear up certain misunderstandings about it. We believe, by laying out future research topics derived from the Excellence Theory, we scholars can add more insight into how public relations and communication management contribute to organizational effectiveness, how to engage stakeholders and publics, and how to establish quality relationship and reputation with stakeholders and publics.

References

Benoit, William. 1995. *Accounts, Excuses and Apologies: A Theory of Image Restoration Strategies*. New York: State University of New York.

Booth, Norman & Julie Matic. 2011. Mapping and leveraging influencers in social media to shape corporate brand perceptions. *Corporate Communications: An International Journal* 16(3). 184–191.

Bortree, Denise S. 2010. Exploring adolescent–organization relationships: A study of effective relationship strategies with adolescent volunteers. *Journal of Public Relations Research* 22(1). 1–25.

Botan, Carl H. & Vincent Hazleton (eds.). 2009. *Public relations theory II*. New York: Routledge.

Botan, Carl H. & Maureen Taylor. 2004. Public relations: State of the field. *Journal of Communication* 54(4). 645–661.

Bowen, Shannon A. 2004. Expansion of ethics as the tenth generic principle of public relations excellence: A Kantian theory and model for managing ethical issues. *Journal of Public Relations Research* 16(1). 65–92.

Bowen, Shannon A. 2006. Autonomy in communication: Inclusion in strategic management and ethical decision making, a comparative case analysis. *Journal of Communication Management* 10. 330–352.

Bowen, Shannon A. 2009. Ethical responsibility and guidelines for managing issues of risk and risk communication. In Robert L. Heath and H. Dan O'Hair (eds.), *Handbook of risk and crisis communication*, 343–363. New York: Routledge.

Bowen, Shannon A. & Tiffany D. Gallicano. 2013. A philosophy of reflective ethical symmetry: Comprehensive historical and future moral approaches in the Excellence Theory. In Krishnamurthy Sriramesh, Ansgar Zerfass & Jeong-Nan Kim (eds.), *Public relations and communication management: Current trends and emerging topics*, 233–239. New York: Routledge.

Bowen, Shannon A., Chun-Ju F. Hung-Baesecke & Yi-Ru R. Chen. 2016. Ethics as a precursor to organization-public relationships: Building trust before and during the OPR model. *Cogent Social Sciences* 2(1). http://doi.org/10.1080/23311886.2016.1141467 (accessed 18 November 2018).

Boyd, Danah & Nicole Ellison. 2007. Social network sites: Definition, history, and scholarship. *Journal of Computer-Mediated Communication* 13. 210–230.

Broom, Glen M., Shawna Casey & James Ritchey. 1997. Toward a concept and theory of organization-public relationships. *Journal of Public Relations Research* 9(2). 83–98.

Broom, Glen, M. & David M. Dozier. 1990. *Using research in public relations: Applications to program management*. Englewood Cliffs, NJ: Prentice Hall.

Cameron, Glen T. 1997. The contingency theory of conflict management in public relations. In *Proceedings of the conference on two-way communication*, 27–48. Oslo: Norwegian Central Government Information Service.

Cancel, Amanda E., Michael A. Mitrook & Glen T. Cameron. 1999. Testing the contingency theory of accommodation in public relations. *Public Relations Review* 25. 171–197.

Cancel, Amanda E., Glen T. Cameron, Lynne M. Sallot & Michael A. Mitrook. 1997. It depends: A contingency theory of accommodation in public relations, *Journal of Public Relations Research* 9. 31–63.

Coombs, W. Timothy. 2009. The future of excellence in public relations and communication management: Challenges for the next generation. *Journal of Communication Management* 13(4). 381–383.

Dess, Gregory G., G. Tom Lumpkin & Alan B. Eisner. 2007. *Strategic management: Texts and cases*, 3rd edn. New York: McGraw-Hill, Irwin.

Dozier, David M., Larissa A. Grunig & James E. Grunig. 1995. *Manager's guide to excellence in public relations and communication management*. Hillsdale, NJ: Lawrence Erlbaum Associates.

Edwards, Lee & Caroline E. M. Hodges (eds.). 2011. *Public relations, society & culture: Theoretical and empirical explorations*. New York: Routledge.

Elwood, William N (ed.). 1995. *Public relations inquiry as rhetorical criticism: Case studies of corporate discourse and social influence*. Santa Barbara, CA: Praeger Publishers.

Ferguson, Mary A. 1984. *Building theory in public relations: Interorganizational relationships*. Paper presented at the convention of the Association for Education in Journalism and Mass Communication, Gainesville, FL. August.

Gallicano, Tiffany D. 2013. Relationship management with the Millennial generation of public relations agency employees. *Public Relations Review* 39(3). 222–225.

Grunig, James E. 1992. *Excellence in public relations and communication management*. Hillsdale, NJ: Lawrence Erlbaum Associates.

Grunig, James E. 2000. Collectivism, collaboration, and societal corporatism as core professional values in public relations. *Journal of Public Relations Research* 12. 23–48.

Grunig, James E. 2006. Furnishing the edifice: Ongoing research on public relations as a strategic management function. *Journal of Public Relations Research* 18. 151–176.

Grunig, James E. 2008. *The international encyclopedia of communication*. https://onlinelibrary. wiley.com/doi/abs/10.1002/9781405186407.wbiece047 (accessed 20 December 2018).

Grunig, James E. 2009. Paradigms of global public relations in an age of digitalization. *PRism* 6(2). http://praxis.massey.ac.nz/prism_on-line_journ.html (accessed 28 November 2018).

Grunig, James E. 2018. Strategic behavioral paradigm. In Robert L. Heath and Winni Johansen (eds.), *The international encyclopedia of strategic communication*. Wiley Online Library. https:// doi.org/10.1002/9781119010722.iesc0171 (accessed 28 November 2018).

Grunig, James E. & Larissa A. Grunig. 1996. *Implications of symmetry for a theory of ethics and social responsibility in public relations*. Paper presented at the meeting of the International Communication Association, Chicago. May.

Grunig, James E. & Larissa A. Grunig. 2008. Excellence theory in public relations: Past, present, and future. In Ansgar Zerfass, Betteke van Ruler & Krishnamurthy Sriramesh (eds.), *Public relations research*, 327–347. Wiesbaden, Germany: VS Verlag für Sozialwissenschaften.

Grunig, James E., Larissa A. Grunig, Krishnamurthy Sriramesh, Yi-Hui Huang & Anastasia Lyra. 1995. Models of public relations in an international setting. *Journal of Public Relations Research* 7(3). 163–186.

Grunig, Larissa A., James E. Grunig & David M. Dozier. 2002. *Excellent public relations and effective organizations*. Mahwah, NJ: Lawrence Erlbaum Associates.

Hatch, Mary J. 1997. *Organization theory: Modern, symbolic and postmodern perspectives*, 3rd edn. Oxford: Oxford University Press.

Heath, Robert L. 1992. The wrangle in the market place: A rhetorical perspective of public relations. In Elizabeth L. Toth & Robert L. Heath (eds.), *Rhetorical and critical approaches to public relations*, 17–36. Hillsdale, NJ: Lawrence Erlbaum Associates.

Hofstede, Geert. 1980. *Culture's Consequences: International Differences in Work-Related Values*. Beverly Hills, CA: Sage.

Holtzhausen, Derina R. & Rosina Voto. 2002. Resistance from the margins: The postmodern public relations practitioner as organizational activist. *Journal of Public Relations Research* 14(1). 57–84.

Hon, Linda C. & James E. Grunig. 1999. *Guidelines for measuring relationships in public relations*. http:// http://painepublishing.com/wp-content/uploads/2013/10/Guidelines_Measuring_ Relationships.pdf (accessed 21 December 2018).

Hong, Soo Yeon & Sung-Un Yang. 2009. Effects of reputation, relational satisfaction, and customer-company identification on positive word-of-mouth intentions. *Journal of Public Relations Research* 21(4). 381–403.

Huang, Yi-Hui. 2001. OPRA: A cross-cultural, multiple-item scale for measuring organization-public relationships. *Journal of Public Relations Research* 13(1). 61–90.

Huang, Yi-Hui, Fang Wu & Qing Huang. 2017. Does research on digital public relations indicate a paradigm shift? An analysis and critique of recent trends. *Telematics and Informatics* 34(7). 1364–1376.

Huang, Yi-Hui & Ying Zhang. 2013. Revisiting organization–public relationship research for the past decade: Theoretical concepts, measures, methodologies, and challenges. *Public Relations Review* 35(3). 181–186.

Hung, Chun-Ju F. 2005. Exploring types of organization–public relationships and their implications for relationship management in public relations. *Journal of Public Relations Research* 17(4). 393–425.

Hung, Chun-Ju F. & Yi-Ru R. Chen. 2009. Types and dimensions of organization–public relationships in greater China. *Public Relations Review* 35(3). 181–186.

Jo, Samsup. 2006. Measurement of organization–public relationships: Validation of measurement using a manufacturer–retailer relationship. *Journal of Public Relations Research* 18(3). 225–248.

Kent, Michael L. & Maureen Taylor. 1998. Building dialogic relationships through the World Wide Web. *Public Relations Review* 24(3). 321–334.

Kent, Michael L. & Maureen Taylor. 2007. Beyond excellence: Extending the generic approach to international public relations: The Case of Bosnia. *Public Relations Review* 33(1). 10–20.

Ki, Eyun-Jung & Linda Hon. 2009. The causal linkages between/among relationship cultivation strategies and relationship quality outcomes. *International Journal of Strategic Communication* 3(4). 242–263.

Ki, Eyun-Jung & Lan Ye. 2017. An assessment of progress in research on global public relations from 2001 to 2014. *Public Relations Review* 43(1). 235–246.

Kim, Jeong-Nam, Chun-ju F. Hung-Baesecke, Sung-Un Yang & James E. Grunig. 2013. A strategic management approach to reputation, relationships, and publics: The research heritage of the Excellence theory. In Craig E. Carroll (ed.), *The handbook of communication and corporate reputation*, 197–212. New York: Wiley-Blackwell.

Kim, Jeong-Nam & James E. Grunig. 2011. Problem solving and communicative action: A situational theory of problem solving. *Journal of communication* 61(1). 120–149.

Kim, Jeong-Nam & Lan Ni. 2013. Two types of public relations problems and integrating formative and evaluative research: A review of research programs within the behavioral, strategic management paradigm. *Journal of Public Relations Research* 25(1). 1–29.

Ledingham, John & Stephen Bruning. 2001. Managing community relationships to maximize mutual benefit: Doing well by doing good. In Robert L. Heath (ed.), *Handbook of public relations*, 527–534. Thousand Oaks, CA: Sage.

Ledingham, John A., Stephen D. Bruning, Dean Thomlison & Cheryl Lesko. 1997. The applicability of the interpersonal relationship dimensions to an organizational context: Toward a theory of relational loyalty a qualitative approach. *Journal of Organizational Culture, Communications and Conflict* 1(1). 23–43.

Leitch, Shirley & David Neilson. 2001. Bringing publics into public relations: New theoretical frameworks for practice. In Robert L. Heath (ed.), *Handbook of public relations*, 127–138. Thousand Oaks, CA: Sage.

L'Etang, Jacquie. 1996. Corporate responsibility and public relations ethics. In Jacquie L'Etang & Magda Pieczka (eds.), *Critical perspectives in public relations*, 82–105. London: International Thomson Business Press.

Li, Charlene & Josh Bernoff. 2011. *Groundswell: Winning in a world transformed by social technologies*. Boston: Harvard Business Review Press.

Lievonen, Matias, Vilma Luoma-aho & J. Bowden. 2018. Negative Engagement. In Kim A. Johnston & Maureen Taylor (eds.), *The Handbook of Communication Engagement*, 531–548. Hoboken, NJ: Wiley-Blackwell.

Lievonen, Matias & Vilma Luoma-aho. 2015. Ethical hateholders and negative engagement. A challenge for organisational communication. In Andrea Catellani, Ansgar Zerfass & Ralph Tench (eds.), *Communication ethics in a connected world: Research in public relations and organisational communication*, 285–303. Brussels: Peter Lang Publishing Group.

Lim, Selina, June Goh & Krishnamurthy Sriramesh. 2005. Applicability of the genetic principles of excellent public relations in a different cultural context: The case study of Singapore. *Journal of Public Relations Research* 17(4). 315–340.

Macnamara, Jim. 2012. The global shadow of functionalism and Excellence Theory: An analysis of Australasian PR. *Public Relations Inquiry* 1(3). 367–402.

McKie, David. 2008. Postmodernism and PR. In Jacquie L'Etang (ed.), *Public relations concepts, practice and* critique, 259–260. London: Sage.

Men, Linjuan R. & Chun-ju F. Hung. 2012. Exploring the roles of organization-public relationships in the strategic management process: Towards an integrated framework. *International Journal of Strategic Communication* 6(2). 151–173

Murphy, Priscilla. 1991. The limits of symmetry: A game theory approach to symmetric and asymmetric public relations. In James E. Grunig and Larissa A. Grunig (eds.), *Public relations research annual* Vol. 3, 115–131. Hillsdale, NJ: Lawrence Erlbaum Associates.

Ni, Lan. 2009. Strategic role of relationship building: Perceived links between employee-organization relationships and globalization strategies. *Journal of Public Relations Research* 21. 100–120.

Ni, Lan, Qi Wang & Bey-Ling Sha. 2018. *Intercultural public relations: Theories for managing relationships and conflicts with strategic publics*. New York: Routledge.

Philips, David & Philip Young. 2009. *Online public relations: A practical guide to developing an online strategy in the world of social media*. London: Kogan Page Publishers.

Pieczka, Magda. 1996. Paradigms, systems theory and public relations. In Jaquie L'Etang & Magda Pieczka (eds.), *Critical perspectives in public relations*, 124–156. London: International Thomson Business Press.

Pieczka, Magda. 2006. Paradigms, systems theory and public relations. In Jaquie L'Etang & Magda Pieczka (eds.), *Public relations: Critical debates and contemporary practice*, 331–358. New York: Routledge.

Plowman, Kenneth. 2005. Conflict, strategic management, and public relations. *Public Relations Review* 31. 131–138.

Sallot, Lynne M., Lisa J. Lyon, Carolina Acosta-Alzuru & Karyn Ogata Jones. 2003. From aardvark to zebra: A new millennium analysis of theory development in public relations academic journals. *Journal of Public Relations Research* 15(1). 27–90.

Schwarz, Andreas & Alexander Fritsch. 2014. Communicating on behalf of global civil society: Management and coordination of public relations in international nongovernmental organizations. *Journal of Public Relations Research* 26(2). 161–183.

Sheldrake, Philip. 2011. *The business of influence: Reframing marketing and PR for the digital age*. Hoboken, NJ: Wiley.

Sriramesh, Krishnamurthy (ed.). 2004. *Public relations in Asia: An anthology*. Singapore: Thomson.

Sriramesh, Krishnamurthy & Dejan Verčič (eds.). 2009. *The global public relations handbook, revised and expanded edition: Theory, research, and practice*, 2nd edn. New York: Routledge.

Steyn, Benita. 2007. Contribution of public relations to organizational strategy formulation. In Elizabeth. L. Toth (ed.), *The future of excellence in public relations and communication management: Challenges for the next generation*, 137–172. Mahwah, NJ: Lawrence Erlbaum Associates.

Taylor, Maureen & Michael L. Kent. 2006. Public relations theory and practice in nation building. In Carl Botan & Vincent Hazleton (eds.), *Public relations theory II*, 341–359. Mahwah, NJ: Lawrence Erlbaum Associates.

Taylor, Maureen & Michael L. Kent. 1999. Challenging assumption of international public relations: When government is the most important public. *Public Relations Review* 25(2). 131–144.

Theunissen, Petra & Wan Norbani Wan Noordin. 2012. Revisiting the concept "dialogue" in public relations. *Public Relations Review* 38(1). 5–13.

Toth, Elizabeth. L. (ed.). 2007. *Excellence in public relations and communication management: Challenges for the next generation*. Mahwah, NJ: Lawrence Erlbaum Associates.

Toth, Elizabeth. L. 2000. From personal to interpersonal influence: A model for relationship management. In John. Ledingham & Stephen Bruning (eds.), *Public relations as relationship management: A relational approach to the study and practice of public relations*, 205–219. Mahwah, NJ: Lawrence Erlbaum Associates.

Van Gorp, Baldwin & Luc Pauwels. 2007. Positioning and role of public relations in large Belgian organizations. *Public Relations Review* 33(3). 301–305.

Valentini, Chiara & Krishnamurthy Sriramesh. 2014. To be, or not to be: Paradoxes in strategic public relations in Italy. *Public Relations Review* 40(1). 3–13.

Vasquez, Gabriel M. 1996. Public relations as negotiation: An issue development perspective. *Journal of Public Relations Research* 8(1). 57–77.

Verčič, Dejan. 2008. Co-orientation model of public relations. In Wolfgang Donsbach (ed.), *International encyclopaedia of communication*, 995–998. New York: Wiley-Blackwell

Verčič, Dejan, Larissa A. Grunig & James E. Grunig. 1996. Global and specific principles of public relations: Evidence from Slovenia. In Hugh M. Culbertson & Ni Chen (eds.), *International public relations: A comparative analysis*, 31–65. Mahwah NJ: Lawrence Erlbaum Associates.

Volk, Sophia C. 2016. A systematic review of 40 Years of public relations evaluation and measurement research: Looking into the past, the present, and future. Public Relations Review 42(5). 962–977.

Waddington, Stephen. 2013. A critical review of the four models of public relations and the Excellence Theory in an era of digital communication. CIPR Chartered Practitioner Paper. https://wadds.co.uk/blog/2018/7/18/a-critical-review-of-excellence-theory-in-an-era-of-digital-communication (accessed 20 November 2018).

Watson, David R. & Lynne M. Sallot. 2001. Public relations practice in Japan: An exploratory study. *Public Relations Review* 27(4). 389–402.

Ye, Lan & Eyun-Jung Ki. 2012. The status of online public relations research: an analysis of published articles in 1992–2009. *Journal of Public Relations Research* 24(5). 409–434

Yun, Seong-Hun. 2006. Toward public relations theory-based study of public diplomacy: Testing the applicability of the excellence study. *Journal of Public Relations Research* 18(4). 287–312.

Zerfass, Ansgar, Piet Verhoeven, Angeles Moreno, Ralph Tench, & Dejan Verčič. 2016. *European communication monitor 2016: Exploring trends in big data, stakeholder engagement and strategic communication: Results of a survey in 43 countries*. Brussels: European Association of Communication Directors.

Krishnamurthy Sriramesh and Jolene Fisher

17 Personal influence in public relations

Abstract: This essay seeks to dispel the popular assumption that public relations is conducted mostly through mass-mediated communication and to highlight the importance of personal influence to the practice. In doing so, it reviews the definition of the term "personal influence," describes its use in public relations practice, and reviews the sparse attention it has received from public relations scholars. In an attempt to dispel another erroneous assumption – that personal influence is only seen in the developing world, such as in Asia – a review of literature is presented chronicling research on this term from various parts of the world. It posits that other disciplines such as mass communication, marketing, and consumer behavior have much more robust scholarship on the use of personal influence. It concludes by offering thoughts on the importance of personal influence to the field and offers avenues for further research.

Keywords: personal influence; personal influence model; personal influence and marketing; ethics and personal influence

1 Introduction

Public relations practice has been erroneously seen almost exclusively as mass-mediated communication. It is easy to ignore the fact that human beings have used personal influence for persuasive purposes since the origin of the human race. Indian emperor Asoka, who ruled greater India (extending from today's Afghanistan and Iran to East India) from 273–232 BC, introduced Buddhism to Sri Lanka, today's Myanmar, and other parts of Central Asia using emissaries including his son and daughter. In ancient and modern times, international diplomacy has used influence that can be termed coercive, attractive, cooperative, or competitive, operationalized through the use of force, economic incentives or pressure, diplomacy, and cultural exchange. In most, if not all, of these instances, personal influence has been, and is being, used. In the field of international diplomacy, the personal influence of ambassadors contributes immeasurably to the success or failure of a diplomatic initiative.

It will be difficult to find many public relations practitioners who would deny that they have used, or are using, personal influence in conducting their public relations activities, whether for lobbying government for media relations or persuading other stakeholders. Yet, personal influence has been neglected by public relations scholarship. This chapter reviews the origins and use of the term "personal influence," chronicles its use in allied disciplines, and examines the current state of personal influence in the public relations body of knowledge. In doing so, it seeks to offer a research

https://doi.org/10.1515/9783110554250-017

agenda that advances our understanding of the term, thereby giving the concept due recognition in public relations scholarship mirroring public relations practice.

2 Review of literature

Although the practice of public relations can be traced back to pre-biblical times in civilizations such as Mesopotamia, ancient Egypt, and the Indus Valley (Sriramesh 2004), "modern" public relations is mostly a 20th century phenomenon (Sriramesh 2009). Public relations scholarship is even younger, having come of age only in the 1970s. After analyzing over 4,100 books and articles on public relations, J. Grunig and Hickson (1976) found only 63 with any research component in them. Concerted efforts at building a scholarly body of knowledge began in the mid-1970s with the early conceptualizations of what later were labeled the "models" of public relations (Grunig, J. 1976) and practitioner roles (Broom and Smith 1979). More than four decades later, the process of building (and expanding) the body of knowledge continues. It is heartening that there are many more scholars contributing to this process than there were in the 1970s and 1980s. These scholars also hail from more diverse cultures, thus helping broaden the cultural horizons of both the profession and scholarship.

Scholarly discussions about the use of personal influence in public relations began only in the late 1980s, based on a study conducted in India (Sriramesh 1988; Sriramesh 1990). Almost simultaneously, two other studies reported the presence of personal influence in public relations practices in Taiwan (Huang 1990) and Greece (Lyra 1991). These studies had set out to look for the presence of the original four models of public relations offered by J. Grunig and Hunt (1984) by seeking to study the models in a setting outside the US, and ended up finding personal influence as a model as reported in J. Grunig et al. (1995). However, since then only sporadic attention has been paid to the concept of personal influence in public relations, which is often seen as a phenomenon that belongs in the "ghetto" of "international" public relations – perhaps because the phenomenon was brought into public relations pedagogy based on studies conducted outside of the United States and Western Europe. Few studies have analyzed its presence in the public relations activities of Western countries although it is very much present in the US, the UK, and Western and Eastern Europe – albeit differently manifested. It is bewildering that personal influence has not received the recognition it merits in public relations scholarship even though most public relations professionals the world over rely on it quite extensively.

3 Definitions and origins of the term *personal influence*

Although these early studies in public relations and the ones that have followed them have confirmed the use of personal influence in public relations activities, none of the studies has offered a definition for the term *personal influence*. This is partly because of the relative novelty of the term to public relations scholarship but also because of the lack of importance accorded this phenomenon by public relations scholars. The term personal influence may be relatively new to the public relations body of knowledge but not to other domains in communication. Relating personal influence to decision-making in the adoption of technological changes, Rogers and Beal (1958: 329) defined personal influence as "those communications contacts which involve[d] a direct face-to-face exchange between the communicator and communicate[d]."

Katz and Lazarsfeld (1955) highlighted the importance of personal influence in consumer decision-making, stating that "personal contact again has considerably greater influence than any other media" (180). Their study proposed that the efficacy of mass-media messages was largely influenced by opinion leaders whose personal networks and influence clearly affected how media messages were perceived and interpreted by audiences. This is popular now as the two-step-flow theory of mass communication, which was the precursor to Everett Rogers' (1962) theory of the diffusion of innovations, which also propounded that interpersonal communication and influence are useful in determining the potential and speed with which new innovations are adopted by people based on endorsements from opinion leaders.

Lazarsfeld, Berelson, and Gaudet (1944) contended that personal networks (family, close friends and close colleagues in the work place) had significant influence on citizens' voting decisions. Based on research conducted in the Federal Republic of Germany, Finkel, Muller, and Opp (1989) found that personal influence played a critical role in both legal and illegal protest behaviors among respondents. When the success of the group is assured, there is a tendency for individuals to "free-ride" and benefit from the group's success by not getting involved personally in a protest, the authors noted. But factors such as personal morals, duty to participate, and the perception that an individual's contributions could make a difference contributed to greater commitment to both illegal and legal protests. Rogers and Beal (1958) noted that the influence that personal networks have on individual decision-making stems from a variety of factors such as similarity in values between the source and receiver of a message, a common level of discourse, accessibility, and individual credibility (as opposed to organizational credibility). The authors stated that "Impersonal sources can usually be more easily avoided, 'turned off,' or ignored than can personal sources" (Rogers and Beal 1958: 329–330). Personal influence, then, may be ignored by the public relations body of knowledge, but it has not been ignored by public relations practice nor by over 60 years of communication scholarship.

4 Personal influence and public relations practice

In a 2012 blog post, Harold Burson, co-founder and president of one of the largest international public relations agencies – Burson-Marsteller (now Burson Cohn & Wolfe) – bemoaned the overemphasis on communication functions in public relations practice, arguing that "too many of us believe the communications part of our job is the totality of what we do" (para. 4). He contended that "[T]he principal purpose of public relations is and has always been persuasion – persuading an individual or group of individuals to a specific course of action" (para. 6). While much of the scholarly literature in public relations focuses on persuasion, it does so in the context of communication via mass-media channels. The role of relationships, and specifically the role of personal influence within those relationships, has often been overlooked.

Persuasion often carries a negative connotation. Clearly persuasion that is undertaken for the purpose of personal gain, and especially if it is at the expense of others, is unethical. However, ethical approaches to persuasion through which mutual benefit is sought are necessary to do much of the work of public relations. We understand building strong relationships as important to achieving public relations goals in large part because relationships build trust and credibility, both of which are necessary when trying to persuade, in a non-normative sense, various stakeholders to take an action, attitude, or stance. Far too little research, however, examines the role and importance of personal influence as part of the relationship-building and persuasion process necessary to achieve successful public relations outcomes.

According to Muzi Falconi (2011), the extant literature looks at personal influence from the perspective of interpersonal influence, as a function of relationship management, or as a fifth model of public relations. Drawing on work from social psychology and interpersonal communication, studies in the first category examine how the specific traits and status of an individual practitioner impact relationship success (Toth 2000). For instance, Schriner (2008) presented the concept of the public role model, specifically in the form of organizational spokespersons, as a way of understanding personal influence in public relations. The spokesperson, who resides at the center of professionalized social networks built through personal influence, requires certain social and communicative skill sets to fulfill their role of maintaining a positive image for the organization.

Studies that focus on personal influence as a dimension of relationship management increasingly acknowledge the "importance of relationships as an indicator of successful public relations" and analyze how strong individual relationships relate to organizational outcomes (Muzi Falconi 2011). Examples include Gallicano's (2009) study of personal influence and management strategies for cultivating personal relationships in the context of a health advocacy organization, and White, Vanc, and Stafford's (2010) examination of the role of personal influence on improving internal communication and employee relationships.

Finally, studies have looked at personal influence as a fifth model of public relations to go along with the more popular four models first offered by J. Grunig and Hunt (1984). The majority of studies that examined the personal influence model have done so in a few countries in Asia, leading to the erroneous assumption that this concept's applicability is relevant only in "more rigid cultures in which power and social class have more bearing on decision making" (Muzi Falconi 2011).

Because relationship management is the primary focus of public relations, it seems obvious that personal influence must play an important role. In practice, personal influence can be seen in key aspects of public relations practice, such as media relations. Public relations practitioners submit that strong relationships with journalists are important to getting their work done (Sriramesh and Takasaki 1999; Sriramesh, Kim, and Takasaki 1999). And in government relations access to key officials is clearly of great importance. Personal influence plays an important role in attracting people to an organization and in strengthening employee relations within it. It also plays a role in building organizational trust with external stakeholders in areas such as public affairs and investor relations. In the current media context, the growth of social media has made personal influence even more relevant to those organizations that have embraced paid influencers and digital brand ambassadors.

According to Muzi Falconi (2011), personal influence as a model of practice "seems to be the most universally adopted, quite contrary to the diffused ethnocentric stereotype that it is mostly practiced in Asia." But despite its strong presence in practice, objections to the concept of personal influence are prevalent in the scholarly field (Valentini 2009). Perhaps it is because personal influence is not seen as a strategic function, or perhaps it is because current perceptions of personal influence conceptualize it as something done "behind closed doors" – hidden and therefore corrupt in some way. In this sense, personal influence is painted as quite the opposite of communication through mass media channels, which, because it takes place in the public sphere, is seen as being more transparent and thus more ethical than personal influence, even though in practice, personal influence is innate to media relations as well. As Valentini (2009) noted, the personal influence model is seen as the most "problematic" in terms of ethical complexities. We of course disagree with this premise. The following section details why this is the case and reviews the state of personal influence in public relations scholarship.

5 Personal influence in public relations scholarship

The concept of relationship and relationship building is clearly linked to the practice of public relations (Johnson 2008). Personal influence plays an important role in building and sustaining relationships with journalists, government officials, public opinion leaders and other stakeholders. Muzi Falconi (2011) and Johnson (2008) emphasize the role of personal influence in the relationship-building process. Strong interpersonal skills, necessary for relationship building, are important for effective public relations practitioners (Toth 2000). Yet little consideration has been given to the importance of personal influence by scholars in the West or in studies focused on a Western context of public relations practice. A series of factors may help explain why this is the case.

The first is the focus on persuasion and the control of messages through mass media channels that dominates public relations research (Muzi Falconi 2011; Yudar-wati 2008). Because in the US most public relations programs are housed in schools of journalism and mass communication, there may be a reluctance to accept the impor-tance of the personal influence model in the field (Wakefield 2013). The potential embarrassment for practitioners caused by the acknowledgement that their personal networks may play as important a role in their careers as other professional competen-cies seems a plausible reason for them to deemphasize the role of personal influence in their practice (Johnson 2008; Muzi Falconi 2011). Such an approach is perplexing because one commonly hears both practitioners and scholar-teachers emphasizing to students the benefits of "networking" to build one's career. Finally, some scholars may worry that acceptance and analysis of the personal influence model within public relations theory might add to the perception that it is a non-scientific, non-strategic field (Muzi Falconi 2011).

But a changing landscape may influence the acknowledgement, and acceptance, of the innate role of personal influence in public relations. Within our current media environment, practitioners have much less ability to maintain control over messag-ing. Thus, the historical emphasis on persuasion and message control must inevitably evolve. We have already seen this shift taking place, with a growing body of scholar-ship emphasizing the role of relationships in the success of public relations practice (J. Grunig and Huang 2000; Muzi Falconi 2011). Muzi Falconi (2010: 3) contended that "the ability to effectively govern relationships, within and amongst networks as well as with society at large, has now become the utmost value, as it reinforces, nurtures and develops the organization's increasingly important 'license to operate'."

Public relations research has almost exclusively focused on the practice of public relations through mass mediated channels from the very beginning. J. Grunig (1976) offered synchronic and diachronic communication as two types of communication that were later expanded to four models of public relations based on two criteria: the *purpose* and *nature* of communication (J. Grunig and Hunt 1984). Scores of other studies replicated J. Grunig's study and confirmed the presence of the four models first in the US and then in some other countries including in Asia. The Excellence Project, which was in the conceptualization stage in the late 1980s, also used the four-model framework for its survey conducted in the US, UK, and Canada. All these studies, however, focused only on public relations through mass mediated channels even though interpersonal communication and relationship building has been the underpinning of public relations practice the world over.

However, anecdotal evidence has long suggested that public relations practice is not limited to the use of mass mediated messages. Even in managing their relationships with stakeholders such as journalists or government officials, public relations people the world over use personal influence. Only the degree to which personal influence is used or how it is manifested may vary depending on socio-cultural and political factors.

An exploratory study of public relations in India was conducted replicating the questionnaire used for testing the models (Sriramesh 1988). The strong role of personal influence in every aspect of public relations in India was confirmed in both that and a subsequent study (Sriramesh 1989). A thorough ethnographic analysis of 18 organizations in Southern India further confirmed the dominance of personal influence in public relations practice in India (Sriramesh 1992). In all three studies, there emerged a worldview of personal influence that was typified in the statement of an interviewee who saw public relations as the art of "developing rapport at the human [personal] level to represent the organization." A predominant percentage of interviewees in the study stated that "ability to network with key individuals" in their organization's environment was the primary characteristic of a successful public relations practitioner. At about the same time, Huang (1990) conducted a study in Taiwan and also discovered personal influence in the form of *gao guanxi*. Lyra (1991) studied public relations in Greece and also reported the presence of personal influence there. All these studies were discussed in a meta-analysis and reported by J. Grunig et al. (1995).

Although personal influence has received some scholarly attention since those early studies, research on the role of personal influence in public relations has remained limited in a number of ways. First, many of these studies were conducted in Asia and it is necessary for the field to acknowledge that personal influence in public relations is certainly not only an "Asian phenomenon." Such an assumption ignores the role of personal influence in public relations in the rest of the world. Further, studies on personal influence are few and far between and therefore such research does not match the actual impact of personal influence in practice. Finally, the impact of a changing media landscape, in which social media is pervasive, have made a theory-based understanding of personal influence increasingly necessary.

6 Personal influence in the West

Wakefield (2013), Muzi Falconi (2008, 2011), Johnson (2008), Reber and Berger (2006), and O'Neil (2003) are representative of the few studies in public relations that have evaluated the presence of personal influence in Western countries. In the United States specifically, the role of personal influence has been downplayed, dismissed, and even disavowed (Sriramesh 2020; Wakefield 2013; Johnson 2008; Muzi Falconi

2011; Toth 2000). In his review of the history of public relations and personal influence in the US, Wakefield (2013: 131) argued that "the prevalence of personal influence through at least 150 years of U.S. society" has been largely ignored even though its role in nation- and community-building are evident. Wakefield (2013: 133) documents the use of personal influence beginning in the early days of the country, noting, "As citizens spread throughout the land and formed agrarian communities, voluntary public relations-type activities helped to develop community pride and solidarity (Olasky 1987; Shain, 1994)." But neither these early activities nor those that followed them have been widely recognized by public relations scholars.

Though neglected in the literature, personal influence is clearly baked into the functioning of public relations both historically and contemporarily. The link between lobbying and personal influence is supported by Johnson (2005), who studied 314 lobbying listings filed in the US by public relations and other agencies that conducted public relations and lobbying activities in the US for Mexican interests in the post-NAFTA period. She found that the "sources of influence" in the lobbying field came predominantly from the personal influence model as opposed to other forms of public relations. Further support comes from Tuite's (2006) study of the roles that Government Relations Professionals (GRPs) performed in maintaining relationships between their organizations and the government of the state of Maryland in the US. The author concluded that the personal influence model (along with the cultural interpreter model) was very frequently used by the GRPs. Wakefield (2013) cited the participation of organizational leaders in industry and community associations, relationships between public relations practitioners and traditional mass and new media sources, and fundraising projects built on relationships with wealthy donors as spaces in which personal influence is certainly at play in the US.

Organizations that have incorporated social media influencers and brand ambassadors into their public relations strategies have already recognized the power of personal influence in the digital sphere. Research on the use of personal influence across new media channels is of growing importance to the field. In a study of Twitter use by CEOs, Hwang (2012) found that CEOs' active use of the platform had positive effects on both the images of CEOs and their organizations. And as audiences' expectations around organizational social media use grow, generating a theoretical understanding of the role of personal influence in the digital sphere should be prioritized.

Although scholars within the US and other Western countries have acknowledged the role of personal influence in areas of the world in which a cultural structure of collectivism and power distance is the norm, they have failed to discern the prevalence of personal influence in more individualistic and egalitarian societies, except for a few studies. Reber and Berger (2006) conducted in-depth interviews with 162 practitioners to identify how public relations practitioners defined "influence" and from where these professionals received influence in their organizations. Their respondents defined influence as the ability to contribute to organizational strategy and decision-making, and found direct influence to occur mostly during times of crises.

Although the authors quoted Berger (2005: 236) that public relations practitioners "must engage in power relations in order to exert influence" in organizations, they never mentioned personal influence as a factor in this process. Only 8.5 percent of respondents reported "personal relationships" as a factor in gaining influence in organizations. Given even a basic understanding of how organizations, in general, operate, these data perhaps offer us a glimpse of an unwillingness to accept the critical role of personal influence rather than its absence.

O'Neil's (2003) study of 300 senior-level public relations practitioners in the US also did not find personal influence as a factor in providing power to public relations within an organization. One has to wonder whether this is because these studies did not look for the presence of personal influence building although both studied "ingratiation" as a factor but only found very weak evidence for that variable. O'Neil noted, however, that self-reporting was "the greatest limitation" of the study and also noted "social desirability" as another potential limitation. As previously noted, acknowledging the importance of personal influence in conducting the work of public relations may engender a sense of general "embarrassment" among practitioners, making them less likely to report on its impacts (Johnson 2008; Muzi Falconi 2011).

The role of personal influence in public relations has also been studied, albeit in a limited way, in some Western European contexts. Based on a study conducted in then newly unified east and west Germany between September and November of 1990, Weimann and Brosius (1994) proposed that personal influence, the mass media, and personal traits "interact rather than compete" in the setting of public agenda. During those early days of unification, the country was grappling with not just the euphoria of the fall of the Berlin Wall but also the reality of funding the hundreds of billions needed to rebuild the infrastructure of the former East Germany. Therefore, setting the public agenda in both east and west Germany was a primary focus for the government on such things as housing, raising taxes to finance unification, unemployment in east Germany, wage disparities between the two, etc. Although the study focused on agenda-setting, it has direct relevance to public relations.

Taylor (2004) found personal influence to be a dominant force in her study of the public relations activities of NGOs in Croatia. Based on a survey and personal interviews with public relations professionals of NGOs and journalists, she concluded that "[P]ersonal influence may best characterize this relational strategy" (Taylor 2004: 157). The author also remarked that "personal relationships have developed as a necessity in public relations" owing to the culture of Croatia (157). Evans and Fill (2000) distinguished between *opinion formers* and *opinion leaders* in conceptualizing their study of communication in the UK car market. Most UK car manufacturers, the authors observed, "tend not to use public relations agencies but prefer to work in-house communicating with both the media and with end-user customers" (Evans and Fill 2000: 381). They found that 80–100 percent of their respondents reported targeting journalists as opinion formers via press releases and events. Although they did not use the term "personal influence," Evans and Fill's (2000) observation clearly points to the use of personal influence in the UK: "[T]he closeness of relationship between PR personnel and journalists is one factor here. Most PR people in car companies are themselves ex-journalists and the network is a fairly close-knit one" (387).

Johnson (2008) interviewed senior managers and executives at large organizations and public relations firms to understand whether and how organizations are capturing and managing the personal relationship networks of their employees. She found that the personal networks and relationships of a candidate are often taken into consideration when hiring managers for public relations positions. Further, participants reported that "relationships with stakeholder publics influence management decisions 'sometimes' to 'always'" (2008: 26). According to Johnson (2008: 25), "everyone interviewed agreed that there is significant potential value to be gained from tapping into stakeholder relationships" in order to benefit the organization, but currently most did not have an organized way to do this. Finding ways to better conceptualize and theorize personal influence and personal relationships within public relations functions may help in achieving this. According to Johnson (2008: 27), "Even though some professionals would rather not acknowledge it, [personal] relationships are a fundamental part of public relations."

White, Vanc, and Stafford (2010) found interpersonal communication to be key to effective internal communication in the context of a multi-campus university in the US. The use of personal influence through face-to-face communication by the university chancellor was found to engender trust, impact employee satisfaction, and help achieve organizational goals. The authors concluded that "both the attributes of the individual and the position (role) that the individual fills are components of personal influence" (2010: 81).

Gallicano (2009: 321) found that personal relationships in the context of a health advocacy organization created successful outcomes for the organization, including "affective commitment, political leverage, social capital, and member recruitment and retention." She also examined a series of interpersonal influence and management strategies for cultivating effective personal relationships. The author noted that the value of the relational outcomes to an organization "seems to be affected in at least some cases by whether people with the personal relationships stay in the organization" (2009: 324). Kent and Taylor (2007) found that in Bosnia interpersonal dimensions were very important to public relations practitioners and that the cultural interpreter model, the press agentry model, and the personal influence model were most prevalent in practice. But in their study the authors argued that "what is more important than understanding the model of public relations practiced (cultural interpreter, personal influence, etc.) is to be able to account for the cultural factors that explain why a model is practiced" (2007: 18).

Ignoring the role of personal influence in public relations scholarship makes it more ethnocentric and less reflective of the field. Scholars in the West have made the argument that it is because of cultural differences around value systems such as collectivism and power distance that we see personal influence emerge in in contexts such as Asia, but not in the West. As we have detailed already, personal influence certainly exists in the practice of public relations in the West, even if it may be manifested in different ways. In Asian contexts, however, neither scholars nor practitioners are resistant to accepting its presence and its usefulness to public relations scholarship.

7 Personal influence in Asia

7.1 The concept of *guanxi*

Most of the studies on personal influence in public relations have been conducted in less than a handful of countries of Asia. A high percentage of these come from China, Hong Kong, and Taiwan. They have referred to personal influence as *guanxi* or *gao guanxi*. X-P. Chen and C. Chen (2004: 306) described *guanxi* as an "indigenous Chinese construct" and defined it as "an informal, particularistic personal connection between two individuals who are bounded [sic] by an implicit psychological contract to follow the social norm of *guanxi* such as maintaining a longterm relationship, mutual commitment, loyalty, and obligation."

The authors stressed the importance of personal influence to trust building, stating that "quality *guanxi* is also characterized by the mutual trust and feeling developed between the two parties through numerous interactions following the self-disclosure, dynamic reciprocity, and long-term equity principles" (2004: 306). The authors further described the various interpretations of this term that itself is a window to the complexity of the term and Chinese culture: "*Guanxi* together can be used as a verb or a noun. As a verb it means to have bearings on; as a noun it denotes a state in which entities (objects, forces, or human beings) are connected" (2004: 306). The authors traced the origin of the term to Confucian philosophy and offered three suggestions to international businesspeople working in China who have to navigate their way through the complexity of *guanxi:* one cannot be impersonal in China; try to establish "common institutional bases" that can serve as platforms for long-term association; rely on local Chinese as "bridges" to the culture.

Lee and Dawes (2005) studied *guanxi* in marketing and described *guan-xi* as consisting of two characters "guan" meaning a gate or a hurdle, and "xi" referring to a relationship, or a connection. So guanxi literally means "pass the gate and get connected." The concept of *guanxi* refers to interpersonal relationships or connections and can be applied not only to kinship and friendship relationships but also to social connections, such as dyadic relationships. Huang (2000) attempted to link personal influence to global public relations by trying to find parallels between Confucianism and the theory of global public relations. Huang noted that traditional Chinese judge their relationships with other individuals based on relationship *hierarchy* as well as relationship *closeness.* She concluded that whereas it may be impossible to eradicate asymmetry in the use of personal influence in Chinese societies, one could bring some element of symmetry to these practices by highlighting "holism" and expanding the purview of "extended family" to "society," social responsibility and public interest; emphasizing disclosure; emphasizing *jen* (humanism); and giving primacy to equality in human relationships.

Chow and Ng (2004) studied *guanxi* among full-time employees enrolled in MBA/EMBA courses in Hong Kong and found that close relations, such as family friends, club members, and school friends, formed the underpinnings for developing *guanxi*, while co-workers or distant family relatives were found to have "distant" relationships with respondents. However, industrialization and modernization meant that "the strength of family bonds is not as strong as in the Confucian tradition" (Chow and Ng 2004: 1089). Gender differences were also found to be important, wherein women tended to have closer relationships with other women, and men with men.

Flora Hung (2004) discussed the role of *guanxi*, face, favor, relational harmony, etc. in the way multinational corporations organized their relationship-building strategies in China. Her qualitative interviews generated some pithy quotes on the significance of relational orientation and personal networking in China. "China is ruled by people," said one respondent, "so relationships are very important" (Flora Hung 2004: 275). The author also found that many of her respondents hid their Chinese cultural idiosyncrasy of practicing *guanxi* when so instructed by their multinational organizations that wanted to be more "professional" and not practice *guanxi*. Sriramesh and Enxi (2004) conducted a survey of different types of organizations in Shanghai and found the strong presence of personal influence. The authors concluded that because of "the deeply entrenched Confucianism philosophy and the emphasis of personal networking ('Guanxi') in China for centuries, the public relations practices in Shanghai are molded by China's relation-centric culture" (Sriramesh and Enxi 2004: 73).

Su, Mitchell, and Sirgy (2007) studied *guanxi* from a stakeholder perspective using a hierarchical stakeholder model of *guanxi*, differentiating between internal and external and primary and secondary stakeholders for *guanxi*. The authors also offered different types of *guanxi*, such as core, major, and peripheral *guanxi*. The authors observed: "*Guanxi* reflects long-term cooperative business relationships, drawing upon a network of resource coalitions and operating within a hierarchical structure" (Su, Mitchell, and Sirgy 2007: 316). Xin and Pearce (1996: 1642) suggested that *guanxi* can be used as a "substitute for reliable government and an established rule of law" based on their study of managers in China from both state-owned and private enterprises. The authors also contended that "private-company executives will seek to build relationships that are deeper in trust (closer *guanxi)* than those sought by executives with structural protection [such as government employees]" (Xin and Pearce 1996: 1645).

The past 20 years have seen a significant increase in the number of public relations scholars from Asia, which has resulted in a wide array of studies on personal influence in public relations from various perspectives. As a result *guanxi* has been studied as relational morality (Tan and Snell 2002), ethical reasoning (Ang and Leong 2000), human resource management (Chen, X-P. and Chen, C. 2004), knowledge transfer (Ramasamy, Goh, and Yeung 2006), corporate governance (Braendle, Gasser, and Null 2005), and relationship marketing (Lee and Dawes 2005; Leung et al. 2005). Chen and Tjosvold (2007) found that guanxi, along with the universal theory of leader-member exchange (LMX) and constructive controversy, plays an important role in building strong relationships between Chinese employees and foreign managers. By using a framework of *guanxi*, foreign managers working in a Chinese context can strengthen collaborations and build stronger work relationships with their local employees.

According to C. Chen, X.-P. Chen, and Huang (2013), there is no universal definition of *guanxi* that is able to truly capture all of its varied dimensions. Thus, the use of the term, specifically as it relates to public relations practice, must be contextualized. For instance, a recent study by Wu, Chen, and Cui (2016: 867) found that while public relations practitioners in Beijing and Hong Kong, "two Chinese societies with a similar Confucian heritage but different institutional and cultural traits", both use *guanxi*-related practices, only practitioners from Beijing see *guanxi* as important when working with government stakeholders. Hou (2016: 633) found that *guanxi* is an "enabling logic" that allows public relations practitioners in China to "draw on particular aspects of *guanxi* (e. g., mutual trust and favor exchange) to facilitate and enable PR practices ... [because] China's market is replete with uncertainty, ambiguity and a lack of integrity, and thus people tend to believe in *guanxi* characterized by mutual trust and obligations to reliable and proper conduct." Her findings showed two main catalysts for the presence of *guanxi* in public relations in China. First, "*guanxi* eases relationship building by rendering mutual trust and commitment between two parties" (Hou 2016: 633). Second, *guanxi* helps "build social capital that is necessary for PR practitioners to operate within "China's vague regulatory system" (Hou 2016: 634).

7.2 The concept of *Cheong*

Several studies have analyzed the influence of personal influence on public relations in South Korea. Not unlike the concept of *guanxi*, the concept of *Cheong* is based on Confucian thought and is a term specific to "the fundamental foundation of Korean relationships" (Berkowitz and Lee 2004: 431). The authors used the concept of *Cheong* to analyze the practice of media relations in Korea, defining *Cheong* as formed through "four key characteristics of interpersonal relationships (Choi 2000): a historical nature; being together; warm heartedness; and absence of reserve" and a concept that has "long-term implications" for relationships, including those between journalists and public relations practitioners (Berkowitz and Lee 2004: 432). The authors found that both journalists and public relations practitioners considered *Cheong* a positive factor in building relationships for media relations. Respondents said that the presence of *Cheong* "emerged through repeated interactions, creating a working relationship between journalists and practitioners that facilitates a flow of information, yet also respects the professional obligations of each party" (Berkowitz and Lee 2004: 434).

Sriramesh, Kim, and Takasaki (1999) found that in South Korean organizations many respondents practiced personal influence regularly in their public relations activities. This is typified by the statement of one respondent: "Personal influence is very important under the *Chaebol* system... if a public relations practitioner has a [sic] acquaintance or the [sic] closeness of friendship with a reporter or gatekeeper, he can ask to take an unfavorable article out or minimize the headline or article." They also reported that public relations professionals regularly sent gifts and gave *Ddukgab* (money for buying Korean cakes) to government officials and media persons as a way of establishing personal influence and relationships. Jo and Kim (2004) studied the relationship between media and organizational public relations in South Korea and noted that personal influence played a key role in the media relations activities of organizations. Organizations deliberately appointed males to conduct media relations activities rather than females because, as one interviewee stated, "male practitioners can drink with journalists" (Jo and Kim 2004: 302) and build personal influence. The authors also noted that "providing monetary gifts, is a habitual aspect of the public relations industry" (Jo and Kim 2004: 302).

Shin and Cameron (2003) studied "informal relations" in South Korea, analyzing the presence of eleven practices used for building personal influence. These ranged from drinking with journalists to golfing/climbing (hiking) or giving free tickets for concerts. Their survey of 150 public relations practitioners and 150 journalists revealed that journalists do not see informal relations as influencing news coverage whereas public relations practitioners felt that personal influence did play a role in news coverage. However, the authors alluded to the press club prevalent in South Korea (as in Japan) as an indicator of the significant role that personal influence plays in news coverage. Kim and Bae (2006) also found that personal influence plays a significant role in the decisions that journalists make in choosing which inputs from public relations practitioners they select for publication. Personal influence, often curried through monetary gifts, played a role prompting the authors to conclude that the "fantasy of objectivity has functioned as a ritual that can only be justified in the news-making process, and news can never be independent from the source–media relations that make it" (Kim and Bae 2006: 244).

We do note that the tradition of gift-giving in South Korea might change after the implementation of the Improper Solicitation and Graft Act in 2016, making giving gifts to journalists illegal (Kim and Heo 2018). The anti-graft law works to ensure "that public officials and relevant persons fulfill their duties uprightly and to secure public confidence in public institutions by forbidding improper solicitations to public officials and relevant persons and by prohibiting them from accepting financial or other advantages" (Kim and Heo 2018: 363). In this regard, it is worth mentioning the 2017 impeachment of South Korean president Park-Guen He amid a web of personal influence peddling that involved Samsung; the tech giant's *de facto* head Lee Jae-yong was among those close to the president who were convicted and jailed for influence peddling and bribery.

Research shows that public relations practitioners in South Korea generally support the anti-graft law as they believe it will lead to stronger public relations ethics (Kim and Heo 2018). According to Kim and Heo (2018: 371), a move away from informal support, which they argue is directly tied to personal influence, will allow practitioners to "focus on their proper duty as public relations practitioners, rather than concern themselves with developing personal networks with journalists." These duties include "formal responsibilities" of media relations, namely writing well-crafted, newsworthy press releases (Kim and Heo 2018: 371). Kim and Heo argued that "the anti-graft law can lead to a critical moment in weakening the personal influence model in Korea," subsequently increasing the focus on the formal responsibility of public relations (2018: 372). It remains to be seen how soon this culture may change.

8 Personal influence in Africa

Africa has been the "silent continent" when it comes to public relations scholarship, despite the high number of multinational companies operating there, the long presence of Inter Governmental Organizations (IGO) on the continent, the expansion of international public relations firms to the region, and the emergence and professionalization of local practice (Kiambi and Nadler 2012; Wu and Baah-Boakye 2009). But analyses of the influence of cultural values and political change on public relations practices in various African countries have begun to provide a more nuanced picture of public relations practice in the region (see, for instance, Molleda and Alhassan 2006; Wu and Baah-Boakyem 2009; Kiambi and Nadler 2012; Holtzhausen, Petersen, and Tindall 2003; and Holtzhausen 2005).

Wu and Baah-Boakyem (2009) surveyed public relations practitioners working at both Ghanaian companies and public relations agencies to analyze the impact of work-related cultural values on public relations practice in Ghana. They found that the personal influence model and cultural interpreter model are the two most frequently practiced in the country. The authors stated that "Public relations practitioners in Ghana have to build good interpersonal relationships with both internal and external publics because building good interpersonal relationship is a key for business success in a collectivist culture" (Wu and Baah-Boaekyem 2009: 83). They also found that the practice of the cultural interpreter model was necessitated by the "multi-cultural characteristic of the Ghanaian culture and the increasing impact of international trade in Ghana," while the practice of the personal influence model speaks to the focus on relationship building (Wu and Baah-Bokeyem 2009: 84).

In Kenya, too, the personal influence and cultural interpreter models are the most frequently practiced models, with the personal influence model used more often.

Kiambi and Nadler noted that "[T]he strong correlation between personal influence model and Hofstede's cultural value of femininity points to the practitioners' strong desire for good interpersonal relationships with colleagues, supervisors, clients and key publics" (2012: 506).

The personal influence and cultural interpreter models, both of which are frequently practiced in Ghana and Kenya, are "indicative of how the public relations model is making a transition to the areas of relationship building and networking with key publics" in countries in Africa (Kiambi and Nadler 2012: 506).

9 Personal influence in other disciplines

Fields such as mass communication, marketing, organizational influence, and consumer behavior have a longer and much more developed body of knowledge on personal influence. Several studies have analyzed the interplay between personal influence and marketing. Interestingly, most of them have been conducted in China (similar to Inter Governmental Organizations (IGO) studies in the field of public relations) and so *guanxi* is again the focus of attention as a synonym for personal influence. Lee and Dawes (2005) studied the relationship between a seller and buyer and stated that personal trust is key to a successful marketing partnership and is affected by three factors: (1) characteristics of the interpersonal relationships (*guanxi*) between a supplier's salesperson and a buying firm's boundary personnel, (2) characteristics of interactions between these two parties, and (3) characteristics of the salesperson (expertise and status).

The authors posited that "a firm's trust in the supplier's salesperson leads to both trust in the supplier and the buying firm's long-term orientation toward the supplier, which is also considered a consequence of trust in the supplier" (Lee and Dawes 2005: 30). They recommended that greater success is assured when doing business with Chinese counterparts if one treats them first as friends because "friendship facilitates business deals" (Lee and Dawes 2005: 52).

Leung et al. (2005) linked personal trust (*xinyong*) with personal influence (*guanxi*) in marketing relationships. They found that *guanxi* had a greater influence on *xinyong* than on satisfaction with the product (their study did not find a significant relationship between trust and satisfaction with the product). The authors further posited that "*xinyong* positioning will create a sustainable partnership relationship between the supplier and the buyer" (Leung et al. 2005: 551). When coupled with product knowledge, *guanxi* would be very helpful for a strong and healthy marketing relationship, and therefore the authors suggested that multinational companies should hire personnel who could establish *guanxi* thereby increasing *xinyong* and thus helping improve the business relationship.

Lee, Pae, and Wong (2001) linked *guanxi* with favors. Linking personal influence with favors is relevant to public relations because, since the early days of conceptualization about the use of personal influence in public relations, the *quid pro quo* nature of personal relationship building has been highlighted (Sriramesh 1992). Lee, Pae, and Wong defined *Guanxi* as "a particularized and personalized relationship based on the reciprocal exchange of favors" (2001: 52). The authors further stated that these favors are rendered through such things as "preferential treatment in dealings, preferential access to limited resources, and increased accessibility to controlled information" (Lee, Pae, and Wong 2001: 52). They identified three types of *guanxi* relationships: expressive tie (eg. family and relatives), mixed tie (seen among friends, same home-town, same school, etc.), and instrumental tie (transactions between a seller and buyer). They noted that *guanxi* in business relationships usually involves reciprocity and social obligations, further reinforcing the notion of *quid pro quo* discussed by studies of personal influence in public relations.

Arias (1998) analyzed *guanxi* from a relationship marketing perspective and pointed out, among other things, a key element of *guanxi*. This phenomenon functions at the individual's level and not at the level of the organization and therefore, the author noted, "[I]f an individual moves to a different organization or department, the connections move with him or her" (Arias 1998: 146). Arias also noted what has already been established in public relations literature: personal influence is not just specific to *guanxi* and China but to many other countries as well. However, the Spanish author displayed his ethnocentricity when he commented that personal influence is a result of "Chinese culture, institutional weakness, and corruption" (1998: 147). Y. Zhang and Z. Zhang (2006) analyzed how *guanxi* at the individual level translates to the organizational level, assessing the influence of *guanxi* on an organization's financial health and overall performance. They observed that, because of China's political system, personal influence with government officials rather than with peers within the organization contributed greatly to an organization's success. They also observed that good *guanxi* alone does not contribute to the financial health of an organization; advertising, product quality, and pricing also played a role.

Zhang (2008) traced the changes in China's approach to public diplomacy since 1949. Research on China's public diplomacy practice has been growing parallel to the country's role on the global stage. The author noted that "the country's international communications have followed a pattern moving from one-way propaganda to one-way public information, then to a mixed-motive model, or a blend of one-way communications and two-way communications" (Zhang 2008: 305). Zhang contended: "As a public relations tactic, the face-to-face meeting is among the most effective ways to bring about attitudinal and opinion change. In addition, the media-forum strategy bears a strong resemblance to Chinese culture: the personal influence model in Asian countries as outlined by J. Grunig et al. (1995)" (Zhang 2008: 312).

Vollenbroek et al. (2014) presented a model on the role of influence in social media and the relationship to the reputation of an organization. They found that the "impact of social media on corporate communications and reputation can be substantial" and that "a correct and conscious treatment of social media influencers can prevent reputation damage and affect the corporate reputation in a positive way" (Vollenberk et al. 2014: 292). The authors noted certain elements that strengthen the influence of an individual in a social media context, including levels of authority, expertise, and how often the individual's content is shared and responded to – indices that were found to be stronger than follower count. Understanding both the elements that feed into successful influence in a social media context, and strategies for building and maintaining organizational relationships with influencers, is of growing relevance to all types of organizations. Studies such as Anspach's (2017: 602), which found that "personal influence, in the form of Facebook's share, like, and comment features, serve as an important heuristic when selecting content on social media" provide further support for the prioritization of research on the role of personal influence in social media contexts.

Nisbet and Kotcher (2009) showed that personal influence is relevant in the context of activism, finding that opinion leaders have an important role to play both in digital and non-digital contexts in climate change campaigns. The power of opinion leaders is indicative of the influence they hold over relational individuals as well as the value they bring in terms of connecting their network to an organization and its cause. The authors stated that "Climate change-related organizations can engage with bloggers using techniques similar to the cultivation of journalists, developing personal relationships while also providing bloggers with content pitches ..." (Nisbet and Kotcher 2009: 341). Because of the challenges of effectively communicating scientific conclusions, the authors argued that organizations must work to train opinion leaders in message framing and talking points to ensure effective message outcomes.

10 Discussion and conclusions

The above literature review gives us a comprehensive overview of personal influence that prompts one overall conclusion: although it is present in practice, personal influence has been largely ignored by the field of public relations. Public relations scholarship has viewed the profession almost exclusively from a mass communication perspective, which is not reflective of public relations practice. Media relations (including social media where relevant) continues to be seen as a core activity for the typical public relations practitioner around the world, and text books keep reinforcing this notion while completely excluding personal influence.

Further, the literature on public relations roles is often described as focusing on the practice at the individual practitioner's level (and the models of public relations that focus on the profession at the organizational level). That has been a useful way of viewing the two bodies of literature, no doubt. However, roles research has restricted its analysis almost exclusively to the mass-mediated activities of practitioners, such as writing press releases, organizing press conferences, writing annual reports, media monitoring, etc. Interpersonal communication – typified by the personal influence model – has been largely ignored. This lacuna has certainly adversely affected the contributions that public relations scholarship can make to practice. The above review of literature also shows that public relations professionals are often more efficacious not merely because they know how to write a good press release or conduct a press conference. Their ability to influence stakeholders both within and outside an organization in more subtle and very interpersonal ways is often of greater value to organizations. The body of knowledge of public relations will only neglect this at its own peril.

Another glaring gap in scholarship is that mutuality in relationships has almost always been viewed from a group (organizational) perspective (e. g. Hon and Grunig, J. 1999) while completely overlooking the fact that it is individuals that make up the group and thus individual decisions are what end up as group decisions. Trust, another relationship factor in public relations literature, has also been seen only from the level of the organization, while *interpersonal trust*, which often results in trust at the organizational level, is completely ignored. Even in the case of members of a dominant coalition, the literature has failed to adequately recognize influence by individual members whose personal characteristics, such as charisma (or political influence), have great influence on decisions of the coalition and its credibility in the eyes of society.

The neglect of individual influence runs parallel to the minimal attention given to the influence of culture by public relations literature (Sriramesh 2020). Individual value systems play a critical role in all organizational activities, but very little research currently exists on whether and how the values held by individual practitioners contribute to effective public relations. It is in this realm that personal influence becomes a key variable for further study – both from a cultural and an intra-organizational perspective. The body of literature has hardly tapped into how culture affects individual values and thereby organizational activities. The same is true of interpersonal theories and small group dynamics. The public relations literature is eerily silent on the integral role that interpersonal communication plays in organizational communication – public relations.

A misperception that it is something unsavory and unethical seems to surround personal influence. It is often perceived as something done surreptitiously (in a manipulative manner) and therefore not in the "public sphere." What appears to be forgotten is that personal influence is integral to many of the core public relations activities that are assumed to be in the "public sphere," such as public affairs (government relations), investor and donor relations, media relations, issues management (including lobbying), etc. Public relations as a field itself has a reputational problem in that most external to it see it as unsavory publicity-oriented activity. We know that, like every activity or phenomenon, public relations and personal influence can be, and are, misused and abused. Do we neglect studying them simply because they are unsavory or unethical? Where is the normative role of scholarship, then? If the symmetrical or mixed-motive model of public relations can be adopted as a normative model, why not personal influence? Only when the positive uses of personal influence are studied and understood can we harness that information, making both the public relations body of knowledge and practice more holistic. After all, public relations practitioners the world over are using personal influence and so it behooves us to study it and provide ways in which the phenomenon can be used ethically.

The ethics of personal influence is often questioned – mostly by critics from the West who point to personal influence as a form of corruption that mostly happens in other societies, such as Asia. However, a deeper understanding of the concept reveals that personal influence (as in the case of *guanxi*) is relationship-oriented, whereas corruption is transaction-oriented (Valentini 2009; Vanhonacker 2004). That is, in many cultures – not just Eastern cultures as revealed by the literature reviewed here – individual relationships are valued and expected even in business settings. If public relations is about relationship management, why has the focus been almost exclusively on relationships at the organizational level? Aren't individual organizational players the ones that are actually engaging in establishing and fostering relationships that "appear" to be at the organizational level? Relationships are rarely built around bribery and corruption, which are transactions.

Critics have also referred to lower levels of economic development and weak institutions such as the judiciary for the popularity of personal influence. However, as we have seen in the literature review, Japan, South Korea, Singapore, Taiwan, and Hong Kong are thriving economies and have quite robust legal systems and relatively low rates of public corruption. Yet, personal influence is predominantly seen in these economies. As Braendle, Gasser, and Null (2005: 391) pointed out, corruption has not been rooted out in Western societies either. Cases of influence peddling by lobbyists and the "revolving door" policy of officials of government in many Western democracies is a case in point. The myth that personal influence is something that happens outside advanced democracies and developed economies is also to be challenged.

Finally, human beings are also spiritual beings. Whether we are religious in our daily life or not, we harbor values that have roots in spirituality because all cultures have roots in the spirituality of religions. This set of values influences our individual value systems and thereby our activities in organizations. For example, corporate social responsibility (CSR) has been viewed in the literature mostly at the organizational level, ignoring that individuals bring their moral bearings (either from religion or spirituality) into decisions about the CSR of organizations. It is high time that the field focused on spirituality in and around organizations and its impact on organizational communication. In doing so, one has to focus more on the individual value systems, which would be a welcome departure from the almost unidirectional approach taken by existing public relations literature, where the focus has been on mass communication.

References

Ang, Swee Hoon & Siew Meng Leong. 2000. Out of the mouths of babes: Business ethics and youths in Asia. *Journal of Business Ethics* 28(2). 129–144.

Anspach, Nicholas M. 2017. The new personal influence: How our Facebook friends influence the news we read. *Political Communication* 34(4). 590–606.

Arias, José Tomás Gómez. 1998. A relationship marketing approach to guanxi. *European Journal of Marketing* 32(1/2). 145–156.

Berger, Bruce K. 2005. Power over, power with, and power to relations: critical reflections on public relations, the dominant coalition, and activism. *Journal of Public Relations Research* 17(1). 5–27.

Berkowitz, Dan & Jonghyuk Lee. 2004. Media relations in Korea: Cheong between journalist and public relation practitioner. *Public Relations Review* 30(4). 431–437.

Braendle, Udo C., Tanja Gasser & Juergen Null. 2005. Corporate governance in China. Is economic growth potential hindered by Guanxi? *Business and Society Review* 110(4). 389–405.

Broom, Glen M. & George D. Smith. 1979. Testing the practitioner's impact on clients. *Public Relations Review* 5(3). 47–59.

Burson, Harold. 2012 July 20. A 'modern' definition of public relations? Why? The Daily FT. http://www.ft.lk/marketing/a-modern-definition-of-public-relations-why/54-99088 (accessed 22 March 2019).

Chen, Nancy Y.F. & Dean Tjosvold. 2007. Guanxi and leader membership relationships between American managers and Chinese employees: Open-minded dialogue as a mediator. *Asia Pacific Journal of Management* 24(2). 171–189.

Chen, Xiao-Ping & Chao C. Chen. 2004. On the intricacies of the chinese guanxi: A process model of guanxi development. *Asia Pacific Journal of Management* 21(3). 305–324.

Chen, Chao C., Xiao-Ping Chen & Shengsheng Huang. 2013. Chinese Guanxi: An integrative review and new directions for future research. *Management and Organization Review* 9(1). 167–207.

Choi, S. C. 2000. *Korean Psychology*. Seoul, Korea: Chung-Ang University Press.

Chow, Irene Hau-Siu & Ignace Ng. 2004. The characteristics of chinese personal ties (Guanxi): Evidence from Hong Kong. *Organization Studies* 25(7). 1075–1093.

Evans, Martin & Chris Fill. 2000. Extending the communication process: The significance of personal influencers in UK motor markets. *International Journal of Advertising* 19(3). 377–396.

Finkel, Steven E., Edward N. Muller & Karl-Dieter Opp. 1989. Personal influence, collective rationality, and mass political action. *The American Political Science Review* 83(3). 885–903.

Gallicano, Tiffany D. 2009. Personal relationship strategies and outcomes in a membership organization. *Journal of Communication Management* 13(4). 310–328.

Grunig, James E. 1976. Organizations and public relations: Testing a communication theory. *Journalism Monographs* 46. 1–59.

Grunig, James E., Larissa A. Grunig, Krishamurthy Sriramesh, Yi-Hui Huang & Anastasia Lyra. 1995. Models of public relations in an international setting. *Journal of Public Relations Research* 7(3). 163–186.

Grunig, James E. & Ronald H. Hickson. 1976. An evaluation of academic research in public relations. *Public Relations Review* 2(1). 31–43.

Grunig, James E. & Yi-Hui Huang. 2000. From organizational effectiveness to relationship indicators: Antecedents of relationships, public relations strategies, and relationship outcomes. In John A. Ledingham & Stephen D. Bruning (eds.), *Public Relations as Relationship Management*, 23–50. New York: Routledge.

Grunig, James E. & Todd Hunt. 1984. *Managing public relations*. New York: Holt, Rinehart, & Winston.

Holtzhausen, Derina R., Barbara K. Petersen & Natalie T. J. Tindall. 2003. Exploding the myth of the Symmetrical/Asymmetrical dichotomy: Public relations models in the new South Africa. *Journal of Public Relations Research* 15(4). 305–341.

Holtzhausen, Derina R. 2005. Public relations practice and political change in South Africa. *Public Relations Review* 31(3). 407–416.

Hon, Linda Childers & James E. Grunig. 1999. *Guidelines for measuring relationships in public relations*. Gainesville, FL: The Institute for Public Relations, Commission on PR Measurement and Evaluation. http://www.instituteforpr.org/wpcontent/uploads/Guidelines_Measuring_Relationships.pdf (accessed 9 September 2019).

Hou, Jenny Zhengye. 2016. The emerging "field" of public relations in China: Multiple interplaying logics and evolving actors' inter-relations. *Public Relations Review* 42. 627–640.

Huang, Yi-Hui. 1990. *Risk communication, models of public relations and anti-nuclear activism: A case study of a nuclear power plant in Taiwan*. College Park, MD: University of Maryland MA thesis.

Huang, Yi-Hui. 2000. The personal influence model and Gao Guanxi in Taiwan Chinese public relations. *Public Relations Review* 26(2). 219–236.

Flora Hung, C. 2004. Cultural influence on relationship cultivation strategies: Mutinational companies in China. *Journal of Communication Management* 8(3). 264–281.

Hwang, Sungwook. 2012. The strategic use of Twitter to manage personal public relations. *Public Relations Review* 38(1). 159–161.

Jo, Samsup & Yungwook Kim. 2004. Media or personal relations: Exploring media relationship dimensions in South Korea. *Journalism and Mass Communication Quarterly* 81(2). 292–306.

Johnson, Melissa. 2005. Mexican public relations in the United States: International public relations in the pre- and post-NAFTAA periods. Paper presented at the annual conference of the International Communication Association, New York, May.

Johnson, Kristin M. 2008. *Knowledge Management and The Personal Influence Model: An Opportunity for Organizational Enhancement*. Gainesville, FL: Institute of Public Relations.

Katz, Elihu & Paul F. Lazarsfeld. 1955. *Personal Influence*. Glencoe, IL: Free Press.

Kiambi, Dane M. & Marjorie K. Nadler. 2012. Public relations in Kenya: An exploration of models and cultural influences. *Public Relations Review* 38. 505–507.

Kim, Yungwook. 1996. *Positive and normative models of public relations and their relationship to job satisfaction among Korean public relations practitioners*. Gainseville, FL: University of Florida MA thesis.

Kim, Yungwook & Jiyang Bae. 2006. Korean practitioners and journalists: Relational influences in news selection. *Public Relations Review* 32(3). 241–245.

Kim, Soo-Yeon & Joohyun Heo. 2018. An exploratory study of transformed media relations dimensions after the implementation of an anti-graft law in Korea. *Public Relations Review* 44(3). 363–373.

Kent, Michael L. & Maureen Taylor. 2007. Beyond excellence: Extending the generic approach to international public relations The case of Bosnia. *Public Relations Review* 33. 10–20.

Lazarsfeld, Paul F., Bernard Berelson & Hazel Gaudet. 1944. *The people's choice. How the voter makes up his mind in a presidential campaign*. New York: Columbia University Press.

Lee, Don Y. & Philip L. Dawes. 2005. Guanxi, trust, and long-term orientation in Chinese business markets. *Journal of International Marketing* 13(2). 28–56.

Lee, Dong-Jin, Jae H. Pae & Y. H. Wong. 2001. A model of close business relationships in China. *European Journal of Marketing* 35(1–2). 51–69.

Leung, Thomas K. P., Kee-hung Lai, Ricky Y. K. Chan & Yuen H. Wong. 2005. The roles of Xinyong and guanxi in Chinese relationship marketing. *European Journal of Marketing* 39(5/6). 528–559.

Lyra, Anastasia. 1991. *Public relations in Greece. Models, roles, and gender.* College Park, MD: University of Maryland MA thesis.

Molleda, Juan-Carlos & Abubakar D. Alhassan. 2006. Professional views on the Nigeria Institute of Public Relations' law and enforcement. *Public Relations Review* 32(1). 66–68.

Muzi Falconi, Toni. 2008. On the little black book syndrome, personal influence, organizational influence and knowledge management. PR Conversation, blog post. http://www.prconversations.com/?p=380 (accessed 6 September 2019).

Muzi Falconi, Toni. 2010. *Global stakeholder relationship governance.* Gainesville, FL: Institute for Public Relations. instituteforpr.org/wp-content/uploads/Global_Stakeholder_Relationship_Governance.pdf (accessed 6 September 2019).

Muzi Falconi, Toni. 2011. Personal influence model. Gainsville, FL: Institute of Public Relations. instituteforpr.org/personal-influence-model/ (accessed 9 September 2019).

Nisbet, Matthew C. & John E. Kotcher. 2009. A two-step flow of influence? Opinion-leader campaigns on climate change. *Science Communication* 30(3). 328–354.

Olasky, Marvin N. 1987. *Corporate public relations: A new historical perspective.* New York: Routledge.

O'Neil, Julie. 2003. An investigation of the sources of influence of corporate public relations practitioners. *Public Relations Review* 29(2). 159–169.

Ramasamy, Bala, K. W. Goh & Matthew C. H. Yeung. 2006. Is guanxi a bridge to knowledge transfer? *Journal of Business Research* 59(1). 130–139.

Reber, Bryan H. & Bruce K. Berger. 2006. Finding influence: Examining the role of influence in public relations practice. *Journal of Communication Management* 10(3). 235–249.

Rhee, Yunna. 2007. Interpersonal communication as an element of symmetrical public relations: A case study. In James E. Grunig, Larissa A. Grunig & Elizabeth L. Toth (eds.), *The Future of excellence in public relations and communication management: challenges for the next generation*, 103–118. Mahwah, NJ: Lawrence Erlbaum Associates.

Rogers, Everett M. 1962. *Diffusion of Innovations.* New York: Free Press.

Rogers, Everett M. & George M. Beal. 1958. The importance of personal influence in the adoption of technological changes. *Social Forces* 36(4). 329–335.

Schriner, Maureen. 2008. The public role model in public relations: An integrated approach to understanding personal influence in the public arena. Institute for Public Relations. https://instituteforpr.org/wp-content/uploads/Maureen Schriner.pdf (accessed 22 March 2019).

Shain, Barry A. 1996. *The myth of American individualism: The Protestant origins of American Political Thought.* Princeton, NJ: Princeton University Press.

Shin, Jae-Hwa & Glen T. Cameron. 2003. Informal relations: A look at personal influence in media relations. *Journal of Communication Management* 7(3). 239–253.

Sriramesh, Krishnamurthy. 1988. Toward a cross-cultural theory of public relations: Preliminary evidence from India. Paper presented at the annual conference of the Association for the Advancement of Policy, Research and Development in the Third World, Myrtle Beach, SC, November.

Sriramesh, Krishnamurthy. 1989. Culture and communication: corporate culture as a determinant of symmetrical communication in organizations. Paper presented to the panel on Symmetrical Communication for Professionals in Development organized by the Association for the Advancement of Policy, Research and Development in the Third World, San Juan, Puerto Rico, November.

Sriramesh, Krishnamurthy. 1990. The impact of societal culture on public relations: An ethnographic study of south Indian organizations. College Park, MD: University of Maryland dissertation.

Sriramesh, Krishnamurthy. 1992. The impact of social and cultural conditioning on public relations. *Public Relations Review* 18. 103–107.

Sriramesh, Krishnamurthy. 2004. *Public relations in Asia: An anthology.* Singapore: Thompson.

Sriramesh, Krishnamurthy. 2009. Globalization and public relations: The past, present and future. *Prism* 6(2).

Sriramesh, Krishnamurthy. 2020. Culture: The "silent" language is also the "neglected" language. In Krishnamurthy Sriramesh & Dejan Verčič (eds.), *The Global Public Relations Handbook: Theory, Research, and Practice,* 28–38. New York: Routledge.

Sriramesh, Krishnamurthy & Mioko Takasaki. 1999. The impact of culture on Japanese public relations. *Journal of Communication Management* 3(4). 337–352.

Sriramesh, Krishnamurthy & Liu Enxi. 2004. Public relations practices and socio-economic factors: A case study of different organizational types in Shanghai. *Journal of Communication Studies* 3(4). 44–76.

Sriramesh, Krishnamurthy, Yungwook Kim & Mioko Takasaki. 1999. Public relations in three Asian cultures: An analysis. *Journal of Public Relations Research* 11(4). 271–292.

Su, Chenting, Ronald K. Mitchell & M. Joseph Sirgy. 2007. Enabling Guanxi Management in China: A Hierarchical Stakeholder Model of Effective Guanxi. *Journal of Business Ethics* 71(3). 301–319.

Tan, Doreen & Stanley R. Snell. 2002. The Third Eye: Exploring Guanxi and Relational Morality in the Workplace, *Journal of Business Ethics* 41(4). 361–384.

Taylor, Maureen. 2004. Exploring public relations in Croatia through relational communication and media richness theories. *Public Relations Review* 30(2). 145–160.

Toth, Elizabeth L. 2000. From personal influence to interpersonal influence: A model for relationship management. In John A. Ledingham & Stephen D. Bruning (eds.), *Public relations as relationship management,* 205–219. Mahwah, NJ: Erlbaum.

Tuite, Leah Simone. 2006. Public relations in a "jolted" political environment: An exploratory study of boundary-spanning government relations professionals in Maryland. https://drum.lib.umd.edu/handle/1903/3716 (accessed 9 September 2019).

Vanhonacker, Wilfried R. 2004. Guanxi Networks in China. *The Chinese Business Review* 31(3). 48–53.

Valentini, Chiara. 2009. The struggle for recognition: Personal influence model, cultural premises and corruption – Understanding societal orientations towards informal relations. In A. Rogojinaru & S. Wolstenholme (eds.), *Current Trends in International Public Relations, Proceeding of EUPRERA Congress 2009,* 365–384. Bucharest: Tritonic.

Vollenbroek, Wouter, Sjoerd de Vries, Efthymios Constantinides & Piet Kommers. 2014. Identification of influences in social media communities. *International Journal of Web Based Communities* 10(3). 280–297.

Wakefield, R. I. 2013. Personal influence and pre-industrial United States: An early relationship model that needs resurgence in U.S. public relations. *Public Relations Review* 39. 131–138.

Weimann, Gabriel & Hans-Bernd Brosius.1994. Is there a two-step flow of agenda-setting? *International Journals of Public Opinion Research* 6(4). 323–341.

White, Candace, Antoaneta Vanc & Gina Stafford. 2010. Internal communication, information satisfaction, and sense of community: The effect of personal influence. *Journal of Public Relations Research* 22(1). 65–84.

Wu, Ming-Yi & Kwame Baah-Boakyem. 2009. Public relations in Ghana: Work-related cultural values and public relations models. *Public Relations Review* 35. 83–85.

Wu, Fang, Zhuo Chen & Di Cui. 2016. Business is business? Stakeholders and power distributions in guanxi-related practices in the Chinese public relations profession: A comparative study of Beijing and Hong Kong. *Public Relations Review* 42. 867–878.

Xin, Katherine R. & Jone L. Pearce. 1996. Guanxi: Connections as substitutes for formal institutional support. *Academy of Management Journal* 39(6). 1641–1658.

Yudarwati, Gregoria A. 2008. Personal influence model of public relations: A case study in Indonesia's mining industry. Presented to the European Public Relations Research and Education Association, Milan, Italy, 16–18 October.

Zhang, Yi & Zigang Zhang. 2006. Guanxi and organizational dynamics in China: A link between individual and organizational levels. *Journal of Business Ethics* 67. 375–392.

Zhang, Juyan. 2008. Making sense of the changes in China's public diplomacy: Direction of information flow and messages. *Place Branding and Public Diplomacy* 4(3). 303–316.

Robert L. Heath, Damion Waymer and Øyvind Ihlen

18 Rhetorical theory of public relations

Abstract: Rhetorical theory of public relations incorporates centuries of strategic discourse practice, ethical judgment and scholarly inquiry to explain the discipline as the negotiation of relatedness through text. Such analysis considers how organizational and societal citizenship employs discourse (layers of contested and co-created meaning) for the strategic purposes of managing relatedness. This theory presumes that textual enactment, what is said and done, is meaningfully influential to others who engage in layered and interconnected rhetorical arenas. This theory acknowledges that such enactments can fall short of rhetors' goals and may have unintended consequences. Such is the case since organizations, groups, and individuals encounter resistance when they assert themselves managerially, operationally, and rhetorically into communities. Public relations requires the enactment of the strategic operations and agency of public, private, non-profit, and commercial marketplaces. Commercial and public policy battles contest standards of trusted and rewardable organizational legitimacy framed as corporate social responsibility. Thus, the chapter argues that rhetorical exigency yearns for resolution: *Rhetorical theory of public relations entails the strategic textual logics with which communities think out loud in search of the relatedness needed for shared governance through individual, group, organizational, and societal agency.*

Keywords: community; conflict; control; controversy; collaboration; cooperation; engagement; legitimacy; relatedness; shared meaning; strategic discourse

1 Introduction

Rhetorical theory of public relations incorporates centuries of strategic discourse practice, ethical judgment, and scholarly inquiry to explain how humans negotiate relatedness through text. Rhetoric occurs when humans use text to relate to one another in varying degrees of association, coordination, harmony, division, and conflict. Rhetoric is the strategic means by which people co-manage uncertainty and controversy to achieve concurrence, conflict resolution, collaboration, coordination, and cooperation; such strategic relatedness allows people to productively and ethically co-manage self-interest, strategic ambiguity, identification, and collective resource management.

Human association (relatedness) cannot occur without co-created meaning. Humans achieve legitimate relatedness by solving problems, aligning interests, building trust, and influencing (enlightening) choices. Humans use text to ethically and legitimately co-manage strategic dialogue and discourse. Thus, rhetoric is the ration-

https://doi.org/10.1515/9783110554250-018

ale for dialogue and discourse as strategic textual processes that resolve conflict and solve problems in ways that facilitate association, relatedness.

Rhetorical theory of public relations is organization-centric. Representing organizations, individuals engage to co-manage, via public relations, issues of all types through layered, interpenetrating community association: Companies, government agencies, NGOs, non-profits, trade associations, front groups, think tanks, trade unions, professional associations, single-issue associations, media reporters and opinion writers, activists, research teams, and such.

Rhetoric is a wrangle: Statement and counterstatement, narrative and counternarrative, competition for advantage, aligned interests, and enlightened choices. Rhetoric facilitates courtship: Invitation to consider opinionated judgements, strategically co-create meaning, and affect relatedness by identification. Enlightenment results as voices advocate that one issue position and solution to some emergent problem is superior to others. Each of these positives can alternatively be a negative, a dysfunction. Dysfunction cannot be attributed to the inherent nature of rhetoric, but its use, the will and purpose of those who seek self-interested advantage.

Rhetoric can empower and enlighten choice as humans struggle with "onwardness," the navigation and management of uncertainty (Heath 2006) and differences of opinion relevant to public relations (Heath, Waymer, and Palenchar 2013). Organization is collective, the strategic means by which individuals develop and implement relational and programmatic solutions needed to navigate the future. At times monologic, it becomes dialogue once statements encounter counterstatement. Thus, humans contest ideas, facts, policies, opinions, attitudes, beliefs, values, ethics, inclusion/exclusion, power/disempowerment, resource management, and shared (or conflicting) interests in the face of decisional ambiguity, uncertainty, and dissent.

Themes such as these reflect a vast and ever-evolving literature that justifies the rhetorical theory of public relations. Since the golden age of Greece, systematic investigation of rhetorical strategies has addressed why meaning matters in human affairs. Humans are inherently rhetorical because they influence one another. Association requires propositional discourse, including courtship, division, merger, and identification. Dialogue can achieve sufficient concurrence so that plans can be developed, relationships forged, and coordinated efforts formulated and implemented in order to manage contingent uncertainty. This literature critically examines rhetoric, including organizational rhetoric, in all of its contexts, purposes and forms, including public relations.

This chapter begins with a prospectus on rhetoric, its intellectual origins and modern updates, to explain the rhetorical heritage which links rhetoric and public relations. Public relations theory explains how humans in and through organizations (of all types) strategically seek, wield, and yield to influence and power. As community members, people struggle for relatedness in public policy, commercial practices, and legitimate acquisition and use of resources. Enter rhetoric, and public relations, as meaning matters to relatedness.

2 Rhetoric: a prospectus

Rhetorical theory of public relations is contextualized as a means of strategic (dis) empowerment, relatedness through text on behalf of organization. Humans' ability to productively associate requires shared meaning. Idiomatic language drives perception, interpretation, identification, attitudes, and ideology. As Kenneth Burke (1969b: 172) mused, "Wherever there is persuasion, there is rhetoric. And wherever there is 'meaning,' there is 'persuasion.'" Organizational rhetors aspire to bring order to matters of choice through language. Co-enacted sensemaking textually addresses the challenges of interest, trust, legitimacy, complexity, resource management, power, and uncertainty (Ihlen and Heath 2018; see also Waeraas 2009). Consequently, rhetoric supports public relations' role in the collective making of meaning by which societies co-manage community in varying degrees of being fully functioning (Heath 2006).

Rhetorical public relations uses textual means strategically to accomplish rhetorical agency by listening to, considering, and responding to others' expressed thoughts and shared information (Heath, Toth, and Waymer 2009). Rhetoric can create shared meaning, jointly solve problems, motivate issue (choice) involvement, answer questions, voice disagreement, counter disagreement, refine choices, express opinions, enlighten decisions, and enact ontological and existential narratives of civic relatedness (Clair et al. 2008; Clair et al. 2011). Enactable norms lead to and result from rhetorical engagement, preferably by successfully resolving differences, achieving mutual benefit, building trust, and bridging management and sociopolitical discourse (Heath 2011).

Caution: Emphasis on the concept of "text" does not limit rhetorical theory to words. All forms of symbolic action (viewed as text) offer the potential for associational influence. Accordingly, Picasso's *Guernica* served as a critical public relations strategy by which Spain's Republican government attracted supporters as it battled Francisco Franco's Nationalists' coup. The Spanish Civil War (1936–1939) was as much a battle of texts as it was of military strategy, alliance, tactics, weaponry, intimidation, death, and destruction. Picasso's mural-sized surrealistic painting, presented at the Paris International Exposition in 1937, helped publicize the atrocity and expressed moral outrage regarding the aerial bombing (by Hitler's bombers) of Guernica in northern Spain (Xifra and Heath 2018).

Similarly textual, Roman carvers created statues of emperors to instil in citizens and slaves the essence of being "Roman." In the USA, organized citizens (especially the United Daughters of the Confederacy) used public relations to help the "South rise again" by erecting statues that honoured confederate soldiers and officers in the spirit of states' rights. Businesses become part of each community's interpretive textuality based on what they do, how they do it, how they affect the community where they operate, and how that community affects them (Heath and Waymer, 2019).

Rhetorical statements include all that is meaningful and attitudinal in context and situation (Heath 2000, 2001a). Rhetoric enables people to analyse situations, investigate problems, seek solutions, generate and weigh facts (as information), express attitudes, state moral judgment, seek agreement, advocate for and oppose policy positions, co-manage issues, polish and repair reputations, and such. Each of these forms of adjustment constitutes a rhetorical problem relevant to a rhetorical situation; what is said and done addresses such problems, in situation.

Rhetorical strategy presumes the engaged textual examination of issues of fact, value, policy position, and identification. It includes the influential nature of relationships and fosters or harms them. It ranges in scope from detailed, complicated discussions of economic policy, for instance, to short statements and even single words. Single words are richly attitudinal, motivational, and judgmental ("war!" "terrorism," "immigrant," "executive compensation," "global warming," "climate change," "energy," "sustainability," "race," "gender"). Once they signal a rich ideological content, words become ideographs (McGee 1980). As Boyd (2018: 143) wrote, powerful terms, ideographs, "possess the power, almost by themselves, to settle arguments."

Rhetorical problems, generated by rhetorical situations, demand resolution. For that reason, rhetorical public relations is a normative professional practice; it is inherently, collaboratively assertive and capable of facilitating and hampering self-governance by addressing problems as the means of benefiting self, at least, and others, at best. Each statement is strategically asserted to advance an interest or interests as a rationale to solve collective problems. For instance, seasoned lobbyists marry their private interests with what they claim to be the public interest (Baumgartner et al. 2009; Ihlen et al. 2018). In political arenas, organized interests seek to build legitimacy by "aligning the self-interested socio-political claims of the organization with a view of the public interest held by at least some influential segments of society" (Oberman 2017: 484). Rhetors counter resistance by asking which competing solutions serve the public interest best. In doing so, organizations inevitably address which solutions best serve their interests. That question may not responsibly consider the interests of others in ways that achieve trust and mutual benefit, but if it fails to do so, others are inspired to continue the debate, pursue the argument, and vanquish narrow self-interest.

The rhetorical paradigm is humans' eternal wrangle over matters, subjective and objective, that inspire, provoke, and taunt. Each rhetor's propositional statements become part of community discourse as voices co-navigate tensions of discord and harmony. Each propositional statement can correct (or confound) others so as to improve collective thought and enlighten collective decision making. Propositional discourse, advocacy, asserts that one idea, conclusion, or opinion is better than others and, when combined like ingredients in a pie, they make some whole discourse better than each part. Such dialogic pressures pose a theoretical challenge to understand instrumental rhetoric and upon that foundation move toward an ontological rhetoric which explicitly fosters dialogue, discourse, and engagement (Czubaroff 2000).

3 Greek origins and modern updates

Foundations of Western rhetorical theory, strategy, and practice reach back 2,500 years to ancient Greece. Although Greece has been applauded for accomplishing the first systematic use and analysis of rhetoric, rhetoric's technical and strategic nature and societal purpose is as ancient as the dawning of human experience. Although rhetoric is the aspiration of deliberative democracy, it is operable in tyranny, autocracy, and organized intimidation. By shared meanings of sound, sight, and action, humans associate with and dissociate from one another in varying degrees of organization: Family, tribe, community, and society. Even cave paintings are rhetoric.

Rhetoric was "invented" by disputatious ancient societies (Lipson and Binkley 2009) and studied by Greek scholars: Plato, Aristotle, and Isocrates. Insights into the nexus of rhetoric and self-governance surfaced in ancient Greece following an era dominated by monologic tyranny. The transition from tyranny required skills (strategy) of rhetoric and belief that such skills (strategizing) can produce successful joint decision-making. (For a discussion of strategy and strategizing, see Heath and Frandsen 2018).

Aristotle (1954) stressed rhetoric's practicality by reasoning that its strategies could be known, perfected, and applied to achieve sound judgment in matters of (1) deliberative politics, (2) forensic judgment, and (3) awarding of public honours. Aristotle did not see rhetoric as an isolated activity limited to elites, but essential to the ethical, fact- and reasoning-based, passionate, and sound political judgment by which citizens searched for moral truth (Johnstone 1980). For Isocrates (1929), these principles became requirements of citizenship. (For a summary of Greeks' and Romans' thoughts on rhetoric, as applicable to public relations, see Conrad 2011; Cheney and Conrad 2018; Heath 2009; Marsh 2012; Meisenbach 2018; Meisenbach and Feldner 2011).

Greek philosophers' lore empowered the Roman Republic's reliance on public fora debate and administrative law. Rhetoricians such as Quintilian (educator) and Cicero (senator) favoured the rhetorical paradigm of the good (moral) person who could speak (and write) with sufficient probative force of fact, reasoning, and language to influence judgment in service of state interests. After the Republic fell, rhetoric consisted of emperors' self-justificatory statements.

Rhetoric is natural. However contrived, it is not some artificial means of social influence. As Burke (1969a) argued, it naturally grows out of division, courtship, merger, and other permutations of human relatedness. Children learn the protocols and agency of strategic messaging quite early. Recognizing that words can get them what they want, children become enculturated by learning text (language and gesture) so that they can negotiate, motivate, express, and perform dozens of other symbolic acts that are relevant to individual, group (including family), organizational, community, and societal agency.

Greek and Roman rhetoricians honed rhetorical technique into a canon designed to answer rhetorical problems and address rhetorical situations in context. Elements of the canon included invention (selection of arguments to be made), arrangement (ordered presentation), style (language specific to audience and purpose), memory (ability to recall needed arguments), and delivery (techniques of presentation). Eventually, the church used rhetoric to propagate the faith, and the marketplace to sell goods.

By the 20th century, especially to counter tyrants and autocrats, rhetoric became firmly established in USA school curricula: Strategic processes of advocacy, argumentation, and accommodation. Millions of students were taught strategies of evidence, reasoning, structure, language, argument, moral appeals, audience adaptation, and delivery. They learned how to use evidence and reasoning to analyse problems experienced by audiences as the rationale for proposing workable, ethical, and practical solutions. Such principles readily translated into advertising and public relations.

4 Rhetorical heritage

Inquiry into rhetoric arises from the sincere belief that communities generate discourse of various qualities and experience constitutive roles as voices aspire, individually and collectively, to create the ideology and co-enact the communication strategies necessary for self-governance and organizational citizenship. Although individual organizations engage strategically in such discourse, the reality is that they do not own it. It occurs at the will and whim of each community. To define and achieve a fully functioning society, layered citizenry of a society aspires not to be exploited, left behind, or denied access to the means of self-governance.

Although stakeholder participation is constructive, even if frustrating for organizations, social-cognitive space is best when populated by those whose mission is the betterment of society, a contestable matter. Rhetoric cannot exist without audience; it presumes multi-vocality, the interdependency of mind, self, and society, as tensions between the individual and the aggregate. Rhetorical theory of public relations inherently requires attention to the values and voices of society as the basis for organizational legitimacy: Corporate social responsibility (Ihlen 2009, 2011b).

As such, text is normative, constitutive and existential. Individuals, as do organizations, "become" as they take on and enact identity-giving and identifying words that create rhetorical substance needed for association and individual, group, and community agency (Campbell 2005). Words facilitate identity, organization, coordination, cooperation, competition, and even damaging and dysfunctional divisions, relationships, and maladjustment. Rhetoric is the textual enactment of deliberative democracy (Palazzo and Scherer 2006).

Such thoughts in the abstract are interesting, but in application, the relevant challenge is to understand how they empower relatedness of interest alignment and coordinated behavior. Such coordination demands the ability to conceptually adjust minds to the objectivity and subjectivity of organization – a business, industry, or even a university, for instance. They can be seen and felt. But their realism/objectivity is not their essence. Neither is their pure subjectivity, which could assume that organizations exist only in text – shared meaning. By these conclusions, rhetorical theory of public relations addresses the tensions of realistic objectivism (epistemology) and subjective realism (constitutive ontology). The objective of intellectual inquiry (as rhetorical practice) is challenged to "fundamentally redefine both the nature of the 'explanatory task' in social and organizational analysis and the contribution that explanatory knowledge can make to our understanding of and participation in emergent socio-organizational forms" (Reed 2005: 1632). Thus, rhetorical theory, as an normative, constitutive, explanatory undertaking, provides insights into how epistemological assumptions are refined into critically subjective assessments that justify normative morality as existentially relevant shared meaning.

5 Nexus of rhetoric and public relations

Laying a cornerstone on which to build a rhetorical theory of public relations, Ihlen (2008, 2010, 2011a, 2015) emphasized the interdependence of rhetorical theory and public relations as means to understand citizens' (companies' and governments') strategic ability to interpret, confront, and respond to rhetorical problems (Bitzer 1968; see Biesecker 1989). Rhetorical problems result when organizations encounter resistance, both the physical realm (such as drought and other severe weather) and discursively (counter-advocacy and counter-narratives). Strategic rhetorical responses to rhetorical problems supply the processes needed for dialogic engagement (Ihlen 2008, 2015; Kent and Taylor 2018; Theunissen and Wan Noordin 2012). Terministic strategies create, sustain, strengthen, or harm societies (their interdependent, component parts) as collective endeavours.

Using that rubric, Heath and Nelson (1986) studied issues management while Cheney and Dionisopoulos (1989) discussed organizational rhetoric and public relations. In the 1990s, additional rhetorical studies enlightened public relations as scholars (Elwood 1995; L'Etang 1996; Toth and Heath 1992) recognized how organizations encounter resistance to their strategic plans (Phillips 2006). Issue debates, shared views of reality, aligned and conflicting interests, and co-created opinions constitute the rationale for public relations.

In the 20th century, public relations theory became a mix of persuasion (Edward Bernays, engineering consent), humanistic/civic journalism (John Hill), and rhetoric (Cutlip 1994: ix: Individuals "make their voices heard in the public forum where thousands of shrill, competing voices daily re-create the Tower of Babel"). Rhetorically oriented scholars argued that propositional advocacy is the rationale by which public relations is empowered by virtue of influence (Heath 2007; Pfau and Wan 2006). As

Porter (2010:132) observed, "the ultimate outcome of public relations efforts will always remain influencing attitudes and ultimately, behaviour. Public relations professionals are paid to advocate ideas and to influence behaviour."

The rhetorical paradigm is dialogue and discourse-driven decision-making. Dialogue is patterned engagement. Discourse is inherently issue-oriented, choice-based, the textual means by which humans debate issues so as to enlighten decisions in the face of contestable, unresolved matters: The challenge of relatedness. Rhetoric is a situated, emergent process by which humans come to share meaning, relate to (see Buber 1970 [1923]; Heath 2001b) and affect one another. Humans manage relatedness by contesting "a shared reality through the word" (Cobley 2008: 660; Craig 1999).

Given the interdependence of rhetoric's and public relations' roles in societal decision-making, three key aspects of rhetoric help explain this relationship: Discourse arenas, choice enlightenment, and terministic enactment – the focus of the next three sections.

6 Discourse arenas

Rhetoric occurs contextually in polyvocal arenas where uncertainty abides. For 2,500 years, government fora, public fora, religious venues, and marketplaces have constituted arenas. Three hundred years ago media provided an arena. Today, they are being reshaped. Expert voices are displaced by artificial intelligence and algorithms that track topic trends, offer advice, and reflect the popularity of expressed opinions (as news content), but not necessarily for their intellectual and moral integrity.

Public relations assumes that individuals are constantly confronted with choices: Where to work, which organizations to support or oppose, what products to buy, which donations to give, plays to attend, issue positions to support or oppose, investments to make, savings to set aside, ailments to treat, foods to eat, decisions to recycle, candidates to support/oppose, and such. Each choice occurs in an arena fraught with efforts to influence decisions and enlighten choices. Corporations address such issues as means for collective resource management.

Discourse arenas are rhetorical situations that arise in physical places and intellectual spaces where interests are defined as issue-driven rhetorical problems and asserted textually to empower and frustrate decision-making that affects relatedness. Zones of engagement produce zones of meaning whereby people share topic-specific knowledge, values, policy preferences, and identifications (including identities). Arenas are shaped by arguments/advocacy, the to and fro of voices seeking to influence and being influenced, and suffering crises (Frandsen and Johansen 2017).

Arenas include physical infrastructures such as fora and hearings, legislative halls, media of all kinds, courtrooms, scientific colloquia, and even streets where protest is enacted. Arenas occur inside organizations, among organizations, both in public and private. Arenas provide infrastructural means of engagement (such as media, but also the ways themes play out in multi-layered conversations) where voices contend over rhetorical problems in rhetorical situations to address the stasis of choices. Arenas presume that parties, alone, cannot demand agreement or control thought and action. Rhetoric taunts us with the need for shared understanding. Paradoxically, understanding and meaning can never truly be shared but can achieve narrative status by which people concur in the knowledge of their past, understand their present, and address the expedience of future behavior.

Such is especially the case given the narrative nature of thought, action, and human association. Although narratives should exhibit fidelity (true to reality) and coherence (internal consistency), both points of judgment are standards, but not guarantees (Fisher 1987; Gergen 1994). Narratives are the temporal rhetorical structuring of identity, even tribal identity, given historical configurations of relatedness. Narratives define and carry forward interpretations of reality, give life a specific form and purpose, and suggest relationships however competing and incompatible. Temporal plot lines of narratives are inherently purposeful for enactment, but must be strategically reinvestigated for their fact and reasoning, value, policy, and identification implications. Such is the nature of human relatedness.

Arenas are place-means of human relatedness (locus of wrangle), issue-driven means of individual and collective decision-making. The motive of arena is the potential means for gaining advantage, even narrow self-interest. Consideration of one interest forces normative consideration of other interests. To feed themselves, and achieve self-protection, people group together. Over time, natural associations become shared interest. That dynamic can ask citizens to serve (bend toward) companies rather than companies bending to serve ordinary people. But arena(s) can bend organizations to serve people.

Today, organizations create and participate in arena-driven rhetorical means of public relations, such as lobbies and business trade associations, by which "public" interests are collectively defined, asserted and evaluated. Thus, workers unite, as do advocates for environmental quality or civil rights. Financial rhetoric occurs in corporatized arenas. Publicly traded companies use arenas to organize for profit by which to court investors. As financial communication, businesses report their financial status to analysts and financial media. They use their websites as means for information-giving and dialogue. They create and publish annual reports. They engage in hearings and industry-trade meetings. Financial discourse features issue-specific discussion that enlightens choice – to buy, sell, or hold.

Scientific discovery is translated by arena engagements into products that produce profit and suffer resistance. For instance, scientists created bisphenol-a (BPA), which became an arena. Internally, businesses engage to commodify invention to gain financial reward through market value of chemical products. They determine products' efficacy and value (scientific arena A). Beyond corporate boundaries, other scientists investigate issues regarding the health and safety of chemical products (scientific arena B). They engage in laboratories, at scientific meetings, and trade associations; scientists and policy experts contest and support published/reported findings, including position papers by NGOs acting on behalf of product safety (regulatory arena A). Such debate may generate governmental hearings (agencies, legislative bodies, courts) (regulatory arena B). Marketing communication and public media eventually discuss scientific conclusions regarding issues of health and safety. Companies that sell soft drinks and water in plastic bottles made with BPA encounter rhetorical problems as consumer resistance (marketing and public communication arena). Finally, health-issue discussions occur among consumers; as maternal arena, mothers who buy such products prefer caution. In the case of BPA, some scientists warn (scientific arena B) that children should not ingest the chemical above a certain level; safe levels are contested at conferences and in published research. Products are marketed as "BPA-free." As the discourse links of rhetorical examination, issue debates range from "sound" science to consumer caution and marketing resistance (Heath et al. 2012).

Text is a hallmark of rhetoric. Strategic presentation does not presume the ability to control, but only to influence thought and action. Although deliberatively strategic, it is emergent. It changes in context as rhetorical problems arise, come under consideration, and concurrence is sought. The wrangle may address a word ("sustainability"), a complex document (colonial Declaration of Independence), as constitutive of organization (i. e., organized religion, Roman Catholic Church), social movement activism (Greenpeace), or commerce (Apple). It is a tension between bending others to an organization's mission, vision, core values, and goals versus bending the organization to others' interests. "Climate change" is only two words, but they are so definitional, attitudinal, judgmental, politicizing, and intimidating that thousands of words are set against one another to define the concept, analyze its socio-political implications, and foment conflict.

Arena presumes rhetoric is collective behaviour. If not consensus, it can accomplish sufficient concurrence for coordinated solutions to complex problems fraught with uncertainty. As much as rhetoricians (and public relations scholars) might aspire to symmetrical outcomes, they recognize that asymmetry is not inherently evil or dysfunctional because it motivates resolution of problems and divisions. Symmetry can stifle progress if agreement and problem-solution are not properly incentivized to contest vistas of differing opinion (Roper 2005). Thus, each rhetor is itself audience to messages presented. The presumed voice of the "audience" is present in the strategic choices made in each rhetor's emergent address. Statements influence those who make them. The dialogic and discursive natures of rhetoric presume that audiences are not passive vessels but thinking beings who speak back as they are spoken to and with. (Kjeldsen 2016 offers a complementary view of audience.)

Arenas as zones of engagement seek zones of meaning. Arenas create opportunities, challenges, and employment for public relations experts. Rhetoric is not some artificial means of social influence. As Burke (1969a) argued, rhetoric grows out of conditions of division, courtship, invitation, integration, merger, and other permutations of relatedness.

7 Choice enlightenment

Rhetorical theory, and thus its support for public relations, examines the means by which choices become enlightened, including facts and reasoning, value judgment, policy formation, and identification (courtship appeals relevant to merger/division) as identity. Rhetoric centres on choice; it addresses stasis (the point at which an issue turns) in rhetorical situations as rhetorical problems. If choice is impossible, then rhetoric has no role. When choice is possible, rhetoric is needed. Choice-making (even personal thought) requires rhetorical advocacy's capacity to enlighten decisions as variously informed, morally charged, passion-driven, interrelated interests.

As normatively emergent strategies, rhetorical statements provide insights as voices examine how positivistic assumptions are refined into critically subjective assessments that justify normative agency of shared meaning and action. As much as rhetoric is assertive (propositional) advocacy, it necessarily is reactionary and even accommodating in anticipation of rejoinder.

Individual choice yearns for enlightenment. People not only must make an infinite number of choices, but long to make the best ones. The "best" choices are those which are more reasonable, moral, functional, normative, instrumental, and even mutually beneficial. Thus, people may or may not be persuaded by what one voice says, but more likely by sustained discourse processes of statement and rejoinder that address interlocking issues: Knowable interpretations of reality, moral judgments, policy preferences, and fulfilling identities and identifications. Listening to others before and during statements is inherent to strategy/strategizing.

Rhetoric is a means for seeking "truth" and sharing "knowledge" but never guarantees either. Facts should become more clearly and precisely understood as they are subjected to reason through statement and counterstatement, but the assumption that fact is evidence of a knowable word-thing relationship is conceptually suspect. Well-reasoned advocacy can be wrong. Facts don't actually reveal themselves, but demand interpretation. Instead of things defining words, the opposite is true; words define by imposing idiom on reality. As recently debated in the USA, is the Confederate battle flag a cherished symbol of Southern heritage, disempowerment, or both?

In this way, rhetorical theory of public relations presumes that emergent discourse requires continuous engagement rather than uncritical adoption of one narrative in preference for others. As corporate histories are the grist of public relations, those constructed narratives necessarily result from and lead to biased interpretations and distorted moral, critically subjective judgments. Discursive matters of fairness, equality, security, and environmental quality are inherently and eternally contestable matters in search of enlightenment.

8 Terministic enactment

Perhaps the most fundamental textual rationale for rhetoric's influence on public relations is Burke's concept of terministic screens. Noting how an art photographer captured "different" images of the same objects by using different coloured lenses, Burke (1968: 46) reasoned that words intervene between observable things and the perceiving mind. Instead of things defining (word-thing relationship) the meanings of words, words define and even attitudinize things. In naming, words point to some characteristics of that which is being observed and ignore others. He emphasized how *"'observations' are but the implications of the particular terminology in terms of which the observation is made"* (italics in original). Idiom becomes ideology. Thus, poverty is a positivistic and morally fraught condition whereby persons lack material possessions and adequate food and shelter, yet discussants might not readily see the myriad factors that can contribute to systemic poverty in a region. As perceptual screens, words define, attitudinize, attribute, motivate, and moralize – at least. Organizations organize to give voice by imposing meaning on reality, but also encounter voice. Terms such as "re-accommodate passengers" can impose order or be evidence of faulty corporate risk and crisis management. Rhetoric fosters lived narratives however positivistically accurate, competing, and morally just.

If order is the goal of collective action, does the rhetoric of public relations foster engagement that accomplishes or frustrates some entity's preferred sense of order: The paradox of order? The search for order is inherently paradoxical. The paradox of the perfect, the positive, for instance, results because sociopolitical ideology is inherently flawed by imperfection; implementation of ideology invariably falls short of the ideal (Heath and Waymer 2009; Waymer 2009; Waymer and Heath 2016).

What became the oil industry originally only produced crude oil which was used without refinement. Eventually, that industry became segmented by specialty (discovery, drilling, production, refining, distribution). Small companies combined to become larger ones. Once Standard Oil of New Jersey dominated the industry. Then, it was broken into parts because of "anti-trust": New term of relatedness. Players in the oil industry adopted identifying names, brands, logos, as voices of the industry. Employees identified by the name of the company/employer, as did retail and wholesale customers. Terministic screens became the constitutive rationale for the industry.

However grand or trivial, text influences choice as agency; text guides interpretable and interpenetrating points of view. Consider workers' apparel, corporate headquarters, executive accoutrements and compensation, as well as industry idioms, reasoning, judgement, insight, and motive. Environmentalists' texts embrace mother polar bears and cubs. Rhetorically, text reveals character/credibility (image, identity, and reputation), form, and language (including figures of language) as ways of strategically thinking collectively and organizing internally and externally; stakeholders engage textually.

Rhetorical figures are not merely ornamental. They provide the argumentative power of paradox, irony, metaphor, and synecdoche. Terms can be descriptive, normative, and relational, even the prepositions "with" and "between." Figures of speech, such as the master tropes (metaphor, metonymy, synecdoche, and irony) are more than mere ornament. Thus, Burke (1941) proclaimed that metaphor is *perspective*, metonymy is *reduction*, synecdoche is *representation*, and irony is *dialectic*. Figures analyse, judge, express, and advocate issue positions. Humans' need for identity and identification constitute a search for order. Order can be enacted terministically (e. g., wearing corporate safety gear, university colours, or a pink pussy cap). Terms, as narrative, provide an understanding of the past and present in order to predict future behavior. Consequently, they can create trained incapacity (Burke 1968 [1931]) and unobtrusive control (Tompkins and Cheney 1985). Trained incapacity results when organizational text unobtrusively shapes and limits the critical thinking of executives, employees, and customers.

The concept of unobtrusive control grew out of Burke's (1969b) discussion of identification's implications for power and control; it uncritically frames organizational influence. Similarly, Edwards' (1980) analysis of successive forms of organizational control – simple, technical and bureaucratic – motivated Tompkins and Cheney (1985) to use the adjective "unobtrusive" to moralize the rhetorical processes by which "dominant premises" uncritically influence organizational members. Once "dominant premises" advocated by management are internalized, they exert control more assuredly than over-the-shoulder supervision or the structuring of work through technology. The same is true for external relatedness where the company assumes that pharmaceutical products' limitations do not need to be exposed and examined because efficacy is sufficient to enlighten doctors' and patients' choice. When companies foster brand loyalty, fealty becomes agentic to moral relatedness.

Organic flaws of language reveal themselves "through the texture of society" as misjudgements and blind spots (Burke 1934: 330) such as gender, age, or racial profiling. Language can produce trained incapacities and dysfunctional identities and identifications that exert unobtrusive control. For that reason, the critical theory of public relations presumes that self-introspection is the first step in the process of taking a public position on matters relevant to collective interests. Statements become self-fulfilling prophecies that lead to a recursive symmetry in judgment that produces incapacity. Lacking introspection, organizational leaderships fail to achieve reflective management.

With textuality come hierarchies and other forms of relatedness, such as those in (and among) a company, denomination, military unit, university, or NGO. Hierarchies are defined and enacted rhetorically as layered identification, association/ disassociation, and merger/division. Terministically defined normatively, businesses enact layers (chief executives, vice presidents, managers, and employees) and disciplines (such as finance, engineering, marketing, public relations). Narratives guide enactment of organization. Text defines identifies of customers, competitors, allies and opponents, regulators, and such.

Battles over terministic interpretations may be as much about moral locus of responsibility and trust than layered battles over truth. Global warming, which can be what Burke called a god-term or a devil-term (powerful terms that positively or negatively predispose judgment and action), becomes motive, the incentive for people to act in its "name" (Heath 1986). If global warming/climate change is "true," that claim drives some citizens' moral judgment, policy preferences, identities, and identifications to reduce carbon emission. If it is "false," the term becomes a rallying cry to resist government control. Scientific judgment is layered expression of societal value and trustworthiness, organizational commitment to expenditure, engineering prowess, and division, department, group, and individual policy. This hierarchy of moral narrative governs how confidently management supports carbon policy and how well a worker tightens a bolt to seal a joint in a pipe or reports an operational problem. Such governing screens are hierarchically normative, trust-based, infinitely reductive, and capable of justifying blame-placing or responsibility-taking.

9 Rhetoric's contribution to public relations theory

This primer explains how the rhetorical heritage shapes our critical thinking about and strategic enactment of public relations as strategic processes invoked to affect relatedness. Rhetoric's foundational contribution to public relations stresses the role that meaning and choice enlightenment play in how humans relate to one another. Given its emphasis on the normative influence of text, rhetoric provides the strategic and critical rationale for those theories of public relations that presume to address differences of opinion. Relatedness is defined and operationalized by conflict, trust, joined decision-making, cooperation, coordination, concurrence, legitimacy, resource management, character/reputation, identification, identity, and aligned interests, at least.

Textuality enables relational enactments which in turn instruct and justify normative choice by which individuals, groups, and organizations become existential through the acquisition of attributional terministic screens. A worker's identity and identification, for instance, become defined by working, a teacher by teaching, a preacher by preaching, an engineer by engineering. So too, organizations become organized by organizing terministically.

The rhetoric of public relations is never static, but dynamic, emergent, and contingent. It is so strategically complex that it defies reduction to a simple formula or model. It is enriched by the acknowledgement that humans' terministically driven ideology constitutes the rationale for effective organization of all types. Ideology affects relatedness as matters of choice yield to enlightening discourse. These matters include naming and attitudinizing and, as argument, strategic analysis of fact, value, policy, and identification, including identity.

Communities and societies constitute inherently polyvocal arenas. Not all members of an organization, community, or society agree or share one set of beliefs, values, policy preferences, identities, and identifications, but association requires sufficient concurrence to accomplish relatedness. Rhetorical theory of public relations informs and critically judges strategic processes by which individuals and groups influence their own and others' decision-making. Ideally, the role of rhetoric is to enlighten collective decision-making.

The arena shift since ancient Greece has moved the locus of rhetorical decision-making from individual humans standing and speaking in judgement of one another's issue positions, to a time when organizations (small to massive, for-profit, and not-for-profit) compete for advantage in a web of zones of engagement and meaning. Upon this foundation, rhetorical theory of public relations presses on with the purpose of explaining how humans can achieve fully functioning society. *Rhetorical theory of public relations entails the dialectical and polyvocal logics of a community thinking out loud in search of societal self-governance through individual, group, and organizational textual agency.*

10 Conclusion

Outcomes of rhetorical engagement and exchange are conditioned by many different factors, including the negotiation of meaning which can take surprising directions (Hoff-Clausen 2018). The antidote for such conditions is not less but more discourse. Let issues be examined under the light of advocacy and the lenses of power-sensitive analysis to illuminate differences in resources, access, and various forms of capital. Any statement prevails as enlightened truth until it suffers rejoinder and is surpassed. Relatedness, by that reasoning, consists of conditions of conflict, compromise, coordination, association/dissociation, courtship, identification, identity, division, and merger.

References

Aristotle. 1954. *Rhetoric*. W. R. Roberts (trans.). New York: Modern Library.

Baumgartner, Frank R., Jeffery M. Berry, Marie Hojnacki, David C. Kimball & Beth L. Leech. 2009. *Lobbying and policy change: Who wins, who loses, and why*. Chicago, IL: University of Chicago Press.

Biesecker, Barbara A. 1989. Rethinking the rhetorical situation from within the thematic of "différance." *Philosophy and Rhetoric* 22(2). 110–130.

Bitzer, Lloyd F. 1968. The rhetorical situation. *Philosophy and Rhetoric* 1(1). 1–14.

Boyd, Josh. 2018. The truth about ideographs: Progress toward understanding and critique. In Øyvind Ihlen & Robert L. Heath (eds.), *Handbook of organizational rhetoric and communication*, 143–154. Malden, MA: Wiley Blackwell.

Buber, Martin. 1970 [1923]. *I and thou*. Walter Kaufmann (trans.). New York: Charles Scribner's Sons.

Burke, Kenneth. 1968 [1931]. *Counter-statement*. Berkeley, CA: University of California Press.

Burke, Kenneth. 1934. The meaning of C. K. Ogden. *New Republic* 78. 328–331.

Burke, Kenneth. 1941. Four master tropes. *Kenyon Review* 3(4). 421–438.

Burke, Kenneth. 1968. *Language as symbolic action*. Berkeley, CA: University of California Press.

Burke, Kenneth. 1969a. *A grammar of motives*. Berkeley, CA: University of California Press.

Burke, Kenneth. 1969b. *A rhetoric of motives*. Berkeley, CA: University of California Press.

Campbell, Karlyn K. 2005. Agency: Promiscous and protean. *Communication and Critical/Cultural Studies* 2(1). 1–19.

Cheney, George & Charles Conrad. 2018. Aristotle, Burke and beyond: Impetus for organizational rhetoric's revival. In Øyvind Ihlen & Robert L. Heath (eds.). *Handbook of organizational rhetoric and communication*, 455–469. Malden, MA: Wiley.

Cheney, George & George Dionisopoulos. 1989. Public relations? No, relations with publics: A rhetorical-organizational approach to contemporary corporate public relations. In Carl Botan & Vincent Hazleton (eds.), *Public relations theory*, 135–158. Hillsdale, NJ: Lawrence Erlbaum.

Clair, Robin. P., Isaac Holyoak, Theon Hill, Prashant Rajan, Elizabeth, L. Angeli, Melissa L. Carrion, Sydney Dillard, Rati Kumar & Shaunak Sastry. 2011. Engaging cultural narratives of the ethnic restaurant: Discursive practices of hybridity, authenticity, and commodification. *Studies in Symbolic Interaction* 37(1). 135–162.

Clair, Robin. P., Megan McConnell, Stephanie Bell, Kyle Hackbarth & Stephanie Mathes. 2008. *Why work: The perceptions of a "real job" and rhetoric of work through the ages*. West Lafayette, IN: Purdue University Press.

Cobley, Paul. 2008. Communication: Definitions and concepts. In Wolfgang Donsbach (ed.), *The international encyclopedia of communication*, 660–666. Malden, MA: Blackwell Publishing.

Conrad, Charles. 2011. *Organizational rhetoric*. Cambridge: Polity Press.

Craig, Robert. 1999. Communication theory as a field. *Communication Theory* 9(2). 119–161.

Cutlip, Scott M. 1994, *The unseen power: Public relations. A history*. Hillsdale, NJ: Lawrence Erlbaum.

Czubaroff, Jeanine. 2000. Dialogic rhetoric: An application of Martin Buber's philosophy of dialogue. *Quarterly Journal of Speech* 86(2). 168–189.

Elwood, William N. 1995. *Public relations inquiry as rhetorical criticism: case studies of corporate discourse and social influence*. Westport, CN: Praeger.

Edwards, Richard. 1980. *Contested terrain*. New York: Basic Books.

Fisher, Walter R. 1987. *Human communication as narration: Toward a philosophy of reason, value, and action*. Columbia, SC: University of South Carolina Press.

Frandsen, Finn & Winni Johansen. 2017. *Organizational crisis communication*. Los Angeles, CA: Sage.

Gergen, Kenneth 1994. *Realities and relationships*. Cambridge, MA: Harvard University Press.

Heath, Robert L. 1986. *Realism and relativism: A perspective on Kenneth Burke*. Macon, GA: Mercer University Press.

Heath, Robert L. 2000. A rhetorical perspective on the values of public relations: Crossroads and pathways toward concurrence. *Journal of Public Relations Research* 12(1). 69–92.

Heath, Robert L. 2001a. A rhetorical enactment rationale for public relations: The good organization communicating well. In Robert L. Heath (ed.), *Handbook of public relations*, 31–50. Thousand Oaks, CA: Sage.

Heath, Robert L. 2001b. Shifting foundations: Public relations as relationship building. In Robert L. Heath (ed.), *Handbook of public relations*, 1–9. Thousand Oaks, CA: Sage.

Heath, Robert L. 2006. Onward into more fog: Thoughts on public relations' research directions. *Journal of Public Relations Research* 18(2). 93–114.

Heath, Robert L. 2007. Management through advocacy: Reflection rather than domination. In Elizabeth L. Toth (ed.), *The future of excellence in public relations and communication management: Challenges for the next generation*, 41–65. Mahwah, NJ: Lawrence Erlbaum.

Heath, Robert L. 2009. The rhetorical tradition: Wrangle in the marketplace. In Robert L. Heath, Elizabeth L. Toth & Damion Waymer (eds.), *Rhetorical and critical approaches to public relations II*, 17–47. New York: Routledge.

Heath, Robert L. 2011. External organizational rhetoric: Bridging management and sociopolitical discourse. *Management Communication Quarterly* 25(3). 415–435.

Heath, Robert L. & Finn Frandsen. 2018. Strategy and strategizing. In Robert L. Heath & Winni Johansen (eds.). *International encyclopedia of strategic communication*, 1587–1606. Malden, MA: John Wiley & Sons.

Heath, Robert L. & Richard A. Nelson. 1986. *Issues management*. Los Angeles, CA: Sage.

Heath, Robert L., Michael J. Palenchar, Katherine A. McComas & Stephanie Proutheau. 2012. Risk management and communication: Pressures and conflicts of a stakeholder approach to corporate social responsibility. In Adam Lindgreen, Paul Kotler, Joelle Vanhamme & Francois Maon (eds.), *A stakeholder approach to corporate social responsibility: Pressures, conflicts, reconciliation*, 121–140. Aldershot, UK: Gower Publishing Limited.

Heath, Robert L. Elizabeth L. Toth & Damion Waymer (eds.). 2009. *Rhetorical and critical approaches to public relations II*. New York: Routledge.

Heath, Robert L. & Damion Waymer. 2009. Activist public relations and the paradox of the positive. In Robert L. Heath, Elizabeth L. Toth & Damion Waymer (eds.), *Rhetorical and critical approaches to public relations II*, 195–215. New York: Routledge.

Heath, Robert L. & Damion Waymer. 2019. Public relations intersections: Statues, monuments, and narrative continuity. *Public Relations Review* 45(5). https://doi.org/10.1016/j.pubrev.2019.03.003

Heath, Robert L., Damion Waymer & Michael J. Palenchar. 2013. Is the universe of democracy, rhetoric, and public relations whole cloth or three separate galaxies? *Public Relations Review* 39(4). 271–279.

Hoff-Clausen, Elizabeth. 2018. Rhetorical agency: What enables and restrains the power of speech? In Øyvind Ihlen & Robert L. Heath (eds.), *Handbook of organizational rhetoric and communication*, 287–299. Malden, MA: Wiley Blackwell.

Ihlen, Øyvind. 2008. Rhetorical theory of public relations. In Wolfgang Donsbach (ed.), *International encyclopedia of communication*, 4395–4397. Malden, MA: Blackwell Publishing.

Ihlen, Øyvind. 2009. Good environmental citizens? The green rhetoric of corporate social responsibility. In Robert L. Heath, Elizabeth L. Toth & Damion Waymer (eds.), *Rhetorical and critical approaches to public relations II*, 360–374. New York: Routledge.

Ihlen, Øyvind. 2010. The cursed sisters: Public relations and rhetoric. In Robert L. Heath (ed.), *The SAGE handbook of public relations*, 2nd edn. 59–70. Thousands Oaks, CA: Sage.

Ihlen, Øyvind. 2011a. On barnyard scrambles: Towards a rhetoric of public relations. *Management Communication Quarterly* 25(3). 423–441.

Ihlen, Øyvind. 2011b. Rhetoric and corporate social responsibility. In Øyvind Ihlen, Jennifer Bartlett & Steve May (eds.), *Handbook of communication and corporate social responsibility*, 147–166. Oxford: Wiley Blackwell.

Ihlen, Øyvind. 2015. Critical rhetoric and public relations. In Jacquie L'Etang, David McKie, Nancy Snow & Jordi Xifra (eds.), *Routledge handbook of critical public relations*, 90–100. London: Routledge.

Ihlen, Øyvind & Robert L. Heath (eds.). 2018. *Handbook of organizational rhetoric and communication*. Malden, MA: Wiley.

Ihlen, Øyvind, Ketil Raknes, Ian Somerville, Chiara Valentini, Charlotte Stachel, Irina Lock, Scott Davidson & Peter Seele. 2018. Framing "the Public Interest": Comparing public lobbying campaigns in four European states. *Journal of Public Interest Communications* 2(1). 107–128 http://journals.fcla.edu/jpic/article/view/105476 (accessed 15 November 2019).

Isocrates. 1929. *Antidosis*. G. Norlin (trans.). Loeb Classical Library. Cambridge, MA: Harvard University Press.

Johnstone, Christopher L. 1980. An Aristotelian trilogy: Ethics, rhetoric, politics, and the search for moral truth. *Philosophy and Rhetoric* 13(1). 1–24.

Kent, Michael L. & Maureen Taylor. 2018. Understanding the rhetoric of dialogue. In Øyvind Ihlen & Robert L. Heath (eds.), *Handbook of organizational rhetoric and communication*, 315–327. Malden, MA: Wiley.

Kjeldsen, Jens E. 2016. Studying rhetorical audiences: A call for qualitative reception studies in argumentation and rhetoric. *Informal Logic* 36(2). 136–158.

L'Etang, Jacquie. 1996. Public relations and rhetoric. In Jacquie L'Etang & Magda Pieczka (eds.), *Critical perspectives in public relations*, 106–123. London: International Thomson Business Press.

Lipson, Carol S. & Roberta A. Binkley (eds.). 2009. *Ancient non-Greek rhetorics*. West Lafayette, IN: Parlor Press.

Marsh, Charles (2012). *Classical rhetoric and modern public relations: An Isocratean model*. New York: Routledge.

Meisenbach, Rebecca J. 2018. New vistas in organizational rhetoric. In Øyvind Ihlen & Robert L. Heath (eds.), *Handbook of organizational rhetoric and communication*, 471–484. Malden, MA: Wiley.

Meisenbach, Rebecca J. & Sandra B. Feldner. 2011. Adopting an attitude of wisdom in organizational rhetoric and practice: Contemplating the ideal and the real. *Management Communication Quarterly* 25(3). 560–568.

McGee, Michael C. 1980. The "ideograph": A link between rhetoric and ideology. *Quarterly Journal of Speech* 66(1). 1–16.

Oberman, William D. 2017. Lobbying resources and strategies. In Phil Harris & Craig S. Fleischer (eds.), *SAGE Handbook of International corporate and public affairs*, 483–497. Los Angeles, CA: SAGE.

Palazzo, Guido & Andreas G. Scherer. 2006. Corporate legitimacy as deliberation: A communicative framework. *Journal of Business Ethics* 66(1). 71–88.

Pfau, Michael & Hua-Hsin Wan. 2006. Persuasion: An intrinsic function of public relations. In Carl H. Botan & Vincent Hazelton Jr. (eds.), *Public Relations Theory II*, 101–136. Mahwah, NJ: Lawrence Erlbaum.

Phillips, Kendall R. 2006. Rhetorical maneuvers: Subjectivity, power, and resistance. *Philosophy and Rhetoric* 39(4). 310–332.

Porter, Lance. 2010. Communicating for the good of the state: A post-symmetrical polemic on persuasion in ethical public relations. *Public Relations Review* 36(2). 127–133.

Reed, Michael. 2005. Reflections on the "realist turn" in organization and management studies. *Journal of Management Studies* 42(8). 1621–1644.

Roper, Juliet (2005). Symmetrical communication: Excellent public relations or a strategy for hegemony? *Journal of Public Relations Research* 17(1). 69–86.

Theunissen, Petra & Wan N. Wan Noordin. 2012. Revisiting the concept "dialogue" in public relations. *Public Relations Review* 38(1). 5–13.

Tompkins, Phillip K. & George Cheney. 1985. Communication and unobtrusive control in contemporary organizations. In Robert D. McPhee & Phillip K. Tompkins (eds.), *Organizational communication: Traditional themes and new directions*, 179–210. Beverly Hills, CA: Sage.

Toth, Elizabeth L. & Robert L. Heath (eds.). 1992. *Rhetorical and critical approaches to public relations*. Hillsdale, NJ: Lawrence Erlbaum.

Waymer, Damion. 2009. Liberty and justice for all? The paradox of governmental rhetoric. *Communication Quarterly* 57. 334–351.

Waeraas, Arild. 2009. On Weber: Legitimacy and legitimation in public relations. In Øyvind Ihlen, Betteke van Ruler & Magnus Fredriksson (eds.), *Public relations and social theory*, 301–322. New York: Routledge.

Xifra, Jordi & Robert L. Heath. 2018. Publicizing atrocity and legitimizing outrage: Picasso's Guernica, *Public Relations Review* 44(1). http://dx.doi.org/10.1016/j.pubrev.2017.10.006

Augustine Pang, Yan Jin, and Glen T. Cameron

19 Contingency theory of strategic conflict management: Explicating a "grand" theory of public relations

Abstract: Since the 1990s, the contingency theory of strategic conflict management has evolved into its own, and emerged as an empirically tested perspective. Coombs (2010) has described the contingency theory as a "grand theory of public relations" (p.41). A "grand theory" is one which "seeks to explain how public relations as a whole operates"; grand theories seek to explain an entire discipline and "can be adapted to specific areas of the discipline" (Coombs 2010: 41). Today, it is one of the top six theories applied in crisis communication research (An and Cheng 2010). The purpose of this chapter is threefold: First, to reassess and recapitulate the theory's explanatory powers in portraying a realistic understanding of how communication is managed between organizations and their diverse publics through enactment of stances. Second, to explicate how the cluster of variables may operate as organizations manage conflicts through the various stages of the strategic conflict management cycle (Wilcox, Cameron, and Reber 2014) and key takeaways for practitioners. Third, to examine new directions of research as the theory develops and its impact on practice.

Keywords: conflict management; crisis; advocacy; accommodation; stance; conflict positioning; emotions

1 Introduction

Since its founding in the 1990s, the contingency theory of strategic conflict management, as it is known now (Pang, Jin, and Cameron 2010a), has emerged as an empirically tested perspective that focuses on how public relations ought to be practiced – that communication could be examined through a continuum whereby organizations practice a variety of stances depending on the circumstance instead of subscribing to straitlaced models; as a "sense-making effort to ground a theory of accommodation in practitioner experience, to challenge certain aspects of the excellence theory..." (Yarbrough et al. 1998: 53).

Contingency theory argues that the organizational response to the communication dilemma at hand ought to be examined through stance movements along a continuum rather than through models. The stance movements along the continuum would determine the position the organization undertakes *"at a given time regarding a given public"* (Cancel, Mitrook, and Cameron 1999: 172; Yarbrough et al. 1998: 40).

https://doi.org/10.1515/9783110554250-019

Coombs (2010: 41) described the contingency theory as a "grand theory of public relations" – one which "seeks to explain how public relations as a whole operates" and "can be adapted to specific areas of the discipline." Contingency theory has since been applied to crisis situations, and today, it is regarded more as a conflict management theory (see Pang, Jin, and Cameron 2010a; Shin, Pang, and Cameron 2013). It is also one of the top six theories applied in crisis communication research, argued An and Cheng (2010).

The purpose of this chapter is threefold: First, to reassess and recapitulate the theory's explanatory powers in portraying a realistic understanding of how communication is managed between organizations and their diverse publics through enactment of stances. Second, to explicate how the cluster of variables may operate as organizations manage conflicts through the various stages of the strategic conflict management cycle (Wilcox, Cameron, and Reber 2014) and key takeaways for practitioners. Third, to examine new directions of research as the theory develops and its impact on practice.

It is hoped that this chapter can help scholars and practitioners view public relations as opportunities to engage in strategic thinking – the process by which the organization uses an occasion as a platform to showcase, reaffirm, reexamine, and reenact its mission, values, and operations (Lerbinger 1997). This involves an examination of the organization's epistemology, hierarchy, and existence (Seeger, Sellnow, and Ulmer 2003).

2 The evolution of the contingency theory: From the continuum of accommodation to strategic conflict management cycle

Organizational thinking on how to practice public relations has, for years, been influenced by the work of the excellence theory. The excellence theory argues that a two-way symmetrical communication between the organization and its publics, where communication flows both ways before deciding on a mutually accepted outcome, is the best way to practice public relations. The two-way symmetrical model has been positioned as normative theory, which stated how organizations should be practicing public relations in what was regarded as the most ethical and effective manner (Grunig, J. and Grunig, L. 1992; Grunig, L. 1996).

The contingency theory argues that a realistic description of how public relations is practiced is through the examination of an organization's stance. Stance is defined as the posture or position the organization assumes. It offers a perspective to examine how one organization relates to a public through the enactment of a given stance toward a given strategic public at a given point in time in a given situation. It further posits how those stances can change, sometimes almost instantaneously, and what can influence the change in stance (Cancel et al. 1997).

As a core construct of the contingency theory, *stance* is measured through a continuum, which has, at one end, advocacy – arguing for self; and at the other end, accommodation – accepting the other party's proposal (see Figure 1).

Advocacy   Accommodation
|--|

Figure 1: The continuum between advocacy and accommodation through which stance is measured in the contingency theory

2.1 "It Depends"

Under the overarching "It Depends" philosophy, Cameron and his colleagues developed the contingency theory by using a continuum from pure advocacy to pure accommodation to represent the stance movement. The contingency theory focuses on the stance of the organization in dealing with a given public, not the outcomes of public relations practice. In the philosophical statement "It Depends," "it" refers to *stance*, which "depends" on circumstances as evidenced in the influence of *contingency factors*, the development of which will be examined in this section.

2.2 Stance: Concept and measurement

Between the two ends of a continuum are a wide range of operational stances and these entail "different degrees of advocacy and accommodation" (Cancel et al. 1997: 37). The contingency theory, from its formation, seeks to understand the dynamics, within and without the organization, that affect an accommodative stance. By understanding these dynamics, it elaborates, specifies the conditions, factors, and forces that undergird such a stance, along a continuum ranging from pure advocacy to pure accommodation. It aims to "offer a structure for better understanding of the dynamics of accommodation as well as the efficacy and ethical implications of accommodation in public relations practice" (Yarbrough et al. 1998: 41).

According to Cameron and his colleagues, stance moves along the continuum and changes, depending on the circumstances. Advocacy and accommodation on the continuum represent the willingness to make concessions or give or offer trade-offs: At one end, the organization pleads its case and at the other makes overtures toward a trade-off or concessions.

2.3 Contingency factors: The circumstance that drives the stance

According to the contingency theory, the stance an organization takes is entangled with different factors. Cameron and his colleagues identified a matrix of 87 contingent factors (see Table 1) based on public relations literature, excellence theory, observations, and grounded theory (Cameron 1997). The contingency theory argues that any of the 87 factors can affect the location of an organization on the continuum "*at a given time* regarding *a given public*" (Cancel, Mitrook, and Cameron 1999: 172; Yarbrough et al. 1998: 40).

Table 1: Variables that affect an organization's response

1. **Organization characteristics**
    A. Open or closed culture
    B. Dispersed widely geographically or centralized
    C. Level of technology the organization uses to produce its product or service
    D. Homogeneity or heterogeneity of officials involved
    E. Age of the organization/value placed on tradition
    F. Speed of growth in the knowledge level the organization uses
    G. Economic stability of the organization
    H. Existence or non-existence of issues management officials or program
    I. Organization's past experiences with the public
    J. Distribution of decision-making power
    K. Formalization: Number of roles or codes defining and limiting the job
    L. Stratification/Hierarchy of positions
    M. Existence or influence of legal department
    N. Business exposure
    O. Corporate culture

2. **Public relations department characteristics**
    A. Total number of practitioners and number of college degrees
    B. Type of past training: Trained in PR or ex-journalists, marketing, etc.
    C. Location of PR department in hierarchy: Independent or under marketing umbrella/ experiencing encroachment of marketing/persuasive mentality
    D. Representation in the Dominant Coalition
    E. Experience level of PR practitioners in dealing with crisis
    F. General communication competency of department
    G. Autonomy of department
    H. Physical placement of department in building (near CEO and other decision-makers or not)
    I. Staff trained in research methods
    J. Amount of funding available for dealing with external publics
    K. Amount of time allowed to use dealing with external publics
    L. Gender: Percentage of female upper-level staff/managers
    M. Potential of department to practice various models of public relations

Tab. 1: (continued)

---

3. **Characteristics of dominant coalition (top management)**
   A. Political values: Conservative or liberal/open or closed to change
   B. Management style: Domineering or laid-back
   C. General altruism level
   D. Support and understanding of PR
   E. Frequency of external contact with publics
   F. Departmental perception of the organization's external environment
   G. Calculation of potential rewards or losses using different strategies with external publics
   H. Degree of line manager involvement in external affairs

---

4. **Internal threats (how much is at stake in the situation)**
   A. Economic loss or gain from implementing various stances
   B. Marring of employees' or stockholder's perception of the company
   C. Marring of the personal reputations of the company decision-makers

---

5. **Individual characteristics (public relations practitioners, domestic coalition, and line managers)**
   A. Training in diplomacy, marketing, journalism, engineering, etc.
   B. Personal ethics
   C. Tolerance or ability to deal with uncertainty
   D. Comfort level with conflict or dissonance
   E. Comfort level with change
   F. Ability to recognize potential and existing problems
   G. Extent of openness to innovation
   H. Extent to which individual can grasp others' worldview
   I. Personality: Dogmatic, authoritarian
   J. Communication competency
   K. Cognitive complexity: Ability to handle complex problems
   L. Predisposition toward negotiations
   M. Predisposition toward altruism
   N. How individuals receive, process, and use information and influence
   O. Familiarity with external public or its representative
   P. Like external public or its representative
   Q. Gender: Female versus male

---

6. **Relationship characteristics**
   A. Level of trust between organization and external public
   B. Dependency of parties involved
   C. Ideological barriers between organization and public

2.3.1 Internal vs. external variables

These factors were initially grouped into *internal variables* related to the characteristics of the organization, and *external variables* regarding the environment and the characteristics of the publics.

2.3.2 Predisposing vs. situational factors

These variables were categorized into predisposing and situational factors. On one hand, *predisposing factors* include the characteristics of dominant coalition, public relations' access to top management, organizational size and culture, and so forth. On the other hand, *situational factors* include characteristics of the external public, perceived urgency and threat, and feasibility of accommodation. Predisposing variables determine an organization's stance before it goes into a situation dealing with a given public, while the combination and variability of situational factors might shift the stance of the organization over time, depending on whether the situational factors are powerful enough to change the predisposing positioned stance on the continuum.

2.3.3 Proscriptive factors

To understand why symmetrical or accommodation stances cannot be taken at some situations, Cameron, Cropp, and Reber (2001) studied the following key *proscriptive factors*: 1) The morality of top management, 2) The position caught in between two contending publics at the same time, and 3) Restriction from regulation and jurisdictions. They were found to preclude an organization from accommodating or even communicating with a public. It is concluded that for those situations, even though an organization seems to take an excellence or "symmetrical" approach, their stance swiftly changes and moves on the continuum of accommodation based on the influence of those proscriptive factors.

2.3.4 Understanding impact of different factors

As the essence of the contingency theory, the matrix of contingent factors provides a systematic spectrum of understanding the dynamics and stance movement in public relations practices and decision-making processes. The approaches to the examination of contingency factors have been 1) *Categorizing* contingency factors as groups according to the way the factors exert influences on public relations practice, primarily for the theory parsimony's purpose, and 2) Further *explicating* specific factors.

As examples of the first approach, Shin, Cameron, and Cropp (2002) conducted a survey of PR practitioners on the perceived importance of contingent factors and their influence in daily public relations practice. Practitioners agreed that the contingency theory reflected their practice reality and organization-related characteristics were found to be most influential. Further, Reber and Cameron (2003) developed a scale to measure some key aspects of contingent factors out of concern for theory parsimony. Through a survey of top public relations practitioners, Reber and Cameron (2003) quantified contingency theory by constructing scales of five theoretical constructs: External threats, external public characteristics, organizational characteristics, public relations department characteristics, and dominant coalition characteristics. Practitioners cited fear of legitimizing activist claims, credibility and commitment of an external public, and the place of public relations in the dominant coalition as contingencies impacting the dialogue with contending publics.

One example of the second approach is in the explication of *threat*, a key factor that exerts internal and external influence on an organizational stance movement. Closely related to the new focus on the role of affective factors in public relations' decision-making process, threats – both internal and external as identified in the original contingency factor matrix – has been used to describe the state of seizure a nation, organization, or individual is in during a crisis. Given its importance and yet-to-explicate status, Jin and Cameron (2007) and Jin, Pang, and Cameron (2012a) conceptually differentiated threats from "risk," "fear," and "conflict," which are the cause and the effect of crisis. A threat appraisal model was proposed by Jin and Cameron (2007) based on the assessments of situational demands and organizational resources (see Figure 2). Jin, Pang and Cameron (2012a) further proposed the explication of the concept of "threat" by expanding, cross-fertilizing, and integrating ideas from an interdisciplinary review of literature, and enumerated the dimensionality of threats such as duration, severity, and type. Jin and Cameron (2007) found that an external and long-term threat combination led to higher situational demands appraisal and more intensive emotional arousal.

Figure 2: Threat appraisal model

3 The development of the contingency theory of strategic conflict management

Although the contingency theory began as a general theory of public relations, over the past two decades, it has developed and deepened into a theory of strategic conflict management. This focus, starting with Reber, Cropp, and Cameron's (2003) case study, which was based on an in-depth analysis of Norfolk Southern's hostile takeover of Conrail, illustrates the dynamism of conflict management in public relations as well as the proscriptions of how an organization handles conflicts. This was one of the first studies that applied the contingency theory to advance the role of public relations beyond its publicity and media relations roots to a crucial place in conflict management. Proscriptive variables (e. g., legal factors, regulatory agencies) further add parsimony to the theory by establishing ground rules that affect a stance toward a public at a given time.

From that point on, the contingency theory has taken the perspective of strategic conflict management. Conflict is a type of public relations situations where one organization's goals conflict with that of another organization or other publics. Not every conflict is a crisis. A conflict can be resolved, or be escalated into a crisis, thus causing reputational and/or operational damages. Over more than a decade, studies using contingency theory have demonstrated its applications in risk communication (e. g., health risk triggered by public health crisis such as SARS news coverage in Singapore and China) (see Jin, Pang, and Cameron 2006, 2007), high-profile conflict resolution (e. g., Shin et al. 2005), and source-reporter relationship (Shin and Cameron 2004), litigation public relations (Reber, Cropp, and Cameron 2001), threat assessment and crisis communication stance movement (Jin and Cameron 2007), just to name a few.

3.1 Conflict positioning and conflict stance in crisis communication

Cameron first coined the term *conflict positioning*, which is the culmination of sound pre-crisis preparations, such as environmental scanning, issues tracking, issues management, and formulation of crisis plans, and are recommended measures organizations should engage in before crises erupt. Taking this concept further, Pang (2006) expanded on the conflict positioning concept by arguing that the key in organizational strategic thinking to position itself favorably in anticipation of crisis is to understand what factors are critical in determining an organization's position, or what Pang calls conflict stance.

As Pang argued, an organization's conflict stance, or stance, which encapsulates organizational thinking, would, in turn, influence its crisis response strategies during the crisis, leading to outcomes that match what the organization had prepared for in the first place. For instance, if a standing rule in an organization's dominant coalition is to forbid communication with its publics, the conflict stance assumed would be one marked by obstinacy and dogged resistance, or advocacy, as described in the contingency theory. The strategy the organization is most likely to employ during the crisis might be one of denial of, or evading of, responsibility. On the other hand, if an organization is predisposed to a more accommodative stance of engaging publics with the aim of working through the crisis with them, it is most likely to employ "accommodative" strategies, such as corrective action, to communicate during the crisis.

Pang (2006) further recommended that a favorable positioning in a crisis involves understanding, first, what factors, within and without the organization, play critical roles in the organization's ability to handle the crisis; second, based on the influence of these factors, what stance is the organization likely to adopt; third, what strategies are likely to be used based on the stance. Knowing the conditions (factors) that facilitate its reaction (stance) and influence its action (strategies) enables the organization to understand what causes the effects of its actions.

The five key factors that influence organizational stance, identified by Pang (2006), are: 1) involvement of the dominant coalition in a crisis; 2) influence and autonomy of public relations in the crisis; 3) influence and role of legal practitioners in the crisis; 4) importance of publics to the organization during the crisis; and 5) the organization's perception of threat in the crisis.

3.2 Explicating the contingency variables across the crisis life cycle

Scholars agree that strategic crisis management is a dynamic, ongoing process, through a life cycle (e. g., Coombs 2010; Seeger, Sellnow, and Ulmer 2003). Using Wilcox, Cameron, and Reber's (2014) proactive-strategic-reactive-recovery framework, we aim to explicate contingency variables across the life cycle (see Figure 3).

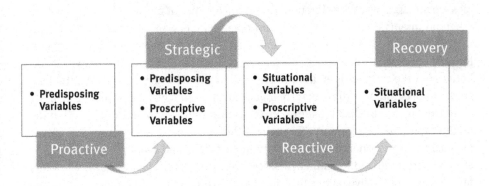

Figure 3: Contingency variables across crisis life cycle

In the first stage of the crisis life cycle, the proactive phase, organizations are encouraged to engage in active online news monitoring and environmental scanning. Here, the predisposing variables are at work. The variables include the size of the organization – a larger organization is assumed to have more resources than a smaller organization; the corporate culture of the organization – an organization with an open culture would be open to adopt new practices; the business exposure the organization has; the corporate communications practitioner's access to the leadership; and the enlightenment of the leadership on the importance of corporate communications. These translate into organizational actions, and encourage the organization towards planning for crisis. At this stage, the focus is to identify, track, and manage potentially conflicting issues online – a crucial part of corporate communications in the Internet age (Gonzalez-Herrero and Smith 2008). Such activities include the development of the company's website, updating important emailing lists and contact databases, a vigilant online media monitoring service, registering all possible domain names, and getting the corporate communications team to familiarize with the virtual world.

In the second stage of the crisis life cycle, the organization engages the online world more actively, identifying and responding to potential threats. Prominent online influencers/opinion leaders are identified; new media technologies such as RSS feeds and Twitter are utilized to establish an online monitoring alert system; a hidden or "dark" website – a site that could be used externally in the event of a crisis to update all constituencies about the issue (Gonzalez-Herrero and Smith 2008: 149) – is created; the tone and language of the online world are taken into consideration; a global mindset is adopted; and an online crisis manual is developed and tested. The authors of this chapter argue that the predisposing factors continue to be considered as part of organizational decision-making. In addition, proscriptive variables assume prominence as the organization considers what factors are acceptable or not in their decision-making.

At the third stage of the crisis life cycle, the contingency theory's situational variables would influence how organizations react to the crisis. These situational variables are the urgency of the situation, the characteristics of the stakeholders involved, potential threats organization faces, and potential costs and benefits to the organization. Organizational actions at the crisis stage include streamlined crisis response for both online and mainstream media, a response from the organization within four hours after the crisis erupts, the involvement of the CEO or member from the leadership to personally address stakeholders, transparent coverage of the crisis on the homepage with a feedback feature, links to third-party endorsements, and tapping on the "dark" site if necessary. Throughout this stage, organizations need to strike a balance between responding to crisis situations swiftly and avoiding too hasty moves that might run into hidden minefields. Therefore, the mindfulness of both situational factors and proscriptive factors (e. g. legal and regulatory considerations) is essential in organizational crisis decision-making.

The last stage is where the organization embarks on several measures to help in its recovery. This includes continuous tracking of how the issue is portrayed in traditional and online media, regularly updating the company's website, evaluating the crisis and reviewing the company's response, and defining the strategies to rebuild the company's reputation. In this, the assessment of situational variables (i. e., how well the organization managed the situation and how lessons gained from the crisis can be used to enhance organizational learning and contribute to crisis preparedness in the future) is essential.

4 Contributions to theory and practice: Important findings from research

So how does the contingency theory inform the practice of public relations? Pang, Jin, and Cameron (2010b) coined the operative phrase: strategic management of communication – in five ways. First, the contingency theory recommends rethinking how public relations can take place – i. e., through the adoption of stances along a continuum instead of adhering to a set model of communication (Pang, Jin, and Cameron 2010b). Instead of viewing communication during crises as the practice of models, with the two-way symmetrical model as the ideal framework, organizations can consider adopting stances, or positions, ranging from advocating its case to accommodating the case to its publics. A model of practice often locks the organization or practitioner into thinking that there is only a set way of communicating when, more often than not, conflict situations are "dynamic" (Seeger 2006: 241). By changing mindsets that public relations can be practiced as the dynamic enactment of stances along a continuum, organizations and practitioners have strategic control to determine how they can manage situations most effectively. It liberates them to think outside the box.

Second, the theory exhorts organizations to engage in strategic analyses before it embarks on public relations practice (Pang, Jin, and Cameron 2010b). Cognizance of the predisposing, situational, and proscriptive variables as posited by the contingency theory would help organizations understand the complex realities they are working in. If public relations is "most effective when it is part of the decision process itself" (Seeger 2006: 236), before organizations or practitioners adopt a stance or position in communication they have to consider how key factors impact their decisions. These factors are critical in reflecting the characteristics, intents, and motivations of the organization (predisposing factors) as well as the external constraints, demands, and realities of a complex public relations situation, especially one involving competitions and conflicts (situational factors). For example, where communication is not possible during the crisis, it may mean that the decision, based on overriding concerns of the organization (proscriptive factors), prevents it from doing so.

Predisposing factors shed light on the decisions that need to be considered *before* organizations and practitioners enter into crisis communication; situational factors illuminate the decisions behind each stance movement *during* crisis communication; proscriptive factors set parameters on why crisis communication may sometimes be curtailed. By understanding the dynamic interactions and interrelations of these factors, organizations and practitioners are able to assess how and why their decisions impact their actions. An example of how strategic analysis can be conducted is presented in Figure 4.

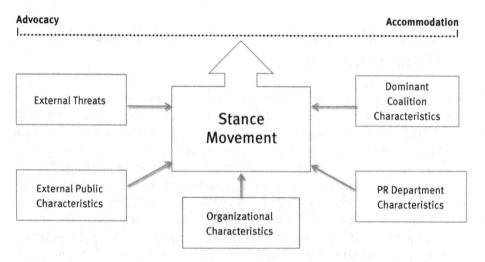

Figure 4: Contingency model of strategic conflict management with five theoretical constructs of contingent variables (Reber and Cameron 2003; Pang 2006)

Third, the theory calls for a strategic assessment of the nature of the publics and the multi-dimensionality of external threats (Pang, Jin, and Cameron: 2010b). It calls for organizations to understand who the publics are, what they want, and how their demands impact organizational prerogatives. For instance, if the organization views the management of publics as paramount, as Seeger (2006) argued, organizations and practitioners would want to take cognizance of the threat involved in the crisis, and the make-up and influence of the publics even as they seek to understand the interplay of factors at work before and as they embark on crisis communication. Thus, understanding the make-up of the organization, incorporating and institutionalizing the involvement of public relations practitioners, and recognizing the dominance of top management collectively play key roles in deciding how the organization should evaluate the importance of publics. Top management may possess organizational dominance, but PR practitioners possess greater expertise to advise top management of the value of stakeholder relationships.

Fourth, while the criticality of the role of the dominant coalition in crises may have been well documented (see Marra 1998; Pauchant and Mitroff 1992; Ray 1999), this is reinforced by the findings of the theory: the character and competence of dominant individuals in top management is one of the most important determinants and constants in managing the unfolding events and the way the organization conducts its crisis communication campaigns, without which a public relations campaign would not have strategic impact among the cacophony of competing voices in the chaotic marketplace (Pang, Jin, and Cameron 2010b). So what kind of leaders are ideal for organizations? It appears that leaders who are involved, open to change, proactive, altruistic, supportive of public relations, and who have been in frequent contact with publics are better placed to lead.

Fifth, given the ambiguity and uncertainty sometimes inherent in a conflict situation (Seeger 2006), organizations seek directions to help them negotiate the minefields while understanding the options open to them. Strategic adoption of stances along the continuum affords organizations a framework to assess the motivations of their positions, and grants them a preview of likely outcomes of their actions (Pang, Jin, and Cameron 2010b). In addressing fluid situations, the organization is given the flexibility to assume different stances to different publics during crisis at a given point in time. Movement along the continuum is never meant to be static. In some situations it may mean having to accommodate, while in others to accommodate on one level and advocate on another, as long as the stances assumed are not used, as Seeger argued, to "avoid disclosing uncomfortable information or closing off further communication" (2006: 242). On some issues, public relations may eventuate on an accommodative note, while on other non-negotiable issues, such as those cited in the proscriptive factors, it may permanently situate on the advocacy mode. Public relations may not always be a win-win situation, but neither must it be a situation where one party wins and the other loses. It is a dynamic process of dialogue and negotiation.

5 New insights for practice and research

Given its nature and major application, contingency theory is a positive theory that describes when and how different types of public relations are practiced and provides a more realistic view of the profession and the "It Depends" reality of public relations practitioners' decision-making process. Contingency theory takes a dynamic view of continuum from the very beginning, in which the organization's stance is influenced by both predisposing and situational factors.

5.1 Introducing emotions in the realistic dynamics

To better understand not only the minds, but also the hearts of key publics, Jin, Pang, and Cameron (2012b) developed a more systematic approach to understanding the responses of audience to crisis situations – the Integrated Crisis Mapping (ICM) model (see Figure 5). The ICM is based on a publics-focused, emotion-driven perspective where responses to different crises are mapped on two continua: The organization's engagement in the crisis and the primary publics' coping strategy. This multi-stage testing found evidence that anxiety is the default emotion that publics feel in crises. The subsequent emotions felt by the publics vary in different quadrants involving different types of crises. As far as coping strategies were concerned, conative coping is more evident than cognitive coping across the four quadrants. Evidence also suggests that conative coping is the external manifestation of the internal cognitive processing that has already taken place. Cognitive coping is thus the *antecedent* of conative coping. Though both the publics and the organizations agreed that the crises were relevant to the organizations' goals, they differed on who should assume more responsibility.

As Jin, Pang, and Cameron (2012b) advocated, audience reception in crises should increasingly dominate crisis research for the simple argument that organizational strategies would be ineffectual if these do not appeal to the hearts and minds of the publics the organizations are trying to reach. Thus, the ICM model, as an extension of the contingency theory, is positioned to understand crisis from the perspectives of the publics so that organizational strategies and responses can be more appropriately targeted and honed.

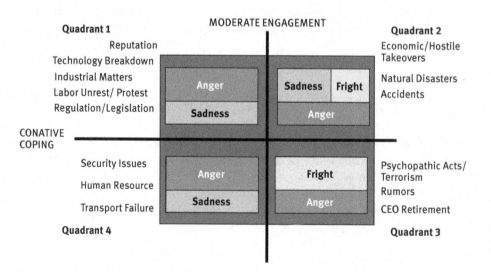

Figure 5: Integrated crisis mapping model

5.2 Identifying and testing ethical variables

Pang, Jin, and Cameron (2010c) unearthed a set of factors, grounded in corporate social responsibility (CSR) and conflict communication literature, called ethical variables that influence the organization's stance before it communicates with its stakeholders: 1) *the role of public relations practitioners*; 2) *the role of top management*; 3) *exposure of organizational business to diversity of cultures*; 4) *government influence and intervention*; 5) *nature of crisis*; and 6) *activism of the stakeholders*. These ethical factors may influence the organization's adoption of an ethical stance toward a given public at a given time from pure advocacy to pure accommodation.

These ethical factors were explored in both the Asian (Pang, Jin, and Ho 2016) and US (Jin, Pang, and Smith 2018) contexts. Public relations practitioners defined an organization's ethical crisis communication as "*communicating with its prioritized publics with accurate and timely crisis information, during the entire crisis cycle, in a transparent, responsible and honest way, which contributes to the overall business strategy and reputational well-being of the organization in the long term.*" They argued that organizations should develop a culture of ethics that permeates the organizations, which makes the consideration of ethical crisis communicate much more straightforward and consistent with the values of the organization.

5.3 Testing the contingency theory in different cultures

So far, the contingency theory has been tested in South Korea (Shin, Park, and Cameron 2006) and in China (Li, Cropp, and Jin 2010), which has indicated the validity and reliability of the contingency theory of strategic conflict management in different cultural contexts.

In South Korea, Shin, Park, and Cameron (2006) conducted a survey to identify which contingent variables Korean public relations practitioners perceived as influential to their practice. Individual-level variables related to the abilities or characteristics of individual professionals were reported as most influential to their practice, such as practitioners' predisposition towards altruism, ability to handle complex problems, communication competency, information use, and personal ethics. The degree of top management's support for public relations was also reported as influential. In China, Li, Cropp, and Jin (2010) examined the influence of each of contingency variables as perceived by Chinese public relations practitioners. Individual characteristics related to conflict management as well as political-social factors were identified as the most influential variables. By forming influential factors and exploring the dimensionality of these factors using factor analysis, the results of this study suggested structural stability of the contingency matrix. Further, the effects of gender and types of organizations were tested on how Chinese practitioners perceive these influences in their public relations practice.

6 Conclusion

The contingency theory has been evolved, modified, tested and improved consistently over the last two decades. J. Grunig argued that when assessing a theory, one way is to examine if "it makes sense of reality (in the case of a positive, or explanatory, theory)" (2006: 152). The contingency theory has thus far offered a perspective supported by empirical foundations.

As a general rule, theory construction is an arduous process, argued Broom (2006). It typically begins with a concept "derived from practice and viewed by practitioners as important" (Broom 2006: 142). Theory construction in an applied field like public relations is made more difficult because it has to resonate with the reality of practitioners.

One of the main critiques on the contingency theory is the large number of contingency factors and the need for a more systematic approach to capturing and predicting the influences of difference factors on stance movement. The interrelationship between contingency factors also needs to be tapped in a deeper sense. Thus far, the contingency factors have either been introduced and examined individually, contributing to the factor matrix, or jointly examined in a pair or so in an experimental setting. However, the gap remains how the different clusters of contingency variables play and interact with each other to influence the decision-making process. Another drawback of the theory, the authors would argue, is that while it is able to describe and analyze organizations' decision-making and stance movements, it is not able to prescribe or determine which is the most appropriate action to take. The last criticism of the theory is that it is not predictive – i. e., it does not indicate what stance assumed would lead to what outcomes.

Despite that, Pang, Jin, and Cameron (2010b) argued that contingency theory was developed to reflect the reality of practice. And even as the insights of the theory are now used to inform practice, the theory actually operates in a continual cycle of how practice informs theory and how theory transforms practice. As the field evolves, so does the theory. The onus is on contingency theorists to continue to capture and reflect this reality.

References

An, Seon-Kyoung & I-Huei Cheng. 2010. Crisis communication research in public relations journals: Tracking research trends over thirty years. In W. Timothy Coombs & Sherry J. Holladay (eds.), *Handbook of Crisis Communication*, 65–90. Malden, MA: Wiley-Blackwell.

Broom, Glen M. 2006. An open system approach to building theory in public relations. *Journal of Public Relations Research* 18(2). 141–150.

Cameron, Glen T. 1997. The contingency theory of conflict management in public relations. *Proceedings of the Norwegian Information Service*. Oslo, Norway.

Cameron, Glen T., Fritz Cropp & Bryan H. Reber. 2001. Getting past platitudes: Factors limiting accommodation in public relations. *Journal of Communication Management* 5(3). 242–261.

Cancel, Amanda E., Glen T. Cameron, Lynne M. Sallot & Michael A. Mitrook, 1997. It depends: A contingency theory of accommodation in public relations. *Journal of Public Relations Research* 9(1). 31–63.

Cancel, Amanda E., Michael A. Mitrook & Glen T. Cameron. 1999. Testing the contingency theory of accommodation in public relations. *Public Relations Review* 25(2). 171–197.

Coombs, W. Timothy. 2010. Parameters for crisis communication. In W. Timothy Coombs & Shelly J. Holladay (eds.), *Handbook of Crisis Communication* 17–53. Malden, MA: Wiley-Blackwell.

Gonzalez-Herrero, Alfonso & Suzanne Smith. 2008. Crisis communications management on the Web: How Internet-based technologies are changing the way public relations professionals handle business crises. *Journal of Contingencies and Crisis Management* 16(3). 143–153.

Grunig, James E. 2006. Furnishing the edifice: Ongoing research on public relations as strategic management function. *Journal of Public Relations Research* 18(2). 151–176.

Grunig, James E. & Larissa A. Grunig. 1992. Models of public relations and communications. In James E. Grunig (ed.), *Excellence in public relations and communication management*, 285–326. Hillsdale, NJ: Lawrence Erlbaum Associates.

Grunig, Larissa A. 1996. Public relations. In Michael B. Salwen & Don W. Stacks (eds.), *An integrated approach to communication theory and research*, 459–477. Mahwah, NJ: Lawrence Erlbaum Associates.

Jin, Yan & Glen T. Cameron. 2007. The effects of threat type and duration on public relations practitioner's cognitive, affective, and conative responses in crisis situations. *Journal of Public Relations Research* 19(3). 255–281.

Jin, Yan, Augustine Pang & Glen T. Cameron. 2006. Strategic communication in crisis governance: Singapore's management of the SARS crisis. *Copenhagen Journal of Asian Studies* 23. 81–104.

Jin, Yan, Augustine Pang & Glen T. Cameron. 2007. Different means to the same end: A comparative contingency analyses of Singapore and China's management of the severe acute respiratory syndrome (SARS) crisis. *Journal of International Communication* 13(1). 39–70.

Jin, Yan, Augustine Pang & Glen T. Cameron. 2012a. Pre-Crisis Threat Assessment: A Cognitive Appraisal Approach to Understanding of the Faces and Fabric of Threats Faced by Organizations. In Bolanie Olaniran, David E. Williams & W. Timothy Coombs (eds.). *Pre Crisis Management: Preparing for the inevitable*, 125–143. New York: Peter Lang.

Jin, Yan, Augustine Pang & Glen T. Cameron. 2012b. Toward a Publics-Driven, Emotion-Based Conceptualization in Crisis Communication: Unearthing Dominant Emotions in Multi-Staged Testing of the Integrated Crisis Mapping (ICM) Model. *Journal of Public Relations Research* 24. 266–298.

Jin, Yan, Augustine Pang & Joshua Smith. 2018. Crisis communication and ethics: The role of public relations. *Journal of Business Strategy* 39(1). 43–52.

Lerbinger, Otto. 1997. *The crisis manager.* Mahwah, NJ: Lawrence Erlbaum Associates.

Li, Chunxiao, Fritz Cropp & Yan Jin. 2010. Identifying Key Influencers of Chinese PR Professionals' Strategic Conflict Management Practice: A National Survey on 86 Contingent Factors in Chinese Context. *Public Relations Review* 36(3). 249–255.

Marra, Francis J. 1998. Crisis communication plans: Poor predictors of excellent crisis public Relations. *Public Relations Review* 24(4). 461–484.

Pang, Augustine. 2006. *Conflict positioning in crisis communication: Integrating contingency stance with image repair strategies.* Columbia, MO: University of Missouri doctoral dissertation.

Pang, Augustine, Yan Jin & Glen T. Cameron. 2006. Do we stand on common ground? A threat appraisal model for terror alerts issued by the Department of Homeland Security. *Journal of Contingencies and Crisis Management* 14(2). 82–96.

Pang, Augustine, Yan Jin & Glen T. Cameron. 2010a. Contingency Theory of Strategic Conflict Management: Directions for the Practice of Crisis Communication from a Decade of Theory Development, Discovery and Dialogue. In W. Timothy Coombs & Shelley J. Holladay (eds.), *Handbook of Crisis Communication*, 527–549. Malden, MA: Wiley-Blackwell.

Pang, Augustine, Yan Jin & Glen T. Cameron. 2010b. Strategic Management of Communication: Insights from the Contingency Theory of Strategic Conflict Management. In Robert L. Heath (ed.), *Sage Handbook of Public Relations*, 17–34. Thousand Oaks, CA: Sage.

Pang, Augustine, Yan Jin & Glen T. Cameron. 2010c. Contingency theory of Strategic Conflict Management: Unearthing factors that influence ethical elocution in crisis communication. *Proceedings of the 13ᵗʰ International Public Relations Research Conference*, 554–573. https://www.iprrc.org/proceedings (accessed 17 March 2020).

Pang, Augustine, Yan Jin & Benjamin Ho. 2016. How crisis managers define ethical crisis communication in Singapore: Identifying organizational factors that influence adoption of ethical stances. *Media Asia* 43(3–4). 191–207.

Pauchant, Thierry C. & Ian I. Mitroff. 1992. *Transforming the crisis-prone organization*. San Francisco: Jossey-Bass.

Ray, Sally J. 1999. *Strategic communication in crisis management*. Westport, CI: Quorum.

Reber, Bryan H., Fritz Cropp & Glen T. Cameron. 2001. Mythic battles: Examining the lawyer-public relations counselor dynamic. *Journal of Public Relations Research* 13(3). 187–218.

Reber, Bryan H., Fritz Cropp & Glen T. Cameron. 2003. Impossible odds: Contributions of legal counsel and public relations practitioners in a hostile bid for Conrail Inc. by Norfolk Southern Corporation. *Journal of Public Relations Research* 15(1). 1–25.

Reber, Bryan H. & Glen T. Cameron. 2003. Measuring contingencies: Using scales to measure public relations practitioner limits to accommodation. *Journalism and Mass Communication Quarterly* 80(2). 431–446.

Seeger, Matthew W. 2006. Best practices in crisis communications. *Journal of Applied Communication Research* 34(3). 232–244.

Seeger, Matthew W., Timothy L. Sellnow & Robert R. Ulmer. 2003. *Communication and organizational crisis*. Westport, CI: Praegar.

Shin, Jae-Hwa & Glen T. Cameron. 2004. Conflict measurements: Analysis of simultaneous inclusion in roles, values, independence, attitudes, and dyadic adjustment. *Public Relations Review* 30(4). 401–410.

Shin, Jae-Hwa, Glen T. Cameron & Fritz Cropp. 2002. Asking what matters most: A national survey of PR professional response to the contingency model. Paper presented at AEJMC, Miami, FL, 7–10 August.

Shin, Jae-Hwa, I-Huei Cheng, Yan Jin & Glen T. Cameron. 2005. Going head to head: Content analysis of high profile conflicts as played out in the press. *Public Relations Review* 31(3). 399–406.

Shin, Jae-Hwa, Augustine Pang & Glen T. Cameron. 2013. Embracing the Strategic Management of Conflict: A Twenty-Year Review of Contingency Theory in Public Relations. In Melike A. Yamanoğlu & B. Pinar Özdemir (eds.), *Halkla İlişkilerin Kazancı Geçmiş Eğilimler Yeni Yönelimler* [Public relations: past trends, new trends], 145–160. Ankara, Turkey: De Ki Basim Yayim.

Shin, Jae-Hwa, Jongmin Park & Glen T. Cameron. 2006. Contingent factors: Modeling generic public relations practice in South Korea. *Public Relations Review* 32. 184–185.

Wilcox, Dennis L., Glen T. Cameron & Bryan H. Reber. 2014. *Public Relations strategies and tactics*. Boston: Allyn & Bacon.

Yarbrough, C. Richard, Glen T. Cameron, Lynne M. Sallot & Allison McWilliams. 1998. Tough calls to make: Contingency theory and the Centennial Olympic Games. *Journal of Communication Management* 3(1). 39–56.

Suwichit (Sean) Chaidaroon and Jenny Zhengye Hou

20 Global public relations: Multi-paradigmatic perspectives, key approaches and future directions

Abstract: To trace the trajectory of global public relations scholarship, this chapter provides an overview of four emerging approaches to understanding public relations in a global context: the Political Economy perspective, the Circuit of Culture model, the Culture-Centred approach, and the Cultural Flows framework. The central tenets, premises, and practical implications of each approach are illustrated. This outline of global public relations scholarship also highlights the fact that public relations practices involve meaning-making, discourse production, and relationship-building, and thus global public relations should expand its scope to include multi-disciplinary perspectives such as political economy, cultural studies, and postcolonialism. By acknowledging the dialectical interplay between globalisation and public relations, this chapter argues that global public relations is both a product of globalisation and an agent that produces economic, political and socio-cultural flows of globalisation.

Keywords: global public relations; political economy; circuit of culture; postcolonialism; cultural flows

1 Introduction

As a managerial profession, public relations practitioners need to manage adeptly the processes of meaning-making and relationship-building with global publics. Hence, global public relations has emerged as a growing body of scholarship because of both increasing research interest and the practical demands of public relations (PR) in multinational agencies, transnational corporations, and international PR associations (e. g., European Monitor Communication, Global Alliance). Initially influenced by US-originated concepts, theories, and principles, mainstream global public relations scholarship is characterised by a tendency towards developing-region or country-specific international public relations scholarship, ranging from European (e. g., Verhoeven et al. 2012; Zerfass et al. 2011), Middle Eastern (e. g., Al-Kandari and Gaither 2011; Kirat 2005), African (e. g., Naude, Froneman, and Atwood 2004; Niemann-Struweg and Meintjes 2008), Oceanian (e. g., Macnamara 2016; Motion and Leitch 1996) and Asian countries (e. g., Chen and Culbertson 2003; Rhee 2002). Among these international public relations studies, a common practice is to apply or test the US-introduced models in non-US contexts in order to seek "best practices" or "generic principles" for global public relations.

https://doi.org/10.1515/9783110554250-020

However, this country-based international public relations scholarship has been vigorously challenged by critical PR scholars (e. g., Edwards and Hodges 2011; Motion and Weaver 2005), who distinguish international PR from global PR in two main aspects (Rittenhofer and Valentini 2015). First, international public relations focuses on studying PR in different geographic locations, which are deemed to be part of a picture of global PR. Instead, global public relations aims to examine how global forces, networks, and dynamics shape public relations not only in a specific country, but also in multinational corporations, institutions and international organisations. Second, through linking or extending US models to non-US contexts, international PR scholarship has reinforced the hegemonic influence of US-centric models, theories, and principles, thus contributing to an ethnocentric view of what PR is or is not. On the contrary, global PR encourages the examination of indigenous culture and local practices that could have otherwise been dismissed in the process of internationalising PR by using US models as a global benchmark or framework.

Bardhan and Weaver (2011) call for a more holistic perspective of studying global public relations, because they have identified three major gaps in the extant body of PR knowledge. First, the current field does not carefully consider globalisation in its full complexities, leaving the phenomenon untheorised and politicised. Second, as culture is becoming more deterritorialised and fragmented, global public relations research needs to address the transnational flows and multicultural PR practices more comprehensively (Rittenhofer and Valentini 2015). Third, diverse paradigmatic approaches to global PR are needed to add nuanced knowledge to this area. Particularly, cautions have been raised as the research tradition of "international" public relations has become predominantly functionalist, organisation-centric, and less culturally oriented (Macnamara 2012).

Against this backdrop, this chapter reviews global public relations scholarship through a dialectical approach to understanding public relations as both a product of globalisation, whereby global economies, politics, technologies and social cultures conjointly shape the identity of PR at a local level, and as an agent of producing globalisation, whereby PR reshapes and drives global flows of economies, politics, technologies, and cultures. Four theoretical perspectives of global public relations have emerged from the recent scholarship and literature:

- A normative approach to global PR, represented by Sriramesh's system perspective based on the interaction of political and economic factors. Through interpreting culture as fixed (located within a nation), objective (identifiable and able to be learnt), and unitary (simplified single version of culture), this approach seeks to explore a broad range of political, economic, and socio-cultural impacts on PR theories, practices, and education (Sriramesh 2009; Sriramesh and Verčič 2009b, 2012).
- A critical cultural approach to global PR, represented by Curtin and Gaither's Circuit of Culture model. Based on a constructivist interpretation of culture, this

approach views global PR as both a site and a vehicle of the production, consumption, circulation, and representation of meaning (Curtin and Gaither 2007).

– A postcolonial approach to global PR, represented by Dutta and his colleagues' social change work (Dutta 2011, 2016; Dutta, Ban, and Pal 2012; Dutta and Pal 2011). While underscoring the history of western theoretical, methodological and cultural domination in the study of public relations, a postcolonial perspective attends to the local resistance to hegemony and the resulting changes and transformations in the process of globalisation.

– A cultural flow approach to global PR, represented by Edwards' (2016, 2018) globalisation framework and Rittenhofer and Valentini's (2015) "practice turn". Built on Appadurai's (1996) five global cultural flows, this approach calls to "unmanage" PR but embraces the complexity, unpredictability, and dynamics of global PR that emerge from various dialectics such as local vs. global, mobility vs. fixity, and hegemony vs. resistance.

Before we delve into great potential offered by each approach to global PR, it is worth clarifying the links between the four approaches. Even though there is no clear-cut timeline for the emergence of the four approaches, Sriramesh's political economy approach appears to be mostly adopted in mainstream global PR studies as it seeks normative practices applicable to global contexts. The other three approaches emerged as criticisms of the dominant approach to global PR. Considering that Sriramesh's political economy approach has mainly targeted PR practices, scholars tend to regard it as a "theory" *of* public relations. Nevertheless, the other three approaches have drawn on theories from anthropology, sociology, and cultural studies to expand the horizon and scope of global PR theory-building. In other words, they offer theories *for* global PR. Additionally, differing from Sriramesh's normative approach that implies how PR "should" be practised in specific cultural contexts (Valentini 2019), the other three approaches appear to be reflective and discursive as they serve as lenses to capture the contingence and fluidity of PR practices in the globalisation process.

To facilitate a comprehensive understanding of the four emerging approaches, what is detailed next is a brief overview of the dominant global public relations theory followed by an illustration of each alternative theoretical approach with its core assumptions, main tenets, and applications in real-world global PR practices. The chapter will conclude with reflections on these emerging trends of global public relations theory-building and their informed future research directions.

2 A brief overview of the dominant global PR theory

Historically, global public relations research emerged in the 1990s in attempts to high-light the influence of national cultures on PR practices (Sriramesh and Verčič 2012). This country-specific international public relations scholarship could be traced back to J. Grunig and his colleagues' landmark Excellence Study, supported by the International Association of Business Communicators (IABC) in 1985 (Dozier, Grunig, L. and Grunig, J. 1995; Grunig, J. 1992; Grunig, L., Grunig, J. and Dozier 2002). Based on investigating over 300 organisations across three countries including the USA, UK, and Canada, these authors proposed the *Excellence Theory of Public Relations*, outlining best-practice principles of public relations applicable on a global scale.

Specifically, Excellence Theory posits that public relations should function at the top management level of an organisation to maximise organisational effectiveness. The crux of the theory advocates a two-way symmetrical model of communication, through which organisations engage in dialogue with stakeholders to build equal and mutually benefical relationships. In particular, Excellence Theory encourages public relations to proactively manage issues from activists and accordingly adjust organisational policies. Efficacious public relations can only be achieved in organisations with participative cultures and less stratified structures. In addition, Excellence Theory promotes diversity, especially enhancing the status of women in the female-dominated profession of PR (Grunig, J. 1992).

On the basis of the above generic principles of PR practices, scholars (e. g. Bowen 2005; Verčič, Grunig, L. and Grunig, J. 1996) endeavoured to add a final principle of ethics and integrity to excellent public relations. They believe that, no matter in what contexts public relations is implemented, a strong organisational commitment to ethical decision-making is the cornerstone of public relations excellence. For example, Bowen (2005: 308) points out that organisations with a rigorous ethics training program and codified decision-making paradigm perform better than those simply desiring to be ethical without investing resources in defining, training, and analysing ethics.

Excellence Theory, along with its subsequent development, has been widely recognised as a mainstream global PR theory and thus been tested in other parts of the world over many years. As Botan and Hazleton (2006: 6) reflect, this dominant theory has "probably done more to develop PR scholarship than any other single school of thought". Excellence Theory provides normative yet concrete guidelines for global PR practices transcending various national, institutional, and organisational contexts. Globally, it enhances the value and legitimacy of public relations through explaining how PR contributes to achieving organisational strategic objectives.

However, it is also the overemphasis on "what" ought to be excellent PR that sparks wide debates and criticisms over Excellence Theory. For example, those international PR studies applying Excellence Theory assume a one-size-fits-all model, and narrowly define "culture" as static "national culture", which is mechanically measured by Hofstede's (1984) four cultural dimensions (i.e., power distance, collectivism/individualm, masculinism/feminism, long-term/short-term). These international public relations studies fail to capture the complexity and dynamics of public relations travelling in multinational contexts (Kenny 2016). Instead of being a quantifiable construct, culture is a multifaceted concept and even holds nuanced meanings among homogeneous cultural groups (Martin and Nakayama 2006). Therefore, it is necessary to build resilient global public relations theories that equip PR practitioners with strategies to cope with multicultural challenges more effectively (Kent and Taylor 2011). What follows next are the four emerging approaches that offer alternative understandings of global public relations.

2.1 A normative approach to global public relations: *The political economy approach*

To fill the research gap from the Excellence Theory tradition, Sriramesh and his colleagues developed a more comprehensive and systematic approach to incorporating political and economic factors in global public relations scholarship (Sriramesh and Verčič 2009b). The primary research effort of these authors was to systematically identify environmental variables that should help us understand PR practices in different countries (Sriramesh and Verčič 2001) and avoid ethnocentrism at the same time. Hence, they adopted a broader definition of culture by incorporating political, economic, and organisational parameters, media systems, and the level of activism, rather than defining national culture as a monolithic whole as Excellence Study does. This approach is, therefore, often referred to as the political economy approach to global public relations.

For instance, Braun (2007) studied the practice of public relations in Bulgaria, focusing on the effects of that country's political environment, and found that a country's political history, the pervading political-philosophical climate, the effects of economic policies created by political bodies, and the effects of political geography heavily influence public relations practices. Additionally, while the political system may be an important environmental factor, media, societal, and activist cultures also influence the practice of public relations in each country. Dhanesh and Sriramesh (2018), for instance, studied a Nestlé food-scare crisis, in which their noodles were found to have monosodium glutamate as an ingredient. Through their analysis, Dhanesh and Sriramesh (2018) concluded that this multinational corporation struggled to cope with the unique media system, the activist pressure, and the vagaries of regulatory enforcement, not to speak of cultural nationalism.

The unique contribution of this political economy approach lies in the fact that it acknowledges the interplay between organisations and publics, with the focus on conflicts, negotiation of expectations, and constraints, by considering the social, economic, and political contexts in which all relevant parties are operating (Duhe and Sriramesh 2009). With this line of inquiry, more conceptualisation efforts and empirical studies have been conducted to investigate and concretely define cultural factors in this political economy framework. The three apparent ones are the economic culture, media culture, and activism culture in each society.

First, to analyse the economic culture of a society, Sriramesh and Duhe (2009) propose that we look into the primary purpose of nation's economic activity and the role of the state in the economy, as well as the structure of the corporate and civil sectors contributing to the economy. For instance, economic activity may vary from driving agricultural sectors, improving gross domestic products, and reducing income gaps to driving digital economy. Yet, these economic activities are driven by the state, the civil sector, and the corporate sector, which should be taken into consideration. Second, to analyse media culture in a society, three factors must be considered: media control, media diffusion, and media access (Sriramesh and Verčič 2009a). PR practitioners in a global context need to identify who influences the media content and the extent to which media are actually consumed by people in the society. Finally, the level of activism in each society plays an important role in global public relations practices. Kim and Sriramesh (2009) attempt to identify the interplay between cultures and activism and conclude that societies with pluralistic political systems and free media that encourage individualism among their populations tend to have a higher level of activism in their communities.

The intersection of economic culture, media culture, and activism culture at least allows us to deviate from the one-size-fits-all approach to global public relations, in that each society could be considered unique and simple national culture alone cannot determine effective global public relations practices. This framework certainly serves as a parsimonious theory for PR practitioners who need to communicate with global stakeholders. Yet, when considered carefully, the political economy approach still implies the differentiation between East and West based on criteria or categories of cultures (i. e. economic development, media, and activism) in this tradition of theoretical development.

2.2 A critical cultural approach to global public relations: *The Circuit of Culture Model*

The second approach to studying and understanding global public relations is based on a constructionist worldview. This critical cultural approach focuses on meaning-making, negotiation, and circulation through various PR activities and practices on a global scale. As Curtin and Gaither (2007: 35) define it, culture is the "process by which meaning is produced, circulated, consumed, commodified, and endlessly reproduced and renegotiated in society". Drawing on du Gay et al.'s (1997) cultural studies, Curtin and Gaither (2007) first introduce the Circuit of Culture Model (CCM) to global public relations and explain how global PR is fundamental to the changing nature of cultures across time and space. As articulated by L'Etang (2006: 388), the "circuit of culture" describes how "meaning is created, modified and reinvented during processes of symbolisation, representation, consumption and identity formation within particular cultural contexts." According to Curtin, Gaither, and Ciszek (2016), CCM comprises five critical and interrelated moments, which collectively and synergistically provide a cultural space where meaning is created, modified, and recreated:

1) Representation. This refers to the location where meanings are encoded to cultural artefacts and similarities and differences between elements of culture are constructed. In order to present differences, representation creates hierarchies and exclusions by "normalising" and "naturalising" some values while "downplaying" or "marginalising" others that do not fit with dominant discourses. Due to representations, stereotypes prevail so that global audiences tend to decode meanings in a patterned and more predicable way.

2) Identity. When audiences identify themselves with the representations of society and culture, the moment of identity occurs. In this sense, identities are meanings accruing to all social networks ranging from publics and organisations to nations.

3) Production. Identities inform future actions such as deciding what kind of products to produce, or what brands to support, thus linking to the moment of production. In the process of production, creators imbue cultural artefacts with meanings, a process often called encoding.

4) Consumption. This moment reflects how cultural artefacts are decoded, interpreted, and evaluated by consumers in their everyday lives, based on varied social and cultural milieux.

5) Regulation. It signifies formal/explicit (e. g., law) and informal/normative (e. g., social mores) norms that determine what kind of meanings are acceptable across different contexts.

The relevance and applications of CCM have been well recognised in global public relations scholarship (e. g., L'Etang 2006; 2008). It provides a framework to understand how PR works with global cultural norms and values to reproduce social hierarchies, simultaneously challenging and resisting dominant discourses or translating them into local contexts. For example, Edwards (2018) clearly unpacked how public relations work is present in all five moments, as a result of which meaning is created, encoded, and travelled through PR campaigns and activities. *Representation* is enabled through PR deliberately attaching discourses and values to products, services, individuals, and organisations. For example, global PR can frame and represent a war as a justified military intervention instead of a crime. Global PR also imputes *identities* to products, services, and cultures that align with a certain type of audience, such that the apparent fit in attributes makes the products more appealing to them (e. g., stereotypical users of most up-to-date iPhones). Global PR decides the *production* of meaning by encoding values to campaigns and circulating meanings in various forms (e. g., a Facebook post may turn into a tweet). Audiences then interpret messages in multiple ways so that PR needs to intervene in their *consumption* by improving the currency and popularity of the campaign and messages, making them more appealing to social and cultural trends. Nonetheless, global PR is subject to *regulations* in order to gain and sustain legitimacy from its operative environment. For example, PR campaigns for a listed public company should adhere to formal rules about information disclosure to prevent insider trading.

Informed by this CCM, PR scholars continue to highlight the role of "culture intermediaries" (Bourdieu 1984) played by global public relations scholarship, practices, and education. L'Etang (2008) emphasised the "diplomatic" function of global public relations that intermediates clashes and negotiations between different cultural values. She invoked Hamilton and Langhorne's (1995: 232) argument: "It has also been remarked of diplomats that they have traditionally been perceived as intermediaries ... The value of a diplomat lay not in any specialist knowledge he might possess, but in his ability to communicate, negotiate and persuade." However, Edwards (2012) cautions that, although global PR practicioners function as cultural intermediaries and promotional workers, the process of "mediation" can also reproduce inequalities and hierarchies through favouring certain values while under-representing others. She explicitly points out that PR people are "symbolically violent" cultural intermediaries because they "generate power for vested interests" (Edwards 2012: 439) without the target audience being fully aware of their manipulation. In addition, Han and Zhang (2009) also adopted CCM to study why the global brand Starbucks was forced to withdraw from China's historical site in Beijing – the Forbidden City (*Zijincheng*). Their study provided a lesson for multinational corporations to strategically appropriate global public relations efforts to local traditions and cultures in order to survive and thrive as an internationally competitive brand.

2.3 A postcolonial approach to global public relations: *Culture-centred framework*

Without a carefully reflective practice, public relations practitioners could materialise and facilitate the new colonial relationships by strengthening the status quo of elites such as transnational corporations (TNCs) and/or international institutions such as the International Monetary Fund, Asian Development Bank, and World Bank, through the production of meaning that consolidates their power while erasing other alternative forms of content (Munshi and Kurian 2005). As Shome and Hedge (2002) explain, this process and product of colonialism has created the intended and/or unintended consequences of power imbalance around the globe, enduring a system that reflects neo-colonisation. Hence, Dutta (2016) calls for a postcolonial investigation of public relations practice and develops a culture-centred approach to global public relations.

Two related issues contribute to the centrality of Dutta's culture-centred approach: subaltern and dialogue. First, Dutta and Pal (2010: 363) explain that subaltern groups are "historically marked by their disconnection from the public spheres of the mainstream, have emerged as markets and as sources of intellectual property for TNCs through the deployment of dialogic tools that increasingly use terms such as listening, empowerment, participation, and development to perpetuate the economic exploitation of the subaltern classes in the global South". Parallel to the postcolonial explanation above, the voices of subalterns have been marginalised, silenced, or erased in the mainstream discursive spaces produced for the social development and public relations objectives by the TNCs and/or other elite organisations through so-called "dialogic communication" that would seemingly empower the marginalised. In essence, their approach to participative communication privileges certain groups, and the subalterns are excluded from the dominant voicing spaces for various political, social, economic and geographical reasons. Hence, the second central issue of the culture-centred approach to global PR is to invite the subalterns to participate in genuine dialogue.

For a positive social change to happen, culture-centred public relations should start with a dialogue that emphasises the agency of local culture. This approach to dialogue differs from our lay understanding of the term in that it starts with a sense of questioning, or a sceptical stance of organisational dialogue in the neoliberalist sense, especially on the dialogue platform that privileges the hegemony (Dutta 2012). Hence, communication in culture-centred public relations is characterised by at least three aspects (Dutta 2016). First, it acknowledges participation as transformative through genuine listening to marginalised voices via an open communication platform that does not privilege the mainstream groups. Second, this reflexive process opens for interrogations, as knowledge or narratives can be reconstructed by the marginalised voices. As Munshi and McKie (2001:16) explain, the "homogenised world view of public relations maintains old colonial legacies that support neo-colonial economic interests." The communicative process of consensus-building that does not allow silenced voices to speak, and recreates the mainstream discourses hence perpetuating colonialism in this sense. Therefore, the more representations of diverse voices, the better for this subaltern approach. Finally, the intervening activities in the knowledge structures are acceptable, as "examining the taken-for-granted assumptions in communicative frameworks offers opportunities for situating these frameworks against the backdrop of neo liberal flows of power" (Dutta 2016: 257).

To illustrate the above dimensions of culture-centred dialogue, we can consider for example the negotiation process of international HIV/AIDS policies. We can see several local HIV/AIDS activist groups around the world and the attempt to develop internationally agreed policies through various international institutions such as the International AIDS Society, International HIV/AIDS Alliance, World Health Organisation etc. When international policies are developed, postcolonial PR practitioners may ask several questions: Who is invited to participate in the policy development? To what extent does the marginalised group have the space to voice its opinions? How is the participation process structured? Is the participation process open for negotiation to allow for changes initiated by the silenced voices? To what extent are the final international policies flexible to incorporate marginalised voices to develop a new version that is more inclusive and less likely to privilege certain groups? The answers to these questions will help determine authenticity of dialogue in the culture-centred global PR process. In general, this global PR approach is primarily applicable to social development in a global context in which it is a moral imperative for PR scholars and practitioners to take this power imbalance into consideration.

2.4 An intersectional approach to global public relations: The framework of *cultural flows*

This approach features a relational and dialectic perspective to study public relations as both a product of globalisation and as producing globalisation. Analysing global PR in this way requires detouring from the normative approach, which promotes integrating a broad range of cultural perspectives into PR theories, practice, and education (Sriramesh 2009; Sriramesh & Verčič 2009b, 2012). It also extends critical-cultural (Curtin and Gaither 2007) and postcolonial approaches (Dutta and Pal 2011; Dutta, Ban, and Pal 2012) to consider various dialectic interplays that characterise globalisation, such as global vs. local, mobility vs. fixity, hegemony vs. resistance, and continuity vs. fluidity. In Edwards' (2018) words, an intersectional approach to global PR entails "unmanaging" PR and globalisation, and instead embracing complexities and dynamics emerging from various intersections among economic, political, and socio-cultural forces at both global and local levels.

In this regard, Appadurai's (1996) global cultural flows can be a robust theoretical framework to capture all kinds of mobility that underpin globalisation and drive cultural movement across different contexts. The global mobility includes: 1) ethnoscapes – the movement of people and ethnic groups; 2) technoscapes – movement of all forms of technology; 3) financescapes – movement of capital; 4) mediascapes – distribution and circulation of information and knowledge; 5) ideoscapes – dissemination of expressly political ideas. Albeit emphasising the "cultural flows", Appadurai also attends to the "locatedness" of lives through which global cultural flows are interpreted, absorbed, or filtered by local agents. Therefore, mobility is often accompanied by fixity, and changes always coupled with continuity. In his framework, imagination is central to all forms of agency to deal with various challenges from globalisation, such as thinking beyond the differences about the world, negotiating new and innovative practices, and challenging existing institutions (Appadurai 1990). Appadurai also views imagination as a source of constructive tension because, while imagination provides impetus for action and change, new practices also inevitably clash with traditional norms of what is right and possible in specific contexts.

Informed by Appadurai's (1996) cultural flows, Edwards (2018) calls to invigorate global PR scholarship in three aspects. First, it is important to understand the ways in which PR is organised as a global industry to either reinforce or disrupt existing global trading structures, such as the dominance of global West and North over global East and South. This is what Edwards (2018) calls PR and global structure. For example, cultural flows have stimulated the growth of PR as a fast-booming industry in non-Western countries. The Chinese local PR brand Bluefocus breaks into Top 10 global PR agencies, thus providing a counter to the West both financially and ideologically. Second, global PR scholarship needs to address the relationship between PR and global culture. In this vein, global PR needs to be understood as a major influence to facilitate the circulation and exchanges between different cultures that are fundamental to globalisation. Distinct from international PR scholarship that frames culture as "fixed" (located within a nation) and "objective" (identifiable and able to be learnt), global PR recognises the fluidity, subjectivity, and fragmentation of cultures. Third, global PR scholarship needs to address the relationship between PR and global discourses, as PR practitioners are skilful discourse technologists (Motion and Leitch 1996) in producing meanings and values that float globally. Nevertheless, the mobility of global PR discourses (e. g., US imperialism) can be countered by moments of fixity (e. g., Chinese Communist Party ideology), which translate global discourses into local contexts through material practices such as events, press releases, interviews, media stories, blogs etc.

As a whole, this intersectional approach to global PR underscores the dialectical interplay between global and local, mobility and fixity, hegemony and resistance, all of which characterise not only globalisation but also global PR scholarship. As such, there is a great need for PR scholars, researchers and practitioners to cast off those linear, transactional models and country-specific narratives, and instead take an open-ended, epistemological approach to understanding why and how PR takes its own form in a particular context. In Rittenhofer and Valentini's (2015) words, the framework of cultural flows does not necessarily encourage us to search for the "best practices" applicable to every country, but rather to construct knowledge and scholarship that warrant a comprehensive understanding and realistic assessment of the actually existing PR practices on a global scale.

3 Discussion, conclusion, and future directions

This chapter has reviewed the recent research trajectory of global public relations scholarship by identifying four key approaches that inform and complement each other: the Political Economy perspective of Global PR, the Circuit of Culture Model, the Culture-Centred Approach, and the Cultural Flows Framework. These four paradigms are not only grounded in extensive research but also provide a practical toolbox for PR practitioners who manage communications with global publics. They allow global PR professionals to critically reflect upon their practices, not only in terms of social and economic effectiveness, but also their ethical stance in dealing with global issues.

Above all, the trail of these approaches to global PR scholarship reflects the dialectical tensions that have been discussed earlier in the introduction. While the Political Economy perspective clearly represents PR as a product of globalisation given that the cultural factors in this paradigm are results of transnational flows, the Circuit of Culture Model as well as the Culture-Centred Approach extend our understanding of PR as an agency reshaping globalisation through meaning-making, negotiation, contestation, and incorporation of marginalised voices of subaltern groups. The Cultural Flows framework, as a more comprehensive and sophisticated approach, highlights the dialectical interplay at the centre of public relations and globalisation. The relationship between PR and globalisation as articulated in the four approaches confirms the idea that PR practice is a meaning-making, social, and cultural process, and that the work of PR in a global context could incorporate international activism, public diplomacy, cultural diplomacy, and international social development, to name a few.

The overview of global PR scholarship provided in this chapter also reflects several gaps in the extant global PR scholarship, which in turn shed light on future theory-building. First, as reflected in the mainstream (normative) literature, there is a strong body of international PR scholarship characterised by culturally specific understandings and describing global influence as from "West to rest" (Edwards 2018: 122). By and large, this kind of international PR scholarship applies US-centric values (e. g., capitalism, democracy, consumerism, self-promotion) as benchmarks to measure how PR practices in non-Western contexts are playing "catch-up" games. Scholarship concerning how global forces, tensions, and dynamics shape PR in specific contexts is lacking. To fill this gap, de-westernising theories, models, and principles becomes imperative to reinvigorate global PR knowledge. For example, some cornerstones of Eastern philosophies, such as *I Ching* (rule of changes) and harmony (co-existence of similarities and differences), could provide new insights into absorbing, harmonising, or even dissolving "Western" influences on local PR practices.

Second, in addition to identifying the negative influence of global PR as hegemonic practices, it is equally important to acknowledge its positive and constructive impacts as manifested in local resistances to hegemony and striving for an equitable future for a globalised world. Only by attending to both sides of influences can we recognise the epistemological inclusiveness and ontological diversity of PR – what it is and does in different social spaces and at different times across the globe. Instead of playing the "catch-up" game from East to West, South to North, the development of "Asian centricity" (Servaes 2016) of public relations could potentially emerge as a powerful force in global public relations scholarship.

Third, beyond the predominant focus on organisational – especially corporate – actors, global PR theories and scholarship need to examine a wide array of actors who practice PR strategically and creatively, such as nation states, NGOs, interest groups, lay publics, and grassroots activists. Through expanding its horizon and territories, global PR scholarship can be readily linked to and also extend influences on other disciplines, including national branding, political sciences, cultural politics, and public diplomacy, thus genuinely improving its visibility and impact on the global stage.

References

Al-Kandari, Ali & T. Kenn Gaither 2011. Arabs, the west and public relations: A critical/cultural study of Arab cultural values. *Public Relations Review* 37(3). 266–273.

Appadurai, Arjun. 1990. Disjuncture and difference in the global cultural economy. *Theory, Culture & Society* 7(2–3). 295–310.

Appadurai, Arjun. 1996. *Modernity at large: Cultural dimensions of globalization*. Minneapolis, MN: University of Minnesota Press.

Bardhan, Nilanjana & C. Kay Weaver (eds.). 2011. *Public relations in global cultural contexts: Multi-paradigmatic perspectives*. New York: Routledge.

Botan, Carl H. & Vincent Hazleton (eds.). 2006. *Public relations theory II*. Mahwah, NJ: Lawrence Erlbaum Associates.

Bourdieu, Pierre. 1984. *Distinction: A social critique of the judgement of taste*. London: Routledge.

Bowen, Shannon A. 2005. Excellence theory. In Robert Heath (ed.), *Encyclopedia of public relations*, 306–308. Thousand Oaks, CA: Sage.

Braun, Sandra L. 2007. The effects of the political environment on public relations in Bulgaria. *Journal of Public Relations Research* 19(3). 199–228.

Chen, Ni & Hugh M. Culbertson. 2003. Public relations in Mainland China: An adolescent with growing pains. In Krishnamurthy Sriramesh & Dejan Verčič (eds.), *The global public relations handbook*, 23–45. Mahwah, NJ: Lawrence Erlbaum Associates.

Curtin, Patricia & T. Kenn Gaither. 2007. International *public relations: Negotiating culture, identity, and power*. Thousand Oaks, CA: Sage.

Curtin, Patricia, T. Kenn Gaither & Erica Ciszek. 2016. Articulating public relations practice and critical/cultural theory through a cultural-economic lens. In Jacquie L'Etang, David McKie, Nancy Snow & Jordi Xifra (eds.), *The Routledge handbook of critical public relations*, 41–53. London: Routledge.

Dhanesh, Ganga S. & Krishnamurthy Sriramesh. 2018. Culture and crisis communication: Nestle India's Maggi noodles case. *Journal of International Management* 24(3). 204–214.

Dozier, David M., Larissa A. Grunig & James E. Grunig. 1995. *Manager's guide to excellence in public relations and communication management*. Mahwah, NJ: Lawrence Erlbaum Associates.

du Gay, Paul, Stuart Hall, Linda Janes, Hugh Mackay & Keith Negus. 1997. *Doing cultural studies: The story of the Sony Walkman*. London: Sage.

Duhe, Sandra C. & Krishnamurthy Sriramesh. 2009. Political economy and global public relations research and practice. In Krishnamurthy Sriramesh & Dejan Verčič (eds.), *The global public relations handbook: Theory, research and practice*, revised and expanded edition, 25–51. New York: Routledge.

Dutta, Mohan J. 2011. *Communicating social change: Structure, culture, and agency*. New York: Routledge.

Dutta, Moha J. 2012. Critical interrogations of global public relations: Power, culture, and agency. In Krishnamurthy Sriramesh & Dejan Verčič (eds.), *Culture and public relations: Links and implications*, 202–217. New York & London: Routledge.

Dutta, Mohan J. 2016. A postcolonial critique of public relations. In Jacquie L'Etang, David McKie, Nancy Snow & Jordi Xifra (eds.), *The Routledge handbook of critical public relations*, 248–260. London: Routledge.

Dutta, Mohan J. & Mahuya Pal. 2010. Dialog theory in marginalized settings: A subaltern studies approach. *Communication Theory* 20(4). 363–386.

Dutta, Mohan J. & Mahuya Pal. 2011. Public relations and marginalization in a global context: A postcolonial critique. In Nilanjana Bardhan & C. Kay Weaver (eds.). *Public relations in global cultural contexts: Multi-paradigmatic perspectives*, 195–225. New York: Routledge.

Dutta, Mohan J., Zhuo Ban & Mahuya Pal. 2012. Engaging worldviews, cultures, and structures through dialogue: The culture-centred approach to public relations. *PRism* 9. http://www.prismjournal.org/fileadmin/9_2/Dutta_Ban_Pal.pdf (accessed 21 August 2018).

Edwards, Lee. 2012. Exploring the role of public relations as a cultural intermediary. *Cultural Sociology* 6(4). 438–454.

Edwards, Lee. 2016. An historical overview of the emergence of critical thinking in PR. In Jacquie L'Etang, David McKie, Nancy Snow & Jordi Xifra (eds.), *The routledge handbook of critical public relations*, 16–27. London: Routledge.

Edwards, Lee. 2018. *Understanding public relations: Theory, culture, society*. London: Sage.

Edwards, Lee & Caroline E. M. Hodges (eds.). 2011. *Public relations, society and culture: Theoretical and empirical exploration*. Abingdon, UK: Routledge.

Grunig, James E. 1992. *Excellence in public relations and communication management*. Hillsdale, NJ: Lawrence Erlbaum Associates.

Grunig, Larissa A, James E Grunig & David M Dozier. 2002. *Excellent public relations and effective organizations: A study of communication management in three countries*. Mahwah, NJ: Lawrence Erlbaum Associates.

Hamilton, Keith & Richard Langhorne. 1995. *The practice of diplomacy: Its evolution, theory, and administration*. New York: Routledge.

Han, Gang & Ai Zhang. 2009. Starbucks is forbidden in the Forbidden City: Blog, circuit of culture and informal public relations campaign in China. *Public Relations Review* 35. 395–401.

Hofstede, Geert. 1984. *Culture's consequences: International differences in work-related values*. Beverly Hills, CA: Sage.

Kenny, Julian. 2016. Excellence Theory and its critics: A literature review critiquing Grunig's strategic management of public relations paradigm. *Asia Pacific Public Relations Journal* 17(2). 78–91.

Kent, Michael & Maureen Taylor. 2011. How intercultural communication theory informs public relations practice in global settings. In Nilanjana Bardhan & C. Kay Weaver (eds.). *Public Relations in Global Cultural Contexts: Multi-paradigmatic Perspectives*, 50–76. New York: Routledge.

Kim, Jeong-Nam & Krishnamurthy Sriramesh. 2009. Activism and public relations. In Krishnamurthy Sriramesh & Dejan Verčič (eds.), *The global public relations handbook: Theory, research and practice*, revised and expanded edition, 79–97. New York: Routledge.

Kirat, Mohamed. 2005. Public relations practice in the Arab World: A critical assessment. *Public Relations Review* 31(3). 323–332.

L'Etang, Jacquie. 2006. Public relations and sport in promotional culture. *Public Relations Review* 32(4). 386–394.

L'Etang, Jacquie. 2008. *Public relations: Concepts, practice and critique*. London & Thousand Oaks, CA: Sage.

Macnamara, Jim. 2012. The global shadow of functionalism and Excellence Theory: An analysis of Australasian PR. *Public Relations Inquiry* 1(3). 367–402.

Macnamara, Jim. 2016. The continuing convergence of journalism and PR: New insights for ethical practice from a three-country study of senior practitioners. *Journalism & Mass Communication Quarterly* 93(1). 118–141.

Martin, Judith N. & Thomas K. Nakayama. 2006. Thinking dialectically about culture and communication. *Communicaiton Theory* 9(1). 1–25.

Motion, Judy & C. Kay Weaver. 2005. A discourse perspective for critical public relations research: Life sciences network and the battle for truth. *Journal of Public Relations Research* 17(1). 49–67.

Motion, Judy & Shirley Leitch. 1996. A discursive perspective from New Zealand: Another world view. *Public Relations Review* 22(3). 297–309.

Munshi, Debashish & David McKie. 2001. Different bodies of knowledge: Diversity and diversi- fication in public relations. *Australian Journal of Communication* 28(3). 11–22.

Munshi, Debashish & Priya Kurian. 2005. Imperializing spin cycles: A postcolonial look at public relations, greenwashing, and the separation of publics. *Public Relations Review* 31(4). 513–520.

Naude, Annelie M. E., Johannes D. Froneman & Roy A. Atwood. 2004. The use of the Internet by ten South African non-governmental organizations – a public relations perspective. *Public Relations Review* 30(1). 87–94.

Niemann-Struweg, Ilse & Corne Meintjes. 2008. The professionalism debate in South African public relations. *Public Relations Review* 34(3). 224–229.

Rhee, Yunna. 2002. Global public relations: A cross-cultural study of the Excellence Theory in South Korea. *Journal of Public Relations Research* 14(3). 159–184.

Rittenhofer, Iris & Chiara Valentini. 2015. A "practice turn" for global public relations: an alternative approach. *Journal of Communication Management* 19(1). 2–19.

Servaes, Jan. 2016. Guanxi in intercultural communication and public relations. *Public Relations Review* 42(3). 459–46.

Shome, Raka & Radha S. Hegde. 2002. Postcolonial approaches to communication: Charting the terrain, engaging the intersections. *Communication Theory* 12(3). 249–270.

Sriramesh, Krishnamurthy. 2009. Globalisation and public relations: The past, present, and the future. *PRism* 6(2). http://www.prismjournal.org/fileadmin/Praxis/Files/globalPR/SRIRAMESH. pdf (accessed 21 August 2018).

Sriramesh, Krishnamurthy & Dejan Verčič. 2001. International public relations: A framework for future research. *Journal of Communication Management* 6(2). 103–117.

Sriramesh, Krishnamurthy & Dejan Verčič. 2009a. Mass media and public relations. In Krishnamurthy Sriramesh & Dejan Verčič (eds.), *The global public relations handbook: Theory, research and practice*, revised and expanded edition, 62–78. New York: Routledge.

Sriramesh, Krishnamurthy & Dejan Verčič (eds.). 2009b. *The global public relations handbook: Theory, research and practice*, revised and expanded edition. New York: Routledge.

Sriramesh, Krishnamurthy & Dejan Verčič. (eds.). 2012. *Culture and public relations: Links and implications*. New York: Routledge.

Sriramesh, Krishnamurthy & Sandra Duhe. 2009. Extending cultural horizons: Political economy and public relations. *Public Relations Review* 35(4). 368–375.

Valentini, Chiara. 2019. Globalization. In Brigitta R. Brunner (ed.), *Public relations theory: Application and understanding*, 125–140. Newark, NJ: Wiley-Blackwell.

Verčič, Dejan, Larissa A. Grunig & James E. Grunig. 1996. Global and specific principles of public relations: Evidence from Slovenia. In Hugh M. Culbertson & Ni Chen (eds.), *International public relations: A comparative analysis*, 31–65. Mahwah, NJ: Lawrence Erlbaum.

Verhoeven, Piet, Ralph Tench, Ansgar Zerfass, Angeles Moreno & Dejan Verčič. 2012. How European PR practitioners handle digital and social media. *Public Relations Review* 38(1). 162–164.

Zerfass, Ansgar, Piet Verhoeven, Ralph Tench, Angeles Moreno & Dejan Verčič. 2011. *European communication monitor 2011: Empirical insights into strategic communication in Europe. Results of a survey in 43 countries*. Brussels: EACD/EUPRERA, Helios Media.

John A. Ledingham

21 Relationship management: Status and theory

Abstract: This chapter presents and discusses the main tenets of relationship management (RM) as a general theory of public relations. The notion of relationship management potentially represents the most comprehensive overhaul of theory and practice in the history of public relations. The emergence of a relationship management paradigm moves the discipline away from crafting communications as the central focus of public relations toward a system for managing the organization-public relationships (OPRs). Within the parameters of a management system, the role of relationship management is to initiate, maintain, and nurture a mutually beneficial relationship between an organization and the publics with which it interacts (Ledingham 2003a). Further, public relations as relationship management function adopts a managerial view in researching, planning, implementing, and evaluating activities. Hence, RM serves as both an organizing concept and, ultimately, a unifying theory of public relations. This chapter reviews the emergence of RM as a general theory of public relations and its core elements, and offers conclusions concerning RM, as well as thoughts regarding the future of public relations profession as RM.

Keywords: relationship; management; mutual benefit; paradigm

1 Introduction

> "Public relations is the ethical and efficient management of an organization-public relationship (OPR), based on common interests and shared goals, over time, in support of benefit for both an organization and the publics with which it interacts."
> Definition of Relationship Management (Ledingham 2003a)

Relationship management (RM) is a term given to the process of managing the relationship between an organization and its publics. Moreover, RM is understood as the "ethical and efficient management" of an organization-public relationship and it is "based on mutual interests and shared goals, over time, to engender benefit both for an organization and key publics" (Ledingham 2003a: 79). The concept has impacted the thinking of scholars, theorists, and progressive practitioners around the world and has brought about a paradigmatic shift in thinking about public relations from a communication-oriented activity toward a relational one. It has been suggested that the emergence of the relational perspective could be traced to five important phases:

1. *The recognition of the central role of relationships in public relations*. Ferguson's (1984) contention was relationships, "not (...) the organization, nor the public,

https://doi.org/10.1515/9783110554250-021

nor the communication process" (ii), should be the central focus of public relations; and it was quickly adopted by scholars, setting the stage for a research
direction that has grown increasingly robust;

2. *The reconceptualization of public relations as a management function.* The idea
    was that organization-public relationships involve processes that can and must
    be managed, and it introduced to public relations principles of management that
    supersede those simply of message production. This coincides with the increas-
    ing dominance in the marketplace of organizations of those trained in the under-
    standing and practice of higher-order management;

3. *The exploration of organization-public relationships.* Scholars began to decon-
    struct organization-public relationships to develop process models of those rela-
    tionships (Broom, Casey, and Richey 1997), to identify the dimensions that com-
    prise them (Ledingham and Bruning 1998), and to link relationships to changes
    among publics in awareness, perceptions, attitudes, and behaviors (Ledingham
    and Bruning 2000).

4. *The increasing theoretical contribution in defining, refining and developing RM.*
    Collections of contributions concerning organization-public relationships
    emerged, including the "Excellence Study" of J. Grunig and Dozier (2000) and
    others, suggesting that the notion of mutuality is key to organizations achieving
    their goals. In addition, a collection was published (Ledingham and Bruning
    2000) with a seminal introduction and chapters concerning the relational per-
    spective and its application to different established public relations organiza-
    tional functions such as crisis and issue management, employee and community
    relations etc. That same volume also included contributions linking interper-
    sonal principles to public relations and a process model of "professional" rela-
    tionships;

5. *The emergence of the notion of "stewardship".* Kelly's (2001) called for steward-
    ship as a component of public relations represents an attempt to take the process
    of public relations beyond evaluation in the traditional four-step management
    model (analyze, plan, implement, and evaluate) and underscores the importance
    of continued monitoring and nurturing of relationships (Ledingham 2003a).

The relational perspective has been explored in the context of various public relations functions, including public affairs (Ledingham 2001), community relations
(Ledingham and Bruning 2001), issues management (Bridges and Nelson 2000),
crisis management (Coombs 2000), and media relations (Ledingham and Bruning
1998, 1999). Within the relational perspective, the role of public relations is to initiate, maintain and nurture mutually beneficial relationships between an organization and its publics (Ledingham 2003a). In this context, communication – once both
the task and the product of public relations – is viewed as "a strategic management
function" charged with supporting organization-public relationships (Dozier 1995:
85). Public relations manages these relationships via communication. Relationships

are in fact "configured and re-configured through communicative processes that can occur in or outside organisational settings" (Valentini 2018: 74). The relational perspective underpinned in the *General Theory of Relationship Management* calls for public relations not only to adopt management processes and procedures, but to look to form new partnerships with publics that emphasize a commonality of interests, shared benefit, and as an appreciation of the role of public relations in contributing to a sence of community (Kruckenberg and Starch 1988, Valentini, Kruckeberg and Starch, 2012).

This chapter reviews the paradigm shift that RM brings to the profession explicating the increasing importance of an organization-public relationships (OPRs), and the system for managing that relationship. OPR essentially is defined as "the patterns of interaction, transaction, exchange, and linkage between an organization and its publics" (Broom, Casey, and Ritchey 2000: 18). The chapter also discusses various theories and how they informed the development of the *General Theory of Relationship Management* in public relations, the subsequent development of knowledge on OPRs, on its typology, and measures for evaluating the impact of RM initiatives. Further, the author offers suggestions for the location of RM within the organizational structure. Finally, the chapter discusses the legacy and main critiques that RM has received across the years.

2 Origins of the relational perspective – from arcane to modern public relations

The industrial revolution brought innovations in production, especially image transferance, that enabled the rise of newspapers that could reach households in developed countries with a rapidity thought impossible prior to the mid-19th Century. Newspapers quickly moved to the top rung of the economic and political ladder in terms of influence. Political careers were created and destroyed by newspaper stories. For example, Theodore Roosevelt became the darling of the American public following the depiction of Teddy and the Rough Riders charging up a hill in San Juan. Sex scandals were a sure way to pump up readership figures. Political leaders caught in an illicit love affair saw their romance reported on the front page of major dailies, above the fold with 72-point headlines, and their careers were destroyed.

Public relations began as an offspring of journalism and clung to those beginnings for nearly a century. The industry was made up of press agents, usually former journalists, seeking to use the media for publicity for their clients. The rationale for press agentry was that the publicity improved the client's image or reputation, notions that are still questionable today. Another reason to employ publicity was to counter negative news reporting. Moreover, press agents did not have to pay the media for the publicity, but the agents charged their client a fee. Thus, the practice was immensely popular with those with journalistic experience, and many were eventually employed by business organizations simply because of a fear of news media.

Like a Rasputin sitting at the right hand of the czar, many of these early press agents, or publicists, developed a good deal of power. However, though press agents insisted that their clients benefited from positive publicity, many of those clients complained that there was no quantifiable evidence of that being the case[1]. Moreover, as the mass media fragmented, the all-powerful effect of media exposure declined. And the lack of accountability of the results of publicity continued to be a problem for individual practitioners, inside organizations, and for public relations firms.

Two factors affected this problem: a lack of journalistic experience, and a lack of appropriate training. Most journalists had majored in journalism, English, and/or business. The preparation may have left something to be desired. For example, the head of the Houston office of Ogilvy & Mather Advertising and Public Relations was once asked where his new hires came from. He named a large local university, specifically the marketing graduates and those with a journalism degree. When asked his opinion of those graduates, he said: "The market graduates are great planners, but they don't want to do anything; and the journalism school grads are wonderful writers, but they don't have anything to say." (Personal conversation, Houston, TX, 1984, at an Advertising Federation luncheon). The second problem was the result of the journalism training. Many journalists had no university-level journalism training and their lack of that training was often accompanied by a deep and abiding lack of ethics. The fact was that most journalism school programs may have offered one or even two public relations courses, but no public relations major. Of course, recent advances in preparation and scholarly and professional credentialing has deeply altered that suituation for the better. At that time, people employed in journalism quickly learned the technical side of the business. Their orientation was toward production, and they came to believe that almost any problem could be solved by a well-written stand-out piece. This "rush to production" method of problem-solving has proven to be ineffective.

Born of the Industrial revolution, production was the public relations practitioner's way of measuring success. In other words, the *output* of the public relations effort – the news releases, brochures, and "earned media" – were treated as they were *outcome*. That is, production was the unit of measurement of achievement rather than the *output* of an initiative. Moreover, corporations struggled with the placement of public relations within the corporate structure. Early practitioners claimed their office should be next door to that of the chief executive officer, a notion that still prevails in some circles. Not surprisingly, it has not proven popular with most

---

1 Meanwhile, the relationship concept was finding a warm welcome in the business world, and by 2004, Customer Relationship Management (CRM), primarily a data collection software program that tracks and compiles sales and customer data, was purchased by Oracle, which has resulted in Oracle holding a 45 % share of that market.

organizations. Academics noted that public relations practitioners, operating primarily at the tactical level, were being left out of discussions about goal-setting, strategic planning and the like. Moreover, the notion of accountability raised by corporations, and advocated by management experts and numerous scholars such as Broom and Dozier (1996), Broom, Casey, and Ritchey (1997), Bruning and Ledingham (2000, 2002), Dozier (1984), Dozier, L. Grunig, and J. Grunig (1995), J. Grunig (1989, 1993) and others as a means of quantifying outcomes, was a notion counter to the prevailing way of conducting public relations at that time. All in all, the demands of organizations for accountability of public relations initiatives resulted in the reconceptualization of public relations as a management function, charged with accounting for the cost of public relations programs in terms compatable with modern management practices.

At that point, the field of public relations, two-thirds of the way through the 20th Century, still found itself seemingly void of leadership capable of finding solutions. Nonetheless, as often happens, the answers came from academia. In 1984, Ferguson reported the results of her content analysis of ten years of public relations articles. She found that most of the activities associated with public relations scholarship concerned tactical skills – writing, publicity, and so on – but were devoid of theory that could guide strategic planning. Ferguson (1984) concluded that scholarship concerning organization-public relationships (OPRs) offered the best potential for building theory. Specifically, she concluded that the core focus of public relations ought not to be communication, but relationships. The relational concept was then incorporated in Cutlip, Center, and Broom's text book (1985, updated 1994) on public relations, which for a decade has been one of the key readings in the field. However, the concept was largely unexplored until the 1990s when the topic "exploded" in terms of the number of publications, a development the eminent scholar James Grunig, though reluctant to abandon established notions of public relations, termed "revolutionary" (2015).

In shifting the evaluation of public relations effectivenss from measures of communication output to those of behavioral outcomes (Broom and Dozier 1996), the relational perspective recognized that public relations is a managerial function in charge of relationships with publics. And, further, the new perspective underscored the findings that the goals of RM are achievable if components and types of organization-public relationships (OPRs) are identified and linked to public attitudes, perceptions, and knowledge. Finally, the system is effective when specific relationship measures exist that are capable of assessing the quality of an OPR. Also, these measures eventually can prove to add value to an organization's public relations function (Ledingham 2003a).

3 Theoretical roots of relationship management

The relationship management perspective in public relations integrates several prem-
ises and ideas from well-known and established theories including Systems Theory,
Stakeholder Theory, Crisis Management Theory, and Social Responsibility Theory.
Below, a short overview and discussion are presented.

3.1 Systems Theory

One of the more important theories in understanding relationship management is
Systems Theory, a theory concerning the study and understanding of the nature of
complex systems. A system is "a complex and highly interlinked network of parts
exhibiting synergistic properties – the whole is greater than the sum of its parts" (Chiukere and Nwoka 2015). Particularly the idea of "open system" as a possible understanding of an organization functioning is relevant in the context of relationship management. An "open" system consists of a set of interdependent units that can adapt to
change either by altering the environment or by altering the unit's interaction with the
environment. Such a system is characterized by taking in energy and information, processing it, and releasing it back into the environment. In this way, a balance or equilibrium is maintained between the system and the environment. An "open" system,
by nature of its flexibility and adaptability, generally results in long-term, mutually
beneficial OPRs. The inability to interact with the environment, to not be open to new
ideas and changes, is a "closed system." A closed system results in isolation and leads
to short-term relationships (see Broom and Sha 2013).

The importance of Systems Theory for relationship management is not simply
found in the advantages of being open, taking in information, and analyzing it for the
good of the organization. Advantages come, for example, in anticipating change in
a system because of a change that has taken place in some other system, or changes
in governmental regulations, or changes in the public's perception of an issue. Being
open to change is part of the process of scan, plan, implement, and evaluate, and
permits the organization to anticipate change, both in one's own organization and
in others. And, the fact is that no organization exists without interaction with other
people and/or other organizations, whether by design or happenstance.

3.2 Stakeholder Theory

Another important theory that has given the ground for the development and justification for a relationship management perspective is Stakeholder Theory. Stakeholder
Theory essentially "outlines how management can satisfy the interests of stakeholders
in a business (...) and addresses moral and ethical values in the management of a busi-

ness or other organization." (Business Dictionary n.d.a). This follows "policies that (1) minimize cost and waste while improving the quality of its products, (2) enhance the skills and satisfaction of its employees, and (3) contribute to the development of the community from which it draws its resources and sustenance" (Business Dictionary n.d.b).

The core of Stakeholder Theory is the notion that, just as an organization must attend to the needs of stockholders, the organization must also understand that the purpose of a business is to create value for stakeholders, and, it could be argued also with publics, not just share- and stockholders. An organization has relationships with any number of stakeholders and publics, inside and outside. Hence, relationship management is a central and core activity in stakeholder management. A great part of "doing" stakeholder relations and OPR is actually communicating back and forth, especially if the organization is involved in a project that stakeholders could put off schedule, or even change, if the organization and stakeholders and publics cannot resolve their differences. However, the major assumption is building mutual and beneficial relationships that allow for genuine engagement with the community.

3.3 Crisis Management

Relationship management is also an important component of crisis management and theorizing in crisis management has expanded the influence of RM paradigm. A crisis is defined as "the perception of an unpredictable event that threatens public's important expectancies of and can seriously impact an organization's performance and generate negative outcomes" (Coombs 2000: 73). The answer to handling a crisis, when possible, is to anticipate it and also to continually monitor public relationships to make certain these relationships are excellent. This includes relationships with other businesses, local government, and all community organizations. A crisis can be so damaging that public relations must always be prepared to deal with it. Also, a crisis that arises from a natural or man-made disaster can be particularly difficult to deal with. Good relationships with public groups could help the management of crises. Coombs, a crisis communication expert, notes that "stakeholders – including publics – and the organization have a connection that binds them together, whether it be grounded in economic, political or social concerns" (and that) "the idea of stakeholder management is nothing more than managing the relationship between an organization and its various stakeholders" (Coombs 2000: 75). He then argues that a strong favourable relationship can protect the relationship in the event of a crisis. Hence, public relations practitioners need to determine how publics perceive a relationship prior to a crisis in order to determine the best course of action in rebuilding positive OPRs. Coombs also suggests that "the relational perspective helps crisis managers to develop effective responses to the crises" (2000: 73).

One of Coombs' many contributions to advancing Relationship Management Theory is the notion of relational history, which he equates with reputation. He posits that a positive relational history can protect an organization in the event of a crisis. Moreover, Coombs offers expert advice on how the management of a pre-crisis relationship – as well as the post-crisis relationship – can mitigate the impact of a crisis through the maintenance of a positive relationship. He further suggests that linkage between publics and relationship history, which he equates with reputation, provides managers with a framework for addressing a crisis when it occurs. He again emphasizes that a positive "relationship history," protects reputation. Moreover, respondents' ratings can indicate which aspects of the relationship need attention least at that point. In addition, a coorientation strategy allows the researcher to compare an organization's perceptions, or ratings of how well the crisis was managed, with the perceptions of how well key publics rated the management of the crisis.

3.4 Social Responsibility Theory

In a broader sense, relationship management is conceptually contributing to Social Responsibility Theory, since it draws upon both Stakeholder Theory and Crisis Management Theory. There is an obvious connection between stakeholders, publics, social responsibility, and relationships. Whereas Stakeholder Theory holds that the purpose of a business is to create value for stakeholders and not solely shareholders, the Social Responsibility perspective suggests that organizational responsibility doesn't stop at the intersection of an organization and stockholders, or even at the point where the organization and various stakeholders and publics interact. Social responsibility holds that organizations are also obligated to contribute positively to the betterment of society, as per the definition of Social Responsibility Theory, "acting with concern and sensitivity, aware of the impact of your actions on others, particularly the disadvantaged" (Entrepreneur Small Business Encyclopedia n.d.).

Social Responsibility Theory argues that there must be a balance between so-called "corporate good" and the welfare of society. However, some businesspeople take the position that the responsibility of a company extends only as far as stockholders. Another popular argument holds that an organization should provide value for society as well. However, this has not always been the case. Some of the USA's largest enterprises were built by people paid barely a living wage. Moreover, whereas stockholders have certain legal rights, and stakeholders have an immediate relationship with an organization, it has been sometime difficult to maintain an acceptable equilibrium between American business and American publics and overall society. However, there are businesses large and small that go far in exceeding any expectation in supporting disadvantaged. Research has shown that organizations that practice social responsibility gain financially as well as in terms of good will and these two influence OPR outcomes.

4 Towards a General Theory of Relationship Management

As can be seen from these different yet well-known and established theories in management literature, the management of relationships is central in many different organizations and contexts. Furthermore, there is a theme that runs through the various descriptions of these relationships and of public relations applications. The theme is *mutuality*. It is reflected in the way each application is approached, and it stands in marked difference from earlier (communication) models of public relations that were based on bringing about change sought by an organization as the primary goal. If public relations is essentially the management of such relationships, public relations is and has a central role in how organizations manage their internal and external environments (Valentini 2017). The relational perspective in public relations not only emphasizes similar managerial concerns, but offers legitimacy to the profession's own identity. As earlier noted, RM can be applied, in custom forms, to the needs of diverse industries (Ledingham 2003a). It is a functioning overview, a philosophy, of part of both giant organizations and minute organizations, of target groups, foundations, charitable organizations, and some not so charitable.

In the process, relationship management has contributed to alleviating two major problems that public relations has faced over the decades: an identity problem and a function problem. Public relations identity problems related to the blurred image that the profession had and still has (see chapters 4 and 6 in this book). Public relations function problems deal with the activities that it entails and the professional competencies of its practitioners, which historically operated at the tactical level, not at the strategic level, and did not follow the basic management processes of scan, plan, implement, or evaluate. As a general theory of public relations, relationship management has dignified and purposively located the public relations profession as one of organization's managerial core functions, having to deal, via communication, with many diverse and complex stakeholders' and publics' needs in light of developing a mutual understanding. Through the years, Relationship Management Theory has functioned as a paradigm for the development of a body of knowledge specifically on the dimensions, qualities, and measures of OPR and more broadly on a set of other strategic activities addressing relationship premises.

5 Types of relationships

Research has shown that there can be different types of relationships that organizations can undertake with different publics, and that therefore different public relations strategies and initiatives must account for. It is important to note that a relationship is the result of joint action by the organization and key members of the public. It is, in that sense, an *outcome,* and not an *output,* thus avoiding many of the difficulties of trying to account for expenditures in terms of outputs.

Among the first, J. Grunig, L. Grunig and Dozier (2002) advanced the notion of two types of relationships, *communal* and *exchange.* A communal relationship is characterized by both parties in the relationship being concerned for the other's interest. In an exchange relationship, one who gives expects to receive back something of equal value. Similarly, Huang (2001) identified five different types of relationships, *exploitive,* that is one side takes advantage of the other, *contractual,* that is limited to agreed-upon terms, *manipulative,* that is an organization serves only its own interests, *convenant,* that is, both sides commit to the common good, and *symbiotic,* that is, both sides are interdependent and work with the public to survive. Further studies have been conducted to test variations based on cultures, contexts, and situations (for example Ni & Wang 2011; Zaharna 2016). Relationships have been broadly placed across a continuum ranging from those which are low in communality, distinguished by their concern for self-interest, to those which are high in communality and make a priority of the other's interests (Hung 2005; Walters and Bortree 2012).

6 Measuring relationships: Dimensions of OPRs

A starting-point to understand and measure organization-public relationships is, indeed, the definition of a relationship and its components or dimensions. In defining a relationship, the key is mutuality – mutual interests, mutual input, and mutual control. But what makes a relationship mutual? Research on this area has focused on identifying, operationalizing, and measuring dimensions of OPR. Dimensions are basically the perceptions of an organization by the key publics or stakeholders with which the organizations interact. Dimensions are important because they provide a way to determine the state of a relationship between an organization and its publics or stakeholders. Dimensions are simplifications, categories that allow us to begin creating order out of chaos. For instance, terms like *trust, openness,* and *caring* have been studied as dimensions describing perceptions of OPRs as defined by publics. As in "XYZ is a company I can trust," or "XYZ is open with me". However, just measuring a public's trust in an organization doesn't describe what the organization needs to do to demonstrate its trustworthiness, and trust may mean different things to different people under different conditions. For example, in one study of an organization and its key publics, Ledingham and Bruning (1998) found that trust, to those public members, meant specifically "I trust company XYZ to do what they say they will do". Another example of the contextual meaning of a dimension is the term *openness.* In the relationship between a manufacturer and its employees, *openness* meant to the employees that the manufacturer "shares its plans for the future with its employees." Having clear definitions and understandings of OPR dimensions are important in that they allow us to compare, for instance, the scores employees give an employer on key dimensions. Poor relationship scores may signal that a strike by employees may be in the offing, or that the sales of a retail store may be not what the store owners have been expecting.

As the relational perspective emerged, a number of scholars began to investigate the notion of relationship dimensions. One of the first studies drew upon the literature of interpersonal communication and other disciplines in identifying the dimensions of reciprocity, trust, mutual legitimacy, openness, mutual satisfaction, and mutual understanding (Grunig, L., Grunig, J. and Ehling 1992). This led to a process in which scholars benchmarked the scores assigned by publics to the dimensions and, in that way, could examine the dimension scores before and after an intervention (an event) to determine the impact of initiatives on the dimensions.

Ledingham, Bruning, Thomlison, and Lesko (1997) also conducted a review of the literature of marketing, management, psychology, and sociology, as well as interpersonal communication, to generate relational dimensions to be used in subsequent research. They initially identified 18 relational dimensions, including investment, commitment, trust, comfort with relational dialectics, cooperation, mutual goals, interdependence, power imbalance, performance satisfaction, comparison, level of alternatives, adaptation, nonretrievable investment, shared technology, summate constructs, structural bonds, social bonds, intimacy, and passion. In subsequent research, Ledingham and Bruning (1998) reduced the relational attributes into the five operationalized dimensions and measured them in a survey questionnaire in which publics were asked to indicate, using a Likert-type scale, their level of agreement with statements concerning a local telecommunication utility. The same strategy was employed regarding the dimensions of openness, interest, involvement and commitment. Respondents were then asked to indicate, using the same type of scale, their perception of the quality of their relationship with the organization. They also were asked demographic questions such as age, gender, number of years as a customer, and household income. After the responses were entered for statistical analysis, linkages were identified between the ratings of the various dimensions and evaluations of the quality of the relationship (Ledingham and Bruning 1998).

In a 1999 article, Bruning and Ledingham identified three distinct groupings of dimensions in responses from publics (those with an interest in the organization) through cluster analysis. Based on the nature of the items, they labeled the clusters *personal*, *professional*, and *community* (see Table 1) and operationalized publics in small groups.

Table 1: OPR dimension clusters

Dimension clusters	Specifications
Personal	How publics feel the organization interacts with individuals
Professional	How publics feel the organization performs its professional services
Community	How the organization is viewed in terms of being a "corporate citizen"

Many other scholars have used the same or very similar method in identifying additional dimensions and their contribution to OPR quality. For example, in a study sponsored by the Public Relations Institute, Hon and J. Grunig (1999) identified the importance of *mutuality* in building positive, long-lasting relationships. Moreover, scholarship has clearly established that the dimensions used in interpersonal relationships can also be found operating in the context of an OPR, and that suggests there may be additional interpersonal strategies that could be useful. It also became clear that cultural characteristics influence OPRs. For example, Huang (2001) identified "renging" and "mianzi" as necessary components of Eastern OPRs.

Scholars then began to explore measurement strategies that, based on changes in dimension scores, would allow practitioners to analyze the impact of programmatic initiatives on relationship state for virtually the first time. Building on earlier managerial role models, Broom and Dozier (1996) were among the first scholars to propose a coorientational approach to determine the level of agreement and accuracy between organizations and publics as indicators of relationship quality. Later, Broom, Casey, and Ritchey (1997) proposed a model of organization-public relationships which included antecedents, characterizations, and consequences of an organization-public relationship. They suggested that "antecedents (...) include perceptions, motives, needs, behaviors (...) posited as contingencies or causes in the formation of relationships (...) [and] are the sources of change pressure or tension (...)" including "properties of exchanges, transactions, communications and other interconnected activities." Consequences of organization-public relationships include "the outputs that have the effect of changing the environment and of achieving, maintaining or changing goal states both inside and outside of the organization" (94). The usefulness of knowing how key publics evaluate their relationships with organizations includes the following:

1. Publics' rating of various dimensions provide an indication of the status of an OPR.
2. Individual scoring of each of a set of dimensions indicates areas that may need attention.
3. Scoring can be used to generate a priority list of dimensions.
4. Helps to refine messaging.
5. Can be used to determine the degree to which strategies are working.
6. Can be used in a coorientation analysis.

Overall, the impact of relational dimensions rests on the ability of scholars to be able to (1) identify the components of an OPR, (2) link those dimensions to OPR quality, (3) compare the status (quality) of the OPR to other OPRs, and (4) be able to determine the results of public relations campaign initiatives on the relative quality of an OPR.

7 Legacy and critique

The first observation concerns the frequency with which the notion of mutuality moved to the front of the stage. There is a plethora of definitions of relationships across disciplines. One of the cornerstones of public relations' relational approach is the normative idea of mutuality as an essential element of quality OPRs. The second observation concerns the increasing interest and rapid dissemination of relational studies. If one of the functions of a theory is to generate research, Relationship Management Theory has continued through the years to provide grounds for public relations researchers exploring antecedents, dimensions, and outcomes of relationship management across contexts, situations, public groups, and cultures. The volume of work was termed an "explosion" by J. Grunig (2015: xxvi), as well as a "revolution" in the thinking of public relations scholars. The flood of informational material challenged traditional public relations thinking causing a bit of reluctance on the part of some, as J. Grunig has candidly admitted, to let go of the notions public relations professionals held dear – including notions such as "image". But, of course, the relational concept strengthened with a spate of journal articles, book chapters, and anthologies. The relational perspective has contributed to the development of important thinking, for instance, around dialogue (Kent and Taylor 1998), engagement (Johnson and Taylor 2018) and social responsibility (Bartlett 2011).

The strength of the relational perspective – and the concepts attendant to it – rests on the ability to resolve issues that have plagued the industry since its inception. Relationship management provides a central focus for public relations practice and scholarship, including a way to measure the change in relationships with publics, and also a means of comparing change across differing situations. In addition, as a management function, public relations can access senior management planning, and will be a beneficiary of the experience of the organization's dominant coalition.

All in all, the notion of relationships as the central focus of public relations has redefined the purpose, operation, and conduct of the discipline. Moreover, the functional embodiment of that concept, relationship management, serves as a unifying theory for the study and practice of public relations. Relationship Management Theory is a normative theory of public relations seeking to benefit publics, to provide guidelines for dealing with crisis, to encourage benefit for society, and to do so not only efficiently but also ethically.

Relationship Management Theory has also raised some concerns. One criticism is that it has only shown "one side of OPR," and that not all OPRs are as positive as Ledingham has shown in the system he developed (Heath 2013). Here critics have noted that relationship management scholarship has not specified any dimension or characteristic that could contribute to negative organization-public relationships. In response, Ledingham (2003a, 2003b) argues that learning how to bring about a negative OPR is of limited interest to organizations and professionals. A more relevant complaint has been directed at those who see public relations as a management function. That is, some public relations professionals feel capable of designing and implementing their campaigns based on their own experience and instincts, without "interference" from management. This has led to situations where the overall policy of an organization and that of public relations differ rather than support each other. The problem is lessening as more organizations and their public relations personnel are coming together under the management umbrella. Much more work needs to be done, however, to understand the complex dynamics of public relationships, power, and organization behaviors.

Another point of critique has to do with accounting for initiatives in terms of outcomes, rather than outputs. Management will very quickly point out that an abundance of produced and disseminated material may be impressive, but is not itself evidence of effective management of OPRs. This problem should be lessened by the inclusion of research methods in many educational programs, and the growing popularity of low-cost, easy-to-understand survey research programs such as Survey Monkey.

8 Conclusions

Relationship management is a system dedicated to an ideal, a plan, and a purpose. As developed by Ledingham (2003a), it is grounded in the literature, builds on prior research, and is explicated in accordance with the guidelines suggested by Littlejohn (1993) and others. And the purpose is a system that benefits public relations practitioners, sponsoring organizations, publics, and society. One of the more interesting matters about relationship management is that, like other processes, it requires more or less the same process to be effective. It needs to scan the environment to determine what is going on, to set goals, and develop plans to reach them, to pre-test concepts, and then implement them, and to evaluate what happened.

As a general theory of public relations, relationship management has become one of the most important theoretical foundations that both normatively and instrumentally drives the work and research in public relations (Ki, Kim & Ledingham 2015). In particular, OPR research has led to a number of important studies and findings addressing empirically the questions that Relationship Management Theory has outlined.

There is no doubt that public relations has been forever changed by the advent of Relationship Management Theory, as evidenced by the sheer abundance of journal articles, book chapters, and anthologies. The relational perspetive is elevating public relations in the organizational structure, and increasingly opening the door to senior management and the organization's dominant coalition. All this comes with the caveat that public relations persons must stop thinking of themselves as journalists, or journalists in residence, or the conscience of the corporation, and adopt the concepts of modern public relations. The successful relationship manager must do that to become a strategic thinker if he/she expects to function at the top level of his/her profession.

The literature of relationship management is abundant and varied with several well-grounded streams of investigation for scholars to build on. It has been suggested that much of the recent published scholarship in this area is simply repetitive or confirmatory. Nonetheless, a close reading of the literature finds new exploration into linkage between relationship management and concepts such as image, reputation, crises, development, and various other issues and elements. Relationship Management Theory provides a means of determining the standing between organizations and their publics, and the comparative contributions of various relational dimensions to a positive relationship. And, as the term implies, the concept brings public relations into the management fold.

The overriding central concept of RM is the notion of mutuality – in terms of input, planning, and execution. Where public relations once concerned itself primarily with achieving its benefits, RM is predicated on mutuality – in philosophy, theory, and in application. Its application strategies are embedded with the notion of mutuality. If followed, RM can bring about a successful partnership between an organization and publics, though the percentages and weights may vary from case to case. RM represents a sea change in the study and practice of an industry that now knows not only what it does, but also what it is.

References

Bartlett, Jennifer L. 2011. Public relations and corporate social responsibility. In Øyvind Ihlen, Jennifer Bartlett & Steve May (eds.), *The handbook of communication and corporate social responsibility*, 67–86. Malden, MA: John Wiley & Sons

Bridges, Janet A. & R. A. Nelson. 2000. Issues management: A relational approach. In John A. Ledingham and Stephen D. Bruning (eds.), *Public relations as relationship management: A relational approach to public relations*, 95–115. Mahwah, NJ: Lawrence Erlbaum Associates.

Broom, Glen M. & David M. Dozier. 1996. *Using research in public relations: Applications to program management*. Englewood Cliffs, NJ: Prentice-Hall.

Broom, Glen M., Shawna Casey & James Ritchey. 1997. Toward a concept and theory of organization-public relationships. *Journal of Public Relations Research* 9(2). 83–98.

Broom, Glen M., Shawna Casey & James Ritchey. 2000. Concept and theory of organization-public relationships. In John A. Ledingham & Stephen D. Bruning (eds.), *Public relations as relationship management: A relational approach to the study and practice of public relations*, 3–22. New York: Routledge.

Broom, Glen M. & Bey-Ling Sha. 2013. *Cutlip and Center's effective public relations*, 11th edn. Harlow, UK: Pearson.

Bruning, Stephen D. & John A. Ledingham. 1999. Relationships between organizations and publics: Development of a multi-dimensional organization-public relationship scale. *Public Relations Review* 25(2). 157–170.

Bruning, Stephen D. & John A. Ledingham. 2000. Organization and key public relationships: Testing the influence of the relationship dimensions in a business-to-business context. In John A. Ledingham & Stephen D. Bruning (eds.), *Public relations as relationship management: A relational approach to public relations*. Mahwah, NJ: Lawrence Erlbaum Associates.

Bruning, Stephen D. & John A Ledingham. 2002. Identifying the comunication behaviors and interaction patterns of agency-client relationships in development and decline. *Journal of Promotion Management* 8(2). 21–34.

Business Dictionary. n.d.a. *Stakeholder theory*. http://www.businessdictionary.com/definition/stakeholder-theory.html (accessed 2 April 2020).

Business Dictionary. n.d.b. *Stakeholder value approach*. http://www.businessdictionary.com/definition/stakeholder-value-approach.html (accessed 2 April 2020).

Chiukere, Cornell C. and Jude Nwoka. 2015. The systems theory of management in modern day organizations – A study of Aldgate Congress Resort Limited Port Harcourt. *International Journal of Scientific and Research Publications* 5(9). 1–7. http://www.ijsrp.org/research-paper-0915.php?rp=P454540 (accessed 26 March 2020).

Coombs, Timothy. 2000. Crisis management: Advantages of a relational perspective. In John Ledingham & Stephen D. Bruning (eds.), *Public relations as relationship management: A relational approach to the study and practice of public relations*, 73–93. New York: Routledge.

Cutlip, Scott M., Allen H. Center & Glen M. Broom. 1994. *Effective public relations*, 7th edn. Englewood Cliffs, NJ: Prentice Hall.

Dozier, David M. 1984. Program evaluation and roles of practitioners. *Public Relations Review* 10(3). 13–21.

Dozier, David M. 1985. *Manager's guide to excellence in public relations and communication management*. Mahwah, NJ: Lawrence Erlbaum Associates.

Dozier, David M., Larissa A. Grunig & James E. Grunig. 1995. *Manager's guide to excellence in public relations and communication management*. Mahwah, NJ: Lawrence Erlbaum Associates.

Entrepreneur Small Business Encyclopedia. n.d. *Social responsibility*. http://entrepreneur.com/encyclopedia/social-responsibility (accessed 30 March 2020).

Ferguson, Mary-Ann. 1984. Building theory in public relations: Inter-organizational relationships as a public relations paradigm. Paper presented at the annual conference of the Association for Education in Journalism and Mass Communication, University of Florida, Gainesville, 5–8 August.

Grunig, James E. 1989. Symmetrical presuppositions as a framework for public relations theory. In Carl H. Botan and Vincent Hazelton (eds.), *Public relations theory*, 17–44. Hillsdale, NJ: Lawrence Erlbaum Associates.

Grunig, James E. 1993. Image and substance: From symbolic to behavioral relationships. *Public Relations Review* 19(2). 121–139.

Grunig, James E. 2015. Foreword. In Eyun-Jung Ki, Jeong-Nam Kim & John A. Ledingham (eds.), *Public relations as relationship management: A relational approach to the study and practice of public relations*, 2nd edn, xxiii–xxvii. New York: Routledge.

Grunig, Larissa A., James E. Grunig & William P. Ehling. 1992. What is an effective organization? In James E. Grunig (ed.), *Excellent public relations and communication management: Contributions to effective organizations*, 65–89. Hillsdale, NJ: Lawrence Erlbaum Associates.

Grunig, Larissa A., James E. Grunig & David M. Dozier. 2002. *Excellent public relations and effective organizations: A study of communication management in three countries*. Mahwah, NJ: Lawrence Erlbaum Associates.

Heath, Robert L. 2013. The journey to understand and champion OPR takes many roads, some not yet well traveled. *Public Relations Review* 39(5). 426–431.

Hon, Linda C. & James E. Grunig. 1999. *Guidelines for measuring relationships in public relations*. Gainesville, FL: The Institute for Public Relations, Commission on PR Measurement and Evaluation. https://www.instituteforpr.org/wp-content/uploads/Guidelines_Measuring_Relationships.pdf (accessed 20 January 2020).

Huang, Yi-Hui. 2001. OPRA: A cross-cultural, multiple-item scale for measuring organization-public relationships. *Journal of Public Relations Research* 13(1). 61–90.

Hung, Flora Chun-Ju. 2005. Exploring types of organization–public relationships and their implications for relationship management in public relations. *Journal of Public Relations Research* 17(4). 393–426.

Johnston, Kim A. & Maureen Taylor. 2018. *The handbook of engagement communication*. Medford, MA: Wiley-Blackwell

Kelly, Kathleen S. 2001. Stewardship: The fifth step in the public relations process. In Robert L. Heath (ed.), *Handbook of public relations*, 279–289. Thousand Oaks, CA: Sage.

Kent, Micheal L. & Maureen Taylor. 1998. Building dialogic relationships through the World Wide Web. *Public Relations Review* 24(3). 321–334.

Ki, Eyun-Jung, Jeong-Nam Kim & John A. Ledingham. 2015. *Public relations as relationship management: A relational approach to the study and practice of public relations*, 2nd edn. New York: Routledge.

Ledingham, John A. 2001. Government and citizenry: Extending the relational perspective of public relations. *Public Relations Review* 27(3). 285–295.

Ledingham, John A. 2003a. Explicating relationship management as a general theory of public relations. *Journal of Public Relations Research* 15(2). 181–198.

Ledingham, John A. 2003b. SMARTS: A relationship process model of public relations. *Business research yearbook*, Vol. 10. 969–973 Saline, MI: McNaughton & Gunn.

Ledingham, John A. & Stephen D. Bruning. 1998. Relationship management and public relations: Dimensions of an organization–public relationship. *Public Relations Review* 24(1). 55–65.

Ledingham, John A. & Stephen D. Bruning. 1999. Managing media relations: Extending the relational perspective of public relations. In Jerry Biberman & Abbass F. Alkhafaji (eds.), *Business research yearbook, Vol. 5*, 644–648. Saline, MI: McNaughton & Gunn.

Ledingham, John A. & Stephen D. Bruning. 2001. Community relations. In Robert L. Heath (ed.), *Handbook of public relations*, 527–534. Thousand Oaks, CA: Sage.

Ledingham, John A. & Stephen D Bruning. 2000. A longitudinal study of organization-public relationships dimensions: Defining the role of communication in the practice of relationship management. In John A. Ledingham and Stephen D. Bruning (eds), *Public relations as relationship management: a relational approach to public relations*. Mahwah, NJ: Laurence Erlbaum Associates.

Ledingham, John A., Stephen D. Bruning & Laurie J. Wilson. 1998. Time as an indicator of the perceptions and behavior of a key public: A work in progress. Paper presented at the Annual Convention of the Association for Education in Journalism and Mass Communication, 5–8 August.

Ledingham, John A., Stephen D. Bruning, Dean T. Thomlison & Cheryl Lesko. 1997. The applicability of interpersonal relationship dimensions to an organizational context: Toward a theory of relational loyalty a qualitative approach. *Academy of Managerial Communications Journal* 1(1). 23–43.

Littlejohn, Stephen W. 1983. *Theories of Human Communication*, 2nd edn. Belmont, CA: Wadsworth.

Mills, Judson & Margaret S. Clark. 1994. Communal and exchange relationships: Controversies and research. In Ralph Erber and Robin Gilmour (eds.), *Theoretical frameworks for personal relationships*, 29–42. Hillsdale, NJ: Lawrence Erlbaum Associates.

Ni, Lan & Qi Wang. 2011. Anxiety and uncertainty management in an intercultural setting: The impact on organization-public relationships. *Journal of Public Relations Research* 23(3). 269–301.

Sallot, Lynne M., Lisa J. Lyon, Carolina Acosta-Alzuru & Karyn Ogata Jones. 2003. From aardvark to zebra: A new millennium analysis of theory development in public relations academic journals. *Journal of Public Relations Research* 15(1). 27–90.

Valentini, Chiara. 2017. Environment. In Craig Scott and Laurie Lewis (eds.), *The international encyclopedia of organizational communication*. Malden, MA: Wiley-Blackwell.

Valentini, Chiara. 2018. 2.1. Communicatively constituted stakeholders: Advancing a communication perspective in stakeholder relations. In Adam Lindgreen, Francois Maon, Joelle Vanhamme, Beatriz Palacios Florencio, Christine Vallaster, Carolyn Stron (eds.), *Engaging with stakeholders. A relational perspective on responsible business*, 65–79. New York: Routledge.

Valentini, Chiara, Dean Kruckberg & Kenneth Starck. 2012. Public relations and community: A persistant convenant. *Public Relations Review* 38(5). 873–879.

Walters, Richard D. & Denise Sevick Bortree. 2012. Advancing relationship management theory: Mapping the continuum of relationship types. *Public Relations Review* 38(1). 123–127

Zaharna, Rhonda. 2016. Beyond the individualism-collectivism divide to relationalism: explicating cultural assumptions in the concept of relationships. *Communication Theory* 26(2). 190–212.

Marina Vujnovic, Dean Kruckeberg, and Kenneth Starck

22 Extending the boundaries of public relations through community-building and organic theories

Abstract: This chapter explicates both community-building and organic theories of public relations. The history, thesis, and main elements of each theory are outlined. The chapter provides basic conceptual definitions and foundations upon which these theories were built. Both theories are predicated on the idea that public relations plays an important role within the larger societal context. Both theories also remind us of the responsibility that public relations has in both the maintenance of and the changes in societal relations. Each theory's main elements and premises are discussed, followed by an examination of their past and current applications and their potential limitations, as well as their future prospects for developing thinking and research within the growing field of critical public relations scholarship. Further, these theories' utility, criticisms, and limitations are discussed. Finally, these theories' current uses and their potential for future research in public relations and beyond are outlined.

Keywords: community-building; community; organic; neoliberalism; social theory; critical theory

> *"In theory, there is no difference between theory and practice. But in practice, there is."*
> — Yogi Berra

1 The value of social and critical theory for public relations theorizing and practice

The study of public relations has long been criticized for its instrumental and managerial approach as espoused by its dominant theory that had begun with J. Grunig and Hunt's (1984) book, *Managing Public Relations*. Unquestionably, that ground-breaking and far-reaching work has evolved into the dominant paradigm of public relations, Excellence Theory, which throughout its history has been met with both embrace and criticism by scholars worldwide. It would be almost impossible to list all of the criticisms of Excellence Theory, especially during the past decade; however, much of this criticism has stemmed from how this dominant paradigm has theorized public relations as a managerial function within an organizational context, rather than as a social phenomenon in and of itself.

This chapter offers an overview of two interrelated theoretical approaches, community-building theory and the organic theory of public relations, whose foundations

https://doi.org/10.1515/9783110554250-022

are laid in the need to see the role of public relations within the larger societal context. Both theories recognize the important role that public relations plays in our societies and remind us about the responsibility that public relations has in both the maintenance of and the changes in societal relations. Each theory's main elements and premises are discussed, followed by an examination of their past and current applications and their potential limitations, as well as their future prospects for developing thinking and research within the growing field of critical public relations scholarship.

Indeed, public relations theory and practice have been experiencing a "paradigmatic shift" (Kuhn 2012) since the late 1990s and early 2000s, when some of the first ideas of postmodern public relations were proposed (Holtzhausen and Voto 2002), signaling a time when more and more scholars would be willing to break out of the modernist, functionalist, managerial view of public relations. Yet, even with this radical proposition, most public relations research stayed surprisingly organization-centric. Ristino (2008) proposed a socio-cultural turn in public relations from a critical-cultural perspective, yet his proposition still saw public relations as an organization-centric managerial communication practice. Recently, Edwards (2018: 9) argued for a socio-cultural approach and more research in which the practice of public relations is seen "as a social and cultural practice in its own right". Her proposition clearly lifts public relations out of the stronghold of the organizational paradigm, arguing that public relations has both a history and a future that has an agency "beyond organizational objectives" (Edwards 2018: 10). She outlines characteristics or assumptions of socio-cultural research in public relations: public relations, even when organization-centric, has consequences on social, political, and cultural life; the relationship between public relations and society is transactional and "mutually constituted" (Edwards 2018: 12); public relations research demands more than simplistic explanations and rigid categorizations; public relations research engages with questions of power in various ways; and public relations research engages with questions about public relations' impact on people's daily lives through qualitative and interpretive methodologies (Edwards 2018: 10–13). By examining the types of societies in which public relations is practiced, how society is changing, the impact of neoliberalism and the role of public relations in neoliberalism's success and by potentially challenging its premises, and with questions of community and common good, Edwards (2018) outlines the socio-cultural turn in public relations scholarship in which an organic theory neatly fits as it has evolved from community-building. However, regardless of these positive developments in thinking about the role and theorizing of public relations, the greatest challenge lies in breaking the dominance of mainstream scholarship that has established public relations as a managerial, strategic function that leads to a perception of public relations as nothing more than organizational propaganda.

Ihlen, van Ruler, and Fredriksson's (2009) book outlined the role of social theory in public relations, arguing for macro (societal), meso (organizational), and micro (individual) levels in which social theory has a central place in public relations theorizing as well as in the methodologies that public relations research employs. Ihlen and van Ruler (2009) argued that most public relations research concerns itself with dyadic relations between an organization and its publics, but not so much with how an organization relates itself to society-at-large. That's not to say that no attempts have been made to theorize public relations from other perspectives. Ihlen and van Ruler (2009) outlined perspectives ranging from rhetorical, communitarian, and sociological to feminist and postmodern. If we had to impose an umbrella term that is based on one commonality, we could call these perspectives critical theory of public relations, which has begun in a critique of the dominant paradigm. Ample evidence exists of the considerable growth of scholarship that has critical perspectives on public relations. L'Etang and Pieczka's (1996) *Critical Perspectives in Public Relations* highlighted scholars who had utilized social and critical theory and provided critiques of the dominant paradigm of public relations. Since then, additional scholarship has appeared in journal articles, books, and edited volumes. More recently, Heath and Xifra (2016) have provided a critique of critical theory in public relations by calling for a different goal – that is, less criticism of public relations for criticism's sake and more scholarship that could provide a true grounding for change.

A critical theory in public relations has been extensively developed, argues Weaver (2016), but she further asserts that a focus on Marxist analysis is surprisingly absent. This contention in many ways supports the argument of Heath and Xifra (2016) that critical theory must move beyond criticism of public relations' dominant paradigm to outline how social, political, and economic structures shape public relations and, alternatively, what role public relations plays, if any, in co-creating those structures. Such scholarship shows that, in some ways, sociological and critical theories that utilize social theory have amassed to a point where a critique of critical theory in public relations might be offered. Edwards (2018), while arguing for a socio-cultural approach to the study of public relations, pays particular attention to the need for the study of public relations practices that occur outside of the organizational framework. Although she acknowledges that public relations has traditionally been seen as a practice within an organizational framework, public relations practices, both historically and today, have equally been a part of social and political life outside of an organizational framework. Lindemann (2011) reminds us of Simmel's (1908) discussion of sociological theory that distinguishes among social theory, mid-range theories, and theories of society. Social theory concerns itself with the roles that human and non-human actors play in society, while mid-range theory limits itself to looking at specific examples. More importantly, and what we are most interested in, are those theories of society that can address historical formations such as pre-modern, modern, and capitalist society. Empirical data gathered in studies using social and mid-range theories have accumulated to help build theories of society. So, indeed, the study of public relations and understanding its role in co-creating social, political, and economic structures are essential in developing a theory of society that could potentially address the historical formation of our present time.

2 Community-building theory

Community-building, as originally developed by Kruckeberg and Starck (1988), is a theory of society that is interested in the role that public relations, as well as organizations through their public relations functions, should play in building their immediate communities and in enhancing the well-being of society-at-large. In community-building theory, several elements deserve special attention: a) the concept of community, b) a concept of community-building, and c) the loss of sense of community that is arguably a result of the growth and proliferation of mass communication.

2.1 The concept of community

Perhaps the most important element of community-building theory is the concept of community itself. This concept has had an important role in the public relations literature, ranging from communitarian (Leeper 1996; Culbertson and Chen 1996; Luoma-aho 2009), community relations (Grunig J. and Hunt 1984; Heath 1997; Wilcox et al. 2003; Wilcox and Cameron 2009; Heath and Ni 2010), corporate social responsibility (Rawlins 2005; Heath & Ni 2010), and community-building perspectives (Kruckeberg and Starck 1988; Starck and Kruckeberg 2001; St. John III 1998; Hallahan 2005). For community-building theory, as first proposed by Kruckeberg and Starck (1988), sociological literature, particularly the Chicago School of Social Thought's conceptualization of community, was at the core of the original community-building conceptual framework. The Chicago School of Thought was a group of sociologists whose work was prominent from just before the start of the 20th Century to the late 1950s. Prominent figures of the Chicago School included the now-famous sociologist Robert E. Park, as well as names such as Erving Goffman and Herbert Blumer. Some of the tenets of their theory were a focus on qualitative and ethnographic methodologies; a focus on complex social interactions in urban settings; an ecological approach, in which they examined parallels between natural and social systems; and, most importantly, the idea of the loss of a sense of community. They also heavily relied on the work of social psychologist George H. Mead and his theory of symbolic interactionism, as well as on the work of John Dewey, who focused on the study of communication and transportation technologies and their impact on society. At the core of the Chicago School's work was the concept of community, in which individuals who form a community share a geographical location, in which they are a *society* with a will to participate in a common life of that community (Burgess 1973). This will to participate in the common life of the community (although a smaller community could be a part of a larger community, even a global community) was key to understanding the Chicago School's definition of community. Together with their concept of community, Kruckeberg and Starck (1988), according to Kruckeberg and Tsetsura (2008: 13–14), used the following ideas to inform their own understanding of community: an individual ordinarily belongs primarily to one community; communication is a key to an individual's life in a community; functional differentiation exists because people have various occupations and fulfill various activities; communities occupy specific geographic areas and develop specific cultural traits; and institutions emerge and become prerequisites for community formation.

2.2 Community-building concept

St. John III used the term "community-building" in an article published in *Public Relations Quarterly* in 1998. He offered an historical view of public relations, especially as it related to nation-building efforts in the United States, and showed how public relations had moved from societal advocacy to corporate advocacy. Furthermore, community-building has often been used simply to refer to types of engagement that organizations seek to increase with various publics, and sometimes has been used as a synonym for community relations. Hallahan (2004) defined community-building as "the integration of people and the organizations they create into a functional collectivity that strives toward common or compatible goals" (Hallahan 2004: 44) and, in 2005, suggested that community-building can take three forms: community involvement, community nurturing, and community organizing (Hallahan 2005: 173–174).

2.3 Loss of sense of community

Valentini, Kruckeberg, and Starck (2012) explained that Chicago School scholars were driven into urban, empirical, sociological research because of their concern with questions of the loss of sense of community. Because of the fast spread of mass media at the time and cheap long-distance communication, people's relationships began to shift away from immediate, geographically defined communities. New societal structures, such as mass media, resulted in the loss of a sense of community.

From this common understanding, Kruckeberg and Starck (1988, 2004) theorized that the main goal of public relations is to restore and maintain sense of community. Public relations practitioners are community-builders who, through communication, should strive to maintain and restore a sense of community. In their 1988 book, they wrote:

> The public relations practitioner's role as a communicator, and more specifically as a communication facilitator, should be his or her highest calling. Being a facilitator of communication in the traditional sense – that is, seeking out and promoting discourse along all avenues – is a role of critical importance today, which can help to build a sense of community among organizations and their geographic publics. (Kruckeberg and Starck 1988: 112)

Therefore, Kruckeberg and Starck (1988, 2004) argue that the main role of public relations is to promote and facilitate communication, with a goal to build a sense of community in their geographic locations. Thus, the work of public relations practitioners is advocacy for community health and for the health of society-at-large. This is why Kruckeberg and Starck (2004) maintained that public relations' best practice should be "an active attempt to restore and maintain a sense of community" (Kruckeberg and Starck 2004: 136), which, if practiced as such, should be regarded as the "highest calling of the public relations practice" (Kruckeberg and Starck 2004: 137). They believe that it is through community-building that public relations practitioners best serve their organizations and society-at-large. Indeed, their argument is, and has always been, that society is organizations' ultimate stakeholder.

2.4 Critiques and further elaborations of the concept of community and community-building

Over the course of the last part of the 20th Century, scholars in sociology and related disciplines have mounted a critique of the Chicago School's concept of community, regarding it as too tied to geographic location, and ultimately making community a static concept (Walsh and High 1999). Calhoun (1978) argued that community includes, not only an organized set of social relationships, but inevitably the structures that work to order those relationships. In that sense, community is everything *but* a static concept. Hamilton (1985) argues that scholars should focus on both the symbolic dimension of community (such as values, moral codes that provide meaning to its members) and the structural dimensions of the community. Hamilton (1985) further argues that organizations as structures aren't really capable of creating meaning, so those organizations that set community-building as a goal might be doomed to failure.

Since Kruckeberg and Starck's (1988) concept of community-building, their thinking on the concept of community has equally evolved in their own work. Kruckeberg and Tsetsura (2008) identified problems with the Chicago School's reliance on geographical space and revised the original community-building theory so that community is no longer tied to a geographical space. They thus revised elements of the definition of community that were proposed by the Chicago School that had been adopted by Kruckeberg and Starck's (1988) community-building theory. Kruckeberg and Valentini (2014) more recently argued for the need to re-think, not only a community-building approach, but also community relations as public relations intended for organizations' immediate geographical communities. Because of the growth of the Internet, which serves as a platform to forge virtual relationships and therefore virtual communities, Kruckeberg and Tsetsura (2008) revised the first element of the definition of community to include multiple communities, although arguing that one of those communities will still be maintained as a primary community with which an individual would identify the most. The second adjustment of the original understanding of community relates to geographical space. Kruckeberg and Tsetsura (2008) acknowledge the existence of virtual spaces and therefore redefine the second element of community as: "people in a community occupy a definable space, whether physical or virtual" (Kruckeberg and Tsetsura (2008: 15). Based on the work of political scientist and historian Benedict Anderson (1983), communities can also be imagined. For example, media play an important role in creating imagined communities that may be removed in space and time. Work of other historians also emphasized a need to look at community beyond geographical boundaries. Therefore, Vujnovic and Kruckeberg (2019) reflect that the changing understanding of community in community-building theory must include a perspective from the work of historians Walsh and High (1999), which suggested that every attempt to examine a community should include contemplation of community as "imagined reality, community as social interaction, and community as process" (Walsh and High 1999: 257). In other words, when theorizing and studying community, public relations theory should include a multi-fold understanding of the phenomenon. Kruckeberg and Tsetsura (2008) include an understanding of globalism and multiculturalism as elements that complicate our understanding of community. For instance, questions emerge about the true possibility of a global community and about how more homogenous communities are changing under the influence of globalization, immigration, and growing multiculturalism. Starck and Kruckeberg (2001) observed that it is this changing landscape of communication technologies in global context that presents a real challenge to community-building, arguing that it is perhaps more important than ever to appreciate the need for the restoration of sense of community. All these elements are of interest to public relations scholars, particularly those in critical public relations scholarship. Critical public relations scholars acknowledge the relations of power among human elements of society. In some sense, ecological elements of the Chicago School are maintained in such understanding of community and community-building. However, as technologies develop and as our world becomes even more complex, power among not only human elements of society, but also human and non-human elements, such as artificial intelligence, might become relevant. Such factors will further challenge the conceptualization of community, community-building, and the idea of the loss of sense of community. Latour (1993) challenged sociologists and other social scientists by exploring the possibility of the agency of non-human elements of society. In a world in which artificial intelligence (AI) is increasingly becoming an everyday phenomenon, we should be open to the fact that our ideas of community, community-building, power, politics, and inclusion will continue to be challenged, both today and in the future.

3 The organic theory of public relations

The organic theory of public relations is likewise a social theory that focuses on commentary and the critique of social relations, with a particular focus on the role of public relations in the larger societal context. Important elements or concepts of the organic theory are: (a) *organic* interrelationships among elements in social systems; (b) the critique of the dominant organization-centric functionalist view of public relations theory and practice; and (c) the critique of power and neoliberal capitalism.

3.1 Organic theory and organic interrelationships among elements in social systems

Vujnovic and Kruckeberg (2005) and Kruckeberg and Vujnovic (2006) developed an organic perspective on public relations, also referred to as an organic model and theory of public relations, which they view as both a critical and ecological theory of public relations. As a critical theory, it is informed by the work of critical political economists of communication such as Mosco (1996, 2009, 2012), Calabrese (2004), and Gibson-Graham (2006). Mosco (2012) suggests that scholars who engage in the study of communication must place it within the context of society, drawing on various connections between and among economy, geography, cultural, and policy studies. Because current social context requires that scholars understand the impact of neoliberal capitalism and the types of inequalities that it creates globally, "organic theory" is, at its core, a critique of neoliberal capitalism. Vujnovic and Kruckeberg (2019) argue that it is a responsibility of public relations to address these inequalities in theory and practice. Ihlen and van Ruler (2009) argued that public relations has been overwhelmingly studied in theory and practice from the managerial and organization-centric approaches. They proposed that public relations should be studied from a social theory perspective and that public relations should offer more theories that have a broader social view, because public relations arguably has a large role to play in shaping our societies. Both social theoretical approaches and critical public relations scholarship have been steadily growing in recent years (Holtzhausen 2007; L'Etang 2004, 2005, 2007; Brunton and Galloway 2016). Although public relations theory and scholarly examination of its practices have not been extensively devoted to a critique of capitalism, scholars such as Weaver (2016) have studied public relations from a Marxist perspective.

The organic theory is also informed by the work of sociologists and social ecologists, ranging from the Chicago School's ecology to Aldo Leopold's (1949) assertions that many historical events were biotic interactions between people and the land. Leopold (1949), for instance, recognized that communities are a foundational concept in the science of ecology. To illustrate the concept of *organic*, we use the work of Lloyd (1901), who proposed an organic theory of society as an answer to the social contract theory that had existed at the time. Because "things participate in their own making" (Lloyd 1901: 579), Lloyd proposed that an organic theory focuses "greater unity of man with himself, as in the character of the individual of today; greater unity of man with his fellow, notably in the development of a conscious internationalism; and greater unity of man with nature in industrialism" (Lloyd 1901: 579). Therefore, the *organic* concept in the organic theory of public relations refers to the recognition of the interconnectedness between and among all the elements in society and the ways in which all things participate in the making and remaking of systems in which we exist. Lloyd's (1901) concept of organic theory, combined with Leopold's (1949) ecological approach to society, further lead to a theoretical approach that Kruckeberg (2007: 24) noted "gives special emphasis to the humane protection of the weak and powerless as well as to the preservation of the physical environment."

For the organic theory of public relations, community is an important concept, but it is not as central as it is in the community-building theory. While community-building theory values the role of public relations in the creation, restoration, and maintenance of the community, an "organic theory" of public relations values organizational participation in the dialogue by listening to the concerns of organizations' communities. In addition, public relations' role is extended to a potential critique of organizations' role in their communities and to the critique of the larger societal relations that may be contributing to these communities' lives (for example, see Vujnovic, Kumar, and Kruckeberg 2007). Thus, one major distinction between community-building theory and organic theory is in the idea of the maintenance of existing networks and communities. Although we agree that maintenance of social relations is important for communities to be able to sustain themselves, we see public relations practitioners more as agents of change. Public relations should prioritize change over maintenance, especially as a means to engage in the critique of established socio-political and economic relations (Vujnovic and Kruckeberg 2019). Similarly to other critical public relations scholarship (Berger 2005; Berger and Reber 2006; L'Etang 1996), the organic theory of public relations is committed to the study of power in both organizational and larger social contexts. Society consists of various publics who are in unequal positions of power to influence change. In addition, non-human elements, such as animals and the physical environment, don't have human agency to speak for themselves, but need to be recognized as "stakeholders" and therefore be a part of public relations' efforts to provide a voice for those on the margins (Vujnovic and Kruckeberg 2019).

3.2 The critique of the dominant organization-centric functionalist view of public relations theory and practice

The organic theory of public relations also emerged through a constant rethinking of the dominant public relations scholarship that stems from the early work of J. Grunig and Hunt (1984). That approach, which is highly functionalist and organization-centered, focuses primarily on the managerial function of public relations in an organizational context. Although J. Grunig (1992) and L. Grunig, J. Grunig, and Dozier (2002), through Excellence Theory, argue for a two-way communicative model and do find organizational impact on society as important, their approach still views organizations as central to that argument. Public relations remains a strategic organizational activity. J. Grunig and L. Grunig (2008), while writing about the trajectory and development of the Excellence Theory, argue that the strategic management function and the integration of public relations in strategic management were key components in integrating so-called middle range theories with a general theory of public relations. Even though elements of postmodernism have been integrated within this dominant paradigm of public relations (see Grunig, L., Grunig, J. and Dozier 2002), critical scholars often maintain that this dominant paradigm is still very much a reflection of modernist and functionalist thinking (Leitch and Neilson 2001; Holtzhausen and Voto 2002). Outside of the realm of scholarly thinking, the results of globalization and corporate dominance over every aspect of life further challenge the theory and practice of public relations (for example, see Kruckeberg and Vujnovic 2017). We see the need for public relations scholarship and theorization to develop in a way that would offer answers to the challenges of a neoliberal age. It is, perhaps, evident that public relations, particularly through its dominant paradigm, has done more to build than to challenge the tenets of neoliberal society. While examining the processes of privatization in the UK economy of the late 1970s and early 1980s and the role of public relations in propagating this privatization, Gray (2012) concluded that 'public relations' has served as an engine for the spread of neoliberalism. However, public relations' growth also emerged as a symptom of neoliberalism because the public relations industry grew due to these new privatization policies. Therefore, he argues, "... growth of PR and the domination of neoliberal ideas can be seen as self-perpetuating" (Gray 2012).

Critical public relations scholars have long offered alternative views to this managerial function of the dominant public relations scholarship (for example, Holtzhausen 2007). Vujnovic (2004) argued that the role of the public relations practitioner in an organizational context should be less that of a manager and more that of an impartial ombudsman. In that context, the public relations practitioner isn't solely responsible to the organization, but rather is a voice for all publics, not just those that are, at a given time, strategically aligned with the organizational interests (Vujnovic and Kruckeberg 2016). Therefore, an organic theory of public relations provides recognition of the importance of *all* social actors in public relations theory and practice. This theory offers public relations a way to interrogate its own responsibility in both the creation and the maintenance of current global neoliberal society. It also offers public relations practitioners a way to think about themselves as agents for change and as a voice for those who otherwise might have none. An organic theory reminds us of the ways in which interdependence among all things begs for a more conscientious approach to our social, political, economic, and cultural realties – that is, to our total existence.

4 Uses and future applications

Both community-building and organic theories of public relations as normative social theories provide a broader societal view of public relations theory and practice. In other words, both theories place public relations in the center of values-driven, ethical communicative practice that has great potential to benefit all stakeholders in any given society. These theories also provide a more inclusive worldview by arguing for a more expansive approach to the definition of a stakeholder, which would include not only distinguished groups that have immediate relationships with a particular organization, but everything and everyone who make up the fabric of society. This more inclusive worldview suggests that those individuals who practice public relations, those organizations that devote their work to public relations practice, and those entities that simply use public relations as one of their communicative strategies should not simply work to advance their bottom lines, but rather work to help build healthier, more just communities/societies. Other scholars in public relations have also argued for a more responsible, less corporate-like approach to public relations through corporate social responsibility (Rawlins 2005) or communitarianism (Leeper 1996). Although these theoretical approaches aren't dominant in public relations scholarship, they have impacted scholarly debates, inspiring research. The value of normative theories is under-appreciated and often misunderstood in traditional empirical research that places greater value on more prescriptive, and thereby easily testable, theoretical approaches. J. Grunig (1992: 12) says a normative theory "prescribes how to do public relations in an ideal situation, and contrasts that theory with our predictions of how public relations generally is practiced". J. Grunig and L. Grunig (1992: 291) say a normative theory is "how things should be or how some activity should be carried out". Importantly, in developing a normative theory, theorists have no obligation to show that an activity actually is conducted in the way the theory describes. They must show only that, if an activity were to be conducted as the theory prescribes, it would be effective. Normative theories are common in fields such as management science, operations research, the economics of decision making, and – to a lesser extent – marketing and organizational communication. (J. Grunig and L. Grunig 1992: 291). In contrast, J. Grunig and L. Grunig say *how* public relations is practiced is a positive (descriptive) theory: "Positive theories describe phenomena, events, or activities as they actually occur" (J. Grunig and L. Grunig 1992: 291). To illustrate, J. Grunig and L. Grunig observe:

> "Most theories in the physical sciences are positive. They describe the rotation of the earth, the nature of the atom, and the origin of the universe. They do not tell the earth how to rotate, how the atom should be structured, or how a new universe could be initiated." (Grunig J. and Grunig L. 1992: 291)

J. Grunig and L. Grunig (1992) caution, however, that, "If that normative theory, in fact, cannot be implemented then it would not be a good theory" (Grunig J. and Grunig, L. 1992: 291). Perhaps a limitation of normative theories, such as community-building and organic theories, is that they cannot provide firm definitions of their concepts because they have to account for change and must argue how things might be, rather than how they are. Normative theories cannot simply observe and describe, providing definitive, more comfortable answers that most researchers and practitioners often seek.

Critics of community-building, such as Cheney and Christensen (2001: 167), argue that community-building is too values-driven and needs to be further developed and articulated or it will remain merely "a slogan". This is often a misunderstanding of normative theory. The very goal of normative theory is to offer a values-driven view of how society ought to be, rather than to explain how things are, which is what the goal of positive theory would be. Normative theories indeed provide values-driven critiques of social relations, offering a view of how these relations can and should be different. In that, both community-building and organic theories of public relations provide a broad view of how the role of public relations could be seen in the larger societal context. That said, community-building has been used to inspire even positivist research (Jin and Lee 2013). Community-building has served as inspiration for numerous research studies, and its impact on helping change the narrative and elicit discussions about the value of social theory for public relations is a real testament to community-building serving as a "persistent covenant" (Valentini, Kruckeberg, and Starck 2012: 873).

The organic theory of public relations is a part of a growing development of critical public relations approaches and is contributing to continued discussions about the consequences of over-represented positivist theoretical approaches in public relations theory and research. An organic theory has been utilized in public relations research relating to the crisis of global climate change and in a study of public health. Galloway and Lynn (2007/2008) embrace an organic framework for inclusion of various voices on the issue of global climate change, arguing that such a framework is better suited for community conversations that could elicit behavior change than is the dominant organization-centered approach. Brunton and Galloway (2016) utilized an organic approach as a more inclusive theoretical approach to the examination of public health issues. These kinds of issues need an approach that embraces a "general public," that is, society-at-large, rather than narrow strategic publics, acknowledging that sometimes "greater good is at stake" (Brunton and Galloway 2016: 163). Brunton and Galloway write: "Organic PR is well-situated to help establish a strong foundation to negotiate outcomes between social actors and healthcare organizations, through acknowledging not only that the answers to wicked problems are elusive, but also that a morally defensible greater good is at stake." (Brunton and Galloway 2016: 163).

Both theories arguably hold an important place in public relations scholarship and practice, and their utility could extend beyond public relations narrowly defined.

Both theories' premises allow individuals and organizations in all walks of life (governmental, nongovernmental, public, private, profit, non-profit) to consider how they adapt to ever-growing changes and to respond to challenges that these changes impose in empathetic and compassionate, as well as socially and environmentally considerate, ways.

Both theories suggest that more scholarship is required and that a practice of public relations is needed that would break from organization-centric and neoliberal paradigms. This need is particularly relevant today when corporate-mindedness has pervaded all walks of life. Auletta's (2018) intricate analysis of the advertising and public relations industries warns about how corporatization of both practices and communication technologies have led to a blurring of the traditional lines that have defined them and how bottom-line approaches dictate how these practices might be defined in the future. We believe that it has never been more important than now to invoke community-building and organic theoretical approaches as theories that have applications even outside of the scope of public relations. We see these theories applied to historical studies about how public relations has been practiced beyond the confines of organizational structures, both domestically and globally. Indeed, without such historical studies, we cannot fully comprehend what community-building and organic theories might be and how they have been and are being practiced, as well as how they might evolve theoretically. Studies of social movements and activism and research that examine what public relations is when used by non-practitioners outside of organizational contexts could also illuminate potentials for community-building and organic theories. However, it is of utmost importance that the ideas espoused by community-building and organic theories gain traction with organizations and individuals everywhere, domestically and globally, so that the practice of public relations becomes less of a tool in the neoliberal capitalism playbook and more a philosophy of "conscientious globalism". In this way, communication practice can emerge to become a tool for social change, in which the idea of unity with others and the environment is not to be used to increase our bottom line, but as an expression of true understanding of our moral duty as agents in achieving a global society that strives toward equality and inclusiveness.

At the core of the argument offered by both community-building and organic theories of public relations is the feeling that this modern condition is not shared by all, that progress hasn't really been shared by all, and, as Colvile (2016) argues, it is isn't always good and, by virtue of being unequal, is inherently unfair. Further, at the core of both theories is the belief that organizations that practice public relations and individuals who practice public relations as communication agents should use their agency to produce meaningful change that could lead to more inclusive and fairer societies. Challenges of our times – for example, climate and global inequalities – require us to seek both theoretical and practical approaches to address these challenges. We believe community-building and organic theories of public relations could help individuals and organizations think about how their actions might alleviate some of the uncertainties that we face as a global community, working to decrease economic, racial, and gender inequalities and discussing in a more inclusive way what progress might mean for us all. That means including those who might have no voice at all, but whose well-being is, indeed, critical for our survival as humanity. As Kotter (2012) argued, the stakes are getting higher and, we should add, with that, the cost to our well-being as a humanity that ultimately shares the same destiny is higher. It, indeed, a moral responsibility of those who have the means and power and, with that, the most agency, to act in a way that would produce the most good for the greatest number.

References

Anderson, Benedict. 1983. *Imagined communities: Reflections on the origins and spread of nationalism*. London: Verso.

Auletta, Ken. 2018. *Frenemies: The epic disruption of the Ad Business (and everything else)*. New York: Penguin Press.

Berger, Bruce K. 2005. Power over, power with, and power to relations: Critical reflections on public relations, the dominant coalition, and activism. *Journal of Public Relations Research* 17(1). 5–28.

Berger, Bruce K. & Bryan H. Reber. 2006. Gaining influence in public relations: The role of resistance in practice. Mahwah, NJ: Lawrence Erlbaum Associates.

Brunton, Margaret A. & Christopher J. Galloway. 2016. The role of "organic public relations" in communicating wicked public health issues. *Journal of Communication Management* 20(2). 162–177.

Burgess, Ernest W. 1973. *On community, family, and delinquency*. Chicago: University of Chicago Press.

Calabrese, Andrew. 2004. Toward a political economy of culture. In Andrew Calabrese & Colin Sparks (eds.), *Toward a political economy of culture: Capitalism and communication in the twenty-first century*, 1–13. Lanham: Rowman and Littlefield.

Calhoun, Craig, J. 1978. History, anthroplogy and the study of communities: Some problems in Macfarlane's proposal. *Social History* 3(3). 363–373.

Cheney, George & Lars Thøger Christensen. 2001. Public relations as contested terrain. In Robert L. Heath (ed.), *Handbook of public relations*, 167–168. Thousand Oaks, CA: Sage.

Colvile, Robert. 2016. *The great acceleration: How the world is getting faster*. New York: Bloomsbury Press.

Culbertson, Hugh M. & Ni Chen. 1996. Communitarianism: A foundation for communication symmetry. *Public Relations Quarterly* 42(3). 36–41.

Edwards, Lee. 2018. *Understanding public relations: Theory, culture and society*. Los Angeles: Sage.

Galloway, Christopher & Margaret Lynn. 2007/2008. Public relations and climate change impacts: Developing a collaborative response. *Prism* 5(1–2): https://researchbank.swinburne.edu.au/items/74a42bc7-8a1e-44e7-811b-ec875d539379/1/ (accessed 21 December 2018).

Gibson-Graham, J. K. 2006. *The end of capitalism (As we knew it): A feminist critique of political economy*. Minneapolis: University of Minnesota Press.

Grunig, James E. 1992. Communication, public relations, and effective organizations: An overview of the book. In James E. Grunig (ed.), *Excellence in public relations and communication management*, 1–30. Hillsdale, NJ: Lawrence Erlbaum Associates.

Grunig, James E. & Larissa A. Grunig. 1992. Models of public relations and communication. In James E. Grunig (ed.), *Excellence in public relations and communication management*, 285–326. Hillsdale, NJ: Lawrence Erlbaum Associates.

Grunig, James E. & Todd Hunt. 1984. *Managing public relations*. New York: Holt, Rinehart and Winston.

Grunig, James E. & Larissa A. Grunig. 2008. Excellence theory in public relations: Past, present and future. In Ansgar Zerfass, Betteke van Ruler & Krishnamurthy Sriramesh (eds.), *Public relations research: European and international perspectives and innovations*, 327–347. Wiesbaden, Germany: VS Verlag fur Sozialwissenschaften.

Grunig, Larissa A., James E. Grunig & David M. Dozier. 2002. Excellent public relations and effective organizations: A study of communication management in three countries. Mahwah, NJ: Lawrence Erlbaum Associates.

Gray, Mark. 2012. The promotional industries: Functions and futures. Public relations as neoliberal. https://prpd2012.wordpress.com/2012/11/23/public-relations-as-neoliberal/ (accessed 20 December 2018).

Hallahan, Kirk. 2004. "Community" as the framework for public relations theory and research. *Communication Yearbook* 28. 44–89.

Hallahan, Kirk. 2005. Community and community building. In Robert L. Heath (ed.), *Encyclopedia of public relations*, 171–174. Thousand Oaks, CA: Sage.

Hamilton, Peter. 1985. Editor's foreword. In A. P. Cohen, *The symbolic construction of community*. London and New York: Routledge.

Heath, Robert L. 1997. *Strategic issues management: Organizations and public policy challenges*. Thousand Oaks, CA: Sage.

Heath, Robert L. & Lan Ni. 2010. Community relations and corporate social responsibility. In Robert L. Heath (ed.), *The SAGE handbook of public relations*, 557–568. Thousand Oaks, CA: Sage.

Heath, Robert L. & Jordi Xifra. 2016. What is critical about critical public relations theory? In Jacquie L'Etang, David McKie, Nancy Snow & Jordi Xifra (eds.), *Routledge handbook of critical public relations*, 200–210. London: Routledge.

Holtzhausen, Derina. 2007. A postmodern critique of public relations theory and practice. *Communicatio* 28(1). 29–38.

Holtzhausen, Derina R. & Rosina Voto. 2002. Resistance from the margins: The postmodern public relations practitioner as organizational activist. *Journal of Public Relations Research* 14(1). 57–84.

Ihlen, Øyvind & Betteke van Ruler. 2009. Introduction: Applying social theory to public relations. In Øyvind Ihlen, Betteke van Ruler & Magnus Fredriksson (eds.), *Public relations and social theory: Key figures and concepts*, 1–20. New York: Routledge.

Ihlen, Øyvind, Betteke van Ruler & Magnus Fredriksson. 2009. *Public relations and social theory: Key figures and concepts*. New York: Routledge.

Jin, Bumsub & Subum Lee. 2013. Enhancing community capacity: Roles of perceived bonding and bridging social capital and public relations in community building. *Public Relations Review* 39. 290–292.

Kotter, John P. 2012. Thoughts on the changing world around us. *Forbes Magazine*. https://www.forbes.com/sites/johnkotter/2012/11/06/thoughts-on-the-changing-world-around-us/#71e94c886e7d (accessed 21 December 2018).

Kruckeberg, Dean. 2007. An "organic model" of public relations: The role of public relations for governments, civil society organizations (CSOs) and corporations in developing and guiding social and cultural policy to build and maintain community in 21st-Century civil society. In Administration of Ulan-Ude Committee of Social Politics (ed.), *Municipal social politics and* the publics: Realities and perspectives: Materials of the International/Scientific Conference, 17–25. Ulan-Ude, Buryatia: Publishing House of Buryatia Scientific Center of Russian Academy of Science.

Kruckeberg, Dean & Kenneth Starck. 1988. *Public relations and community: A reconstructed theory.* New York: Praeger.

Kruckeberg, Dean & Kenneth Starck. 2004. The role and ethics of community building for consumer products and services. *Journal of Promotion Management* 10(1&2). 133–146.

Kruckeberg, Dean & Katerina Tsetsura. 2008. The "Chicago School" in the global community: Concept explication for communication theories and practices. *Asian Communication Research* 3. 9–30.

Kruckeberg, Dean & Marina Vujnovic. 2017. The future of the global public relations industry in a 21ˢᵗ century era of de-globalization. Paper presented at the Public Relations Division Post-Conference of the International Communication Association, San Diego, 30 May.

Kruckeberg, Dean & Marina Vujnovic. 2006. Toward an "organic model" of public relations in public diplomacy. Paper presented at the 9ᵗʰ Annual International Public Relations Research Conference, Miami, 9–12 March.

Kruckeberg, Dean & Chiara Valentini. 2014. Conceptualization of community and community-building in a globalized world. Paper presented at the 100ᵗʰ Annual Convention of the National Communication Association, Chicago, 20–23 November.

Kuhn, Thomas. 2012. *The structure of scientific revolutions*, 4ᵗʰ edn. Chicago: University of Chicago Press.

Latour, Bruno. 1993. *We have never been modern.* Cambridge, MA: Harvard University Press.

Leeper, Kathie A. 1996. Public relations ethics and communitarianism: A preliminary investigation. *Public Relations Review* 22(2). 163–179.

Leitch, Shirley & David Neilson. 2001. Bringing publics into public relations; New theoretical frameworks for practice. In Robert L. Heath (ed.), *Handbook of public relations*, 127–138. Thousand Oaks, CA: Sage.

Leopold, Aldo. 1949. *A Sand County almanac and sketches here and there.* London: Oxford University Press.

L'Etang, Jacquie. 1996. Corporate responsibility and public relations ethics. In Jacquie L'Etang & Magda Pieczka (eds.), *Critical perspectives in public relations.* 82–105. London: International Thompson Business Press.

L'Etang, Jacquie. 2004. The myth of the "ethical guardian": An examination of its origins, potency and illusions. *Journal of Communication Management* 8(1). 53–67.

L'Etang, Jacquie. 2005. Critical public relations: Some reflections. *Public Relations Review* 31(4). 521–526.

L'Etang, Jacquie. 2007. Public relations and tourism. Critical reflections and a research agenda. *Public Relations Review* 33(1). 68–76.

L'Etang, Jacquie & Magda Pieczka. 1996. *Critical perspectives in public relations.* London: International Thompson Business Press.

Lindemann, Gesa. 2011. On Latour's social theory and theory of society, and his contribution to saving the world. *Human Studies* 34(1). 93–110. https://www.jstor.org/stable/41478457 (accessed 26 March 2020).

Lloyd, Alfred H. 1901. The organic theory of society. Passing of the contract theory. *American Journal of Sociology* 6(5). 577–601.

Luoma-aho, Vilma. 2009. On Putnam: Bowling together—Applying Putnam's theories of community and social capital to public relations. In Oyvind Ihlen, Betteke van Ruler & Magnus Fredriksson (eds.), *Public relations and social theory: Key figures and concepts*, 231–251. New York: Routledge.

Mosco, Vincent. 1996. *The political economy of communication*. London, Thousand Oaks, CA, & New Delhi: Sage.

Mosco, Vincent. 2009. *The political economy of communication*, 2nd edn. London & Thousand Oaks, CA: Sage.

Mosco, Vincent. 2012. Marx is back, but which one? On knowledge labour and media practice. *Triple C: Communication, Capitalism & Critique* 10(2). 570–576.

Rawlins, Brad L. 2005. Corporate social responsibility, in Robert L. Heath (ed.), *Encyclopedia of public relations*, Vol. 1. 210–214. Thousand Oaks, CA: Sage.

Ristino, Robert J. 2008. The sociocultural model of public relations/communications management practice: A critical-cultural perspective. *International Journal of Strategic Communication* 2(1). https://doi.org/10.1080/15531180701816585 (accessed 20 December 2018).

Simmel, Georg. 1908. *Soziologie. Untersuchungen über die Formen der Vergesellschaftung.* [Sociology: inquiries into the construction of social forms]. Leipzig: Duncker & Humblot.

St. John III, Burton. 1998. Public relations as community-building: Then and now. *Public Relations Quarterly* 43(1). 34–40.

Starck, Kenneth & Dean Kruckeberg. 2001. Public relations and community: A reconstructed theory revisited. In Robert L. Heath (ed.), *Handbook of public relations*, 51–59. Thousand Oaks, CA: Sage.

Valentini, Chiara, Dean Kruckeberg & Kenneth Starck. 2012. Public relations and community: A persistent covenant. *Public Relations Review* 38(5). 873–879.

Vujnovic, Marina. 2004. *The public relations practitioner as ombudsman – A reconstructed model.* Unpublished master's thesis. Cedar Falls, IA: University of Northern Iowa.

Vujnovic, Marina & Dean Kruckeberg. 2005. Imperative for an Arab Model of public relations as a framework for diplomatic, corporate and nongovernmental organization relations. *Public Relations Review* 31(3). 338–343.

Vujnovic, Marina & Dean Kruckeberg. 2016. In the bind between theory and practice. In Brigitta R. Brunner (ed.), *The moral compass of public relations*. 137–148. New York: Routledge.

Vujnovic, Marina & Dean Kruckeberg. 2019. Community. In Brigitta Brunner (ed.), *Public relations theory. Application and understanding*. Hoboken, NJ: Wiley & Sons.

Vujnovic, Marina, Anup Kumar & Dean Kruckeberg. 2007. An "organic theory" as a social theory of public relations: A case study from India. Paper presented at the 10th Annual International Public Relations Research Conference, Miami, 8–11 March.

Walsh, John C. & Steven High. 1999. Rethinking the concept of community. *Social History* 32(64). 255–273.

Weaver, C. Kay. 2016. A Marxist primer for critical public relations scholarship. *Media International Australia* 160(1). 43–52.

Wilcox, Dennis L. & Glen T. Cameron. 2009. *Public relations: Strategies and tactics*, 9th edn. Boston: Allyn & Bacon.

Wilcox, Dennis L., Glen T. Cameron, Philip H. Ault & Warren K. Agee. 2003. *Public relations: Strategies and tactics*, 7th edn. Boston: Allyn & Bacon.

Anne Lane

23 Dialogic theory

Abstract: Dialogue is a prominent feature of much contemporary research and the-ory-building in public relations. This prominence could be associated with the rise of co-creational perspectives on the relationships between organizations and stake-holders, and the desire of scholars and practitioners to better understand the type of communication this requires. This chapter provides an overview of the concept of dialogue including its history, its implicit role within early public relations theories, its more recent emergence as a discrete concept, a discussion of its defining charac-teristics, and a review of relevant critiques. Using Kent and Taylor's 2002 article as a guiding framework, dialogue is shown to be much more than two-way communica-tion. The unique properties of dialogue are ideally suited to provide a foundation for the increasingly interactive and equitable forms of public relations that are emerging as we enter the third decade of the new millennium.

Keywords: dialogue; dialogic turn; principles; critiques

1 Introduction

Dialogue is becoming more and more important in public relations research and the development of theory in the discipline. This growth is perhaps allied to the increasing interest public relations has in finding ways to operate that challenge the supremacy of communication that accepts – and even reinforces – traditional organization-cen-tric perspectives and the existence of power differentials. However, the potential of dialogue to contribute to the theory and practice of public relations has not yet fully been realized, largely because of the continuing lack of consensus over what dialogue actually means.

Dialogue is a word that everyone thinks they understand, a "primitive term" (Chaffee 1991: 62) that is so self-evident it seems not to need definition. Surely every-body knows dialogue means two-way communication? But there is more to dialogue than that. Dialogue has been a topic of philosophical discussion for over 2,000 years (Anderson, Baxter, and Cissna 2004). In recent times, it has also emerged as a phe-nomenon of interest to the field of public relations. This is perhaps not surprising given the potential alignment between the discipline's focus on relationship manage-ment and engagement, at the heart of which must be two-way communication. From an academic and theoretical perspective though, true dialogue is not *just* two-way communication: it is a form of two-way communication characterized by the positive orientation of participants to each other, and to the communication in which they are engaged.

https://doi.org/10.1515/9783110554250-023

This chapter presents a brief history of the evolution of the dialogic theory of public relations and its links to the wider philosophical discussion of dialogue as a concept. The connections between dialogic theory of public relations and other public relations theories are identified and explored, and critiques are acknowledged. The chapter concludes with suggestions of how dialogic theory might evolve in the field of public relations.

2 The origins of a dialogic theory of public relations

The use of the term "dialogic theory of public relations" could be regarded as misleading, given that there is, in fact, no single and agreed theoretical conceptualization of dialogue in the field. This is despite the large and growing interest in dialogue in public relations as evidenced by the 17,100 academic journal articles containing both terms noted on Google Scholar since 2013 – including 3,410 in the first four months of 2019 alone. However, there has been some progress toward articulating aspects of a dialogic theory of public relations.

The article generally credited with introducing dialogue to public relations was published by Kent and Taylor (2002). In this paper, Kent and Taylor drew on the work of Pearson (1989b) and others to develop their earlier discussions (Kent and Taylor 1998) of the use of the Internet to build dialogic relationships. In both of their articles, Kent and Taylor incorporate ideas originally found in the work of dialogic theorists and philosophers. To understand the connections between these foundational concepts and the resulting principles of dialogue presented in Kent and Taylor (2002), the next section of this chapter presents an overview of the wider philosophical roots of dialogue.

2.1 A brief history of dialogue

Dialogue has been a topic of interest since the time of Socrates (Zappen 2004). At the risk of over-simplifying a delicate and nuanced concept, Socratic dialogue consists of a series of enquiries and responses between two participants through which one (the teacher or more learned person) encourages the other (the student) to develop their knowledge and understanding of a subject by explaining it (Kahn 1998). In conducting these enquiries, both participants learn more about the topic, and come to share a deeper appreciation of each other (Kahn 1998; see also more recent uses of Socratic dialogue in Morrell 2004; Paul and Elder 2007).

In the mid-20th century there was a marked resurgence of interest in both the philosophy of dialogue and its application in practice. Specialists in the field of dialogue (such as those featured in Anderson, Baxter, and Cissna 2004) consistently focus on the work of that time of theorists and scholars like Bakhtin (1981), Bohm (2006), Buber (1958), Freire (1990), Gadamer (1980a), and Rogers (1961). Each of these key scholars takes a slightly different perspective on dialogue.

Buber's work on the philosophy of dialogue in the mid-20th century marked the beginning of a concentrated study of the concept by academics from a range of fields, including theoretical physics and education. Buber was among the first to conceptualize dialogue holistically, that is, seeing dialogue as a phenomenon whose whole is greater than the sum of its part(icipant)s (see, for example, Buber 1965). He acknowledged the duality of the roles of participants in the development of his classic *I-Thou* binary (Buber 1958).

In these binaries, the *I* represents the observer, the perspective of one of the participants. The *I-Thou* is the connection made physically between that individual and aspects of the divine, which Buber felt could be found in animals, objects, and art, as well as in people. This type of dialogue is respectful and appreciative of the other participant. In contrast, the *I-It* dialogue is based on a perception of the other participant as some *thing*, to be engaged with to benefit the *I*. The main points gleaned from a review of Buber's work on dialogue are firstly that it involves two participants, the *I* and another. This *I* may perceive the other as equal or even superior (*Thou*) or inferior (*It*). This perception affects the orientation of the *I* to the other participant; *Thou* is respected – cherished even – while the *It* is objectified and manipulated to suit the desires of the *I*. Buber positions this latter type of dialogue based on an objectification of the other participant as vastly inferior.

Rogers worked in the field of counselling and psychotherapy and his perspective on dialogue derived from the interaction between the participants of doctor and patient. He argued that the doctor in these interactions is motivated by an empathetic desire to help patients by "mirroring back" their experiences to them, and reworking those experiences in a way that is healthier for the patient (Rogers 1961). The patient is motivated by their desire to share their current (flawed) understanding of their situation with their counsellor, whom they trust to improve their perceptions, thereby resolving uncomfortable internal conflict (Rogers 1961). Thus, the orientation of the participants to each other is one of care, concern, mutual respect, and empathy. Rogers (1961) insisted that warmth, genuineness, and empathy are necessary for dialogue to be effectively implemented.

Gadamer's work reinforced Buber's ideas concerning the duality of participants in dialogue, but also introduced some new ideas. Based on his deep interest in the structure of Plato's discourses (Gadamer 1980a; Grondin 2003), Gadamer positioned dialogue as being the exchange of arguments between two participants to resolve an issue – that is, as a dialectic. He identified the existence of return communication between participants as part of dialogue, and proposed that dialogue is both the communicative action taken by participants and its result (Gadamer 1980b, 1989).

Bakhtin similarly understood dialogue as instances of speech communication and responsiveness or reply, labelling the whole event as "the utterance" (Bakhtin 1981, 1986).

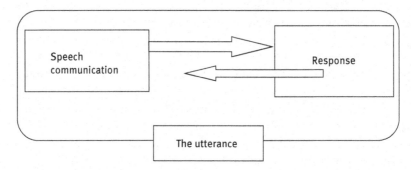

Figure 1: Bakhtin's utterance model of dialogue (Source: Devised from extant literature for this chapter)

To Bakhtin, the utterance was a way to generate empathy and understanding between participants, creating a platform on which they could develop mutually acceptable solutions to problems (Cissna and Anderson 1994; Hamilton and Wills-Toker 2006).

Bohm saw dialogue as "a stream of meaning flowing among and through us and between us" (Bohm, Factor, and Garrett 1991: 27). His work on dialogue positions it as a holistic process involving repeated interactions between participants, rather than as the sum of those interactions (Bohm 1985; Stewart, Zediker, and Black 2004). Bohm (2006) and others (Bohm, Factor, and Garrett 1991) are advocates of a concept they label Dialogue (note the capitalization). "Capital D" Dialogue is a specific form of group interaction "in which collective learning takes place and out of which a sense of increased harmony, fellowship and creativity can arise" (Bohm, Factor, and Garrett 1991: 2). As The Dialogue Group (cited in The Center for Whole Communities 2006) puts it, "In Dialogue [sic] we are interested in creating a fuller picture of reality rather than breaking it down into fragments or part, as happens in discussion. In Dialogue we do not try to convince others of our point of view. There is no emphasis on winning, but rather on learning, collaboration and the synthesis of points of view."

Freire, on the other hand, saw dialogue as the archetypal exercise of democratic interchange between citizens in preference to the domination of oppressor over oppressed (see, for example, Freire 1990). Freire's perspective positioned dialogue as an inclusive, transformative event, significant in the establishment and functioning of a truly democratic state. Freire's perspective was also that the power differentials that generated the need for such dialogue were in themselves anathema to dialogue. Thus, dialogue not only allowed the entry of previously disadvantaged citizenry to the political arena, it dismantled that arena and prevented its perpetuation.

Freire's work is one of the few that acknowledges that dialogue does not only take place within a positive context, and that it can in fact be conducted within an environment in which participants are actively hostile to each other. However, his perspective was that once the citizenry had been taught how to undertake dialogue "properly", they were equipped with the weapons to take on the dominant hegemony and thus overthrow it. In this there are echoes of Habermas' (1984) theory of communicative action, in which he proposed that societal decision-making could achieve the best results through highly structured interactions leading to joint agreement between participants, based on the quality of the argumentation undertaken.

A detailed review of the work of these – and other – dialogic theorists and scholars is beyond the scope of this chapter. However, what can be determined from such a review is that dialogue consists of two-way communication carried out between two or more participants, each/all of whom are positively oriented toward each other and the process of communication in which they are involved. A secondary but important sub-theme is that there are forms of two-way communication that do not demonstrate such positive orientations, such as Buber's *I-It*, and Bohm's non-capitalized dialogue, that are inescapably inferior. This distinction might be captured through reference to the differences between dialogue and authentic or *true* dialogue (Gadamer 1975/2006; Pearson 1989a; Theunissen and Wan Noordin 2011).

3 Dialogue in public relations

The translation of dialogue to the field of organizational studies began in the mid-1980s. At this time there was a widespread change in organizational theory as functionalist paradigms were challenged by the rise of alternative perspectives, particularly those that introduced the viewpoint of stakeholders as independent, powerful entities (see, for example, Albert and Whetten 1985, who proposed that stakeholders[1] have a significant role of in the co-creation of organizational identity). Functionalist approaches were no longer seen as being entirely appropriate to help organizations understand newly emergent stakeholder perspectives; and to incorporate stakeholder needs in organizational behavior. The subjective views and perspectives of stakeholders were repositioned as being important in determining organizational behavior; contrary stakeholders were accommodated, rather than being addressed as deviants to be corrected (cf. with systems theory, as in Spicer 1997). A new relational perspective on organizational theory emerged, one that introduced the idea that stakeholders

---

1 In this chapter I follow the lead of Hallahan (2000) and others, and use the term "stakeholders" to refer to groups and individuals that are defined by their connection to an organisation, whereas publics are stakeholders who are also connected to an issue. I refer to dialogue with stakeholders as there is no need to have a specific issue at its heart.

were not organizational playthings, and could in fact drive organizational change. The relational paradigm proposed that organizations and stakeholders are inextricably intertwined in relationships based on mutual dependency; stakeholders were therefore seen as partners with organizations in the achievement of organizational objectives (Post, Preston, and Sauter-Sachs 2002).

This more inclusive approach in organizational theory to incorporating stakeholder influences on the operation of organizations was also reflected in the emergence of new perspectives on public relations. Public relations practitioners were no longer seen as "the former journalist-as-hired-gun" (Kent 2008: 18) to fire communication "magic bullets" that defined their role under the functionalist/instrumentalist paradigm. Instead public relations practitioners were seen as being responsible for the development and enhancement of newly prioritized relationships with stakeholders (see, for example, Dozier 1984; Ferguson 1984).

The relational turn in public relations generated more interest in the type of communication required to achieve mutually beneficial relationships between organizations and their stakeholders. As Pieczka (2011: 110) concluded, "Although relationships are built from communication as well as other kinds of action (for example, product or policy related ones), communication occupies a privileged position". Dialogue was positioned within the relational paradigm as the communication method of choice (Bruning, Dials, and Shirka 2008; Bruning and Ledingham 1999). Indeed, the two concepts are often conflated, as in McAllister-Spooner and Kent's (2009: 223) assertion that "Dialogic communication is relational".

3.1 Links to two-way communication

Forms of two-way communication that have been linked to dialogue in the public relations literature include deliberation, debate, and conversation. Escobar (2009) and others (including Barnes, Newman, and Sullivan 2004; Kim, J. and Kim, E. J. 2008; Roberts 1997) assert that dialogue has an important place in the conduct of deliberative or participatory democracy. Drawing on the work of Buber, Bakhtin, Gadamer, Freire, Bohm and Habermas, Escobar (2009: 52–53) acknowledges the prescriptive nature of much dialogue theorizing and distinguishes between two forms of dialogue: the "collaborative non-polarised discourse" he labels "dialogue$_1$"; and the "relational space" of "dialogue$_2$". He notes that it is the former that features most strongly in the managerial and organizational context, while the latter is more relevant to abstract theoretical discussion and consideration, following the lead of Habermas (1984, 1989) in conceptualizing the contribution of dialogue to an idealized "public sphere".

Others, including Heath (2001), have equated dialogue in public relations with the conduct of debates or, as he terms it, rhetorical dialogue. In this conceptualization, "dialogue consists of statement and counterstatement" (Heath 2000: 74). This reflects to a certain extent the two-way communication already identified as being at the heart of dialogue. However, Kent and Taylor (2002: 27, echoing the work of Karlberg [1996]) refute the conflation of dialogue with debate, seeing the latter term as referring to a "clash of ideas" rather than the "lover-like" desire to benefit the other which they see as the nature of dialogue. In adopting this understanding of dialogue as "a conversation between lovers where each has his or her own desires but seeks the other's good" Kent and Taylor (2002: 27) maintain the perspectives proposed in the work of the dialogue theorists discussed previously in this chapter.

Heath (2000: 69) also ties in dialogue to the notion of public discourse, which he describes as being the communicative means "through which ideas are contested, issues are examined, and decisions are made collaboratively". Similarly, Weaver, Motion, and Roper (2006), Leeper (1996) and others writing in the public relations literature connect dialogue with discourse as being the expression of views on a topic during a process of refinement and concession-making *en route* to the making of mutually acceptable decisions by participants. This acknowledges the potential outcome of dialogue in public relations as collaborative decision-making, also echoing the precepts of the dialogue theorists discussed in Section 2 of this chapter.

Another set of discussions of dialogue in public relations sees it as a type of conversation between participants (Grunig J. 2009; Kelleher 2009; Pearson 1991). These discussions see conversation as an important means by which two parties communicate verbally *en route* to achieving mutual understanding of each other and the given topic of discussion. This again echoes the normative precepts of dialogue, and indicates why the concepts of conversation and dialogue are sometimes conflated. For the purposes of public relations practice however, the restriction of communication in conversation to the spoken word means it is often positioned as a form of dialogue, or a means by which dialogue is undertaken (as in Pearson 1991, for example).

Scholars (such as Leeper 1996; Woodward 2000) followed Pearson's lead and began to consider the relevance of dialogue to the context of public relations. Some, such as Fitzpatrick and Gauthier (2001), Kent and Taylor (2002), and Steinmann and Zerfass (1993), also adopted Pearson's perspective on the ethical superiority of dialogue in public relations, again assuming the existence of attributes in this communication that are appropriate to the concept of normative dialogue. This prescriptive premise is a common theme running throughout much of the literature that covers the relevance of dialogue to public relations. For Pearson and others of his school of thought, dialogue in public relations is understood holistically as two-way communication leading to one specific type of outcome: that of change by both participants leading to mutual benefit (although this perspective is not unchallenged: see, for example, Edgett 2002; Stoker and Tusinski 2006). This understanding then provides a framework to articulate how dialogue ought to be practiced in public relations (as in Kent and Taylor 2002).

3.2 J. Grunig and Hunt's two-way models

It is arguably not unconnected to the changing zeitgeist of the mid-1980s that J. Grunig and Hunt (1984) developed their influential four-part model of public relations practice at this time (see chapter 15 in this book for a full discussion of the models). Their acknowledgement of the co-existence of one-way and new two-way forms of communication reflected the transition from the functionalist to the relational paradigm in public relations. Given that two-way communication is inherent to the conduct of dialogue – although as stated previously, not all two-way communication is dialogue – then the rise of the relational perspective might therefore be directly linked to increasing levels of interest in dialogue as a key concept in public relations.

The two-way models of communication developed by J. Grunig and Hunt (1984) recognize that communication *with* stakeholders using two-way communication rather than communicating *to* them using monologue was an important part of the way public relations changed in the first half of the 20th century. In this they echo the two-way communication between pairs of participants that was found to be an identifying characteristic of dialogue in the previous section of this chapter. However, it does not necessarily mean that the two-way models of public relations demonstrate the occurrence of dialogue. Communication may be two-way in nature without demonstrating any of the other defining characteristics of dialogue.

The two-way symmetric model of public relations describes a situation where an organization allows its stakeholders to influence its decision-making. The model hinges on the conduct of communication between organizations and their stakeholders that is characterized by the free and equal two-way flow of information between participants, leading to mutual understanding and responsiveness (Grunig J. 1984; Grunig J. and Hunt 1984). Thus, dialogue is potentially at the heart of this model, which also demonstrates the prescriptive approach to the co-creation of meaning between participants as identified in the previous review of dialogue theorists' work.

The ethical aspect of the prescriptive approach is also evident in J. Grunig and Hunt's (1984) positioning of the two-way symmetric model as the ideal, aspirational form of public relations because of its putative ethical superiority over other communication types. J. Grunig based this assertion on what he saw as the inherently ethical approach engendered by communication based on "negotiation and compromise" (Grunig J. 1993: 146–147). Other researchers, such as Pearson (1989a, 1991), have reached similar conclusions about the altruistic nature of dialogue-based two-way symmetric public relations. Perhaps more pragmatically, J. Grunig, L. Grunig, and Ehling (1992) subsequently suggested that the ethical superiority of this model would enhance organizational effectiveness. They determined that excellence in communication was predicated by the use of the two-way symmetric public relations model, and that "only excellent public relations departments would contribute to bottom-line organizational effectiveness" (Grunig, L., Grunig, J. and Ehling 1992: 71).

Some scholars (for example, Podnar and Golob 2009; Theunissen and Wan Noordin 2011) have equated dialogue only with the two-way symmetric model of public relations, basing their distinction on the fact that the asymmetric variation involves persuasion and is therefore inherently unethical. Following the lead of J. Grunig and Hunt (1984) and Pearson (1991) among others, this school of thought suggests that dialogue only occurs where it can be shown that the organization has changed its behavior to accommodate the needs of its stakeholders.

J. Grunig noted the commonality of the two-way process of communication in both the asymmetric and the symmetric models when concluding that the ethical distinction between them should be based on their outcome, rather than on the process of two-way communication they shared (Grunig J. and Grunig L. 1992). J. Grunig's contention was that the point of distinction was the extent to which this process admitted the participants involved to the decision-making process on the topic being discussed (limited in the asymmetric model); to him, this is what gave the symmetric model its ethical superiority. It might be argued, therefore, that both models have a process of two-way communication at their core but linked to different outcomes. If this is the case, then the a/symmetry or im/balance lies not in the conduct of communication, but in the differences in the power over decision-making between participants, and the degree to which the more powerful participants cede that power. Yet, arguably, the asymmetric model still provides organizations with the opportunity to enhance their respect for – and understanding of – their stakeholders, which was noted as one of the defining characteristics of dialogue in the review of dialogue literature earlier in this chapter.

These conclusions begin to hint at ideas of significance in the carrying out of dialogue in public relations. First, and perhaps most significantly, there is a clear understanding in the literature that power is antithetical to the conduct of dialogue (as in Bohm 2006; Pearson 1989a, for example). As a result, none of the theories of dialogue incorporate any reference to power. Yet power has long been understood to be one of the major factors, concerns, or influences on the practice of public relations, whether it be perceived as an inherent fact to be accepted and worked with, or as an obstacle to organizational communicative authenticity and sustainability to be overcome (Edwards 2006; Grunig J. 2000). Second, there seems to be a suggestion in the literature that aspects of two-way communication in public relations practice might align with some of the characteristics of dialogue as identified in the literature.

As noted previously there is a persistent trend in public relations of conflating the concept of dialogue with that of the two-way symmetric model of public relations (Leeper 1996; Theunissen and Wan Noordin 2011). This has resulted in the critiques of symmetry being applied to dialogue *per se*: for example, critics (such as Brown 2006; Leitch and Neilson 1997; Stoker and Tusinski 2006) feel that the idea of conducting dialogue along the lines proposed in the two-way symmetric model is naïve, overly idealistic, and has no place in the real-world practice of public relations. They suggest that organizations, faced with the day-to-day reality of communication with their stakeholders, strongly question what advantage is to be gained by spending time and effort in a quest for mutual responsiveness that seems doomed to failure from the outset. As Leitch and Neilson (1997: 20) put it, "That organizations may rightly perceive there to be no advantage in adapting to the 'environment' through compromises with their publics is one reason that the symmetrical approach may not be adopted." Because of this uncritical equation of dialogue with the two-way symmetrical model of public relations, the existence of other forms of dialogue has been glossed over, and the value of continuing consideration of dialogue has been lost in the criticism of symmetrical approaches.

3.3 The relational turn revisited

The focus on theorizing of relationship management in public relations that occurred in the late 1990s (Botan and Taylor 2004) provided a natural "home" for the continuing (albeit largely hidden) discussion of the relevance of dialogue to public relations (McAllister-Spooner and Kent 2009). For example, Taylor, Kent, and White (2001: 264) looked at activist websites "to determine the extent to which they use dialogue effectively to build organization-public relationships"; and one of the most significant books on the role of relationship management in public relations (Ledingham and Bruning 2000) contains repeated mentions of the word "dialogue" and an entire chapter by Thomlison (2000) devoted to interpersonal dialogic communication.

The relational perspective positions dialogue as the two-way communication that occurs between organizations and their stakeholders. The outcome of such communication is (enhanced) mutual understanding between the participants, resulting in improved relationships between the two. Within the public relations context, better and enriched relationships are often deemed to equate to organizationally desirable behavior by stakeholders, such as becoming or remaining customers (see, for example, Ledingham and Bruning 1998).

3.4 The dialogic turn

In the late 20th century, a social "dialogic turn" (Aubert and Soler 2006; Escobar 2009; Gómez, Puigvert, and Flecha 2011) became evident in a number of fields. The impact of this dialogic turn appeared in the organizational management literature (for example, dialogue as a key tool in the discipline of Team Learning as part of developing a learning organization as suggested by Senge 1990) at about the same time as it began to emerge as a distinct phenomenon of interest in its own right in the public relations literature.

A review of literature on dialogue in public relations indicates a divergence in perspectives occurring at this point, with two distinct schools of thought emerging. The relational perspective (as in Bales and Forstner 1992; Ledingham 2003) demonstrates the legacy of the relational paradigm, and sees dialogue as a catch-all label for two-way communication between organizations and stakeholders. It is held that simply undertaking such communication and achieving better understanding of other participants is enough to enhance relationships between the parties. Because of these improved relationships, stakeholders may undertake organizationally desirable behavior (Ledingham and Bruning 2000).

The second school of thought (of which Kent and Taylor are prominent advocates) sees dialogue as a very specific kind of holistic construct deserving of theoretical development in its own right. The emergence of dialogue as a discrete theoretical construct with relevance to public relations has been described as signaling the start of a dialogic turn in public relations (Kent 2008). However, it has yet to result in a fully articulated theory of dialogue in the discipline, and dialogue, despite its putative significance to public relations, remains poorly understood in the field and lacks clear theoretical underpinning (Pieczka 2011).

4 Antecedents of a dialogic theory of public relations

The person most often credited with focusing the spotlight of academic attention on dialogue within public relations is Pearson (1989a, 1990, 1991), whose "work on dialogue as a practical public relations strategy is the earliest substantive treatment of the concept", according to Kent and Taylor (2002: 21) (see also Botan and Taylor 2004: 653). Specifically, Pearson (1991) articulated a construct of dialogue that used respectful and truthful two-way communication between organizations and stakeholders allowing public relations practitioners to achieve balance between "partisan" benefits for a client and "nonpartisan" mutual benefits (presumably mutual in terms of benefit to client and stakeholders). In doing so, Pearson (1989a) characterized dialogue as being ethical in its conduct and its outcome. This led him to claim that *ipso facto* dialogue as he understood it was ethically superior to other forms of communication. In this it is possible to determine echoes of the work of dialogue theorists on the concept of normative dialogue as discussed previously in this chapter. Indeed Pearson (1989a: 128) concluded that managing communication between organizations and stakeholders so that it comes as close as possible to what could be construed as dialogue is "the core ethical responsibility of public relations from which all other obligations follow". In adopting this stance, Pearson perpetuated the attribution of normative status to such forms of public relations first mooted in the promotion of the two-way symmetric model by J. Grunig and Hunt (1984) (see also Grunig J. and Grunig, L. 1992; Pearson 1991: 71).

5 Principles of dialogue in public relations

In their 2002 paper, Kent and Taylor made one of the greatest contributions so far to the development of a dialogic theory of public relations when they articulated their principles of dialogue in public relations. They presented five principles and sub-principles which they felt described the context in which Pearson-esque *true* dialogue can take place. In doing so they drew on the work of Buber and Rogers, with additional reference to brief extracts of the work of Johannesen and Stewart. Although no direct connections were drawn from these theorists to the principles of dialogue that Kent and Taylor (2002) proposed, comparing their ideas to those developed by the dialogue theorists whose work was reviewed earlier in this chapter shows these principles clearly equate to the characteristics of true dialogue.

5.1 Mutuality

This principle covers the inextricably intertwined nature of the co-dependency between organizations and their stakeholders, and recognizes that changes made by either organizations or their stakeholders can have effects on each other. This is very similar to Bakhtin's (1981) notion that the outcome of dialogue is change and accommodation by both parties involved. In addition, if the mutual accommodation between organizations and stakeholders were shown to lead to the development of new ideas and content shared by both participants, then this would represent the type of outcome for dialogue espoused by Bohm (2006).

5.2 Propinquity

This principle looks at the "process of dialogic exchanges" (Kent and Taylor 2002: 26). The first requirement is that dialogue must take place at a time *before* any decisions have been made so that input from all parties can be considered. In this, it resembles Gadamer's (1980a) perception that dialogue should be used to achieve shared understanding of an idea (or perhaps an issue in the public relations context) before decisions on it can be made. Kent and Taylor (2002) argue that a dialogue underpinned by the principle of propinquity must consider the history of the participants as well as provide the basis for future and ongoing relationships between them. Participants in dialogue should not try to maintain positions of neutrality but instead be prepared to find themselves developing a fondness for the others. Finally, dialogue must be taken seriously and adequately resourced. Kent and Taylor (2002) conclude that organizations that embrace propinquity in their dialogue can benefit from knowing in advance about likely issues with upcoming decisions (although whether this benefit results in the organization being better prepared to persuade dissidents, or being able to accommodate their objections, is not specified).

5.3 Empathy

The empathic or sympathetic principle of dialogue refers to the ability of participants in dialogue to show supportiveness and collegiality, as well as to demonstrate confirmation of others. "The practice of confirmation refers to acknowledging the voice of the other in spite of one's ability to ignore it" (Kent and Taylor 2002: 27) and is regarded as being vital in building trust between participants. Kent and Taylor (2002) conclude that empathy/sympathy has been the foundation of the relational approach to public relations for years, and suggest that a sympathetic orientation to stakeholders improves an organization's relationships with them. The significance of empathy between participants in dialogue is a major aspect of the work of Rogers (1961).

5.4 Risk

Dialogue is acknowledged as being risky for participants as it involves making oneself vulnerable through disclosure; it can result in unanticipated consequences; and it requires the acknowledgement of others who might otherwise be regarded as strange or undesirable. The idea of dialogue generating positive outcomes from tense and potentially hostile interactions was also addressed in the work of Freire (1990), who noted that – from the perspective of the marginalized – this interaction was highly desirable, and allowed input from informed but largely ignored contributors. Kent and Taylor (2002: 29) suggest that this dialogic risk is acceptable to organizations as it can "create understanding to minimize uncertainty and misunderstandings", and thus improve relationships between organizations and stakeholders.

5.5 Commitment

The final principle proposed by Kent and Taylor (2002) is commitment. They describe commitment as being built on foundations of genuineness (being honest and forthright), commitment to mutual benefit and understanding between all participants, and a desire to understand the other and reach mutually satisfying positions. These characteristics echo those espoused by Buber (1958) in his *I-Thou* interaction, and by Bohm (2006) and Rogers (1961) in their respective philosophies of dialogue. Kent and Taylor (2002: 30) suggest that commitment like this is also something that is familiar to public relations practitioners, who "often [have] to negotiate relationships with publics holding diverse positions".

Since the articulation of these principles, the integration of dialogue with public relations has continued. Discussions have been particularly evident in scholarly articles on the role of dialogue conducted via the internet and social media (see, for example, Kelleher 2009; Smith 2010) although there is some dispute over whether the phenomenon of interest in some of these studies is, in fact, true dialogue or just two-way communication (Kent 2017). Dialogue has also been recognized as having a significant role in engagement (Lane and Kent 2018; Taylor and Kent 2014), which is emerging as a new potential paradigm for public relations theory and practice.

6 Critiques of dialogue in public relations

Despite Kent and Taylor's development of a clear normative concept of dialogue in public relations, there appears to be a significant dearth of discussion of its actual implementation in practice. Pieczka (2011: 108) notes that interest in dialogue in public relations has remained at the level of the normative concept, and has not translated into "developing expert dialogic tools or spaces in which public relations experts routinely use such tools". Kent and Taylor (2002) themselves go further and state that not only is operationalizing this form of dialogue difficult, it might not even be possible. This suggests that perhaps constraints exist that make the implementation of dialogue in public relations problematic.

This conclusion was supported by Woodward's (2000: 260) comment that "public relations scholars (...) demonstrate that public relations practice is inherently directed toward dialogue, even in those instances when practitioners fall short of this norm". In this statement he suggests that the abstract academic idea of dialogue has been clearly articulated as a normative, aspirational concept, which practitioners are perhaps aware of but find difficulty in attaining. In a study by Crase, Dollery, and Wallis (2005), the authors conclude that many actual instances of two-way communication, which they refer to as consultation, are often "sub-optimal" in their implementation. In other words, these instances deviate from the optimal or normative ideal, which Crase, Dollery, and Wallis (2005) describe in terms that closely reflect the normative concept of true dialogue identified in the literature.

Research by Lane and Bartlett (2016) showed a number of situational forces and pressures in the conduct of public relations practice often preclude the conduct of true dialogue. These impediments include a lack of time and the need to work to deadlines, plus the existence of hostile participant attitudes to each other and the process of communication in which they were engaged. Lane and Bartlett (2016: 4088) concluded "Either public relations practitioners should be given training and resources to overcome the constraints they experience in undertaking dialogue, or the concept of dialogue itself needs to be retheorized to acknowledge its position as an unattainable ideal." These findings echo the conclusions of others, such as

Peters (2007: 125), who describes dialogue as "a jealous god (...) demanding and difficult".

The question for contemporary practitioners therefore is, should we continue to strive for the unattainable heights of true dialogue on the assumption that it is not only desirable but superlative; or should we admit defeat before we begin and limit ourselves to creating situations that foster the conduct of the best forms of two-way communication we can manage in each situation?

7 Conclusion

This chapter has laid out a road map of the journey from the scholarly theorizing of dialogue in Ancient Greece to the beginning of the development of a dialogic theory of public relations. It has traced the links between academic concepts of dialogue and the dominant theories of public relations in recent decades, particularly symmetry and relationship management. Dialogue has been shown as a means by which public relations academics and practitioners can address the challenge of how to develop communication approaches that empower stakeholders, while still allowing organizations to achieve the goals required to ensure their success. Dialogue's strength lies in its adaptability and relevance to so many of the aims and ambitions we set ourselves in contemporary public relations, from managing and enhancing relationships to the co-creation of perspectives between organizations and stakeholders. A dialogic approach to conceptualizing the role and practice of public relations in the 21st century allows for the development of less organization-centric positioning, and allows us to fully embrace the promise of public relations as boundary-spanning engagement facilitators. However, this chapter has also shown that the practice of true dialogue, demonstrating the five principles articulated in the seminal work of Kent and Taylor (2002) is not easy, and might not even be possible. This leaves the theorizing of dialogue in public relations at a crossroads – should we persist in maintaining the distinction between true dialogue and two-way communication? If so, how do we progress with a goal that is impossible to achieve in the complexity and confusion of contemporary public relations practice? If not, what is the future for the concept of true dialogue? Should it be abandoned as a dated and impractical form of communication, as redundant and impossible to achieve as the use of the passenger pigeon to carry messages? Or should it be maintained as a relic, a shining exemplar of the passing of a golden age of dialogue that might never, in fact, have existed?

References

Albert, Stuart & David A. Whetten. 1985. Organizational identity. In Larry L. Cummings & Barry M. Staw (eds.), *Research in Organizational Behavior*, 263–295. Greenwich, CT: JAI Press.

Anderson, Rob, Leslie A. Baxter & Kenneth N. Cissna (eds.). 2004. *Dialogue: Theorizing difference in communication studies*. Thousand Oaks, CA: Sage.

Aubert, Adriana & Marta Soler. 2006. Dialogism: The dialogic turn in the social sciences. In Joe L. Kincheloe & Raymond A. Horn (eds.), *The Praeger Hanbook of Education and Psychology*, 521–529. Westport, CT: Greenwood Press.

Bakhtin, Mikhail. 1981. *The dialogic imagination: four essays by M. M. Bakhtin*. Craig Emerson & Michael Holquist (trans.). Austin, TX: University of Texas Press.

Bakhtin, Mikhail. 1986. *Speech genres and other late essays*. Victor W. McGee (trans.). Austin, TX: University of Texas Press.

Bales, Jack & Gordon Forstner. 1992. Building dialogue into the public consultation process. *Public Relations Quarterly* 37(3). 31–35.

Barnes, Marian, Janet Newman & Helen Sullivan. 2004. Power, participation, and political renewal: theoretical perspectives on public participation under New Labour in Britain. *Social Politics* 11(2). 267–279.

Bohm, David. 1985. *Unfolding meaning: A weekend of dialogue with David Bohm*. New York: Routledge.

Bohm, David. 2006. *On Dialogue*. Abingdon, UK: Routledge.

Bohm, David, Donald Factor & Peter Garrett. 1991. Dialogue – a proposal. http://www.david-bohm. net/dialogue/dialogue_proposal.html (accessed 26 March 2020).

Botan, Carl & Maureen Taylor. 2004. Public relations: state of the field. *Journal of Communication* 54(4). 645–661.

Brown, Robert E. 2006. Myth of symmetry: public relations as cultural styles. *Public Relations Review* 32. 206–212.

Bruning, Stephen D., Melissa Dials & Amanda Shirka. 2008. Using dialogue to build organization-public relationships, engage publics, and positively affect organizational outcomes. *Public Relations Review* 34(1). 25–31.

Bruning, Stephen D. & John A. Ledingham. 1999. Relationships between organizations and publics: development of a multi-dimensional organization-public relationship scale. *Public Relations Review* 25(2). 157–170.

Buber, Martin. 1958. *I and Thou*. Robert G. Smith (trans.). Edinburgh: T. & T. Clark.

Buber, Martin. 1965. *The knowledge of man: a philosophy of the interhuman*. Maurice Friedman & Ronald G. Smith (trans.). New York: Harper and Row.

Chaffee, Steven H. 1991. *Explication*. Communication Concepts 1. Newbury Park, CA: Sage.

Cissna, Kenneth N. & Rob Anderson. 1994. Communication and the ground of dialogue. In Rob Anderson, Kenneth N. Cissna & Ronald C. Arnett (eds.). *The reach of dialogue: confirmation, voice, and community*, 9–30. Cresskill, NJ: Hampton Press.

Crase, Lin, Brian Dollery & Joe Wallis. 2005. Community consultation in public policy: the case of the Murray-Darling Basin of Australia. *Australian Journal of Political Science* 40(1). 221–237.

Dozier, David. 1984. Program evaluation and roles of practitioners. *Public Relations Review* 10(2). 13–21.

Edgett, Ruth. 2002. Toward an ethical framework for advocacy in public relations. *Journal of Public Relations Research* 14(1). 1–26.

Edwards, Lee. 2006. Rethinking power in public relations. *Public Relations Review* 32(2). 229–231.

Escobar, Oliver. 2009. The dialogic turn: dialogue for deliberation. *In-Spire Journal of Law, Politics and Societies* 4(2). 42–70.

Ferguson, Mary A. 1984. Building theory in public relations: interorganizational relationships as a public relations paradigm. Paper presented at the Public Relations Division, Association for Education in Journalism and Mass Communication Annual Convention, Gainesville, 5–8 August.

Fitzpatrick, Kathy & Candace Gauthier. 2001. Toward a professional responsibility theory of public relations ethics. *Journal of Mass Media Ethics* 16(2). 193–212.

Freire, Paolo. 1990. *Pedagogy of the oppressed*. Myra Bergman Ramos (trans.). New York: Continuum.

Gadamer, Hans-Georg. 1975/2006. *Truth and method*, 2nd edn. New York: Continuum.

Gadamer, Hans-Georg. 1980a. *Dialogue and dialectic: eight hermeneutical studies on Plato*. Philip C. Smith (trans.). New Haven, CT: Yale University Press.

Gadamer, Hans-Georg. 1980b. Practical philosophy as a model of the human sciences. *Research in Phenomenology* 9. 74–85.

Gadamer, Hans-Georg. 1989. Text and interpretation. Dennis J. Schmidt & Richard E. Palmer (trans.). In Diane P. Michelfelder & Richard E. Palmer (eds.), *Dialogue and deconstruction: the Gadamer-Derrida encounter*. Albany, NY: State University of New York Press.

Gómez, Aitor, Lídia Puigvert & Ramón Flecha. 2011. Critical communicative methodology: informing real social transformation through research. *Qualitative Inquiry* 17(3). 235–245.

Grondin, Jean. 2003. *Hans-Georg Gadamer: a biography*. Joel Weinsheimer (trans.). New Haven, CT: Yale University Press.

Grunig, James E. 1984. Organizations, environments and models. *Public Relations Research and Education* 1(1). 6–29.

Grunig, James E. 1993. Public relations and international affairs: Effects, ethics and responsibility. *Journal of International Affairs* 47(1). 137–162.

Grunig, James E. 2000. Collectivism, collaboration, and societal corporatism as core professional values in public relations. *Journal of Public Relations Research* 12(1). 23–48.

Grunig, James E. 2009. Paradigms of global public relations in an age of digitalisation. *PRism* 6(2). 1–19.

Grunig, James E. & Larissa A. Grunig. 1992. Models of public relations and communication. In James E. Grunig (ed.), *Excellence in public relations and communication management*, 285–325. Hillsdale, NJ: Lawrence Erlbaum Associates.

Grunig, James E. & Todd Hunt. 1984. *Managing public relations*. New York: Holt, Rinehart & Winston.

Grunig, Larissa A., James E. Grunig & Wilbur Ehling. 1992. What is an effective organization? In James E. Grunig & David Dozier (eds.), *Excellence in public relations and communication management*, 65–90. Hillsdale, NJ: Lawrence Erlbaum Associates.

Habermas, Jürgen. 1984. *The theory of communicative action – volume 1: Reason and the rationalization of society*. Thomas McCarthy (trans.). Boston: Beacon Press.

Habermas, Jürgen. 1989. *The structural transformation of the public sphere: An inquiry into a category of bourgeois society*. Thomas Burger & Frederick Lawrence (trans.). Cambridge, MA: MIT Press.

Hallahan, Kirk. 2000. Inactive publics: the forgotten publics in public relations. *Public Relations Review* 26. 499–515.

Hamilton, Jennifer D. & Caitlin Wills-Toker. 2006. Reconceptualizing dialogue in environmental public participation. *Policy Studies Journal* 34(4). 755–775.

Heath, Robert. L. 2000. A rhetorical perspective on the value of public relations: crossroads and pathways toward concurrence. *Journal of Public Relations Research* 12(1). 69–91.

Heath, Robert. L. 2001. A rhetorical enactment rationale for public relations. In Robert L. Heath (ed.), *The Handbook of Public Relations*, 31–50. Thousand Oaks, CA: Sage.

Kahn, Charles. H. 1998. *Plato and the Socratic dialogue: The philosophical use of a literary form*. Cambridge: Cambridge University Press.

Karlberg, Michael. 1996. Remembering the public in public relations research: From theoretical to operational symmetry. *Journal of Public Relations Research* 8. 263–278.

Kelleher, Tom. 2009. Conversational voice, communicated commitment, and public relations outcomes in interactive online communication. *Journal of Communication* 59(1). 172–188.

Kent, Michael. L. 2008. The dialogic turn in public relations: toward a theory of dialogic practice. Paper presented at the The 94th annual convention of the National Communication Association, San Diego, 21–24 November. http://www.allacademic.com/meta/p256510_index.html (accessed 6 January 2009)

Kent, Michael L. 2017. Keynote presentation. Paper presented at the annual international conference of the Public Relations Society of China, Wuhan, 27–30 October.

Kent, Michael L. & Maureen Taylor. 1998. Building dialogic relationships through the World Wide Web. *Public Relations Review* 24(3). 321–334.

Kent, Michael. L. & Maureen Taylor. 2002. Toward a dialogic theory of public relations. *Public Relations Review* 28. 21–37.

Kim, Joohan & Eun Joo Kim. 2008. Theorizing dialogic deliberation: everyday political talk as communicative action and dialogue. *Communication Theory* 18. 51–70.

Lane, Anne B. & Jennifer L. Bartlett. 2016. Why dialogic principles don't make it in practice – And what we can do about it. *International Journal of Communication* 10. 4074–4094.

Lane, Anne B. & Michael L. Kent. 2018. Dialogic engagement. In Kim A. Johnston & Maureen Taylor (eds.), *The Handbook of Communication Engagement*, 61–72. Thousand Oaks, CA: Wiley.

Ledingham, John A. 2003. Explicating relationship management as a general theory of public relations. *Journal of Public Relations Research* 15(2). 181–198.

Ledingham, John A. & Stephen D. Bruning. 1998. Relationship management in public relations: dimensions of an organization–public relationship. *Public Relations Review* 24(1). 55–65.

Ledingham, John A. & Stephen D. Bruning (eds.). 2000. *Public relations as relationship management: A relational approach to the study and practice of public relations.* Mahwah, NJ: Lawrence Erlbaum Associates.

Leeper, Roy. 1996. Moral objectivity, Jurgen Habermas's discourse ethics, and public relations. *Public Relations Review* 22(2). 133–151.

Leitch, Shirley & David Neilson. 1997. Reframing public relations: New directions for theory and practice. *Australian Journal of Communication* 24(2). 17–32.

McAllister-Spooner, Sheila M. & Michael L. Kent. 2009. Dialogic public relations and resource dependency: New Jersey community colleges as models for web site effectiveness. *Atlantic Journal of Communication* 17(4). 220–239.

Morrell, Kevin. 2004. Socratic dialogue as a tool for teaching business ethics. *Journal of Business Ethics* 53(4). 383–392.

Paul, Richard & Linda Elder. 2007. Critical thinking: The art of Socratic questioning. *Journal of Developmental Education* 31(1). 36–37.

Pearson, Ron. 1989a. Business ethics as communication ethics: public relations practice and the idea of dialogue. In Carl Botan & Vince Hazleton (eds.), *Public Relations Theory*, 111–134. Hillsdale, NJ: Lawrence Erlbaum Associates.

Pearson, Ron. 1989b. *A theory of public relations ethics.* Athens, OH: Ohio University PhD thesis.

Pearson, Ron. 1990. Ethical Values or Strategic Values? The Two Faces of Systems Theory in Public Relations. *Public Relations Research Annual* 2(1–4). 219–234.

Pearson, Ron. 1991. Beyond ethical relativism in public relations: Coorientation, rules and the idea of communication symmetry. In James E. Grunig & Larissa A. Grunig (eds.), *Public Relations Research Annual* 1, 67–86. Hillsdale, NJ: Lawrence Erlbaum Associates.

Peters, John D. 2007. Media as conversation, conversation as media. In James Curran & David Morley (eds.), *Media and cultural theory*, 115–126. London: Routledge.

Pieczka, Magda. 2011. Public relations as dialogic expertise? *Journal of Communication Management* 15(2). 108–124.

Podnar, Klement & Urša Golob. 2009. Reconstruction of public relations history through publications in Public Opinion Quarterly. *Management* 13(1). 55–76.

Post, James E., Lee E. Preston & Sybille Sauter-Sachs. 2002. *Redefining the corporation: Stakeholder management and organizational wealth*. Stanford, CA: Stanford University Press.

Roberts, Nora C. 1997. Public deliberation: an alternative approach to crafting policy and setting direction. *Public Administration Review* 57(2). 124–132.

Rogers, Carl R. 1961. *On becoming a person: a therapist's view of psychotherapy*. London: Constable.

Senge, Peter. 1990. *The fifth discipline*. New York: Doubleday.

Smith, Brian G. 2010. Socially distributing public relations: Twitter, Haiti, and interactivity in social media. *Public Relations Review* 36(4). 329–335.

Spicer, Christopher. 1997. Establishing the organizational setting: Systems theory and beyond. *Organizational public relations: A political perspective*, 53–76. Mahwah, NJ: Lawrence Erlbaum Associates.

Steinmann, Horst & Ansgar Zerfass. 1993. FOCUS: Corporate Dialogue – a new perspective for public relations. *Business Ethics: A European Review* 2(2). 58–63.

Stewart, John, Karen E. Zediker & Laura Black. 2004. Chapter 2: Relationships among philosophies of dialogue. In Rob Anderson, Leslie A. Baxter & Kenneth N. Cissna (eds.), *Dialogue: Theorizing difference in communication studies*, 21–38. Thousand Oaks, CA: Sage.

Stoker, Kevin L. & Kati Tusinski. 2006. Reconsidering public relations' infatuation with dialogue: why engagement can be more ethical than symmetry and reciprocity. *Journal of Mass Media Ethics* 21(2&3). 156–176.

Taylor, Maureen & Michael L. Kent. 2014. Dialogic engagement: Clarifying foundational concepts. *Journal of Public Relations Research* 26(5). 384–398.

Taylor, Maureen, Michael L. Kent & William J. White. 2001. How activist organizations are using the Internet to build relationships. *Public Relations Review* 27(3). 263–284.

The Center for Whole Communities. 2006. A Brief Orientation to Dialogue. http://measuresofhealth. net/pdf/brief_orientation_dialogue.pdf (accessed 31 March 2020).

Theunissen, Petra & Wan Norbani Wan Noordin. 2011. Revisiting the concept "dialogue" in public relations. *Public Relations Review* 38. 5–13.

Thomlison, T. Dean. 2000. An interpersonal primer with implications for public relations. In John A. Ledingham & Stephen D. Bruning (eds.), *Public relations as relationship management: A relational approach to the study and practice of public relations*, 177–204. Mahwah, NJ: Lawrence Erlbaum Associates.

Weaver, Kay, Judy Motion & Juliet Roper. 2006. From propaganda to discourse (and back again): truth, power, the public interest, and public relations. In Jacquie L'Etang & Magda Pieczka (eds.), *Public relations: Critical debates and contemporary practice*, 7–21. Mahwah, NJ: Lawrence Erlbaum Associates.

Woodward, Wayne D. 2000. Transactional philosophy as a basis for dialogue in public relations. *Journal of Public Relations Research* 12(3). 255–275.

Zappen, James P. 2004. *The rebirth of dialogue: Bakhtin, Socrates, and the rhetorical tradition*. New York, NY: SUNY Press.

Jeong-Nam Kim, Lisa Tam, and Myoung-Gi Chon

24 A conceptual genealogy of the situational theory of problem solving: Reconceptualizing communication for strategic behavioral communication management

Abstract: The situational theory of problem solving (STOPS) was constructed with the premise that communicative behaviors are purposive and epiphenomenal to problem solving. It inherits from the situational theory of publics (STP) the assumption that communication is not just what senders do to change receivers' attitudes and behaviors – rather, communication is what individuals do to cope with problematic life situations. While STP explains the role of information in decision making, STOPS explains communicative behaviors of publics in the context of problematic situations. The shift of focus from decisional situations to problematic situations provides scholars with a new theoretical foundation to conceptualize public relations. STOPS has shifted the focus of public relations theory from generating media effects to influence the general public to understanding why and how individuals become motivated to organize into issue-specific publics. STOPS has been widely applied to multiple contexts, including health communication, employee communication, environmental communication, crisis communication, and public diplomacy.

Keywords: communication management; communicative behaviors; problem solving; publics; situational theory

1 Conceptual and empirical development of the situational theory of problem solving

The situational theory of publics (hereafter STP) is one of the oldest public relations theories. Based on a conceptualization of previous views on publics (Dewey 1927), STP was constructed with the premise that publics are groups of individuals who face a similar problem and engage in information behaviors to solve the problem (Grunig J. 1976, 1997). It assumes that publics are not passive recipients of information but active individuals who engage in information behaviors to solve their problems. First developed in the 1960s by James E. Grunig for his dissertation, in which he examined why Colombian farmers use information in decisional situations, STP used three situational variables (i.e., problem recognition, level of involvement, and constraint recognition) to predict information processing and information seeking. STP has been widely used as

https://doi.org/10.1515/9783110554250-024

a framework to guide the segmentation of publics (i. e., active publics, aware publics, latent publics, and non-publics).

As an extension of STP, the situational theory of problem solving (STOPS) similarly proposes that publics are issue-specific and situational and can be used as a framework to understand how and why individuals become motivated to organize into publics. Publics and their motivated problem-solving efforts could originate from their problem recognition in personal life contexts or from their recognition of a problem caused by organizational behaviors (Kim and Grunig J. 2011). In essence, publics are problem solvers who arise themselves and seek opportunities or approach organizations for problem resolution. STOPS explains and assists a variety of problem solvers, ranging from individuals and organized groups, such as activist publics, to institutions or organizations, such as governments or corporations, in solving problems based on the premise of communicative action as a purposive coping tool and the nature of situational publics as problem solvers.

While a decision maker is likely to seek information for their decisional choices, the communicative action of a problem solver shows not only information acquisition behaviors but also information selection and transmission to cope with the problem (Kim and Krishna 2014). While a decision maker seeks information to make decisions to maximize satisfactory outcomes within the boundaries of constraints, a problem solver solves a problem by seeking, choosing, and propagating information about the problem. A decision maker does not always need to transmit information; a problem solver tends to do so for effective problem solving.

As organizations or organized publics are frequently constrained by limited resources, STOPS guides problem solvers to cope and communicate better with the knowledge of their communicative partners to gain opportunities and resources for problem resolution. Specifically, STOPS provides a conceptual framework and practical procedures to help organizations to identify, segment, and prioritize strategic publics from non-publics in whom they invest resources to build relationships with in order to inform organizational decisions (Kim, Ni, and Sha 2008). STOPS not only explains the origins, processes, and nature of the situational communicative behaviors of individuals and groups (i. e., public-initiated public relations [PPR] problems), but also the communicative behaviors of organizations (i. e., organization-initiated public relations [OPR] problems) (Kim and Ni 2013). Like individuals, organizations also exhibit motivated communicative behaviors as problem solvers.

Since it was first published as a dissertation (Kim 2006) and a journal article (Kim and Grunig J. 2011), STOPS has been further conceptually and empirically developed as a generalized theory which both resembles and differs from STP. The conceptual evolvement of STOPS has led to the development of associated concepts. It also has theoretical implications for further theory development, and practical applications for the public relations industry. As a foundational framework, STOPS can be applied to a variety of communication research and practical settings to inform public rela-

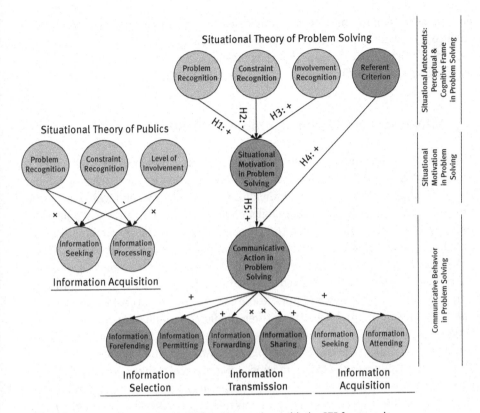

Figure 1: Theoretical framework of STOPS and comparison with the STP framework (Kim & Grunig J. 2011: 121)

tions practices (see Grunig J. and Kim 2017 for a comprehensive review on publics and the application of STOPS).

1.1 Theoretical framework

STOPS, as a communication theory developed based on the premise of problem solving, is a generalized extension of STP. It proposes the conditions under which individuals are motivated to solve problems through communicative behaviors. The framework explains that individuals' *situational motivation in problem solving* can be explained by three perceptual variables: *problem recognition, constraint recognition,* and *involvement recognition*. Together with the *referent criterion*, a variable originally dropped in STP that refers to relevant prior experiences of success in dealing with similar problems, *situational motivation in problem solving* could predict *communicative action in problem solving* (CAPS), which explains individuals' activeness in *information acquisition, information selection,* and *information transmission*. It explains and predicts not only how and why individuals *seek* information to cope with a problem, but also how and why they *select* and *transmit* information to solve the problem either individually or collectively (cf. STP; Grunig J. 2003). Figure 1 outlines the STOPS framework (cf. STP in Figure 1) published in Kim and J. Grunig (2011).

1.2 Situational motivation in problem solving

To explain *why* individuals are motivated to engage in communicative behaviors in problem solving, STOPS proposes that there are situational antecedents which are the perceptual triggers motivating individuals' situational communicative action in problem solving. Individuals' situational motivation in problem solving begins when they face a subjective life situation (i. e., problem). Three variables predict the situational motivation in problem solving. First, *problem recognition* is triggered when an individual faces a problem and recognizes it as affecting them. Second, *involvement recognition* refers to one's perceived connection between oneself and the problem. Third, *constraint recognition* is defined as the extent of perceived obstacles preventing one from solving the problem. These three predictor variables explain individuals' situational motivation in problem solving, mediating the effects between the predictor variables and subsequent CAPS. *Situational motivation in problem solving* is a mediator variable defined as the extent to which an individual thinks about and becomes curious to gather, select, and give more information about the problem. It represents "a state of situation-specific cognitive and epistemic readiness to make problem-solving efforts – that is, to decrease the perceived discrepancy between the expected and experiential states" (Kim and Grunig J. 2011: 132).

The *referent criterion*, a variable which was originally dropped from STP, was reintroduced to STOPS to predict CAPS. Defined as "any knowledge or subjective judgmental system that influences the way one approaches problem solving," a referent criterion provides decision guidelines or cues based on individuals' prior knowledge or experience of a problem (Kim and Grunig J. 2011: 130). It is expected that individuals with more referent criterion will be more active in CAPS.

1.3 Communicative action in problem solving

Both STP and STOPS are built on the premise that communication is a *purposive* behavior as individuals cope with a problematic life situation which is *situational*. When an individual is motivated to solve a problem they will engage in communicative action as a coping mechanism. STOPS introduces CAPS as a generalized outcome variable which describes individuals' activeness in communicative behaviors in terms of information seeking, selecting and sharing to solve the problem. While STP is limited to information processing (attending or ignoring) and information seeking (active or inactive), STOPS extends the framework into information acquisition, information selection, and information transmission, each of which is classified into two sub-dimensions: either active or passive.

The shift from the decision-making approach (i. e., STP) to the problem-solving approach (i. e., STOPS) to communication extends from seeking information to making a decision to select and give information to others in order to mobilize resources to cope with the problem. Information acquisition, which is classified into two dimensions, information seeking (active/proactive) and information attending (passive/reactive), refers to a problem solver's action to turn to external sources for information. Information seeking is planned, whereas information attending is unplanned. Yet, the two sub-dimensions are not mutually exclusive. Active problem solvers are high in both information seeking and information attending; they do not only proactively seek information but also attend to information when given. On the other hand, passive problem solvers are only high in information attending, meaning that they only attend to the information given to them.

STOPS posits that problem solvers select certain types and sources of information based on the preferences they have developed over time. Hence, information selection refers to a problem solver's process of evaluating information in terms of its value and relevance to the problem. It is classified into two sub-dimensions: information forefending (active) and information permitting (passive). Information forefending is defined as the extent to which a problem solver rejects and/or approach certain information. When a problem solver is active about a problem they will be discriminatory about the value and relevance of the information received. On the other hand, information permitting refers to a problem solver's acceptance and sharing of any information encountered as long as it is related to the problem of their current interest. When a problem solver is not active about a problem they will have little regard for the value or relevance of the information received. However, information permitting is not equivalent to the lack of information selection – permitting information is often present at the early phase of problem solving. Depending on the presence of one's subscription of referent criteria, information forefending, which refers to the systematic and specific selection of information, tends to occur at the later phase of problem solving when the purpose of information selection is to reduce information overload or inconsistency.

When individuals are confronted with a problem to solve (as opposed to a decision to make), they will not only be consumers of information but tend to give information to others to mobilize resources to solve the problem collectively (i. e., creating an active public). They will be motivated to engage in giving information to others about the problem. The active dimension of information transmission is known as information forwarding, which refers to disseminating information to others even without being asked. The less active dimension is known as information sharing, which refers to only sharing information when asked.

Figure 2 shows the difference between STP and STOPS in extending the study of situational communicative action from information acquisition to include information selection and information transmission. Problem recognition activates the internal inquiring stage when an individual recognizes a problem as affecting them based on the knowledge that they already hold. As the problem solver encounters the problem, they enter the external inquiring stage as they become active in acquiring external information about the problem. STOPS also suggests that individuals enter the cognitive and collective stage of effectuating when they apply a framework of selectivity to evaluate the value and relevance of information to the given problem, and actively transmit this information to others – that is, reproducing their problem perception and motivation with their chosen information and emerging referent criteria. An individual becomes an active public when they cope with the problem by sharing information about it with others. The communicative action of information transmission can lead to the collective effectuating stage, as active publics organize themselves into an activist public to cope collectively with the problem.

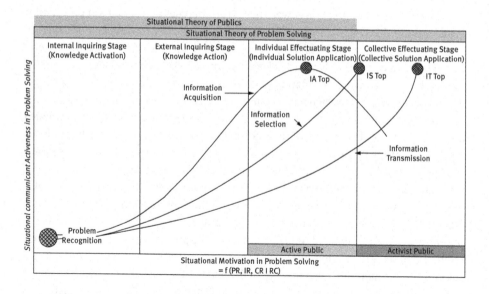

Figure 2: STP and STOPS (Kim and Grunig J. 2011: 121)

2 Application of STOPS

Scholars have been using the STOPS framework to understand *why* and *how* people become active in communicative action in the context of controversial social issues. In addition to the application of the general STOPS framework, existing research has used the variables in various communication contexts, including health communication (Kim and Lee 2014), employee communication (Park, Kim, and Krishna 2014) and crisis communication (Kim, Miller and Chon 2016). New concepts, such as problem-chain recognition effects (Kim, Shen, and Morgan 2011) and lacuna publics (Kim and Krishna 2014), have been developed to explore phenomena associated with understanding publics and their behaviors. The earliest application of STOPS can be found in public segmentation research for the classification of publics (Kim, Grunig, J. and Ni 2010). In the context of strategic communication, identifying and segmenting strategic publics based on their characteristics is critical for organizations to understand the motivations behind which publics rise for or against them.

2.1 Public segmentation

Using three situational variables (problem recognition, constraint recognition, and involvement recognition), the summation method is proposed in STOPS for the purpose of public segmentation (Kim 2011). Because organizations are constrained by limited resources, a systematic approach to public segmentation is necessary for them to identify and prioritize strategic publics in whom they invest resources to build relationships (Kim, Ni, and Sha 2008). A population within an issue or a problem can be divided into four types of groups: active publics, aware publics, latent publics, and non-publics. The summation method in the STOPS framework allows practitioners and researchers to better understand strategic publics who show active communicative behaviors. Figure 3 shows the types of publics within an issue (Kim 2011).

- **Nonpublic (0):**
  has no consequence.
- **Latent Public (1):**
  a consequence creates a problem but has not detected the problem yet.
- **Aware Public (2):**
  has recognised the problem.
- **Active Public (3):**
  has started working for solving the problem and creating an issue. (*Individual Effectuating* Phase)
- **Activist Public (3):**
  has organised to discuss about the problem and do something about it with others.

  (*Collective Effectuating* Phase)

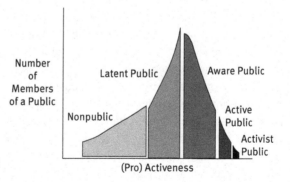

Figure 3: Types of publics within an issue (Kim 2011: 2)

2.2 Public segmentation and crisis communication

Using the six dependent variables of STOPS (i. e., the CAPS model), Ni and Kim (2009) introduced a taxonomy for public segmentation focusing on active and aware publics (i. e., the summation method II). Using the summation method to segment the four types of publics is a good starting point to understand the differences in publics in terms of the communicative behaviors they exhibit to cope with a given problem. According to Kim, Grunig, J. and Ni (2010), communicative behavior, as an instrumental tool for problem solving, should be conceptualized as comprising three dimensions: information acquisition, information selection, and information transmission. Ni and Kim (2009) propose using the history of problem solving (i. e., information seeking and attending), the extent of activeness (i. e., information forwarding and sharing), and openness to approaches in problem solving (i. e., information forefending and permitting) to segment active and aware publics into eight groups. This new theoretical framework, summation method II, was further tested in a crisis communication context to identify publics (Kim, Miller, and Chon 2016). Using survey data, Chon and Kim (2016) used both summation methods I and II to identify key publics in a government crisis. The CAPS model was used to understand and predict crisis communication behaviors of publics in an organizational crisis (Kim 2016). In the context of crisis communication, the CAPS model has therefore been used as a theoretical framework to segment active publics and predict their communicative action.

2.3 Hot-issue publics and lacuna publics

The STOPS framework and the CAPS model have been applied to study controversial social issues. Specifically, one type of public has attracted much interest: hot-issue publics. Hot-issue publics are defined as those who are "active only on a single problem that involves nearly everyone in the population and that has received extensive media coverage" (Grunig J. 1997: 13). Hot-issue publics are unique – they arise due to external sources, such as media coverage (exogenously), while most other publics arise due to internal sources (endogenously) (Chen, Hung-Baesecke, and Kim 2017). Although hot-issue publics are likely to dissipate when media coverage subsidies, some of them, if not properly handled, will remain single-issue publics (Aldoory and J. Grunig 2012). It is also likely that some of them will become chronic-issue publics; if they find new evidence about the problem they can turn the issue into a hot issue again (Kim et al. 2015). Based on the STOPS model, a study was also conducted to examine the communicative action of hot-issue publics in South Korea regarding United States (US) beef imports by testing the impact of cross-situational variables (e. g., political interest, protest participation, and demographics) and situational variables (Chen, Hung-Baesecke, and Kim 2017). More recently, Kim and Krishna (2014) proposed lacuna publics, a subtype of active publics on controversial issues. As group extremism in the networked society is threatening social advancement, research on lacuna publics shows how active publics with deficient knowledge are engaged in active communicative behaviors on controversial issues.

2.4 Health communication

The STOPS framework and the CAPS model have also been applied to health communication. In the context of organ donation, Kim, Shen, and Morgan (2011) demonstrated the applicability of STOPS for strategic planning in health campaigns. Their study proposed a new concept known as problem-chain recognition effects, which suggests that an anchor issue (e. g., organ donation) leads individuals to seek or attend to information about a related issue (e. g., shortage of bone-marrow donation). Another topic to which STOPS and CAPS have been applied is cybercoping. Defined as behaviors of information forwarding and information seeking for problem solving in health-related problems, information seeking and forwarding were used as independent variables to predict coping processes and outcomes (Kim and Lee 2014). The findings related to cybercoping show that active information behaviors online can assist patients with chronic diseases and caregivers of dementia patients in coping with health problems (Jeong, Kim, and Chon 2018; Kim and Lee 2014). In a recent study on the anti-vaccine movement, STOPS was used as a theoretical framework to explore how people become active in communicative behaviors and indicate behavioral intentions to be vaccinated (Krishna 2017). The findings indicated that people with low trust in the Center for Disease Control and Prevention and a lack of knowledge about vaccines were less likely to use vaccines and become active in communicating about vaccines.

2.5 Employee communication

With its origin in the strategic behavioral paradigm, the STOPS framework and the CAPS model are closely associated with the relationship-centered approach to public relations. In light of this, Kim and Rhee (2011) explored the relationship between employees' perceived relationship quality with their organization and their communicative behaviors about the organization. They identified that positive relationship quality could predict two types of employees' advocacy behaviors: positive megaphoning and scouting. Megaphoning, which can be positive or negative, refers to the extent to which employees are engaged in positive or negative external communication behaviors about their organization. It is defined as "the likelihood of employees' voluntary information forwarding or information sharing about organizational strengths (accomplishments) or weaknesses (problems)" (Kim and Rhee 2011: 246). In addition, scouting is defined as the voluntary communication efforts made by employees to bring relevant information to the organization. The findings suggest that organizations build and cultivate positive relationships with employees to encourage them to become micro-boundary spanners between organizations and their publics by engaging in positive megaphoning and scouting. Park, Kim, and Krishna (2014) found that positive organization-employee relationships could motivate employees' voluntary intrapreneurship and scouting. To build and cultivate positive relationships, Lee and Kim's (2017) study found that organizations' authentic behavioral efforts are critical to employees' evaluation of their relationships with their organization and subsequent communicative behaviors.

2.6 Public diplomacy

Public diplomacy, as opposed to traditional diplomacy, stresses the importance of building relationships with foreign publics (as opposed to foreign governments). The CAPS model has been applied as an analytical foundation to examine foreign publics' communicative behaviors relating to foreign countries. Vibber and Kim (2015) suggest that foreign publics' communicative behaviors about countries could create chain-networked effects; in particular, their experiences in foreign countries could be used as a basis on which to evaluate those countries. Vibber's (2014) study on international students proposes that these students' perceived relationship quality could predict their megaphoning behaviors about their host countries. These megaphoning behaviors, in turn, would affect how their families and friends in their home countries perceive those host countries. The STOPS framework also offers insights as to why and how foreign publics engage in positive or negative megaphoning about foreign countries.

3 Practical implications

Theoretically, STOPS has been applied to a variety of contexts. In a practical context, STOPS is particularly invaluable in guiding strategy in the practice of public relations. Based on the strategic behavioral paradigm of public relations, Kim and Ni (2013) classify public relations problems into two types: organization-initiated public relations (OPR) problems and public-initiated public relations (PPR) problems.

PPR problems arise when publics sense a problem caused by organizational decisions or actions. In this situation, publics, especially active publics, would be motivated to engage in active communicative behaviors to increase others' situational motivation in problem solving (i.e., problem recognition, involvement recognition and constraint recognition). Through communicative behaviors, these publics cope with the problem by also turning others into active publics. These active publics may also turn into activist publics as they mobilize resources to cope collectively with the problem. The STOPS framework can be used as a guideline as to how to decrease these active publics' situational motivation in problem solving, such as decreasing their problem recognition by working with them to decrease the impact of organizational decisions and actions on them. Figure 4 shows the conceptualization of PPR problems as organizations work to decrease publics' situational motivation in problem solving.

	High Involvement (HI)		Low Involvement (LI)	
	Behavior Type	Type of Public	Behavior Type	Type of Public
Problem-Facing Behavior (PF): Hi PR/Lo CR	HIPF	**Activist/Active**	LIPF	**Aware/Active**
Constrained Behavior (CB): Hi PR/Hi CR	HICB	**Aware/Active**	LICB	**Latent/Aware**
Routine Behavior (RB): Lo PR/Lo CR	HIRB	**Active (Reinforcing)**	LIRB	**None/Latent**
Fatalistic Behavior (FB): Lo PR/Hi CR	HIFB	**Latent**	LIFB	**None**

Figure 4: Conceptualization of PPR problems (Kim and Ni 2013: 4)

While PPR problems require organizations to decrease publics' situational motivation in problem solving, OPR problems arise when organizations sense that there is a problem preventing them from meeting organizational objectives. Thus, OPR problems begin with organizations' problem recognition. For example, the Center for Disease Control and Prevention may identify increasing cancer rates in the population as a problem preventing them from meeting their mission of preventing cancer. Thus, it will be interested in creating publics around the issue. In OPR problems, public relations intervention is used to increase publics' problem perception and encourage communicative behaviors about the issue. The STOPS framework provides organizations with guidelines on how to increase publics' situational motivation by carrying out communication efforts that increase their problem recognition and involvement recognition and decrease their constraint recognition. Figure 5 shows the conceptualization of OPR problems (Kim and Ni 2013).

	High Involvement (HI)		Low Involvement (LI)	
	Behavior Type	Type of Public	Behavior Type	Type of Public
Problem-Facing Behavior (PF): Hi PR/Lo CR	HIPF	**Activist/Active**	LIPF	**Aware/Active**
Constrained Behavior (CB): Hi PR/Hi CR	HICB	**Aware/Active**	LICB	**Latent/Aware**
Routine Behavior (RB): Lo PR/Lo CR	HIRB	**Active** (Reinforcing)	LIRB	**None/Latent**
Fatalistic Behavior (FB): Lo PR/Hi CR	HIFB	**Latent**	LIFB	**None**

Organization-Initiated PR Problem

Figure 5: Conceptualization of OPR problems (Kim and Ni 2013: 4)

4 Limitations and future directions

Existing research that has applied the STOPS framework has shown the applicability of the framework to understand a variety of different social phenomena. As a relatively new communication theory, STOPS has made connections between publics' motivation for problem solving and communicative action. In today's digitally networked society, STOPS can be used to provide a lens to understand problematic situations and publics' communicative action. Furthermore, scholars and practitioners may develop applied frameworks based on STOPS to examine cognitive factors and communicative action behind the rise of publics. One of the limitations of STOPS is its positivist focus. However, recent research studies that have applied STOPS from an interpretivist perspective have extended the use of STOPS for developing a more thorough understanding of why people become active in communication behaviors, and its effects on organizations (Poroli and Huang 2018).

While STOPS has been extensively used and published, it is expected that it will continue to evolve. In the context of public segmentation, STOPS will continue to be a useful framework for identifying strategic publics and their communicative behaviors in socially problematic situations. For example, using situational variables and cross-situational variables as a synthetic approach could be a new direction based on which researchers can predict strategic publics who show active communication behaviors in an organizational crisis. In risk communication, STOPS may contribute to segmenting strategic publics and their communicative action regarding controversial issues such as nuclear and environmental issues. As coping with health problems is significant to health communication, the STOPS framework also offers a model to predict publics' information behaviors. When dealing with predictions of disease spread (e.g., Ebola and MERS), individuals tend to be active in seeking information to reduce uncertainty. In times of public health crises, STOPS can be used to explain and predict communicative action of publics coping with a given crisis. In disaster communication, the STOPS framework could be used to predict and manage disaster resilience, specifically identifying active publics (i.e., focal communicants) in disastrous situations and using them to diffuse disaster literacy to inactive publics (i.e., peripheral communicants).

In crisis and risk communication, future research could be conducted to understand publics' activism and flaming behaviors in cyberspace. In particular, STOPS can be used to explain why people are active in controversial issues and their communication behaviors in the networked society. Due to the prevalence of social media, people have attempted to solve social problems through collective action in cyberspace. Although social media could be analyzed, latent factors – that is, individuals' perceptual and cognitive factors – still need to be explored using theoretical frameworks like STOPS to understand and predict individuals' communication behaviors in a problematic situation. In a recent study, the STOPS framework was used to predict why and how individuals engage in collective action in social media and offline activism (Chon and Park 2020). It was found that their collective action on social media was associated with offline activism on controversial societal issues such as gun control, illegal immigration, and police brutality issues in the US. Following this study, possible research topics include identifying activist publics and their communicative action in social media. STOPS was also applied to explain flaming behaviors in cyberspace (Kim and Kim 2009); a conceptual model could be used to explore Internet users' likelihood of engaging in flaming behaviors about a problem-causing entity and situation.

In addition, the concept of communicative behaviors can be further explored. The concepts of megaphoning and scouting, originally developed as dependent variables in the STOPS framework, may be applied to understand consumers in the private sector and citizens in the public sector under the lens of the strategic behavioral paradigm. Existing research proposes a concept called lay consumer informatics that should be further explored. In the digital world, digital publics play a vital role in generating and diffusing information. The concepts of megaphoning and scouting could be used to explore how they impact organizational reputation and authentic branding. Consequently, new frameworks developed based on STOPS have emerged, suggesting an association between organization–public relationship quality and megaphoning behaviors. STOPS should also be used to identify the extent to which the frameworks are applicable to different sectors, such as non-profit organizations and government agencies, given their differences in missions and need for public support. As non-profit organizations need publics' support, megaphoning and scouting of publics toward the organizations should be studied to identify how best to manage relationships to maximize organizational outcomes. As for government agencies, citizens' support in crises or risk situations is required to encourage supportive behaviors. Megaphoning is a useful concept in predicting how citizens can advocate for government agencies (i. e., advocacy megaphoning for the organization experiencing an issue) in problematic situations. In the context of public diplomacy, in which relationships are multi-level (e. g., individuals' relationships with foreign individuals, foreign organizations, and foreign countries), it is possible that individuals are engaged in both positive and negative megaphoning (Tam, Kim, and Kim 2018). Thus, it may be worth using the STOPS framework and the CAPS model to examine how individuals' relationships with and communicative behaviors relating to foreign countries are shaped by their variety of different experiences associated with those countries.

References

Aldoory, Linda & James E Grunig. 2012. The rise and fall of hot-issue publics: Relationships that develop from media coverage of events and crises. *International Journal of Strategic Communication* 6(1). 93–108.

Chen, Yi-Ru Regina, Chun-Ju Flora Hung-Baesecke & Jeong-Nam Kim. 2017. Identifying active hot-issue communicators and subgroup identifiers. *Journalism & Mass Communication Quarterly* 94(1). 124–147.

Chon, Myoung-Gi. 2016. *Social media activism and activist publics: Testing an integrative model of activism on contentious issues*. Louisiana State University PhD dissertation.

Chon, Myoung-Gi & Jeong-Nam Kim. 2016. Understanding active publics and their communicative action through public segmentation: Applying situational theory of problem solving to public segmentation in an organizational crisis situation. *Journal of Public Relations* 20(3). 113–138.

Chon, M.-G., & Park, H. 2020. Social Media Activism in the Digital Age: Testing an Integrative Model of Activism on Contentious Issues. *Journalism & Mass Communication Quarterly* 97(1). 72–97. https://doi.org/10.1177/1077699019835896

Dewey, John. 1927. *The public and its problems*. New York: Holt.

Grunig, James E. 1976. Communication behaviors occurring in decision and non-decision situations. *Journalism Quarterly* 53. 252–263.

Grunig, James E. 1997. A situational theory of publics: Conceptual history, recent challenges and new research. In D. Moss, T. MacManus & D. Verčič (eds.), *Public relations research: An international perspective*, 3–48. London: International Thomson Business.

Grunig, James E. 2003. Constructing public relations theory and practice. In Brenda Devin, Steven H. Chaffee & Lois Foreman-Wernet (eds.), *Communication, another kind of horse race: Essays honoring Richard F. Carter*, 85–115. Creskill, NJ: Hampton Press.

Grunig, James E. & Jeong-Nam Kim. 2017. Publics approaches to segmentation in health and risk messaging. In Roxanne Parrott (ed.), *Encyclopedia of Health and Risk Message Design and Processing*. New York: Oxford University Press. https://oxfordre.com/communication/view/10.1093/acrefore/9780190228613.001.0001/acrefore-9780190228613-e-322 (accessed 28 March 2020).

Jeong, Jae-Seon, Young Kim & Myoung-Gi Chon. 2018. Who Is Caring for the Caregiver? The Role of Cybercoping for Dementia Caregivers. *Health Communication* 33(1). 5–13.

Kim, Jeong-Nam. 2006. *Communicant activeness, cognitive entrepreneurship, and a situational theory of problem solving*. College Park, MD: University of Maryland.

Kim, Jeong-Nam. 2011. Public segmentation using situational theory of problem solving: Illustrating summation method and testing segmented public profiles. *PRism* 8 https://www.prismjournal. org/uploads/1/2/5/6/125661607/v8-no2-c1.pdf (accessed 28 March 2020.)

Kim, Jeong-Nam & James E. Grunig. 2011. Problem solving and communicative action: A situational theory of problem solving. *Journal of Communication* 61(1). 120–149.

Kim, Jeong-Nam & Lan Ni. 2013. Two types of public relations problems and integrating formative and evaluative research: A review of research programs within the behavioral, strategic management paradigm. *Journal of Public Relations Research* 25(1). 1–29.

Kim, Jeong-Nam, James E. Grunig & Lan Ni. 2010. Reconceptualizing the communicative action of publics: Acquisition, selection, and transmission of information in problematic situations. *International Journal of Strategic Communication* 4(2). 126–154.

Kim, Jeong-Nam & Jang-Yul Kim. 2009. *Mr. Hyde logged in: A theoretical account of situation-triggered flaming*. Chicago: National Communication Association.

Kim, Jeong-Nam & Arunima Krishna. 2014. Publics and lay informatics: A review of the situational theory of problem solving. In Elisia L. Cohen (ed.), *Communication Yearbook*, Vol. 38, 71–105. New York: Routledge.

Kim, Jeong-Nam & Seungyoon Lee. 2014. Communication and cybercoping: coping with chronic illness through communicative action in online support networks. *Journal of Health Communication* 19(7). 775–794.

Kim, Jeong-Nam, Lan Ni & Bey-Ling Sha. 2008. Breaking down the stakeholder environment: Explicating approaches to the segmentation of publics for public relations research. *Journalism & Mass Communication Quarterly* 85(4). 751–768.

Kim, Jeong-Nam & Yunna Rhee. 2011. Strategic thinking about employee communication behavior (ECB) in public relations: Testing the models of megaphoning and scouting effects in Korea. *Journal of Public Relations Research* 23(3). 243–268.

Kim, Jeong-Nam, Hongmei Shen & Susan E. Morgan. 2011. Information behaviors and problem chain recognition effect: Applying situational theory of problem solving in organ donation issues. *Health Communication* 26(2). 171–84.

Kim, Soojin, Jeong-Nam Kim, Laishan Tam & Kwang Tae Kim. 2015. Inquiring into activist publics in chronic environmental issues: use of the mutual-gains approach for breaking a deadlock. *Journal of Public Affairs* 15(4). 404–422.

Kim, Young. 2016. Understanding publics' perception and behaviors in crisis communication: Effects of crisis news framing and publics' acquisition, selection, and transmission of information in crisis situations. *Journal of Public Relations Research* 28(1). 1–16.

Kim, Young, Andrea Miller & Myoung-Gi Chon. 2016. Communicating with key publics in crisis communication: The synthetic approach to the public segmentation in CAPS (Communicative Action in Problem Solving). *Journal of Contingencies and Crisis Management* 24(2). 82–94.

Krishna, Arunima. 2017. Motivation with misinformation: Conceptualizing lacuna individuals and publics as knowledge-deficient, issue-negative activists. *Journal of Public Relations Research*. 29(4). 176–193.

Lee, Yeunjae & Jeong-Nam Kim. 2017. Authentic enterprise, organization-employee relationship, and employee-generated managerial assets. *Journal of Communication Management* 21(3). 236–253.

Ni, Lan & Jeong-Nam Kim. 2009. Classifying publics: Communication behaviors and problem-solving characteristics in controversial issues. *International Journal of Strategic Communication* 3(4). 217–241.

Park, Soo Hyun, Jeong-Nam Kim & Arunima Krishna. 2014. Bottom-up building of an innovative organization: Motivating employee intrapreneurship and scouting and their strategic value. *Management Communication Quarterly* 28(4). 531–560.

Poroli, Alessandro & Lei Vincent Huang. 2018. Spillover effects of a University crisis: A qualitative investigation using situational theory of problem solving. *Journalism and Mass Communication Quarterly* 95(4). 1128–1149.

Tam, Lisa, Jarim Kim & Jeong-Nam Kim. 2018. The origins of distant voicing: Examining relational dimensions in public diplomacy and their effects on megaphoning. *Public Relations Review* 44(3). 407–418.

Vibber, Kelly. 2014. *Advocates or adversaries? An exploration of communicative actions of within-border foreign publics and their affect on the host country's soft power.* West Lafayette, IN: Purdue University PhD dissertation.

Vibber, Kelly & Jeong-Nam Kim. 2015. Diplomacy in the globalized world: Focusing internally to build relationships externally. In G. J. Golan, S.-U. Yang & D. F. Kinsey (eds.), *International public relations and public diplomacy: Communication and engagement*, 131–146. New York: Peter Lang Publishing.

Part IV – **Recent Theorizing in Public Relations**

Vincent Hazleton and Emilie Tydings

25 The strategic application of social capital theory in public relations

Abstract: Social capital is a theory of increasing interest among public relations schol-ars. Social capital is the ability that organizations have to create, maintain, and use rela-tionships to achieve organizational goals. Scholarship is largely focused on theoretical rather than practical applications. Basic elements of social capital theory are reviewed and explained. Three extra theoretic constructs are proposed to advance social capital theory and facilitate its use as a practical theory for the community of public relations professionals. The concepts are goals, goal compatibility, and interdependence. These concepts provide an enhanced theoretical structure that links public relations or com-munication strategies to the formation, maintenance, and expenditure of social capi-tal to achieve organizational goals. Finally, the potential of social capital theory as an alternative to contemporary research on organization-public relationships is discussed.

Keywords: social capital; public relations strategy; goal compatibility; interdepend-ence; organization public relationships

1 Introduction

Social capital theory is concerned with both the dynamics and the outcomes of social relationships. Hazleton and Kennan (2000, 2006) define social capital as the ability that organizations have to create, maintain, and use relationships to achieve organi-zational goals. Relationships are multi-dimensional and given the centrality of rela-tionships to the study of public relations, social capital is of theoretic and potentially practical importance. Applications of social capital to our understanding of public relations are clear and direct. Public relations practitioners are those with the capac-ity to cultivate, maintain, and spend social capital on behalf of their organizations in an effort to cultivate functional public relationships. For example, the relationships established with media and other publics constitutes a deposit of social capital, which the organizations may expend to secure fair media coverage, gather information, and build alliances with other groups or organizations.

This chapter has several distinct goals. First it reviews applications of social capital theory to public relations. Second, it identifies key elements of social capital theory that are relevant to public relations. Third, it describes the dimensional char-acteristics of social capital. Fourth, it examines the limits of social capital theory in strategic public relations. Fifth, it identifies additional theoretic concepts which are necessary for the strategic use of social capital in public relations. Finally, the utility of this model for both strategic practice and research is discussed.

https://doi.org/10.1515/9783110554250-025

2 Applications of social capital theory to public relations

Despite what we see as enormous potential, social capital theory has not generated a large body of practical and applied public relations research. Perhaps this is because of the scope of potential applications. Following the initial publication of Hazleton and Kennan (2000), several PR scholars (Ihlen 2005; Luoma-aho 2005, 2009) have published theoretical essays addressing the potential of the theory. For instance, Ilhen (2005) used the work of sociologist Nan Lin (2002) to add depth to Bourdieu's conceptualization of social capital. Ilhen emphasized ideas related to creation and strength of network connections. But he distinguishes between "expressive actions", which focus on the creation of social capital, and "instrumental actions", which focus on the use of social capital to achieve organizational goals. Finally, he ties these activities to the creation and exercise of power.

Luoma-aho (2009) links social capital to the popular research of Robert Putnam (1995, 2000) on civic engagement in the United States and Italy. From this perspective, social capital is conceptualized as a public good that public relations helps to create through community-building (see chapter 22 in this book). Two different types of social capital, *bonding* and *bridging*, play important roles from this perspective. Bonding social capital is necessary in the creation of coherent and effective organizations and bridging social capital provides the links between groups. It is bridging social capital which is most necessary and useful in the creation of community. Trust is the product of public relations which makes social capital possible and effective. Later on, Luoma-aho (2013) has used this perspective to look at corporate reputations. She describes a reciprocal relationship between social capital and corporate reputation. Social capital is useful in establishing good reputations and good reputations facilitate the development of additional social capital.

Diversely, Maureen Taylor and her colleagues (Taylor 2011; Sommerfeldt and Taylor 2011; Sommerfeldt 2013; Yang and Taylor 2013), have focused on concepts of dialogue and social networks as expressions of social capital. In their model, social capital is a necessary condition for the development and maintenance of civil society. Dialogue represented as face-to-face interaction is the primary and most effective means of establishing social capital rather than mediated forms of communication traditionally associated with public relations. Kent and Taylor (2002) describe dialogue as being based on the acknowledgement of the diverse values of others, facilitation of participation, and an emphasis on mutual benefit with like-minded individuals. They have gathered data supporting their conceptualization through a variety of network studies of NGOs and government agencies.

The notion of social capital has also offered reflections relevant to studies about internal and organizational matters. Kennan and Hazleton (2006), in their essay on internal communication, claimed that reduced transaction costs were a likely social capital outcome of good internal communication. In an organizational case study, Fussell, Harrison-Rexrode, Kennan, and Hazleton (2007) found support for this claim and a significant relationship to organizational outcomes. In their study, trust served as a predictor of both transaction costs and organizational outcomes. In addition, the social capital components of access, timing, and network ties were significantly associated with transaction costs and organizational outcomes.

Perhaps the most studied area is social capital in relation to social media communications and civic engagement. Several public relations scholars have looked at the role of social media in social capital processes. Putnam (2000) argued that increased uses of social media leads to decreases in civic engagement. Kennan and Hazleton (2006) on the other hand observed that social media might facilitate the maintenance and activation of existing stores of social capital. Kennan, Hazleton, Janoske, and Short (2008) examined channel preferences for undergraduate students and found that social media were reported to be useful in building social capital with individuals not available for face-to-face interaction. Zhang and Abitol (2014), examined data from a Pew internet usage survey and found that general internet usage did not influence social capital, but strategic internet usage did have a positive influence on social capital. They also found that face-to-face communication was the only channel to have a positive impact on trust, and higher usage of social media did lead to lower levels of civic engagement.

More recently Dodd, Brummet, and Hazleton (2015), using data from the General Population Survey of the Census bureau, compared the frequencies of civic engagement behaviors reported by public relations specialists and public relations managers to the frequencies of these behaviors in the general survey population. The data indicated that public relations professionals are more likely to participate in civic engagement behaviors than the general U.S. population, and differences were found between public relations roles (manager/technician) for three researcher-created subcategories of civic engagement behaviors: political involvement, participation in voluntary organizations, and personal interaction. Managers were found to be more likely to engage in personal interactions, and specialists were found to be more likely to engage in political organizations and voluntary organizations. While diverse in focus, attempts to demonstrate the potential value of social capital theory to public relations have yielded useful and interesting results. In the next section of this essay we explore some theoretical issues deriving from social capital that pose problems for public relations scholarship.

3 Key elements of social capital

According to Portes (1998), social capital is based upon the fundamental assumption that group involvement and participation can be beneficial to individuals and groups. It would be fair to say that this not a new or unique idea. What is unique and beneficial from a strategic public relations perspective is its link to other forms of capital: financial capital, human capital, and symbolic capital. Social capital is something that can be acquired, stored, and expended, and used to facilitate action that can result in a competitive advantage for individuals, groups, and organizations. Social capital activities may produce increases in social capital or may produce financial capital, human capital, or intellectual capital. Most importantly, the account balance of available social capital emerges from the communication among individuals, groups, and organizations that allows them to successfully form, maintain, and utilize relationships.

Several scholars have contributed to the contemporary emergence of social capital as a significant theory. The earliest included Bourdieu (1979, 1980, 1985) and Coleman (1988a, 1988b, 1990, 1993, 1994a, 1994b). Other scholars contributing to the contemporary interest in social capital are Fukuyama (1995) and Putnam (1993, 1995, 2000).

Bourdieu (1986) defined social capital in terms of social networks as "the aggregate of the actual or potential resources which are linked to possession of a durable network of more or less institutionalized relationships of mutual acquaintance or recognition" (248). Bourdieu's definition is important because it distinguishes between two critical theoretical and practical elements: (1) the social relationship itself that allows a variety of actors to access resources held by their associates, and (2) the amount and quality of those resources. Outcomes are always constrained by the resources that actors possess.

Coleman (1988a: 98; 1990) defines social capital functionally as "a variety of entities with two elements in common: they all consist of some aspect of social structures, and they facilitate certain action of actors ± whether persons or corporate actors ± within the structure" (1990: 302). Specifically, it is changes in the relations between actors that produce social capital (Coleman 1988a; Baker 1990). Such changes are accomplished through communication.

Fukuyama (1995), a social economist, sees the central feature of social capital as trust. However, the focus of his analysis is viewing social capital as a cultural and social phenomenon that provides outcomes such as relative advantage and reduced transaction costs through the creation, maintenance, and expenditure of social relationships. He explains, for example, the economic success of the United States as a function of the willingness of Americans to trust others.

Putnam (1993, 1995, 2000), interested in the decline of civic engagement in the United States and other countries, contributed to the popularization of social capital. He viewed social capital as a public good expressed through social and political organizations. Among his contributions is a distinction between bonding and bridging forms of social capital.

4 Dimensions of social capital

Most theorists acknowledge that social capital is best viewed as a multiple dimensional construct. Nahapiet and Goshal (1998) proposed a multidimensional model consisting of structural, relational, and cognitive dimensions. Hazleton and Kennan (2000) proposed an alternative three-dimensional model of social capital. The three dimensions are a relational dimension, a structural dimension, and a communication dimension. They argued that communication is a necessary condition for the formation, maintenance, and utilization of social capital. The relational dimensions consist of three components (Hazleton and Kennan 2000; Kennan and Hazleton 2006): (1) expectations and obligations, (2) trust, and (3) identification (see Figure 1).

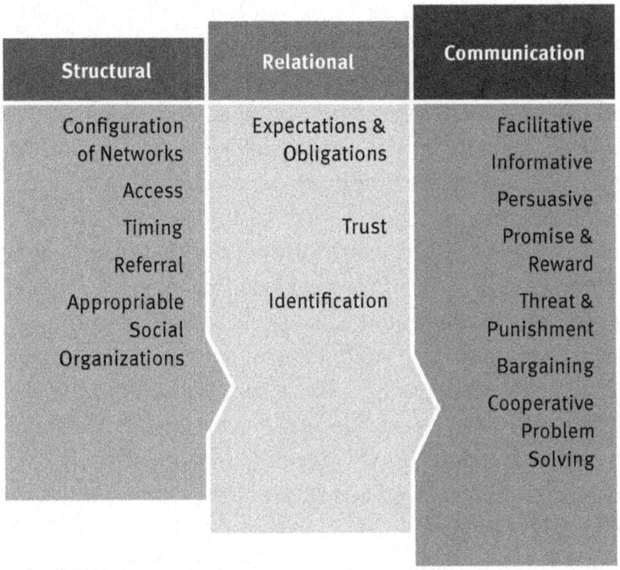

Structural	Relational	Communication
Configuration of Networks	Expectations & Obligations	Facilitative
Access		Informative
Timing		Persuasive
Referral	Trust	Promise & Reward
Appropriable Social Organizations	Identification	Threat & Punishment
		Bargaining
		Cooperative Problem Solving

Figure 1: Dimensions of social capital theory

Expectations and obligations (Coleman 1988a) have been defined as central features of the social capital relationship. The amount and nature of both are central features in understanding an organization's relations with its internal publics and clarifies the role of communication in building excellent public relations. Expectations and obligations are created through the communicative exchange and they both contain actor beliefs about past and future exchanges. As Coleman (1988a) explains:

> If A does something for B and assumes that B will reciprocate in the future, an expectation is established in A and an obligation incurred on the part of B. This obligation can be conceived as a credit slip held by A for the fulfillment of an obligation by B. These credit slips constitute a relational deposit that has a value that A can spend to accomplish various goals and objectives – unless, of course, the actor who has the obligation defaults on the debt. (1988a: 102)

Whether or not B repays A depends on several factors. One of these factors is the motivation to meet obligations through resource allocation (Portes 1998). Two different relational consequences of communication are important to the motivational model: trust and identification. Both help us to understand motivation regarding retiring relational debt.

Trust is the primary relational feature of social capital in Coleman's (1998a) formulation and the most frequently studied concept linked to other social outcomes from a social capital perspective (Portes 1998). Trust on the part of an actor supplying resources assumes the "anticipated cooperation" (Burt and Knez 1996) of the actor seeking resources. Organizational trust becomes an "orientation toward risk" and an "orientation toward other people and toward society as a whole" (Kramer 1999: 573). Rousseau, Sitkin, Burt, and Camerer (1998) after reviewing numerous definitions of trust define it in the following statement: "Trust is a psychological state comprising the intention to accept vulnerability based upon the positive expectations of the intentions or behavior of another" (1998: 395).

Trust as a basic component of social capital may be further clarified. Trust may be fragile or resilient. Fragile trust is a characteristic of weak relationships. It is dependent on the immediate likelihood of rewards, and it is not likely to survive where benefits and costs are not perceived as equal. The willingness of mere acquaintances to expend large amounts of time or resources to help those they do not know well is rare. Effort rather than the value of resources is a dominant factor in such situations. Information is easily given and does not necessarily result in lost opportunity costs to people giving it. Information is widely recognized as the most common exchange when social capital relationships are fragile.

Alternative forms of behavior, rather than social capital, may be used when cooperation or assistance is necessary, but relationships are fragile. When high risk or investment costs are present and relationships are fragile, formal communication exchanges that constitute a public obligation may be required (Leanna and Van Buren 1999). This is referred to as "contracting." This does not lead to a deeper level of association, and does not lead to an exchange if the reward structure is not clarified through some contractual arrangement.

Resilient trust is based on stronger and more numerous links and is not likely to be disrupted by occasional unequal exchanges (Leanna and Van Buren 1999). Further, resilient trust reflects a transaction based on a handshake rather than a complex set of requirements embodied in a written contract. Resilient trust requires little maintenance because it inheres in a history characterized by stable, principled, and ethical interactions. However, resilient trust is easily destroyed through thoughtless acts that can immediately and irrevocably destroy the relationship.

Identification refers to the extent to which actors view themselves as connected to other actors. Portes (1998) identifies two forms of identification. First is bounded solidarity. Grounded in Marx's concept of emergent class consciousness (Marx 1967 [1894]; Marx and Engels (1947 [1848]), the production of social capital is a product of the emergent awareness of a common fate. Originally, the concept referred to situations bounded by community. That is, individuals who are residents of a community sense their connectedness in terms of goals, values, and beliefs, and identify with each other on that basis. Out-group members are identified based on their lack of solidarity with a particular community. This concept must be expanded, however. It is possible for motivation to seek solidarity to cross social boundaries where contextual factors drive together groups, forming alliances previously impossible.

The second form of identification arises when A and B hold membership in a common social structure. Unlike the bounded solidarity situation, the expectation of repayment is not dependent on a perceived common fate, but on norms operational within the community. This is embodied in the concept of reciprocity. Reciprocity is a widely recognized social concept and not limited to social capital theory. In some instances, the actual repayment to A may come not from B but from the broader community. For example, the benefit to an employer who regularly hires workers with special needs and provides them with appropriate accommodations may not come directly from those employees. Rather, the reward emanates from the approval of the broader community of employees in that organization. This type of social capital outcome seems to be embedded in assumptions of many corporate social responsibility programs.

Structure affects access to other actors and is a necessary condition for the development and utilization of social capital. Communication scholars have a long history of interest in communication networks (Farace, Monge, and Russell 1977; Monge 1987). Elements of configuration such as network density, hierarchy, and connectivity are all structural components that affect the ability to create social capital. In addition to traditional network concepts, Hazleton and Kennan (2000; Kennan and Hazleton 2006) identify several other elements of networks as structural features of social capital.

Burt (1992) identifies three features of networks relevant to social capital: access, timing, and referral. Access describes the opportunity to send or receive messages, as well as knowledge of the appropriate network channels to use in social capital formation, maintenance, and expenditure. Knowledge of formal and informal networks facilitates both strategic choices and the efficiency of communication. Knowing whom to talk with about what is important, and it reflects what people know and intuitively understand about the nature and character of their networks (Garfinkel 1967).

Timing is a consequence of both knowledge and network structures. However, all other factors being equal, organizations that can communicate more quickly and in an appropriate chronological frame are likely to possess an organizational advantage. For example, an organization that encounters a new market competitor can only succeed if the response is immediate and if information about this challenge is available in a chronological frame that enables effective decision making. Beyond this, however, the issue has to do with when the response should occur. When, for example, should the market response occur?

Referrals indicate the network processes that provide information to actors about availability and accessibility of additional network ties. That is, some networks are more open and accessible than others. Also, inclusion in one network can make membership of other networks possible. Networks with high referral potential are more likely to produce more social capital from more different relationships than networks with low referral potential. The final feature of network structure has to do with Coleman's idea of the appropriable social organization (1988a). This concept describes the ability of networks or organizations formed for one purpose to be utilized for other purposes. Fukuyama (1995), for example, describes the transfer of trust from family and religious affiliations into work situations. Coleman (1990) shows social capital formed in personal relationships is appropriated for business purposes. Burt (1992) describes how social capital that emerged in personal relationships was then expended to create organizations.

Applications of these concepts to our understanding of public relations are clear and direct. Public relations practitioners are those with the capacity to cultivate, maintain, and spend social capital on behalf of their organizations in an effort to cultivate functional public relationships. For example, the relationships established with media and other publics constitutes a deposit of social capital, which the organizations may expend to secure fair media coverage, gather information, and build alliances with other groups or organizations. Thus, access, referral, timing, and the appropriable social organization as basic characteristics of networks may be used to better understand how public relations works, and it also affords the opportunity to create a series of metrics that can help assess the effectiveness of the public relations practitioner. Similarly, the connectedness of practitioners to networks is likely to be an indicator of the influence of public relations on behalf of the organization. Ties to the dominant hierarchy alone are not likely to produce excellent public relations. Rather, excellent public relations are best conceptualized by understanding the nature of the social capital accessible by the organization, including the practitioner, and the manner in which available social capital is expended to achieve important goals and objectives. This perspective offers something unique: a conceptualization of excellent public relations as a distinctively communication-grounded phenomenon that produces a commodity that can be observed and measured and that can be connected directly to the organization's efforts to succeed.

Communication, as a visible and manifest activity, provides the process through which public relationships are accomplished. As such, human communication provides the symbolic mechanism through which social capital is acquired and the mechanism through which it is expended in ways designed to produce desired public relations outcomes. Communication is not a dichotomous variable. Its mere presence or absence cannot account for social capital formation. Although its presence may be necessary for social capital formation and use, a careful explanation will require theories that explain and describe variations in communication content and strategy. One particular means of viewing the communication is provided by Hazleton (1992, 1993, 1998), who advances a set of public relations strategies that could be connected to social capital creation, maintenance, and expenditure. Hazleton proposes a taxonomy of seven public relations strategies: facilitative, informative, persuasive, promise and reward, threat and punishment, bargaining, and cooperative problem solving.

According to Hazleton, strategy refers to a family of message tactics that possess common manifest characteristics. Strategy selection begins with consideration of the characteristics of audiences and objectives at the level of both organizational goals and communication goals that directly reference the audiences for communication. Strategies are chosen based on assumptions that they will be effective.

Page (1998, 2000a, 2000b, 2000c, 2003; Page and Hazleton 1999; Werder 2003, 2004, 2005), in a series of studies, has explored the use of the public relations strategies identified by Hazleton. Her research demonstrates both the utility and validity of the strategy taxonomy for studying public relations communication, demonstrating empirical linkages between perceived attributes of publics, and perceived public relations effectiveness. One would expect that a public relations strategy will systematically vary with social capital processes. Some of these strategies are associated with the formation of social capital, whereas others either drain the available stock of social capital or inhibit its development. Different public relations strategies are likely to characterize differing levels and types of social capital.

Several examples of strategies influencing production and expenditure of social capital are provided below. Facilitative strategies that enable others to overcome constraints and achieve their goals clearly have implications for social capital formation. They are likely to produce a sense of obligation (social capital) in those receiving assistance. Both bargaining and promise and reward are more likely to be used in situations where trust is fragile rather than resilient – that is, when resilient trust is in demand. On the other hand, effective and fair use of some of these strategies over time may create more social capital and facilitate the use of additional communication strategies.

Communication, in addition to laying the foundation for the emergence of social capital, is also the mechanism whereby the available stock of social capital can be accessed and expended to further individual, group, and organizational goals and objectives. Informative strategies, cooperative problem-solving strategies, and persuasive strategies may all be useful in the transformation of social capital into other forms of capital (Coleman 1988a), as communicators indicate their needs and goals to employees or other publics with a sense of obligation to the organization. Communication is a primary concept in the theory of social capital.

5 Limits of social capital theory in strategic public relations

There are a number of practical limits to the strategic application of social capital theory. As Hazleton and Kennan noted (2000), social capital outcomes are characterized by unspecified obligations, uncertain time horizons, and potential violations of reciprocity expectations (Bourdieu 1979, 1980). First, one does not know exactly how actors might construe their obligations based on social capital, and hence the type of outcomes that can emerge are contextually embedded. Second, it is difficult to understand when obligations will be repaid (uncertain time horizons). When can one expect an obligation to be repaid or whether actors perceive reasons for reciprocating at all? Finally, actors may violate reciprocity expectations. Most simply put, an actor loans an acquaintance $20. The actor expects that the loan will be repaid promptly. The acquaintance seeks to meet the obligation by offering to buy lunch in some unspecified time frame. While the intent is to repay the obligation, the manner in which the obligation is to be met fails to meet conventional expectations.

One must also understand that financial obligations are more fungible, whereas social capital obligations are less fungible. A financial debt generally can be sold or passed on to another individual or organization. Unlike financial or economic obligations, social capital is rooted in and constrained by the particular relationship in which it emerges. One could not tell Bob that he ought to buy Ed lunch because Ed had bought Sam lunch last Tuesday. The relationship and the social capital exist only between Bob and Ed and within a particular context. Such transfers are possible, but they cannot occur without the approval of the obligated party.

Investments of any type of capital involve the possibility of losses of capital. There is no common metric for assessing the cost or returns of social capital investments. Business biases predispose researchers and theorists to try and express both cost and returns as economic capital. More consideration should be given to the development of alternative metrics.

The possession of social capital does not necessarily mean that it will be effectively maintained or spent. Little attention has been paid to how actors maintain existing stores of social capital or the actions which actors take to produce returns from existing stores of social capital. Like economic capital, social capital is not always used wisely and can produce negative consequences for actors (Portes and Landolt 1996). Criminal organizations, criminal conspiracies, and victimless crimes such as prostitution and drug use can be explained using social capital theory. Social capital is best understood as potential, and its utilization recognized as influence.

Finally, in its current form, social capital theory is best described as a descriptive or explanatory theory. When an organization or individual (A) with expectations seeks to exploit a store of social capital in an organization or individual with obligations (B), there is a probability (Y) that the actions of B will fail to meet the expectations of

A. This poses a correlational relationship between social capital and public relations outcomes rather than a causal relationship. This suggests the possibility of mediating factors which may enhance or mitigate social capital outcomes but are not currently recognized as relevant to the theory.

6 Extra theoretic concepts for the strategic use of social capital

The transformation of social capital theory from an explanatory and descriptive theory to a predictive theory requires additional theoretic constructs. In this chapter, we identify three constructs central to public relations which provide a framework for selecting public relations strategies useful in the creation, maintenance, and transformation or use of social capital. We argue that these constructs will advance social capital theory as a strategic theory. These constructs are goals, interdependence, and goal compatibility (see Figure 2).

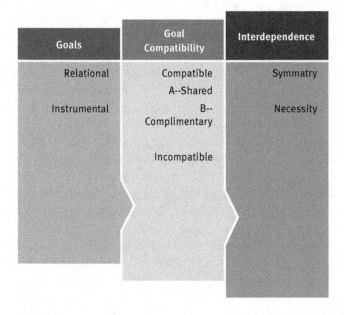

Figure 2: Social capital extra theoretical concepts

6.1 On goals

Hazleton and Long (1987) proposed that achievement of organizational goals is the primary purpose of public relations. Goals are a central concept to the social sciences and specifically theories of organization because they directly reference intentionality in human behavior (Mohr 1973). Simon (1964) defines goals as "value premises that can serve as inputs to decisions" (3). While the purpose of public relations is to help organizations achieve their goals, it is important to recognize that others also have their own goals. It is easier to secure cooperation when goals are shared than when they are not shared.

6.2 Types of goals

Hazleton (2006) has identified two different types of public relations goals: instrumental goals and relational goals. Instrumental goals directly reference the communicator in terms of outcomes or action and are aligned with the traditional concepts of organizational mission or purpose. Instrumental goals are those that we commonly identify as the organization's bottom line and would include concepts such as market share, return on investment, profit, and cost. Communicators who achieve their instrumental goals are generally assumed to be effective.

Relational goals, on the other hand, reference the connection by communication of two or more communicators. Generally, in democratic societies the successful achievement of instrumental goals requires the cooperation of others, which may only be acquired legally and ethically through communication. A different criterion for effectiveness is used to judge communication in the achievement of relational goals. Successful relational communication is considered to be appropriate (Hazleton 2006). We would further propose that appropriateness is an important characteristic of communication in the creation, maintenance, and utilization of social capital.

Logic, consistency, and necessity are not necessary characteristics that explain goals. It is merely important to observe that communicators have goals that influence public relations. Further, goals alone are inadequate to predict intentions or behavior. Goals are situationally operant and relevant. Perrow (1961) distinguishes between official goals, "which are vague and general," (855) and operative goals, which "designate the ends sought through actual operating policies." The expression of official goals as operative goals is constrained and bounded by the priorities of multiple goals and the multiple alternatives made available in the environment for achieving goals. Specifically, it is the relationship between the goals of communicators which is most important. This relationship is expressed in terms of judgments of interdependence and goal compatibility.

6.3 On goal compatibility

Goal compatibility references the extent to which goals of communicators conflict with each other. This can be conceptualized as a continuum. At one end of the continuum goals are totally incompatible. If one party achieves their goals the other cannot achieve theirs. Communication avoidance and conflict are likely when goals are incompatible. At the other end of the continuum, organizations and publics may share the same goals. When goals are shared, both communication and cooperation are logical consequences. However, goal compatibility does not necessitate that interactants share common goals. Goals may also be considered compatible when they are complimentary. Goals are considered complementary when the achievement of goals by one communicator facilitates the achievement of goals by other communicators. Again, communication and cooperation are logical consequences of complementary goals.

In the middle of the continuum goals are neither compatible or incompatible. They are on their face irrelevant and independent. Obviously, goal compatibility influences the potential for both conflict and cooperation. The middle of the compatibility continuum may be of particular theoretic interest. When communicator goals are independent the potential for bargaining is likely to emerge. Reciprocal exchanges of assistance and support toward goal achievement, which enhance the potential for developing social capital, may make sense when both parties are helped, and neither is harmed

6.4 On interdependence

Interdependence references the extent to which communicators may influence each other's goals achievement or potential for goals achievement through action or words. McCann and Ferry (1979) describe interdependence as occurring when "actions taken by one referent system affects the actions or outcomes of another referent system" (113). Interdependence as a concept is also embedded in the stakeholder approach to public relations. Freeman (1984) defines a stakeholder as "any group or individual who can affect or is affected by the achievement of the firm's objectives" (25). Coombs (2007) acknowledges the connection to stakeholder theories and suggests that interdependence may be useful in defining relationships. While it is not certain that interdependence defines or is an appropriate measure of relationships, it is proposed that perceptions of interdependence are a powerful source of motivation for relationship formation and maintenance. Analytically it may be useful to segment and consider the dependence of each party on an interaction relative to the other parties.

Dependence is a traditional variable recommended as useful in identifying priorities among publics. In general, introductory public relations texts recommend that organizations should communicate with those stakeholders whose cooperation is required to achieve goals, and that levels of dependency can be used to prioritize stakeholders in terms of importance. Priority should be given to those you are most dependent upon. This seems to be a very simple idea, but in a world in which all communicators have goals it becomes more complex. The goals and dependencies of stakeholders on organizations should also be considered. The interactive complexity of interdependence is embedded in concepts of symmetry and necessity that are explained below.

First, dependence relationships may be considered symmetrical or asymmetrical. Relationships are asymmetrical when communicator A is dependent upon communicator B for goal achievement, but communicator B is not dependent upon communicator A for goal achievement. In this case, communicator B may be said to have power over communicator A. When communicator A is dependent upon communicator B for goal achievement and communicator B is equally dependent on communicator A for goal achievement, the relationship is symmetrical. The concept of symmetry implies a motivation for cooperation.

The concept of necessity references the importance of particular communicators to goal achievement. It only becomes meaningful when at least one communicator is dependent upon another in a population for goal achievement. For any given goal of communicator A there may be one or more potential communicators B whose cooperation or support is necessary for goal achievement. Necessity is viewed as a continuum along which levels of necessity are normally distributed. At the far end of the necessity continuum, communicators are independent. This suggests that for any given goal there is a small number of communicators whose support and cooperation is critical, and an equally small number who may be considered irrelevant.

—Sometimes, the support of a specific and limited set of communicators is not necessary for goal achievement. In some cases, there is a large population of possible communicators B where the cooperation and support of any member or set of members of the population is sufficient for goal achievement by A. This idea helps to explain and understand the prevalence of more general campaigns to improve organizational images and reputations. When communicators are mutually interdependent and have common goals, cooperative behavior and the development of positive relationships is a natural consequence.

Therefore, in principle, when planning a campaign, practitioners should identify all the necessary and sufficient stakeholders and publics whose cooperation and support will lead to goal achievement. However, there are other factors that need to be taken into consideration in selecting others with whom you will need to communicate. Perhaps the most important of these is goal compatibility. Figure 3 visually depicts how the three social capital constructs inform the selection of public relations strategies.

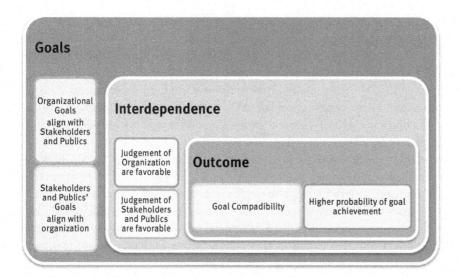

Figure 3: Social capital theoretical predictors

There is an additional factor that is important; however; its influence is tactical rather than strategic. The ability of any actor to repay social capital obligations is clearly dependent upon the resources available in a given situation. Thus, resources are mediating rather than causal factors. But they should not be ignored.

7 Future research and strategic application of social capital theory

Social capital still represents an under-theorized and under-researched theory of great practical value to both the academic and professional public relations communities. While there are numerous directions which research and theory development can take, there are some which may be of greater value to the strategic practice of public relations.

First, we would encourage research which explores the nature and character of the expectations and obligations that are common to public relationships. Research into concepts such as brand loyalty may already provide a useful framework for some of this research. Research on organization-public relationships has focused almost exclusively on perceptions of organizations by publics. Research is limited in explaining how organizations care about publics. In contrast, expectations and obligations may include cognitive, affective, and behavioral components, providing a much richer theoretical framework. For instance, perceptions and reactions to corporate social responsibility may be linked to concepts of both goal compatibility and interdependence. Future research could be relevant in this regard.

The research described in this chapter may be a necessary condition for the development of useful and meaningful social capital metrics. Since social capital is not a dichotomous variable, research that tries to address and describe variances in social capital among various populations would be useful in this respect. Because of the theoretic scope and multidimensional nature of social capital theory, there are likely be multiple useful metrics.

The nature of both workplace relationships and professional relationships are also promising areas of research. To what extent do professionals strategically build and maintain social relationships to achieve personal and organizational goals? Recent research by Dodd, Brummette, and Hazleton (2015) showed that public relations technicians were more likely than the general population to engage in civic activities associated with social capital. Is this a strategic process characteristic of organizations or merely a characteristic of people that are attracted to the practice of public relations? The use of personal social capital to benefit the organization is a promising area of research. It necessarily involves the willingness of actors to recognize transfers as appropriate in meeting obligations and expectations. On a more practical level for the academic community, to what extent can skills related to social capital development and use be learned or taught?

At the meso or organizational level of operation, we think that there are likely to be differences in the character of expectations of publics and the perceived obligations of organizations to those publics. It seems common sense to recognize that our relationships with organizations are different than our relationships with other people. We suspect that most organization-public relationships (OPRs) are characterized by weak ties. We do believe that strong ties are possible, but it is likely that they are rare. Following this logic, we believe that social capital theory represents a potentially valuable alternative to the study of organization-public relationships. Broom and his students (1997) argued that good OPR theories would involve more than the study of perceptions on the part of publics. Social capital theories include structural and communication dimensions that can provide the basis for a view of OPR consistent with the recommendations of Ferguson (1984) and Broom (1997) and his colleagues.

As noted earlier, social capital outcomes have been viewed by some theorists as limited and non-fungible. The most common return on social capital investments appears to be "information" and this is viewed as related to "weak ties." We have also observed social capital outcomes of high economic value from what might be characterized as relationships with weak ties. High levels of goal compatibility and interdependence may account for such outcomes. The extra-theoretic concepts of goals, goal compatibility, interdependence, and resources allow for numerous research studies that address the frequency of various social capital outcomes.

Communication is a manifest and observable component of public relations. The richest area of research possibilities related to social capital theory and strategic public relations lies in exploring the relationship among communication, social capital formation, social capital maintenance, and social capital outcomes. While our personal interest is in the strategies identified by Hazleton and his colleagues, other models of strategic communication may be theoretically valuable. The work on dialogic communication of Taylor and her colleagues in relation to social capital and civil society is a line of research that clearly should be extended.

The study of the role of social capital in strategic public relations is still in its early stages. It is gradually moving from theoretical speculation to practical research that can be of value to communities of practice. It is likely that interest in social capital will grow among both scholars and practitioners in coming years. It complements other approaches to public relations. It does not necessarily replace them.

References

Baker, Wayne E. 1990. Market networks and corporate behavior. *American Journal of Sociology* 96. 589–625.

Bourdieu, Pierre. 1979. Les trois etats du capital culturel. *Actes de la Recherche en Sciences Sociales* 30. 3–6.

Bourdieu, Pierre. 1980. Le capital social: notes provisoires. *Actes de la Recherche en Sciences Sociales* 31. 2–3.

Bourdieu, Pierre. 1985. The social space and genesis of groups. *Theory and Society* 14(6). 723–744. doi:10.1177/053901885024002001 (accessed 16 April 2020).

Bourdieu, Pierre. 1986. The forms of capital. In John G. Richardson (ed.), *Handbook of Theory and Research for the Sociology of Education*, 241–258. New York: Greenwood.

Broom, Glen M., Shawna Casey & James Ritchey. 1997. Toward a concept and theory of organization-public relationships. *Journal of Public Relations Research* 9(2). 83–98.

Burt, Ronald S. 1992. *Structural Holes: The Social Structure of Competition*. Cambridge, MA: Harvard University Press.

Burt, Ronald S. & Mark Knez. 1996. Trust and third-party gossip. In R. M. Kramer & T. R. Tyler (eds.), *Trust in organizations: Frontiers of Theory & Research*, 68–89. Thousand Oaks, CA: Sage.

Coleman, James S. 1988a. Social capital in the creation of human capital. *American Journal of Sociology* 94. 95–120. doi:10.1086/228943 (accessed 16 April 2020).

Coleman, James S. 1988b. The creation and destruction of social capital: Implications for the law. *Notre Dame Journal of Law, Ethics, and Public Policy* 3. 375–404.

Coleman, James S. 1990. *Foundations of Social Theory*. Cambridge, MA: Belknap Press.

Coleman, James S. 1993. The rational reconstruction of society. *American Sociological Review* 58. 1–15.

Coleman, James S. 1994a. A rational choice perspective on economic sociology. In N. J. Smelser & R. Swedberg (eds.), *Handbook of Economic Sociology*, 166–180. Princeton, NJ: Princeton University Press.

Coleman, James S. 1994b. The realization of effective norms. In R. Collins (ed.), *Four Sociological Traditions: Selected Readings*, 171–189. New York: Oxford University Press. doi:10.1057/palgrave.crr.1550049 (accessed 16 April 2020).

Coombs, W. Timothy. 2007. Protecting organization reputations during a crisis: The development and application of situational crisis communication theory. *Corporate Reputation Review* 10(3). 163–176.

Dodd, Melissa, John Brummette & Vincent Hazleton. 2015. A social capital approach: An examination of Putnams's civic engagement and public relations roles. *Public Relations Review* 41(4). 472–479.

Farace, Richard V., Peter R. Monge & Hamish H. Russell. 1977. *Communicating and organizing.* Reading, MA: Addison-Wesley.

Ferguson, Mary Ann. 1984. Building theory in public relations: Interorganizational relationships as a public relations paradigm. Paper presented at annual conference of the Association for Education in Journalism and Mass Communication, Gainesville, 5–8 August.

Freeman, R. Edward. 1984. *Strategic Management: A Stakeholder Approach.* Boston: Pittman.

Fukuyama, Francis. 1995. *Trust: The Social Virtues and the Creation of Prosperity.* New York: The Free Press.

Fussell, Hilary, Jill Harrison-Rexrode, William R. Kennan & Vincent Hazleton. (2006). The relationship between social capital, transaction costs, and organizational outcomes: A case study. *Corporate communications: An international journal* 11(2). 148–161.

Garfinkel, Harold. 1967. *Studies in ethnomethodology.* Englewood Cliffs, NJ: Prentice Hall.

Hazleton, Vincent. 1992. Toward a systems theory of public relations. In Horst Avenarius & Wolfgang Ambrecht (eds.), *Ist Public Relations eine Wissenschaft?*, 33–46. Berlin: Westdeutscher Verlag.

Hazleton, Vincent. 1993. Symbolic resources: Processes in the development and use of symbolic resources. In Horst Avenarius, Wolfgang Armbrecht & Ulf Zabel (eds.), *Image und PR*, 87–100. Berlin: Westdeutscher Verlag.

Hazleton, Vincent. 1998. Implications of a theory of public relations competence for crisis communication: Balancing concerns for effectiveness and appropriateness. Paper presented at the annual meeting of the National Communication Association, New York, 21–24 November.

Hazleton, Vincent. 2006. Toward a theory of public relations competence. In Carl H. Botan & Vincent Hazleton (eds.), *Public Relations Theory II*, 199–222. London: Lawrence Erlbaum Associates.

Hazleton, Vincent & William Kennan. 2000. Relationships as social capital: Reconceptualizing the bottom line. *Corporate Communication: An International Journal* 5. 81–86.

Hazleton, Vincent & Larry W. Long. 1987. Public relations: A theoretical and practical response. *Public Relations Review* 13(2). 3–13. doi:10.1016/S0363-8111(87)80034-6 (accessed 16 April 2020).

Ihlen, Øyvind. 2005. The power of social capital: Adapting Bourdieu to the study of public relations. *Public Relations Review* 31(4). 492–496.

Kennan, William R. & Vincent Hazleton. 2006. Internal public relations, social capital, and the role of effective organizational communication. In Carl H. Botan & Vincent Hazleton (eds), *Public Relations Theory II*, 273–296. London: Lawrence Erlbaum Associates.

Kennan, William. R., Vincent Hazleton, Melissa Janoske & Melissa Short. 2008. The influence of new communication technologies on undergraduate preferences for social capital formation, maintenance, and expenditure. *Public Relations Journal* 2(2). 1–21.

Kent, Michael L. & Maureen Taylor. 2002. Toward a dialogic theory of public relations. *Public Relations Review* 28. 21–27.

Kramer, Roderick M. 1999. Trust and distrust in organizations: Emerging perspectives, enduring questions. *Annual Review of Psychology* 50. 569–598.

Leanna, Carrie R. & Harry J. Van Buren III. 1999. Organizational social capital and employment practices. *Academy of Management Review* 24(3). 538–555.

Lin, Nan. 2002. *Social Capital: A Theory of Social Structure and Action.* New York: Cambridge University Press.

Luoma-aho, Vilma. 2005. *Faith-holder as social capital of Finnish public organizations.* University of Jyväskylä doctoral dissertation. http://urn.fi/URN:ISBN:951-39-2262-6 (accessed 17 January 2018).

Luoma-aho, Vilma. 2009. Bowling together: Applying Robert Putnam's theories of community and social capital to public relations. In O. Ihlen & M. Fredricksson (eds.), *Social Theory on PR*, 231–251. Routledge/Lawrence Erlbaum.

Luoma-aho, Vilma. 2013. Corporate reputation and the theory of social capital. In Craig E. Carroll (ed.), *The Handbook of Communication and Corporate Reputation*, 279–292. Oxford: John Wiley & Sons.

Luoma-aho, Vilma. 2018. On Putnam: Bowling Together – Applying Putnam's Theories of Community and Social Capital to Public Relations. In Øyvind Ihlen & Magnus Fredriksson (eds.), *Public Relations and Social Theory: Key Figures, Concepts and Developments*, 195–214. New York: Routledge.

Marx, Karl. 1967 [1894]. *Capital* (3). New York: International.

Marx, Karl & Frederick Engels. 1947 [1848]. *The German Ideology*. New York: International.

McCann, Joseph E. & Diane L. Ferry. 1979. An approach for assessing and managing inter-unit interdependence. *Acadamy of Management Review* 4(1). 113–119. doi:10.5465/AMR.1979. 4289199 (accessed 16 April 2020).

Mohr, Lawrence B. 1973. The concept of organizational goal. *American Political Science Review* 67(2). 470–481. doi:10.2307/1958777 (accessed 16 April 2020).

Monge, Peter R. 1987. The network level of analysis. In Charles R. Berger & Steven H. Chaffee (eds.), *The Handbook of Communication Science*, 239–270. Newbury Park, CA: Sage.

Nahapiet, Janine & Sumantra Ghoshal. 1998. Social capital, intellectual capital and the organizational advantage. *Academy of Management Review* 23(2). 242–266.

Page, Kelly G. 1998. *An empirical analysis of factors influencing public relations strategy use and effectiveness*. Radford, VA: Radford University master's thesis.

Page, Kelly G. 2000a. An exploratory analysis of goal compatibility between organizations and publics. Paper presented at the meeting of the Public Relations Division of the Southern States Communication Association, New Orleans, 29 March–2 April.

Page, Kelly G. 2000b. Prioritizing relations: Exploring goal compatibility between organizations and publics. Paper presented at the meeting of the Public Relations Division of the International Communication Association, Acapulco, June.

Page, Kelly G. 2000c. Determining message objectives: An analysis of public relations strategy use in press releases. Paper presented at the meeting of the Public Relations Division of the Association for Education in Journalism and Mass Communication, Phoenix, 9–12 August.

Page, Kelly G. 2003. Responding to activism: An experimental analysis of public relations strategy influence on beliefs, attitudes, and behavioral intentions. Paper presented at the meeting of the Public Relations Division of the International Communication Association. San Diego, 23–27 May.

Page, Kelly & Vincent Hazleton. 1999. An empirical analysis of factors influencing public relations strategy selection and effectiveness. Paper presented to the annual meeting of the International Communication Association, San Francisco, 27 May–1 June.

Perrow, Charles. 1961. The analysis of goals in complex organizations. *American Sociological Review* 26(6). 854–866.

Portes, Alejandro. 1998. Social capital: Its origins and applications in modern society. *Annual Review of Sociology* (24). 1–24. doi:10.1146/annurev.soc.24.1.1 (accessed 16 April 2020).

Portes, Alejandro & Patricia Landolt. 1996. Unsolved mysteries: The Tocqueville files II. *The American Prospect* 7(26). http://www.prospect.org/print/V7/26/26-cnt2.html.

Putnam, Robert D. 1993. The prosperous community: social capital and public life. *American Prospect* (13). 35–42.

Putnam, Robert D. 1995. Bowling alone: America's declining social capital. *Journal of Democracy* (6). 65–78.

Putnam, Robert D. 2000. Bowling alone: The collapse and revival of American community. New York: Simon & Schuster.

Rousseau, Denise M., Sim B. Stikin, Ronald S. Burt & Colin Camerer. 1998. Not so different after all: A cross-discipline view of trust. *Academy of Management Review* 23(3). 393–404.

Simon, Herbert A. 1964. On the concept of organizational goal. *Administrative Science Quarterly* 9(1). 1–22. doi:10.2307/2391519 (accessed 16 April 2020).

Sommerfeldt, Erich J. 2013. The civility of social capital: Public relations in the public sphere, civil society, and democracy. *Public Relations Review* 39. 280–289. doi:10.1016/j.pubrev.2012.12.004 (accessed 16 April 2020).

Sommerfeldt, Erich J. & Maureen Taylor. 2011. A social capital approach to improving public relations' efficacy: Diagnosing internal constraints on external communication. *Public Relations Review* 37(3). 197–206.

Taylor, Maureen. 2011. Building social capital through rhetoric and public relations. *Management Communication Quarterly* 25(3). 436–454.

Werder, Kelly Page. 2003. An empirical analysis of the influence of perceived attributes of publics on public relations strategy use and effectiveness. Paper presented at the meeting of the Public Relations Division of the Association for Education in Journalism and Mass Communication, Kansas City, 30 July–2 August.

Werder, Kelly Page. 2004. Responding to activism: An experimental analysis of public relations strategy influence on attributes of publics. Paper presented at the meeting of the Public Relations Division of the Association for Education in Journalism and Mass Communication, Toronto, 4–7 August.

Werder, Kelly Page. 2005. An empirical analysis of the influence of perceived attributes of publics on public relations strategy use and effectiveness. *Journal of Public Relations Research* 17. 217–266.

Yang, Aimee & Maureen Taylor. 2013. The relationship between the professionalization of public relations, societal social capital and democracy: Evidence from a cross-national study. *Public Relations Review* 39. 257–270. doi:10.1016/j.pubrev.2013.08.002 (accessed 16 April 2020).

Zhang, Weiwu & Alan Abitbol. 2014. The role of public relations in social capital and civic engagement. *Communication Faculty Publication* 45. 644–680.

Magnus Fredriksson, Sara Ivarsson, and Josef Pallas

26 Ideas of public relations in the light of Scandinavian institutionalism

Abstract: The aim of this chapter is to show how Scandinavian institutionalism can help us better understand public relations. The core argument is that public relations, rather than a *function* or *role*, is to be understood as a (management) *idea*. Public relations is then one of many other recipes, techniques and models organizations act to incorporate in their formal structures to foster what they believe is better management. This means that we will approach public relations as something negotiated, questioned, resisted and transformed as it moves from one context to another. It will then, by necessity, become different things in different organizations and change over time.

Keywords: carriers; ideas; public relations; Scandinavian institutionalism; translation

1 Introduction

The aim of this chapter is to flesh out how Scandinavian institutionalism can help us better understand public relations and to contribute to the increasing stream of research focusing on public relations as a socially embedded activity (Edwards 2018; Ihlen and Fredriksson 2018). Central to our argument is that public relations, rather than a *function* or *role*, is to be understood as a (management) *idea*. Public relations is then one of many other recipes, techniques and models organizations act to incorporate in their formal structures to foster, what they believe is, better management. This means that we will approach public relations as something negotiated, questioned, resisted and transformed as it moves from one context to another. It will then, by necessity, become different things in different organizations and change over time.

To support our argument we will use the first part of our chapter to introduce the foundations of Scandinavian institutionalism and then develop our discussion around four central conceptualizations including ideas, carriers, re- and de-contextualizations and, finally, ecology of translations.

2 Institutionalisms

Scandinavian institutionalism belongs to the family of organizational institutionalism (sometimes labelled neo-institutional theory), which is not so much a theory but rather an approach. It offers a diversified toolbox for analyses of organizations

https://doi.org/10.1515/9783110554250-026

and their institutional contexts. It appeared in the middle of the 1970s as a challenge to rationalist perspectives on organizations, and over the years it has become the dominating framework for organizational analyses. One of its key contributions is the insight that organizations, irrespective of mission, operations, size etc., have a tendency to be become very much alike and demonstrate a great deal of conformity in structures, procedures and activities (Meyer and Rowan 1977). Such structural conformity (isomorphism in the language of institutional theorists) is explained by coercive, mimetic and normative processes through which organizations adapt to institutional expectations in their quest for social acceptance (Greenwood et al. 2017). To explain the pressures institutions exercise vis-à-vis organizations, institutional theorists operate with notions such as legitimacy and rationalized myths (Meyer and Rowan 1977), isomorphism, (DiMaggio and Powell 1983) and, more recently, logics (Thornton, Ocasio, and Lounsbury 2012). The underlying argument binding these notions together is based on extensive empirical observations of similarities, standardization and stability that appear in the wake of diffusion of global models across the social landscape (Grinsven, Heusinkveld, and Cornelissen 2016).

2.1 Institutional approaches to public relations

It is easy to see how myths, legitimacy and other concepts offered by organizational institutionalism could be utilized to study public relations. Surprisingly little has been done, however. There are examples of conceptual papers (e. g. Frandsen and Johansen 2013; Fredriksson and Pallas 2011, 2014; Fredriksson, Pallas, and Wehmeier 2013; Sandhu 2009) and empirical analyses (e. g. Bartlett, Tywoniak, and Hatcher 2007; Le and Bartlett 2014; Merkelsen 2013; Wehmeier 2006). But the overall impression is that public relations scholars avoid institutional theory. As pointed out by Spicer (1997), one reason for this is the lack of agency and autonomy institutional theory attribute to organizations. In his book, Spicer refers to Aldrich (1992, in Spicer 1997: 169), who stated that "most of the verbs used to describe organization-environment relations carry the connotation that environments dominate or overpower organizations ... organizational structures may be: imposed, authorized, induced, acquired, imprinted or incorporated". Overall, this means that conventional organizational institutionalism leaves little leeway and discretion for organizational members to actively relate to and enact the structural pressures and expectations in which they are embedded. Accordingly, organizational institutionalism has been seen as irrelevant for a field dominated by research referring to management and strategy.

The critique of over-determinism in institutional theory has been articulated both within and outside the neo-institutional field (Alvesson and Spicer 2018) and it is relevant. There is a tendency among institutionalists to oversee the motives and skills of actors and how they relate to the institutions they are embedded in. As a number of empirical studies have shown, actors can indeed influence the structural properties of their environments. Actors both individually and collectively are capable of creating new, changing and disturbing existing institutional arrangements. However, one needs to be cautious about how far the notion of agency can be pushed. Even if there is room for agency, creativity, change and disruption, actors can never step outside the social contexts of which they are a part. It is therefore necessary not to overstate the liberties and maneuvering space available to the actors (Lawrence, Suddaby, and Leca 2009).

3 Scandinavian institutionalism

Scandinavian institutionalism is a response to the critique faced by organizational institutionalism. It highlights organizational variations and distinctiveness and rests on an ambition to explain how stable institutions change over time and how actors play an important role as change agents when they encounter and interact with institutions. This is done, however, without losing track of the institutional conditions actors are embedded in. There are always rules and norms that stipulate what an organization in a specific institutional context can or cannot do (Boxenbaum and Strandgaard Pedersen 2009).

The interest in change was a result of empirical observations done in the 1980s, when an increasing number of organizations started to implement techniques and models to gain what they argued was better management. Many of the models were introduced as whole-cut solutions for how organizations ought to perform their activities efficiently. Markedly often, they were labelled with acronyms such as TQM (Total Quality Management) and MBO (Management by Objectives). Scandinavian institutionalists showed a certain interest in public sector organizations and how they incorporated private sector management models in their formal structures (Boxenbaum and Strandgaard Pedersen 2009) – a movement later labelled NPM (New Public Management) (Hood 1991).

These and other studies showed that there are strong pressures on organizations to adhere to management fashions (Abrahamson 1996), but that the models seldom fit. So to some extent the apparent application of new models were ceremonial, as suggested by previous applications of institutional theory (Meyer and Rowan 1977), but it was also evident that organizations, as they struggle with new concepts and models, made changes to what they do and how they do it. So the models had consequences and effects but they tended to be others than those expected and desired (Sahlin-Andersson 1996).

To find the tools that could help them to put together this puzzle, Scandinavian institutionalists turned to sociology of science (Callon 1986) and actor network theory (Latour 1986). What these approaches offered was a possibility to explain: why and how organizations pick up and incorporate management models in terms of *ideas*; the significance of *carriers* involved in the transformation and distribution of ideas into and between new contexts; the processes in which ideas get *translated* so they gain relevance in the contexts into which they get introduced (Czarniawska and Joerges 1996).

3.1 Ideas as prototypes, templates and bundles

Ideas are narratives (Czarniawska and Joerges 1996) connecting causes and effects, providing actors with (1) descriptions of a universal problem, relevant across sectors, fields and organizations, and (2) solutions to these problems (Höllerer, Walgenbach, and Drori 2017). Hence, ideas define what is appropriate and provide organizations with motives and justifications to act, make decisions and communicate. In addition, they call out roles, identities and behaviours, defining certain actors and/or activities as more or less valuable than others (Zilber 2016). Ideas can come in different shapes and formats and level of abstraction. Ideas, while varying between being clearly defined in relation to general rationalities or logics and appearing as ambiguous and imprecise, allow organizations (elsewhere) to make their own interpretations both in terms of which ideas to pay attention to, and how to incorporate them into their activities (Waldorff 2013). This notion is especially important as it allows us to think of ideas as rationalized manifestations of institutions that are only for a given period of time defined as relevant and important to implement (i. e. fashion) (Abrahamson 1996). And as such, ideas only partially bear inscriptions of the underlying values, practices and preferences of the context in which they were originally formulated. Instead, for ideas to become attractive (i. e. defined as necessary to comply with) the format and content of these ideas need to remain fuzzy and open to interpretations on their way through the institutional landscape (Czarniawska and Sevón 1996).

Of certain interest for us, studying public relations, are management ideas relating to aspects of organizational life such as leadership, administration, production and communication. They come in a wide variety, but one example, analysed by Morris and Lancaster (2006), is the spread and implementation of LEAN management into the British construction industry. From the beginning a principle for waste management utilized by Japanese car manufactures in the 1950s, it was later picked up by management scholars and consultants. The latter gave the idea its name as it was packaged, distributed and introduced to organizations outside Japan and outside the car industry. The model grew in popularity, and over time LEAN has become an overarching principle for a number of other management ideas utilized in manufacturing including quality management and just-in-time. It didn't stop there, however. Over time, LEAN has travelled to other sectors and been adapted in service industries, hospitals, government agencies and kindergartens, as well as communications departments (Andersen and Røvik 2015).

Management ideas have become a recurring feature in organizational life and, as in the case of LEAN, they often appear as *prototypes* (Wedlin and Sahlin 2017) or as *recipes* (Røvik 2008). These are models or exemplars, imitated and put into practice. They are commonly promoted to appeal to management and leaders and they provide users with pre-packaged solutions to general problems, such as productivity, quality, diversity or communication. Other ideas travel as *templates* and function as reference when actors assess, evaluate or benchmark their own or others' activities. Instead of providing a solution to a general problem (as prototypes), templates proscribe how success is to be measured. They provide actors with indicators, scales and references used as a currency when organizations are valuated. One example is Times Higher Education (THE), an international ranking system for universities. It is based on a set of "performance indicators" (e. g. learning environment, research reputation, citations, international outlook and industry income) to measure teaching excellence. Over time it has become the standard reference when universities are rated and it is evident that the system has influenced the beliefs of what a good university *is* among actors both inside and outside the sector of higher education (Wedlin 2006). As in higher education, the influence of audits and templates have increased over time – a development strongly linked to what Power (1997) describes as "audit society".

Symbols and rhetoric are central for our understanding of ideas and how they make way across contexts (Brown, Ainsworth, and Grant 2012; Özen 2013). They are often bundled together with other elements, however, and according to Pallas, Fredriksson, and Wedlin (2016) symbols are complemented by at least three additional elements that help ideas come across. These include *artefacts* (objects associated with certain specifications, conventions or standards), *routines* (compilations of activities, actions or procedures) and *relations* (professions, roles or identities associated with certain norms values and/or activities). Each of these elements has its own qualities, but as they are closely related and associated with each other, they can individually motive organizations to adopt the entire idea. So, for instance, when universities introduce specialized social media units or set up vice-chancellor's blogs, it will most likely lead to adoption of professional values, practices and relations that are seen as necessary and legitimate in the field of social media (Lövgren 2017).

3.2 Ideas that flow

There seems to be a never-ending stream of models, prototypes and templates for managers to choose from. In some cases they are short-lived fads with limited distribution, picked up only by a small number of organizations who rapidly change to another. Others become popular in very specific contexts, whereas additional others get widely distributed. In order to identify the characteristics of ideas "that flow" and become widespread, much effort has been made to chart the origins and the qualities or properties of popular ideas. From a rationalist position, the suggestion would probably be that the best idea is "the one that is best fitted to solve organizations' problems". That is to say, ideas that work. Accordingly, the most widely distributed ideas are also the best ideas. For this there is little support, however. Røvik (2002), in his study of ideas that have gained wide distribution (e. g. MBO and TQM), found that popular management literature, consultants and others make frequent references to successful organizations when they promote an idea. The ideas are presented as a main contributor to the success, and other organizations are offered radical improvements if they go along and adapt these ideas. However, there is usually very little evidence or detailed descriptions of how the implemented ideas can help organizations to become more efficient and productive. Rather, the promotion and implementation of management ideas rest upon anecdotes and selective success stories. What seems to explain the popularity of certain management ideas is not their inherent qualities, but other characteristics such as from whom the ideas get support and how they are packaged and presented. From this, Wedlin and Sahlin (2017: 105) come to the conclusion that it "appears to be not so much a case of ideas flowing widely because they are powerful, but rather of ideas becoming powerful as they circulate".

3.3 Carriers

Ideas don't move from one place to another without support. They need help to get transferred, re-localized and presented in new contexts. This highlights the significance of actors, or *carriers*, who operate as promotors of ideas. They can appear in a number of different characters (Hedmo, Sahlin-Andersson, and Wedlin 2005), but theoretically it is possible to discern two main categories (a) those who are unaware of their role as carrier, and (b) those who actively seek to pick up, transform and distribute ideas. The last can in turn be divided into two subcategories: a) those who mainly function as intermediaries between different contexts, and b) those who act in their own interest and promote ideas to gain economic, political or social advantages (Sahlin-Andersson and Engwall 2002).

Unaware carriers are those who move between contexts and unintentionally bring ideas to settings where they haven't been present before –for instance, when organizations expand their operations to other countries and bring new ways to produce and market their products. The move can also be from one sector to another – as when corporations start to operate hospitals, homes for the elderly, schools or other services previously provided by public sector organizations. In other cases, the move of ideas is embedded in work of individuals – such as when students study abroad and bring with them ideas that they later introduce in organizations for which they start to work. Similar "transfers of ideas" can also be seen when individuals change work from one organization to another, from one type of organization to another (e. g. from private to public sector), or when individuals change professions (e. g. when a journalist leaves her work to join the PR industry).

News and business media, researchers, publishers, expert committees, international organizations, educators and others are examples of intermediators (Sahlin-Andersson and Engwall 2002). One of their key roles is to make ideas travel from one context to another. However, these types of carriers are attentive to their position and they make extensive efforts to nourish and protect their (as least symbolic) independence. Much of what they do and how they are perceived by others implies autonomy and impartiality, qualities that would be lost if they were perceived as self-promoters. This is the result of intermediators frequently functioning as role models for organizations; Meyer (1996) accordingly described them as "others" (compare with "significant others" in the work of Mead) to portray their position. Heavily involved in the distribution of ideas, they select some and disregard others, and they present, interpret, support, transform and promote ideas. They are not involved in the applications, however, and they don't take responsibility for how the ideas are utilized or the outcome.

This is done by the third category of carriers. A category that includes consultants, trade associations, unions, interest groups and others whose self-interest is tied to the utilization of certain ideas. Gaining attention and getting organizations to adopt their idea(s) is linked to advantages and/or resources for themselves or others with whom they are affiliated or represent. For consultants it means revenues and probably additional customers if organizations buy their idea, concept or model, start to use it and tell others. Trade associations and unions, on the other hand, act to secure and extend their members' influence; certain ideas or models might be more helpful than others and therefore promoted. One example is "self-governing groups", an idea influenced by LEAN and presented as an alternative to assembly lines in the car industry. It was vigorously supported by the Swedish trade union of car workers in the 1980s, as it was believed to provide their members with extended responsibilities, variations in tasks and autonomy (Docherty and Huzzard 2003).

3.4 Translations as de- and re-contextualization

The causes and motives for carriers to introduce ideas and for organizations to adopt them vary, but both processes involve movement and transformation. It is a form of *translation* to make ideas fit for different settings and purposes. The meaning of translation here exceeds its linguistic interpretation and refers to processes of negotiation, displacement, (re)invention and (re)creation, and it plays out as two interdependent activities: *de-* and *re*-contextualization.

De-contextualization entails the removal of local peculiarities and other elements that can cause hesitance or resistance when ideas are to be relocated (Czarniawska and Joerges 1996). To what degree actors are aware of the alterations they make varies, but it is a common operation and in general it means that ideas become theorized and made abstract. A frequent feature is that ideas are presented as a cure-all solution with universal reach. For instance, ideas are commonly staged as a solution with reference to the general category "organization" rather than the more specific "car manufacturer" or "hospital". In addition, Røvik (2002) showed the importance of ideas to be connected to rationality, efficiency, development and other cornerstones of modernity. For instance, by social authorization (the association of ideas and individuals/ organizations producing good results or being recognized for other deeds) and dramatization (ideas as pioneering and fundamentally different, commonly associated with an inventor who had to struggle long and hard to get approval for an innovation). There is more to de-contextualization than rhetoric and narratives, however, as it also implies materialization and physical transformation. To be able to travel, ideas are translated into objects or routines, emphasising how ideas both have immaterial and material aspects, and how the two are heavily interwoven (Czarniawska and Joerges 1996; Pallas, Fredriksson, and Wedlin 2016).

The supply of ideas is extensive and in most cases they pass settings without making any impression. When they do make an impression it is often the result of imitation and identification linked to perceptions and categorizations. By seeing itself as being of a certain kind, an organization will more easily pay attention to some ideas than others. The mechanisms behind this are the inabilities to see things one can't relate to or things one can't place in already established compartments. In addition, organizations, as social actors in general, have an urge to be alike; when others start to make use of a certain technique, model or process it mobilizes wishes and desires to follow the leader. The probability of this happening increases if the other is a prestigious, leading or well-known actor, or if it is an actor the organization relates to. The adaptation of ideas is then not so much about efficiency or best practice and the question of how to solve a problem, but more about identity, fashion and appropriateness, as well as the question, "What does an organization like us do in a situation like this?" (Sevón 1996). The answer to the question isn't necessarily imitation, however, as processes of identity formation also include elements of distinction and being different. Adoption of new ideas is thus a process where organizations actively notice, select and embrace widely spread solutions whereas others are abandoned without further notice (Czarniawska and Joerges 1996).

4 Ideas of public relations

Taking our point of departure in Scandinavian institutionalism, we argue that public relations is a management idea. Not a *role* or *function,* nor a *profession,* but a narrative that organizations refer to when they encounter particular situations involving communicative problems or possibilities. This means that public relations isn't static, consistent or coherent, but something volatile and that actors can perform under different labels. There are situations when an activity must be performed under certain conditions to fulfil the validity claims that are at play to gain acceptance and do its work – as when a "referee" awards a soccer team a "penalty kick". This doesn't apply to public relations. Public relations doesn't have a set of fixed qualities someone must fulfil to gain acceptance – not even in situations when there are formal regulations about how it ought to be practiced. In Nigeria, for instance, public relations practition-ers must be accredited by the state but still struggle with its work content and domains (Fashakin 2018). As an idea, public relations rather provides organizations with solu-tions for how to encounter situations and what communicative artefacts, activities, routines, postures, competences, relations and symbols these circumstances pre-suppose. Public relations can then be a number of different things, and it will differ between organizations and over time.

Exactly what these qualities are remain a question for empirical investigation. The work of Boltanski and Thévenot (2006), as well as Edwards (2018), Ewen (1996) and empirical accounts by Fashakin (2018), Jackall (1988), Kjeldsen (2013) and Lövgren (2017), indicate that the idea(s) of public relations relate to shifts in public opinions, (negative) publicity, (lack of) attention, respect, stakeholders' approval and unclear identity. That is, issues that are thought of as to be solved by communicative efforts, control, consistency and promotion. It is accordingly difficult to clearly separate public relations from other concepts, roles or functions claiming their relevance for different aspects of organizations' communication, or to refer to public relations as a given set of activities, positions, objects, attributes or criteria. In practice, it means that the distinctions between public relations and "strategic communication", "corpo-rate communication" or "marketing", cherished by some scholars, are in most cases irrelevant and more a question of history, culture, ideology, meaning systems, values and resources (cf. Halff and Gregory 2014; Verčič et al. 2001). Suggesting that while actors are free to infuse meaning in ideas and practices, one has to remember that actors, ideas and practices are embedded within a broader discourse and cultural framework that both enables and constrains actions and meanings (Zilber 2006).

4.1 Public relations – something many can adhere to

Not all ideas are picked up by organizations. Many of them circulate without being noticed or make their way into specific organizational contexts. In most sectors and fields, actors refer to recipes, prototypes and models unknown outside these contexts. Public relations is not one of these ideas. Over time it has become widely spread and made its entrance into most fields and sectors, including business, government, the public sector, non-government sector, sports, culture and religion, as well as fiction and public opinion. To gain this position, to become something organizations refer to and make the effort to translate, an idea must adhere to a set of cherished and recurring qualities. Without solutions to widely experienced problems or recognizable characteristics an idea won't be noticeable or distinguishable and then it will circulate without further attention. The spread of general recipes for publicity can serve to illustrate how the idea of public relations has gained wide application and how this has been supported by the distribution of templates, including recognizable and easy to understand recommendations, to-do-lists, etc. (cf. Lövgren 2017). The narrative on public relations thus includes qualities and features that together make it familiar to actors in different contexts, and something that they can adhere to.

This broad distribution implies that we need to understand public relations not only in an organizational context but in relation to broader society (Pallas and Kvarnström 2018). It is evident that "public relations" and probably even more so "PR" are frequently used as references, arguments or insults in diverse settings. The idea is represented in news media, fiction and management literature. Both scholars and professional bodies do their best to promote the idea, and students and practitioners make their contribution. All of them are thereby involved in the packaging, carrying and diffusion of the idea(s). Their common contribution doesn't necessarily means that all are aware of their involvement, nor that there is a common understanding they refer to, but irrespective of that, all of them make their contribution.

4.2 Re-contextualization of public relations

Public relations has been carried across different contexts and stood the test of time. We can therefore expect its narrative to be highly homogenized and standardized, referring to a set of established principles, values and preferences. It is then plausible to assume that the implementation of public relations will exhibit a great deal of similarities and commonalities. Given the fact that organizations are exposed to a general idea of what public relations is, how it operates, how it should be organized and staffed, and what can be achieved by it.

At the same time, we can expect slightly different ideas of public relations appearing in different contexts. Because, even if the idea refers to some general features and qualities, it will always undergo transformations as it travels. The idea an organization encounter is then marked by its journey between different carriers and organizations, and two organizations will therefore encounter partly different ideas. In combination with differences in how the ideas are interpreted and understood, as well as differences in organizational configurations, public relations will appear in different versions across organizations. At least three parameters are at play here. First, organizations are conservative constructs set up to create security, continuity and predictability infused with rules, norms and values emanating from their different purposes and assignments. Accordingly, idea(s) of public relations evoke negotiations, resistance and hesitations leading to variations in the way they get implemented in organizations (Pallas, Fredriksson, and Wedlin 2016). That is to say, already-existing conditions will make different spaces for the features public relations has to offer. Second, there are differences resulting from whom public relations is introduced. Communications departments, marketing departments and board of managers will see different things, and thereby suggest different applications as they introduce public relations for co-workers. Third, time must also be taken into account. Organizations establishing their public relations departments at different times will encounter partly different ideas, and there will be variations in the services consultancies present and provide for an organization over time (cf. Tyllström 2013).

All these aspects have proven to be relevant when understanding differences between organizations, but they are also at play when differences in the same organizations must be explained. Even if organizations tend to share ideas about central activities, it is evidently the case that interpretations, labels and practices also differ between departments, sections or levels in organizations. Of primary relevance here is the professional background among organizational members, and how differences in professional identities bring people to understand, make sense and foster ideas differently (cf. Pallas, Fredriksson, and Wedlin 2016). In line with this, Lövgren (2017) could show how a shared recipe regarding communication was manifested in organizations promoting branding, reputation, visibility, centralization, coordination and integration, underscoring how organizations embrace widely distributed ideas. At the same time, however, he could also show that there were extensive differences in how the idea was embraced locally. At day-to-day events, the idea promoted by management had little impact on actual activities. Instead it was the competences, personal values, ambitions, experiences among communicators and the (eventual) support they got from professional groups that guided work throughout the organizations. As the configurations of professional groups differed so did the work with communication (see also Grandien and Johansson 2016).

Organizational configurations are then central if we want to understand differences both between and within organizations, but as Salomonsen, Frandsen, and Johansen (2016) and others have shown, dissimilarities also come from the embeddedness of public relations. Public relations doesn't travel as a conduit on its own across time and space; it is strongly intertwined with other ideas. The role and position assigned to public relations is then the result of how it intermingles with other ideas or to what extent it can show relevance when organizations encounter problems not necessarily in the realm of communication. This is evident in the work of Bartlett, Tywoniak, and Hacher (2007) and their study of public relations in the Australian banking system. Rather than being a response to a self-experienced communication problem, it emerges as the result of pressures from external actors, demanding more and better communication from banks regarding their CSR activities. This in turn urged public relations practitioners to take advantage of the situation by offering solutions to the upcoming problems. In practice it meant that public relations became interwoven in institutional contexts where it hadn't been applied before. This in turn meant that it had to be adapted to ideas of what it means to communicate responsibly. This included changes in its rationale from giving priority to publicity and avoiding attention to promoting interaction and responsiveness.

5 Conclusion: public relations in an ecology of translations

Referring to public relations as an idea highlights how it is institutionally constrained and follows taken-for-granted rules, norms and ideas about how to communicate. It also discloses how the idea is locally translated and takes on different forms in different contexts. In addition, it points out that public relations is open to many alternative interpretations, and finally that the idea is strong as it has stood the test of time and has the ability to change patterns of how organizations operate, communicate and perform.

Each of these aspects are in themselves central for us if we want to understand how public relations is practiced in different contexts. Each of them can be empirically investigated and contribute to our knowledge of why, how, when and by whom public relations is applied. It isn't until these aspects are investigated in the light of each other, however, that we can fully provide a detailed and extensive description of the phenomenon. That is to say, it isn't until we see public relations interwoven in what Wedlin and Sahlin (2017) described as an *ecology of translations* that we are able to fully explore the dynamics that emerge when public relations is set in the interactions between institutions, actors, activities, time and place.

Taking these conditions seriously could do two things for research on public relations. First, it can provide the field with stimulating perspectives and new questions regarding the ideational and ideological driving forces, what frames and legitimation there are that mobilize translation of public relations, how, when and why public relations influences organizational processes, actors, identity, artefacts etc., and what sorts of consequences this idea might have regarding organizational activities such as decision-making, knowledge production, control etc. Second, it can make research on public relations relevant outside its own limited domains. As argued by, for instance, Cornelissen, Durand, Fiss, Lammers, and Vaara (2015), communication is a central component of institutions and organizations. Taking institutional perspectives seriously and getting involved in broader analyses of the conditions, processes and activities of public relations can then inform our understanding of the role(s) of public relations when institutions and organizations emerge, sustain and change, and how this plays out in the intersection of ideas, actors, activities, time and space.

References

Abrahamson, Eric. 1996. Management Fashion. *The Academy of Management Review* 21(1). 254–285. doi:10.2307/258636 (accessed 1 April 2020).

Alvesson, Mats & André Spicer. 2018. Neo-Institutional Theory and Organization Studies: A Mid-Life Crisis? *Organization Studies* 40(2). 199–218. doi:10.1177/0170840618772610 (accessed 1 April 2020).

Andersen, Hege & Kjell Arne Røvik. 2015. Lost in translation: a case-study of the travel of lean thinking in a hospital. *BMC health services research* 15(1). 401–409. doi:10.1186/s12913-015-1081-z (accessed 1 April 2020).

Bartlett, Jennifer, Stephane Tywoniak & Caroline Hatcher. 2007. Public relations professional practice and the institutionalisation of CSR. *Journal of communication Management* 11(4). 281–299.

Boltanski, Luc & Laurent Thévenot. 2006. *On Justification: Economies of Worth*. Princeton: Princeton University Press.

Boxenbaum, Eva & Jesper Strandgaard Pedersen. 2009. Scandinavian institutionalism – a case of institutional work. In Thomas B. Lawrence, Roy Suddaby & Bernard Leca (eds.), *Institutional Work. Actors and Agency in Institutional Studies of Organizations*, 178–204. Cambridge: Cambridge University Press.

Brown, Andrew D., Susane Ainsworth & David Grant. 2012. The Rhetoric of Institutional Change. *Organization Studies* 33(3). 297–321.

Callon, Michael. 1986. Some Elements of a Sociology of Translation: Domestication of the Scallops and the Fishermen of St Brieuc Bay. In John Law (ed.), *Power, Action and Belief. A New Sociology of Knowledge?*, 196–233. London: Routledge & Kegan Paul.

Cornelissen, Joep P., Rodolphe Durand, Peer C. Fiss, John C. Lammers & Eero Vaara. 2015. Putting Communication Front and Center in Institutional Theory and Analysis. *Academy of Management Review* 40(1). 10–27.

Czarniawska, Barbara & Bernward Joerges. 1996. Travels of Ideas. In Barbara Czarniawska & Guje Sevón (eds.), *Translating Organizational Change*, 13–48. Berlin: Walter de Gruyter.

Czarniawska, Barbara & Guje Sevón. 1996. Introduction. In Barbara Czarniawska & Guje Sevón (eds.), *Translating Organizational Change*, 1–12. Berlin: Walter de Gruyter.

DiMaggio, Paul J. & Walter W. Powell. 1983. The Iron Cage Revisited: Institutional Isomorphism and Collective Rationality in Organizational Fields. *American Sociological Review* 48(2). 147–160. doi:10.2307/2095101

Docherty, Peter & Tony Huzzard. 2003. Marknads-, management-och medarbetartrender 1985–2005 [Market-, management- and co-worker trends 1985–2005]. In Casten von Otter (ed.), *Ute och inne i svenskt arbetsliv. Forskare analyserar och spekulerar om trender i framtidens arbete.* [Non-fashion and fashion in Swedish worklife. Scholars analyses and speculate about trends in future work] 135–157. Stockholm: Arbetslivsinstitutet.

Edwards, Lee. 2018. *Understanding public relations. Theory, culture and society*. London: Sage.

Ewen, Stuart. 1996. *PR!: a social history of spin*. New York: Basic Books.

Fashakin, Oludotun Kayode. 2018. *An institutional approach to public relations professional project. A case study of Nigeria*. Aarhus, Denmark: Aarhus University PhD dissertation.

Frandsen, Finn & Winni Johansen. 2013. Public relations and the new institutionalism: In search of a theoretical framework. *Public Relations Inquiry* 2(2). 205–221.

Fredriksson, Magnus & Josef Pallas. 2011. Regler, normer och föreställningar. Ett neoinstitutionellt perspektiv på strategisk kommunikation [Rules, norms and ideas. an institutional perspective on strategic communication]. In Jesper Falkheimer & Mats Heide (eds.), *Strategisk kommunikation. Forskning och praktik* [Strategic communication: research and practice], 45–63. Lund, Sweden: Studentlitteratur.

Fredriksson, Magnus & Josef Pallas. 2014. Strategic communication as institutional work. In Derina Holtzhausen & Ansgar Zerfass (eds.), *Handbook of strategic communication*. London: Routledge.

Fredriksson, Magnus, Josef Pallas & Stefan Wehmeier. 2013. Institutional Perspectives on Public Relations. *Public Relations Inquiry* 2(3). 183–203.

Grandien, Christina & Catrin Johansson. 2016. Organizing and Disorganizing Strategic Communication: Discursive Institutional Change Dynamics in Two Communication Departments. *Inter-*

national Journal of Strategic Communication 10(4). 332–351. doi:10.1080/1553118X.2016.
1196692 (accessed 1 April 2020).

Greenwood, Royston, Christine Oliver, Thomas B. Lawrence & Renate E. Meyer. 2017. Introduction:
Into the Fourth Decade. In Royston Greenwood, Christine Oliver, Thomas B Lawrence & Renate E
Meyer (eds.), *The Sage handbook of organizational institutionalism*, 1–23. London, Thousands
Oaks, New Dehli & Singapore: Sage.

Grinsven, Marlieke, Stefan Heusinkveld & Joep Cornelissen. 2016. Translating Management
Concepts: Towards a Typology of Alternative Approaches. *International Journal of Management
Reviews* 18(3). 271–289. doi:doi:10.1111/ijmr.12106 (accessed 1 April 2020).

Halff, Gregor & Anne Gregory. 2014. Toward an historically informed Asian model of public relations.
Public Relations Review 40(3). 397–407. doi:https://doi.org/10.1016/j.pubrev.2014.02.028
(accessed 1 April 2020).

Hedmo, Tina, Kerstin Sahlin-Andersson & Linda Wedlin. 2005. Field of Imitation: The Global
Expansion of Management Education. In Barbara Czarniawska & Goje Sevón (eds.), *Global
Ideas: How Ideas, Objects and Practices Travel in the Global Economy*, 190–212. Malmö: Libris.

Hood, Christopher. 1991. A public management for all seasons? *Public Administration* 69(1). 3–19.

Höllerer, Markus A., Peter Walgenbach & Gili Drori. 2017. The Consequences of Globalization for
Institutions and Organizations. In Royston Greenwood, Christine Oliver, Thomas B. Lawrence
& Renate E. Meyer (eds.), *The Sage handbook of organizational institutionalism*, 214–242.
London, Thousands Oaks, New Dehli & Singapore: Sage.

Ihlen, Øyvind & Magnus Fredriksson. 2018. *Public relations and social theory: key figures, concepts
and developments*, 2nd edn. New York: Routledge.

Jackall, Robert. 1988. *Moral Mazes: The World of Corporate Managers*. New York: Oxford University
Press.

Kjeldsen, Anna Karina. 2013. *Forandring eller fernis: museale translationer af strategisk
kommunikation. Et studie af institutionaliseringen af strategisk kommunikation i tre danske
kunstmuseer* [Change or polish: translations of strategic communication in museums. A study
of how strategic communication is institutionalized in three Danish art museums]. Aarhus,
Denmark: Aarhus Universitet dissertation.

Latour, Bruno. 1986. The powers of association. In John Law (ed.), *Power, Action and Belief. A New
Sociology of Knowledge?*, 264–280. London: Routledge & Kegan Paul.

Lawrence, Thomas B., Roy Suddaby & Bernard Leca (eds.). 2009. *Institutional Work. Actors and
Agency in Institutional Studies of Organizations*. Cambridge: Cambridge University Press.

Le, Jenny & Jennifer L. Bartlett. 2014. Managing impressions during institutional change – The role
of organisational accounts in legitimation. *Public Relations Inquiry* 3(3). 341–360.

Lövgren, Daniel. 2017. *Dancing Together Alone: Inconsistencies and Contradictions of Strategic
Communication in Swedish Universities*. Uppsala, Sweden: Uppsala University dissertation.

Merkelsen, Henrik. 2013. Legitimacy and reputation in the institutional field of food safety: A public
relations case study. *Public Relations Inquiry* 2(2). 243–265. doi:10.1177/2046147x13485368
(accessed 1 April 2020).

Meyer, John W. 1996. Otherhood: The Promulgation and Transmission of Ideas in the Modern
Organizational Environment. In Barbara Czarniawska and Guje Sevón (eds.), *Translating
Organizational Change*, 241–252. Berlin: Walter de Gruyter.

Meyer, John W. & Brian Rowan. 1977. Institutionalized Organizations: Formal Structure as Myth and
Ceremony. *American Journal of Sociology* 83(2). 340–363.

Morris, Timothy & Zoë Lancaster. 2006. Translating management ideas. *Organization Studies* 27(2).
207–233.

Özen, Şükrü. 2013. Rhetorical Variations in the Cross-national Diffusion of Management Practices:
A Comparison of Turkey and the US. In Gili Drori, Markus A Höllerer & Peter Walgenbach (eds.),

Global Themes and Local Variations in Organization and Management, 119–132. New York and London: Routledge.

Pallas, Josef, Magnus Fredriksson & Linda Wedlin. 2016. Translating institutional logics: When the media logic meets professions. *Organization Studies* 37(11), 1661–1684. doi:10.1177/0170840616655485 (accessed 1 April 2020).

Pallas, Josef & Emilia Kvarnström. 2018. On Meyer. Public relations in a Context of World Society, Soft Actors and Rationlized De-coupling. In Øyvind Ihlen & Magnus Fredrikson (eds.), *Public Relations and Social Theory. Key figures, concepts and developments*. New York: Routledge.

Power, Michael. 1997. *Audit Society: Rituals of Verification*. Oxford: Oxford University Press.

Røvik, Kjell Arne. 2002. The secrets of the winners: Management ideas that flow. In Kerstin Sahlin-Andersson & Lars Engwall (eds.), *The Expansion of Management Knowledge: Carriers, Flows, and Sources*, 113–144. Stanford, CA: Stanford University Press.

Røvik, Kjell Arne. 2008. *Managementsamhället: Trender och idéer på 2000-talet* [Management society: trends and ideas in the 21st century]. Stockholm: Liber.

Sahlin-Andersson, Kerstin. 1996. Imitating by Editing Success: The Construction of Organizational Fields. In Barbara Czarniawska & Guje Sevón (eds.), *Translating Organizational Change*, 69–92. Berlin: Walter de Gruyter.

Sahlin-Andersson, Kerstin & Lars Engwall. 2002. The Dynamics of Management Knowledge Expansion. In Kerstin Sahlin-Andersson & Lars Engwall (eds.), *The Expansion of Management Knowledge. Carriers, Flows, and Sources*, 277–296. Stanford, CA: Stanford University Press.

Salomonsen, Heidi Houlberg, Finn Frandsen & Winni Johansen. 2016. Civil Servant Involvement in the Strategic Communication of Central Government Organizations: Mediatization and Functional Politicization. *International Journal of Strategic Communication* 10(3). 207–221. doi:10.1080/1553118X.2016.1176568 (accessed 1 April 2020).

Sandhu, Swaran. 2009. Strategic Communication: An Institutional Perspective. *International Journal of Strategic Communication* 3(2). 72–92.

Sevón, Guje. 1996. Organizational Imitation in Identity Transformation. In Barbara Czarniawska & Guje Sevón (eds.), *Translating Organizational Change*, 49–68. Berlin: Walter de Gruyter.

Spicer, Christopher. 1997. *Organizational Public Relations. A Political Perspective*. Mahwah, NJ: Lawrence Erlbaum Associates.

Thornton, Patricia H., William Ocasio & Michael Lounsbury. 2012. *The Institutional Logics Perspective: A New Approach to Culture, Structure and Process*. Oxford: Oxford University Press.

Tyllström, Anna. 2013. *Legitimacy for sale: Constructing a market for PR consultancy*. Uppsala, Sweden: Uppsala University dissertation.

Waldorff, Susanne Boch. 2013. What is the Meaning of Public Sector Health? Translating Discourse into New Organizational Practices. *Journal of Change Management* 13(3). 283–307. doi:10.1080/14697017.2013.822673 (accessed 1 April 2020).

Wedlin, Linda. 2006. *Ranking Business Schools: Forming Fields, Identities, and Boundaries in International Management Education*. Northhampton, MA: Edward Elgar.

Wedlin, Linda & Kerstin Sahlin. 2017. The Imitation and Translation of Management Ideas. In Royston Greenwood, Christine Oliver, Thomas B Lawrence & Renate E Meyer (eds.), *The Sage handbook of organizational institutionalism*, 102–127. London, Thousands Oaks, New Dehli & Singapore: Sage.

Wehmeier, Stefan. 2006. Dancers in the dark: The myth of rationality in public relations. *Public Relations Review* 32(3). 213–220. doi:10.1016/j.pubrev.2006.05.018 (accessed 1 April 2020).

Verčič, Dejan, Betteke van Ruler, Gerhard Bütschi & Bertil Flodin. 2001. On the definition of public relations: a European view. *Public Relations Review* 27(4). 373–387. doi:http://dx.doi.org/10.1016/S0363-8111(01)00095-9 (accessed 1 April 2020).

Zilber, Tammar B. 2006. The work of the symbolic in institutional processes: Translations of rational myths in Israeli high tech. *Academy of Management Journal* 49(2). 281–303.

Zilber, Tammar B. 2016. How Institutional Logics Matter: A Bottom-Up Exploration. In Joel Gehmann, Michael Lounsbury & Royston Greenwood (eds.), *How Institutions Matter!* Research in the Sociology of Organizations Volume 48A, 137–155. Bingley, UK: Emerald Group Publishing.

Ian Somerville
27 Public relations and Actor-Network Theory

Abstract: Today we live in a time characterised by uncertainty, hybridity and complexity. A time when the powerful dualisms that characterised previous eras; nature/society, human/machine, male/female, etc. are being problematized in a fundamental way. This chapter discusses the significance of actor-network theory (ANT) as a guide to researching the liminal times in which we live. More particularly, it explores the usefulness of ANT for understanding contemporary public relations. The chapter is divided into several sections and proceeds as follows: it discusses ANT's philosophical approach; its relation to social theory; the strengths and limitations of ANT; what public relations scholars have produced to date by approaching public relations through ANT; and what it offers for future public relations scholarship.

Keywords: actor-network theory; public relations; law; Latour; ethnomethodology

1 Introduction

Within the sociology of science and technology studies (STS), actor-network-theory (ANT) has become a highly influential approach that "seeks to explain social order not through an essentialized notion of 'the social' but through the networks of connections among human agents, technologies, and objects" (Couldry 2008: 93). From an ANT perspective, all entities (human, technological, textual or "natural") are important "social" actors that can all acquire power through placing themselves at the centre of a network. A couple of points need to be noted. First, clearly the concept of actor is much broader here than that of conventional sociological network theories where "actor" generally refers to humans with agency. Second, the idea of a "network" is conceived of as an assemblage of these diverse actors, existing in constantly shifting interactions and relations. Networks and the connections routed through them are contingent and emerge historically, the job of ANT is primarily to trace and describe them. Couldry (2008: 94) notes that "ANT seems perfectly placed to generate a theory of the role(s) of media and communication technologies in contemporary societies. (...) Yet this connection has been surprisingly little explored". The same could also be said for attempts to deploy ANT in theorising public relations. However, ANT has to date been so little explored in public relations scholarship that one can count specific publications on the topic on the fingers of one hand (Somerville 1999; Verhoeven 2009 [updated 2018]; Luoma-aho and Paloviita 2010; Schölzel and Nothhaft 2016). In a similar way that Couldry (2008) does for media studies, we might speculate about an explanation for this lack of attention paid to ANT in public relations scholarship. It could be for different reasons. First, it may be that ANT itself is not a significant or

https://doi.org/10.1515/9783110554250-027

coherent approach. Second, it could be that, while it might have great explanatory value as a perspective in science and technology studies (or even as an important contribution to sociological theory), ANT's applicability to public relations is limited. The third possibility is that ANT may be a fruitful approach to theorising public relations, but that this task needs to be engaged in more comprehensively that has been the case up to now. This chapter explores the significance of ANT and its usefulness for the theorisation (or to use an ANT term, the *re-description*) of public relations. In the sections below we will discuss ANT's philosophical approach, its relation to social theory, the strengths and limitations of ANT, what public relations scholars have produced to date by approaching public relations through ANT, and what it offers for future public relations scholarship.

2 ANT as a philosophical approach

ANT's key philosophical premise involves a rejection of the "modern episteme", which it is claimed creates a world where humans are centre-stage and which marginalises and excludes non-human entities. Latour (1993: 10) suggests that this dichotomising "modern critical stance" creates "two entirely distinct ontological zones: that of human beings on the one hand; that of nonhumans on the other" and establishes "a partition between a natural world that has always been there, a society with predictable and stable interests and stakes, and a discourse that is independent of both reference and society" (1993: 11). The irony, as Latour (1993) is fond of pointing out, is that, while the modern way of thinking is characterised by this concern with strict boundaries between humans and non-humans, contemporary life is actually characterised by the increasing proliferation of social/technology and nature/culture hybrids. Actor-network theory according to Latour (1993) is an "amodern" (or "non-modern") approach to thinking about the different realms which constitute experience, the human/social, the technological, the natural world etc. It is this ontological position, which rejects a fundamental distinction between human and non-human actors, which distinguishes the actor-network approach. This position puts ANT at odds with the foundational assumption of most social science theory and hence public relations theory, which – whether from the functionalist perspective, or indeed from the "critical school" – is rooted in, as ANT theorists would see it, modern dichotomising social science thinking. A functionalist approach assumes that human/social consensus is achievable and that it is a good thing. The "critical" perspective asks who benefits from this consensus, and problematises the idea that it is always desirable, especially if it comes at the price of the domination of one group by another. Ontologically, much of thinking from theorists in both camps assumes the primacy of the human/social and usually accepts the traditional "modern" dichotomies of nature/society, human/machine etc. that ANT challenges.

To (re)describe the world from an actor-network standpoint there are three key theoretical premises which must be adhered to in order to attempt to escape from the language constraints of the "modern episteme"; *generalised agnosticism, generalised symmetry, free association* (Michael 1996; Somerville 1999). Generalised agnosticism requires an analytic impartiality to whatever actors are being described, all are treated as essentially equal in respect to their causality or agency within the network. Generalised symmetry involves the use of an abstract and neutral vocabulary to understand and draw out the conflicting viewpoints of actors, that is, human and non-humans are analysed with the same conceptual and terminological framework. Free association repudiates *a priori* distinctions between the social, the natural and the technological and focuses attention on the relations between entities. ANT emphasises the interconnectedness of the heterogeneous elements that make up a network and this interconnectedness is elucidated in the pivotal process of *translation* (Callon 1986). For Callon and Latour (1981), translation rests on the idea that actors within networks will try to redefine the meaning of other actors, "speak" on their behalf, and *enrol* (manipulate or force) the other actors into positions with them. When an actor's strategy is successful and it has organised other actors in the network for its own benefit it can be said to have translated them. A key result of the process of translation is the "black-boxing" (or acceptance/agreement) of knowledge, the establishing of a "fact" that is so unquestioned and stable that it can be ignored within that system. Latour (1999: 304) describes black-boxing as "the way scientific and technical work is made invisible by its own success ... Thus, paradoxically, the more science and technology succeed, the more opaque and obscure they become". The actor-network perspective stresses the *contingency* of networks, that is, they are not determined, permanent, or universal. The aim of ANT's narratology is to carefully expose and *describe* the work which is being done at the "local" level in order to maintain the network, to generate associations, to enrol and translate. The approach avoids appealing to overarching, general analytical constructs (e. g. class, pathology, interests), rather it is an approach which is grounded, observational and ethnographic. ANT aims to focus our attention on the relations between actors in a network, as it attempts to pry open black boxes by providing comprehensive accounts (redescriptions) of their structures, workings, and origins and development. Law (2008: 141) explains that ANT treats

> everything in the social and natural worlds as a continuously generated effect of the webs of relations within which they are located. It assumes that nothing has reality or form outside the enactment of those relations. (...) Like other material-semiotic approaches, the actor-network approach thus describes the enactment of materially and discursively heterogeneous relations that produce and reshuffle all kinds of actors including objects, subjects, human beings, machines, animals, 'nature', ideas, organisations, inequalities, scale and sizes, and geographical arrangements.

What does this attempt to (re)present and (re)describe networks look like in practice? Banks (2011: 1) offers an ANT (re)description of the #occupyalbany event (part of the wider *#occupy* campaign) in which he was involved:

> After several hours, the IT working group resolves that 4G hotspots will not cooperate with their encampment. The 4G signal refuses to visit the park with the same regularity as the activists. Without the 4G signal, those in the park are unable to reach their fellow activists, computers, protest signs, and supplies located throughout the Hudson Valley region. (...) They devise an assemblage of signal repeaters and routers that will provide a more reliable stream of data that will show up on time to general assemblies, and in sufficient numbers. The working group believes that the attendance of broadband Internet will allow the geographically and temporally dispersed occupiers to be enrolled within the larger actor-network of Occupy Albany (...) and keep the occupation going through the winter.

Elsewhere Banks points out that he is deliberately deploying generalised symmetry in relation to his terminology in this narrative – that is, using the same language to describe human and non-human entities. It is the relationships between wifi hardware, 4G signals and people that is being examined and described here, with the different actors (nodes in the network) and the relations between them all viewed as essential and important elements in a contingent assemblage. The careful reader may detect that perhaps only the human actors are ascribed "intentionality" but all actors are described as possessing agency. This is an issue we will return to later but the key point is that ANT narratology proceeds by avoiding the construction of hierarchies of importance and demonstrates that "social" events are always made up of a multiplicity of human and non-human elements. The above example highlights some of the key features of ANT as a "method", and this might be a good point to reflect on the relationship between the approach and other social theories because in many ways it is its focus on "method" which is at the heart of ANT's dispute with, and departure from, the assumptions of much social theory.

3 Actor-network theory and social theory

As we noted, ANT is a philosophical approach out of which has grown a research tradition and which uses, as Law (2008: 141) puts it, "a disparate family of material-semiotic tools, sensibilities and methods of analysis". We will return to this idea of a material-semiotic method below, but for now it is worth noting ANT's relationship with social theory more widely. Its key role in STS has already been noted and it is fair to say that its impact on organisation studies has been influential for the many scholars in that field who have welcomed the insights generated by ANT. Thus, for Inns and Jones (1996: 118) the "actor-network metaphor", in giving equal importance to human and non-human elements in organisations, radically alters perspectives on organisational research and "offers a way out of the cage of thought and language constructed by the dominance of a few paradigms within the subject". ANT has also had an influence on cultural anthropology, particularly in work trying to capture the perspectives of indigenous peoples and their relationships to the natural, social and political worlds. For example De La Cadena's (2010: 364) ethnographic work on Latin American indigenous politics notes that "current indigenous movements, propose a different political practice, plural not because of its enactment by bodies marked by gender, race, ethnicity or sexuality (as multiculturalism would have it), but because they conjure nonhumans as actors in the political arena." De La Cadena's discussion of *tirakuna* or "earth-beings" (mountains, soil, water, etc.) expands the notion of politics. Politics is usually conceptualised as disputes between "rational human beings" about who has the power to represent others vis-à-vis the state. However, for De La Cadena an ANT sensibility helps transform the notion of politics to "cosmopolitics", where non-human actors can become central agents in day-to-day struggles, just as it transforms for Inns and Jones (1996) what we mean by the concept "organisation".

ANT is sceptical about the possibility of social *science* or more specifically of scientific sociology, and Latour (2005) in particular is implacably opposed to the attempt to reduce social life to scientific explanations in the manner of a Durkheim, for example. Although this will be expanded on in the final two sections of this chapter, it is worth briefly pointing to the significance of this ANT criticism for public relations scholarship. Most attempts to theorise public relations have been built upon traditional social theory foundations (Prior-Miller 2009) but there have been increasing calls for public relations researchers to embrace the insights and methods of cultural anthropology (L'Etang 2012) or the socio-cultural turn more generally (Edwards and Hodges 2011). These approaches challenge the functionalism of previous public relations scholarship not just theoretically and politically, but additionally in respect to methodology they push to make ethnography more central in the study of public relations practice. This emerging "critical school" in public relations theory has been successfully building upon the insights of authors like Bourdieu and Foucault to engage in the task of developing a more nuanced understanding and explanation of the role public relations plays in contemporary societies. In this context it is difficult to ignore the emergence and influence of ANT, which purports to offer radical critiques of traditional social theory and anthropology and which may offer new directions in how to understand and research public relations.

We should acknowledge that, in assessing the relationship between ANT and social theory, the first issue we must confront is that all of the key ANT theorists, Latour, Callon and Law, deny that ANT is actually a theory. Callon (1999: 194) writes, "ANT is not a theory. It is this that gives it both its strength and its adaptability". Law (2008: 141) explains more precisely what it means to say that the actor-network approach is not a theory:

> Theories usually try to explain why something happens, but actor-network theory is descriptive rather than foundational in explanatory terms, which means that it is a disappointment for those seeking strong accounts. Instead it tells stories about 'how' relations assemble or don't. As a

form, one of several, of material semiotics, it is better understood as a toolkit for telling interesting stories about, and interfering in, those relations.

Mol (2010: 257) also attempts to clarify the rationale behind the reluctance to describe ANT as a theory: "ANT is not a theory: there is no coherence to it. (...) It rather takes the form of a repertoire. If you link up with it you learn sensitising terms, ways of asking questions and techniques for turning issues inside out or upside down". Law and Singleton (2013: 485) attempt to explain how ANT works "on" and "in" the world and argue that it is "best understood as a *sensibility*, a set of empirical interferences in the world". ANT "is a sensibility to the messy practices of relationality and materiality of the world. Along with this sensibility comes a wariness of the large-scale claims common in social theory: these usually seem too simple" (Law 2008: 141). This sensibility is empirically sensitive, first, to the *heterogeneity* of the world, second, to its *relationality*, and third, to the way in which it is *unfolding and uncertain (Law and Singleton 2013)*. It is this focus on heterogeneity and relationality which leads to the most startling claim of ANT: that human and non-human actors can be understood alike as similar elements in a web of relations. Law acknowledges that this is unacceptable to many social theorists but notes that "the issue of humanism and non-humanism, is primarily a metaphysical quarrel perhaps all we can do is note the difference and move on" (Law 2008: 152). It would be wrong to suggest that Law has no interest in the how webs of relations impact on humans, but for him ANT is primarily concerned with exploring the enactment of existing realities (ontology) and the construction of knowledge (epistemology) and exploring them from the ground up. Grand theoretical claims are of little interest to ANT researchers who focus not on abstractions but always seeks to remain grounded in empirical case studies. This is why ANT theorists deny that ANT is a "theory". The serious point that underlies this position is the idea, particularly promoted by Latour (2005), that ANT's approach is similar to the research tradition of ethnomethodology, a tradition which also challenges many assumptions of conventional social theory. ANT is concerned with the social more as an ethnomethodological idea rather than a social scientific concept. However, ethnomethodology is primarily concerned with the sense-making activities and accounts people give of their own lives and opposes the theories and methods of "traditional" and "critical" sociology with its "scientific" pretensions and assumptions about what constitutes "social" life. Ethnomethodology is largely an empirical enterprise that is concerned with human social ordering; ANT's positioning of itself as primarily an (ethno)methodological approach expands the empirical orientation to a wider focus on the ordering of human and non-human entities and how they relate to each other in networks.

The central metaphor of the "network" is deliberately deployed by ANT theorists to emphasize its distance from the "systems" approach central to much social theory. Although not exceptional in this focus on networks – Castells (2009) among many others has highlighted the move to the "network society" – it must also be stressed that ANT conceives of networks differently from social network theorists. Today everywhere there is the "net", "networking", the "social network", etc., but we should beware of "network-conflation" no matter how powerful the urge (Venturini, Munk, and Jacomy 2016: 4). Digital networks, actor-network theory, social network analysis, etc. are not all understanding "networks" in the same way, and even recent developments in "relational sociology", which emphasises the importance of networks and takes "a heterogeneity of human and non-human actors into account", are still crucially different from ANT in respect to the (lack of) agency non-human actors are understood to have (Mützel 2009: 872–4). As one would expect, sociologists wish to ensure that the "social" will always remain privileged, as Silverstone (1994: 84–85) puts it, "the natural, the economic and the technical, in their obduracy or their malleability, have no significance except through social action ... the notion of network does not add much to that of system". Such a view is fundamentally at odds with ANT and indeed Latour (1993, 1999) in particular is overtly critical of what he regards as the narrowness of ideas of the "social" in both sociology and systems theory. He is particularly scathing about the mechanistic and functionalist "open-systems theory" approach so influential in public relations theory, with its "implicit assumption that the organisation is centre stage" (Gregory 2000: 274), has distinct boundaries, and operates within the social realm. The ANT "project" according to Callon and Latour (1981: 285–286) should be seen as "directing our attention not to the social but towards the processes by which an actor creates lasting asymmetries".

4 Strengths and limitations of ANT

Those claiming to do ANT research vary, sometimes quite widely, in what they say ANT is, and indeed ANT is celebrated as changing, complex and multiple (Mol 2010). Trying to make sense of the various strands of ANT research can be confusing at times, but it is fair to say that broadly speaking there are common elements to the ANT approach. As noted above, the most important ontological pre-supposition of ANT is that our world can be understand as made up of actor-networks (also described as "assemblages" or "associations") constructed out of entities (social, natural, technological, textual) that all potentially possess agency and that all exist in chains of relations. This foundational assumption of ANT is vitally important and it is accompanied by a sustained attack on thinking that does not acknowledge the materiality of existence, such as the more radical forms of social constructivism and poststructuralism. ANT argues that social constructivism reifies the social. If we reify the social, assume it has a concrete material reality, we end up in a tautology of explaining social "facts" with social "facts", or social "things" by reference to social "things", and we miss all the other "things" and "facts" that are assembled into, and constitute our experience of, the "social" realm. In order to capture complexity, uncertainty and hybridity, ANT proposes a "sociology of associations" rather than a "sociology of the social" (Latour

2005). ANT as a "material-semiotic" method proposes to trace simultaneously the connections or relations between things and concepts. Firmly constructivist, but opposed to radical social constructivism, with its inherent dualism, ANT is determined to include the agency of the non-human at the centre of contemporary research. This insistence on material semiotics (Law 2008) should be regarded as a key strength of the approach and an antidote to some of the intellectual excesses of post-structuralism with its assertions that there are only "texts" (Derrida) or "ideas" (Baudrillard). The ANT approach produces a determination to always "follow the actors" and results in rich, data-laden accounts, which, as noted above, share the strengths of ethnomethodology, with its empirically driven, "grounded", explorations of how things come to be ordered the way they are. Linked to this, a second major strength of the ANT perspective is its problematizing of concepts like *social structure* and *power* and challenging their use as "taken for granted" explanations of phenomena. This focus on the empirical grounding of research, the determination to explore the materiality of experience and the challenge to be conceptually rigorous, (e. g. to always fully explain notions like "structure" and "power") are key strengths of approach.

ANT then, is dedicated to challenging taken-for-granted assumptions, shaking our complacency about everyday and technical language, prying open black boxes and disputing "settled" issues by (re)describing them. ANT is hard to pin down precisely because it is constantly changing, challenging assumptions and ignoring boundaries in an attempt to engage with the richness of experience. As one would expect of an approach which seems counter-intuitive and confrontational, ANT has been subject to a range of criticisms. Key among these are: first, its narrowness as a research programme; second, its anti-humanism; and third, what is usually referred to as its political conservativism.

First, there is the accusation that ANT is much more interested in mapping the establishment of networks than in the long-term consequences of networks. Winner (1993: 368) criticises the ANT approach in STS, suggesting it is limited to explaining how technologies arise and how particular views and devices prevail within a range of alternatives, while "the consequences of prevailing are seldom a focus of study". The critique has some merit to the extent that much existing ANT research does not sufficiently develop accounts of consequences, but to be fair neither does it necessarily exclude this task for the researcher. The second key criticism levelled at ANT is that it is an amoral and anti-humanist approach. While this charge of immorality is clearly related to Winner's accusation that the approach has no interest in examining consequences, it has also been raised in response to ANT's efforts to challenge the dualist "modern critical stance" that requires a heuristic flattening in relation to all entities in a network. Elder-Vass (2015: 102) praises ANT's attack on dualistic understandings of the social versus the "natural" world, its insistence that "nonhuman actors make a contribution to outcomes that are traditionally treated as social, and its demand that when we do invoke the 'social,' we must trace the connections that the term implies rather than taking them for granted". As we have noted, a key strength of ANT lies in this insistence that the empirical focus is inclusive of a multiplicity of material objects as well as humans, ideas and texts. However, while it seems absurd to deny that the natural, the textual and the technological influence and impact on other entities, including humans, it also seems absurd to deny that human agency has consequences in the world in way that other entities cannot, and at the heart of this lies questions of morality. Latour (1993: 130) responds to the accusations of ANT's "immorality" by stating:

> Refusing to explain the closure of a controversy by its consequences does not mean we are indifferent to the possibility of judgement, but only that we refuse to accept judgements that transcend the situation ... In order to make a diagnosis or a decision about the absurdity, the danger, the amorality or the unrealism of an innovation, one must first describe the network.

While some might read the above as an admirable determination to retain a solidly empirical focus, others may see the response as dodging the question. I see it as doing both, and in many ways this is an unresolvable dilemma for ANT, for moral judgements necessarily always "transcend the situation". Couldry (2008: 101) outlines a third important criticism that is sometimes levelled at ANT, and in doing so crystallizes the main criticisms of the approach;

> For all its intellectual radicalism, ANT comes charged with a heavy load of political conservatism that is, I would argue, directly linked to its professed disinterest in human agency. Power differentials between human actors matter in a way that power differentials (if that is the right term) between nonhumans do not: they have social consequences that are linked to how these differences are interpreted and how they affect the various agents' ability to have their interpretations of the world stick.

Latour (2005), of course, does implicitly address this point when he argues against focusing on the *causal significance* of social structures in social/human events, and instead insists the researcher should focus on producing (re)descriptions that only trace the *connections* between actors. Some may be more satisfied with Latour's argument than others, but he does seem prepared to accept the political consequences when he notes that this perspective means that "there is no society, no social realm, and no social ties" (2005: 108). From a political point of view, the lack of explanatory ability here regarding the impacts of social forces does seems problematic. How might this accusation of ANT's political quietism to be responded to? Is this critique of ANTs political conservativism valid? Tkacz (2011: 2) in his defence of ANT notes:

> The task of the ANT researcher is not to discover the hidden power structure that works over a set of relations, but to describe the way certain relations are stabilised, made durable, how certain asymmetries are formed. In this regard ANT has a lot more in common with a Foucaultian (1972) approach to power than a Marxist one. ANT certainly speaks of power and of force, of stability, durability and perhaps even structures or structuring devices and tendencies. However, it does not speak of 'power structures' understood in the sense of an overarching edifice that bears upon

an individual. ... To invoke an overarching power structure would be to deny the distributed character of power.

This is a crucial point. ANT is not denying the potential significance of existing power structures – although it does wish to move beyond the structure/individual autonomy dead-end (Tkacz 2011), where this sort of debate tends to lead. For Tkacz, the ANT researcher must first describe the network before moving on to take up political positions, although we must acknowledge that ANT as an (ethno)methodological approach, dedicated to (re)description, has never shown much inclination to do that.

5 Doing ANT in/on PR: How has ANT helped expand the focus of PR research?

As noted in the introduction, to date there is a rather limited amount of work by public relations scholars using ANT, by Somerville (1999), Verhoeven (2009[2018]), Luoma-aho and Paloviita (2010) and Schölzel and Nothhaft (2016). This section will discuss some of the lessons from that work, before the final section identifies how this might contribute to public relations' research agenda. Somerville's (1999) article largely restricted itself to outlining ANT's distinctive philosophical approach, explaining some of its key terminological and conceptual departures from "traditional" and "critical" social science thinking, and calling for public relations scholars to follow their colleagues in organisation studies in exploring how ANT might be usefully engaged with.

Verhoeven (2009) offers a comprehensive discussion of Latour's thinking and its potential for public relations research. He focuses on a whole range of key concepts and particularly adroitly differentiates ANT's constructivism from social constructivism. What does this mean for studying an "organisation", for example? It means we study the relations/interactions not just between humans, but rather the transient network of relations/interactions between technologies, people, their ideas, texts, and the natural environment, all of which under certain conditions stabilise into an entity we can call an "organisation". Verhoeven (2009: 179) notes that adopting an ANT approach to studying public relations practices "not only means to follow public relations people in action; it means especially to accept the basic principles of ANT, most of them being incommensurable with the functionalist and normative perspectives that are dominant in the field." Therefore, in an ANT-inspired approach, the key questions that one investigates are around the role that public relations practitioners play alongside scientists, IT systems, politicians, nature, texts, economists, machines, journalists, facts, "publics", etc. in constructing "reality". Focusing on public relations people leads us to question what their role is, how and why they acquired this role and how they relate to other actors (actants). Verhoeven also helpfully develops an interesting case study on controversies around Schiphol Airport, Amsterdam, which from an ANT perspective are not just controversies around risk and air safety but also around group formation, action and causality, objects and agency, and the construction of facts. For Verhoeven, the empirical work of the ANT researcher is to follow the actors and reveal their network of relations, to "make visible the construction of partisan and non-partisan interests and the way they are brought into the collective [and] show the role of public relations people in those construction processes of the inside and outside boundaries of the issue at stake" (Verhoeven 2009: 175). His case study illustrates that concepts like *translation* can usefully be deployed to understand how public relations practitioners might enrol other actors into networks, or be enrolled into networks, which establish facts around the issue of risk.

The process of translation is also central to the study by Luoma-aho and Paloviita (2010), which brings many insights of ANT and stakeholder theory together in an interesting analysis of the strategic communication of three organisations in the Finnish corporate sector. Their starting point is the conceptualisation of the corporation as a "socio-technical system" and their cases specifically focus on how "non-human entities such as infrastructure, technology, and market trends contributed to translating masses into opposing the corporation or leveraging wide support for it" (Luoma-aho and Paloviita 2010: 50). They don't argue that we should treat non-human entities as essentially similar to other stakeholders or that they always have equivalent agency to humans, but that researchers recognise more clearly their capacity to make a difference and study it more carefully. They note that most existing stakeholder literature acknowledges and includes the sociocultural, political and legal spheres, but has tended to marginalise the technological, the spatiotemporal and the ecological. Yet, as they demonstrate in their three organisational case studies, non-human entities (particularly IT systems and natural environments) come to the fore in a range of issues and crises for corporate actors and an analysis of their role in translating other entities into networks of influence is required if stakeholder theory is to capture the multiple, complex world made up of human and non-human entities.

A concern to capture and interrogate this multiple complexity also lies at the heart of Schölzel and Nothhaft's (2016) study which is both a carefully argued methodological discussion and a fascinating analysis of a controversy in the German political sphere. Their starting point is that ANT's concern with tracing processes and relationships around the "establishment of facts" is particularly useful for empirical public relations research. Indeed they state that few attempts are made "to capture the complexity, fragility as well as resilience, of the concept of 'fact' in public discourse [and this] tendency masks out a crucial part of what public relations does" (Schölzel and Nothhaft 2016: 54). In an era when political spokepersons readily articulate the notion of "alternative facts", focusing attention of how facts are established seems particularly apposite. Facts are always established, or *fabricated*, in specific processes, and as Schölzel and Nothhaft (2016: 56) note, this involves a whole array of actors' (or actants') "arguments, observations, instruments with which observations are recorded (i.e. drawings, graphics, statistics, tables, texts etc.) as well as human allies as authorities." Fabrication should be understood here as the process by which information is stabilised, then translated into knowledge and finally, once it is beyond argument and even the memory of any dispute forgotten, "black-boxed" as fact (Latour 1999). Schölzel and Nothhaft's (2016) analysis of the controversy over plagiarism which eventually destroyed the political career of the German politician Guttenberg describes the complex and diverse network including "facts", "activists", "the wiki platform", "a plagiarised PhD thesis", "German politicians", etc. that eventually broke open the black box of this public figure. Their use of ANT to explore the agency of facts in a controversy, the influence of technological actors and to reconceptualise the notion of "the public" as rhizomatic networks offers interesting insights that are missed by observing the process through a conventional public relations theory lens. The case of Guttenberg was not simply the story of a politician caught committing wrongdoing and forced to resign – that was the outcome – but focusing on the controversy, tracing the movements of the various actors, reveals much about the resilience, vulnerability and uncertainty of the complex networks that make up the realm of political public relations.

What the public relations research above reveals, and actor-network research more generally illustrates, is that one cannot really do ANT unless one works through qualitative case studies. What is also clear from work to date is that the emphasis on a *constructivist* (not social constructivist) approach opens up new possibilities for the public relations researcher to understand and address the complexity of relations and interaction which are overlooked by more functionalist accounts of public relations. Somerville (1999) has previously noted that typically in studies of environmental crisis communication public relations researchers tend to focus their description and analysis on human/social actors, but tend to ignore the non-human (Cheney 1992; L'Etang 1996). Therefore in describing, for example, the 2010 Deepwater Horizon BP oil spill catastrophe, the actor-network theorist would focus attention on an actor not because it is human, or because of its size, but because it has the most significant role in a particular network at a particular time. Yet from an actor-network perspective, "the relevant actors within the network include: the sea; the 'public'; the oil company; the hazardous waste; and the environmentalists. In actor network accounts it will be assumed that the sea, or the hazardous waste, are important actors possessing agency and sometimes managing to place themselves at the centre of the network" (Somerville 1999: 11). ANT draws our attention to the reality that an actor-network exists in a constant state of economic, political, cultural and physical flux, and actor-network theory provides a tool for public relations researchers by which a complex and sophisticated account, of causation, agency and significance, may be constructed.

6 Conclusions and future directions

The central ANT concept of *translation*, the idea that actors within networks will try to redefine the meaning of other actors, "speak" on their behalf, and *enrol* (manipulate or force) the other actors into positions with them, is an idea that public relations researchers may usefully employ to reflect on how public relations actors attempt to organise (or are organised by) other actors into positions which benefit them or their organisation. Callon and Latour (1981: 40) note: "By translation we understand all the negotiations, intrigues, calculations, acts of persuasion and violence thanks to which an actor or force takes or causes to be conferred on itself authority to speak or act on behalf of another actor or force. 'Our interests are the same', 'do what I want', 'you cannot succeed without going through me'". Such research requires a reorientation toward a more ethnomethodological approach in following public relations practitioners' interactions with a range of actors (human, technical, natural and textual) and tracing the success/failure of enrolment strategies across the networks they inhabit. Such a methodological approach has already been partially called for, with L'Etang's (2012) plea for more anthropological and ethnographic research, but of course ANT moves this research into new ontological and epistemological directions beyond the "social". Or as Latour (2005) would have it, it reassembles the "social", and broadens its scope to include how the interacting influences of humans, texts, ideas, hybrids and material objects must all be taken into account by public relations researchers in their studies.

A key area for public relations researchers to explore is the role of the public relations professional in the establishing of "facts" in our contemporary mediatised, promotional and contested communication environment. Studying the process of "the establishment of facts" and of "blackboxing" is central to the analysis of controversies in the political, social and business realms. For Couldry (2008: 93) ANT's profound insight is in how it helps us see "how networks come to be established as normal, regular, and, gradually, as natural … This … although not unique to ANT (it is central also to the work of Pierre Bourdieu) is especially relevant to an understanding of media's social dynamics". This insight also has important implications because understanding public relations work as a process of "naturalisation" is central to understanding public relations. Indeed Latour and Woolgar's point that "the result of the construction of a fact is that it appears unconstructed by anyone" (1979: 240) is significant for critical public relations studies, for you cannot produce persuasive regimes of truth without "establishing" facts. Highlighting this "uncovering" work of ANT provides in some ways a riposte to accusations of ANT's political quietism. Clearly ANT can offer at least the opportunity to provide substantive political critique by "de-naturalizing" social formations (Alcadipani and Hassard 2010) and, in this sense, its approach to deconstructing power can usefully be compared to the work of Foucault. It is also this attention to the empirical that enables the approach to go some way toward avoiding the charge that it does not engage with the issue of power. Law and Singleton (2013) note that the ANT sensibility is "a way of looking for *unexpected forms of power* and how these work. (...) power is not a monolithic structure. It's not even the *effect* of a monolithic structure (...) through an ANT sensibility to multiplicity, power emerges as an effect of *masses of little overlapping and variably successful practices*" (Law and Singleton 2013: 499).

ANT has a number of features which make it a distinctive research approach. First, it is not a theory (in the strictest sense). Law and Singleton (2013) refer to it as a sensibility, but it can also be described as more of a methodological or narratological approach. Second, it claims to resist and challenge many of the foundational assumptions of "modernity". Third, of necessity therefore it attempts to develop a "non-modern" terminology with which to construct its alternative narratology; this involves questioning whether even using the term *actor* is the best way to proceed (*actant* has been deployed as a less anthropocentric term). This clearly differentiates it from most public relations theories today, which reflect the ontological and epistemological assumptions of modernity. From the ANT perspective this means that those theorising public relations tend to take for granted an anthropocentrism which privileges the human and the social in a dualism which marginalises the non-human and the non-social. ANT challenges this dichotomy in the sense that it questions its hierarchical nature and claims to offer a more coherent way of (re)describing or narrating a complex world filled with "quasi-objects", constructed from human and nonhuman elements.

What is the significance of this rejection of the "modern Constitution", as Latour (1993) puts it, for public relations scholarship? Well, adopting an ANT approach would clearly be a dramatic departure from much current theorizing for the field. Up to now, almost all approaches to theorising public relations belongs to the modern episteme where the human/social is central. Botan and Hazleton (1989: 3) note that the role of public relations theory is "to identify and explain the theoretic roots appropriate to the study of public relations as a social science". This suggests that virtually all scholarly perspectives on public relations, even those that we think of as being in conceptual or political conflict with one another, such as functionalist/systems or "critical school" socio-cultural approaches, share many similar foundational assumptions which ANT challenges, contests or rejects. It does so by emphasising networks, not systems, and by turning its attention to all entities in a network, human and non-human. An expanded vision/understanding of the complexity of the world in which we all work, relate and interact helps to guard against treating non-human entities as mere props on the set of a human drama. Is ANT a useful guide to the liminal times in which we live? It certainly advertises itself as such, and its criticisms and challenges of classical dichotomies do force us to think anew about epistemological and ontological questions which motivate our research. As Restivo (2011: 523) notes in "a world of hybrids, monsters, and uncertainties it should not surprise us that Latour has produced theories and concepts that are themselves hybrids, monsters and embodiments of uncertainty". On the face of it, there does not seem to be much for practitioners to take from ANT, but in fact it is an approach which is keenly focused on practice(s) even if it fundamentally about redescribing practice through practicing redescription. For public relations professionals, as for public relations scholars, ANT raises awareness that they exist in a wide network of relationships, not just with humans but with technologies, texts and natural entities, all of which are entangled with and impact upon public relations work in a myriad of significant ways.

References

Alcadipani, Rafael & John Hassard. 2010. Actor-Network Theory, organizations and critique: towards a politics of organizing. *Organization* 17(4). 419–435.

Banks, David. 2011. A brief summary of actor network theory. *Cyborgology.* https://thesocietypages. org/cyborgology/2011/12/02/a-brief-summary-of-actor-network-theory/ (accessed 23 February 2018).

Botan, Carl H. & Vincent Hazleton (eds.). 1989. *Public Relations Theory.* Hillsdale, NJ: Lawrence Erlbaum Associates.,

Callon, Michel. 1986. The sociology of an actor-network: The case of the electric vehicle. In Michel Callon, Arie Rip & John Law (eds.), *Mapping the Dynamics of Science and Technology: Sociology of Science in the Real World*, 19–34. London: Macmillan.

Callon, Michel. 1999. Actor-Network Theory – The Market Test. *The Sociological Review* 47(1). 181–195.

Callon, Michel & Bruno Latour. 1981. Unscrewing the big Leviathan. In Karin D. Knorr-Cetina & Michael Mulkay (eds.), *Advances in Social Theory and Methodology*, 275–303. London: Routledge and Kegan Paul.

Castells, Manuel. 2009. *Communication power.* Oxford: Oxford University Press.

Cheney, George. 1992. The corporate person (re)presents itself. In Elizabeth L. Toth & Robert L. Heath (eds.), *Rhetorical and Critical Approaches to Public Relations*, 165–183. Hillsdale, NJ: Lawrence Erlbaum Associates.

Couldry, Nick. 2008. *Actor network theory and media: do they connect and on what terms?* In Andreas Hepp, Friedrich Krotz, Shaun Moores & Carsten Winter (eds.), *Connectivity, Networks and Flows: Conceptualizing Contemporary Communications*, 93–110. Cresskill, NJ: Hampton Press.

de la Cadena, Marisol. 2010. Indigenous cosmopolitics in the Andes: Conceptual reflections beyond "politics". *Cultural Anthropology* 25(2). 334–370.

Edwards, Lee & Caroline Hodges. 2011. Introduction: Implications of a radical socio-cultural 'turn' in public relations scholarship. In Lee Edwards & Caroline Hodges, (eds.), *Public relations, society and culture: Theoretical and empirical explorations*, 1–14. London: Routledge.

Elder-Vass, Dave. 2015. Disassembling Actor-Network Theory. Philosophy of the Social Sciences 45(1). 100–121.

Gregory, Anne. 2000. Systems theories and public relations practice. *Journal of Communication Management* 4(3). 266–277.

Inns, Dawn & Philip Jones. 1996. Metaphor in organisation theory: following in the footsteps of the poet? In David Grant & Cliff Oswick (eds.), *Metaphor and Organisations*, 110–126. London: Sage.

Latour, Bruno & Steve Woolgar. 1979. *Laboratory Life.* Beverly Hills, CA: Sage Publications.

Latour, Bruno. 1993. *We Have Never Been Modern.* Brighton, UK: Harvester Wheatsheaf.

Latour, Bruno. 1999. *Pandora's Hope: Essays on the Reality of Science Studies*. Cambridge, MA: Harvard University Press.

Latour, Bruno. 2005. *Reassembling the Social: An Introduction to Actor-Network-Theory*. New York: Oxford University Press.

Law, John. 1992. Notes on the theory of the actor-network: ordering, strategy and heterogeneity. *Systems Practice* 5. 379–393.

Law, John. 2008. Actor-Network Theory and material semiotics. In Bryan Turner, (ed.), *The New Blackwell Companion to Social Theory*, 3rd edn., 141–158. Oxford: Blackwell.

Law, John & Vicky Singleton. 2013. ANT and Politics: Working in and on the world. *Qualitative Sociology* 36(4). 485–502.

L'Etang, Jacquie. 1996. Public relations as rhetoric. In Jacquie L'Etang & Magda Pieczka (eds.), *Critical Perspectives in Public Relations*, 106–123. London: Thomson Business Press.

L'Etang, Jacquie. 2012. Public relations, culture and anthropology – towards an ethnographic research agenda. *Journal of Public Relations Research* 24(2). 165–183.

Luoma-aho, Vilma & Ari Paloviita. 2010. Actor-networking stakeholder theory for today's corporate communications. *Corporate Communications: An International Journal* 15(1). 49–67.

Michael, Mike. 1996. *Constructing Idenitities*. London: Sage.

Mol, Ann-Marie. 2010. Actor-Network Theory: sensitive terms and enduring tensions. *Kölner Zeitschrift für Soziologie und Sozialpsychologie. Sonderheft* 50. 253–269.

Mützel, Sophie. 2009. Networks as culturally constituted processes: A comparison of relational sociology and actor-network theory. *Current Sociology* 57(6). 871–887.

Prior-Miller, Marcia. 1989. Four major social scientific theories and their value to the public relations researcher. In Carl Botan & Vincent Hazleton (eds.), *Public Relations Theory*, 67–81. Hillsdale, NJ: Lawrence Erlbaum Associates.

Restivo, Sal. 2011. Bruno Latour: The Once and Future Philosopher. In George Ritzer & Jeffrey Stepnisky (eds.), *The Wiley-Blackwell Companion to Major Social Theorists*, Vol. 2, 520–540. Malden: Blackwell Publishing.

Schölzel, Hagan & Howard Nothhaft. 2016. The establishment of facts in public discourse: Actor-Network-Theory as a methodological approach in PR-research. *Public Relations Inquiry* 5(1). 53–69.

Silverstone, Roger. 1994. *Television and everyday life*. London: Routledge.

Somerville, Ian. 1999. Agency versus identity: Actor-network-theory meets public relations. *Corporate Communications: An International Journal* 4(1). 6–13.

Tkacz, Nathaniel. 2011. In Defence of ANT. *Journal of Peer Production* 1–6. http://peerproduction. net/issues/issue-0/debate-ant-and-power/in-defence-of-ant/ (accessed 2 April 2020).

Venturini, Tommaso, Anders Munk & Mathieu Jacomy. 2016. Actor-Network VS Network Analysis VS Digital Networks: Are We Talking About the Same Networks? In David Ribes & Janet Vertesi (eds.), *Digital STS: A Handbook and Field Guide*, 510–524. Princeton, NJ: Princeton University Press.

Verhoeven, Piet. 2009. On Latour: Actor-Network-Theory (ANT) and Public Relations. In Oyvind Ihlen, Betteke Van Ruler & Magnus Fredriksson (eds.), *Public Relations and Social Theory: Key Figures and Concepts*, 166–186. London: Routledge.

Verhoeven, Piet. 2018. On Bruno Latour: Actor-Networks, Modes of Existence and Public Relations. In Oyvind Ihlen, Betteke Van Ruler & Magnus Fredriksson (eds.), *Public Relations and Social Theory: Key Figures and Concepts*, 166–186. London: Routledge.

Winner, Langdon. 1993. Social Constructivism: Opening the Black Box and Finding It Empty. *Science as Culture* 3(3). 427–452.

Laura Olkkonen and Vilma Luoma-aho

28 Public relations and expectation theory: Introducing Relationship Expectation Theory (RET) for public relations

Abstract: Expectations provide organizations with information and cues about their stakeholders' and publics' values, interests, experiences, and knowledge. This chapter argues for a move that takes expectations beyond the current cursory level for different areas of public relations – reputation management, corporate responsibility, issues management, and legitimacy – toward explicit theoretical understanding and models for addressing expectations. The chapter introduces expectations as an intersecting phenomenon in public relations research and builds postulations for theorizing expectations in public relations by reviewing theories that address expectations in relationships, and by exploring different conceptual meanings of expectations. As a result, the chapter introduces Relationship Expectation Theory (RET), which places expectations in the domain of public relations. RET acknowledges different expectation types, the context of organizational relations, and organizations' limited ability to influence expectations.

Keywords: expectations; expectancies; Relationship Expectation Theory

1 Introduction

This chapter discusses the relevance of existing expectation theories for public relations and sets forth Relationship Expectation Theory (RET) to explain expectations in the context of public relations. In existing research of public relations, expectations are widely referred to as factors explaining reputations, corporate responsibility, relationships, legitimacy, and trust, which are some of the most important and widely studied areas of research in the field (Olkkonen and Luoma-aho 2015; Olkkonen 2015a). Expectations are further connected to central areas of the public relations function, such as issues management (e. g., Jaques 2009; Reichart 2003), relationship management (e. g., Coombs 2000; Ledingham 2003), reputation management (e. g., Eisenegger 2009; Fombrun and Rindova 1998), and crisis management (e. g., Coombs 2000; Brønn 2012) (see Olkkonen and Luoma-aho 2014 for a review). The ability to identify stakeholder expectations is also important for public relations practitioners (e. g., Global Alliance for Public Relations and Communication Management 2012), and the field itself continues to face pressing expectations stemming from its history in unethical practices such as manipulation (e. g., L'Etang and Pieczka 2006; L'Etang et al. 2016). In essence, public relations is expected to prove that it can and will add

https://doi.org/10.1515/9783110554250-028

value for society at large – and bring transparency to the related practices, interests, and tensions.

Expectations relate to public relations research and practice especially in the sense that expectations provide organizations with information and cues about their stakeholders' and publics' values, interests, experiences, and knowledge. In other words, by understanding the expectations that stakeholders and publics have at a given point of time, organizations can assess their potential impacts on relationships, and possibly also learn about signals that assist in anticipating expectations' future direction. Considering the importance of expectations across many areas of public relations theory and practice, we argue in this chapter that expectations are best understood with explicit theoretical understanding and by employing models that explain how they unfold in various stages of relationships.

To build our argument and theory, we begin the chapter by discussing how expectations are currently connected to public relations research. Second, we review predominantly micro-level theories on expectations to explain how expectations affect the very core area of public relations: relationships. This review provides a comprehensive examination of expectations in relationships, starting from relationship entry (social exchange theory and expectancy value theory), moving on to interaction in relationships (symbolic interactionism and expectation states theory) and finally to relationship outcomes and continuation (expectancy disconfirmation theory, the gap model, and expectancy violations theory). In the third step, we dissect the concept of expectations by elaborating on the different meanings attached to it. For this, we review literature from social psychology, interpersonal communication, and customer management research to build a strong understanding of the concept of expectations –the fundamental building block for our theory development (cf. Walker and Avant 2011; Gioia, Corley, and Hamilton 2013). The concept, as we demonstrate, includes positive and negative, as well as predictive and normative, elements.

Toward the end, the chapter presents our theorization of expectations in public relations as two-fold assessments of the outcomes the stakeholders or publics value and the confidence they place in an organization. We formulate our synthesis as Relationship Expectation Theory, which acknowledges different types of expectations, the context of organizational relations, and organizations' limited ability to influence expectations, especially when they are based on values. We suggest that by theorizing expectations in public relations, we can add to the stream of public relations research that focuses on less organization-centric approaches and sees stakeholders and publics as cocreators of relationships, meaning, and communication (Botan & Taylor 2004). We also discuss expectation analysis from a practical perspective and assess how it can connect to areas such as organizational monitoring and listening, with overarching connections to more strategic (and sometimes suspicious) attempts to prime and frame communication. We conclude that theorizing expectations can connect with various areas of public relations and give depth to understanding public relations and organization-stakeholder dynamics. RET is a future-oriented theory that gives insight into how expectations form and what components need to be analyzed to evaluate their future direction.

2 Expectations in public relations

Expectations appear across many areas of academic research on public relations. Expectations can be mentioned, for example, as one of the factors that organizations should try to identify and monitor to keep abreast or ahead of changes in their environment, along with attitudes, values, and norms (Heath and Bowen 2002; Ledingham 2003). The concept is likely to be familiar to scholars of issues management, as expectations can result in urgent issues when left unanswered (e. g., Jaques 2009; Reichart 2003). Scholars of relationship management may refer to expectations as the makings of the "relationship history" between an organization and its stakeholders, which is shaped by met and unmet expectations (Coombs 2000), or as factors that can induce changes in relationships or even cause relationships to end (Coombs 2000; Ledingham 2003). For scholars of reputation management, expectations can unfold as assessments of organizational ability (e. g., Eisenegger 2009). Mismatched or misinterpreted expectations also can appear in crisis management literature, this time as potential causes of crises (Brønn 2012; Coombs 2000).

In a systematic review of several decades of public relations literature (Olkkonen & Luoma-aho 2015), expectations were connected to the following seven concepts: reputation, responsibility, relationship, legitimacy, satisfaction, trust, and identity. Next, we elaborate on each of them. When expectations are used to explain *reputations*, an organization's reputation is defined as the ability or capacity to fulfill the expectations posed by stakeholders or publics, or as an assessment of how well the organization is meeting expectations (e. g., Coombs 2007; de Quevedo-Puente, de la Fuente-Sabaté, and Delgado-García 2007; Westhues and Einwiller 2006). Furthermore, exceeding expectations can be seen as a way to strengthen or improve reputation; whereas failing to meet expectations can be seen as a source for reputational threats (e. g., Brønn 2012; de Quevedo-Puente de la Fuente-Sabaté, and Delgado 2007). *Responsibility* can be explained as conformance to societal expectations or as anticipation of societal expectations (e. g., Golob, Jancic, and Lah 2009; Westhues and Einwiller 2006), much in the same vein as *legitimacy*, which can be defined as societal support for organizational actions that result from congruence with societal expectations and norms (e. g., Barnett 2007; Johansen & Nielsen 2012).

In terms of organization-stakeholder relations, expectations are mentioned as factors that start *relationships* (Broom, Casey, and Richey 1997), as well as factors that affect relationships after they are formed; for example, in the sense that relationships include an interchange of needs, expectations, and fulfillment (Ledingham 2003).

Furthermore, relationship management can be treated as a tool for aligning or reconciling organizational behavior with the expectations of stakeholders or publics (e. g., Bruning and Galloway 2003). In relation to *satisfaction*, expectations are factors that contribute to why relationships end, particularly as dissatisfaction can result from unfulfilled expectations (e. g., Jo 2006; Ledingham, Bruning, and Wilson 1999). In addition to satisfaction in relationships, expectations are connected to satisfaction attached to products and services (e. g., Brønn 2012).

Expectations are further connected to stakeholder *trust* in the sense that trust can be seen as reinforcing future positive expectations and generating a feeling of satisfaction; that is, a feeling that expectations and experiences meet (e. g., Kramer 2010). Trust can be seen as a willingness to rely on another based on a positive expectation (e. g., Poppo and Schepker 2010). Finally, research that connects expectations with *identity* call for congruence between organizational identity and expectations; mismatches between expectations and organizational conduct are seen as future threats for identity (e. g., Illia et al. 2004).

The examples above show how many areas of research expectations touch upon in the public relations literature. As a whole, the connections to issues management, relationship management, reputation management, crisis management, and to the concepts of reputation, responsibility, relationship, legitimacy, satisfaction, trust, and identity, give hints regarding which areas of public relations could possibly be understood better by clarifying expectations at a theoretical and conceptual level in the academic research. Expectations are an intersecting phenomenon in public relations because they not only explain individual areas and concepts, but also often interlink two or more concepts; for example, expectations of responsibility can be connected to how reputations are assessed (e. g., Berens and van Riel 2004; Ponzi, Fombrun, and Gardberg 2011).

Despite the way expectations intersect important areas of public relations research and practice, expectations are mainly used to explain other concepts and, perhaps, for this reason, expectations' role in existing research is often cursory. From this perspective, it is not surprising that public relations scholars seldom use or develop theoretical models for addressing expectations. Thus, we now turn our attention to making (theoretical) sense of expectations' role in one of the broadest areas of the field: relationships.

3 Theory on expectations in relationships

There is wide agreement that the specific focus on relationships between organizations and their publics is the defining factor that sets public relations apart from other fields (e. g., Botan & Taylor 2004), even to the extent that relationship management could serve as a general theory of public relations (Ledingham 2003). While more factors affect relationships than expectations (e. g., Thomlison 2000), we dedicate this section to explaining expectations' relevance to relationships. Moreover, we step outside the scope of existing public relations research in our search for a more solid theoretical foundation for expectations. This is done by discussing different theoretical perspectives that place expectations in relationships: we present theories and models that relate to different phases of relationships and their formation, starting from relationship entry, moving on to interaction in relationships, and finally to relationship outcomes and continuation. Table 1 presents an overview of the theories and models discussed in this section. We present each theory or model briefly; the aim is not to discuss the theories exhaustively or to present a comprehensive list of theories, but rather to demonstrate expectations' theoretical relevance for relationships.

Table 1: Theories that place expectations in relationships

Relationship stage	Theories contributing	Brief description of how expectations are addressed
ENTRY	Social exchange theory (Homans 1961; Blau 1964)	Decision to engage in a relationship is influenced by an evaluation of the expected costs and rewards.
	Expectancy value theory (Atkinson 1957)	Motivation is an interplay between what is considered valuable and whether the outcome can be achieved.
INTERACTION	Symbolic interaction (Blumer 1969)	Meanings, roles, and cues that are given in an interaction invoke expectations of others' and own behavior.
	Expectation states theory (Berger & Zelditch 1998)	Assessments and anticipations of others lead to performance expectations that shape hierarchy and behavior.
OUTCOME; CONTINUATION	Expectancy disconfirmation theory (Oliver 1980)	Satisfaction depends on a comparison or an assessment that is made based on how well the initial expectations were met.
	The gap model (Zeithaml, Parasuraman, and Berry 1990)	Discrepancies between initial expectations and perceived performance explain how (dis)satisfaction occurs.
	Expectancy violations theory (Burgoon 1993)	Emotional experience and expression can be explained with positively or negatively confirmed or violated expectations.

3.1 Relationship entry: Social exchange theory and expectancy value theory

The decision to engage in a relationship is an assessment process in which relational partners assess possible outcomes, the requirements the relationship puts on them, and how motivated they are to interact. These dynamics are explained by the social exchange theory (Homans 1961; Blau 1964) and the expectancy-value theory (Atkinson 1957; Wigfield and Eccles 2000) from social and educational psychology.

Social exchange theory (Homans 1961; Blau 1964) is a major theoretical perspective in social psychology that explains the social behavior and interaction of relational partners as reciprocal or negotiated exchanges (Cook and Rice 2013). Essentially, the social exchange theory takes interest in the tangible or intangible "exchange" between relational partners that is understood to depend on an assessment of expected costs and rewards (Cook and Rice 2013). The theory rests on assumptions that actors engage with others when they have a desired goal they want to obtain. When actors engage with others, there are always some costs, and choosing to engage depends on weighing the expected costs with the possible rewards (Blau 1964). Rewards can be understood in different ways, depending on what the actor finds valuable. For example, acceptance, approval, respect, prestige, compliance, or power are examples of social rewards (Blau 1964: 100). Equally, costs can take many forms, starting from investment of time and effort, to material resources and opportunities that are lost while engaging in a certain relationship (Blau 1964; Homans 1961). If the costs of interaction are expected to exceed the potential benefits and rewards, or if the expected rewards are higher in some other (competing) relationship, actors can refrain from forming a relationship in the first place. Within the domain of public relations, the social exchange theory has been applied to argue for a relational theory for public relations (Ledingham 2001), with some reference to the importance of expectations in relationships.

Expectancy-value theory (Atkinson 1957; Wigfield and Eccles 2000) suggests that the assessments made by individuals are influenced by what is considered valuable and whether they think they can achieve that outcome. Expectancy-value theory relates strongly to motivation both in terms of motivation to succeed and motivation to avoid failure (Wigfield, Tonks, and Klauda 2009). Although one of the main domains for the expectancy-value theory is educational psychology, the theory also includes applications to, for example, the broad area of work motivation (e. g., Van Eerde and Thierry 1996). Recently, the expectancy-value theory has also been connected to stakeholder participation (Purvis, Zagenczyk, and McCray 2015), which brings the theory closer to an organization's relationships with its central stakeholders and publics. In their study of stakeholder participation, Purvis, Zagenczyk, and McCray (2015) suggested that expectations influence whether stakeholders are motivated to participate in a project, and whether they will help or harm the completion of the project. Within public relations research, the expectancy-value theory has been applied to explain, for example, preferences for corporate responsibility practices (David, Kline, and

Dai 2005), yet without specifically focusing the study on expectations. As we see it, the value of the expectancy-value theory to public relations is that it explains how individuals assess what they can achieve by engaging in something, and how the expectations they make based on this assessment further impact their motivation in a relationship.

3.2 Relationship interaction: Symbolic interactionism and expectation states theory

Once the relationship has begun, the relational partners organize their interaction, roles, and dynamics. This phase of relationship development is explained by symbolic interactionism (Blumer 1969) and expectation states theory (Berger and Zelditch 1998).

Symbolic interactionism (Blumer 1969) explains society as "a web of communication or interaction, the reciprocal influence of persons taking each other into account as they act" (Stryker and Vryan 2006: 3). The word "symbolic" refers to the meanings, roles, and cues developed while interacting with another—interacting is not only about reacting to each other's actions, but about interpreting and defining those actions (Blumer 1969). Stryker and Vryan (2006) explain the role of expectations in symbolic interactionism as follows:

> Interacting persons recognize and label one another as occupants of positions, invoking linked expectations. They label themselves, invoking expectations for their own behavior. On entering situations, people define who they and others in the situation are and what the situation itself is, and they use these definitions to organize their behavior. Interaction can validate these definitions; it can also challenge them. Interactions are often venues for bargaining or conflict over alternative definitions, for battles over whose definitions will hold and organize the interaction. (Stryker & Vryan 2006: 23)

In the context of public relations, Hallahan (1999) has discussed symbolic interactionism in connection to framing and persuasion. He mentions expectations as factors affecting not only how frames are interpreted, but also as products of framing – a certain type of framing can create certain expectations (Hallahan 1999).

Expectation states theory originates from observations about differences in participation, evaluation, and influence across members of (small) groups, and how status hierarchies that stem from differences in prestige and power can explain them (Berger and Zelditch 1998; Correll and Ridgeway 2006). As Correll and Ridgeway (2006) describe, expectation states theory explains how members of groups with a collective task or a goal make assessments and anticipations of other members of the group, leading to performance expectations that, once developed, shape the group's hierarchy and behavior in a self-fulfilling manner (Correll and Ridgeway 2006: 31). Expectation states theory relates mostly to group dynamics, and how some members are given more chances to speak, suggest, and decide – often implicitly and unconsciously – while others are given fewer opportunities. As organizations and their stakeholders or publics are not task-oriented groups as such, the relevance of expectation states theory for public relations is limited. However, task orientation can gain relevance when organizations seek collective action and engagement with their stakeholders and publics. Thus, we see value in how expectation states theory recognizes status characteristics, such as background and expertise, as antecedents for expectations on interaction, how input is valued, and how others are heard in the process (cf. Correll and Ridgeway 2006).

Overall, theories that explain expectations in relationship interaction become relevant especially from the perspective of stakeholder categorizations and how different voices are heard. Furthermore, these theories can have relevance for stakeholder engagement and collaboration, as the theories are about assessing the relational partner's behavior and characteristics.

3.3 Relationship outcomes and continuation: Expectancy disconfirmation theory, the gap model, and expectancy violations theory

Once the relationship is underway, the actors engaged in it assess whether the relationship is meeting their expectations. These confirmations and discrepancies have been addressed by both the expectancy disconfirmation theory (Oliver 1980) and the gap model (Zeithaml, Parasuraman, and Berry 1990) in customer satisfaction literature, and by expectancy violations theory (Burgoon 1993) in interpersonal communication.

Expectancy disconfirmation theory explains how customer satisfaction depends on a comparison or an assessment of a product or a service, based on how well the initial expectations were met (Oliver 1980). Disconfirmation refers to "a subjective post-usage comparison" (Lankton and Mcknight 2012: 89). A similar argument is posed by *the gap model* that explains dissatisfaction as discrepancy (i. e., a gap) between initial expectations and perceived performance (Zeithaml, Parasuraman, and Berry 1990). Expectation gaps can originate from multiple sources: not knowing what is expected, offering a quality that does not meet expectations, not meeting expectations with performance, or promising something that cannot be delivered (Zeithaml, Parasuraman, and Berry 1990). In the field of public relations, Brønn (2012) has used the gap model in connection with corporate responsibility communication, reputation management, and risk management – with considerable attention given to expectations and how their violations potentially hurt organizations.

According to *expectancy violations theory*, expectations can be either confirmed or violated – positively or negatively. In the case of positive violation, the enacted behavior is more positive than initially expected, and, in the case of negative violation, the enacted behavior is more negative than initially expected (Burgoon 1993). The theory poses that these violations explain emotional experience and expression in relationships. For example, a violation of expectations can distract attention from the original situation or issue, as the violation leads to emotional responses and a need to make sense of the violation, as well as to evaluate its consequences (Burgoon 1993). In public relations research, expectancy violations theory has been applied to predict how publics react to organizations' attempts to mimic interpersonal communication on social media (Sung and Kim 2014).

To sum up the reviewed theories relating to relationship outcomes and continuation, the expectations formulated in the beginning of the relationship affect how the relationship is evaluated and whether it is perceived as worth continuing. Fulfilling positive expectations, for example, by delivering good quality and keeping promises, generally leads to positive assessments of the relationship. When gaps or violations occur, they can pose threats to the continuation of the relationship.

We conclude this section by noting how expectations connect to relationships in different contexts such as social groups, work, customer relations, and interpersonal communication. For the most part, these micro-level theories explain interpersonal relationships; however, some examples illustrating how these theories apply in the context of public relations exist. Therefore, while theoretical understanding of expectations is making its way into public relations research, we propose there is a further need to theorize how expectations play out specifically in organization-stakeholder relations. Thus, we move on to discuss the concept of expectations.

4 Defining expectations

Concepts are the building blocks in theory construction (Walker and Avant 2011; Gioia, Corley, and Hamilton 2013); therefore, we continue our theoretical endeavor from the conceptual level of defining expectations. Considering how often and how widely expectations are connected to public relations, existing literature gives us surprisingly few actual definitions of expectations in public relations (Olkkonen 2017; Olkkonen 2015a; Olkkonen and Luoma-aho 2015). Often, the role of expectations is cursory in that it explains other concepts and relations between concepts; for example, that meeting expectations of corporate responsibility is crucial for maintaining reputations and legitimacy (Olkkonen 2017). Therefore, to offer a solid foundation for building theory on expectations in public relations, we take another step outside the scope of public relations, this time by reviewing literature on customer management and customer satisfaction, which are areas with detailed conceptual insight on expectations and illustrative introductions to the positive and negative elements of expectations.

Customer management and customer satisfaction research offers not one but several definitions to understand the full range of expectations. Using this background, expectations can be seen as a dynamic phenomenon where different factors can affect the final formation of an expectation (see, e. g., Miller 1977; Summers and Granbois 1977; Swan, Trawick, and Carroll 1982; Woodruff, Cadotte, and Jenkins 1983; Zeithaml, Berry, and Parasuraman 1993; also Olkkonen and Luoma-aho 2015). These factors have been suggested to create different *expectation types* that have different origins (Summers and Granbois 1977; Woodruff, Cadotte, and Jenkins 1983). The types suggested are abundant, some dealing with values, such as "normative" (Summers and Granbois 1977) or "ideal" expectations (Miller 1977), while some rest on the information that is available, such as "precise" or "realistic" expectations (Ojasalo 2001). Furthermore, previous experience is recognized as a factor for expectation formation, for example, in "experience-based" expectations (Woodruff, Cadotte, and Jenkins 1983). Finally, expectations can be driven by personal interest as suggested in "deserved" (Miller 1977) or "desired" expectations (Swan, Trawick, and Carroll 1982).

Based on an extensive review of customer management and customer satisfaction literature (Olkkonen and Luoma-aho 2015), we have previously categorized expectations into four streams that explain the range of different expectation types:

1. *Value-based expectations* (Miller 1977; Summers and Granbois 1977): Normative expectations that indicate an ideal state based on what is valued or wished for. Value-based expectations are the most difficult to fulfill due to their idealistic and sometimes unrealistic nature. Also referred to as "ideal" or "should" expectations.

2. *Information-based expectations* (Miller 1977; Ojasalo 2001): Expectations based on what is known and what information is available or unavailable. Information-based expectations can be influenced by both explicit facts and implicit cues. Moreover, information-based expectations may become unrealistic or fuzzy based on imprecise or lack of information. Also referred to as "precise," "realistic," "explicit," and "official" expectations.

3. *Experience-based expectations* (Miller 1977; Summers and Granbois 1977; Swan, Trawick, and Carroll 1982; Woodruff, Cadotte, and Jenkins 1983; Zeithaml, Berry, and Parasuraman 1993): Expectations based on direct or indirect previous experiences that guide what is believed to be possible. Experience-based expectations indicate a likelihood similar to predictive expectations, or they result from comparisons with similar brands or organizations. Prior experiences can raise or lower these expectations to avoid future disappointments. Also referred to as "brand-based," "comparative," or "minimum tolerance" expectations.

4. *Personal interest-based expectations* (Miller 1977; Swan, Trawick, and Carroll 1982; Zeithaml, Berry, and Parasuraman 1993): Expectations that are primarily influenced by personal evaluations of gains and assessments of what is deserved, based on desires, or the effort and resources invested. These expectations are a challenge for brands and organizations as they can cause some information to be filtered out when it does not match personal interests. Also referred to as "desired," "deserved," or "unofficial" expectations.

Each of the four categories gives different conceptual explanations to expectations. These categories add to the previous understanding of public relations literature, not only by explaining the many ways expectations form, but also by drawing attention to how the assessment of fulfilled or violated expectations is actually very different depending on the expectation type. Most importantly, while value- and interest-based expectations are, presumably, always positive hopes, wishes, or demands as they are based on what should or ought to be, information- and experience-based expectations can take both positive and negative forms. For example, if prior experience has been a disappointment, an expectation based on probability might predict the disappointment to repeat itself. This connects not only to how not meeting positive expectations can lead to reputational losses, but also how meeting negative expectations might actively build or maintain an unfavorable reputation or, for example, cause damage to legitimacy. Moreover, when understood as negative anticipations, expectations can help to decipher why stakeholders and publics sometimes display pessimism or cynicism toward organizations. We suggest that understanding the different expectation types and, furthermore, understanding expectations as positive and negative, as well as normative and predictive, constructs explains more profoundly how they influence public relations.

The conceptual understanding of expectations, in addition to what we have presented in the previous sections, sets the stage for formulating our own theorization of expectations in the specific context of public relations. The next section articulates the postulations for this theorization.

5 Relationship Expectation Theory (RET)

So far, we have discussed theories and models that address expectations in relationships, and articulated the different ways expectations are understood at a conceptual level. Our earlier work suggested that organizations can make sense of expectations by analyzing the outcomes the stakeholders or publics value and the confidence they place in an organization (see the Expectation Grid first introduced by Olkkonen and Luoma-aho 2015; empirically tested and revised by Olkkonen 2015a, 2015b; see also Olkkonen 2017). We draw on this background but take a step forward by elaborating on what we mean with an interplay between valued outcomes (normative assessment) and confidence placed on an organization (organization-specific assessment). We draw from the previous sections to build three postulations for our theory to explain expectations in public relations: the Relationship Expectation Theory.

Social exchange theory and expectancy value theory connect with value- and interest-based expectation types, as these theories explain how the prospect of valuable outcomes and rewards affect relationships, especially in their formation stage. Although social exchange theory and expectancy value theory are mainly micro level theories, we assume that expectation formation is universal for all relationships where humans are involved (cf. Thomlison 2000). Therefore, values and interests represent the outcomes that stakeholders and publics are looking for in a relationship and, vice versa, are seeking to avoid. Based on this, we formulate the first postulation for theorizing expectations in public relations:

> Postulation 1: Stakeholders and publics assess desirable and undesirable outcomes when they form expectations for organizations, and these assessments are influenced by values and interest.

Values and interests are relatively static in that they remain the same when stakeholders and publics assess different organizations; thus, they are the baseline for forming expectations. As we have argued elsewhere (Olkkonen 2015a; Olkkonen and Luoma-aho 2015), value- and interest-based expectations guide the normative assessment of expectation formation, and they vary depending on what is desirable and why – bound by both individual and cultural variance. Hence, values can, for example, range from economic to societal values, and interests can be anything from very limited self-interest to utilitarianism. We also argue that organizations can influence value- and interest-based expectations only to a limited extent; for example, by taking part in the discussions that shape societal values and trends. In essence, our first postulation implies that both positive and negative outcomes are assessed when stakeholders and publics form expectations for organizations.

When we examine expectations beyond their normative dimension, we can again refer to social exchange theory and expectancy value theory in how they explain the impact of expected costs and probabilities on relationships. Similarly, in symbolic interaction and expectation states theory relationships are affected by how we judge and anticipate others' behavior and characteristics. Expectancy disconfirmation theory, the gap model, and expectancy violations theory are also relevant as they explain how relationship outcomes are assessed based on whether expectations prove to be true. In terms of expectation types, information and experience-based expectations deal mostly with this predictive side of expectation formation. Based on these arguments, our next postulation is:

> Postulation 2: When expectations are attached to specific organizations, stakeholders' and publics' values and interests are weighed against experience and information about an organization's ability and willingness to deliver preferred outcomes.

As predictive expectations derive mostly from experience and available (direct or indirect) information, organizations have more direct influence over them, for example, if their communication matches the actual actions that the organization takes. This is what we have described earlier as the organization-specific assessment, which is actually embedded in the normative assessment as it takes a reference point in values and interests (Olkkonen 2015a; Olkkonen and Luoma-aho 2015). However, compared to the normative assessment, the organization-specific assessment is more dynamic and predictive: it is close to the actual target of expectations and describes how likely it is to attain preferred outcomes in the case of a specific organization. Essentially, the organization-specific assessment can result in positive or negative expectations, as the stakeholders assess how likely it is that their expectations will be fulfilled; that is, how willing and able the organization is perceived to meet their values and interests. The organization-specific assessment can turn an expectation negative if the organization is perceived as unwilling or unable either to offer an outcome that is valued or to prevent an outcome that is not valued. Hence, the importance of our second postulation is that stakeholders and publics can form both positive and negative expectations for organizations and their conduct.

The two embedded assessments – normative assessment of different outcomes and organization-specific assessment dealing with confidence in a particular organization – make expectations *"positive or negative future-oriented assessments of an organization's ability and willingness that form in the interplay between normative and predictive factors"* (Olkkonen 2015a: 60). In other words, expectations form an interplay between the outcomes the stakeholders and publics value and the confidence they place in an organization. What we pause to argue here is that expectations are not to be treated too lightly in academic research of public relations, as they are a complex phenomenon with significant implications for relationships. Their complex nature holds whether we talk about establishing relationships, interacting in them, or judging when they are satisfying and worth continuing. Thus, we push for a need to articulate a theory for expectations in public relations that inevitably includes interplay between preferred outcomes (values and interests) and confidence in a particular organization (influenced by information and experience). This leads us to the third and final postulation for RET:

> *Postulation 3: The interplay between normative and organization-specific assessments results in positive and negative expectations attached to organizations.*

Our interpretation of the different expectation types, based on both conceptual and empirical work (Luoma-aho and Olkkonen 2016; Olkkonen 2015a, 2015b, 2017; Olkkonen and Luoma-aho 2015) is that the normative and (organization-specific) predictive interplay can lead to optimistic, hopeful, cynical, or pessimistic expectations. We next elaborate on each by following Figure 1, a visualization of how we draw together our three postulations to formulate the Relationships Expectation Theory (RET) for public relations.

The two axes of Figure 1 are based on the first two postulations: the vertical axis portrays the assessment of outcomes, which can be viewed positively or negatively by stakeholders and publics, and the horizontal axis represents stakeholders' or publics' assessments of whether an organization is perceived able and willing to deliver the outcomes. As a result, organizations may face two types of positive and two types of negative expectations. As illustrated in the figure, RET acknowledges two types of

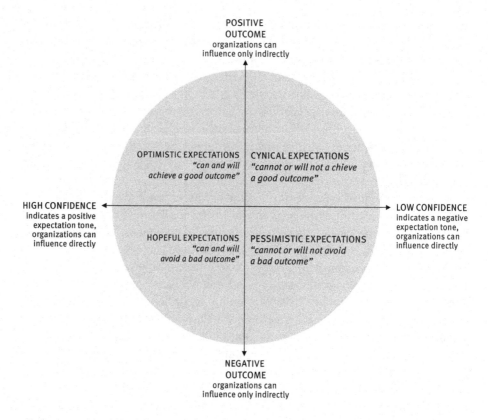

Figure 1: Relationship Expectation Theory (RET) for public relations (adapted from Olkkonen & Luoma-aho 2015)

positive expectations: *optimistic* and *hopeful*. When stakeholders or publics have optimistic expectations, they anticipate that the organization is willing and able to offer outcomes they value. This is perhaps most easily visible in communicating values, mission, and organizational purpose; when these meet with stakeholder values and interests, expectations are optimistic. The other positive expectation type is hopeful, which indicates an anticipation that the organization is willing and able to prevent an outcome the stakeholder or public perceives as negative. This could be, for example, an organization's good reputation in tackling social challenges or maintaining high environmental standards despite possible risks. The difference between these two is the outcome that is assessed. An optimistic expectation is connected to a positive outcome (and its delivery); whereas a hopeful expectation is connected to a negative outcome (and its prevention). Overall, positive expectations are a sign of confidence and trust in the organization; hence, their violation is also likely to violate the confidence and trust invested in them.

Figure 1 further presents two negative expectations: *cynical* and *pessimistic*. When expectations are negative, confidence in the organization's willingness and ability is low. Cynical expectations indicate an anticipation that the organization is unwilling or unable to offer outcomes that stakeholders and publics perceive as positive. This could be the result of, for example, greenwashing, lip service, or window-dressing, which leave stakeholders dissatisfied and expecting further disappointments. A pessimistic expectation indicates an anticipation that the organization is unwilling or unable to prevent an outcome that the stakeholder perceives as negative. An example of a pessimistic expectation could relate to, for example, discrimination, pollution, or privacy. The difference between cynical and pessimistic expectations again is the outcome.

As the vertical axis shows, our formulation of RET acknowledges that organizations can influence expectations only to a limited extent, especially in relation to the normative assessment guided by values and interests. Organizations' influence over the information and experiences that shape expectations is more direct and they can, for example, attempt to frame their communication, seek for a fit between what is done and what is communicated, and find ways to include and engage their stakeholders in their actions. However, the line between direct and indirect influence is not clear-cut, as even every information-based and experience-based expectation takes a comparison point in the value-based and interest-based expectations.

The added value of Relationship Expectation Theory when compared to existing theoretical knowledge of expectations in public relations is that it (1) takes into account that expectations are multi-dimensional rather than one-dimensional constructs, (2) connects the understanding of expectations to the context of a specific organization and the confidence invested in it, and (3) recognizes that organizations can influence expectations only to a limited extent.

If we were to apply expectation mapping and analysis to the function of public relations, overlapping areas could include relationship management, including monitoring and listening. Furthermore, mapping and analyzing expectations could take on a more strategic role in public relations, relating to priming expectations to a realistic level, framing communication to make it meaningful, and ensuring satisfaction with sufficient disclosure and dialogue (cf. Luoma-aho, Canel, and Olkkonen 2020). Earlier, we have suggested comprehensive strategic monitoring, mapping, and analysis of stakeholder expectations as activities of *expectation management* that we describe as an organization's ability to manage its own understanding of what is expected of it, especially in terms of different expectation types and their differences in relevance and priority (Luoma-aho and Olkkonen 2016; Olkkonen and Luoma-aho 2015; Olkkonen and Luoma-aho 2014; Olkkonen 2015a). Although management can refer to control, which consequently can raise critical questions for the (hidden) intentions of expectation analysis, we argue that in the current communication environment it is impossible to manipulate or control stakeholders' or publics' expectations. However, we acknowledge the ambiguity and pitfalls of the term, which calls for a need for further discussion on what organizations ideally should "do" with their knowledge of expectations. Whether we call it management, analysis, or mapping, RET gives structure to organizations' understanding of expectations.

The next section concludes our exploration of expectations and discusses the relevance of RET for the future of public relations research.

6 Concluding remarks

Relationships are central to public relations, and expectations affect them in every stage from the beginning to the end. This chapter has reviewed theories that address expectations in relationships and discussed their relevance for public relations. Furthermore, the chapter used the different conceptual dimensions of expectations as building blocks to theorize expectations in public relations. We formulated Relationship Expectation Theory as an emerging theory of expectations in public relations that treats expectations as multidimensional constructs, connects the understanding of expectations to the context of a specific organization and the confidence invested in it, and recognizes that organizations can influence expectations only to a limited extent.

RET explains how expectations form in an interplay between the outcomes the stakeholders or publics value and the confidence they place on an organization. As such, RET rests on understanding expectation formation as a two-fold assessment process of normative assessment and organization-specific assessment. We argue that our theory responds to the apparent interest of current public relations research in expectations as factors affecting reputations, corporate responsibility, relationship management, organizational legitimacy, stakeholder satisfaction, trust, organizational identity, and issues management. Importantly, the urgency of understanding expectations is likely not to diminish in the increasingly complex environment in which organizations practicing public relations are embedded: stakeholders and publics can organize unexpectedly (e. g., Aldoory and Grunig J. 2012); opinions and experiences can be shared visibly, effortlessly, and potentially virally (e. g., Pang, Begam Binte Abul Hassan and Chee Yang Chong 2014); and value-polarization can cause conflicts between diverging expectations (e. g., Wettstein and Baur 2016). As a result, there are many reasons why organizations may face expectations and expectation gaps that call for urgent attention and potentially cause serious damage to organizations and their relationships with stakeholders and publics. RET offers a theoretical frame to continue exploring specifically how expectations affect organizations in a complex environment.

As to the limitations related to RET, we note that the expectations organizations face are not likely to be a homogenous cluster even within a single stakeholder group (Olkkonen 2015b). Therefore, the reality of expectation mapping is likely to be messy, as well as laborious, involving intensive analysis. As noted during the testing and revision of our earlier model (Olkkonen 2015a, 2015b), the four expectation types represent extremities, because in reality stakeholders might display caution in their expectations rather than, for example, pure optimism or cynicism. Furthermore, expectations often seem to be interconnected; the optimism or hopes in positive expectations can be overturned by the simultaneous impact of negative expectations (Olkkonen 2015b). This can happen, if the organization's good deeds are perceived as insufficient to counteract (broader) negative trends. Moreover, expectations can change over time as relationships evolve. Therefore, our categorizations are likely to reflect passing stages, not fixed states, which calls for longitudinal studies that can capture the dynamics of evolving expectations.

RET also sets some critical considerations for the practice of public relations. We have proposed expectation management (as management of the knowledge extracted from expectations) as a possible supplementing task for public relations practice, but management can also take the form of control and manipulation. Attempts to control, manipulate, or artificially create and steer expectations could become another suspicious and potentially unethical area that the field has been accused of containing (e. g., L'Etang 2006; L'Etang et al. 2016). On the other hand, it can be questioned to what extent organizations have actual possibilities and power to shape expectations, especially as the normative assessment is influenced by values and interests. Relating to power, a relevant question is: Who gets to voice their expectations and to whose expectations should organizations respond? These are some of the potential critical questions for future research.

Based on what we have presented in this chapter, expectations are an emerging and intersecting theme in public relations, and one that is likely to increase in importance. Public relations as a practice is increasingly interested in predicting stakeholders' and publics' mindsets, values, and preferences to be able to safeguard their reputations, to prevent communication from backfiring, and to work with stakeholders to achieve shared goals. Moreover, recent developments such as algorithms and big data give organizations increasing opportunities to monitor their audiences. A thorough understanding of expectations can give public relations research and practice predictive power in an increasingly unpredictable world of interlinked relations, networks, and shifting power relations. Thus, we argue that Relationship Expectation Theory is a step toward understanding the future of public relations, especially when stakeholders and publics are seen as cocreators of relationships, meaning, and communication.

References

Aldoory, Linda & James E. Grunig. 2012. The rise and fall of hot-issue publics: Relationships that develop from media coverage of events and crises. *International Journal of Strategic Communication* 6(1). 93–108.

Atkinson, John William. 1957. Motivational determinants of risk taking behavior. *Psychological Review* 64. 359–372.

Barnett, Michael L. 2007. Tarred and untarred by the same brush: Exploring interdependence in the volatility of stock returns. *Corporate Reputation Review* 10(1). 3–21.

Berger, Joseph & Morris Zelditch, Jr. 1998. *Status, power, and legitimacy: Strategies and theories.* New Brunswick, NJ: Transaction

Berens, Guido & Cees B. M. van Riel. 2004. Corporate associations in the academic literature: Three main streams of thought in the reputation measurement literature. *Corporate Reputation Review* 7(2). 161–178.

Blau, Peter Michael. 1964. *Exchange and power in social life.* New York: John Wiley.

Blumer, Herbert. 1969. *Symbolic Interactionism: Perspective and Method.* Englewood Cliffs, NJ: Prentice-Hall.

Botan, Carl H., & Maureen Taylor. 2004. Public relations: State of the field. *Journal of Communication* 54(4). 645–661.

Brønn, Peggy Simcic. 2012. Adapting the PZB service quality model to reputation risk analysis and the implications for CSR communication. *Journal of Communication Management* 16(1). 77–91.

Broom, Glen M., Shawna Casey & James Richey. 1997. Toward a concept and theory of organization-public relationships. *Journal of Public Relations Research* 9(2). 83–98.

Bruning, Stephen D. & Tara Galloway. 2003. Expanding the organization-public relationship scale: Exploring the role that structural and personal commitment play in organization-public relationships. *Public Relations Review* 29(3). 309–319.

Burgoon, Judee K. 1993. Interpersonal expectations, expectancy violations, and emotional communication. *Journal of Language and Social Psychology* 12(1–2). 30–48.

Coombs, W. Timothy. 2000. Crisis management: Advantages of a relational perspective. In John A. Ledingham & Stephen D. Bruning (eds.), *Public Relations as Relationship Management*, 73–93. Mahwah, NJ: Lawrence Erlbaum Associates.

Coombs, W. Timothy. 2007. Protecting organization reputations during a crisis: The development and application of situational crisis communication theory. *Corporate Reputation Review* 10(3). 163–176.

Cook, Karen S. & Eric Rice. 2013. Social exchange theory. In John DeLamater & Amanda Ward (eds.), *Handbook of Social Psychology*, 2nd edn., 61–88. Dordrecht, Netherlands: Springer.

Correll, Shelley J. & Cecilia. L. Ridgeway. 2006. Expectation states theory. In John Delamater (eds.), *Handbook of social psychology*, 29–52. New York: Springer.

David, Prabu, Susan Kline & Yang Dai. 2005. Corporate social responsibility practices, corporate identity, and purchase intention: A dual-process model. *Journal of Public Relations Research* 17(3). 291–313.

de Quevedo-Puente, Esther, Juan Manuel de la Fuente-Sabaté & Juan Bautista Delgado-García. 2007. Corporate social performance and corporate reputation: Two interwoven perspectives. *Corporate Reputation Review* 10(1). 60–72.

Eisenegger, Mark. 2009. Trust and reputation in the age of globalization. In Joachim Klewes & Robert Wreschniok (eds.), *Reputation Capital*, 11–22. Berlin: Springer.

Fombrun, Charles J. & Violina Rindova. 1998. Reputation management in global 1000 firms: A benchmarking study. *Corporate Reputation Review* 1(3). 205–212.

Gioia, Dennis A., Kevin G. Corley & Aimee L. Hamilton. 2013. Seeking qualitative rigor in inductive research: Notes on the Gioia methodology. *Organizational Research Methods* 16(1). 15–31.

Global Alliance for Public Relations and Communication Management. 2012. The Melbourne Mandate. A Call to Action for New Areas of Value in Public Relations and Communication Management. https://globalalliancepr.org/melbourne-mandate (accessed 2 April 2020).

Golob, Urša, Zlatko Jancic & Borut Marko Lah. 2009. Corporate social responsibility and transparent pricing in the case of the euro changeover. *Corporate Communications: An International Journal* 14(4). 456–469.

Hallahan, Kirk. 1999. Seven models of framing: Implications for public relations. *Journal of Public Relations Research* 11(3). 205–242.

Heath, Robert L. & Shannon A. Bowen. 2002. The public relations philosophy of John W. Hill: Bricks in the foundation of issues management. *Journal of Public Affairs* 2(4). 230–246.

Homans, George Caspar. 1961. *Social behavior: Its elementary forms*. New York: Harcourt Brace.

Illia, Laura, Evelyn Schmid, Irene Fischbach, Robert Hangartner & Roberto Rivola. 2004. An issues management perspective on corporate identity: The case of a regulatory agency. *Corporate Reputation Review* 7(1). 10–21.

Jaques, Tony. 2009. Issues and crisis management: Quicksand in the definitional landscape. *Public Relations Review* 35(3). 280–286.

Jo, Samsup. 2006. Measurement of organization-public relationships: Validation of measurement using a manufacturer-retailer relationship. *Journal of Public Relations Research* 18(3). 225–248.

Johansen, Trine Susanne & Anne Ellerup Nielsen. 2012. CSR in corporate self-storying: Legitimacy as a question of differentiation and conformity. *Corporate Communications: An International Journal* 17(4). 434–448.

Kramer, Roderick M. 2010. Collective trust within organizations: Conceptual foundations and empirical insights. *Corporate Reputation Review* 13(2). 82–97.

Lankton, Nancy K. & D. Harrison McKnight. 2012. Examining two expectation disconfirmation theory models: assimilation and asymmetry effects. *Journal of the Association for Information Systems* 13(2). 88–115.

Ledingham, John A. 2001. Government-community relationships: Extending the relational theory of public relations. *Public Relations Review* 27(3). 285–295.

Ledingham, John A. 2003. Explicating relationship management as a general theory of public relations. *Journal of Public Relations Research* 15(2). 181–198.

Ledingham, John A., Stephen D. Bruning & Laurie J. Wilson. 1999. Time as an indicator of the perceptions and behavior of members of a key public: Monitoring and predicting organization-public relationships. *Journal of Public Relations Research* 11(2). 167–183.

Luoma-aho, Vilma, María-José Canel & Laura Olkkonen. 2020. Public sector communication and citizen expectations and satisfaction. In Vilma Luoma-aho & María-José Canel (eds.), *Handbook of Public Sector Communication*. New York: Wiley Blackwell.

Luoma-aho, Vilma & Laura Olkkonen. 2016. Expectation management. In C. E. Carroll (ed.), *The SAGE Encyclopedia of Corporate Reputation* I, 303–306. Thousand Oaks, CA: Sage.

L'Etang, Jacquie. 2006. Public relations and propaganda: Conceptual issues, methodological problems, and public relations discourse. In Jacquie L'Etang & Magda Pieczka (eds.), *Public relations: Critical debates and contemporary practice*, 23–40. Mahwah, NJ: Lawrence Erlbaum Associates.

L'Etang, Jacquie, David McKie, Nancy Snow & Jordi Xifra. 2016. The Routledge handbook of critical public relations. London & New York: Routledge.

L'Etang, Jacquie & Magda Pieczka (eds.). 2006. *Public relations: Critical debates and contemporary practice*. Mahwah, NJ: Lawrence Erlbaum Associates.

Miller, John A. 1977. Studying satisfaction, modifying models, eliciting expectations, posing problems, and making meaningful measurements. In H. Keith Hunt (ed.), *Conceptualization and Measurement of Consumer Satisfaction and Dissatisfaction*, 72–91. Cambridge, MA: Marketing Science Institute.

Ojasalo, Jukka. 2001. Managing customer expectations in professional services. *Managing Service Quality* 11(3). 200–212.

Oliver, Richard L. 1980. A cognitive model of the antecedents and consequences of satisfaction decisions. *Journal of Marketing Research* 17. 460–469.

Olkkonen, Laura. 2015a. *Stakeholder expectations: Conceptual foundations and empirical analysis.* Jyväskylä, Finland: University of Jyväskylä doctoral dissertation.

Olkkonen, Laura. 2015b. Audience enabling as corporate responsibility for media organizations. *Journal of Media Ethics* 30(4). 268–288.

Olkkonen, Laura. 2017. A conceptual foundation for expectations of corporate responsibility. *Corporate Communications: An International Journal* 22(1). 19–35.

Olkkonen, Laura & Vilma Luoma-aho. 2014. Public relations as expectation management? *Journal of Communication Management* 18(3). 222–239.

Olkkonen, Laura & Vilma Luoma-aho. 2015. Broadening the concept of expectations in public relations. *Journal of Public Relations Research* 27(1). 81–99.

Pang, Augustine, Nasrath Begam Binte Abul Hassan & Aaron Chee Yang Chong. 2014. Negotiating crisis in the social media environment: Evolution of crises online, gaining credibility offline. *Corporate Communications: An International Journal* 19(1). 96–118.

Ponzi, Leonard J., Charles J. Fombrun & Naomi A. Gardberg. 2011. RepTrak™ Pulse: Conceptualizing and validating a short-form measure of corporate reputation. *Corporate Reputation Review* 14(1). 15–35.

Poppo, Laura & Donald J. Schepker. 2010. Repairing public trust in organizations. *Corporate Reputation Review* 13(2). 124–141.

Purvis, Russell L., Thomas J. Zagenczyk & Gordon E. McCray. 2015. What's in it for me? Using expectancy theory and climate to explain stakeholder participation, its direction and intensity. *International Journal of Project Management* 33(1). 3–14.

Reichart, Joel. 2003. A theoretical exploration of expectational gaps in the corporate issue construct. *Corporate Reputation Review* 6(1). 58–69.

Stryker, Sheldon & Kevin D. Vryan. 2006. The symbolic interactionist frame. In John Delamater (ed.), *Handbook of social psychology*, 3–28. New York: Springer.

Summers, John O. & Donald H. Granbois. 1977. Predictive and normative expectations in consumer dissatisfaction and complaining behavior. *Advances in Consumer Research* 4(1). 155–158.

Sung, Kang-Hoon & Sora Kim. 2014. I want to be your friend: The effects of organizations' interpersonal approaches on social networking sites. *Journal of Public Relations Research* 26(3). 235–255.

Swan, John E., I. Fredrick Trawick & Maxwell G. Carroll. 1982. Satisfaction related to predictive, desired expectations: a field study. In Ralph L. Day & J. Keith Hunt (eds.), *New Findings on Consumer Satisfaction and Complaining*, 15–22. Bloomington, IN: Indiana University Press.

Thomlison, T. Dean. 2000. An interpersonal primer with implications for public relations. In John A. Ledingham & Stephen D. Bruning (eds.), *Public relations as relationship management: A relational approach to the study and practice of public relations*, 177–203. Mahwah, NJ: Lawrence Erlbaum Associates.

Van Eerde, Wendelien & Henk Thierry. 1996. Vroom's expectancy models and work-related criteria: A meta-analysis. *Journal of Applied Psychology* 81. 575–586.

Walker, Lorraine Olszewski & Kay Coalson Avant. 2011. *Strategies for theory construction in nursing*, 5th edn. Upper Saddle River, NJ: Prentice Hall.

Westhues, Martina & Sabine Einwiller. 2006. Corporate foundations: Their role for corporate social responsibility. *Corporate Reputation Review* 9(2). 144–153.

Wettstein, Florian & Dorothea Baur. 2016. "Why should we care about marriage equality?" Political advocacy as a part of corporate responsibility. *Journal of Business Ethics* 138(2). 199–213.

Wigfield, Allan & Jacquelynne S. Eccles. 2000. Expectancy-value theory of achievement motivation. *Contemporary Educational Psychology* 25(1). 68–81.

Wigfield, Allan, Stephen Tonks, & Susan Lutz Klauda. 2009. Expectancy-value theory. In Kathryn R. Wentzel & Allan Wigfield (eds.), *Handbook of Motivation at School*, 55–76. New York: Routledge.

Woodruff, Robert B., Ernest R. Cadotte & Roger L. Jenkins. 1983. Modeling consumer satisfaction processes using experience-based norms. *Journal of Marketing Research* 20(3). 296–304.
Zeithaml, Valarie A., Leonard L. Berry & A. Parasuraman. 1993. The nature and determinants of customer expectations of service. *Journal of the Academy of Marketing Science* 21(1). 1–12.
Zeithaml, Valarie A., A. Parasuraman & Leonard L. Berry. 1990. *Delivering quality service*. New York: Free Press.

Patricia A. Curtin

29 Public relations and cultural theories

Abstract: This chapter offers an overview of the nexus of public relations and cultural theories. Scholars almost universally recognize the close relationship between culture and public relations, yet only relatively recently have cultural theories been introduced and used. Early functionalistic approaches saw culture instrumentally, using cultural indices to operationalize it as a predictive variable. Around 2000, the socio-cultural turn saw the adoption of social constructivist theory and ethnographic methods from cultural anthropology. Culture was understood as a system of subjectively defined meanings, often at the micro level of analysis. Much early research, however, was shallow, although a few notable exceptions emerged. Critical/cultural approaches introduced the notion of culture as constitutive of meaning. Diversity, process, and power became central concepts, as did cultural capital, with practitioners serving as cultural intermediaries. Postmodern and postcolonial perspectives encouraged reflection on the role of capitalist culture in practice and questioning of the neoliberal economic basis of globalization. Future work is needed that examines public relations as an intercultural process extending beyond the "us-them" and private-public binaries to engage with cultural flows, active diverse publics, and networks and technologies as active agents.

Keywords: organizational culture; corporate culture; societal culture; cultural indices; cultural anthropology; cultural intermediaries; cultural studies

1 Introduction

Much scholarship has demonstrated that public relations is an ancient, worldwide practice that was and is shaped by micro-, meso-, and macro-cultural forces (Wakefield 2010). Additionally, the public relations profession itself has a culture and many subcultures; practitioners work to create cultural meanings that connect with publics; and publics are active audiences who create their own cultural meanings. The relationship of culture to public relations is "incontrovertible" (Sriramesh 2010: 698); in fact, "cultural constructs don't affect public relations practice; they are the essence of public relations practice" (Curtin and Gaither 2007: 12).

How culture connects with public relations, however, depends to some extent on the definition of culture used. Simply put, organizational culture may be defined as the norms, vision, and values that guide organizational behavior – the spoken and unspoken rules that define how things are done in an organization. Corporate culture is a subset of organizational culture, encompassing for-profit organizations in which neoliberal economic values often heavily influence the culture. Societal culture may

https://doi.org/10.1515/9783110554250-029

be defined in anthropological terms as the shared norms and values of a social group, resulting in particular behaviors. Cultural studies defines culture as a way of ordinary life that is constitutive of meaning, rather than separate from it.

Despite the long-standing connection between the two fields, the purposeful integration of public relations with these varying definitions of culture and cultural theories is a relatively new phenomenon and remains underdeveloped (McKie 2001), although it is an area of study undergoing rapid expansion. This examination of the nexus of public relations and cultural theories takes a loosely historical perspective, albeit a necessarily short one. It begins with an overview of work that embeds the public relations profession in organizational culture first and foremost, then examines later studies marking the socio-cultural turn in public relations scholarship, such as those connecting practice to cultural anthropology; critical/cultural approaches that incorporate culture as constitutive of meaning; postmodernism and postcolonialism and the role of public relations practice in capitalist culture; and public diplomacy, particularly cultural diplomacy. The chapter concludes with suggestions for future areas of research.

2 Organizational culture and public relations

Much of the purposeful joining of public relations and cultural theories can be traced to the 1980s and the privileging of organizational culture's influence on public relations practice. The next section outlines how the two main strands of organizational public relations theories – excellence theory and relationship management theory – and the role of culture in shaping practice in a proposed universally applicable fashion, and it then uses culture as a predictive variable in studies.

2.1 Excellence theory

U.S. scholars, funded by the International Association of Business Communicators, developed the Excellence Project in the late 1980s and early 1990s. Their work, based in a functionalist systems theory perspective, was premised on the concept of public relations as a product and agent of organizational culture. From survey data gathered from respondents in the United States, Canada, and the United Kingdom, J. Grunig, L. Grunig, and Dozier (2002) developed a normative theory of excellent public relations practice, outlining the ideal conditions under which public relations could be effectively practiced within an organization (see chapter 16 in this book). Because the theory was based in organizational structures and functions, they argued that organizational culture plays a much more formative role than does societal culture in shaping how public relations is practiced. Although the team of excellence researchers stressed that its work encompassed corporations, nonprofit organizations, government agencies, and associations (Sriramesh, Grunig, J. and Buffington 1992), later work tended to reduce organizational culture to corporate culture, treating these two as synonymous and establishing a dominant neoliberal economic approach.

The excellence study researchers, borrowing from an early anthropologic perspective, defined culture as a set of organizational rules (e. g., Goodenough 1956), both implicit and explicit, established by the organization's dominant coalition. Because the researchers viewed culture as an organizational attribute, it became a variable in their study that predicted whether the culture would support excellent (i. e., effective) public relations practice. They measured culture along two dimensions: authoritarian and participative. Authoritarian culture was characterized as competitive and hierarchical, with a highly centralized and controlled decision-making authority. Conversely, participatory culture encompassed decentralized management and an environment in which employees felt a sense of teamwork and shared in decision making. Although it was expected that participatory culture would be a necessary precondition of what the researchers termed excellent public relations practice, they found that participatory culture was not, by itself, a necessary nor sufficient condition for excellence (Sriramesh, Grunig, J. and Dozier 1996). It did, however, leave the door open to change from within, which authoritarian cultures did not. Participatory culture, then, was deemed a factor that nurtured excellent public relations practice, although it did not guarantee it. The Excellence Project resulted in ten generic principles of effective public relations practice. The researchers claimed these principles did not vary across societal or national cultures, resulting in a global theory of public relations (Grunig, J., Grunig, L. and Dozier 2002).

2.2 Relationship management theory

A closely related approach grounded in organizational management theory is relationship management theory (see chapter 21 in this book). Similar to excellence theory, one normative goal of relationship management theory is to develop an organizational culture that propagates and maintains mutually beneficial relationships between organizations and their publics (Ledingham 2009). Briefly, the outcomes of these mutually beneficial relations can be measured in terms of trust, satisfaction, control mutuality, and commitment. These relationship outcomes are held to be universal, providing an organization-centered theory of public relations practice applicable worldwide. Because these relationships outcomes "are culturally constrained, culturally sensitive, and operate in an environment in which goals are achieved in distinct cultural settings" (Ledingham 2009: 226), culture is treated as a measurable variable in how relationships are managed for mutual benefit.

2.3 Applying organization-centered theories cross-culturally using cultural indices

Similarly, although the excellence study did not measure societal culture as a predictive variable, researchers suggested it was one of five environmental factors that could influence how excellent public relations was practiced, the other four being political ideology, economic system, activism, and media systems (Verčič, Grunig, L. and Grunig, J. 1996). Subsequent studies collapsed those five factors into three: a country's infrastructure, media environment, and societal culture (Sriramesh and Verčič 2009). The result was a proliferation of research designed to elucidate the global-local dialectic by discovering particular socio-cultural factors serving as contextual influences. Subsequent studies suggested the addition of variables such as *guanxi* (social influence networks) for Chinese practice, *wa* (harmony) for Japanese (Sriramesh 2009), and Confucianism for Korean (Rhee 2002). Similarly, in terms of relationship management theory, Huang (2001) suggested adding face and favor as variables to account for Eastern-based practice.

To measure societal culture as a variable, many proponents of excellence theory and relationship management theory have adopted social psychologist Hofstede's cultural dimensions (1984). Hofstede developed his indices from an organizational management perspective, which made it a natural fit with organization-centered public relations based theories, although more global perspectives have occasionally used it as well. He defined culture as the unwritten rules governing the society, knowledge of which defines one as a member of a culture. Using a factor analysis of data from a survey of IBM employees in 40 countries from 1967 to 1973, Hofstede identified four dimensions as descriptive of societal-level cultural differences. The first, individualism/collectivism, quantifies national cultures according to their degree of group integration, that is whether members tend to identify in terms of self or the group. The second dimension, uncertainty avoidance, measures national tolerance for ambiguity as opposed to a strong felt need for principles to counter uncertainty. Power distance provides a national measure of acceptance of social hierarchy and unequal power distribution. The masculinity/femininity dimension quantifies assertiveness and achievement versus cooperation and modesty.

Hofstede later extended his research to 76 countries and added two more dimensions: long-term orientation, which refers to an underlying Confucian philosophy of honoring tradition versus preparing for the future, and indulgence versus self-restraint, which can be loosely construed as immediate gratification versus suppressing gratification through strict cultural norms. Scores for each country on each dimension can be compared. For example, East Asian and Latin American countries tend to rate highly on power distance and are accepting of social hierarchies, whereas Scandinavian countries tend to rate much lower on this measure.

Public relations theorists (e. g., Men and Tsai 2012; Zaharna 2001) have used cultural indices developed by anthropologists as well, such as Edward Hall's (1966) dimensions of high- and low-context cultures and polychronic versus monochronic attitudes toward time. In high-context cultures, communication tends to be implicit and in-person; in low-context cultures, communication tends to be explicit and often mediated. In monochronic cultures, time is linear and appointments are strictly scheduled; in polychromic cultures, people often are doing several things at once, and personal relations take precedence over schedule keeping. From Hall's perspective, culture was not only key to verbal and nonverbal communication, but also to perception of meaning. Public relations theorists have applied Hall's concepts less frequently than they have Hofstede's, perhaps because his concepts were based on his observations as head of the Foreign Service Institute, established post-World War II to train people in intercultural competence, making them more suited to applied public relations research (e. g., Ihator 2000) than to more purely theoretical endeavors.

Culbertson and Chen, in their (1996) volume examining international public relations practice, suggested using Hofstede's indices in addition to the basic foundations of excellence theory. Despite the inherent danger of stereotyping in using such measures, their model of a country-by-country case study approach employing the "country=culture logic" (Bardhan 2012: 19) was replicated in the majority of subsequent book-length treatments that appeared between 2002 and 2006 addressing global or international practice (e. g., Moss and DeSanto 2002; Parkinson and Ekachai 2006; Tilson and Alozie 2004). In response to globalization trends of increasing information and population flows, public relations scholars also began examining how practice and cultures engage as part of a global process in flux, particularly in times of crisis. Taylor's (2000) examination of possible Coca-Cola contamination in Europe used Hofstede's power distance and uncertainty avoidance indices to elucidate varying public reactions to the crisis in different nations. Molleda's (2010) concept of cross-national conflict shifting examines how transnational organizations handle crises that often spread through global information channels and may trigger global networks of activists. He states that such conflict can result from differing cultural notions of what is ethical, and transnational organizations must balance their responses to be both coordinated yet culturally appropriate. Although this approach implies a process orientation, it is based on excellence theory and often applies Hofstede's indices as measurable cultural variables.

2.4 Criticisms of organization-centered approaches

Excellence theory and relationship management theory are predicated on the assumption that a model developed in Western nations based on Western organizational practices is applicable to the rest of the world, with only minor contextual differences coming into play. By privileging organizational culture over societal culture and relying on national indices to provide a context for organizational practice, excellence theory and relationship management theory have downplayed the interplay of culture across levels of analysis and the large role that societal culture can play in shaping or possibly constraining organizational culture.

Additionally, by defining culture as a variable that can be quantitatively measured, excellence theory takes an instrumental approach to culture, reducing its complexities (L'Etang 2012). A number of criticisms of using national cultural indices have emerged. A case study of a crisis involving a Scandinavian company operating in the Middle East demonstrated that while Hofstede and Hall's constructs helped delineate broad trends at the macrosocial level, they did not account for increasing global hybridization or suggest a solution outside of pure cultural relativism (Gaither and Curtin 2008). Because the indices are reductionist, they treat national cultures as monolithic and stable, erasing subtleties and creating homogeneity out of multiple identity facets, such as race/ethnicity, religion, and gender orientation (Xifra and McKie 2011). Despite these criticisms, excellence theory was the dominant theory in terms of public relations and culture in the early 2000s, and relationship management theory remains a dominant approach today.

These organization-centered perspectives, however, sparked a call for work that examined culture from the bottom up and how it organically influenced the development of public relations in different micro-, meso-, and macro-cultures, leading to what has been termed the *socio-cultural turn* in public relations research (Edwards 2018). Although the cultural turn in most communication studies dates to about the 1970s, it was a latecomer to public relations because of the dominance of excellence theory throughout the 1990s (L'Etang et al. 2016).

3 The socio-cultural turn in public relations

Critical/cultural public relations theorists suggest that culture has been undertheorized in public relations research, with culture operationalized as a static and geopolitically bound variable that can be generalized to large populations rather than examined as a site of contested meanings (Bardhan and Weaver 2011). Resistance built to theory that used North America as the benchmark and North American-based businesses as the focus of study in the face of global network flows and the rise of multilateral institutions, such as the World Trade Organization, and international non-governmental organizations, such as Médecins Sans Frontiéres. Equally troubling was the scant attention paid to micro-cultures and their relationship to public relations practice. To address these concerns, a number of competing but complementary theoretical approaches emerged in the 1990s, mainly in Europe and Australia/ New Zealand, and spread to other areas of the world after the turn of the century. These culture-centered approaches included social constructivism, critical/cultural studies, and postcolonialism.

3.1 Public relations and cultural social constructivism

Social constructivism draws on cultural anthropology, particularly Geertz's (1973) notion of human-created webs of significance and the prominence of ritual, and Goffman's (1959) micro-sociological theory, addressing the rules and processes by which people structure their everyday lives, to propose that meaning resides not in an essentialized external reality but in cultures' created and shared social realities; therefore, nothing can be understood apart from its social context.

3.1.1 Banks' social-interpretive theory of multicultural public relations

Banks (1995) developed what he termed a social-interpretive theory of multicultural public relations, taking a rhetorical approach to the intersection of public relations and cultural theory. His perspective differed sharply from excellence theory in that he viewed culture as a system of subjectively defined meanings, resulting in theory that embraced cultural diversity rather than reducing culture to measurable indices. His theory provided publics with a much more active role in interpreting organizational messages within their own cultural frameworks. Although his work affirmed multiple cultural identities and stressed the role of interpersonal communication (Bardhan 2011), it relied on organizational structure and the role of organizational leaders in establishing an organizational culture that would support multicultural practice (McKie and Munshi 2007).

Banks' theory of public relations practice as tied to diverse communities and understandings, then, is in its own way as idealistic as the excellence theory it was competing with, relying on enlightened organizational leadership to be successful. Banks' contribution was to propose that culture created diverse perspectives among active audiences that public relations practice had to account for, but his theory did little to present a pragmatic way of addressing that diversity. While his approach was a step toward defining culture as a construct, it remains a normative ideal that does not take into account unequal distributions of power and the need to empower certain publics (Bardhan 2011).

Banks' multicultural theory gained little traction at the time it was introduced. Later efforts within this theoretical tradition were less organization-centered, noting that public relations both comprises cultures and is a practice that engages with various cultures. This broader social-constructionist approach examines the cultures of agency life, in-house departments, and professional organizations as well as how people make sense of public relations communications in their everyday lives (L'Etang 2012). The focus is on cultural difference and diversity as localized phenomena within microcultures.

3.1.2 Cultural anthropology and public relations practices

Despite the promising insights that could result from the application of cultural anthropology to public relations practice, limited rhetorical work (e. g., Gordon 1997; Leichty 2003) has examined the shared cultural meanings that have accumulated around public relations practitioners and practice and how those meanings contribute to how the profession and its place in society are understood. A few participant observation studies have examined professional cultures in settings such as a public relations department within a government agency (Filby and Willmott 1988), an intern acculturating into a firm (Bremner 2012), and during professional training programs (Pieczka 2002).

Ethnographic approaches received a boost in 2012 with the publication of a special edition of *Public Relations Review*, edited by L'Etang, Hodges, and Pieczka (2012), as well as an essay by L'Etang (2012) in the *Journal of Public Relations Research* outlining the contributions that more cultural anthropologic approaches could make to public relations scholarship. Included in the special edition of *Public Relations Review* was one of the first, and only, autoethnographic pieces, which self-reflexively deconstructed the application of theory to practice in a public relations campaign, revealing much about the strained relationship between public relations theory and practice within a microculture (James 2012).

Other ethnographic work, including in-depth interviews as well as participant observation, often consists of cross-cultural studies or studies done by expats returning to their home culture. Some early ethnographic work was notable for its lack of rigor, constituting what has been termed *blitzkrieg ethnography* (L'Etang 2012), and is therefore of questionable value. More substantive work in the area includes Terry's (2005) study of practice in Kazakhstan, which she concluded was a tool of power wielded by the elite. Bardhan's (2003) examination of public relations in India was a sharp rebuke of the generic principles of excellence theory. Braun's (2007) in-depth interviews with Bulgarian practitioners revealed the role of historicity and political environment in shaping conceptions of public relations as similar to propaganda and relying heavily on personal influence. A small research subset has also looked at crisis communication cross-culturally to demonstrate the primacy of shared cultural meanings in shaping practice (e. g., Zhao, Falkheimer, and Heide 2017).

Many other areas of scholarship exist that would benefit from applying cultural theory and methods to public relations, but they remain woefully under-researched. For example, little extant research explores how framing theory could be used in public relations campaigns to foster shared realities within a culture (Johansson 2007). Similarly, while marketing has long used ethnographic research to inform practice (Chong 2010), such as Sony's play stores where consumers are observed interacting with products to determine how they relate to them in their everyday lives, applied public relations scholarship has lagged behind (L'Etang 2012). Industry leader Brian Solis (2011: 3) has observed that "social media is less about technology and more about anthropology, sociology, and ethnography," but research has yet to fully explore these conceptual connections as they apply to what is arguably the forefront of public relations practice. The fact that participant observation can be incredibly time-consuming if done correctly may be partly to blame for the dearth of more anthropological cultural research in public relations areas.

3.2 Public relations and critical/cultural studies approaches

The 1990s marked the integration of critical/cultural approaches with public relations theory and scholarship. Many of these approaches built on the Birmingham Centre's concept of culture as constitutive of meaning, not separate from it (Williams, 1981): culture in this sense "is the process by which meaning is produced, circulated, consumed, commodified, and endlessly reproduced and renegotiated in society" (Curtin and Gaither 2007: 35). From this perspective, it is impossible to disengage public relations practice from culture.

Critical/cultural public relations scholarship first appeared in Europe in the 1990s, most notably through the efforts of L'Etang and Pieczka (1996), but encountered considerable resistance from the proponents of the dominant excellence theory. A nucleus of critical scholarship grew in the United Kingdom and New Zealand. After the turn of the century, critical/cultural approaches gained momentum and spread into other areas of Europe and Australasia and somewhat less so into North America. Much work appeared around the world at approximately the same time (i.e., mid-2000s), suggesting that scholars were working in isolation from each other but with a similar end goal in mind (L'Etang 2012). Critical approaches in general and critical/cultural approaches in particular remain, however, a somewhat marginalized area of study in many journals (*Public Relations Inquiry* being a notable exception). The work also has yet to be well received at many conferences and or in some regions of the world (Pompper 2005; Waymer 2012). Yet as a practice embedded throughout socio-cultural systems, public relations has both contributed to the maintenance of social order and cultural norms while possessing the capacity to work for change (Edwards 2018; Liu and Pompper 2012). More critical approaches, then, have firmly tied issues of cultural norms to issues of diversity, raising awareness of the links between culture, race, and ethnicity (Pompper 2005; Waymer 2012) and how societies react to these linkages in order to maintain social order (Liu and Pompper 2012).

3.2.1 Discourse, power, culture, and public relations

Power plays a significant role in all critical perspectives of how culture creates and sustains public relations practices (see chapter 7 in this book). Instead of the early Marxist concept of power as an oppressive, negative force, critical public relations scholars have often adopted Foucault's conception of power as residing in relationships between or among things, but not a quality of the things themselves. Within this conceptualization, power has the capacity to be positive and productive, and power can be successfully resisted, as evidenced by countercultures and activist publics, among others. Critical/cultural approaches, then, unlike excellence theory, place power relations and flows squarely at the center of inquiry, which allows for a full and nuanced examination of a variety of cultures, such as employee subcultures, localized cultures of professional practice, and global campaigns undertaken by multinational entities. Motion and Leitch (1996, 2009) developed Foucault's thought within public relations, and their work, along with that of Weaver, often uses case studies to demonstrate how practice uses discourse to construct socio-cultural notions of truth, such as the discourse surrounding genetic engineering and modification (e. g., Henderson, Cheney, and Weaver 2015; Motion and Weaver 2005; Weaver 2010;), and the way that discourse functions ideologically. Practitioners, then, "draw on existing systems, norms and values to claim authority for particular perspectives of the world – or, more specifically, for the perspectives of their clients" in order to structure knowledge (Edwards 2018: 60).

A discourse-centered approach is at the heart of the cultural-economic model (CEM) proposed by Curtin and Gaither (2006). The model is based on the circuit of culture developed by scholars at the Open University in the United Kingdom, which was first applied to public relations scholarship by Weaver (2001). The model brings together five moments (regulation, production, consumption, identity, and representation) that are conjoined in articulations, creating spaces of shared cultural meanings. These articulations can be localized or widespread, allowing for examination of constitutive discourse at the micro-, meso, and macro-cultural levels. Within this model, public relations activity is envisioned not as a linear transmission of information from an organization to a public and back, but instead as a dynamic, non-linear process in which meanings are continuously negotiated and renegotiated. Some of these articulated meanings resonate, proving remarkably long-lived and widely adopted, gaining the appearance of historical fact. Culture, then, is central to public relations practice, and economic forces can be viewed as cultural, discursive constructs that in turn shape culture (Curtin and Gaither 2006).

This perspective provides a flexible framework for considering public relations practices that remain contextually bound but not constrained, balancing structure and agency. The CEM thus allows for cultural nuance but does not devolve into full cultural relevancy because of the structure provided within the five moments. The emphasis is on process within structure – a hallmark of a number of emerging critical approaches to public relations and cultural theories (Curtin, Gaither, and Ciszek 2016). Within this model, practitioners serve as cultural intermediaries.

3.2.2 Practitioners as cultural intermediaries

Many critical scholars have borrowed Bourdieu's (1984) notion that public relations practitioners act as *cultural intermediaries*. Bourdieu trained as an anthropologist before turning to sociology, and he coined the term to refer to a specific sector of an emerging social class that deals with cultural capital (Ihlen 2009). In some public relations scholarship, the term has come to have a meaning similar to boundary spanner, although it encompasses much more than is usually implied in a boundary spanner role. Rather than being a communication conduit who spans the boundary between an organization and its publics, cultural intermediaries create shared meanings between producers and consumers (Hodges 2006). Of fundamental import, therefore, is that cultural intermediaries be culturally literate or fluent in cultural capital because they are themselves producers of culture (Edwards 2018). Some scholars have suggested that social media have made public relations practitioners cultural curators rather than cultural intermediaries, with content deriving from consumers and not just practitioners (Tombleson and Wolf 2017). Such characterization, however, fundamentally changes the practitioner role back to one of simply transmission of information, rather than as an active shaper of content and strategy that uses consumer discourse as an entry point into shared meanings.

3.3 Postmodern and postcolonial approaches

Postmodernist thought was first developed in conjunction with public relations by Mickey (1997), but similar to Banks' (1995) sociocultural theory, it gained little traction at the time because of the dominance of excellence theory and more functionalist approaches. Postmodernism privileges the situational and thus emphasizes the local aspects of culture: "Public relations will be best understood in the way it is practiced in a particular environment and at a particular time. In that way, public relations will reflect the diversity of the societies in which it is practiced" (Holtzhausen 2000: 107). Postmodern approaches can easily devolve into cultural relativism, but they share with postcolonialism two major constructs that inform the nexus of public relations and cultural theories. The first is the need for self-reflexivity; the second is their examination of the culture of capitalism and the role it has played in global public relations practice (McKie 2001).

Postcolonialism is rooted in the thought of two literary theorists, Said (1978) and Spivak (1988), but its principles have informed a branch of public relations scholarship that overlaps with critical views of culture and theories of globalization. In particular, scholars have examined the role of corporate, capitalist cultures in globalization, such as how privileging a culture of neoliberalism has encouraged public relations as a managerial science and pursuit, silenced subaltern voices, and helped create activist publics (Dutta 2009; McKie and Munshi 2007, 2009). Such approaches decry the ethnocentricity inherent in many transnational corporations' public relations endeavors and the resulting colonization of the global South by the global North.

Dutta and Pal (2011) label their postcolonial approach a *culture-centered* one; similar to the cultural-economic model described above, it positions culture as constitutive of meaning, power relations as inherent to those meanings, and integrates structure and agency. The constraining role of structure within a neoliberal culture is readily apparent in their approach: their stance positions public relations practices as almost solely Western-corporate based and used to maintain U.S. hegemony, forming an "elite network of control" (Dutta 2016: 249). Less apparent in their approach is agency, which they appear to grant solely to self-reflective researchers who recognize and overcome cultural imperialism. The goal is to encourage participatory communication and allow dialogue to flourish, resulting in mutual understanding and the redressing of global inequities (Dutta 2016). In this sense, Dutta's culture-centered approach appears to be more a political-economic model of global practice that relies on a few, enlightened activist researchers to redress the structural wrongs of neoliberal economics.

For both postmodern and postcolonial approaches, then, the role of the research is to enact cultural change through self-reflexive practice. Whereas postmodernism foregrounds local, situated cultures, postcolonialism often privileges larger, economic structural constraints on culture. Postmodernism calls for practitioners to be internal activists within their organizations (Holtzhausen 2000, 2011), while postcolonialism calls for activism that privileges subaltern voices and gives them power in the face of capitalist culture (Dutta and Pal 2011).

4 Public diplomacy

Delineating the intersection of cross-cultural public relations and public diplomacy, first outlined by Signitzer and Coombs (1992), lies outside the scope of this chapter except to note that much public diplomacy employs public relations techniques to bring about greater cultural understanding and thus deserves short mention here. The relationship between the two has been explored from all the theoretical approaches outlined above, including excellence and relationship management theories and nation-based cultural indices (Golan and Yang 2015), ethnographic studies rooted in cultural anthropological perspectives (L'Etang 2009), and critical examinations of public diplomacy as serving the interests of capitalistic culture only (Dutta and Pal 2011).

Many public diplomacy efforts are state-sponsored, inviting a comparison of national cultures through indices such as Hofstede's (Golan and Yang 2015) and leaving them open to critique that public diplomacy has become the main carrier of neoliberal intent (Dutta and Pal 2011). Yet public diplomacy takes many forms, and much cultural diplomatic outreach is more localized, such as sister city programs and grassroots cultural exchanges. These approaches combine mediated and interpersonal public relations communication channels with the goal of increased cross-cultural understanding, yet they remain understudied and undertheorized in the literature.

5 Future research

In sum, work to date demonstrates that the integration of cultural theory into public relations theory and practice has provided numerous insights. Organizational-level approaches, such as excellence theory and relationship management theory, provide normative guidance to practitioners that not only prescribes everyday functions but can also help, to some extent, mitigate crisis and risk. Using cultural indices, such as those of Hofstede and Hall, can lend broad, macro-level insights to transnational organizations, helping avoid some of the larger cultural miscues in communication despite lacking specific contextual insights. Integrating cultural anthropology approaches allows greater insight into the lived experience of practitioners and also those of publics and how they make use of public relations campaign materials in their everyday lives.

Interrogating culture as a concept in public relations allows us to grapple with the notion that, at least at the micro-level, almost all public relations work involves cross-cultural, or intercultural, communication (Rittenhofer and Valentini 2015: 7). Publics are fluid, constructing multiple and diverse meanings and identities that require cultural fluency to reach and engage. Cultural approaches encourage public relations theorists to explore the value of cultural capital and the role that practice plays in society by creating spaces of shared meanings shaped by political and economic forces. In doing so, they make us question the role of agency in public relations work, which brings with it concomitant examination of the role of activists and social movements. In this way, cultural theories help us look at public relations as a process that intertwines the public and private spheres.

Much work remains to be done to explore the nexus of public relations and cultural theories. What follows is a brief outline of a few promising areas for future research.

The little extant research tends to cluster by level of analysis: the microcultural or more cultural anthropology in approach, the meso-cultural level focused on organization management, or the macro-cultural level privileging structural forces and state players acting within geopolitical boundaries. This theorizing reinforces the global-local dichotomy, creating a binary approach that may ill inform practice in today's networked and hybridized world.

Appadurai (1996), a socio-cultural sociologist, explores a multidimensional sense of cultural flows in the five "scapes" of his global cultural economy – the technoscape (mediated information flows and cultural interactions), the ethnoscape (migrations of peoples and cultures across geopolitical boundaries), the financescape (flows of capital), the mediascape (media constructions of a global world), and the ideoscape (ideological flows). For Appadurai (1996), these global flows are marked by disjunctures in practice, which he (1996: 31) characterized as "a form of negotiation between sites of agency and globally defined fields of possibility." Disjunctures shape the possibilities within which "discourse and practice inform each other" (Edwards 2011: 34), allowing for the emergence of the unexpected as the lines between global and local are blurred.

Appadurai's thought invites public relations scholars and practitioners to reconfigure their ways of approaching public relations practice (Edwards 2011; Rittenhofer and Valentini 2015: 10), yet little work has built directly on Appardurai's thought to date. Likewise, little work has robustly addressed Castells' (1996) elucidation of the networked society, although both his and Appardurai's notions of networked global flows are compatible with some critical/cultural approaches to public relations theory and practice.

The blending of social and cultural approaches also invites an increasing examination of cultures of diversity within public relations, using queer theory and intersectional approaches. Such non-binary theories embrace the local-global dialectic in its richness, favoring process over product and disruptions over metanarratives. Public relations culture and its role in constructing culture is better understood from these non-reductionist perspectives. Similarly, Latour's (2005) actor-network theory, which emphasizes the role of nonhuman actors in networks of meaning, holds great promise for extending how we theorize public relations in terms of culture in diverse, networked globalized/localized flows.

Although the history of using cultural theories in conjunction with public relations is fairly recent, the research trajectory is on a strong upward trend that will benefit from greater appreciation of how cultural theories inform public relations practice.

References

Appadurai, Arjun. 1996. *Modernity at large*. Minneapolis, MN: University of Minnesota Press.
Banks, Stephen. 1995. *Multicultural public relations: A socio-interpretive approach*. Thousand Oaks, CA: Sage.
Bardhan, Nilanjana R. 2003. Rupturing public relations metanarratives: The example of India. *Journal of Public Relations Research* 15. 225–248.
Bardhan, Nilanjana R. 2011. Culture, communication, and third culture building in public relations within global flux. In Nilanjana Bardhan & C. Kay Weaver (eds.), *Public relations in global cultural contexts: Multi-paradigmatic perspectives*, 77–107. New York: Routledge.
Bardhan, Nilanjana R. 2012. Culture as a "traveling" variable in transnational public relations: A dialectical approach. In Damion Waymer (ed.), *Culture, social class, and race in public relations*, 13–30. New York: Lexington Books.

Bardhan, Nilanjana, and C. Kay Weaver. 2011. *Public relations in global cultural contexts: Multi-paradigmatic approaches.* New York: Routledge.

Bourdieu, Pierre. 1984. *Distinction: A social critique of the judgement of taste.* R. Nice (trans.). Cambridge, MA: Harvard University Press.

Braun, Sandra L. 2007. The effects of the political environment on public relations in Bulgaria. *Journal of Public Relations Research* 19. 199–228.

Bremner, Stephen. 2012. Socialization and acquisition of professional discourse: A case study in the PR industry. *Written Communication* 29(1). 7–32.

Castells, Manuel. 1996. *The rise of the network society.* Oxford: Blackwell.

Chong, Josephine L. L. 2010. Evaluating the impact of Arnould and Wallendorf's (1994) market-oriented ethnography. *Journal of Business Research* 63(12). 1295–1300.

Culbertson, Hugh & Ni Chen. (eds.). 1996. International *public relations: A comparative analysis.* Mahwah, NJ: Lawrence Erlbaum.

Curtin, Patricia A. & T. Kenn Gaither. 2006. Privileging identity, difference, and power: The circuit of culture as a basis for public relations practice. *Journal of Public Relations Research* 17(2). 91–115.

Curtin, Patricia A. & T. Kenn Gaither. 2007. International *public relations: Negotiating culture, identity, and power.* Thousand Oaks, CA: Sage.

Curtin, Patricia A., T. Kenn Gaither & Erica Ciszek. 2016. Articulating public relations practice and critical/cultural theory through a cultural-economic lens. In Jacquie L'Etang, David McKie, Nancy Snow & Jordi Xifra (eds.), *The Routledge handbook of critical public relations*, 41–53. London: Routledge.

Dutta, Mohan J. 2016. A postcolonial critique of public relations. In Jacquie L'Etang, David McKie, Nancy Snow & Jordi Xifra (eds.), *The Routledge handbook of critical public relations*, 248–260. London: Routledge.

Dutta, Mohan J. 2009. On Spivak: Theorizing resistance – applying Gayatri Chakravorty Spivak in public relations. In Øyvind Ihlen, Betteke van Ruler & Magnus Fredriksson (eds.), *Public relations and social theory: Key figures and concepts*, 278–300. London: Routledge.

Dutta, Mohan J. & Mahuya Pal. 2011. Public relations and marginalization in a global context: A postcolonial critique. In Nilanjana Bardhan & C. Kay Weaver (eds.), *Public relations in global cultural contexts: Multi-paradigmatic approaches*, 195–225. New York: Routledge.

Edwards, Lee. 2011. Critical perspectives in global public relations. In Nilanjana Bardhan & C. Kay Weaver (eds.), *Public relations in global cultural contexts: Multi-paradigmatic approaches*, 29–49. New York: Routledge.

Edwards, Lee. 2018. *Understanding public relations: Theory, culture and society.* London: Sage.

Filby, Ivan & Hugh Wilmott. 1988. Ideologies and contradictions in a public relations department: The seduction and impotence of living myth. *Organization Studies* 9(3). 335–349.

Gaither, T. Kenn. & Patricia A. Curtin. 2008. Examining the heuristic value of models of international public relations practice: A case study of the Arla Foods crisis. *Journal of Public Relations Research* 20(1). 115–137.

Geertz, Clifford. 1973. *The interpretation of cultures.* New York: Basic Books.

Goffman, Erving. 1959. *Presentation of self in everyday life.* New York: Doubleday.

Golan, Guy J. & Sung-Un Yang. 2015. Introduction: The integrated public diplomacy perspective. In Guy J. Golan, Sung-Un Yang & Dennis F. Kinsey (eds.), *International public relations and public diplomacy: Communication and engagement*, 1–12. New York: Peter Lang.

Goodenough, Ward. 1956. Residence rules. *Southwestern Journal of Anthropology* 12(1). 22–37.

Gordon, Joye C. 1997. Interpreting definitions of public relations: Self assessment and a symbolic interactionist based alternative. *Public Relations Review* 23(1). 57–66.

Grunig, James E., Larissa A. Grunig & David M. Dozier. 2002. *Excellent public relations and effective organizations: A study of communication management in three countries*. Mahwah, NJ: Lawrence Erlbaum Associates.

Hall, Edward T. 1966. *The hidden dimension*. Garden City, NY: Doubleday.

Henderson, Alison, George Cheney & C. Kay Weaver. 2015. The role of employee identification and organizational identity in strategic communication and organizational issues management about genetic modification. *International Journal of Business Communication* 52(1). 12–41.

Hodges, Caroline. 2006. "PRP culture": A framework for exploring public relations practitioners as cultural intermediaries. *Journal of Communication Management* 10(1). 80–93.

Hofstede, Geertz. 1984. *Culture's consequences*. Beverly Hills, CA: Sage.

Holtzhausen, Derina. 2000. Postmodern values in public relations. *Journal of Public Relations Research* 12(1). 93–114.

Holtzhausen, Derina. 2011. The need for a postmodern turn in global public relations. In Nilanjana Bardhan, and C. Kay Weaver (eds.), *Public relations in global cultural contexts: Multi-paradigmatic approaches*, 140–166. New York: Routledge.

Huang, Yi-Hui. 2001. OPRA: A cross-cultural, multiple-item scale for measuring organization-public relationships, *Journal of Public Relations Research* 13(1). 61–90.

Ihator, Augustine. 2000. Understanding the cultural patterns of the world – An imperative in implementing international PR programs. *Public Relations Quarterly* Winter. 38–44.

Ihlen, Øyvind. 2009. On Bourdieu: Public relations in field struggles. In Øyvind Ihlen, Betteke van Ruler & Magnus Fredriksson (eds.), *Public relations and social theory: Key figures and concepts*, 62–82. London: Routledge.

James, Melanie. 2012. Autoethnography: The story of applying a conceptual framework for intentional positioning to public relations practice. *Public Relations Review* 38(4). 555–564.

Johansson, Catrin. 2007. Goffman's sociology: An inspiring resource for developing public relations theory. *Public Relations Review* 33(3). 275–280.

Latour, Bruno. 2005. *Reassembling the social: An introduction to actor-network-theory*. Oxford: Oxford University Press.

Ledingham, John A. 2009. Cross-cultural public relations: A review of existing models with suggestions for a post-industrial public relations pyramid. *Journal of Promotion Management* 14(3–4). 225–241.

Leichty, Greg. 2003. The cultural tribes of public relations. *Journal of Public Relations Research* 15(4). 277–304.

L'Etang, Jacquie. 2009. Public relations and diplomacy in a globalized world: An issue of public communication. *American Behavioral Scientist* 53(4). 607–626.

L'Etang, Jacquie. 2012. Public relations, culture and anthropology – towards an ethnographic research agenda. *Journal of Public Relations Research* 24. 165–183.

L'Etang, Jacquie, Caroline Hodges & Magda Pieczka 2012. Culture and places: Ethnography in public relations spaces. *Public Relations Review* 38. 519–521.

L'Etang, Jacquie, David McKie, Nancy Snow & Jordi Xifra (eds.). 2016. *The Routledge handbook of critical public relations*. London: Routledge.

L'Etang, Jacquie & Magda Pieczka. 1996. *Critical perspectives in public relations*. London: International Thomson Business Press.

Liu, Brooke Fisher & Donnalyn Pompper. 2012. The crisis with no name: Defining the interplay of culture, ethnicity, and race on organizational issues and media outcomes. *Journal of Applied Communication* 40(2). 127–146.

McKie, David. 2001. Updating public relations: "New science," research paradigms, and uneven development. In Robert L. Heath (ed.), *Handbook of public relations*, 75–91. Thousand Oaks, CA: Sage.

McKie, David & Debashish Munshi. 2007. *Reconfiguring public relations: Ecology, equity, and enterprise*. London: Routledge.

McKie, David & Debashish Munshi. 2009. Theoretical black holes: A partial A to Z of missing critical thought in public relations. In Robert L. Heath, Elizabeth L. Toth & Damion Waymer (eds.), *Rhetorical and critical approaches to public relations II*, 61–75. New York: Routledge.

Men, Rita Linjuan & Wan-Hsui Sunny Tsai. 2012. How companies cultivate relationships with publics on social networking sites: Evidence from China and the United States. *Public Relations Review* 38(5). 723–730.

Mickey, Thomas J. 1997. A postmodern view of public relations: Sign and reality. *Public Relations Review* 23(3). 271–284.

Molleda, Juan-Carlos. 2010. Cross-national conflict shifting: A transnational crisis perspective in global public relations. In Robert L. Heath (ed.), *The Sage handbook of public relations*, 2nd edn., 679–690. Thousand Oaks, CA: Sage.

Moss, Danny & Barbara DeSanto (eds.). 2002. *Public relations cases: International perspectives*. London: Routledge.

Motion, Judith M. & Shirley Leitch. 1996. A discursive perspective from New Zealand: Another world view. *Public Relations Review* 22. 29–309.

Motion, Judith M. & Shirley Leitch. 2009. On Foucault: A toolbox for public relations. In Øyvind Ihlen, Betteke van Ruler & Magnus Fredriksson (eds.), *Public relations and social theory: Key figures and concepts*, 83–101. New York: Routledge.

Motion, Judith M. & C. Kay Weaver. 2005. A discourse model for critical public relations research: The Life Sciences Network and the battle for truth. *Journal of Public Relations Research* 17(1). 49–67.

Parkinson, Michael & Dee Ekachai (eds.). 2006. International *and intercultural public relations: A campaign case approach*. Boston, MA: Allyn & Bacon.

Pieczka, Magda. 2002. Public relations expertise deconstructed. *Media, Culture & Society* 24. 301–323.

Pompper, Donnalyn. 2005. "Difference" in public relations research: A case for introducing critical race theory. *Journal of Public Relations Research* 17(2). 139–169.

Rhee, Yunna. 2002. Global public relations: A cross-cultural study of excellence theory in South Korea. *Journal of Public Relations Research* 14(3). 159–184.

Rittenhofer, Iris & Chiara Valentini. 2015. A "practice turn" for global public relations: an alternative approach. *Journal of Communication Management* 19(1). 2–19.

Said, Edward W. 1978. *Orientalism*. London: Routledge & Kegan Paul.

Signitzer, Benno H. & Timothy Coombs. 1992. Public relations and public diplomacy: Conceptual convergences. *Public Relations Review* 18(2). 137–147.

Solis, Brian. 2011. *Engage!, Revised and updated: The complete guide for brands and businesses to build, cultivate, and measure success in the new web*. Hoboken, NJ: John Wiley & Sons.

Spivak, Gayatri C. 1988. Can the subaltern speak? In Cary Nelson & Lawrence Grossberg (eds.), *Marxism and the interpretation of culture*, 271–313. London: Macmillan.

Sriramesh, Krishnamurthy. 2009. The relationship between culture and public relations. In Sriramesh Krishnamurthy & Dejan Verčič (eds.), *The global public relations handbook: Theory, research, and practice*, 52–67. London: Routledge.

Sriramesh, Krishnamurthy. 2010. Globalization and public relations: Opportunities for growth and reformulation. In Robert L. Heath (ed.), *The Sage handbook of public relations*, 2nd edn., 691–707. Thousand Oaks, CA: Sage.

Sriramesh, Krishnamurthy, James E. Grunig & J. Buffington. 1992. Corporate culture and public relations. In James E. Grunig (ed.), *Excellence in public relations and communications management: Contributions to effective organizations*, 577–596. Hillsdale, NJ: Lawrence Erlbaum Associates.

Sriramesh, Krishnamurthy, James E. Grunig & David M. Dozier. 1996. Observation and measurement of two dimensions of organizational culture and their relationship to public relations. *Journal of Public Relations Research* 8(4). 229–261.

Sriramesh, Krishnamurthy & Dejan Verčič (eds.). 2009. *The global public relations handbook: Theory, research, and practice*. London: Routledge.

Taylor, Maureen. 2000. Cultural variance as a challenge to global public relations: A case study of the Coca-Cola scare in Europe. *Public Relations Review* 26. 277–293.

Terry, Valerie. 2005. Postcard from the Steppes: A snapshot of public relations and culture in Kazakhstan. *Public Relations Review* 31. 31–36.

Tilson, Donn James & Emmanuel C. Alozie. 2004. *Toward the common good: Perspectives in international public relations*. Boston: Allyn & Bacon.

Tombleson, Bridget & Katharina Wolf. 2017. Rethinking the circuit of culture: How participatory culture has transformed cross-cultural communication. *Public Relations Review* 43(1). 14–25.

Verčič, Dejan, Larissa A. Grunig & James E. Grunig. 1996. Global and specific principles of public relations: Evidence from Slovenia. In Hugh Culberson and Ni Chen (eds.), *International public relations: A comparative analysis*, 31–66. Mahwah, NJ: Lawrence Erlbaum Associates.

Wakefield, Robert I. 2010. Why culture is still essential in discussions about global public relations. In Robert L. Heath (ed.), *The Sage handbook of public relations*, 2nd edn., 659–670. Thousand Oaks, CA: Sage.

Waymer, Damion. 2012. Culture, social class, and race in public relations: An introduction. In Damion Waymer (ed.), *Culture, social class, and race in public relations*, 1–11. Lanham, MD: Lexington Books.

Weaver, C. Kay. 2001. Dressing for battle in the new global economy: Putting power, identity, and discourse into public relations theory. *Management Communication Quarterly* 15(2). 279–288.

Weaver, C. Kay. 2010. Carnivalesque activism as a public relations genre: A case study of the New Zealand group Mothers Against Genetic Engineering. *Public Relations Review* 36. 35–41.

Williams, Raymond. 1981. *Culture*. London: Fontana.

Xifra, Jordi & David McKie. 2011. Desolidifying culture: Bauman, liquid theory, and race. *Journal of Public Relations Research* 23(4). 397–411.

Zaharna, Rhonda S. 2001. "In-awareness" approach to international public relations. *Public Relations Review* 27(2). 135–148.

Zhao, Hui, Jesper Falkheimer & Mats Heide. 2017. Revisiting a social constructionist approach to crisis communication – Investigating contemporary crises in China. *International Journal of Strategic Communication* 11(5). 364–378.

Shannon A. Bowen and Nandini Bhalla

30 Ethical theories and public relations: Global issues and challenges

Abstract: This chapter discusses the ethical issues and challenges for public relations from an organizational perspective in an increasingly global environment. We introduce the overarching concepts of normative (ideal) and positive (descriptive) ethics, followed by the two most prominent forms of normative ethics: utilitarianism and deontology. We discuss the use of these frameworks in public relations and global contexts, offering numerous topics and perspectives on ethics studies from management and closely related areas to enlarge our approach to ethics and moral problem-solving in the communication management discipline.

Keywords: ethics; moral philosophy; deontology; duty; respect; intention; utilitarianism; virtue; rights; responsibility

1 Introduction

Ethics is essential in communication. As a management function, public relations is charged with communicating in a global environment swirling with different cultural traditions, beliefs, and value systems. In that environment it is important to understand the numerous ethical challenges that must be faced, as well as how rigorous forms of ethics can help identify universal truths that transcend cross-cultural differences of tradition and temporal norms. Unfailingly, ethics plays a role in public relations activities that impact, change or address social, cultural, and political environments around the globe. Even in a more tactical situation, the choices of what, when, where, and how to communicate are ethical choices. Ethics is a sense of morality or guidelines of wrong and right behavior and action that govern both personal and social behavior. Philosophers argued that ethics exist not only in the personal and social sense but also in a universal, more normative capacity, similar to a law of physics. Philosophers pointed out that ethics exist in and of themselves outside of man-made constraints or society.

Public relations, as a management function, is situated within the realm of the management literature, but also as a part of business ethics in a global society. It is the pursuit of universal, principled ethics that can help public relations in an international or global environment by transcending the challenges of the everyday, mundane, culture-bound bias to seek an analytical, consistent, and rational means of decision-making. Although ethical decision-making systems based on a rational or egalitarian approach are not infallible, they are labeled "universal" because they seek underlying moral principles that most reasonable people will agree should be valued

https://doi.org/10.1515/9783110554250-030

and upheld. These universal truths are concepts such as honesty, fairness, dignity, transparency, authenticity, good intention, and similar.

Ethical challenges in public relations can range from defining issues and facts to listening to challenges, from honesty and disclosure to conflicts of interest and the myriad choices that come with the exercise of power and influence. The list of ethical problems that can be encountered by a public relations professional is endless. Ethics can offer no quick answers, but a means of thorough analysis to help examine problems. We offer a review of literature and unique issues in global ethics and offer a summary model to assist in analyses of ethical problems. Ethical problems in public relations can range from clients asking for exaggerated news value (relatively common) to the withholding of essential safety or risk information about a product or service (less common but quite serious). Puffery in the news and fake news are all too common in today's public relations environment. And scandals such as Pacific Gas and Electric withholding vital safety information on harmful or deadly heavy water disposal illustrate the dangerous side of what can happen when the public relations professional is less than an ethical steward. But first, we introduce the overarching theory that can help analyze ethical challenges: the concepts of normative (ideal) and positive (descriptive) ethics, along with the primary theories and tests in each paradigm.

2 Normative and positive ethics

Moral philosophy or the study of ethics is largely divided into two realms: Normative ethics and positive ethics. Normative ethics emphasizes the best possible solutions, or normative goals, guiding how an organization or person (a moral agent) should resolve moral dilemmas. Normative ethics seeks to base decisions on universal moral principles that are rational and understandable, rather than those that are situation- or culture-specific and would be less applicable to other situations. Normative ethics teach us what values underlie the best decision and can be universalized. Positive ethics are useful for description and case analyses, yet normative ethics are arguably more valuable in offering the ability to resolve ethical problems. Positive ethics is largely used in the area of business management and is concerned with actual behavior in real organizations (O'Fallon and Butterfield 2005; Hunt 1993). In the public relations literature, a normative model for issues management was offered by Bowen (2004, 2005) by introducing a rational means of analyzing an ethical decision to create an ideal resolution.

The universal moral theory provided by normative ethics offers a powerful framework that can be employed for understanding ethics in a global environment. Two normative ethical theories, each discussed in more detail below, provide frameworks for use in analyses: utilitarianism (consequence-based reasoning and analytics) and deontology (principle-based reasoning and analytics). These forms of normative analysis offer a way to optimize ethical decision-making in public relations, lessen bias, and offer consistency over time.

2.1 Utilitarianism

In a utilitarian approach, ethical decisions are determined when the outcomes or consequences are deemed to provide more good outcomes than negative outcomes. The consequentialist approach often results in a public good for the majority of people. The utility of a decision is what the decision does in terms of creating consequences or outcome. In *act* utilitarianism, a decision is ethical if it creates the greatest good for the greatest number of people while minimizing harms (Elliott 2007). Mill, the progenitor of utilitarian theory, derived the classic test of "the greatest good for the greatest number" as a way to maximize ethical outcomes and potential benefits for society (Mill 1969 [1874]).

The decision resolution or alternative that creates the greatest amount of positive outcome and minimizes harms is therefore the ethical course of action. In the arguably more powerful form called *rule* utilitarianism, a decision should be considered as a rule or law to be implemented for all people, considering the consequences of similar decisions in the past (Christians 2007).

In both act and rule utilitarianism, there are caveats. Because these types of decisions always benefit the majority, they must be carefully weighed against the prospective harm to a minority (Elliott 2007). Additionally, any time the decision-makers ask to predict future consequences, unanticipated outcomes could arise. Utilitarian types of decisions often reduce people to numbers, and close balances of numbers changing could suddenly alter a decision. Finally, utilitarianism is a normative framework of ethics that is based on potential outcomes rather than on moral principles themselves, a concept to which many philosophers object – because, they argue, what is the point of creating ethics without considering morals? These drawbacks do not render act or rule utilitarianism useless, only limited. Act and rule utilitarianism are particularly helpful in decisions that need to serve the public interest, such as designing a reward system for an organization. The limitations of utilitarian theory mean that a more powerful and rigorous framework of normative ethics is needed; now we turn to deontology.

2.2 Deontology

Deontology is a normative form of duty-based ethics developed by the philosopher Immanuel Kant (1704–1824). Based on the ancient virtue ethics of Greece, in which character and arguing for truth was the ultimate goal, deontology developed along those lines but to maximize rationality and moral duty (Peck 2007). Kant thought a way to make virtue ethics more applicable and testable by anyone who was rational, basing his philosophy on equality, rather than formal education, social station, breeding, or affluence.

Deontology holds that all moral decision-makers can reason rationally, therefore all are equal and, in addition, are equally obligated to behave morally through virtue of that reason. Aside from rationality, deontology also requires moral autonomy or objective independence and moral judgment (Kant 1964 [1785]). Kant realized that, through the very nature of being human, complete objectivity is not possible. However, he encouraged decision-makers to consider numerous viewpoints, gathering information from all perspectives to a decision, and regarding that decision with as much objectivity as possible in order to arrive at a decision based on reason alone. Fairness and justice are sought (Rawls 1972). In this framework of normative decision-making, the moral autonomy required rules out bias, selfishness, capriciousness, and cultural norms that so often entertain moral decision-making (Bowen 2006).

2.2.1 Categorical imperatives

Kant (1994 [1785]) designed a three-pronged test of decisions in order to help ensure that universal moral principles were maintained, and to help reveal any unrealized areas of bias or logic decision-making. Kant (1930) offered a normative framework that should result in rigorous and analytical ethical decisions when all three conditions are met.

2.2.2 First categorical imperative: Universal duty

In this form, Kant (1964) dictates that the decision-maker ask: What is the universal moral standard that all rational decision-makers could impose as a perpetual law? In this statement, ethics are universalized because the decision-maker must weigh the merit and impact of a decision from all perspectives and time periods (Sullivan 1989). This form of the categorical imperative is meant to seek a universal moral truth that takes one out of time and place, self-interest, and situational bias. If a potential decision could be viewed by all rational beings from any perspective, maintaining a universal principle, the decision-maker moves to the second form of the test.

2.2.3 Second categorical imperative: Ends not means

Eschewing selfishness and not using other people as a means to one's own ends but respecting them as of value in and of themselves is demanded (Baron 1995). This second form of the categorical imperative demands that dignity and respect be offered to all parties around the decision (Sullivan 1989). Radical equality is in this form of the categorical imperative, regardless of education, social status, race, class, affluence, or cultural norms (Baron 1995). If the decision maintains dignity and respect for others by treating as valuable and considering the rational merit of their views, this test has been passed.

2.2.4 Third categorical imperative: Good will

The third and final form of the categorical imperative may be the most difficult to satisfy because it asked the decision-maker to test the intention driving the decision (Ross 1930). Kant (1994) asked: Is the decision made from a basis of good will and good intention alone? This highest test of deontology may require reflection and rational assessment of motives, yet offers ethical decisions that are valuable *prima facie* (on the face).

When a potential decision passes the three tests of the categorical imperative, it is deemed ethical, as this approach is thought to be the most rigorous framework in ethics (Singer 1994). Although not infallible, deontology provides the most sophisticated ethical framework available for resolving dilemmas in public relations.

2.3 Implementation in public relations practice

Scholars who study the implementation of ethics in public relations find that the practice is primarily deontological. Wright (1985) found that, although public relations professionals start their careers in a utilitarian manner, their beliefs become more deontological as they progress toward management roles. By the time public relations professionals have a number of years of experience and responsibility in the field, their beliefs are primarily deontological (Wright 1985, 1989; Bowen 2005). However, the field is still nascent with regard to ethical training.

Studies (Pratt and Rentner 1989; Bowen and Prescott 2015) found that public relations textbooks only infrequently and superficially mention ethics, and do not devote detail to the topic other than mentioning it as a standard of professionalism. Pratt and McLaughlin (1989) and Pratt and Rentner (1989) argued that the US public relations education system failed to address ethics in a theoretical, meaningful, systematic, and philosophical way. An exception is McElreath (1997), which introduced a normative approach to systematic and ethical public relations campaigns, as well as books that followed in the public relations management area (Hansen-Horn and Neff 2008; Bowen, Rawlins, and Martin 2019). An international study comparing systems of teaching ethics in public relations found that the European approach was more critical of the field and offered a more solid basis in deontological rational thought than did the US approach (Bowen and Erzikova 2013).

Jiang and Bowen (2011), in studying 50 international activist groups, also identified a heavy preference for deontological ethics among the activists. Despite their work in the public interest, activist groups were definitive in their preference for deontology. Wright (1985) also found that public relations executives were highly preferential of deontological ethics. Pratt, Im, and Montague (1994) also found that public relations professionals express a preference for deontological ethics, likely due to the complex and often global nature of the challenges involved. For example, the use of low-paid "sweatshop" labor caused a public relations crisis for Nike, who eventually had to agree to examine the conditions at contractors it used in Asia (Locke 2003). Such examples are too common when public relations professionals fail to adequately address or predict ethical expectations of stakeholders.

Studying public relations professionals in the dominant coalition of global organizations, Bowen (2002) found that as global-level responsibility increased, so did preference for deontological ethics over utilitarian forms. A global study (Bowen et al. 2006) found that the longer someone worked in public relations, the more likely he or she was to act in an ethics advisor capacity to senior management, or to build internal ethical values throughout the organization. Those who acted as ethics counselors or values managers were likely to use a deontological view of ethics (Bowen et al. 2006). Another study (Bowen 2006) found those public relations managers who displayed high degrees of independence, objectivity, or moral autonomy were more likely to be included in the strategic decision-making core of their organizations than those who held less moral autonomy. With a values orientation, the public relations professional may have to "go around" roadblocks to air ethical concerns (Neill and Barnes 2018). Still, many public relations professionals either do not have access to counsel top management on ethics, do not have the necessary knowledge to do so, or do not have the moral autonomy or courage to do so (Bowen 2008; Neill 2016), leading to infamous scandals. For example, the Toyota crisis was attributed in large part to having no public relations counsel at the top of the organization to help prevent the crisis or to assist in ethical resolution (Bowen and Zheng 2015). The same could be said for the VW emissions scandal that resulted in fines and enormous recalls worldwide (Bowen, Stacks, and Wright 2017).

Ethical failures such as the false Congressional hearing testimony authored by Hill and Knowlton leading to the Gulf War (Grunig J. 1993), or the British Petroleum CEO complaining about media intrusion while the Deep Water Horizon oil spill crisis plodded on (Atkinson 2013), or the failure of United Airlines to apologize for dragging a bloodied paying customer off a plane in favor of crew using the seat (Benoit 2018), are common examples. Had an ethical analysis been conducted at these organizations, outcomes would have been altered in favor of ethical responsibility; public relations would have been far more effective in each case. Using the ethical standards of honesty, contextual disclosure, candor, respect, and good intent offered in moral philosophy (Bowen 2010, 2016) could have prevented some of the largest public relations problems of our age.

Now that the normative forms of ethical analysis have been reviewed, we turn to exploring the areas that are common sources of ethical problems and the factors that influence how we understand ethics in public relations. We offer Table 1 to summarize the normative approaches to ethics, and the factors that can influence ethical behavior.

Table 1: Summary guidelines for ethical considerations

Normative ethics (basic): Utilitarianism: Greater good for greatest number; minimizing harms.
Normative ethics (complex): Deontology: Duty and rational autonomy to uphold universal moral principle. *Categorical imperative 1: Universal duty* *Categorical imperative 2: Ends not means* *Categorical imperative 3: Good will or good intent alone based on virtue*   = must pass all 3 categorical imperative tests

Individual factors in ethics:	Organizational and situational factors:
– Gender	– Organizational culture and climate (executive
– Age	management influence)
– Moral philosophy and value orientation (incl.	– Code of ethics
societal norms)	– Opportunity: rewards, sanctions
– Education	– Organization size and level
– Work experience	– Cross-cultural dimensions
– Religion/spirituality	
– Personality, beliefs, and values	

3 Factors in ethics and organization

As a strategic management function, public relations is placed within the business management literature; public relations needs to understand and counsel on the problems and ethical ramifications of global business in today's complex world. We use a seminal meta-study (Loe, Ferrell, and Mansfield 2000) to offer an overview of those ethical challenges and add literature relevant to public relations ethics. Based on theoretical ethical decision-making models, as well as empirical research, we review factors likely to present ethical problems or to challenge individual, organizational, (Loe, Ferrell, and Mansfield 2000) and global ethical decision-making in public relations.

3.1 Individual factors in ethics

Individual factors include personal attributes, which an individual possesses due to birth (e. g., nationality, sex, age, etc.) and uniquely impact an individual's decision-making. Individual factors also include variables that result from social surroundings and upbringing or environment. These factors can alter how a public relations professional defines and approaches ethical problems, and what is considered important in the decision-making process.

3.1.1 Gender

Marques and Azevedo-Pereira (2009) found that gender is the most significant predictor of ethical judgment: men made stricter ethical judgments than did women. Studies by Eweje and Brunton (2010) and Herington and Weaven (2008) also supported gender as a key variable in ethical decision-making. Yet in public relations, women are less likely to hold the CCO level position than men and have less access to the CEO, meaning they will have to use influence strategies of working across the executive suite (O'Rourke, Spangler, and Woods 2018) or using other means of influence (Neill and Barnes 2018).

3.1.2 Age

Wright (1985) surveyed public relations practitioners to examine the impact of age differences on moral and ethical values. Findings revealed that age has a progressive effect on moral values among public relations practitioners, particularly in the areas of basic morality and basic honesty. The older practitioners (age 36–66) appeared to have higher standards of morality than the younger practitioners (age 22–35). Kim and Choi (2003) surveyed public relations practitioners and found that Generation X appeared to have a lesser belief in being responsible for the public and clients than Baby Boomers.

3.1.3 Moral philosophy and value orientation

Much research has been conducted on various forms of moral philosophy in strategic or global business from widely varying perspectives (cf. Hunt and Vasquez-Parraga 1993; Mayo and Marks 1990; Cyriac and Dharmaraj 1994; Hegarty and Sims 1978; Marta, Singhapakdi, and Kraft 2008). In general, literature revealed that ethical decision-making is related to individuals' moral philosophy and is also based on individuals' age, professional experience, or industry type (Loe, Ferrell, and Mansfield

2000), yet the overriding factor was an institutionalized values orientation (Goodpaster 2007). In the public relations literature, similar results were found: a values orientation must be present in order for organizations to define issues as ethical problems in need of resolution (Bowen 2015).

3.1.4 Education

O'Fallon and Butterfield (2005) stated that the research "generally indicates that more education, employment or work experience is positively related to ethical decision-making" (387). Cagle and Baucus (2006) found that studying corporate ethics scandals is positively related to students' ethical decision-making, emphasizing the importance and effectiveness of ethics instruction in influencing students' attitudes. In addition, studying case studies led to positive views of the ethics of businesspeople (Cagle and Bacus 2006). These findings mirror studies in specific areas of public relations as reported by Wright (1989) and Bowen (2009), concluding that demand exists for more ethics education in public relations. Bowen and Erzikova (2013) reported that students with a philosophical orientation in studying public relations ethics were more prepared to face challenges than those who simply relied on professionalism or codes of ethics. This area is such an important one in public relations education that the Commission on Public Relations Education recommended a required course in public relations ethics for all students of the subject (Commission on Public Relations Education 2017).

3.1.5 Work experience

Higher work experience was related to higher ethical judgment, as experienced individuals appeared to be more ethically oriented and had the greater ethical intention (Eweje and Brunton 2010; Valentine and Rittenburg 2007). In contrast, Pierce and Sweeney (2010) found the relationship between the length of experience and ethicality is not simply positive or negative, but more complex, as it varies with the number of years of experience and other factors. Years of experience in public relations has been found to play a role in how often individuals engage in ethical counsel (Bowen et al. 2006), how deontological the views of public relations practitioners are (Wright 1985), and how likely the communicator is to label a problem ethical as opposed to legal (Bowen 2008).

3.1.6 Religion/spirituality

Religiosity is an important cultural value that can influence the ethical perception of managers (Ho 2010). Vitell et al. (2009) supported the belief that religion positively influences ethical decision-making. In contrast, Kurpis, Beqiri, and Helgeson (2008) reported that the commitment to moral self-improvement was more strongly associated with an individual's rating of the importance of ethics than with religiosity. These factors are positively related to the moral autonomy required by deontological ethics that are also prevalent in public relations ethics (Bowen 2004).

3.1.7 Personality, beliefs, and values

Individuals with an internal locus of control consistently had more ethical sensitivity (awareness of ethical issues) (Chan and Leung 2006) and were more likely to select ethical options than people with an external locus of control (M. Street and V. Street 2006). Ruedy and Scheweitzer (2010) found that highly mindful individuals felt a requirement to uphold higher moral standards; those with high mindfulness care more about how ethical they *are*, but less about how they are *perceived*. Mindfulness is correlated to the moral autonomy required by deontology, as well as the ability of a public relations professional to act as an activist or resister (Berger and Reber 2006) when ethically required to confront management.

3.2 Organizational and situational factors

3.2.1 Culture and climate (executive management influence)

Research has found a pervasive influence of culture and climate in the adaptation of ethics in organizational settings (Loe, Ferrell, and Mansfield 2000). Findings in this area strongly support the theoretical and managerial beliefs that managing the culture of the organization contributes to managing organizational ethics (Armstrong, Williams, and Barrett 2004; Moberg and Caldwell 2007). Sriramesh, J. Grunig, and Buffington (1992) explained that "culture is the glue that holds excellent organizations together and keeps mediocre organizations mediocre" (577). In researching the topic of organizational culture, Bowen (2004) identified many factors, such as emphasis on ethics, rewarding ethical behavior, participative management, symmetrical communication based on dialogue, a counseling role, ethics training, and a codified organizational values approach, that create a conducive environment in an organization for ethical decision-making. An organizational culture that encourages ethical decision-making is essential for public relations to operate as an ethical counsel (Bowen 2015).

3.2.2 Code of ethics

The research has found a positive correlation between the code of ethics and ethical decision-making. Employees in an organization with a written code of ethics were less likely to accept ethically questionable situations than those at organizations without one (McKinney, Emerson, and Neubert 2010). In contrast, O'Leary and Stewart (2007) and Rottig, Koufteros, and Umphress (2011) suggested that the mere presence of codes of ethics cannot ensure ethical behavior. Kim and Choi (2003) surveyed public relations practitioners and also found that older practitioners expressed a higher level of agreement with the PRSA Code of Ethics than did younger practitioners. Public relations researchers find that codes of ethics alone are not enough to spur ethical behavior (Baker and Martinson 2002), are unenforceable (Wright 1993), or lead to marginal outcomes (Bivins 1989).

3.2.3 Opportunity: rewards; sanctions

Overall, the literature suggested that the behavioral impact of sanctions and rewards is significant, based on the consequences of unethical decision-making (Craft 2013; Hegarty and Sims 1978; Hayibor and Wasieleski 2009; Premeaux 2004). Opportunity, rewards, and sanctions are consistent with normative utilitarian theory because they are based on outcomes of ethical (or unethical) behavior. Public relations research findings are consistent: offering rewards for ethical decision-making as a means of reinforcing the identification and resolution of ethical problems (Men and Bowen 2017; Bowen 2015).

3.2.4 Organization size and level

There are comparatively fewer studies examining the relationship between organization size and ethical decision-making and they have contradictory results (Craft 2013). Longenecker et al. (2006) conducted a 17-year longitudinal study and surveyed over 5,000 business professionals; there was no statistical difference between the ethical standards of large versus small businesses and they reported an upward trajectory over time of ethical standards. Organization size is considered one component of creating a positive organizational culture using symmetrical communication (Sriramesh, Grunig, J. and Buffington 1992; Grunig J. 1992; Grunig L. 1992). Perhaps a large and unwieldy organization size played into the ethical failures at Wells Fargo Bank, which created thousands of "fake" accounts to inflate sales staff figures (Cavico and Mujtaba 2017). Again, the public relations response to this crisis was slow, seemed insincere, and attempted to scapegoat employees rather than take an analytical look at organizational failures using utilitarianism or deontology.

3.2.5 Cross-cultural dimensions

Bartels (1967) was a pioneer in identifying the role of culture, such as customs, religion, law, and national identity among others, in ethical decision-making. Hofstede's (1984, 1991) dimensions of culture are often used in these studies: masculinity, power distance, uncertainty avoidance, individualism, and collectivism. Studies noted the importance of an individual's cultural norms in influencing perceptions of ethical situations (Ferrell and Gresham 1985; Hunt and Vitell 1986, 1992; Hegarty and Sims 1978; Sims 2009). Ho (2010) reported that cultural differences could explain differences in ethical perceptions, especially when one cultural group attributes moral significance to something that another culture group does not. It is important to keep these differences in mind when working in a global public relations environment.

Public relations professionals who engage in global business will undoubtedly face these ethical challenges, as well as those from different international standards. Who can forget the case of Volkswagen installing a "defeat device" in its cars to falsify emissions data during US air quality tests? The public relations mistakes at Volkswagen were the ethical failure of allowing such devious engineering practices, failing to anticipate the reaction of stakeholders and publics to such blatant deception, and failing to issue honest communication as soon as questions arose (Bowen, Stacks, and Wright 2017).

Yet differences in understanding an action as being unethical might differ across different countries. For example, Carter (2000) argued that certain kinds of bribery that act as "grease" payments or facilitating payments are actually legal in certain countries. In most countries, bribery has generally been eschewed and declared illegal; however, it still poses a challenge to communication managers who must work across international systems in which bribery is commonplace. For example, Walmart generated a public relations crisis and has seen falling stock process since news broke of its bribery of Mexican officials to open more Walmart stores (Derr 2012). Walmart's headquarters in Arkansas shut down the internal investigation into bribery allegations, rather than handle the matter ethically, and will face fines and loss of credibility.

In this concise overview, we have touched on many of the ethical issues that create problems for public relations professionals. In fact, there are more ethical problems and thornier challenges than one chapter can address. The standards of utilitarianism and deontology offer guidelines to help analyze exceptionally complex ethical issues that public relations professionals in a global environment consistently address. In summary, we refer the reader to Table 1, which outlines the ethical frameworks available to help unravel both the consequences and the duties inherent in such multifaceted dilemmas of public relations.

4 Importance of public relations ethics and conclusions

Ethical decision-makers should consider the normative ethic underlying decisions along with the positive implementation of that decision. Act and rule utilitarianism can help weight specific consequences to assess actions in light of public interest. Considering each of the areas listed above in terms of international and global ethical guidelines allows the public relations professional to determine true public interest; or, how to serve the greatest good for the greatest number of people through strategic communication management. Guarding against infringing upon the rights of a minority is essential, and anticipating unforeseen consequences can help insulate an organization from the default inherent in a utilitarian normative ethics paradigm.

Normative ethics or deontology offers a more powerful and rigorous paradigm for application to a complex ethical dilemma or those not based exclusively in the public interest or consequence. Competing rights or multiple wrongs often provide the complex types of scenarios that can only be analyzed by the deontological approach. Deontology, heavily based in rights, duties, moral autonomy, and rationality, seeks a radical equality, for all decision-makers are equally obligated under a universal moral principle to do the right thing regardless of personal gratification, self-interest, cultural norms, or other biasing factors.

Of course, there are limitations with applying normative theories of ethics. The increasingly global environment discussed above offers numerous factors that can impact value systems, making finding universal moral norms and universally "good" outcomes a challenge. The information environment can also offer limitations because both forms of normative ethics require that the decision-maker is aware of all relevant information to examine duties or potential outcomes. In situations with an imperfect information environment, unknowns, or limited access to accurate data, these theories of ethics can become challenging. In such situations, it is best to combine both forms of normative ethics to examine as much is known about the situation. Despite these challenges, using analytical, normative forms of ethics leads to better, more responsible, less biased, and more consistent outcomes over time that can help organizations build relationships.

Public relations can create value for an organization through building understanding, resolving problems, and preventing crises through the enactment of ethical analyses using the philosophies presented above. In doing so, public relations enters a normative role for society: As Bowen (2010) argued, a greater social good is created through facilitating understanding in publics, stakeholders, organizations, governments, and cross-culturally; offering greater responsibility, consideration of consequences, and rectitude toward the public interest; providing a shared space in which ethical examination is encouraged; and fostering rational thought, duty, equality, autonomy, dignity, and good intent. Using the ethical theories detailed above allows public relations to help organizations face and understand the numerous challenges we have delineated above, as well as perform an ethical social role and face problems as opportunities to enhance ethics.

References

Armstrong, Robert W., Robert J. Williams & J. Douglas Barrett. 2004. The impact of banality, risky shift and escalating commitment on ethical decision making. *Journal of Business Ethics* 55. 365–370. doi:10.1023/B:BUSI.0000043491.10007.9a (accessed 2 April 2020).

Atkinson, Ted. 2013. Blood Petroleum: True Blood, the BP Oil Spill, and Fictions of Energy/Culture. *Journal of American Studies* 47(1). 213–229.

Baker, Sherry & David L. Martinson. 2002. Out of the red-light district: Five principles for ethically provocative public relations. *Public Relations Quarterly* 47(3). 15–19.

Baron, Marcia W. 1995. *Kantian ethics almost without apology.* Ithaca, NY: Cornell University Press.

Bartels, Robert. 1967. A model for ethics in marketing. *The Journal of Marketing* 31 (January). 20–26.

Benoit, William. L. 2018. Crisis and image repair at united airlines: Fly the unfriendly skies. *Journal of International Crisis and Risk Communication Research* 1(1). 11–26. https://doi.org/10.30658/jicrcr.1.1.2 (accessed 2 April 2020).

Berger, Bruce & Brian Reber. 2006. *Gaining influence in public relations: The role of resistance in practice.* Mahwah, NJ: Lawrence Erlbaum.

Bivins, Thomas. 1989. Are public relations texts covering ethics adequately? *Journal of Mass Media Ethics* 4(1). 39–52.

Bowen, Shannon A. 2002. Elite executives in issues management: The role of ethical paradigms in decision making. *Journal of Public Affairs* 2(4). 270–283.

Bowen, Shannon A. 2004. Organizational factors encouraging ethical decision making: An exploration into the case of an exemplar. *Journal of Business Ethics* 52(4). 311–324.

Bowen, Shannon A. 2005. A practical model for ethical decision making in issues management and public relations. *Journal of Public Relations Research* 17(3). 191–216.

Bowen, Shannon A. 2006. Autonomy in communication: Inclusion in strategic management and ethical decision-making, a comparative case analysis. *Journal of Communication Management* 10(4). 330–352.

Bowen, Shannon A. 2008. A state of neglect: Public relations as corporate conscience or ethics counsel. *Journal of Public Relations Research* 20(3). 271–296.

Bowen, Shannon A. 2009. All glamour, no substance? How public relations majors and potential majors in an exemplar program view the industry and function. *Public Relations Review* 35. 402–410.

Bowen, Shannon A. 2010. The nature of good in public relations: What should be its normative ethic? In R. L. Heath (ed.), *Handbook of public relations*, 569–583. Thousand Oaks, CA: Sage.

Bowen, Shannon A. 2015. Exploring the role of the dominant coalition in creating an ethical culture for internal stakeholders. *Public Relations Journal* 9(1). 1–23. https://prjournal.instituteforpr.org/wp-content/uploads/2015v09n01Bowen.pdf (accessed 4 April 2020).

Bowen, Shannon A. 2016. Clarifying ethics terms in public relations from A to V, authenticity to virtue. BledCom special issue of PR review sleeping (with the) media: Media relations. *Public Relations Review*, 42. 564–572. http://dx.doi.org/10.1016/j.pubrev.2016.03.012 (accessed 2 April 2020).

Bowen, Shannon. A., Robert L. Heath, Jaesub Lee, Graham Painter, Frank J. Agraz, David McKie & Margalit Toledano. 2006. *The business of truth: A guide to ethical communication perspective*. San Francisco: International Association of Business Communicators Research Foundation.

Bowen, Shannon A. & Elina Erzikova. 2013. The international divide in public relations ethics education: Advocacy versus autonomy. *Public Relations Journal* 7(1).1–41.

Bowen, Shannon A. & Paul Prescott. 2015. Kant's contribution to the ethics of communication. *Ethical Space: The International Journal of Communication Ethics* 12(2). 38–44.

Bowen, Shannon A. & Yue Zheng. 2015. Auto recall crisis, framing, and ethical response: Toyota's missteps. *Public Relations Review* 41(1). 40–49. http://www.sciencedirect.com/science/article/pii/S036381111400160X (accessed 4 April 2020).

Bowen, Shannon A., Don W. Stacks & Donald K. Wright. 2017. VW emissions scandal: An example of bad public relations on a worldwide scale and the defeat device that defeated a worldwide reputation. In J. V. Turk, J. Paluszek & J. Valin (eds.), *Public relations case studies from around the world*, 2nd edn. 3–21. New York: Peter Lang Publishing.

Bowen, Shannon. A., Brad Rawlins & Thomas R. Martin. 2019. *An overview of the public relations function*, 2nd edn. New York: Business Expert Press.

Cagle, Julie A. & Melissa S. Baucus. 2006. Case studies of ethics scandals: Effects on ethical perceptions of finance students. *Journal of Business Ethics* 64(3). 213–229.

Carter, Craig R. 2000. Ethical issues in international buyer-supplier relationships: a dyadic examination. *Journal of operations management* 18(2). 191–208.

Cavico, Frank J. & Bahaudin G. Mujtaba. 2017. Wells Fargo's fake accounts scandal and its legal and ethical implications for management. *SAM Advanced Management Journal* 82(2). 4–19.

Chan, Samuel Y. S. & Philomena Leung. 2006. The effects of accounting students' ethical reasoning and personal factors on their ethical sensitivity. *Managerial Auditing Journal* 27(4). 436–457. doi:10.1108/02686900610661432 (accessed 2 April 2020).

Christians, Clifford G. 2007. Utilitarianism in media ethics and its discontents. *Journal of Mass Media Ethics* 22(2). 113–131. doi:10.1080/08900520701315640 (accessed 2 April 2020).

Commission on Public Relations Education. 2017. *Fast forward: The 2017 report on undergraduate public relations education*. http://www.commissionpred.org/commission-reports/fast-forward-foundations-future-state-educators-practitioners/ (accessed 4 April 2020).

Craft, Jana L. 2013. A review of the empirical ethical decision-making literature: 2004–2011. *Journal of Business Ethics* 117(2). 221–259.

Cyriac, K. & Raj Dharmaraj. 1994. Machiavellianism in Indian management. *Journal of Business Ethics* 13(4). 281–286. doi:10.1007/BF00871674 (accessed 2 April 2020).

Derr, Cammi L. 2012. Ethics and leadership. *Journal of Leadership, Accountability and Ethics* 9(6). 66–71.

Eweje, Gabriel & Margaret Brunton. 2010. Ethical perceptions of business students in a New Zealand university: Do gender, age and work experience matter? *Business Ethics: A European Review* 79(1). 95–111. doi:10.111 1/j.1467-8608.2009.0158 1.x (accessed 2 April 2020).

Elliott, Deni. 2007. Getting Mill right. *Journal of Mass Media Ethics* 22(2–3). 100–112.

Ferrell, Odies C. & Larry G. Gresham.1985. A contingency framework for understanding ethical decision making in marketing. *Journal of marketing* 49(3). 87–96.

Goodpaster, Kenneth E. 2007. *Conscience and corporate culture*. New York: Blackwell.

Grunig, James E. 1992. Symmetrical systems of internal communication. In James E. Grunig (ed.), *Excellence in public relations and communication management*, 531–575. Hillsdale, NJ: Lawrence Erlbaum.

Grunig, James. E. 1993. Public relations and international affairs: Effects, ethics and responsibility. *Journal of International Affairs* 47.137–162.

Grunig, Larissa A. 1992. How public relations/communication departments should adapt to the structure and environment of an organization … and what they actually do. In James E. Grunig (ed.), *Excellence in public relations and communication management*, 467–481. Hillsdale, NJ: Lawrence Erlbaum.

Hansen-Horn, Tricia & Bonita Dostal Neff. 2008. *Public relations: From theory to practice*. Boston: Pearson Allyn & Bacon.

Hayibor, Sefa & David M. Wasieleski. 2009. Effects of the use of the availability heuristic on ethical decision-making in organizations. *Journal of Business Ethics* 84(1). 151–165.

Hegarty, W. Harvey & Henry P. Sims. 1978. Some determinants of unethical decision behavior: An experiment. *Journal of Applied Psychology* 63(4). 451–547. doi:10.1037/0021-9010.63.4.451 (accessed 2 April 2020).

Herington, Carmel & Scott Weaven. 2008. Improving consistency for DIT results using cluster analysis. *Journal of Business Ethics* 80(3). 499–514. doi:10.1007/s10551-007-9451-z (accessed 2 April 2020).

Ho, Jo Ann. 2010. Ethical perception: are differences between ethnic groups situation dependent? *Business Ethics: A European Review* 19(2). 154–182. doi:10.1111/j.1467-8608.2010.01583.x (accessed 2 April 2020).

Hofstede, Geert. 1984. *Culture's consequences: international differences in work-related values*. Abridged edition. Beverly Hills, CA: Sage.

Hofstede, Geert. 1991. *Cultures and organizations: software of the mind*. London: McGraw Hill.

Hunt, Shelby. D. 1993. Objectivity in marketing theory and research. *The Journal of Marketing* 57(2). 76–91.

Hunt, Shelby D. & Arturo Z. Vasquez-Parraga. 1993. Organizational consequences, marketing ethics, and salesforce supervision. *Journal of Marketing Research* 30(1). 78–90.

Hunt, Shelby D. & Scott Vitell. 1986. A general theory of marketing ethics. *Journal of Macromarketing* 6(1). 5–16.

Jiang, Hua & Shannon A. Bowen. 2011. Ethical decision making in issues management within activist groups. *Public Relations Journal* 5(1). 1–21. https://prjournal.instituteforpr.org/wp-content/uploads/Ethical-Decision.pdf (accessed 4 April 2020).

Kant, Immanuel. 1930. *Lectures on ethics*. Louis Infield (trans.). Cambridge: Hackett.

Kant, Immanuel. 1964 [1785]. *Groundwork of the metaphysic of morals*. H. J. Paton (trans.). New York: Harper & Row.

Kant, Immanuel. 1994 [1785/1797]. *Ethic philosophy*. J. W. Ellington (trans.). Cambridge: Hackett.

Kim, Yungwook & Youjin Choi. 2003. Ethical standards appear to change with age and ideology: A survey of practitioners. *Public Relations Review* 29(1). 79–89.

Kurpis, Lada V., Mirjeta S. Beqiri & James G. Helgeson. 2008. The effects of commitment to moral self-improvement and religiosity on ethics of business students. *Journal of Business Ethics* 80(3). 447–463.

Locke, Richard M. 2003. The Promise and Perils of Globalization: The Case of Nike, Inc. In Thomas A. Kochan and Richard Schmalensee (eds.), *Management: Inventing and Delivering Its Future*, 39–70. Cambridge, MA: MIT Press.

Loe, Terry W., Linda Ferrell & Phylis Mansfield. 2000. A review of empirical studies assessing ethical decision making in business. *Journal of Business Ethics* 25(3). 185–204.

Longenecker, Justin G., Carlos W. Moore, J. William Petty, Leslie E. Palich & Joseph A. McKinney. 2006. Ethical attitudes in small businesses and large corporations: Theory and empirical findings from a tracking study spanning three decades. *Journal of Small Business Management* 44(2). 167–183. doi:10.111l/j.l540-627X.2006.00162.x (accessed 2 April 2020).

Marques, Pedro Augusto & José Azevedo-Pereira. 2009. Ethical ideology and ethical judgments in the Portuguese accounting profession. *Journal of Business Ethics* 86(2). 227–242. doi:10.1007/s10551-008-9845-6 (accessed 2 April 2020).

Marta, Janet, Anusorn Singhapakdi & Kenneth Kraft. 2008. Personal characteristics underlying ethical decisions in marketing situations: A survey of small business managers. *Journal of Small Business Management* 46(4). 589–606. doi:10.1111/j.1540-627X.2008.00258.x (accessed 2 April 2020).

Mayo, Michael A. & Lawrence J. Marks. 1990. An empirical investigation of a general theory of marketing ethics. *Journal of the Academy of Marketing Science* 18(2). 163–171.

McElreath, Michael P. 1997. *Managing systematic and ethical public relations campaigns*, 2nd edn. New York: Brown and Benchmark.

McKinney, Joseph A., Tisha L. Emerson & Mitchell J. Neubert. 2010. The effects of ethical codes on ethical perceptions of actions toward stakeholders. *Journal of Business Ethics* 97(4). 505–516. doi:10.1007/s10551-010-0521-2 (accessed 2 April 2020).

Men, Rita L. & Shannon A. Bowen. 2017. *Excellence in internal communication management*. New York: Business Expert Press.

Moberg, Dennis & David F. Caldwell. 2007. An exploratory investigation of the effect of ethical culture in activating moral imagination. *Journal of Business Ethics* 73(2). 193–204. doi:10.1007/s10551-006-9190-6 (accessed 2 April 2020).

Mill, John Stuart. 1969 [1874]. Nature. In J. M. Robson (ed.), *Essays on ethics, religion and society*, 375–402. Toronto: University of Toronto Press.

Neill, Marlene S. 2016. Accredited vs. non-accredited: How accreditation impacts perceptions and readiness to provide ethics counsel. *Public Relations Review* 42. 856–866. doi:10.1016/j.pubrev.2016.08.002 (accessed 2 April 2020).

Neill, Marlene S. & Barnes, Amy O. 2018. *Public relations ethics: Senior P.R. pros tell us how to speak up and keep your job*. New York: Business Expert Press.

O'Fallon, Michael J. & Kenneth D. Butterfield. 2005. A review of the empirical ethical decision-making literature: 1996–2003. *Journal of Business Ethics* 59(4). 375–413.

O'Leary, Conor & Jenny Stewart. 2007. Governance factors affecting internal auditors' ethical decision-making: An exploratory study. *Managerial Auditing Journal* 22(8). 787–808.

O'Rourke, James S. IV, James Spangler & Richard Woods. 2018. Total integration: Working across the c-suite. In Roger Bolton, Don W. Stacks & Eliot Mizrachi (eds.), *The new era of the CCO: The essential role of communication in a volatile world*. 107–122. New York: Business Expert Press.

Peck, Lee Anne. 2007. Sapere Aude! The importance of a moral education in Kant's doctrine of virtue. *Journal of Mass Media Ethics* 22(2–3). 208–214.

Pierce, Bernard & Breda Sweeney. 2010. The relationship between demographic variables and ethical decision making of trainee accountants. *International Journal of Auditing* 14(1). 79–99.

Pratt, Cornelius B. & Gerald W. McLaughlin. 1989. Ethical inclinations of public relations majors. *Journal of Mass Media Ethics* 4(1). 68–91.

Pratt, Catherine A. & Terry Lynn Rentner. 1989. What's really being taught about ethical behavior. *Public Relations Review* 15(1). 53–66.

Pratt, Corneilius B., SungHoon Im & Scarlett N. Montague. 1994. Investigating the application of deontology among U.S. public relations practitioners. *Journal of Public Relations Research* 6(4). 241–266.

Premeaux, Shane. F. 2004. The link between management behavior and ethical philosophy in the wake of the Enron convictions. *Journal of Business Ethics* 85(1). 13–25. doi:10.1007/s10551-0 (accessed 2 April 2020).

Rawls, John. 1972. *A Theory of Justice*. Cambridge, MA: Harvard University Press.

Ross, William David. 1930. *The right and the good*. Oxford: Oxford University Press.

Rottig, Daniel, Xenophon Koufteros & Elizabeth Umphress 2011. Formal infrastructure and ethical decision making: An empirical investigation and implications for supply management. *Decision Sciences Journal* 42(1). 163–204. doi:10.1111/j.1540-5915.2010.003 (accessed 2 April 2020).

Ruedy, Nicole E. & Maurice E. Schweitzer. 2010. In the moment: The effect of mindfulness on ethical decision making. *Journal of Business Ethics* 95(1). 73–87. doi:10.1007/s10551-011-079 (accessed 2 April 2020).

Sims, Randi. L. 2009. Collective versus individualist national cultures: Comparing Taiwan and U.S. employee attitudes toward unethical business practices. *Business & Society* 48 (1). 39–59. doi:10.1177/0007650307299224 (accessed 2 April 2020).

Singer, Peter. 1994. *Ethics*. Oxford: Oxford University Press.

Sriramesh, Krishnamurthy, James E. Grunig & Jody Buffington. 1992. Corporate culture and public relations. In James E. Grunig (ed.), *Excellence in public relations and communication management*. 577–595. Hillsdale, NJ: Lawrence Erlbaum.

Street, Marc & Vera L. Street. 2006. The effects of escalating commitment on ethical decision-making. *Journal of Business Ethics* 64(4). 343–356. doi:10.1007/s10551/005-5836-z. (accessed 2 April 2020).

Sullivan, Roger J. 1989. *Immanuel Kant's Moral Theory*. Cambridge University Press, Cambridge.

Valentine, Sean R. & Terri L. Rittenburg. 2007. The ethical decision making of men and women executives in international business situations. *Journal of Business Ethics* 71(2). 125–134. doi:10.1007/s10551-006-9129-y (accessed 2 April 2020).

Vitell, Scott John, Mark N. Bing, H. Kristl Davison, Anthony P. Ammeter, Bart L. Garner, & Milorad M. Novicevic. 2009. Religiosity and moral identity: The mediating role of self-control. *Journal of Business Ethics* 88(4). 601–613. doi:10.1007/s10551-008-9980-0 (accessed 2 April 2020).

Wright, Donald. K. 1985. Can age predict the moral values of public relations practitioners? *Public Relations Review* 11(1). 51–60.

Wright, Donald. K. 1989. Ethics research in public relations: An overview. *Public Relations Review* 15(2). 3–5. doi:10.1016/S0363-8111(89)80049-9 (accessed 2 April 2020).

Wright, Donald. K. 1993. Enforcement dilemma: Voluntary nature of public relations codes. *Public Relations Review* 19(1). 13–20.

Afterwords

Clea Bourne and Lee Edwards

31 Critical reflections on the field

Abstract: In this chapter, we argue that the effect of public relations on society merits further attention from scholars and practitioners. In particular, the advent of digitisation, algorithmic technologies and AI more generally, have been under-examined. In these areas, greater reflexivity and scrutiny of how such tools are used in the industry, and the ways they might perpetuate or challenge in-built biases, is sorely needed. In a communications landscape characterised by the co-existence of digital utopias, post-truth politics and fake news, we suggest that the challenges raised by these new technologies relate to two key issues: voice and diversity, both of which are deeply affected by digital technologies. The industry's capacity to adequately reflect on its role in enhancing or limiting these inequalities depends on adopting a renewed ethics in pedagogy and practice that adequately equips practitioners with the reflective and analytical skills to not only use digital technologies, but also to account for their effects as part of the arsenal of communications tactics in the 21st century.

Keywords: digital; Artificial Intelligence; algorithms; ethics; voice; diversity

1 Introduction

The "industrialisation" of public relations (PR) has been marked by the growth and spread of this industry across the globe, so that today PR firms count among some of the most wealthy and influential global conglomerates in existence. According to industry research, the global PR industry grew by 5 % in 2018, with the top 250 public relations firms reporting fee income of around US$12.3bn in 2018, up from US$11.7bn the previous year (Sudhaman 2019). While industry growth is positive from a commercial perspective, it is also significant because of the impact that PR has on society. This is a dimension of the profession's work that attracts somewhat less attention in scholarship than commercial effects, but in this chapter, we argue that the contemporary communications environment, and the rise in particular of digital technologies, including artificial intelligence (AI), mean that recognising and accounting for the societal impact of strategic communications work is increasingly important.

Existing scholarship does recognise the social role played by PR in a range of arenas. For example, PR campaigns by international development agencies have encouraged the acceptance of global programmes for immunisation against diseases such as polio and measles, although each of these campaigns has suffered PR setbacks (Curtin and Gaither 2007; Jacobson 2012). Not-for-profit organisations depend heavily on PR to raise awareness of issues such as food security, climate change and various forms of social inequality. In financial markets, PR has encouraged new forms

https://doi.org/10.1515/9783110554250-031

of borrowing and banking that change the way consumers understand and engage with financial systems and institutions (Brodsky and Oakes 2017; Marous 2019). PR has helped to package the BRIC nations as an investment idea, thus changing the shape of investment markets as well as international political relations (Bourne 2015). Likewise, governments and supranationals, such as the World Bank, have used PR techniques to globalise the tenets of neoliberalism, a political ideology associated with free trade and minimal government intervention in business (Miller and Dinan 2007).

The quality of democracy has been directly affected by public relations through its use in historical civil rights struggles in the US and elsewhere, including the NAACP, and contemporary movements such as Everyday Sexism, #MeToo, Black Lives Matter and Stand with Standing Rock. Across the global south, PR has been fundamental to the visibility of causes such as the Landless movement in Brazil, Cuba Solidarity Campaign, the Umbrella Movement in Hong Kong, and the #FeesMustFall movement in South Africa. On a global scale, PR has supported activists' response to the global financial crisis and ensuing recession, through movements and projects such as Occupy, Jubilee Debt and the Robin Hood Tax, and to ongoing environmental movements (Bourne 2017; Demetrious 2019; Moscato 2019; Straughan 2004).

Less positively, communications professionals have contributed to serious infringements of rights and freedoms. For example, Southern Publicity Association, one of the first formal public relations companies in the US, played a significant role in the revival of the Ku Klux Klan in the 1920s (Cutlip 1994), while almost 100 years later, in the digital era, public relations and marketing tactics using big data have been key to successfully disseminating disinformation that has distorted the political, social and electoral landscape in a range of countries since 2010 (Briant 2018; Ong and Cabanes 2018; Wasserman 2017). Public relations companies have provided support for industries such as tobacco, oil and pharmaceuticals, where the main objective has been to protect profit rather than the public interest and tactics have included rhetorical manipulation of facts, "astroturfing" (creating artificial grassroots organisations), and avoiding regulatory controls by using social media for promotion (Greenberg, Knight, and Westersund 2011; Kozinets 2019; Shir-Raz & Avraham 2017). At the organisational level, public relations has also been implicated in organisational activities designed to silence opposition in order to protect their legitimacy (Dimitrov 2018).

Despite this clear role in constructing the democratic and social health of the societies we inhabit, commercial and professional priorities tend to focus on securing influence within organisations and on their behalf, rather than reflecting on and learning from the consequences of these broader effects. This was recently evident in PR's failure to acknowledge its role in the 2008 financial crisis, following years of promoting financial markets as never-ending "boom" – "and to hell with bust" (Pitcher 2008: 69). Similarly, industry associations have actively obscured the occupation's history and current role in the production and circulation of disinformation, neatly allocating responsibility to other groups such as digital platforms (Facebook in particular) and media-illiterate audiences (Edwards 2020). And in response to economic stagnation in many developed countries during the post-crisis decade, the digital world, and AI in particular, have been positioned by PR practitioners as the necessary "shot in the arm" for mature economies. While the race is now on for technological and commercial supremacy in these fields (Bourne, 2019), the necessary optimism for reinvigorating growth through digital innovations is increasingly accompanied by recognition of the attendant problems such innovations have wrought across society and the public sphere – including digital disruption of communication channels and the rapid spread of emotive content and "fake news".

These examples of PR practice show that social in/justice is often a focus, outcome or side effect of the work practitioners do. However, the chances of introspection by the profession are usually scarce, because PR is constantly called on to address more pressing issues. We suggest that this somewhat casual approach to the effects of practice must be addressed, so that social in/justice is given a more prominent place in both practical and academic analyses. The professional, ethical and social challenges of this complex era deserve urgent attention, considered not only in terms of the impact they have on organisations, but also taking into account the "work" they do in wider society.

2 Digital utopias and the post-truth era: Landscapes of practice

2.1 Digital utopias

Accounting for PR's current influence in wider society begins with understanding new landscapes of PR practice based on platform capitalism. Data has become pivotal to modern capitalism as a means of maintaining economic growth in the face of sluggish production. Digital platforms have emerged as a new business model for extracting, circulating and controlling vast amounts of data (Beer 2019; Srnicek 2017). It is not the data itself that is powerful, but the analytical insights, which are presented as the means by which "hidden" value might be unearthed; helping people manage their health, relationships, creditworthiness, voting, and other behaviours (Beer 2019).

Central to this data-based capitalism is speed, which is partly enabled through the feeling of acceleration being cultivated by the data analytics industry, and in particular through the burgeoning world of artificial intelligence, or AI. AI includes a host of activities, including cognitive robotics and human-agent–robot interaction (Dignum 2018). However, much of what we currently call AI is "machine learning", where machines are taught through complex algorithms, enabled by greater 21st-century computing power. The PR industry's response to data and AI has been to "ready" practitioners for associated demand for skills. Those intermediaries who are most able to work with digital platforms and AI tools, locate value in data, narrate and then attach meaning to data, are increasingly influential (Beer 2019: 28). Thus, digital capability promises greater professional influence and legitimacy for PR practitioners, advertisers and marketers who enthusiastically embrace digital technologies (Valentini 2015) for new approaches to stakeholder relations, audience targeting, content generation and programme evaluation. One UK industry survey estimates that at least 150 AI tools are now actively used in PR (Slee 2018).

Throughout the 2000s, the PR profession was particularly optimistic about social media's potential to improve direct relations with stakeholders, by bypassing the media's gatekeeping role. A more participatory culture had arisen, in which active, engaged consumers became media content producers themselves (Hutchins and Tindall 2016). As platform capitalism's "speed" imperative closed the temporal gap between production and consumption of messages and ideas, PR's utopian ideal was a more one-to-one exchange of knowledge and ideas between organisations and their publics (Valentini 2015). By the 2010s, PR practitioners had convinced many client organisations to create their own digital media centres, enabling companies with "good stories to tell" to do their own storytelling (Lieb 2017: 1). Content production could be augmented and automated through computational algorithms and AI software, able to turn data into stories. In addition, digital techniques presented more quantifiable measures, offering a solution to the evaluation conundrum that has plagued the PR industry in particular (Royle and Laing 2014; Zerfass, Verčič, and Volk 2017).

AI will mean PR's impact on society is felt in new ways and we argue that it constitutes an urgent location for reflexive critique. PR's utopian views of digital technologies have already led to complacency over the impact of the industry's use of digital platforms and technologies on the public sphere. Digitisation and participatory culture forced newsrooms to downsize, weakening the media's gatekeeper role, while forcing journalists to draw on (possibly biased and unchecked) PR content. Meanwhile, content production can only become more personalised by data-tracking consumers, employees and other stakeholders. Greater personalisation encouraged more investors to financially capitalise on algorithms in order to manipulate public sentiment. On social media platforms, this has resulted in clustering groups of people together to feed them select information via search engine bias, thus creating digital echo chambers or "filter bubbles" (Bakir and McStay 2018). Beyond social media, AI technologies now datafy people's emotions, tracking them while they browse computer devices, shop or simply walk through the streets, in order to develop supposedly appropriate responses to marketing campaigns (McStay 2016).

Grey areas include the ability of targeted audiences to choose whether or not their data is shared; their ability to understand who their data is being shared with, for how long and for what purpose; and more broadly, the desirability of having promotional content increasingly inserted into what used to be private space (Edwards 2018b). The ethics of using data services to scrape audience data are scarcely raised in the PR industry, which suggests that questions such as these are largely neglected by practitioners. Moreover, other uses of digital technologies such as the deployment of bots and algorithms, which directly affect the quality of political and social life, remain under-examined. This includes the impact of AI technologies and filter bubbles on the spread of "fake news" and "post-truth" politics, as discussed in the next section.

2.2 Post-truth and fake news

The rise of fake news marked the profession's first outward acknowledgement of a visible dent in PR's digital utopia. One of the hallmarks of post-truth politics is the level of heated emotion and sheer noise it produces. This noise sucks in audience time and attention, making fake news a highly effective form of misdirection in today's public sphere. It helps to enforce our silence by redirecting public attention away from controversial issues.

Fake news does not just take the form of text-based storytelling. Equally troubling are developments such as "deep fake videos" which can now be developed with machine learning. Public scepticism about PR tools such as press releases is not as well-developed for content such as social media videos, which are often more emotive than written communication, evoking warmth, empathy, sadness, and/or anger. Today, anyone from state-backed propagandists to trolls can access AI technologies to create "deep fake videos" (Schwartz 2018). AI technologies can alter what a speaker says in an existing video, combine two disparate videos, or create artificial video material from scratch. Deep fake video can thus skew information and manipulate beliefs, creating wider chasms between communities and between the powerful and the marginalised (Schwartz 2018).

Research shows that audiences are at best sceptical about the credibility of news generally, and while fake news may be actively assessed for its veracity using a range of cues, any notion of a singular "truth" is increasingly questionable (Waisbord 2018). The integration of digital techniques into online publicity – for example, increasing affective content to maximise shareability; automating circulation via algorithms; and the use of bots to enhance circulation – also increase audience tendencies to use online popularity cues such as likes and shares as a justification for circulating news, fake or otherwise. The end result is that the quality of public debate about critical social and political issues is undermined.

While some journalists point to the connection between PR and fake news on digital platforms, the PR industry has been rushing to position itself as the antidote to fake news (Czarnecki 2017). Industry narratives suggest that PR practitioners can be a trusted source of information for both journalists and audiences, protecting organisations from the threat of fake news and providing support and toolkits for audiences and organisations who want to verify the news they consume (e. g. Chartered Institute of Public Relations 2017; Public Relations and Communications Association 2017;

Staunton 2017). However, such narratives are optimistic to say the least, given that they implicitly deny the long heritage of disinformation that has characterised the PR industry. They also ignore the fact that mainstream communication strategies and tactics are directly implicated in the current disinformation crisis. Cambridge Analytica deployed widely used marketing techniques to pursue its clients' objectives, and was heralded by the marketing industry as an exemplary model of practice only a year before its fall from grace (Nix 2016). Ong and Cabanes (2018) show that, in the Philippines, a subcultural promotional industry has been constructed around fake news, and the new "disinformation architects" that populate this industry are practitioners whose day jobs are in the mainstream industries. These facts provide incontrovertible evidence that the industry's public approach to the post-truth era and the disinformation debate is at best ignorant and at worst actively misleading (Valentini, 2020).

3 Social in/justice – voice, ethics, diversity

As noted in our introduction, the significance of these new landscapes for public relations relates not only to their impact on organisations, but also to their effects on various forms of social in/justice. In this section we discuss two main areas where such effects appear: issues of voice and diversity.

3.1 Voice

For PR to support social justice, it has to be able to facilitate voice for marginalised groups. Voice that matters is more than simply speaking out; it is articulated in a context where it is understood as a valuable intervention in society, and as such it is inextricably linked to a politicised form of recognition and the redistribution of power (Couldry 2010; Edwards 2018b; Honneth 1996). Couldry and Powell (2014: 4) maintain, however, that "something similar to 'voice' is required in this new world" of algorithmic-driven automation, because the value of voice is "not immediately compatible with a world saturated with the automated aggregation of analytic mechanisms that are not, even in principle, open to any continuous human interpretation or review".

Issues to do with voice in the digital age are further exacerbated by the introduction of digital data banks, which have proved to exacerbate inequalities across all societies where these technologies operate. For example, AI programs designed to police criminal activity, recruit employees and issue loans have all been shown to incorporate bias against women and people of colour (Cossins 2018: 12; Eubanks 2017). Following Couldry and Powell (2014), these new systems, with their automatic sensing and calculative logic, eliminate the accountability of voice as a subjective form of expression.

3.2 Diversity

PR professionals cannot successfully intervene in the spaces where AI algorithms exhibit bias and erode human rights if the profession itself does not represent society. Digital platforms are not "neutral" technologies, their design is purposeful, exhibiting bias and eroding human rights (Noble 2018). This is painfully obvious to those living in liminal or marginalised space (digital or material) and vulnerable to exclusion, but for those who are not subjected to it, it is notoriously easy to ignore or mistake for a "natural" state of affairs. Indeed, the faith in numbers that neoliberalism fosters through its reification of quantifiable data leads to an even stronger belief that whatever is produced by data is a reflection of the "real" world (Kennedy 2016). It follows that, unless the public relations profession includes practitioners who are familiar with the lived experience of marginalisation, it will remain blissfully unaware of the implications of its work for some of the most vulnerable groups in society. The state of affairs is exacerbated if the majority of PR practitioners lack the capacity to design and/or work with digital architectures and user experience, because they will be unable to intervene in such spaces, even if they wanted to.

In other words, as long as diversity is limited in the PR profession, then the use – and continued promotion – of digital technologies in promotion is far more likely to perpetuate social *in*justice than support social justice. Currently, diversity is in a parlous state: data shows that the PR profession in many countries has failed to make progress on diversity in class, race or gender. One UK professional survey found that, in 2019, 92 % of respondents classified themselves as white, compared to 88 % the previous year. The gender pay gap between men and women had also increased over the two previous years. Meanwhile, 28 % of respondents had attended fee-paying schools – four times higher than the national UK average, and a significant rise on the 16 % figure reported in the same survey in 2015/16 (Chartered Institute of Public Relations 2019). At the same time, professional bodies have cited the profession's lack of self-awareness of the disadvantages many face on entering the PR profession, or progressing in their careers (Sudhaman 2017).

Around the world, digital skills attainment has emerged as a new area of socio-economic exclusion. Young people raised in households with access to broadband, smart phones, tablets and other devices have significant advantages when they move through the education system and into the job market. Considering the PR profession reports a lack of digital skills as its biggest recruiting gap (Chartered Institute of Public Relations 2019), it is worth asking whether the ever-expanding range of digital skills required in the PR sector may even be exacerbating well-meant efforts to diversify the profession. PR's professional bodies have also failed to acknowledge that algorithmic technologies adopted by HR departments and recruitment firms (designed to screen by postal district, education, and turn of phrase) inevitably create bias in PR's own recruitment processes, potentially contributing to the backward slide in diversity in the PR profession in different parts of the world.

4 A renewed ethics in pedagogy and practice?

As practitioners and academics have already recognised, there is no doubt that future PR professionals must have the practical ability to navigate persuasion architecture in its contemporary form. Plentiful analysis exists on the lack of data skills, limited understanding of new technologies, and challenges associated with grasping complex and emergent communication and information ecologies (Chartered Institute of Public Relations 2019; European Communication Monitor 2016). This kind of research high-lights the new skill sets required to live up to PR's professional promise to its clients of mitigating risk and increasing engagement with audiences. In addition, we argue that new knowledge must incorporate critiques of data-driven utopias that refuse to abstract data from reality. Rather, such approaches will insist on situating the development and use of data – whether for the purposes of creating fake news, client stories or algorithmic interventions – in its social and political context.

Inevitably, this would lead to a pedagogy that instils in students an ethical sensibility going beyond decision-making models and generic principles that cannot be applied to practice. On the contrary, PR ethics needs to be taught in a way that reaches beyond the immediate realm of persuasion, to draw on the context for and consequences of communication in the wider world, so that future practitioners are aware of the impact they have when they engage with persuasion architecture. Beyond public relations, ethical debates focused on the different dimensions of the digital age are common. They consider, among other things, the ethics of big data, the notion of consent, the trajectory of AI and algorithmic technologies, and ethical dilemmas around specific applications, such as driverless cars or the spread of surveillance technologies. Within the field, however, such discussions are notable for their absence, and their inclusion in both pedagogy and practice is long overdue.

Ethical viewpoints, practices and procedures within PR have always been complex and inconsistent: ethics is acknowledged as important, yet *managing* ethics in PR is limited and poorly communicated (Jackson and Moloney 2019: 88). So, how might ethics debates be changing in the digital age? We suggest there are two main areas of concern. First, and as Jackson and Moloney (2019) argue, the effect of PR's involvement in/exposure to digitalisation and technological convergence, facilitated by the abundance of social media platforms, means that consumers now occupy the same communicative spaces as companies, products and brands. Inviting customers to engage and integrate organisational presence into their private worlds through effective – and often unobtrusive – "targeting", simultaneously invites their input into organisational operations. Consumers and other stakeholders have more opportunity to fact-check and opine on moral standards of companies in public spaces and in real time (Jackson and Moloney 2019). The question then arises as to whose ethical critique counts, whose is ignored, and what the basis is for such judgements. At its most fundamental, this is a question of voice. It offers the possibility of a more democratic way of managing organisations as social actors, where society (manifest as customers, consumers and communities) enjoys a level of recognition that validates the importance of its input. How democratic public relations is depends on the breadth of voices taken into account, and the degree to which engaging with their critique is performative rather than genuine (Edwards 2016).

The second arena of change relates to the structure of the "persuasion architecture" that PR practitioners use in the course of their work. Constructed by Amazon, Google, Facebook and other digital advertising platforms (Tufekci 2017), this architecture, as noted above, is built on platforms that deploy algorithms with a baked-in bias against minoritised groups. Using these algorithms, intermediaries from advertising, marketing, PR and data-science professions can isolate citizens in digital "filter bubbles", while spreading disinformation and triggering crises in digital privacy. In the process, practitioners buy into the discriminatory structure of promotion in the digital age. While promotion has always been biased towards "useful" audiences, ignoring those whose "market value" is limited (Aronczyk, Edwards, and Kantola 2017), the digital age runs the risk of masking this bias under the guise of myths that celebrate universal access to voice via platforms and networks that know no boundaries. It thereby lulls PR practitioners into a false sense of ethical security, believing that their practices no longer perpetuate social inequalities. This situation raises questions of personal and professional ethics for practitioners. Furnished with the knowledge of actual effects of practice, rather than what the industry would like practice to be and do, questions of ethical practice can extend beyond the acceptability of work for a client or industry, to questions of whether and how practices could be adjusted to work around the limitations of persuasion architecture and mitigate discrimination.

As Sloane (2018) argues, a focus on "ethics" and "bias" does not necessitate an acknowledgement of the historic patterns of unequal power structures, discrimination and multi-faceted social inequalities that *cause* algorithmic and data "bias". Nonetheless, moving PR's ethical debate into the digital realm inevitably exposes many of the weaknesses in the field's past approach to ethics. It draws the ethical gaze from the present towards the past, in the struggle to understand how the profession's own history leads to its current role in bias and discrimination. That said, much of PR's association with the digital realm and AI remains a "black box", and in-depth investigations of practice are still necessary if we are to unpick how the profession's history is shaping its present and future. Therefore, we agree with Jackson and Moloney's (2019: 98) observation that PR could "benefit from ethnographic and observational work", which would go behind the public personas currently presented by the PR profession, to understand the new and existing ethical tensions inherent to 21st century PR work, and how it shapes professional identity within the context of everyday practice.

5 Conclusion

A renewed ethics in pedagogy and practice requires a significant rewrite of the current curriculum for public relations and communications science. The lack of ability to learn from history, and the absence of ethical training that addresses contemporary issues, all leave practitioners ill-equipped to deal with the constantly changing communication landscape, characterised by shades of grey, rather than black and white oppositions. Noble argues that bias in algorithmically driven culture should be a wake-up call for people living in the margins – we argue that it, alongside the rest of the complex digital communications landscape, should *also* be a wake-up call for the PR profession.

From a practical perspective, and as data scientists become increasingly influential intermediaries (Beer 2019), entry-level PR roles may increasingly require pattern recognition, visual verification and linguistic analysis as part of the skill set for detecting "fake news" and disinformation, for example. But PR education should also incorporate compulsory courses in critical thinking, inequalities, data studies and critique. If *all* voices matter (Couldry 2010), then PR must "challenge the distance" that neoliberal logic installs between marginalised voices and those who possess the practical resources and symbolic status to command a (digital) platform for recognition. An ethical public relations practice must avoid giving the public the *impression* of voice (see, e. g., Cronin 2018), while allowing corporate elites to use algorithmically driven communication to retreat from meaningful interactions. An ethical public relations must further commit to transparency, by specifying the human agency behind AI-led communications. The profession needs to engage with, and actively value, dissenting voices offering resistance to platform capitalism and its associated discourses. Finally, existing discussions of social media as a tool for media relations and stakeholder engagement in PR (e. g. Cronin 2018; Hutchins and Tindall 2016; Motion et al., 2016) need to expand to consider the broader meaning of platform capitalism, data science, algorithmic tracking technologies and AI. Some useful foundations for this digital scholarship have already been laid (e. g. Bourne 2019; Collister 2016; Moore 2018), but more needs to be done.

The resulting knowledge would enable practitioners to address the complex and urgent challenges presented by today's "wicked problems": deeply material, global political-economic, environmental and social issues such as climate change, migration, and the changing global balance of power. All these problems are shaped by the communicative landscape in which PR operates, and communication is fundamental to any attempt to resolve them, as well as to combating movements that could lead to the destruction, rather than the preservation, of humanity (Willis 2016). Communicators deeply affect how these problems unfold, are understood, and are dealt with in practice. As we have argued, normative models of communication, which put the organisation at the centre of events, are manifestly unsuitable for the environments in which practitioners now operate and the tools they deploy. Solutions, including communicative solutions, must mirror the complex causes, multiple dependencies and networked effects of the problems themselves – but must also accommodate the difficult ethical issues that inevitably arise around voice, diversity and, ultimately, the profession's ability to contribute to social justice in the contemporary world.

References

Aronczyk, Melissa, Lee Edwards & Anu Kantola. 2017. Apprehending public relations as a promotional industry. *Public Relations Inquiry* 6(2). 139–155.

Bakir, Vian & Andrew McStay. 2018. Fake news and the economy of emotions. *Digital Journalism* 6. 154–175.

Beer, David. 2019. *The data gaze: Capitalism, power and perception*. Thousand Oaks, CA: Sage.

Bourne, Clea. 2015. Thought Leadership as a trust strategy in global markets: Goldman Sachs' promotion of the 'BRICs' in the marketplace of ideas. *Journal of Public Relations Research* 27(4). 322–336. doi:10.1080/1062726X.2015.1027772 (accessed 3 April 2020).

Bourne, Clea. 2017. *Trust, power and public relations in financial markets*. Abigdon, UK: Routledge.

Bourne, Clea. 2019. AI cheerleaders: Public relations, neoliberalism and artificial intelligence. *Public Relations Inquiry* 8(2). 109–125.

Briant, Emma. 2018. *Building a stronger and more secure democracy in a digital age: A response to recent interim reports and proposals by: U.S. Senate Select Committee on Intelligence; & U.K. Parliament Digital, Culture, Media and Sport Select Committee Inquiry into Fake News*. https://www.academia.edu/37402706/_Building_a_stronger_and_more_secure_democracy_ in_a_digital_age_A_Response_to_Recent_Interim_Reports_and_Proposals_on_Fake_News_ September_2018_(accessed 18 December 2019).

Brodsky, Laura & Liz Oakes. 2017. *Data sharing and open banking*, McKinsey. https://www. mckinsey.com/industries/financial-services/our-insights/data-sharing-and-open-banking (accessed 18 December 2019).

Chartered Institute of Public Relations. 2017. *"PR must elevate the importance of ethics" – CIPR welcomes fake news inquiry*. http://newsroom.cipr.co.uk/pr-must-elevate-the-importance-of- ethics---cipr-welcomes-fake-news-inquiry/ (accessed 18 December 2019).

Chartered Institute of Public Relations. 2019. *'We're building a profession of white, public school alumni' – CIPR State of the Profession 2019*. https://newsroom.cipr.co.uk/were-building-a- profession-of-white-public-school-alumni--cipr-state-of-the-profession-2019/ (accessed 18 December 2019).

Collister, Simon. 2016. Algorithmic public relations: Materiality, technology and power in a post- hegemonic world. In Jacquie L'Etang, David McKie, Nancy Snow, & Jordi Xifra (eds.), *The Routledge handbook of public relations*, 360–371. London: Routledge.

Cossins, Daniel. 2018. Discriminating algorithms: 5 times AI showed prejudice. *New Scientist* 12 April. https://www.newscientist.com/article/2166207-discriminating-algorithms-5-times-ai- showed-prejudice (accessed 6 April 2020).

Couldry, Nick. 2010. *Why voice matters: Culture and politics after neoliberalism*. London: Sage.

Couldry, Nick & Alison Powell. 2014. Big data from the bottom up. *Big Data and Society* 1(2). doi:10.1177/2053951714539277 (accessed 3 April 2020).

Cronin, Anne M. 2018. *Public relations capitalism: Promotional culture, publics and commercial democracy*. Basingstoke, UK: Palgrave Macmillan.

Curtin, Patricia A. & T. Kenn Gaither. 2007. Examining the heuristic value of models of international public relations practice: A case study of the Arla foods crisis. *Journal of Public Relations Research* 20(1). 115–137.

Cutlip, Scott M. 1994. *Public relations: The unseen power. A history*. Hillsdale, NJ: Lawrence Erlbaum Associates.

Czarnecki, Sean. 2017. Arthur W. Page Society renews pledge to always tell the truth. *PR Week* 7 April. https://www.prweek.com/article/1430021/arthur-w-page-society-renews-pledge-always-tell-truth (accessed 6 April 2020).

Demetrious, Kristin. 2019. 'Energy wars': Global PR and public debate in the 21st century. *Public Relationns Inquiry* 8(1). 7–22. doi:10.1177/2046147X18804283 (accessed 3 April 2020).

Dignum, Virginia. 2018. *What we talk about when we talk about Artificial Intelligence*. https://medium.com/@virginiadignum/what-we-talk-about-when-we-talk-about-artificial-intelligence-13423a294160 (accessed 18 December 2019).

Dimitrov, Roumen. 2018. *Strategic silence: Public relations and indirect communication*. Abingdon, UK: Routledge.

Edwards, Lee. 2016. The role of public relations in deliberative systems. *Journal of Communication* 66(1). 60–81. doi:10.1111/jcom.12199 (accessed 3 April 2020).

Edwards, Lee. 2020. Organised lying and professional legitimacy: Public relations' accountability in the disinformation debate. *European Journal of Communication*. In press.

Edwards, Lee. 2018b. *Understanding public relations: Theory, culture and society*. London: Sage.

Eubanks, Virginia. 2017. *Automating Inequality*. New York: St Martin's Press.

European Communication Monitor. 2016. *European Communication Monitor 2016: Exploring trends in big data, stakeholder engagement and strategic cmmunication*. http://www.communicationmonitor.eu/2016/06/13/ecm-european-communication-monitor-2016-big-data-algorithms-social-media-influencer-strategic-communication-automated-pr/ (accessed 18 December 2019).

Greenberg, Josh, Graham Knight & Elizabeth Westersund. 2011. Spinning climate change: Corporate and NGO public relations strategies in Canada and the United States. *International Communication Gazette* 73(1–2). 65–82.

Honneth, Axel. 1996. *The struggle for recognition: The moral grammar of social conflicts*. Cambridge: Polity Press.

Hutchins, Amber & Natalie T. J. Tindall. 2016. New media, new media relations: Building relations with bloggers, citizen journalists and engaged publics. In Amber Hutchins & Natalie T. J. Tindall (eds.), *Public relations and participatory culture: Fandom, social media and community engagement*, 103–116. Abingdon, UK: Routledge.

Jackson, Daniel & Kevin Moloney. 2019. 'Uneasy lies the head that wears a crown'. A qualitative study of ethical PR practice in the United Kingdom. *Public Relations Inquiry* 8(1). 87–101.

Jacobson, Robert M. 2012. Vaccinations: A public health triumph and a public relations tragedy. *Minnesota Medicine* 95(8). 36–40.

Kennedy, Helen. 2016. *Post, mine, repeat: Social media data mining becomes ordinary*. London: Palgrave Macmillan.

Kozinets, Robert. 2019. *How social media is helping Big Tobacco hook a new generation of smokers*. https://theconversation.com/how-social-media-is-helping-big-tobacco-hook-a-new-generation-of-smokers-112911 (accessed 18 December 2019).

Lieb, Rebecca. 2017. *Content: The atomic particle of marketing*. London: Kogan Page.

Marous, Jim. 2019. *Top 10 Retail Banking Trends and Predictions For 2019*. https://thefinancialbrand.com/78423/2019-top-banking-trends-predictions-outlook-digital-fintech-data-ai-cx-payments-tech/ (accessed 18 December 2019.

McStay, Andrew John. 2016. *Digital Advertising*. London: Palgrave.

Miller, David & William Dinan. 2007. *A century of spin: How public relations became the cutting edge of corporate power*. London: Pluto Press.

Moore, Simon. 2018. *Public relations and individuality: Fate, technology and autonomy*. Abingdon, UK: Routledge.

Moscato, Derek. 2019. The metanarrative of rural environmentalism: Rhetorical activism in Bold Nebraska's Harvest the Hope. *Public Relations Inquiry* 8(1). 23–47. doi:10.1177/204614 7X18810733 (accessed 3 April 2020).

Motion, Judy, Robert L. Heath & Shirley Leitch. 2016. *Social media and public relations: Fake friends and powerful publics*. Abingdon, UK: Routledge.

Nix, Alexander. 2016. Cambridge Analytica: The power of Big Data and psychographics. https://www.youtube.com/watch?v=n8Dd5aVXLCc (accessed 6 April 2020).

Noble, Safiya U. 2018. *Algorithms of oppression: How search engines reinforce racism*. New York: New York University Press.

Ong, Jonathan Corpus & Jason Vincent A. Cabañes. 2018. *Architects of Networked Disinformation: Behind the Scenes of Troll Accounts and Fake News Production in the Philippines*. https://newtontechfordev.com/wp-content/uploads/2018/02/ARCHITECTS-OF-NETWORKED-DISINFORMATION-FULL-REPORT.pdf (accessed 18 December 2019).

Pitcher, George. 2008. Financial PR is no scapegoat. *Profile 69*.

Public Relations and Communications Association. 2017. *Public Relations and Communications Association (PRCA) response to the Culture, Media and Sports Committee's 'Fake News' Inquiry*. https://www.prca.org.uk/sites/default/files/PRCA%20Response%20to%20Fake%20News%20Inquiry.pdf (accessed 18 December 2019).

Royle, Jo & Audrey Laing. 2014. The Digital Marketing Skills Gap: Developing a digital marketer model for the communications industries. *International Journal of Information Management* 34. 65–73.

Schwartz, Oscar. 2018. You thought fake news was bad? Deep fakes are where truth goes to die. *The Guardian*. https://www.theguardian.com/technology/2018/nov/12/deep-fakes-fake-news-truth (accessed 18 December 2019).

Shir-Raz, Yaffa & Eli Avraham. 2017. Under the regulation radar: PR strategies of pharmaceutical companies in countries where direct advertising of prescription drugs is banned – The Israeli case. *Public Relations Review* 43. 382–391. doi:10.1016/j.pubrev.2017.01.003 (accessed 3 April 2020).

Slee, Dan. 2018. Robot Comms: What public sector comms people need to know about artificial intelligence. *Influence Online* 2 July. https://influenceonline.co.uk/2018/07/02/robot-comms-what-public-sector-comms-people-need-to-know-about-artificial-intelligence/ (accessed 6 April 2020).

Sloane, Mona. 2018. *Making artificial intelligence socially just: Why the current focus on ethics is not enough*. http://blogs.lse.ac.uk/politicsandpolicy/artificial-intelligence-and-society-ethics/ (accessed 18 December 2019).

Srnicek, Nick. 2017. *Platform Capitalism*. Cambridge: Polity Press.

Staunton, James. 2017. Opinion: Fake news is good news for communicators. http://www.gorkana.com/2017/09/instinctif-partners-james-staunton-opinion-fake-news-good-news/ (accessed 18 December 2019).

Straughan, Dulcie M. 2004. 'Lift every voice and sing': The public relations efforts of the NAACP, 1960–1965. *Public Relations Review* 30. 49–60.

Sudhaman, Arun. 2017. 'Inclusion may well be a pipe dream': PR industry grapples with pivotal challenge. https://www.holmesreport.com/latest/article/%27inclusion-may-well-be-a-pipe-dream%27-pr-industry-grapples-with-pivotal-challenge (accessed 18 December 2019).

Sudhaman, Arun. 2019. *2019 agency rankings: Global PR industry growth holds steady at 5 %*. https://www.holmesreport.com/long-reads/article/2019-agency-rankings-global-pr-industry-growth-holds-steady-at-5 (accessed 18 December 2019).

Tufekci, Zeynep. 2017. *We're building a dystopia just to make people click on ads*. https://ted2srt.org/talks/zeynep_tufekci_we_re_building_a_dystopia_just_to_make_people_click_on_ads (accessed 18 December 2019).

Valentini, Chiara. 2020. Trust research in public relations: An assessment of its conceptual, theoretical and methodological foundations. *Corporate Communications: an International Journal* 25.

Valentini, Chiara. 2015. Is using social media 'good' for public relations? A critical reflection. *Public Relations Review* 41. 170–177.

Waisbord, Silvio. 2018. Truth is what happens to news: On journalism, fake news and post-truth. *Journalism Studies* 19(13). 1866–1878. doi:10.1080/1461670X.2018.1492881 (accessed 3 April 2020).

Wasserman, Herman. 2017. Fake news from Africa: Panics, politics and paradigms. *Journalism* December. doi:10.1177/1464884917746861 (accessed 3 April 2020).

Willis, Paul. 2016. From humble inquiry to humble intelligence: Confronting wicked problems and augmenting public relations. *Public Relations Review* 42(2). 306–313. doi:10.1016/j.pubrev.2015.05.007 (accessed 3 April 2020).

Zerfass, Ansgar, Dejan Verčič & Sophia Charlotte Volk. 2017. Communication evaluation and measurement skills: Skills, practices and utilization in European organizations. *Corporate Communications: An International Journal* 22(1). 2–18.

Chiara Valentini

32 Mapping public relations theory: Concluding reflections and future directions

Abstract: This chapter reviews and discusses the status of public relations theory. It does so by offering the editor's own reading and interpretation of public relations theory as discussed in this handbook. Specifically, a typology for classifying public relations theories is presented, and then used to conduct a meta-level theoretical analysis of the theories presented in Part III. The typology is based on three major theoretical objectives (normative, descriptive, and instrumental), and three perspectives (managerial, public, and conceptual). Concluding reflections on the status of public relations theory and suggestions for the future direction of research are offered.

Keywords: public relations theory; heuristic typology; theoretical perspectives; theoretical objectives; theorizing

> *"He who loves practice without theory is like the sailor who boards ship without a rudder and compass and never knows where he may cast." Leonardo da Vinci*

1 Introduction

Over 500 years ago, the Italian artist and scientist Leonardo da Vinci already recognized that practice without theory is useless. Not only has public relations as a professionalized practice grown in relevance in today's societies, but its body of knowledge has also expanded, and it is gaining momentum through further theorizing. But why bother to reflect on public relations theory? Perhaps it is because "executing effective public relations starts with knowing and understanding the public relations theory that helps define the practice" (Toth and Dozier 2018: 71). But a theory is much more than that; as Brunner (2019) noted, it helps people to see new and valuable things (Littlejohn 1999), and helps in predicting or explaining future outcomes (Griffin et al. 2015). Although public relations has earned a role – albeit sometimes negative – in organizational and societal matters, it has not yet attained an adequate status among the broad scientific community; I believe it can and should realize such a place. There is already evidence that public relations scholars are increasingly engaging with socially important objectives, questions, and debates that intersect different disciplinary traditions, principal specialties, methodologies, and schools of thought (for examples see Adi 2019; Brunner 2016; Johnston 2016; Johnston and Taylor 2018). These actions illustrate that public relations can also contribute to the understanding

https://doi.org/10.1515/9783110554250-032

of, and offer a contribution to, solving diverse problems. As the contributors of this handbook have shown, public relations is a multi-faced profession handling many different communication and non-communication activities. It is a profession with own identity, but is often not clearly understood or accepted by others. It is trying to bring value to how organizations of any kind, including publics as well as stakehold-ers, engage in different types of relations and conversations. In order to pay tribute to the fact that public relations has evolved from a managerial practice into a more comprehensive research field, and now comprises a collection of theories, models, and thinking – what we can refer to as public relations theory – we must first reflect upon what kind of theories we have.

This concluding chapter thus intends to offer the editor's own reading and inter-pretation of public relations theory as discussed in this handbook. This handbook presents a variety of theories, theoretical approaches, and paradigms that contrast and sometimes collide one with another. This may give the impression that public relations theory is chaotic. Yet, it could also be interpreted as a healthy academic effort by a field attempting to challenge its own assumptions and ideas through mul-tiple views and philosophical perspectives.

Scholars tend to be familiar with the specific theories they use in their own research. Yet, rarely do they think about the purpose, definition, or meaning of theory itself, especially in a field like public relations, that disagrees on its own theoretical foundations and the research questions it should address. Recognizing public rela-tions theory as an essentially contested field, subject to multiple competing interpre-tations, this chapter presents a meta-level theoretical analysis of the theories consid-ered classical public relations (Part III). This exercise is a parsimonious attempt to wrap up the contributions of this volume, and thus bears the limits of the discussed public relations theories.

To embark on this endeavor, it is important to start by summarizing the most important challenges to contemporary public relations theory, which number at least three. First, although multiple paradigms and perspectives have been explored, espe-cially in recent years, public relations theory is still lacking a widely accepted norma-tive foundation (Brunner 2019; Botan and Hazleton 1989). For many years, excellence theory has dominated public relations research, but rhetorical theory, dialogic theory, contingency theory, and community-building theory have also taken their share of attention as first-order public relations theories. Interpretivist approaches have also emerged as new forces in scholarly theorizing efforts, but no specific public relations theory has yet emerged from that standpoint. Second, public relations theory is still weak in terms of descriptive and empirical analyses of the diverse forms of public/ stakeholder–organization interactions. Most research has crystalized around the pos-itivist idea of an organization managing relationships with specific active publics at a single point in time; there has not been much research on intra- and inter-organiza-tional relations, nor much about stakeholder relations or organizationS-stakeholderS relationships (Heath 2013; Sommerfeldt and Kent 2015, Valentini et al. 2012). Third, if the discipline needs to advance, we must then consider theorizing about theories and concepts themselves as an important scientific outcome. Although some developments on this subject have appeared (Coombs and Holliday 2019; Ferguson 2018; Grunig J. 2006; Heath 2006; Ledingham 2003), they are too few and limited in scope.

This concluding chapter addresses the third challenge by mapping these developments as discussed in this handbook, and putting them into a "typology of theories". Summarizing and drawing parallels is always a difficult exercise, and often falls short of adequately representing the types of sophisticated thinking that underpins each of the different theoretical approaches presented in this volume. Yet, such an exercise is badly needed if the uncertainty regarding the actual scope of public relations theories is to be reduced. While I tried to embark on this process of mapping and classifying with a detached, objective vision, my knowledge of the field and my academic background have undoubtedly influenced the way I see and understand these theories. That is to say, I do not expect that all of the contributors to this volume will agree with my classification of their work into the categories described in the heuristic typology I propose.

2 Mapping public relations theory: a typology

The proposed typology for mapping the theoretical body of knowledge in public relations takes its point of departure from a similar analytical approach used for classifying major public relations theories addressing globalization (cf. Valentini 2019), and is inspired by early stakeholder management literature (Donaldson and Preston 1995; Friedman and Miles 2006; Steurer 2006). The proposed typology is a heuristic attempt to organize theories by their theoretical objectives – which can be normative, descriptive, or instrumental – and by their perspectives – which, in this analysis, I chose to classify as managerial, public, or conceptual (see Table 1). It has been argued that combining objectives and perspectives in analyzing a field's theories can offer a more systematic and in-depth approach to learning about the actual scope of a field's theoretical development (Steurer 2006). The first dimension, the theoretical objective, responds to the ontological question of what kind of knowledge a theory offers. Normative theories are essentially theories about how the world should be or work. They display clear similarities with the deductive method, in that their intention is to apply general principles (often based on ethical considerations) to specific cases. Typically, the two types of normative elements are referred to as the *normativity of outcomes* and the *normativity of justification,* with the former considered to have a superior moral foundation (Friedman and Miles 2006). Descriptive theories, also known as positive theories, are theories about how the world actually is or works (Grunig J. and Grunig L. 1992). These theories tend to show similarities to the inductive approach, since, differently than normative theories, they try to derive general principles and conclusions by examining individual cases. Instrumental theories, on the other hand, are theories about how the world would be if something happens or is done. Instrumental theories, also known as prescriptive theories, essentially examine *ceteris paribus* connections, and offer guidelines that describe what to do in order to achieve specific outcomes (Donaldson and Preston 1995). Instrumental theories thus concern both the normative/deductive and the descriptive/inductive approach, but their characteristic element is a focus on causalities through linking means and ends (Steurer 2006).

The second dimension of the typology is the theoretical perspective. This refers to the thematic width of a theory, and essentially it examines the specific problems underlined in the theoretical premises. In this analysis of public relations theory, I propose to use managerial, public, and conceptual perspectives. As has been noted on several occasions (e. g. Ihlen and Verhoeven 2009; Edwards 2018; Valentini and Edwards 2019), the field has expanded significantly from a narrow view of public relations as the management of symbols and meanings for corporations and powerful entities to include a broader view of public relations as a cultural, social, and public practice dealing with the negotiation of both meaning and behavior. Reviewing the key conceptual foundations in public relations literature, Coombs and Holladay (2019) found that the three main concepts are organizations, publics, and relationships. Ihlen and Verhoeven (2009) identified a number of other relevant concepts in addition to relationships, such as trust, legitimacy, understanding, and reflections. In several ways, it is thus possible to see a pattern among early scholarly discussions on the core public relations concepts and perspectives, resulting in the conclusion that it is possible to classify the diverse body of public relations theories into managerial, public, and conceptual perspectives. Similar perspectives have also been employed in management literature interested in stakeholder theory (Donaldson and Preston 1995; Friedman and Miles 2006; Steurer 2006), which I would argue shares a high degree of similarity in research questions – at least those concerning stakeholders – with public relations. My choice of a managerial perspective rather than an organizational one relies on the fact that the former term includes an organizational perspective, but is not limited to it; it is thus best suited to capture the socio-cultural turn of public relations, which would fit too tightly under the umbrella of "organization". In the proposed typology, a public perspective has a broad view, and captures a range of different actors such as stakeholders, stake-seekers and stake-watchers (Fassin 2009), influencers, claimants, collaborators and recipients (Miles 2017), non-publics, and the general public (Hallahan 2000). Finally, I chose not to focus on a specific concept, and thus used a conceptual perspective in order to open up the discussion to a wider set of concepts, not limited to relationship, trust, legitimacy, etc.

Ultimately, the managerial perspective focuses on how public relations deals with publics, stakeholders, and society, while the public perspective analyzes how publics, stakeholders, and society try to influence organizations and any kind of organized entity for which public relations operates, and the conceptual perspective explores how particular concepts such as trust, power, legitimacy, mutuality, symmetry, or dialogue relate to public relations practice or theory. The three perspectives proposed here are an attempt to complement and expand the scope of analysis of other reviews of public relations theories, by providing not just managerial reflections but also public and conceptual reflections on the object of public relations theory in a more systematic and parsimonious manner. In the next section, I apply this typology to the theories presented in Part III of this handbook.

Table 1: A typology of classification for public relations theory (modified from Steurer 2006: 62)

			Public relations theory perspectives		
			Managerial	*Public*	*Conceptual*
Public relations theory objectives	*Normative*	Focus	Interprets the function of public relations regarding publics and wider society	Interprets the function and legitimacy of publics and their claims	Interprets the normative characteristic of concept X and its significance for public relations practice/theory
		Main question	Why and how should public relations deal with publics and societal matters?	What makes publics legitimate, and how should they try to accomplish their interests?	What issues of concept X should public relations and publics take into account?
	Descriptive	Focus	Describes public relations characteristics, practices, and behaviors regarding publics and society	Describes public characteristics and behaviors regarding issues and organizations	Describes how particular issues of concept X play a role in public relations practice/theory
		Main question	How does public relations actually deal with publics and societal matters?	What do publics expect or claim, and how do they actually try to achieve their claims?	Which issues of concept X do public relations and/or publics take into account?
	Instrumental	Focus	Analyses the connection between public relations practice and public relations goals	Analyses the connection between a public's strategy and its ability to meet the public's claims	Analyses the connection between public relations practice/theory and the realization of concept X
		Main question	How can public relations practice contribute to an organization's performance?	How can publics best accomplish their claims?	To what extent can concept X be achieved through public relations practice?
	Overall	Focus	Public relations in/for organizations/causes	Publics'/stakeholders' claims and public relations practice	Concept X and public relations practice/theory
		Main question	How does public relations relate to publics or an issue?	How do publics address organizations?	How does concept X relate to public relations practice/theory?

3 The status of public relations theory

In part III of this volume, twelve theories, two of which are further elaborations of old theories, were presented and discussed in ten chapters. By focusing on the main features as described by the authors, it is possible to extrapolate their theoretical objectives and perspectives. As Table 2 shows, most of these public relations theories are normative or descriptive, and predominantly take a managerial perspective.

Table 2: Mapping classical public relations theories by theoretical objectives and perspectives

Theories	Theoretical objectives	Theoretical perspectives
Excellence theory	Normative	Managerial
Relationship management theory	Normative	Managerial
Community-building theory	Normative	Conceptual
Organic theory of public relations	Normative	Conceptual
Dialogic theory of public relations	Normative	Conceptual
Rhetorical theory of public relations	Normative, descriptive	Managerial, public
Four models of public relations	Descriptive	Managerial
Personal influence model of public relations	Descriptive	Managerial
Contingency theory of strategic conflict management	Descriptive	Managerial, public
Global public relations theory	Descriptive	Conceptual
Situational theory of publics	Instrumental	Public
Situational theory of problem-solving	Instrumental	Public

While not a surprise, a managerial perspective emphasizes specific professional or organizational characteristics and managerial behaviors regarding publics and stakeholders (descriptive), or identifies connections or the lack of them to the achievement of traditional public relations goals (instrumental), or interprets the function of public relations, including the identification of moral or philosophical guidelines (normative). Given the historical legacy of public relations as a form of publicity and even propaganda, many scholars may have attempted to "redeem" its identity by elaborating on its practice and function through ethical and moral lenses. This is perhaps a plausible explanation for the great amount of attention given to managerial and normative theories.

J. Grunig and L. Grunig (1992) do not shy away from saying that *Excellence theory* should be considered the grand theory of public relations, as its objective is to guide the practice of public relations professionals toward what they consider "excellence", thus underlining both its normative and managerial grounds. On the same line, *Relationship management theory* can be considered a normative theory with a managerial perspective, as it takes its own foundation from Systems theory, Stakeholder theory, Social responsibility theory, and Crisis management theory, and interprets the function of public relations in light of these theories and the practice of managing relationships with publics and stakeholders. While relationship management has been recognized as one of – if not *the* – central paradigms of public relations (cf. Ferguson 2018), the theory underpinned by Ledingham in chapter 21 offers a moral, ethical ground for practicing public relations based on the management of public concerns.

Community-building theory and the *Organic theory of public relations* are also normative theories, in that they try to guide the practice of public relations from a different viewpoint, which is through the lenses of two concepts, and thus their perspective is considered conceptual. A normative theory with a conceptual perspective discusses public relations problems from a particular concept's vantage point and searches for a moral or theoretical ground for public relations, or explores how public relations relates to a particular concept (Steurer 2006). While *Community-building theory* and the *Organic theory of public relations* are grounded on the concepts of community and organic, they consider the public relations, organizational, and societal interests from the perspective of these concepts, and from the theory of society.

The *Dialogic theory of public relations* is another theory of this kind. It is a normative theory, since it offers moral grounds to practice public relations in honest and ethical ways while trying to create effective organization-public communications (Kent 2003). It also discusses the moral foundations of ethical communication through the lenses of dialogue and dialogic communication, and thus searches for a moral ground for public relations through the concept of dialogue. Hence, it is classified as a conceptual perspective.

Another example of a normative theory is the *Rhetorical theory of public relations*, the main purpose of which is to explain how humans can achieve a fully functioning society. Yet, the same theory also offers many descriptive elements, based on observations and rhetorical literature, on how humans communicate and try to influence each other. This theory contains some elements of a real-life description; thus, its theoretical objective is hybrid. Furthermore, this theory addresses both managerial and public perspectives. While Heath, Waymer, and Ihlen claim (see Chapter 18 in this book) that the *Rhetorical theory of public relations* is essentially organization-centric, thus emphasizing the managerial perspective, they later acknowledge that any social actor can use rhetoric to influence the communication dynamic through the use of discourse enactments. Thus, this theory is constructed to respond to both managerial (public relations, organizations) and public (any other social actor) perspectives.

Moving on to descriptive theories, earlier J. Grunig and L. Grunig (1992) argued that the *Four models of public relations* represents a good example of a descriptive public relations theory, since its foundations are confirmed by diverse empirical studies showing that public relations is performed according these models. In the same line, the *Personal influence model of public relations*, sometimes referred as the fifth model of public relations, can be considered a descriptive theory for similar reasons. Both the four models and the personal influence model show a managerial perspective, in that they describe how the management of public relations is actually done. Another descriptive theory is the *Global public relations theory* by Verčič and Sriramesh, which is essentially a spin-off of the Excellence Project. This theory briefly tries to explain how societal, cultural, and system elements – such as media, activism, and civil society – affect the practice of public relations. Therefore, it can be considered a descriptive theory with a conceptual perspective, because it describes how particular elements characterizing the concept "global" (media, culture, politics, activism, etc.) play a role in public relations practice.

An example of a special descriptive theory is the *Contingency theory of strategic conflict management*. It is descriptive because it explains how organizations or publics can influence each other through the communication of different stances. The theory describes how such stances change along a continuum, depending on the situation and the communication recipient. Yet, the theory also contains some core norma-tive reflections, in that it recommends a rethinking of how public relations can take place. Nonetheless, this theory has been classified as descriptive in this typology, as its core assumptions were developed through many empirical studies, and its main features were thus inductively derived. Concerning the theoretical perspective, this theory responds to both managerial and public concerns, albeit that the theory was primarily developed to address managerial ones. The explicative power of this theory is much broader than that of public relations and organizations. Focusing on describ-ing stance movements, it can explain how any social actor or organized entity could use such stances to influence the other. As a result, contingency theory is considered a descriptive, yet managerial- and public-oriented, theory.

Only two classical theories have an instrumental perspective. The *Situational theory of public* and the *Situational theory of problem solving* represent good illustra-tions of two instrumental theories, since both examine the communicative behaviors of publics to forecast possible actions, and thus link the "means and ends". Both theories, in fact, analyse the connection between a public's strategy/behavior and its ability to influence an organization. Because these theories take a public's viewpoint, they can be considered to have a public perspective, as their primary role is under-standing how publics and stakeholders can affect an organization.

4 Concluding reflections and future directions

Three major conclusions merit being mentioned here. First, public relations theory consists of a discrete amount of theories dealing with normative, descriptive, and instrumental objectives, albeit normative and descriptive scopes are predominant. Perhaps it is now time to move toward developing instrumental theories. As Wehmeier (2009) noted, if public relations theory ought to address professional problems, we must generate theories that can help professionals to handle them. Thus, we must focus more on theories of the middle range, particularly those of an instrumental nature. For example, specialized areas of public relations, such as crisis communication, have developed a set of instrumental theories that can serve this purpose. We must look behind the crises and imminent issues and also address broader societal and public concerns by expanding our toolkit of instrumental theories; for example, to address compelling questions on societal and geo-cultural matters such as climate change, terrorism, health outbreaks, immigration, conflict, use of natural resources, etc. What kind of a role does public relations have as an organizing function in these bigger problems? Does it hinder or facilitate them? How? Instrumental theories could then analyse the connection between public relations practice/theory and the specific issue or question at stake, and offer guidelines that describe what to expect if certain actions are taken.

Second, most public relations theories have a managerial outlook. This is not surprising, given that most of theories in this volume are either about defining the identity and function of public relations, or assisting in its practice. Yet, there are also some conceptual perspectives in public relations theory, and, if we consider part IV of this volume, we could argue that many of the recent theorizing efforts are essentially conceptual: that is, they try to borrow and adapt a concept from a discipline and apply it to public relations problems. What is actually needed is a public perspective on public relations theory. For example, what kind of public relations theory can we develop out of the recent work on social advocacy, activism, and community? What can we theorize about public behaviors and influencing strategies? These are examples of new areas that have only been briefly explored. Empirical studies – for example, on employee whistleblowing (Greenwood 2015), voicing (Tam et al. 2018), public negative engagement (Lievonen et al. 2018) and other topics – are increasing in number, but there is a fundamental gap in theory development here. It is time to move from empirical case studies to theory.

Third, most classical public relations theories are western-centric; that is, they are highly influenced by western thinking and theorizing practices. While it could be argued that normative theories should essentially be able to normatively explain public relations practice across cultures, empirical case studies show often they fall short of completely explaning the phenonmenon. Yet, alternative, non-western theories from public relations are essentially non-existent. There is a substantial gap in theorizing from the non-western world in this discipline. Theories addressing public relations from a non-western perspective would be of great value across the full range of normative, descriptive, instrumental objectives and managerial, public, and conceptual perspectives.

To add to this, I would argue that an understanding of public relations as an *organizing* function, as I described in the Introduction to this handbook, rather than an *organizational* function, may turn to be more useful in helping the scientific community to theorize beyond the western, capitalist view of public relations. The idea of organizing can also dissolve the dichotomy between theory and practice, as the identity of public relations is defined by what it does and what it produces, and this is not fixed or structured, but flexible (Langenberg and Wesseling 2016). Many of the theories presented in Part III appear to have in common an emphasis on agency, rather than on the loci of function. They essentially expose what public relations can do through communication, and thus somehow illustrate the back-and-forth movement and translation between the actions of public relations and their interpretation, which is essentially the idea of organizing (Weick 1979). The rethinking of public relations as an organizing function also calls for more reflection on the actual impact, and added value, of this profession on and for organizations, publics, and societies. This could be a fruitful approach to develop a consistent narrative across schools of thought, and a grand theory of public relations.

Public relations scholars may not agree on the best theory, nor even on what can be considered a theory *of* or *for* public relations, yet this overview of public relations theory through a typology of classification hopes to shed some light on which type of theories are still needed to better understand certain aspects of public relations (Brunner 2018; Grunig J. 1992). A brief disclaimer is needed here. As with most typologies, this classification typology, based on theoretical objectives and perspectives, has to be understood as a simplified review, derived from a selection of the important tenets of each theory. Obviously, reality is not always as orderly as theory would hope. Many public relations theories often follow more than one objective, and identifying which of the three perspectives a theory uses can be difficult. Likewise, the typology falls short in showing theoretical interactions, and these can be productive efforts in theorizing. Regarding other biases of the proposed typology as a classification instrument, it has been noted in management literature that several theories with an instrumental approach also have a normative core as well, and that several normative theories derive their managerial insights from empirical case studies, and thus through direct observations (Steurer 2006; Freeman 1999). There is no reason for not seeing similar challenges in classifying public relations theory, as much of what characterizes public relations also characterizes the management of stakeholder relations – albeit from a communication angle. Despite the limits of this systematic and, at times, simplistic approach to classifying public relations theory, I believe this typology and the exercise performed here can capture, in its very simplicity, the essence of what public relations theory is today, and show in what direction scholars should steer in the future.

In conclusion, I hope the reader will find it enlightening and useful to look at the different theoretical approaches, models, and concepts that are collected in this volume. Public relations as an *organizing* function takes place at multiple levels: organizational, societal, and even individual. Much of what public relations does, provokes, or responds to is communicatively embedded, which is why we should not forget the communication origin of public relations. A communication perspective emphasizes both the constitutive nature of communicating and the process of meaning creation (van Ruler 2018). Through this lens, communication becomes the means by which public relations professionals convey meanings and ideas toward publics and stakeholders, for instance via campaigns and messaging. Communication can also be a means of developing an understanding of different environments by monitoring, observing, and analyzing people's communicative behaviors (Valentini 2018), which organizations, clients, and communities may expect to be advised on. Communication can thus be not only a result, a campaign, a message, content, etc., but also an antecedent for understanding complexity and public and stakeholder interests. Furthermore, communication can be a process for creating meanings, structures, and practices, particularly because communication can be performative in constituting a reality, or simply institutionalizing practices and activities in organizations (Valentini 2018). I think this is important, and we should not forget it when trying to advance public relations notions, and trying to theorize about problems and issues that affect the profession.

As stated in the Introduction chapter, public relations is essentially a profession in the "business" of social influence. It has a specific focus and purpose, albeit that agreement on what this should be is still contested. Yet in my view, the beauty of this discipline is exactly the diversity of its methodological and theoretical premises, and its increasing curiosity about exploring and expanding its own boundaries. It is also important to note that, although the contributors to this volume have reviewed and discussed their topic thoroughly, there is more that could be gained from others who could not be included in this handbook. Some of these recent studies are inspiring, and should be taken into consideration, as they could lead to new theorizing in the near future.

References

Adi, Ana. 2019. *Protest public relations. Communicating dissent and activism*. New York: Routledge.

Botan Carl H. & Vincent Hazleton. 1989. *Public Relations Theory*, Vol. I. Hillsdale, NJ: Lawrence Erlbaum Associates.

Brunner, Brigitta R. 2016. *The moral compass of public relations*. New York: Routledge.

Brunner, Brigitta R. 2019. *Public relations theory: Application and practice*. Medford, MA: Wiley Blackwell.

Coombs, W. Timothy. 2010. Parameters for crisis communication. In Timothy W. Coombs & Shelly J. Holladay (eds.), *Handbook of Crisis Communication*, 17–53. Malden, MA: Wiley-Blackwell.

Coombs, Timothy W. & Sherry J. Holladay. 2019. The conceptual heritage of public relations: Using public memory to explore constraints and liberation. *Journal of Communication Management* 23(4). 375–392.

Donaldson Thomas and Lee E. Preston 1995. The stakeholder theory of corporation: Concepts, evidence, and implications. *The Academy of Management Review* 20(1). 65–91.

Edwards, Lee. 2018. *Understanding public relation. Theory, culture and society*. London: Sage.

Fassin, Yves. 2008. The stakeholder model redefined. *Journal of Business Ethics* 84(1). 113–135.

Ferguson, Mary Ann. 2018. Building theory in public relations: Interorganizational relationships as a public relations paradigm. *Journal of Public Relations Research* 30(4). 164–178.

Freeman, Edward R. 1999. Divergent stakeholder theory. *Academy of Management Review* 24(2). 233–236.

Friedman, Andrew L. & Samantha Miles. 2006. *Stakeholders: Theory and Practice*. Oxford: Oxford University Press.

Greenwood, Cary A. 2015. Whistleblowing in the Fortune 1000: What practitioners told us about wrongdoing in corporations in a pilot study. *Public Relations Review* 41(4). 490–500.

Griffin, Em, Andrew Ledbetter & Glenn Sparks. 2015. *A first look at communication theory*, 9th edn. New York: McGraw Hill Education.

Grunig, James E. 1992. *Excellence in public relations and communication management*. Hillsdale, NJ: Lawrence Erlbaum Associates.

Grunig, James E. 2006. Furnishing the edifice: Ongoing research on public relations as a strategic management function. *Journal of Public Relations Research* 18(2). 151–176.

Grunig, James E. & Larissa A. Grunig. 1992. Models of public relations and communications. In James E. Grunig (ed.), *Excellence in public relations and communication management*, 285–326. Hillsdale, NJ: Lawrence Erlbaum Associates.

Hallahan, Kirk. 2000. Inactive publics: The forgotten publics in public relations. *Public Relations Review* 26(4). 499–515.

Heath, Robert L. 2006. Onward into more fog: Thoughts on public relations research directions. *Journal of Public Relations Research* 18(2). 93–114.

Heath, Robert L. 2013. The journey to understand and champion OPR takes many roads, some not yet well traveled. *Public Relations Review* 39(5). 426–431.

Ihlen, Øyvind & Piet Verhoeven. 2009. Conclusions on the domain, context, concepts, issues, and empirical venues of public relations. In Øyvind Ihlen, Magnus Fredriksson & Betteke van Ruler (eds.), *Public relations and social theory: Key figures and concepts*, 322–340. New York: Routledge.

Johnston, Jane. 2016. *Public relations and the public interest*. New York: Routledge.

Johnston, Kim & Maureen Taylor. 2018. *The handbook of communication engagement*. Medford, MA: Wiley Blackwell.

Kent, Michael. 2003. The relationship between web site design and organizational responsiveness to stakeholders. *Public Relations Review* 29. 63–77.

Langenberg, Suzan & Hans Wesseling. 2016. Making sense of Weick's organising. A philosophical exploration. *Philosophy of Management* 15(3). 221–240.

Ledingham, John A. 2003. Explicating relationship management as a general theory of public relations. *Journal of Public Relations Research* 15(2). 181–198.

Lievonen, Matias, Vilma Luoma-aho & Jana Bowden. 2018. Negative engagement. In Kim Johnston & Maureen Taylor (eds.), *The handbook of communication engagement*, 531–548. Medford, MA: Wiley Blackwell.

Littlejohn, Stephen W. 1999. *Theories of human communication*. Belmont, CA: Wadsworth.

Miles, Samantha. 2017. Chapter 2: Stakeholder theory classification, definitions and essential contestability. In David M. Wasieleski & James Weber (eds.), *Stakeholder management*, 21–48. Bingley, UK: Emerald Publishing.

Sommerfeldt, Erich J. & Michael L. Kent. 2015. Civil society, networks, and relationship management: Beyond the organization–public dyad. *International Journal of Strategic Communication* 9(3). 235–252.

Steurer, Reinhard. 2006. Mapping stakeholder theory anew: From the 'stakeholder theory of the firm' to three perspectives on business–society relations. *Business Strategy and the Environment* 15. 55–69.

Tam, Lisa, Jarim Kim & Jeong-Nam Kim. 2018. The origin of distant voicing: Examining relational dimensions in public diplomacy and their effects on megaphoning. *Public Relations Review* 44(3). 407–418.

Toth, Elizabeth L. & David M. Dozier. 2018. Theory: The ever-evolving foundation for why we do what we do. In *Commission for Public Relations Education, Fast forward: Foundations + future state. Educators + practitioners*, 71–77. New York: Commission for Public Relations Education.

Valentini, Chiara. 2018. Communicatively constituted stakeholders: Advancing a communication perspective in stakeholder relations. In Adam Lindgreen, Francois Maon, Joelle Vanhamme, Beatriz Palacios Florencio, Christine Strong & Carolyn Vallaster (eds.), *Engaging with Stakeholders: A Relational Perspective on Responsible Business*, 65–79. New York: Routledge.

Valentini, Chiara. 2019. Globalization. In Brigitta R. Brunner (ed.), *Public Relations Theory: Applications and Understanding*, 125–140. Hoboken, NJ: Wiley.

Valentini, Chiara & Lee Edwards. 2019. Theories in public relations: Reflections and future directions. *Public Relations Inquiry* 8(3). 195–200.

Valentini, Chiara, Dean Kruckeberg & Kenneth Starck. 2012. Public relations and community: A persistent covenant. *Public Relations Review* 38(5). 873–879.

van Ruler, Betteke. 2018. Communication theory: An underrated pillar on which strategic communication rests. *International Journal of Strategic Communication* 12(4). 367–381.

Wehmeier, Stefan. 2009. Out of the fog into the future: Directions of public relations theory building, research, and practice. *Canadian Journal of Communication* 34. 265–282.

Weick, Karl E. 1979. *The Social Psychology of Organizing*, 2nd edn. New York: McGraw-Hill.

Contributors to this volume

Linda Aldoory, PhD, is Associate Dean for Research and Programming for the College of Arts and Humanities and Professor in Communication at the University of Maryland, USA. She is former Endowed Director of the Herschel S. Horowitz Center for Health Literacy, and founder and former Director of the Center for Health Communication Research at Maryland. She is also a former editor of the *Journal of Public Relations Research*. Aldoory's research focuses on health public relations and campaigns for underserved health populations. She has worked in public relations for over 20 years and has consulted for the CDC, FDA, and USDA.

Jennifer Bartlett, PhD, is an Associate Professor in the QUT Business School specializing in CSR, legitimacy, public relations, and corporate communication. Much of her research work is focused around the role of communication in building and managing organizational legitimacy. She is one of the editors of the award-winning Wiley Blackwell *Handbook of Communication and Corporate Social Responsibility*, which is the seminal work on communication and CSR. She is a Fellow of the Public Relations Institute of Australia and past Chair of the Public Relations division of ICA (International Communication Association).

Nandini Bhalla, PhD, is an assistant professor in the School of Journalism and Mass Communications at Washington and Lee University, USA. Her scholarship interests are Corporate Social Responsibility (CSR), global public relations, intercultural relationships, and media representations of yoga. Nandini is a Page Legacy Scholar (2018) and her work has appeared in various journals including *Public Relations Review*, *International Journal of Strategic Communication*, *International Journal of Communication*, and *Corporate Communications: An International Journal*, among others. She has received multiple awards for her research including The Inez Kaiser Graduate Students of Color Award from the Public Relations Division of AEJMC.

Clea Bourne, PhD, is a Senior Lecturer in the Department of Media, Communications and Cultural Studies at Goldsmiths, University of London. Her research interests span the different ways that 21st century economies are strategically communicated and mediatized through various actors, practices, and discourses. Her current research explores the public legitimization of discourses surrounding artificial intelligence and new technologies. Clea's work has been published in a range of journals and edited collections. She is the author of *Trust, Power and Public Relations in Financial Markets* (Routledge, 2017), and is currently working on her second monograph for Palgrave-Macmillan's Professional Discourses series.

Shannon A. Bowen, PhD, professor, University of South Carolina, USA, focuses on ethics within the highest levels of organizations, specifically the application of Kantian deontological ethics in communication. She is a former editor of *Ethical Space: The International Journal of Communication Ethics*, board member of the International Public Relations Research Conference (IPRRC), the Arthur W. Page Society, and a regular columnist for *PRWeek*. Professionally, she worked on Capitol Hill and as an analyst at a research firm. Ethics is featured in her 100+ publications, and she has been honored with numerous awards such as the Jackson Jackson & Wagner Behavioral Science Research Prize, the Leadership in Scholarship Award, and the Robert L. Heath Award. Recent books include, *An Overview of the Public Relations Function* (2nd ed.) and *Excellence in Internal Communication Management* by Business Expert Press.

https://doi.org/10.1515/9783110554250-033

Glen T. Cameron, PhD, is professor emeritus and the Maxine Wilson Gregory Chair in Journalism Research at the Missouri School of Journalism, USA. He also is founder and co-director of the Health Communication Research Center at the University of Missouri. Cameron has a joint appointment in Family and Community Medicine. He has received many academic awards and honours. In statistical analyses of journalism and mass communication scholarship, Cameron is cited as the most published researcher nationally in major refereed journals over the past five years. In 1996, he received the Pathfinder Award from the Institute for Public Relations Research & Education.

Craig E. Carroll, PhD, University of Texas at Austin, is Lecturer of Management in the Department of Strategy and Environment at Rice University's Jones Graduate School of Business, USA. He also serves as the Executive Director of The Observatory on Corporate Reputation, a research think-tank devoted to the corporate affairs and communications functions, and as Leader of the Communications Institute for The Conference Board's Center for Marketing and Communication and on the advisory council for the Future Trends Forum with Fundacion de la Innovacion. He has published three research compendiums on corporate reputation, over 20 scholarly articles, and serves on the editorial board of several scholarly journals in corporate communication. His research examines the role of communication and media in creating social change through organizations.

Suwichit (Sean) Chaidaroon, PhD, is Senior Lecturer in Strategic Communication at the National University of Singapore. His research focuses on the intersection between public relations and organizational communication, especially in the global and digital contexts. His work has been published in several international peer-reviewed journals, edited volumes, and academic handbooks in communication and marketing fields. He reviews for leading journals in public relations, business communication, and marketing disciplines, and has served on the research committee for the Association for Business Communication.

Yi-Ru Regina Chen, PhD, is an Associate Professor of public relations at Hong Kong Baptist University. Her research areas include strategic communication, social media engagement and gamification, government affairs, corporate social responsibility, and creating shared values. She has published in leading communication, new media, and behavioral change journals, including *International Journal of Communication, Information, Communication & Society, American Behavioral Scientist, Journal of Medical Internet Research, Journal of Public Relations Research*, and *Public Relations Review*.

Myoung-Gi Chon, PhD, is an assistant professor in public relations at the School of Communication and Journalism, Auburn University, USA. He is interested in understanding communicative behaviours of publics to solve problematic situations. His research interest focuses on risk-crisis, employee, and health communication. He also expands his research interest to public diplomacy by exploring how public relations theories can be applied to international issues.

Patricia A. Curtin is professor and associate dean for undergraduate affairs in the School of Journalism and Communication at the University of Oregon, USA. Her research encompasses cross-cultural public relations, public relations history, and development of critical/postmodern approaches to public relations theory, particularly the cultural-economic model. She is the author of two books and numerous peer-reviewed book chapters and journal articles. She is a former Chair of AEJMC's Public Relations Division and has chaired AEJMC's Research and Publications Committees, serving two terms on the organization's board of directors. She reviews for several international journals and conferences.

Audra Diers-Lawson, PhD, is a senior lecturer of Public Relations at Leeds Beckett University's Business School in the United Kingdom. Her research interests focus on risk and crisis communication, stakeholder relationship management, and cross-cultural research. Her work has appeared in international peer-reviewed journals, edited volumes, handbooks, and international encyclopedias. Her book *Crisis Communication: Managing Stakeholder Relationships* offers a comprehensive review of the literature on issues and crisis communication. She is the chair for the Crisis Division of ECREA and editor for *Journal of International Crisis and Risk Communication*, and serves as a reviewer and/or on the editorial boards of several other publications.

Lee Edwards, PhD, is Associate Professor in the Department of Media and Communications at the London School of Economics and Political Science, UK. She teaches and researches public relations from a socio-cultural perspective, and is particularly interested in the relationship between public relations, inequalities, social justice, and democracy. She has published over 60 theoretical and empirical articles and book chapters on a range of topics, including public relations as a cultural intermediary, diversity in public relations, and public relations and democracy. Her authored and edited books include *Public Relations and Society: The Generative Power of History* (Routledge, 2019, with Ian Somerville and Øyvind Ihlen), *Understanding Public Relations: Theory, Culture and Society* (Sage, 2018), *Power, Diversity and Public Relations* (Routledge, 2014), and *Public Relations, Society and Culture: Theoretical and Empirical Explorations* (Routledge, 2011, with Caroline Hodges).

Michael Etter, PhD, is Senior Lecturer at King's Business School, King's College London. His research interest focuses on new information and communication technologies and the changes they bring to social evaluations of organizations, such as organizational reputation, legitimacy, and stigma. His research has appeared in international journals such as *Academy of Management Review, Academy of Management Annals, Journal of Management Studies, Business and Society, Journal of Business Ethics, International Journal of Strategic Communication, Journal of Communication Management, Public Relations Review*.

Johanna Fawkes, PhD, was Principal Research Fellow at the University of Huddersfield, UK (2016–2018), leading an international team to produce a Global Capability Framework for Public Relations and Communications Management in conjunction with the Global Alliance. From 1990, she developed undergraduate, postgraduate and doctoral degrees in public relations in three UK Universities and in Australia (2011–2016), following a career in public sector communication. She has delivered keynote speeches and published widely on public relations and ethics. Her book, *Public Relations Ethics and Professionalism; The Shadow of Excellence*, was published by Routledge in 2015 (paperback 2017). She is working on a sequel.

Jolene Fisher, PhD, is an assistant professor in the Department of Advertising, Public Relations and Media Design at the University of Colorado Boulder, USA. Her research interests lie at the intersection of strategic communication, new media, and social change. Her current work investigates the use of digital games as organizational tools for education, community building, and engagement. Her research has been published in the journals *Communication, Culture & Critique, International Communication Gazette*, and *Media, Culture & Society*, among others. She received her doctoral degree from the University of Oregon.

Magnus Fredriksson, PhD, is associate professor in Media and Communication Studies at University of Gothenburg, Sweden. His research focuses on ideas of communication in general and in public sector contexts in particular. He is the co-editor of *Public Relations and Social Theory* (Routledge, 2018) and his research has been published in *European Journal of Communication, Management*

Communication Quarterly, Organization Studies, Public Administration, Public Relations Inquiry and elsewhere.

James E. Grunig, PhD, is professor emeritus of communication at the University of Maryland, USA. He has published six books and more than 250 other publications. He has won six major awards in public relations. He was the founding co-editor of the *Journal of Public Relations Research* and has been awarded honorary doctorates by universities in Peru, Romania, Turkey, and Canada. His research over more than 50 years has included communication and development, publics, public relations behavior of organizations, public relations and strategic management, excellence in public relations, organization-public relationships, reputation, employee communication, ethics and responsibility, and science communication.

Vincent Hazleton, PhD, APR, Fellow PRSA is an independent scholar residing in Radford, Virginia, USA. Vincent earned a BA in Speech and Theatre from the University of Science and Arts of Oklahoma, USA. He earned an MA and PhD in Communication from the University of Oklahoma. His research interests include social capital, public relations theory, social influence, and the sociology of knowledge. He has studied social capital for over 20 years and published a variety of journal articles on the topic. He is the co-editor of two books on Public Relations Theory. Vincent has been a member of the Public Relations Society of America since 1980, and has served in leadership positions at local, regional, and national levels.

Robert L. Heath, PhD, University of Illinois, 1971, is professor emeritus at the University of Houston. He is author or editor of 23 books, including handbooks and master collections, and 272 articles in major journals, chapters in leading edited books, and encyclopedia entries. In addition to strategic issues management, he has written on rhetorical theory, social movements, communication theory, public relations, organizational communication, crisis communication, risk communication, terrorism, corporate social responsibility, investor relations, engagement, public interest, and reputation management. His most recent books are the *International Encyclopedia of Strategic Communication* and the *Handbook of Organizational Rhetoric and Communication*.

Sherry J. Holladay, PhD, is professor of Communication at Texas A&M University in College Station, Texas, USA. Her research addresses strategic communication in crisis communication, issues management, corporate social responsibility and irresponsibility, and activism. Her work has appeared in *Public Relations Review, Management Communication Quarterly, Journal of Communication Management, and International Journal of Strategic Communication*. She is co-editor of the *Handbook of Crisis Communication* and co-author of *It's Not Just PR: Public Relations in Society, Public Relations Strategies and Applications: Managing Influence,* and *Managing Corporate Social Responsibility*.

Jenny Zhengye Hou, PhD, is a Senior Lecturer in Strategic Communication at Queensland University of Technology, Australia. Her research revolves around strategic communication and institutional sociology, fake news in the digital age, and the PR-journalism interrelationship. Her work has appeared in *Public Relations Review, Journalism & Mass Communication Quarterly, Journal of Business and Technical Communication, Communication Research and Practice, Asia Pacific Public Relations Journal,* and *PRism*. In 2017, Jenny was awarded Public Relations Educator Fellowship by the Plank Centre for Leadership in Public Relations. In 2019, she was awarded The Arthur W. Page Centre Legacy Scholar Grant.

Chun-Ju Flora Hung-Baesecke, PhD, will join the University of Technology Sydney, Australia in 2021. She is currently the Chair of the Public Relations Division and a board member in International

Communication Association and a member of the Arthur W. Page Society. Flora is on the editorial boards of *Public Relations Review, Journal of Public Relations Research, International Journal of Strategic Communication*, and *Public Relations Journal*. She has won several awards at international conferences and publishes in various international refereed journals, book chapters, and research reports. In 2018, together with two scholars in China, Flora co-edited the first comprehensive collection on public relations theory in Greater China.

Bree Hurst, PhD, is a Senior Lecturer in Public Relations at the QUT Business School. Bree's ongoing research seeks to provide rich insights into how organisations can address the complex task of managing their impacts on communities, society, and the environment. Her research is largely centred around the interrelated topics of social licence to operate, social impact, corporate responsibility, stakeholder engagement, and organisational communication. Bree has had her work published in a number of academic journals and award-winning handbooks.

Øyvind Ihlen, PhD, is professor at the Department of Media and Communication, University of Oslo, Norway, and co-director of POLKOM – Centre for the Study of Political Communication. He has over 120 publications, including *Public Relations and Social Theory: Key Figures and Concepts* (2009, 2nd expanded edition 2018, with Magnus Fredriksson), the award-winning edited *Handbook of Communication and Corporate Social Responsibility* (2011, with Jennifer Bartlett and Steve May), and *Handbook of Organizational Rhetoric* (2018, with Robert L. Heath). Ihlen was President of the European Public Relations Education and Research Association (EUPRERA) 2016–2017. His research focuses on strategic communication/public relations, using theories of rhetoric and sociology.

Sara Ivarsson is a PhD student at the Department of Journalism, Media and Communication, University of Gothenburg. Her research interests encompass public sector communication.

Yan Jin, PhD, is the Georgia Athletic Association Professor in Grady College of Journalism and Mass Communication and the Assistant Department Head of Advertising and Public Relations at the University of Georgia (UGA). She is also the Associate Director of UGA's Center for Health & Risk Communication. Her primary research programs are in the areas of crisis communication and strategic health risk communication. She has authored over 80 peer-reviewed journal articles and is a member of the editorial board of *Communication Research, Public Relations Review, Journal of Public Relations Research*, and *Journal of International Crisis and Risk Communication Research*.

Jeong-Nam Kim is the Gaylord Family Endowed Chair in Public Relations and Strategic Communication at the Gaylord College of Journalism and Mass Communication at the University of Oklahoma, USA. Kim investigates "public behavior" and its implications for social dynamics from a communication perspective. He has theorized on lay citizens' communicative actions in individual life and in response to social problems. He is working to conceptualize the communicative-cognitive interface of lay publics in personal and social problems. His work identifies both opportunities and challenges generated by lay publics and how their communicative actions either contribute to or detract from a civil society.

Dean Kruckeberg, APR, Fellow PRSA, is co-author of *This Is PR: The Realities of Public Relations; Public Relations and Community: A Reconstructed Theory*, and *Transparency, Public Relations, and the Mass Media: Combating the Hidden Influences in News Coverage Worldwide*. He is co-editor of *Strategic Communications in Russia: Public Relations* and *Advertising and Public Relations in the Gulf Cooperation Council Countries: An Arab Perspective*. His honors include the PRSA Atlas Award for Lifetime Achievement in International Public Relations, the PRSA Outstanding Educator Award, the Pathfinder

Award of the Institute for Public Relations, and the Jackson Jackson & Wagner Behavioral Research Prize. He has lectured and performed research worldwide.

Anne Lane, PhD, is Public Relations Subject Area Coordinator in QUT's Business School. She teaches courses in public relations theory, techniques, and management; and community consultation and engagement. Her research centers on the uses, potential, and limitations of stakeholder engagement and dialogue. She has presented to industry on topics including storytelling for business. She reviews for several international peer-review journals and conferences. Anne has published over 20 peer-reviewed academic journal articles and conference papers; had articles in *The Conversation* and *Smart Business*; and made guest appearances on ABC news radio around Australia.

John A. Ledingham, PhD, is professor emeritus at Capital University in Columbus, Ohio, USA. His research interests are focused on public relations as relationship management and stakeholder relations. Dr. Ledingham is the author of more than 60 scholarly articles, conference papers, and book chapters. He is also editor of two collections of scholarly works. Dr. Ledingham has served as principal and co-principal investigator on numerous grants from a variety of sources. He is a graduate of Ohio State University, 1980.

Vilma Luoma-aho, PhD, is full professor of Corporate Communication and Vice Dean of Research at JSBE, University of Jyväskylä, School of Business and Economics, and visiting professor at IULM University, Milan, Italy. She has published widely on stakeholder engagement and social media in journals including *Journal of Communication Management, Computers in Human Behavior,* and *International Journal of Strategic Communication.* Currently she leads an Academy of Finland-funded research project on young people's agency on social media, and is editing the forthcoming *Handbook of Public Sector Communication* (Wiley-Blackwell).

Jim Macnamara, PhD, is Distinguished Professor of Public Communication in the School of Communication at the University of Technology Sydney, Australia. He is also a Visiting Professor at the London School of Economics and Political Science, Media and Communications Department, and a Visiting Professor at the London College of Communication. He is internationally recognized for his research into evaluation of public communication and organizational listening, and is the author of more than 70 academic journal articles and book chapters and 16 books including *Organizational Listening: The Missing Essential in Public Communication* and *Evaluating Public Communication: Exploring New Models, Standards, and Best Practice.*

Grazia Murtarelli, PhD, is assistant professor of Corporate Communication at Università IULM in Milan, Italy, where she teaches Digital Communication Management and Web Analytics. Her research focuses on the analysis of online scenario and, more specifically, on the following issues: social media-based relationship management, online dialogue strategies, digital visual engagement processes and social media measurement and evaluation. She is Public Relations Student & Early Career Representative at International Communication Association. She is also a faculty affiliate of the Center of Research for Strategic Communication at Università IULM.

Lan Ni, PhD, Professor, Valenti School of Communication at the University of Houston, USA, focuses on intercultural public relations, understanding and segmentation of publics, relationship management, conflict management, and community engagement with diverse publics. She has been awarded multiple research grants from major national and regional funding agencies, such as NSF, published numerous journal articles and chapters, and is the lead author of *Intercultural Public Relations: Theories for Managing Relationships and Conflicts with Strategic Publics* (Routledge, 2018). She currently serves as the senior associate editor of *Journal of Public Relations Research* and associate editor of *Negotiation and Conflict Management Research*.

Laura Olkkonen is a Postdoctoral Researcher in the School of Business and Management at LUT University and Docent of Corporate Communication at Jyväskylä University School of Business and Economics, Finland. She is an expert on business-society relations and CSR communication, and has published her research in journals such as *Journal of Public Relations Research*, *Corporate Communications: An International Journal*, and *Public Relations Inquiry*. She teaches sustainable business and stakeholder relations, and acts as a local coordinator of the UN's Principles for Responsible Management Education at LUT.

Josef Pallas, PhD, professor, Department of Business Studies, Uppsala University, Sweden. His research focuses on the expansion, dynamics, and consequences of mediatization in a context of governance of public sector organizations in general and universities, governmental agencies, and municipalities in particular. He is the co-editor of *Corporate Governance in Action* (Routledge, 2018) *Organizations and Media: Organizing in a Mediatized World* (Routledge 2014), and *Det styrda universitet?* (Makadam 2017). His work has been published in journals such as *European Journal of Communication*, *International Journal of Strategic Communication*, *Media, Culture and Society*, *Organization Studies*, *Public Administration* and others.

Augustine Pang, PhD, is professor of Communication Management (Practice) at the Lee Kong Chian School of Business, Singapore Management University (SMU). He is also the Academic Director, MSc in Communication Management and Member of University Tribunal. His research interests include crisis management and communication, image management and repair, media management, and corporate communication management. He has published more than 110 refereed journal articles, book chapters, proceedings and case studies. In 2015, he was inducted as a member of the Arthur W Page Society (US). He is Fellow of SMU Academy, and an Honorary Fellow at Hong Kong Polytechnic University.

Thomas Pleil, PhD, is Professor of Public Relations at Darmstadt University of Applied Sciences (h_da), Germany. His research focuses on online communications and social media, lifelong learning, digital transformation, and transformative research. He is founder of a BSc program in Online Communication and Director of the Institute for Communication and Media at h_da. Thomas is part of larger teams in state-funded research projects on digital transformation, sustainability, and the future of work. As a co-founder of Steinbeis Transfer Centre Flux, he is a sparring partner for organizations and companies on change, lifelong learning, and communications.

Natalia Rodríguez-Salcedo, PhD, earned a double degree in Journalism and in Advertising and Public Relations. She is deputy director of the Marketing and Media Management department, and deputy director of the Master's Degree in Corporate Reputation at the School of Communication of Universidad de Navarra, Spain, where she has been teaching since 2001. She has co-authored two books and published several chapters and articles on the history of public relations in Spain.

Stefania Romenti, Ph.D., is associate professor in Strategic communication and PR at Università IULM in Milan, Italy, and Chair of the Master of Science in Strategic Communication (English Language) and Rectors' Proxy to Sustainability and Social Responsibility. She is the Director of the Executive Master in Corporate Public Relations (Università IULM) and Adjunct Professor at IE Business School in Madrid in Measuring Intangibles and KPIs in Communication. She is the Founder and Director of the Research Center in Strategic Communication (CECOMS) and the President-Elect of the European Association of

Public Relations Education and Research Association (EUPRERA). She centers her research on strategic communication, corporate reputation, stakeholder management and engagement, dialogue, social media, measurement, and evaluation.

Betteke van Ruler, PhD, is professor emerita of Communication Science and Corporate Communication at the University of Amsterdam, Netherlands. Her research focuses on the practice of communication management, its professionalization and theoretical foundations. She was awarded the honorary title of Officer in the Civil Order of Orange-Nassau by the Queen for her work in bridging the gap between academic theory and practice. Van Ruler has been Chair of the Department of Communication Science of the University of Amsterdam. She is Past President of the European Public Relations Education and Research Association (EUPRERA) and Past Chair of the Public Relations Division of the International Communication Association (ICA) as well as Fellow of the ICA. She is published in numerous peer-reviewed journals and wrote many books for communication professionals.

Ian Somerville, PhD, is Head of the School of Media, Communication and Sociology at the University of Leicester, UK. His research has been published in a range of international communication, public relations, sociology, and politics journals. His most recent book is *Public Relations, Society and the Generative Power of History* (co-edited with Lee Edwards and Øyvind Ihlen, Routledge, 2019). He is currently a member of the editorial boards of *Public Relations Review, Public Relations Inquiry* and the *Journal of Media and Communication*.

Erich J. Sommerfeldt, PhD, is an associate professor in the Department of Communication at the University of Maryland, USA. Sommerfeldt has authored dozens of articles and book chapters on the role of public relations in civil society, public diplomacy, and development initiatives. He is a two-time winner of the Best Article of the Year Award from the Public Relations Division of the National Communication Association. He has participated in civil society research projects in developing nations around the world, and has lectured on public affairs evaluation methods to the US Department of Defense Information School, the US Air Force, US Army Reserve, and NATO.

Krishnamurthy Sriramesh, PhD, is Professor of Public Relations and Director of Master of Arts in Corporate Communication at the University of Colorado, Boulder, USA. His research focuses on topics such as global public relations, the impact of culture on public relations, and CSR. He has taught public relations at universities in Asia, Australasia, Europe, and North America, and has received several awards for excellence in teaching and research, including the prestigious Pathfinder Award from the Institute of Public Relations (in 2004). He has co-edited several books, published over 100 research articles and book chapters, and presented more than 100 conference papers and presentations in over 30 countries.

Kenneth Starck, PhD, is Professor Emeritus at the University of Iowa, USA, where he served 17 years as director of the School of Journalism and Mass Communication. He also served four years as dean of the Zayed University College of Communication and Media Sciences, United Arab Emirates. His research interests center on media freedom and responsibility. He has lectured in more than a dozen countries and has held Fulbright professorships in China and Romania, as well as extended academic appointments in Finland and Germany. He is co-author of *Backtalk: Press Councils in America* and *Public Relations and Community: A Reconstructed Theory* and author of *The Dragon's Pupils: A China Odyssey*.

Elina R. Tachkova is a PhD candidate at the Department of Communication at Texas A&M University, USA. Her research focuses on the nature of crises and how organizational crisis response strategies affect stakeholder perceptions and reputation following a crisis. Her dissertation examines the relationship between scandals and crises and the communicative implications it poses for crisis communication research and practice. Elina's work has appeared in edited volumes and international peer-reviewed journals including *Journal of Communication Management* and *Corporate Communication: An International Journal*.

Lisa Tam, PhD, Purdue University, USA, is Lecturer of Advertising and Public Relations at the QUT Business School in Brisbane, Australia. Her research focuses on (a) public relations and integrated communication, (b) relational approach to public diplomacy, and (c) construct development and measurement. In addition to academic research, she also works on commercially funded research in collaboration with industry partners.

Elizabeth L. Toth, PhD, professor, Department of Communication at the University of Maryland, USA, has published more than 80 refereed journal articles, book chapters, monographs, and conference papers on public relations. She co-authored, edited, and co-edited eight books including *Women and Public Relations: How Gender Influences Practice*; and *The Gender Challenge to Media: Diverse Voices from the Field*. She was editor of the *Journal of Public Relations Research*. She received the Institute for Public Relations Pathfinder Award and the PRSA Jackson, Jackson & Wagner Behavioral Science Prize. She is past president of the Association for Education in Journalism and Mass Communication.

Katerina Tsetsura, PhD, is Gaylord Family Professor at the University of Oklahoma, USA. Tsetsura is internationally known for her work in global public relations and media transparency. She is the author of over 80 peer-reviewed publications and co-author of *Transparency, Public Relations, and the Mass Media: Combating the Hidden Influences in News Coverage Worldwide*. Tsetsura is a past chair of the PR Divisions of ICA and NCA and serves on the editorial boards of *Communication Theory, International Journal of Strategic Communication,* and *Public Relations Review,* among others. In 2018, Tsetsura received the PRSA Outstanding Public Relations Educator Award.

Emilie Tydings is a consultant on Public Relations and Organizational Development residing in Dublin, Virginia, USA. She studied Communication at the University of Colorado and earned an MS degree in Corporate Communication at Radford University, Virginia, USA. She has collaborated on a variety of research projects related to social capital, public relations theory, and public relations practitioners with Vincent Hazleton.

Chiara Valentini, PhD, is Professor of Corporate Communication at Jyväskylä University School of Business and Economics (JSBE), Jyväskylä, Finland and adjunct professor at IULM University, Milan, Italy. Her research interest focuses on strategic public relations, stakeholder relationship management, government communication, and digital communications. Her work has appeared in several international peer-reviewed journals, edited volumes, handbooks and international encyclopaedias. She is a former Secretary, Vice-Chair, and Chair of ICA Public Relations Division. She reviews for several international peer-review journals and is a member of the editorial boards of *Corporate Communication: An International Journal, Journal of Public Interest Communication, International Journal of Strategic Communication, Public Relations Inquiry* and *Public Relations Review*.

Marina Vujnovic, PhD, is an Associate Professor of Journalism in the Department of Communication at Monmouth University, USA. A native of Croatia, Dr. Vujnovic came to the USA in 2003 to pursue her graduate education in journalism and mass communication. Before that, she worked as a journalist and then a research assistant at the University of Zagreb. She also worked as a PR practitioner for Cyprus-based PR agency Action Global Communications. She received her MA in Communication from the University of Northern Iowa, and her PhD at the University of Iowa in 2008. She is author of *Forging the Bubikopf Nation: Journalism, Gender and Modernity in Interwar Yugoslavia*, co-author of *Participatory Journalism: Guarding Open Gates at Online Newspapers*, and co-editor of *Globalizing Cultures: Theories, Paradigms, Actions*.

Tom Watson, PhD, is Emeritus Professor in the Faculty of Media & Communications at Bournemouth University, UK. He was the founder of the International History of Public Relations Conference (2010 onwards) and edited the seven-volume *National Perspectives on the Development of Public Relations: Other Voices* series for Palgrave Macmillan (2014–2017). Tom has written extensively on the history and historiography of public relations.

Damion Waymer, PhD, Purdue University, is Professor and Chairperson of the Department of Advertising and Public Relations at the University of Alabama, USA. He is an authority on issues of diversity, race, class, and gender in the context of public relations, issues management, corporate social responsibility (CSR), and strategic communication research. His research appears in outlets such as *Journal of Applied Communication Research, Journal of Public Relations Research, Management Communication Quarterly*, and *Public Relations Review*.

C. Kay Weaver, PhD, is Professor and Dean of the School of Graduate Research at the University of Waikato in New Zealand. She focuses much of her research on the socio-cultural role of public relations and strategic communication, and promotes the value of critical theories in this endeavor. She is co-editor of *Public relations in global contexts* (2011) and has published in *Public Relations Review, Journal of Public Relations Research, Media Culture & Society, New Media and Society* and the *Journal of Applied Communication Research*, among other journals.

Gareth T. Williams is a doctoral candidate in the Department of Communication at the University of Maryland, USA. His studies include issues management, risk communication and digital studies in the arts and humanities. Also a communication strategist and public relations practitioner, Williams recently participated in efforts to improve cybersecurity practices in US power utilities. His previous work supported scientific, programmatic, public, and legislative communications by federal and state agencies and industry and non-profit associations. Clients include the US Department of Energy, US Department of Homeland Security, NASA, US-China Clean Energy Research Center, and American Public Power Association.

Peter Winkler, PhD, is Professor of Organizational Communication at the University of Salzburg, Austria. His research interest focuses on communicative approaches to organizational theory, digitization, and responsibility. His work has appeared in several edited volumes and handbooks as well as in international peer-reviewed journals such as *Business & Society, International Journal of Strategic Communication, Management Communication Quarterly, Science, Technology & Human Values*, and *Social Studies of Science*.

Index

https://doi.org/10.1515/9783110554250-034